The New Naturalist

A Survey of British Natural History

British Warblers

D1465257

Editors

Kenneth Mellanby, C.B.E., Sc.D.
S. M. Walters, M.A., Ph.D.
Prof. Richard West, F.R.S., F.G.S.

Photographic editor

Eric Hosking, O.B.E., F.R.P.S.

The aim of this series is to interest the general reader
in the wild life of Britain by recapturing the enquiring
spirit of the old naturalists. The Editors believe that
the natural pride of the British public in the native fauna
and flora, to which must be added concern for their
conservation, is best fostered by maintaining a high
standard of accuracy combined with clarity of exposition
in presenting the results of modern scientific research.

The New Naturalist

BRITISH WARBLERS

Eric Simms D.F.C., M.A.

COLLINS
8 Grafton Street, London

William Collins Sons & Co Ltd
London · Glasgow · Sydney · Auckland
Toronto · Johannesburg

To

Joan and George Burton

First published 1985
© Eric Simms 1985

ISBN 0 00 219404 x (limpback)
ISBN 0 00 219810 x (hardback)

Text set by Ace Filmsetting Ltd, Frome, Somerset
Illustrations originated by Alpha Reprographics Ltd, Harefield, Middlesex
Printed and bound in Great Britain by
Butler & Tanner Ltd, Frome, Somerset

Contents

Colour Plates

Editor's Preface

As has been well documented, the tendency in the New Naturalist series has been towards books concerned with groups of birds. The specialist nature of detailed treatments of species has thus been combined with a broader survey of the taxonomic group to which they belong. The relationships of the component species, and their peculiar characteristics and distinctions, reveal ways of considering their origins and ecology.

Warblers please everyone. Even the mildly interested naturalist cannot but experience an uplift of his or her spirits on hearing the year's first Chiffchaff or Willow Warbler, whose March arrival and northward spread through Britain signal the onset of spring. Their varied and felicitous songs form a sound background to our countryside in early summer, and have been the inspiration of poets and musicians. Return migration in the autumn brings vagrants like Pallas's Warbler blown off course from mainland Europe, to test the serious 'birder'. Conservationists find reward in their work to protect some of the rarest species, such as the resident Dartford Warbler, whose population is receding, and the migratory Savi's Warbler, a recent coloniser of Britain following an expansion of its European range.

We are fortunate to have as the author of this study Mr Eric Simms, already represented in the series by his *Woodland Birds* (1971) and *British Thrushes* (1978). Drawing on a lifetime of experience as a communicator, in the form of teaching, lecturing, broadcasting and writing, he has made a comprehensive presentation of one of his favourite bird families. With an underlying interest in the effect of Man's history on bird life, he has made particular studies of woodland, moors, wetlands, heaths and suburbs. The remarkable (for migrant birds) ubiquity of the warblers has interested him, and in this book he deals with habitat in some detail.

Always in the front line of research into recording methods, Mr Simms has an informed approach to vocalization, and the songs of the various species are the subject of not merely sonagrams, but also a more emotional response by the author as listener.

The identification of warblers presents a number of challenges. An important feature of this book is a section of plates by Mr Ian Wallace, whose great experience of field identification has enabled him to paint each warbler species with accuracy and realism, and to achieve results of great artistic beauty.

Many years of personal observation of warblers, in Britain and Europe, as well as in their winter quarters, have enabled Mr Simms to make an enlightened analysis of the scientific work of myriad other ornithologists. Serious ornithologists will appreciate a bibliography containing over a thousand entries, as well as statistical tables covering important aspects of warbler biology. The more general reader will appreciate that the text is not peppered relentlessly with such numerical details, but rather addresses itself to an appreciation of the manner in which warblers occupy our natural, and unnatural, countryside. The author's own delight in these birds is conveyed by his engaging text, which will be the source of a wider understanding, not only of warblers themselves, but also of the dynamics and balance of faunal communities.

Crispin Fisher

Author's Foreword

I perhaps first became aware of the family of warblers when at about the age of twelve I spent many hours endeavouring to identify a Willow Warbler singing high up in a swamp cypress in Kew Gardens. Without sound recordings to consult or field glasses to help a sight-identification it was only by a long process of elimination that I finally satisfied myself as to the identity of the elusive singer. There were distinct advantages in this since as a boy I was taught patience and care in both looking and listening. In fact, the calls and songs of birds were to give me both aesthetic pleasure and material for much investigation and enquiry. From 1921–40 I lived on the edge of Ladbroke Square in North Kensington in London, a private open space three hectares in size and liberally sprinkled with tall trees, dense shrubberies and cared-for lawns, where I listed no fewer than 63 species of bird. These included six species of migrant warbler: Chiffchaff, Willow Warbler, Blackcap, Garden Warbler, Whitethroat and Lesser Whitethroat, all birds that occurred annually in spring or autumn. This encouraged me to extend my researches to Holland Park, Hampstead Heath and Richmond Park, the woodlands, ancient hedgerows and heaths of Surrey and Sussex, Epping Forest, the River Thames from estuary to Oxford, Beddington Sewage Farm and London's reservoirs and gravel pits. To reach these haunts of warblers and other birds I cycled out in the early morning before school, at weekends and during the holidays. In due course I visited many parts of the British Isles and Europe, Africa and the New World and for the last 35 years have tape recorded the vocalizations of many species. I was early in my life attracted to the thrushes which were constantly around my home – five species appeared in Ladbroke Square – and this interest was to lead to the writing of a book devoted especially to them.

Warblers, in fact, bear a close relationship to the thrushes and so it was natural for me to extend my interests to another family which was described by Thomas Bewick as forming 'a very considerable portion of those numerous tribes of singing birds, with which this island so plentifully abounds.' Agile and lively in their movements and with cheerful notes, reeling songs or soothing melodies the warblers afford pleasure in themselves while their often skulking and retiring habits provide the ornithologist with a remarkable challenge. Detailed studies of some warbler species have revealed likenesses and dissimilarities which have helped us to understand more about this family of birds. Most of us can recall days on which a warbler has by its utterance, manner or sheer rarity brought us pleasure: the first Chiffchaff of spring, a displaying Wood Warbler, the song flight of a Whitethroat, the mimicries of a Marsh Warbler or a tired diminutive Pallas's Warbler in a seaside tamarisk. Perhaps providing less of an inspiration to the poets than the Nightingale, Skylark or Cuckoo, yet the warbler has not been ignored by the more discerning or better informed of the creative writers. Take these words of John Clare, the Northampton poet:

> 'The happy whitethroat on the sweeing bough
> Swayed by the impulse of the gadding wind
> That ushers in the showers of April – now
> Singeth right joyously . . . '

The great Order of birds known as the *Passeriformes* embraces a Sub-order *Oscines* – the music-makers, consisting largely of Old World insect-ivorous birds each with ten flight feathers in the wing. The first members of that Suborder emerged some forty million years ago, while the warblers along with the wagtails and shrikes can be traced back as families for about half that time. Eight genera are represented on the British and Irish list of birds containing some 45 or 46 species; at the time of writing one species still awaits ratification. For anyone who seeks to widen their knowledge of a delightful and rewarding group of birds the research material is both wide and varied.

This book has been greatly enriched by the accurate and sympathetic drawings and paintings of warblers by Ian Wallace and these reflect his vast experience and extensive journeyings in search of them. Eric Hosking has kindly provided many of his outstanding photographs of different warbler species and for their illustrations I must also thank: J. B. and S. Bottomley for Blackcap and Chiffchaff outside the breeding season; Richard Vaughan for Goldcrest display; Felicia Elwell for Whitethroat habitat and Dr Leo Batten, with whom I have spent many happy hours watching birds in the field, for his Firecrest and its English habitat. Many other habitat photographs were taken by myself.

A work of this kind inevitably rests on a foundation of other research and writings and I propose to list the more important sources here rather than in the bibliography at the end. The references as they are noted in the text are shown in parentheses at the end of each one. I must mention, firstly, the Midland steelmaster Henry Eliot Howard who wrote *The British Warblers* (Howard 1907–14), which was a classic, as well as his pioneering *Territory in Bird Life* (Howard 1948). It is impossible to pay a high enough tribute to the late Kenneth Williamson, who transcribed his unique knowledge of the warblers into three *Identification Guides*, pub-lished by the British Trust for Ornithology, which have remained con-stantly by my side just as they must have occupied many a well-worn place at all the bird observatories. These Guides are 1. *The Genera* Cettia, Locustella, Acrocephalus and Hippolais; 2. *The Genus* Phylloscopus, and 3. *The Genus* Sylvia (Williamson 1976). Other books that I have widely consulted are *The Birds of the British Isles* by Dr David Bannerman and G. E. Lodge (Bannerman 1954), *The Handbook of British Birds* by H. F. Witherby, F. C. R. Jourdain, N. F. Ticehurst and B. W. Tucker (*The Handbook* 1946), the *Atlas of European Birds* by Dr K. H. Voous (Voous 1961), *The Atlas of Breeding Birds in Britain and Ireland* compiled by Dr J. T. R. Sharrock for the B.T.O. (*The Atlas* 1976), as well as Dr Sharrock's own *Scarce Migrant Birds in Britain and Ireland* (Sharrock 1974) and with E. M. Sharrock *Rare Birds in Britain and Ireland* (Sharrock and Sharrock 1976). I would also like to mention Dr Colin Harrison's *A Field*

Guide to the Nests, Eggs and Nestlings of British and European Birds (Harrison 1975) and his *An Atlas of the Birds of the Western Palaearctic* (Harrison 1982). Finally amongst the books are Professor C. Vaurie's *The Birds of the Palearctic Fauna: A Systematic Reference* (Vaurie 1959) and C. B. Ticehurst's *A Systematic Review of the Genus Phylloscopus* (Ticehurst 1938).

Certain scientific papers have been widely consulted as well and these include the annual accounts of population changes from the Common Birds Census of the B.T.O. in *Bird Study* as well as the following: by J. H. Elgood, R. E. Sharland and P. Ward, *Palaearctic migrants in Nigeria, Ibis* 108:84–116 (Elgood et al 1966); by R. E. Moreau, *Problems of Mediterranean–Sahara migration, Ibis* 103a:373–427 (Moreau 1961); by D. J. Pearson, *The wintering and migration of Palearctic migrants at Kampala, southern Uganda, Ibis* 114:43–60 (Pearson 1972); by D. J. Pearson and G. C. Backhurst, *The southward migration of Palearctic birds over Ngulia, Kenya, Ibis* 118:78–105 (Pearson and Backhurst 1976) and by C. Vaurie, *Systematic notes on Palaearctic birds No. 9 and 10, Sylviinae,* 1685, 1691 (Vaurie 1954).

I am very grateful to the editors of *British Birds,* the *Ibis* and *Bird Study* for permission to reproduce maps, diagrams, figures, tables and sonagrams that have appeared in their journals and I wish to pay a special tribute in this respect to Dr J. T. R. Sharrock, Dr Janet Kear and Robert Hudson for much help and many kindnesses. I also appreciate the approval granted to me by the British Trust for Ornithology to use the migration divide map for Blackcaps first published in *Identification for Ringers 3 The Genus Sylvia.* I am greatly indebted to Dr Colin Bibby, who allowed me to use material from *The Ibis* on Cetti's and Dartford Warblers and from *Bird Study* on Reed and Sedge Warblers, to Mme Françoise Dowsett-Lemaire for my use of her sonagrams of Marsh Warbler imitations published in the *Ibis,* to Peter J. Grant and Bob Scott for their illustration of the wings of Willow Warbler and Chiffchaff in *Bird Study* and to Iain H. Leach for his map of winter Blackcap records and one figure from a paper of his, also in *Bird Study.*

I have made use of a number of sonagrams obtained from sound recordings to illustrate this book. Most of them are from my own recordings but I am grateful to the British Broadcasting Corporation for their agreement to the use for this purpose of those recordings that are BBC copyright, having been obtained when I was a member of their staff, or were made by Dr Ludwig Koch, Roger Perry or Robin Prytherch. S/Ldr V. C. Lewis most generously made available six recordings from his fine set of warbler tapes in *British Bird Vocabulary* for copying and conversion into sonagrams for this book. Professor W. H. Thorpe and Cambridge University Press also kindly gave me authority to reproduce from *Bird-Song* the sonagrams for Grasshopper and Savi's Warblers. Through the kindness and good offices of Ronald Kettle, the Curator of the British Library of Wildlife Sounds, I was able to listen to many sources of material while he was also responsible for dubbing all the selected recordings on to a master tape. This tape was then sent to Joan Hall-Craggs of the Sub-Department of Animal Behaviour at Madingley for conversion by her into sonagrams. She had previously broadcast with me in two series of BBC radio programmes on animal communication that I presented and given me much practical help. I cannot sufficiently express to her my deep appreciation for all the time and loving care which she devoted to the production of such clear and invaluable sonagrams.

This is the third New Naturalist volume that it has been my privilege to write. The first, *Woodland Birds*, referred to in the present text with the reference (Simms 1971), was written at the direct invitation of the late James Fisher on behalf of the Editors of the series and I am delighted that Crispin, the son of my old friend, has watched over this book on behalf of the publishers. *Woodland Birds* enabled me to examine in some depth the environment in which trees are able to grow including the background of geology, soils and climate as well as the origins and history of British and Irish woodlands and their birds from Pliocene times to the present day. It seemed entirely logical to follow it with a second New Naturalist on *British Thrushes* many of whose species evolved in and still occupy woodland habitats. Since warblers are related to thrushes I believed that a book about the British warblers would complement the two earlier volumes. I hoped to be able to assemble a great deal of material not previously brought together, to include much personal observation on behaviour and vocalizations and to examine the different genera and individual species occurring in the British Isles.

To achieve these four aims I have devoted three broad introductory chapters to the warblers of the Old and New Worlds and those of Britain with several chapters examining, comparing and contrasting members of each genus and a series of single chapters for each breeding species. However, the Fan-tailed Warbler as the only member of its genus represented – and a non-breeding one at that – does earn itself a chapter on its own. Each chapter on a breeding species reviews in detail the appearance and plumage, measurements, range, numbers, habitats, past histories, diet, calls and songs, breeding season, nests and nest-sites, clutches, broods, success, predation, out of nesting season activities, migrations and so on. Other chapters are devoted to the rare migrant warblers and vagrants that have occurred in the British Isles, grouped according to their genera. The final chapter looks at certain aspects of warbler populations and possible changes in the future in numbers and distribution according to biotic factors, the effects of climate and other influences. There is a bibliography with more than a thousand references which, apart from the references given in the Foreword, covers chapter by chapter all the other publications mentioned in the text. A selected list of sound recordings is also provided at the end.

It has been a great pleasure to write this book but the exercise, rewarding as it has been, has also served to underline the deficiencies in our knowledge of many aspects of life in the family of warblers, especially on inter-specific relationships, habitat requirements, moult and migration. The purpose of this book has been to provide where possible some insight into the lives of a very pleasing and fascinating group of small songbirds. The omissions in the text are themselves signposts towards those fields of study and endeavour which remain virgin and unexplored terrain. Some members of the group have been well studied, others not so deeply but all pose many unanswered questions. To have spent so much of my life among the members of what Sir William Jardine in 1839 called 'a family of smaller species, abounding in numbers, and extremely interesting' has been a privilege and blessing for which as a naturalist I remain extremely grateful.

Introducing the Warblers   CHAPTER   I

To anyone with an awakening interest in ornithology the warblers may seem a very daunting group – 'little green or brown jobs' as they have irreverently been dubbed! To the budding botanist the umbellifers or grasses may seem just as difficult a group to cope with. Yet with an increasing knowledge of their habitats, plumages, vocalizations and behaviour one not only appreciates the wide variety that exists among the warblers but also comes closer to getting to terms with their identification. Some will always remain difficult and there is no point in minimising the problems: others even when examined in the hand remain enigmas. The warblers of the Old World occupy a wide range of habitats so that during the summer examples may be found in most parts of Europe; indeed some may be the dominant species in an ecosystem. It is not difficult to find even a small area of the British Isles where one can hear singers that include the typical warblers of the *Sylvia* genus as well as members of the reed and leaf warblers. I know a lake in the English Midlands which is surrounded by trees and grassland where I can listen to Blackcap, Willow Warbler, Sedge and Grasshopper Warbler all in song at the same time – representatives of four different genera of Old World warbler. Although less successful in spreading across the surface of the Earth than the true thrushes of the genus *Turdus*, to which they are closely allied, the Old World warblers have still occupied a fair amount of the land surface and continue to expand their range.

This is a book about the warblers that occur in the British Isles, but it also includes references to the warblers of the whole Holarctic Zone. Many of these are not yet on the British list so the British species can be seen against a background on which the latter birds are also depicted. In this way I hope to provide a rather wider account of each genus and its distribution through the world. The name 'warbler' is itself derived from the verb 'to warble' which means 'to sing or utter in a trilling, vibratory or quavering manner, to modulate, to carol or to produce any melodious succession of pleasing sounds' – apt descriptions of the territorial utterances of many of the warblers of the Old World. The origin of the word seems to be from the Middle English *werbelen* or the Old French *werbler* – to sing or play on a musical instrument. The Dutch *wervelen* appears to be its counterpart in Holland. Because of the origin of the name I make no apology for devoting more space to the bio-acoustic features of this subfamily than other authors might do! Vocal communication in birds and other animals has been a study of mine from childhood and from 1950, when I was appointed to direct the BBC's wildlife sound recording projects, I have personally captured on tape many of the calls and songs of British and Continental warblers. This special bias in the present volume will I hope give it an extra appeal not only in the written accounts but through the sonagrams that I have included.

The name 'warbler' is the substantive term applied to many species which belong to the subfamily *Sylviinae* of the *Muscicapidae* in the sub-order *Oscines* of that great order of perching birds known as the *Passeri-formes*. The family *Muscicapidae* embraces many Old World species of songbird with ten primaries and a primarily insect-eating habit. The sub-families include the *Turdinae* which were featured in my earlier New Naturalist volume *British Thrushes*, the *Polioptilinae* or gnat-catchers and gnat-wrens of the New World which are closely allied to the Old World warblers, the *Muscicapinae* or Old World flycatchers and fantails and the *Sylviinae* or Old World warblers, kinglets including the Goldcrest and Firecrest, tit-warblers (*Leptopoecile*) and fern-bird (*Bowdleria*).

It is important to make clear that the Old World warblers with which this book is concerned, which carry ten primaries, are different from the New World, American or wood warblers (*Parulidae*) which have only nine. It may, however, be of interest to say something about the New World warblers since a number of species have appeared from time to time in the British Isles. The wood warblers of the American continent are small, often brightly coloured, insectivorous and mainly migratory birds which rarely warble and rely more on their plumages for advertisement. They occupy a wide range of habitats including broad-leaved and coniferous woodland, tropical rainforests, swamps and marshes, scrub and agricultural land and desert environments. To have witnessed as I have the passage of many of these birds northward in spring up the American continent is to enjoy one of Nature's greatest and most thrilling experiences. Warblers of many species sweep up through North Carolina in late April from the West Indies, Central and even South America as they move up to their breeding grounds. On a day of heavy movement it is possible to see at least one third of all the species of wood warbler that breed east of the Rocky Mountains. Edwin Way Teale (1955) described a car journey that he made for more than a hundred miles in North Carolina in late April 'and there were warblers, pockets of warblers, trees swarming with warblers, warblers beyond count, along the way.' Among the northern species of wood warbler there is often sexual or seasonal dimorphism but in a number of tropical species both sexes retain bright colouring through the whole year. Many moult in the autumn into dull, rather similar plumages which make identification rather difficult. The American warblers of the *Parulidae* also seem to show some affinity with emberizine finches and certain tanagers. There are about 113 species of some 26 genera that range from Alaska south to Argentina. Half of the genera are primarily North American or West Indian and most of the northern species are migratory by nature.

The largest genus of the *Parulidae* is that of *Dendroica* which includes some twenty-seven species, five of which have made their way to the British Isles, as well as Kirtland's Warbler, which breeds in an area of jack pines only 160 km long and 100 km wide in peninsular Michigan, and winters in the Bahamas. There are also eleven species of *Vermivora* warblers of northern and central America which are related to *Dendroica* and these include the Tennessee Warbler – another vagrant to the British Isles. There are just over twenty species of the genus *Basileuterus* which are tropical birds living from Mexico south to Argentina. Some species are well adapted to the capture of flying insects – those of the genus *Setophaga* (one species of which has reached our shores), as well as *Myioborus* both known as 'redstarts' but having few features in common with the Old World redstarts *Phoenicurus*; the three species of the genus *Wilsonia* are yellow with various blackish markings of the face or head. The yellow-throats *Geothlypis* are scrub and wetland dwellers, while three members of the genus *Seiurus* include the Ovenbird and Northern Waterthrush, both of which are ground-walkers in what is primarily a tree-dwelling family. One species that I much admired when I lived in the southern United States was the golden-yellow Prothonotary Warbler *Protonotaria citrea* – named after the brilliant orange-yellow robe of the Papal Secretary – which I saw nesting in holes in rotten trees in the wooded swamps of the Deep South. Another interesting wood warbler is the Black-and-white Warbler *Mniotilta varia* which scales trees rather in the manner of a treecreeper.

The wood warblers were described by Roger Tory Peterson (1947) as 'the "butterflies" of the bird world – bright-coloured mites' and all with one exception are smaller than sparrows, have thin bills, rounded tails and rictal bristles. Most eat insects but a few species will take berries and fruit in the winter. Some species hawk for insects on the wing, others forage under leaves for insects and their eggs or spiders, others climb the bark, forage in trees of all kinds as well as scrub and grassland or feed on the ground. Most of the males have high, rather persistent songs but the atypical Yellow-breasted Chat *Icteria virens* is quite a good mimic and a few wood warblers have richer tones or song-flights for greater advertisement. The nests may be open cups or roofed with side entrances from almost at ground level to the tops of the tree canopies. They are built almost entirely by the females and the eggs that they lay are whitish, tinged with blue, green or brown especially at the broader end. The northern migratory species lay from 4–5 eggs and are usually single-brooded while smaller clutches are laid in the tropics. Incubation is carried out by the female which may be fed on the nest. The incubation period is from 11–14 days, or 16 in tropical species. For the migratory breeders the fledging period is from 8–10 days and from 12–14 for the non-migratory species of Central America.

The American wood warblers that have reached the British Isles are as follows:

Black-and-white Warbler	*Mniotilta varia*
Tennessee Warbler	*Vermivora peregrina*
Northern Parula (Parula Warbler)	*Parula americana*
Yellow Warbler	*Dendroica petechia*
Cape May Warbler	*D. tigrina*
Magnolia Warbler	*D. magnolia*
Yellow-rumped (Myrtle) Warbler	*D. coronata*
Blackpoll Warbler	*D. striata*
American Redstart	*Setophaga ruticilla*
Ovenbird	*Seiurus aurocapillus*
Northern Waterthrush	*S. novaeboracensis*
Common Yellowthroat	*Geothlypis tricas*
Hooded Warbler	*Wilsonia citrina*

In 1976 no fewer than eleven or twelve Blackpoll Warblers were recorded in the British Isles and a Yellow-rumped Warbler wintered in Devon in January 1955. The arrival of migratory North American warblers and other land birds in Britain and Ireland is spasmodic, but records have increased in recent years. They are mostly made in the autumn, and involve long-distance migrants en route from breeding grounds in eastern North America to South America or the West Indies. The weather conditions associated with the arrival of Nearctic birds in Britain and Ireland have been discussed by Elkins (1977, 1979). He was able to show that 'there is a definite relationship of vagrancy to the strong west or southwest winds of warm sectors' with a disorientation of migrants occurring with frontal zones creating fast eastward-moving waves to assist multiple crossings: this proposal has the support of the arrival dates of 75% of the vagrants. The crossings may be initiated anywhere between Nova Scotia and Bermuda while the birds are migrating south, although some may have been on a random dispersal or reversed passage. The 1976 influx of Blackpoll Warblers was unprecedented, and the Grey-cheeked Thrush and Nighthawk were involved in the same movement. It is possible that some birds may have been shipborne (Durand 1963, 1972), since a Blackpoll Warbler which reached the Ocean Terminal in Southampton in the autumn of 1961, aboard the RMS Queen Elizabeth, sailed with the ship on her return and died halfway across the Atlantic. It is quite possible that other Nearctic warblers and their allies may also turn up in time. Chandler S. Robbins (1980) predicted that in descending order of probability the following species might appear as vagrants in Europe: Connecticut Warbler *Oporornis agilis*, Black-throated Blue Warbler *Dendroica caerulescens*, Canada Warbler *Wilsonia canadensis*, Orange-crowned Warbler *Vermivora celata*, Palm Warbler *Dendroica palmarum* (now in Category D of the British and Irish list but not in the Full List), Mourning Warbler *Oporornis philadelphia*, Magnolia Warbler *Dendroica magnolia* and Cape May Warbler *D. tigrina* (the last two species arrived not long afterwards and are on the Full List), Black-throated Green Warbler *D. virens*, Blue-winged Warbler *Vermivora pinus*, Prairie Warbler *Dendroica discolor*, Wilson's Warbler *Wilsonia pusilla*, Bay-breasted Warbler *Dendroica castanea* as well as the Ruby-crowned Kinglet *Regulus calendula* and Golden-crowned Kinglet *Regulus satrapa*.

The Old World warblers are very different from those of the New World. They are on the whole better singers. After a whole summer listening, for example, to the thin double notes of the Blackpoll Warbler, the even-pitched and repeated 'tweet-tweet' of the Prothonotary Warbler, the 'beee-bsss' of the Blue-winged Warbler and the 'zeeee-up' of the Parula Warbler, I began to long for the pure soprano runs of the Blackcap, the sustained warblings of the Garden Warbler and the falling cadences of the Willow Warbler. The *Parulidae* are probably quite an ancient family of songbirds and may well have evolved in what was tropical North America. North America was cut off from South America in the Tertiary Period by areas of sea which may have been in existence for several million years. For millions of years the southern part of the northern isolated area was tropical in character and a fauna appeared that was distinct from that of tropical South America. Ernst Mayr and other ornithologists were of the opinion that several families of New World birds evolved there – vultures (New World), limpkins, trogons, mockingbirds, thrashers, vireos and the wood warblers. It can be said that the *Parulidae* have done very well but the *Sylviidae* or Old World warblers, an older and separate group, have produced three times as many living species.

COLOUR PLATES

Plate 1

Depicted here are the four tree warblers *Hippolais* known to occur in Britain and the two largest members of the reed warblers *Acrocephalus*. All are uncommon or rare. The first quartet consists of two short-winged species with olive to grey-brown upperparts and essentially dull white underparts and one short-winged and one long-winged species with mainly greenish upperparts and typically yellow underparts. Of the first pair, the Booted Warbler (1) is always small and (atypically for its genus) weak-billed – prompting confusion even with Bonelli's Warbler – but the Olivaceous Warbler (2) can be as big as the Icterine Warbler (3), with the most prominent bill of all four. The Icterine carries the most distinctive plumage characteristic of all – a bright wing panel (of overlapping yellow fringes on the tertials and secondaries) – but a few of the usually duller Melodious Warbler (4) may show such a mark. Confusion is best removed by the last's short wing point. For discussion, see p. 251. The Great Reed Warbler (5) and the Thick-billed Warbler (6) are the biggest, most hulking warblers to reach Britain. They differ most in head pattern, rump and tail colour – noticeably reddish in the latter – and flight silhouette. See also Fig. 111.

Plate 2

Shown here are eight warblers of three genera; all breed regularly at least occasionally in Britain. First met, the Garden Warbler (1) can suggest many other species but with experience, its gentle face, dark eyes, stubby bill and domed crown give it a distinctive head. The Reed Warbler (2) also provokes much confusion with its uniformly-coloured congeners. Its indistinct supercilium and always warm plumage tones are less helpful than its relative abundance in southern reed-beds. The Sedge Warbler (3, juvenile; 4, adult) is the most common and widespread *Acrocephalus*. Its dark crown, almost white supercilium, streaked back and tawny rump give it a distinctive appearance. Usually more olive, even greener above than the Reed, the Marsh Warbler (5) differs also in a more marked face pattern, paler underparts and structure. The larger of the two 'grasshopper' warblers here is the Savi's Warbler (6), similarly coloured to a dark Reed but with a fuller, more graduated tail and reeling song; see Chapter 13. A silent Grasshopper Warbler's (7) main characteristic is its softly streaked plumage but sadly this varies in colour tones, bringing it in confusion with the two other rare streaked *Locustella* (in Plate 3). Happily the miniature nightingale that is Cetti's Warbler (8) has a distinctive tail-cock to display its blotched undertail coverts.

Plate 3

Illustrated here are eight more warblers of three genera; only the Moustached has ever bred and most of the others are true rarities. Of the four *Acrocephalus*, the Aquatic Warbler (1) is distinctive, with its long-striped head and bright yellow-buff appearance – beware, however, wishful thinking over a young Sedge (see Plate 2). The Blyth's Reed Warbler (2) comes closest to the Marsh in general appearance but its greyer tones, short wing-point and distinctive postures (see p. 238) assist separation. The Paddyfield Warbler (3) resembles the brightest Reed; its thicker bill and full supercilium allow diagnosis. Closely convergent with the Sedge, the Moustached Warbler (4) presents a formidable challenge in field identification. Its plumage presents, however, even stronger contrasts and more rufous tones; the bird's habit of tail cocking is also helpful. Next come three more 'grasshopper warblers'. The River Warbler (5) is uniformly cold-toned above and more mottled than streaked below. The Pallas's Grasshopper Warbler (6) recalls a Sedge before any congener but its tail pattern is unique and its call quite different; see also p. 132. The Lanceolated Warbler (7) is the 'shrew' of British warblers, able to hide in a grass tuft. Its pipit-like streaking is the most complete of its genus. Last here is the tiny, neurotic Fan-tailed Warbler (8). At close range, its yellow bill and eye patch create a distinctively pale face. When cocked, its tail shows the marked tippets well.

PLATE

4

1. Subalpine Warbler (♂)   4. Marmora's Warbler (♂)   7. Rüppell's Warbler (♂)
2. Subalpine Warbler (♀)   5. Orphean Warbler (♂)   8. Barred Warbler (juvenile)
3. Spectacled Warbler (♂)   6. Sardinian Warbler (♂)   9. Desert Warbler

Plate 4

Presented here are nine uncommon or rare members of the genus *Sylvia*, the first seven vagrants from the Mediterranean region. The Subalpine Warbler is very distinctive as an adult male (1), but as a female or immature (2), it is not – sporting an eye-ring like the Spectacled Warbler (3) and otherwise provoking confusion with several other small congeners around the Mediterranean – and the last word on its diagnosis may never be written; see p. 119. The male Spectacled looks like a miniature Common Whitethroat; its mate and young are far less easy, see also p. 119. Happily, the Marmora's Warbler (4, male) is, well seen, an easy bird. With the mien of the Dartford (see plate 5), it is the swarthiest of all warblers. The female may momentarily suggest a Sardinian Warbler. Dark and almost thrush-like at times, the Orphean Warbler (5) has no confusion species in Europe. Smaller and slimmer than the whitethroats, the male Sardinian Warbler (6) is also distinctive but the much duller female is another trap for the unwary, see p. 117. Almost as big as the Common Whitethroat, the Rüppell's Warbler (7, male) wears the only black throat among British warblers but beware confusing the red-eyed female with a Sardinian. Actually larger than the Orphean (but not looking so), the Barred Warbler (8, immature) – with its soft grey-blue-buff look and dull wing bars – is soon learnt. Smallest and palest of its genus, the Desert Warbler (9) is unmistakable. At any range, only its reddish tail catches the eye.

Plate 5

Displayed here are four leaf warblers *Phylloscopus* and the remaining four *Sylvia* of Britain; all but one breed. The male Blackcap (1) is easy, often confiding and always sporting his black cap. The female's hat is red-brown. The Bonelli's Warbler (2) is difficult, dogged by pale Chiffchaffs (see below and Plate 6) and even the Booted Warbler (see Plate 1), but close observation will show its tit-like bill, pale rump and greener wings. Second largest and plumpest in its genus, the Wood Warbler (3) sports the only clear divide in underpart tones of any *Phylloscopus*. The white belly catches the eye. Potentially the most confusing warbler of all – with its wide racial variation – the Chiffchaff (4, southern morph) is worth long study. Always dingy, its dark bill and legs and frequently pale eye-ring form the best quick clues; see also Fig. 139. Commonest of all warblers, the Willow

Warbler (5) is a cleaner bird than the southern Chiffchaff, with a paler bill base, longer supercilium and wing, and usually paler legs; see also Fig. 135. With its dusky mask and duller plumage, the Lesser Whitethroat (6) differs distinctly from the once much commoner Whitethroat (7, male; 8, female) but in immature plumage, the rufous wing margins of the latter provide a better mark. Beware especially young Whitethroats in autumn; they can suggest both an *Acrocephalus* and other rare *Sylvias*. At close range in good light, the male Dartford Warbler (9) is colourful. Otherwise he and his mate can present just dark whirring wings ahead of a 'pencil' tail.

Plate 6

Portrayed here are the last ten warblers on the British list and one vagrant race of the Chiffchaff. Only the two 'crests' *Regulus* breed; the leaf warblers all fall in the 'adored rarity' class. The northeastern form of the Chiffchaff (1) often wears a good supercilium and an obvious wing bar, promoting serious confusion with the Greenish Warbler (2). Without a clear call transcription (see p. 333), many claims of the latter fail but its more rakish appearance is actually distinctive (and it does not wag its tail). Also confused with the Greenish are the larger Arctic Warbler (3) and the supposedly greener and yellower Green Warbler (4). The last is clearly another bogey bird but the Arctic – robust, energetic, with straw-coloured legs, whatever state its supercilium and wing-bars are in – needs no neurosis; see p. 331. The Pallas's Warbler (5) can hide its rump but that little square is totally diagnostic, however much the rest of the plumage pattern echoes those of the Yellow-browed Warbler (6) and the Firecrest (9); see also Fig. 159. The front wing bar of the Yellow-browed may wear off but its pale tertial fringes should prevent any confusion with large, wing-barred congeners. Usually found in ground cover, the Radde's Warbler (10) and the Dusky Warbler (11) were once thought virtually inseparable. Close study of the head is the answer, with Radde's showing the strongest bill and boldest head marks of its genus. The Dusky twitches; see Fig. 162. Both minute, the Goldcrest (7 adult, 8 juvenile, of British race) and the Firecrest (9) look alike when silhouetted amongst high foliage but the latter shows its full beauty instantly in good light. No British warbler is more breathtaking and any confusion with the small, striped *Phylloscopi* does not last.

The Old World Warblers CHAPTER 2

As a family the Old World warblers go back at least twenty million years. Warblers with their delicate skeletons are not as easily fossilized as the larger birds. It seems that the earliest fossil warbler was that of a typical warbler of the *Sylvia* genus recovered in France while a fossil Whitethroat has been recorded for Ice Age England (Fisher 1966). The Ice Ages of the Pleistocene period that began about a million years ago saw the disappearance of a number of bird species like the large flightless birds of prey. Yet a very large proportion of the birds which were alive in that period still exist somewhere in Europe. Indeed K. Lambrecht (1933) showed that only six of the 182 Ice Age bird species were absent from modern Europe. This showed a remarkable resilience and persistence in the European avifauna. The Palaearctic region is a zoogeographical area comprising the British Isles, the whole of Europe, Africa north of the Sahara Desert, and Asia north of the Himalayas and the Yangtze Kiang; it embraces all that part of the Old World which was under arctic conditions during the Quaternary glaciations which ended some ten thousand years ago. The Neotropical region of Central and South America holds about half the world's more than 8000 bird species either as nesters or winter visitors. In its variety the Ethiopian region of Africa south of the Sahara comes next. The fauna of

Fig. 1
Three Nearctic wood warblers (left to right); Myrtle Warbler, American Redstart, Black-and-White Warbler; all in first autumn plumage. Some of the New World warblers are more strikingly marked than the Old World warblers. (D. I. M. Wallace)

the Oriental Region between Africa and Australasia is less rich. Sometimes the Nearctic region which covers North America to the north of the tropics is joined to the Palaearctic to form a region known as the Holarctic. The birdlife is not uniform, nor is it static, so sub-divisions have been added for the Arctic, Siberia, Mongolia and so on.

In the middle of the Tertiary period, from around 20–40 million years ago, a tropical African avifauna existed in Europe (Cracraft 1973), but a general cooling in the European climate may well have pushed these tropical families south and into Africa. This would have coincided with the main evolution of Palaearctic genera and families. Today in that region there are some 500 passerine species placed in some 116 genera. However,

whereas a warbler like the Fan-tailed *Cisticola juncidis* is an African element
in the European avifauna and is classified by Voous (1960) as an Indo-
African faunal type, the European warblers are not of tropical origin but
'belong to genera whose evolutionary centres are clearly Palaearctic'
(Snow 1978). The map, for example, shows the outer breeding limits of

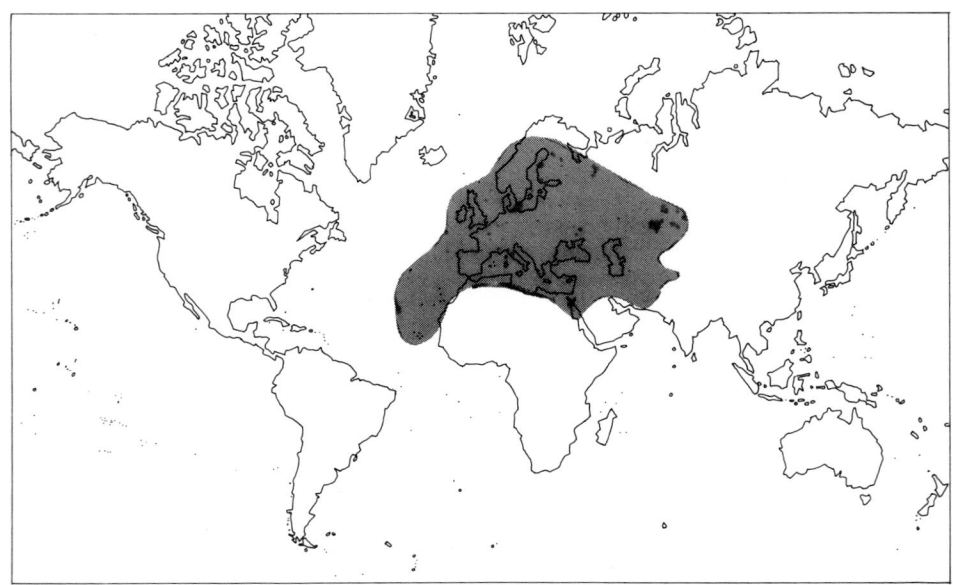

Fig. 2
*Outer breeding limits of
18* Sylvia *species.*

eighteen species of *Sylvia*, typical warblers. Yet the Old World warblers
appear to attain their greatest diversity in tropical Africa with around 134
species compared with the much smaller number of about 85 in tropical
Asia. The more than 100 Palaearctic species appear to be less diversified but
Voous (1977) was of the opinion that all of them 'probably have a Sino-
Himalayan or Indo-African root.' The Palaearctic species are much more
generalized and simple in their structure and habits than those in the tropics
which have acquired long insect-gathering bills and build ingenious, complex and often suspended nests. Dome-shaped nests, which are characteristic of relatives in the tropics such as the flycatcher-warblers *Seicercus*,
could have proved invaluable in ensuring the survival of *Phylloscopus*
warblers in colder and more temperate climatic conditions. The *Phylloscopus* leaf warblers, *Locustella* grasshopper warblers and *Acrocephalus* reed
warblers probably originated from Asia and the typical *Sylvia* warblers
and *Hippolais* tree warblers around the Mediterranean Sea.

Table 1 shows the genera of the Old World warblers and the zoogeographical regions of the world. For the purpose of this list I have not
included the subfamily *Malurinae* or Australian wren babblers, or *Polioptilinae* the gnat-catchers and gnat-wrens of the New World. *Abroscopus* is
sometimes merged with *Seicercus* and *Chloropeta* is sometimes excluded.
Sharp boundaries cannot be drawn at the subfamily level but the table may
provide a useful guide.

Genera of the Old World Warblers   Table 1

Tesia (Ground warblers)	Incana (Socotra Grass Warbler)
Psamathia (Palau Bush Warbler)	Drymocichla (Red-winged Grey Warbler)
Cettia (Bush warblers)	Orthotomus (Tailor birds)
Bradypterus (Bush/scrub warblers)	Bathmocercus (Rufous warblers)
Cisticola (Cisticolas)	Artisornis (Forest warblers)
Prinia (Prinias)	Scepomycter (Mrs Moreau's Warbler)
Scotocerca (Streaked Scrub Warbler)	Eminia (Grey-capped Warbler)
Rhopophilus (Chinese Warbler)	Camaroptera (Camaropteras)
Locustella (Grasshopper warblers)	Euryptila (Kopje Warbler)
Megalurus (Grass warblers and Marshbirds)	Hypergerus (Oriole warblers)
Acrocephalus (Reed warblers)	Eremomela (Eremomelas)
Nesillas (Tsikirity/Comoro/Aldabra warblers)	Sylvietta (Crombecs)
Thamnornis (Kiritika)	Calamocichla (Madagascan Swamp Warbler)
Chloropeta (Yellow warblers)	Parisoma (Tit-warblers)
Hippolais (Tree warblers)	Randia (Rand's Warbler)
Sylvia (Typical warblers)	Chaetornis (Bristled Grass Warbler)
Abroscopus (Flycatcher-warblers)	Schoenicola (Broad-tailed Warbler)
Phylloscopus (Leaf warblers)	Bowdleria (Fernbird)
Seicercus (Flycatcher-warblers)	Megalurulus (New Caledonian Grass Warbler)
Regulus (Kinglets)	Cichlornis (Thicket warblers)
Leptopoecile (Tit-warblers)	Ortygocichla (Long-legged Warbler)
Apalis (Apalises)	Buettikoferella (Buettikofer's Warbler)
Graminicola (Large Grass Warbler)	Hylia (Green Hylia)
Sphenoeacus (Grassbirds)	Lamprolia (Silktail)
Dromaeocercus (Emu-tails)	

All the systematic classification of the Old World warblers has been fraught with difficulties and still remains controversial. The subfamily is generally understood to include the kinglets *Regulus* with both Goldcrest and Firecrest, later subjects of chapters in this book, two species of tit warblers *Leptopoecile*, goldcrest-like birds of scrub in central Asia and China, and the swamp-living fernbirds *Bowdleria* of New Zealand which with a number of species are beyond the scope of this volume.

In general the Old World warblers range in size from small (19 cm in the Great Reed Warbler) to very small (9 cm in Pallas's Warbler and the kinglets). They are on the whole rather plainly coloured with browns, greens, greys and sometimes yellows predominating. In most species the sexes tend to look alike but a few species, including the Blackcap, Rüppell's and Subalpine Warblers, reveal clear differences, and there are sexual differences too in the kinglets. There are many instances in which species resemble each other and their separation will depend upon small specific characters such as wing formulae and emargination of primary feathers being determined in the hand. In general the warblers occupy a very wide range of habitats from broad-leaved and coniferous trees to scrub, wetlands with or without reeds, grasslands, *maquis*, heathland and semi-desert. They forage constantly for insects and their eggs and larvae, spiders and other invertebrates. The bills of many are adapted to insect diets, but competition may be avoided by different feeding techniques or spacing, and some species become frugivorous in the autumn. The Old World warblers tend to live alone or in pairs but they may join up in flocks of other warblers or small passerines such as tits. While on their territories, the males of most species have clear audible territorial songs but others have buzzing songs in dense cover, simple repetitions of notes and are markedly mimetic. There are many interesting displays which are revealed among the Old World warblers, although they are somewhat stereotyped in form. Among the Sylviid warblers when reproductive fighting takes place the bill is not usually raised as in the families of thrushes, starlings and cardueline finches but it is often raised in courtship, and in this the warblers do resemble the thrushes (Andrew 1961). The lowering of the bill in male courtship can lead to the collection of nest-material and this has been reported for much of the *Sylvia*, *Acrocephalus* and *Locustella* groups. In the Whitethroat, copulation is immediately preceded by bill-lowering and in the young Garden Warbler (Sauer 1956) the movement is also accompanied by lateral tremblings of the bill which seem to be nest-material inserting movements. The vibrating of the wings is a very common form of male courtship in at least twenty-seven bird families and it has been recorded in all the *Sylviinae* for which observations exist. Old World warblers can also be seen raising their feathers and spreading their tails in reproductive fighting, the latter behaviour being a feature of the Parulid warblers as well. Simple crest-raising in male courtship has been observed in the Old World warblers and kinglets while a general raising of the feathers is regular in the typical *Sylvia* warblers and reed and leaf warblers. Crouching, wing-quivering and tail raising can be seen in species such as the Willow and Marsh Warblers. Wing-quivering often accompanies displays at nest-sites and may be marked by special notes as well.

Song is quite common among courtship displays of both the Old and New World warblers and this is probably adaptive in birds which live in dense cover. It tends to be softer in the presence of a female than the vocalization from a solitary male. Among the warblers it is very variable and matches the low subsong produced early in the breeding season. Mimicry is less common in birds whose songs are of a stereotyped kind, but it is a feature of many species that sing alone and do not employ display movements like the *Acrocephalus* warblers (Andrew 1961). Dr David Lack (1940) undertook a wide review of courtship feeding in birds – a piece of behaviour in which the begging movements of the young bird reappear in the adult. It has been recorded for the Old World warblers but appears to be uncommon and where it occurs it is described in the later chapters on individual species. Similarly, distraction displays to lure predators including man away from nests or young have been observed in these warblers. There are instances of a male Spectacled Warbler leading a cat some 40 m away from its young (Gibb 1947) and a Willow Warbler feigning injury before both a man and a tractor (Robertson 1954).

The Old World warblers will build their nests in dense foliage in trees and shrubs, sometimes in the field layer or ground zone and sometimes attached to the vertical stems of plants. The nests are generally cups open to the sky, purse-shaped or domed structures with side entrances. Some are simple platforms of twigs, roots or grass, lined with feathers or plant down, while others are cleverly woven structures slung between reeds, sedges or other plants. The nests of some are woven together with spider's webs. The males in certain species build 'cock's nests'. Tailor-birds *Orthotomus* stitch the edges of large hanging leaves together to form a fold in which the nest can be placed. The eggs tend to be rather standard in appearance with a ground colour of whitish, buffish, pinkish or greenish hue and very fine spots, sometimes zoned around the larger ends of the eggs. Clutches of at least 3–10 eggs may occur but in the British Isles, apart from the kinglets, the clutch-size is more likely to lie between 4–6. In some species such as the Leaf Warblers incubation is the responsibility of the female but in other genera, including those of the typical and Reed Warblers, both parents may be involved and it is normal for them also to feed and care for the young.

Relying very much on an insect diet, the Old World warblers may be resident where conditions permit, but most of those breeding in Europe

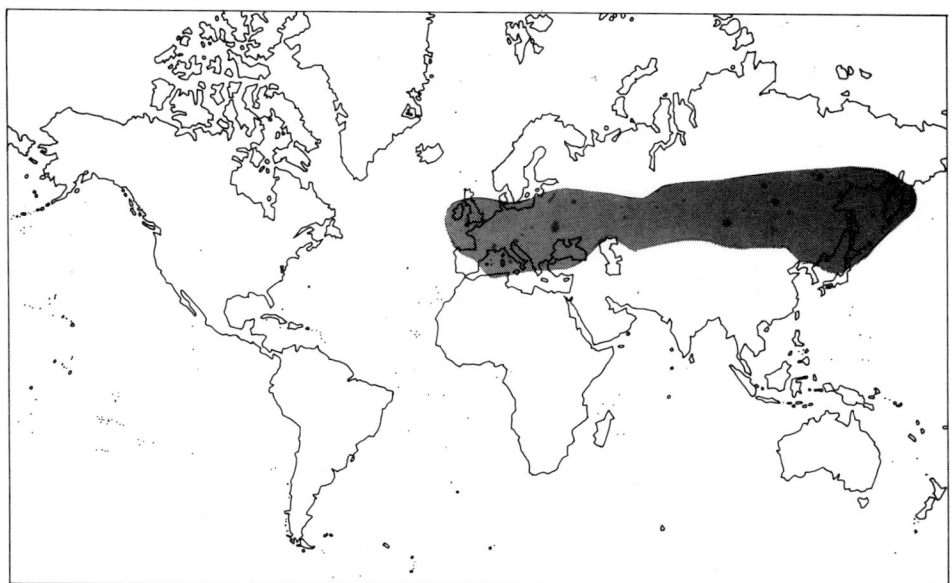

and the British Isles are migratory; they spend the winter months mainly in tropical Africa but also in parts of Asia. Some warblers carry out tremendously long journeys: Willow Warblers nesting in eastern Siberia have to reach their winter quarters in East Africa, while the Arctic Warbler travels from Fenno-Scandia to Indonesia and the Philippines. During the Ice Ages a greater proportion of birds of European origin would have crossed into Africa than does now, although the total number moving was probably smaller since much of Europe was quite unable to accommodate passerine birds. Nearly 50% of European Russia and more than half of the remainder of Europe was in the grip of ice or was covered with tundra so that the overall number of birds feeding on insects and relying on trees and shrubs would have been far smaller. Many found refuge in the winter north of the Sahara Desert, which was an area with a Mediterranean vegetative cover while the desert itself was much less wide and arid than it is today. Many of the migrants would also have had to face much shorter flights than they do in the twentieth century. Between each glaciation

Fig. 3
Outer breeding limits of Locustella *species.*

there would have been an amelioration in the climate and the improved weather conditions would have allowed trees to advance to the north again. Indeed between the second and third glaciations, broad-leaved trees advanced north almost to the White Sea. The third glaciation brought the ice as far south as Dollis Hill in north-west London (where my garden on the London Eocene clay was topped with glacial gravel); as it advanced south it succeeded in pushing birdlife out of most of Europe. If the birds now present in our broad-leaved woods such as the Blackcap, Whitethroat, Garden and Wood Warbler were present in the British Isles at this time they would have been badly affected. R. E. Moreau (1954) wrote that 'for most land-birds the post-Pliocene history has been a series of compressions and expansions of range on an enormous scale.'

The subfamily *Sylviinae* is made up of just over 300 species ranging chiefly as breeding birds throughout the Old World. Over 30 species are known to breed in Europe, over 150 in Africa and over 20 each in southeast Asia and Australia: one even straddles both the Old and New Worlds. Two genera are represented in the latter – *Regulus* and *Phylloscopus*; in the latter genus the Arctic Warbler, which was a Palaearctic bird, crossed from Siberia into Alaska after the Ice Ages but winters in the tropics of the Far East in the Old World. If we look at the breeding European warblers we find that there are twelve species in the genus *Sylvia* (typical warblers), seven in *Acrocephalus* (reed warblers), six in *Phylloscopus* (leaf warblers), five in *Hippolais* (tree warblers), three in *Locustella* (grasshopper warblers), two in *Regulus* (kinglets), and one each in *Cettia* and *Cisticola* (grass warblers). The current list of warblers for the British Isles includes eighteen breeding species and twenty-seven migrants and vagrants. Many of the European genera have sibling species – Chiffchaff and Willow Warbler, Reed and Marsh Warbler – which are best separated by their vocalizations and differences in habitat and behaviour.

The typical *Sylvia* warblers belong to quite a large genus which has differentiated chiefly in body size, with the Mediterranean species being generally smaller with longer legs and tails and the temperate ones rather larger in size. The body length of the more southern species ranges from 12–15 cm (the last figure being exceptional in the case of the Orphean Warbler) and an average length (taken from ten Mediterranean warblers) is 13 cm. The range of temperate species lies between 13.5–15 cm for body length with an average (for five warbler species) of 14.1 cm. The nominate *Sylvia* group includes some of the best known warblers such as the Blackcap, Garden Warbler and Whitethroat; all are active birds with rounded graduated tails. They frequent woodland, tall vegetation, and scrub, both luxuriant and desert. Most have two characteristic notes – a harsh churring sound and a sharp 'tacc' note – as well as sweet and pleasant warbled songs. All the members of the genus build open, rather loose nests tucked into a fork in twigs or herbage and rarely attached to vegetation. Some nests are close to the ground. Males often construct trial nests which could be just reflections of their internal breeding drive but have uses as decoys to confuse predators or as roosting platforms. The male often helps to build the nest and incubate the eggs, usually four or five in number, and both parents feed the young with insects brought in their bills. The young are usually naked and their mouth colour varies from orange to yellow or pink. Two dark spots at the base of the tongue are typical.

Another European genus of warblers is that of *Locustella* – the grass-hopper warblers which are named because many possess rather undistinguished buzzing or reeling songs that suggest certain kinds of grasshopper or bush-cricket. In fact, four species have songs of this type and three have more orthodox utterances. The genus consists of rather plain, brownish birds which are extremely shy by nature. They have round, almost graduated tails which appear heavy in flight – an activity that they normally avoid. They also have indistinct whitish eye-stripes. In general, grasshopper warblers live in dense scrub and thick ground cover, usually in wet or moist areas where they walk or run mouse-like through the vegetation, but the males may appear in exposed sites to sing territorial songs. B. Leisler (1977) has shown that the evolution of a walking locomotor pattern in this genus was an innovation of great significance, since it allowed birds to occupy and exploit dense ground zones covered with thick vegetation. The River and Grasshopper Warblers have a narrow gait and have become excellent walkers on the ground, slipping under and between obstacles without difficulty. Savi's Warbler has a wide gait and so tends to hop in slightly waterlogged conditions from stem to stem. The genus reveals considerable freedom of rotary movement in the joints of the hindlimbs and this permits greater ease of turning and creeping movements while the comparatively long femora and rather short tarsometatarsi are all well suited for walking actions. This use of the legs opens up a special habitat to a migratory insect-eating group while the rather narrow pointed wings are an adaptation for migratory flights. The genus has also differentiated itself by body size and occupies somewhat different habitats by species. The nests are over water, or on or near the ground, but in luxuriant cover where approach is difficult. They are often rather loosely built but tend to have deep cups. Both nest-building and incubation may be by both parents or by the female alone. The eggs number from 4–7 in the genus and incubation takes from 12–15 days. The young carry down on their heads and backs as well as having yellow mouths and gape flanges and three dark spots on the tongue.

The group-name of bush warblers is sometimes given to two species which are on the British list – Cetti's and the Fan-tailed Warblers – and to the Graceful Prinia *Prinia gracilis* (see Table 2) and the Streaked Scrub Warbler *Scotocerca inquieta* (see Table 2) which are not. Cetti's Warbler *Cettia cetti* is the only European member of a genus of some ten species which live in Asia. It has recently arrived as a breeding species in Britain where it frequents low moist cover. The genus *Cettia* is marked by long soft plumage, strongly rounded tails, thin narrow bills and a broad first primary about half as long as the second. The songs are loud and arresting. The females build bulky loosely-constructed nests where they incubate from 3–5 eggs. Polygyny is not unknown. The Fan-tailed Warbler *Cisticola juncidis* – a vagrant to the British Isles – belongs to a very large genus of so-called grass warblers of the Old World. Most of the species live in Africa where they occupy habitats of a grassy nature, but some can be found from the Mediterranean across Asia to Japan and south to Australia. They are primarily skulking birds of grassy fields and marshes, with simple songs which may first draw an observer's attention, since they are small, often dark-striped brownish birds. Their globe- or purse-shaped nests of plant fibre, down and cobwebs are amongst the most perfect examples of bird architecture. A loose connection of allied genera that is sometimes made by students of taxonomy not only includes *Cettia* and *Cisticola* but also *Bradypterus* – the bush warblers of scrub and marshes in the tropics and subtropics of Asia and Africa, while *Megalurus* – the canegrass warblers of Australia and southern Asia (see Table 1) – are often included as well.

The genus *Acrocephalus* – the reed warblers – contains over a score of species that inhabit wetlands and marshy places, including dense reedbeds, throughout the Old World, although the Sedge Warbler *A. schoenobaenus* can now be found in bushy places such as young conifer plantations, away from water. All the species tend to be brown or cinnamon-coloured above – some are clearly streaked on the back – and paler below with rounded tails. They form quite a difficult group but this is not an uncommon feature of the warblers. The Reed Warbler *A. scirpaceus* seems to differ in one respect from the rest. Birds scratch their heads in one of two ways – indirectly, in which a bird lowers one wing and brings up the leg on the same side and over the shoulder to the head, or directly in which the bird brings the foot straight up to the head without any previous movement of the wing (Simmons 1957). It was pointed out by Dr K. E. L. Simmons (1974) 'that, as an anomaly among all sylviids known, *A. scirpaceus* is "scratching directly".' It has been the differentiation in bill, legs and feet in the *Acrocephalus* species that has affected the adaptive radiation of this genus – something that will be more fully discussed in the chapters on individual species. The call notes tend to be rather similar and the songs harsh and repetitive but some may contain mimicries and in this last respect the Marsh Warbler *A. palustris* excels in variety, musical quality and imitations of other birds. These reed warblers are skulking by nature but can be seen singing from quite prominent perches. The nests are well-shaped cups woven around or bound to vertical stems of reeds, sedges and other plants. The eggs are of two types – finely mottled or boldly blotched. Clutches vary in size from 3–7 eggs and incubation, which may be by the female alone or by both parents, lasts from 11–15 days according to species. The nestlings are bare of down, have orange or yellowish mouths with yellowish gape flanges and two black spots at the base of the tongue. In the reedy marshes of Africa this genus appears to be replaced by the swamp warblers of the genus *Calamocichla*. By one of the African Rift Valley lakes I found the Greater Swamp Warbler *C. gracilirostris*, which is quite common in reeds – a habitat which also attracts *Acrocephalus* warblers as a wintering area.

The tree or *Hippolais* warblers are small warblers breeding in trees and bushes. They are uniformly coloured in greys, greens or yellows. They have broad, flat bills, square tails and high foreheads which help to distinguish them from the leaf warblers *Phylloscopus*. When excited they often raise the feathers on the crowns of their heads. As a genus *Hippolais* is close to *Acrocephalus*. The various species can best be separated by their distinctive, varied and babbling kinds of song, some of which are mimetic. The nests are deep cups in shrubs or small trees or even in the ground zone vegetation. The eggs are 4–6 in number, smooth and glossy and of a characteristic pink colour with delicate spotting. Incubation can be by the female alone or by both sexes and lasts from 12–13 days. The young are without down, have yellow mouths and gape flanges and two dark spots on the tongue.

It is possible to group the more than thirty species of the genus *Phylloscopus* – the leaf warblers – into clusters of species (Marshall and Pantuwattana 1969, Williamson 1976) but little is known about the inter-relationships. The leaf warblers are very small greenish or yellowish warblers that can be found almost everywhere in the Old World, breeding in the cooler parts of Eurasia and with many wintering in the tropics. Some species and forms are resident, some live high in the Himalayas and other mountain ranges in south-central Asia and descend to lower levels in winter and many are highly migratory. They often feed in the canopies of both broad-leaved and coniferous trees and may be rather difficult to observe. It is often necessary to establish recognition by songs and behaviour. When seen they reveal slightly forked tails and often flick their wings and tails. Songs range from the double notes of the Chiffchaff *Phylloscopus collybita* and Crowned Leaf Warbler, to the three notes of the Pale-legged Leaf Warbler *Phylloscopus tenellipes*, four or five of the Dusky Warbler *Phylloscopus fuscatus*, five or six of the Sulphur-bellied *Phylloscopus griseolus* and Tickell's *Phylloscopus affinis* Warbler and to various buzzes, trills, shivering sequences, cadences and plaintive notes of the more advanced singers. The Wood Warbler *Phylloscopus sibilatrix* has two types of song. The taxonomic position of the last species is in some doubt and Gaston (1974) was of the opinion that it might be in the process of forming an incipient genus.

The leaf warblers breed near trees and shrubs and construct domed nests with side entrances on or near the ground. The nests are generally very well concealed in low plants or dead leaves in the field layer or ground zone. The female builds the nest and incubates the eggs over a period of 13–14 days; the clutch size ranges from 3–9 eggs. Both parents usually tend the young but female Chiffchaffs seem to work harder than the males. The young have some thin greyish down on the head and shoulders, and mouths coloured yellow or orange.

The Goldcrests and Firecrests – *Regulus*, or kinglets – have been in the past placed in a different subfamily but they are now treated as members of the *Sylviinae*. Once linked to the tits *Paridae* they still remain slightly odd members of the Old World warbler group. They have rather loose, soft and fluffy plumages and dramatic head patterns and crests. There are two species in the Old World (three if the Formosan Firecrest is regarded as a true species and not a race of the Firecrest), and two in the New World. These are Europe's smallest birds, denizens of coniferous forests and sometimes broad-leaved forests, building the daintiest of moss and cobweb nests at great heights above the ground. They feed on minute insects and spiders and will join up in the winter with parties of tits and other birds to forage through the woodlands. Their songs and calls are extremely high-pitched. The female carries out the incubation alone and sits on the clutch which varies in size from 7–13 eggs for from 14–17 days. The young are tended by both parents. One curious feature of the genus *Regulus* are the arrangements by which the nostrils near the base of the bill with an operculum are partially covered by a single stiff feather, but the Ruby-crowned Kinglet of the New World has bristles.

In summing up we can say that the Old World warblers are small or very small, generally migratory birds with thin bills adapted for eating insects, although a few species may turn to berries and fruits in the autumn. Some have evolved physical traits, feeding techniques and migratory habits to exploit a range of different habitats. The sexes are generally similar in colour. These warblers differ from the thrushes and Old World flycatchers in having unspotted young. The tarsus may be scutellate or booted, and rictal bristles may be missing, slightly or strongly developed. In the *Sylvia* and *Phylloscopus* warblers some species undergo a complete moult between the end of the breeding season and the start of migration, while in others the post-nuptial moult is only partial and the feathers in the wings and tail are not replaced until the birds reach their wintering areas. *Hippolais* warblers largely moult in their winter quarters but the Booted Warbler *Hippolais caligata* seems to renew the body plumage before migration. In *Acrocephalus* there is some variation in moult with Reed Warblers enjoying a complete moult in Africa and the Sedge Warbler after a partial post-nuptial moult completing the process in Africa. Most *Locustella* warblers when adult seem not to undergo a complete moult until they reach their winter home. Kinglets in Europe appear to have an autumn moult. Fuller accounts of moult in individual species will appear in later chapters.

Dr K. H. Voous (1977) drew up an invaluable list of Holarctic bird species grouped in suborders, families, genera and species. He admitted more families than some other authors were prepared to do. In this Sylviid list he begins with species of tropical origin and closes with species which were 'supposed evolutionary newcomers in temperate and boreal regions that have found means to survive the Pleistocene glacial periods.' There are 105 species of 17 genera.

Table 2   *Warblers of the Holarctic region and the zoogeographical regions that they occupy*

Key:	P = Palaearctic region	N = Nearctic
	E = Ethiopian	O = Oriental
	A = Australasian	

Tesia castaneocoronata	Tesia or Chestnut-headed Ground Warbler PO
Cettia squameiceps	Short-tailed or Scaly-headed Bush Warbler PO
C. diphone	Chinese Bush Warbler POA
C. fortipes	Strong-footed Bush Warbler PO
C. major	Large Bush Warbler PO
C. flavolivacea	Aberrant Bush Warbler PO
C. acanthizoides	Verraux's Bush Warbler PO
C. brunnifrons	Rufous-capped Bush Warbler PO
C. cetti	Cetti's Warbler PO
Bradypterus thoracicus	Spotted Bush Warbler PO
B. major	Large-billed Bush Warbler PO
B. tacsanowskius	Chinese Bush Warbler PO
B. luteoventris	Brown Bush Warbler PO
Cisticola juncidis	Fan-tailed Warbler PEOA
Prinia gracilis	Graceful Prinia PEO
P. inornata	Plain Prinia O
P. criniger	Brown Hill Prinia O
P. atrogularis	Black-throated Prinia PO
Scotocerca inquieta	Streaked Scrub Warbler PO
Rhopophilus pekinensis	White-browed Chinese Warbler P

Key:	P = Palaearctic region	N = Nearctic
	E = Ethiopian	O = Oriental
	A = Australasian	

Locustella certhiola	Pallas's Grasshopper Warbler PO
L. ochotensis	Middendorff's Grasshopper Warbler PO
L. lanceolata	Lanceolated Warbler PO
L. naevia	Grasshopper Warbler PEO
L. fluviatilis	River Warbler PE
L. luscinioides	Savi's Warbler PE
L. fasciolata	Gray's Grasshopper Warbler POA
Megalurus pryeri	Japanese Marsh Warbler PO
Acrocephalus melanopogon	Moustached Warbler PEO
A. paludicola	Aquatic Warbler PE
A. schoenobaenus	Sedge Warbler PEO
A. sorgophilus	Chinese Sedge Warbler or Speckled Reed Warbler PO
A. bistrigiceps	Von Schrenck's or Black-browed Reed Warbler PO
A. concinens	Blunt-winged Paddyfield Warbler or Swinhoe's Reed Warbler PO
A. agricola	Paddyfield Warbler PO
A. dumetorum	Blyth's Reed Warbler PEO
A. brevipennis	Cape Verde Islands Cane Warbler P
A. palustris	Marsh Warbler PE
A. scirpaceus	Reed Warbler PE
A. stentoreus	Clamorous Reed Warbler PEO
A. arundinaceus	Great Reed Warbler PEOA
A. aëdon	Thick-billed Warbler PO
Hippolais pallida	Olivaceous Warbler PE
H. caligata	Booted Warbler PO
H. languida	Upcher's Warbler PO
H. olivetorum	Olive-tree Warbler PE
H. icterina	Icterine Warbler PE
H. polyglotta	Melodious Warbler PE
Sylvia sarda	Marmora's Warbler P
S. undata	Dartford Warbler P
S. deserticola	Tristram's Warbler P
S. conspicillata	Spectacled Warbler P
S. cantillans	Subalpine Warbler PE
S. mystacea	Ménétries's Warbler PE
S. melanocephala	Sardinian Warbler PE
S. melanothorax	Cyprus Warbler P
S. rüppelli	Rüppell's Warbler PE
S. nana	Desert Warbler PO
S. leucomelaena	Arabian or Blanford's Warbler E
S. hortensis	Orphean Warbler PEO
S. nisoria	Barred Warbler PEO
S. curruca	Lesser Whitethroat PEO
S. communis	Whitethroat PEO
S. borin	Garden Warbler PE
S. atricapilla	Blackcap PE

Key: P = Palaearctic region   N = Nearctic
            E = Ethiopian   O = Oriental
            A = Australasian

Seicercus burkii	Yellow-eyed Flycatcher Warbler PO
Abroscopus albogularis	White-throated Flycatcher Warbler PO
A. schisticeps	Black-faced Flycatcher Warbler PO
Phylloscopus umbrovirens	Brown Woodland Warbler PO
Ph. ricketti	Slater's or Black-browed Leaf Warbler POA
Ph. cantator	Yellow-faced or Black-browed Leaf Warbler PO
Ph. davisoni	Oates's Leaf Warbler PO
Ph. reguloides	Blyth's Crowned Leaf Warbler PO
Ph. coronatus	Eastern Crowned Leaf Warbler PO
Ph. occipitalis	Western Crowned Leaf Warbler PO
Ph. tenellipes	Pale-legged Leaf Warbler PO
Ph. tytleri	Slender-billed Leaf Warbler PO
Ph. nitidus	Green or Bright-green Leaf Warbler PO
Ph. plumbeitarsus	Two-barred Greenish Warbler PO
Ph. trochiloides	Greenish Warbler PO
Ph. magnirostris	Large-billed Leaf Warbler PO
Ph. borealis	Arctic Warbler NPO
Ph. pulcher	Orange-barred Leaf Warbler PO
Ph. maculipennis	Ashy-throated or Grey-faced Leaf Warbler PO
Ph. proregulus	Pallas's Warbler PO
Ph. subviridis	Brooks's Leaf Warbler PO
Ph. inornatus	Yellow-browed Warbler PO
Ph. schwarzi	Radde's Warbler PO
Ph. armandii	Milne-Edwards's or Buff-browed Leaf Warbler PO
Ph. fuscatus	Dusky Warbler PO
Ph. fuligiventer	Smoky Warbler O
Ph. griseolus	Sulphur-bellied Warbler PO
Ph. affinis	Tickell's or Chinese Leaf Warbler PO (includes *subaffinis* Ogilvie-Grant's Warbler)
Ph. bonelli	Bonelli's Warbler PE
Ph. sibilatrix	Wood Warbler PE
Ph. neglectus	Plain Leaf Warbler PO
Ph. sindianus	Mountain Chiffchaff PO
Ph. collybita	Chiffchaff PEO
Ph. trochilus	Willow Warbler PE
Regulus calendula	Ruby-crowned Kinglet N
R. regulus	Goldcrest PO
R. ignicapillus	Firecrest P
R. satrapa	Golden-crowned Kinglet N
Leptopoecile sophiae	White-browed Tit Warbler PO
L. elegans	Crested Tit Warbler PO

Warblers in the British Isles CHAPTER 3

When Europe lay in the severest and most extensive grip of the Ice Ages there were virtually no trees growing north of the Alps, the Pyrenees and the Black Sea so that there were no woodland birds and consequently no warblers. During the last glaciation, when the ice sheet descended across Britain and Ireland only to the English Midlands, mid-Wales and the River Shannon estuary in Ireland, the tundra which covered south-eastern England experienced a mid-winter temperature of around − 20°C and a mid-summer one of 7°C. The land was still under permafrost and among the alpine and northern-flowering plants the tallest vegetation would have been that of dwarf willows and birch trees. Much of Europe was occupied by steppe country and as the ice eventually retreated large areas of that continent and Asia became grassy and bushy, ranging from the high cold steppes of Mongolia and Tibet to the low-lying warmer steppes of the Turkestan-Mediterranean regions. Many grazing animals roamed over the steppes and there were large numbers of rodents and the predators that fed upon them. Avian species typical of the low steppes of southern Europe and southwest Asia probably included the Moustached and Cetti's Warblers, Blyth's Reed Warbler, the Booted Warbler and Sardinian Warbler. Others may have survived the Ice Ages around the more temperate regions of the Mediterranean and Asia and many would have occupied the riverine vegetation – Savi's, Grasshopper, Sedge, Reed, Great Reed and Barred Warblers and both Common and Lesser Whitethroats. The British Isles were probably too waterlogged and damp for typical steppe country to form. Today the continental steppes represent a giant kind of ecotone between the northern forested taiga and the southern deserts.

North of the steppes lies a broad belt of coniferous trees – the taiga – and the Siberian taiga covers a region a third or more larger than the area of the United States. The coniferous trees are, for example, firs, larches and pines or 'cedars' with a mixture of deciduous trees such as alder, rowan, willow and birch growing on heathy and often damp ground. If the taiga is burned or otherwise destroyed, birch and aspen, for example, will grow readily in the light conditions but are doomed to eventual shading out by the conifers. The undergrowth of the taiga consists of dwarf willows, juniper, *Vaccinium*, rose, meadowsweet and sedges. Because the Russian taiga advanced northwards fairly soon after the end of the Ice Ages its existing plants and wildlife are considerably older than those of the northern coniferous forest regions of Europe. Indeed some of the Siberian taiga birds, by moving westwards in due course, helped to repair the losses in the European area. Typical warblers of the taiga are the Arctic, Greenish and perhaps Radde's Warbler.

With improving conditions in Europe birds based in the Mediterranean region that moved northwards into Europe include the Blackcap, Garden Warbler, Aquatic and Marsh Warblers, Icterine, Wood and Bonelli's

Warblers. Birds of the Mediterranean type now embrace the following warblers: Melodious, Olivaceous, Olive-tree, Orphean, Spectacled, Sub-alpine, Dartford, Marmora's and Rüppell's. Palaearctic warblers typical of the cooler, more temperate and subtropical regions are the River Warbler, Paddyfield Warbler, Willow Warbler, Chiffchaff and Goldcrest.

In the British Isles in the pre-Boreal climatic phase that started about 8000–7500 BC, with warmer summers following on the cold tundra period, birch trees pushed northwards on the heels of the retreating arctic heaths. Scots pine was soon to follow and smaller amounts of oak, hazel, elm and alder. In the early period when birch was dominant there would have been a particular avifauna in the woods. By looking at the present birdlife in Fenno-Scandian birchwoods, where the Willow Warbler is the commonest bird, we find that the characteristic species in that ecosystem in pre-Boreal Britain would almost certainly have contained Meadow Pipit, Redwing, Ring Ouzel, Fieldfare, Reed Bunting and Redpoll. The Northern Willow Warbler of Lapland belongs to a different race from that of Britain so some racial divergence was able to take place. The Garden Warbler breeds further north in Europe than the Blackcap but the former species is not a common bird in Lapland. Each year the date on which the snow cover disappeared from the ground would have been crucially important so that the breeding of Willow Warblers, for example, would have varied from year to year. However, since it is light which is the most important factor regu-lating bird activities in the Arctic (Armstrong 1954), it is not possible to deduce exactly the differences which probably existed between the birch-woods of Britain today and those of Fenno-Scandia.

In mid-Boreal times, around 6000 BC, the ground dried out and, although birch held on strongly in Wales, Scotland and northern Ireland, Scots pine made considerable advances through England. In the end a large part of the British Isles was colonized by pine but today only a few relics of this Boreal forest survive in Scotland. Several species of bird are confined to these coniferous forests but Willow Warblers and Goldcrests are common. I have always enjoyed walking through these pinewoods amongst trees nearly three hundred years old with their orange-red boles and domed, bottle-green canopies, or amongst the younger trees shaped like cones or pyramids. The air is redolent with the scent of resin and the ground below the trees is green with ling or bell-heather, blaeberry and cowberry; here orchids and chickweed wintergreen flourish in the spaces between the trees. The region is full of the sweet songs of Willow Warblers in the birch scrub, the trillings of Crested Tits, the thin refrains of Goldcrests, the robust ditties of Chaffinches as well as snatches of song from Whinchats, Redstarts and Meadow Pipits. Crossbills fly over with deep 'tyoop-tyoop' calls, Ospreys pass on their way to fish in the lochs or rivers, Buzzards soar on broad pinions as one walks through the pine forests which provide a link with the Ice Ages. Here I have spent some of the happiest hours of my life and 'for perfect peace there is a tiny little-known lochan where I can listen to a gentle chain of Goldcrest's songs and the soothing plop of trout rising in an ever-widening ripple of activity' (Simms 1979). Even among the pines planted and growing on the sandy heaths of southern England the Willow Warbler and Goldcrest are common, drawn to these areas of birch and conifer.

Between 5500–2500 BC, still with a sustained high temperature but growing moister, brought about by the cutting of the land bridge with the Continent and a change in air flow (Stamp 1946), broad-leaved trees achieved dominance over the Scots pine and birch. Sessile and pedunculate oaks, limes, ash, elms and alders advanced northwards. Later arrivals included beech, hornbeam, whitebeam, field maple and poplars which remained on the whole confined to lowland Britain. Oak flourished on the clays and loams of England and in the highlands, and ash, beech and yew on thin chalk and limestone soils. Ireland was separated early from Britain and the flora and fauna are marked by notable absentees. The native trees do not, of course, include those species that failed to move out of their bridgehead in southeast England. There are about fifty species of bird that breed regularly in Britain that cannot be found in Ireland; the missing warblers are the Reed, Marsh and Dartford Warblers and Lesser Whitethroat and among the new colonists the Firecrest, and Cetti's and Savi's Warblers. The common breeding warblers in Ireland are Grasshopper, Sedge and Willow Warblers, Whitethroat, Blackcap and Goldcrest while Garden and Wood Warbler occur in smaller numbers. The bird species that would have come north with the returning broad-leaved woodlands are likely to have included the woodpeckers, Nuthatch, Wryneck, Kite, Nightingale, Hawfinch, Great and Marsh Tits and three warblers that form an important part of the bird community – Garden and Wood Warblers and Blackcap. Some of the species such as the Willow Warbler which were brought in with pine and birch adapted themselves to fully broad-leaved woods, while the Goldcrest, despite appearing in oakwoods for example, still remained tied to conifers for actual nesting. With the advent of the wetter Atlantic period, oak forest became the most significant woodland climax type in the British Isles and with the subsequent weather conditions would have remained so if man had not directly intervened.

For the ornithologist early morning is the best time to study and enjoy the warbler species that breed in the British Isles. An English pedunculate oakwood in spring is an attractive place. It is starred with yellow celandines and silvery wood anemones while creamy primroses and great cerulean swaths of bluebells carpet the ground. I well remember mornings spent in a Midland wood waiting to anticipate the passage of dawn as it swept across the British Isles from northeast to southwest. Robin, Blackbird and Song Thrush were the earliest singers and on one late May morning I noted the first warbler – a Garden Warbler – at 0311 hrs (GMT), then a Blackcap at 0318, Chiffchaff at 0325 and Willow Warbler at 0346. As the number of singers grew and the dawn chorus began to swell in volume so individual performers tended to be swamped by the noise. That latter morning dawn was at 0356 GMT. In the sessile oakwoods of highland Britain Wood Warblers sing alongside Pied Flycatchers and Redstarts and in May 1968 I found Wood Warblers the commonest singing birds in the sessile woods near Morar on the west coast of Scotland. They are also common in sessile woods in Wales and on Deeside in Scotland. Irish sessile woods have a rich field layer like that of an English lowland pedunculate wood and here the Willow Warbler is regular and 'the Chiffchaff is common in sessile woods although in general it is absent from other woods of this species in Britain' (Simms 1971). After a study of hundreds of woods in the British Isles I remain convinced that if all other things are equal it is not the species of oak that affects the size and variety of the bird communities present but rather 'the actual structure and formation of the wood, the distribution, age and height of the trees and the composition and richness of the shrub layer.' The pedunculate oak can support up to 227 different kinds of herbivore: moths and their larvae, bugs, thrips, mites, aphids and beetles thus provide a rich food resource for insectivorous birds. Ash woods, especially in Ireland, will contain Willow Warblers and Chiffchaffs in some numbers although the ash tree has a thin invertebrate fauna with only 22 kinds of insect and mite. I have found beech woods rich in Blackcaps, Willow Warblers, Chiffchaffs and Wood Warblers while Scottish alderwoods often contain numbers of Willow Warblers and Goldcrests.

With the loss of many of our broad-leaved woods, scrub – the growth of young trees amongst other shrubs, plants and rough grass – has an important part to play in the ecology of many of our warbler species. Scrub is a habitat or ecotone halfway between forest and prairie and is rich in hawthorn and other spiny shrubs, such as blackthorn and rose, hazel, elder and young oaks and ashes. Woodland scrub is dynamic in its nature and will eventually become forest. It is often the home of Whitethroats of both species, Willow Warblers and, where grassy, Grasshopper Warblers as well. It is possible that in the first place Whitethroats and Willow Warblers were birds of scrub that colonized the woodlands rather than being refugees from the felled forests. Old overgrown hedgerows and coppiced woods also formed a scrub habitat. Similarly the new conifer plantations of the state forests in their thicket stage before brashing were of a scrubby nature and here it was possible to trace a succession of warblers of grassland, scrub and finally mature woodland.

From about 700–550 BC even wetter conditions prevailed in the British Isles and in many areas pine and birch gave way to large areas of blanket-bog – a climatic soil type where the rainfall is high and the surface remains waterlogged. From around 400–1200 AD, northern Europe and Britain enjoyed a milder climate when grapes were widely harvested in England, but another cold period from 1200 AD led to an increase in the blanketbog cover. Since then the weather has been up and down but a mean rise in temperature between 1900 and the middle of the twentieth century saw such species as Garden and Wood Warbler, Chiffchaff and Whitethroat advancing into northwest Scotland, and the westward movement of Siberian species. (More recent changes are discussed in Chapter 35 of the present volume.)

To find the *Acrocephalus* warblers one needs to visit the damp habitats and wetlands – the fenny wildernesses of mere and scrub which attract the Sedge Warblers, the osier-beds and sedgy ditches where the Marsh Warblers sing and those ecotones of mixed swamp and shrubby growth where I have heard Grasshopper and Savi's Warblers reeling away, the short snatches of declaimed song from Cetti's Warblers, the contralto notes of Garden Warblers in the thorns and perhaps in the distance the monotonous chatters of Reed Warblers among the reed fronds. These watery landscapes and wild places are rare and cherished habitats indeed – survivors of the great fens drained by Vermuyden and other engineers, now growing cereals or sugar-beet and still shrinking bit by bit each year. Some have been preserved as nature reserves where many of the old wetland species of bird have lived on, or like Minsmere consist of land once deliberately flooded to stop invasion. To seek out the wetland warblers among the bending, hissing reeds and the clumps of thorny scrub, with the scent of damp rotting vegetation and black ooze in one's nostrils, is a rare experience indeed and yet the 'slodgers' or fenmen regarded these watery regions as home.

It is also just as rewarding to walk across the heathlands of southern England – an equally rare and precious habitat. They are somewhat barren areas on rather acid soils and unfold towards the horizon as flat-topped plains covered in pale ling and purple bell-heather while gorse, bracken, tough grasses and occasional self-sown pine or birch grow like a thick stubble across the landscape. The better-drained regions support the trees while the boggier parts hold scarce plants and dragonflies. These heaths are the home of uncommon butterflies, rare reptiles and that shy, skulking and outstandingly vulnerable bird, the Dartford Warbler. Once

The habitats occupied by sixteen species of British breeding warbler   Table 3

Species	Broad-leaved wood or scrub	Boreal pine forest	Conifer plantation Thicket	Conifer plantation Mature	Mixed woods	Heath, with birch	Wet land	Farm land	Hedgerow	Urban	Total
Willow Warbler	●	●	●	●	●	●		●	●	●	9
Whitethroat	●	●	●			●		●	●	●	7
Garden Warbler	●		●		●			●	●	●	6
Goldcrest	●	●	●	●	●					●	6
Chiffchaff	●		●		●			●	●		5
Grasshopper Warbler	●		●			●	●		●		5
Sedge Warbler			●				●	●	●		4
Blackcap	●				●			●		●	4
Firecrest	●			●	●						3
Lesser Whitethroat	●		●						●		3
Wood Warbler	●					●					2
Marsh Warbler							●	●			2
Cetti's Warbler							●				1
Reed Warbler							●				1
Savi's Warbler							●				1
Dartford Warbler						●					1

resident on many of the commons south of London – the bird was separated
in 1787 at Bexley Heath near Dartford – and on some to the north of the
capital the Dartford Warbler was forced to retreat as London grew out-
wards, destroying the heaths and bringing noise and disturbance. It could
not adapt because of the specific nature of its habitat. If one is fortunate
enough to visit a heath on a sunny morning when the Dartford Warbler is
launching himself upwards in song the experience is a captivating one
indeed. However, London and other cities have not proved a total desert
for all warbler species. Willow Warblers nest along disused railway tracks,
on allotments and sometimes in the central Royal Parks where Blackcaps
may also hold territories, encouraged by the Clean Air Acts which have
brought benefit to the insect species on which they feed. Sedge Warbler
and Whitethroat have bred at the disused Surrey Docks and even the Reed
Warbler, once common along the River Thames, breeds at Lonsdale Road
and Barns Elm Reservoirs in Surrey near the river. Further out from the
city centre the typical and leaf warblers are better represented.

The situation among the warblers of the British Isles is a dynamic one
with sometimes traditional species declining through factors outside the
country as well as inside, lost birds returning and new ones arriving. This
is part of the fascination of the study of warblers and for that matter any
group of birds. Table 3 (p. 33) illustrates the adaptability or success shown
by British warblers in occupying different kinds of habitat. Ten habitats are
included, and the final column on the right of the table which gives the
total actually occupied by the different species of warbler is a factor of
success.

From Table 3 one can see that the Willow Warbler is able to exploit the
greatest number of potential habitats in the British Isles and the Reed,
Cetti's, Savi's and Dartford Warblers the least number. The table is not an
indication of total numbers since the Firecrest, for example, has a figure as
low as 3 but there is no shortage of Norway spruce plantations which are
the most favoured habitat. Any species in the British Isles which scores 2
or 1 must be regarded as vulnerable, and where the total number of pairs
for three of these species is under 600 their fragile position is clearly shown.
Table 4 gives some indication of the total number of pairs of the sixteen
species of warbler breeding in Britain and Ireland.

Table 4   *Total numbers of breeding pairs of warblers in the British Isles*

Species	Population ranges		
Willow Warbler	3,000,000	Cetti's Warbler	60
Goldcrest	1,000,000	Firecrest	15
Whitethroat	500,000–700,000	Savi's Warbler	5
Chiffchaff	300,000		
Sedge Warbler	300,000		
Blackcap	200,000		
Garden Warbler	60,000–100,000		
Reed Warbler	40,000–80,000		
Wood Warbler	30,000–60,000		
Lesser Whitethroat	25,000–50,000		
Grasshopper Warbler	25,000		
Dartford Warbler	500	(based on *The Atlas* (1976),	
Marsh Warbler	50–80	Parslow (1973) and *British Birds*)	

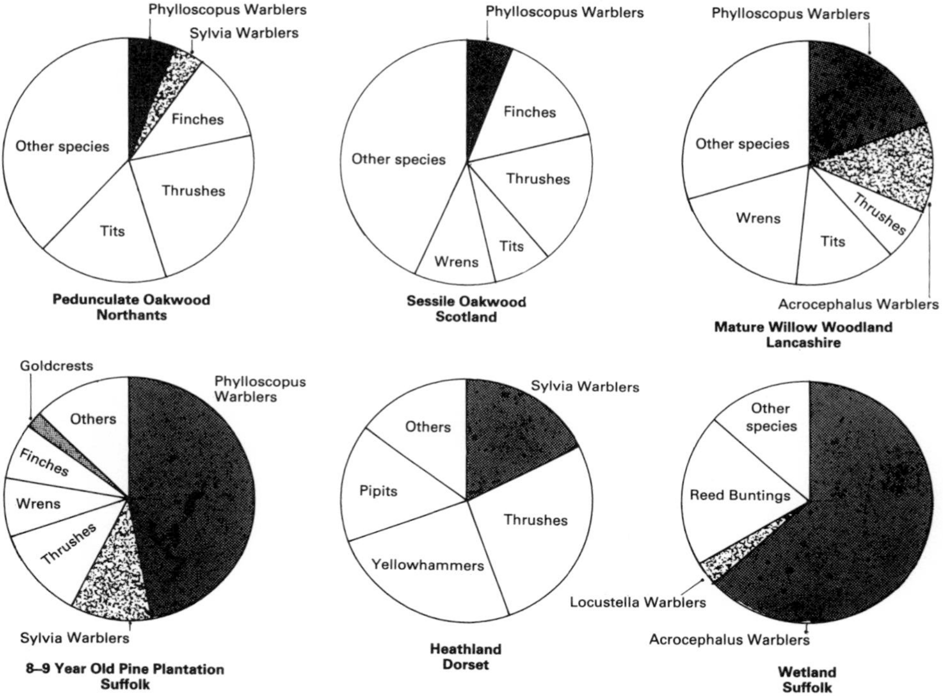

Pedunculate Oakwood Northants

Phylloscopus Warblers
Sylvia Warblers
Finches
Other species
Thrushes
Tits

Sessile Oakwood Scotland

Phylloscopus Warblers
Finches
Other species
Thrushes
Tits
Wrens

Mature Willow Woodland Lancashire

Phylloscopus Warblers
Other species
Wrens
Thrushes
Tits
Acrocephalus Warblers

8–9 Year Old Pine Plantation Suffolk

Goldcrests
Others
Phylloscopus Warblers
Finches
Wrens
Thrushes
Sylvia Warblers

Heathland Dorset

Sylvia Warblers
Others
Pipits
Thrushes
Yellowhammers
Locustella Warblers

Wetland Suffolk

Other species
Reed Buntings
Locustella Warblers
Acrocephalus Warblers

Fig. 4 (*above*)
*Dominance (percentage of total pairs)
for different habitats (after Simms 1971
and unpublished, and Wilson 1978).*

Fig. 5
*Distribution of singing males of 7 warbler
species in a Lincolnshire conifer
plantation with some broad-leaved
scrub. (Eric Simms)*

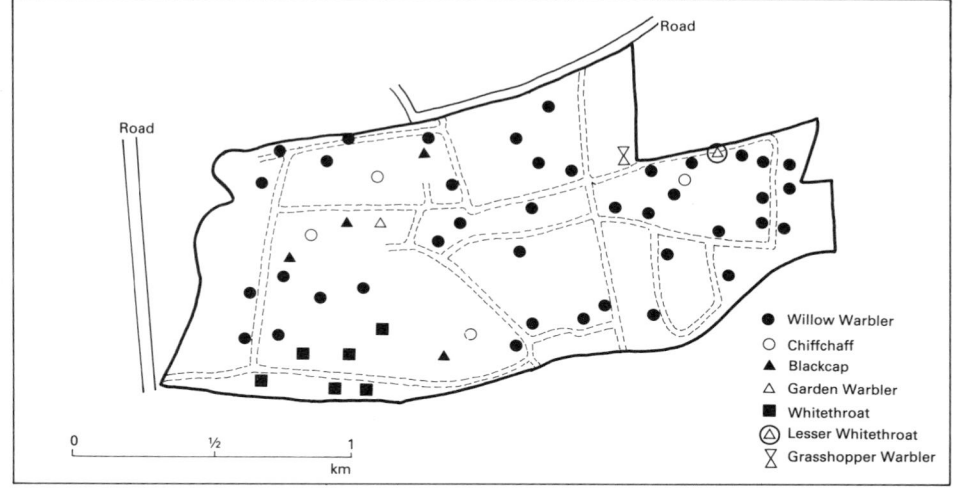

Road
Road

● Willow Warbler
○ Chiffchaff
▲ Blackcap
△ Garden Warbler
■ Whitethroat
⊘ Lesser Whitethroat
⋈ Grasshopper Warbler

0   ½   1
km

Table 5 Scientific and vernacular names of British warblers

Breeding species	Scientific name	French name	German name	Swedish name	Dutch name
Cetti's Warbler	Cettia cetti	Bouscarle de Cetti	Seidensänger	Cettisångare	Cetti's zanger
Grasshopper Warbler	Locustella naevia	Locustelle tachetée	Feldschwirl	Gräshoppsångare	Sprinkhaanrietzanger
Savi's Warbler	Locustella luscinioides	Locustelle luscinoïde	Rohrschwirl	Vassångare	Snor
Moustached Warbler	Acrocephalus melanopogon	Lusciniole à moustaches	Tamariskensänger	Tamarisksångare	Zwartkoprietzanger
Sedge Warbler	Acrocephalus schoenobaenus	Phragmite des joncs	Schilfrohrsänger	Sävsångare	Rietzanger
Marsh Warbler	Acrocephalus palustris	Rousserolle verderolle	Sumpfrohrsänger	Kärrsångare	Bosrietzanger
Reed Warbler	Acrocephalus scirpaceus	Rousserolle effarvatte	Teichrohrsänger	Rörsångare	Kleine karekiet
Dartford Warbler	Sylvia undata	Fauvette pitchou	Provencegrasmücke	Provencesångare	Provencegrasmus
Lesser Whitethroat	Sylvia curruca	Fauvette babillarde	Klappergrasmücke	Ärtsångare	Braamsluiper
Whitethroat	Sylvia communis	Fauvette grisette	Dorngrasmücke	Törnsångare	Grasmus
Garden Warbler	Sylvia borin	Fauvette des jardins	Gartengrasmücke	Trädgårdssångare	Tuinfluiter
Blackcap	Sylvia atricapilla	Fauvette à tête noire	Mönchsgrasmücke	Svarthätta	Zwartkop
Wood Warbler	Phylloscopus sibilatrix	Pouillot siffleur	Waldlaubsänger	Grönsångare	Fluiter
Chiffchaff	Phylloscopus collybita	Pouillot véloce	Zilpzalp	Gransångare	Tjiftjaf
Willow Warbler	Phylloscopus trochilus	Pouillot fitis	Fitis	Lövsångare	Fitis
Goldcrest	Regulus regulus	Roitelet huppé	Wintergoldhähnchen	Kungsfågel	Goudhaantje
Firecrest	Regulus ignicapillus	Roitelet à triple bandeau	Sommergoldhähnchen	Brandkronad kungsfågel	Vuurgoudhaantje

Migrant and vagrant species

Fan-tailed Warbler	Cisticola juncidis	Cisticole des joncs	Cistensänger	Grässångare	Waaierstaartrietzanger
Pallas's Grasshopper Warbler	Locustella certhiola	Locustelle de Pallas	Streifenschwirl	Starrsångare	Siberische snor
Lanceolated Warbler	Locustella lanceolata	Locustelle lancéolée	Strichelschwirl	Träsksångare	Temminck's rietzanger
River Warbler	Locustella fluviatilis	Locustelle fluviatile	Schlagschwirl	Flodsångare	Kreketzanger
Aquatic Warbler	Acrocephalus paludicola	Phragmite aquatique	Binsenrohrsänger	Vattensångare	Waterrietzanger
Paddyfield Warbler	Acrocephalus agricola	Rousserolle isabelle	Feldrohrsänger		
Blyth's Reed Warbler	Acrocephalus dumetorum	Rousserolle des buissons	Buschrohrsänger	Busksångare	Blyth's kleine karekiet

Breeding species	Scientific name	French name	German name	Swedish name	Dutch name
Great Reed Warbler	Acrocephalus arundinaceus	Rousserolle turdoïde	Drosselrohrsänger	Trastsångare	Grote karekiet
Thick-billed Warbler	Acrocephalus aëdon	Rousserolle à gros bec	Dickschnabelsänger		Vale spotvogel
Olivaceous Warbler	Hippolais pallida	Hypolaïs pâle	Blasspötter	Blek gulsångare	
Booted Warbler	Hippolais caligata	Hypolaïs russe	Buschspötter		
Icterine Warbler	Hippolais icterina	Hypolaïs icterine	Gelbspötter	Gulsångare	Spotvogel
Melodious Warbler	Hippolais polyglotta	Hypolaïs polyglotte	Orpheusspötter	Polyglottsångare	Orpheusspotvogel
Marmora's Warbler	Sylvia sarda	Fauvette sarde	Sardengrasmücke	Sardinsk sångare	Sardijnse
Spectacled Warbler	Sylvia conspicillata	Fauvette à lunettes	Brillengrasmücke	Glasögonsångare	Brilgrasmus
Subalpine Warbler	Sylvia cantillans	Fauvette passerinette	Bartgrasmücke	Vitskäggsångare	Baardgrasmus
Sardinian Warbler	Sylvia melanocephala	Fauvette mélanocéphale	Schwarzkopfgrasmücke	Sammetshätta	Kleine zwartkop-grasmus
Rüppell's Warbler	Sylvia rüppelli	Fauvette masquée	Maskengrasmücke	Svarthaked sångare	Rüppell's grasmus
Desert Warbler	Sylvia nana	Fauvette naine	Wustengrasmücke		
Orphean Warbler	Sylvia hortensis	Fauvette orphée	Orpheusgrasmücke	Mästersångare	Grote zwartkop
Barred Warbler	Sylvia nisoria	Fauvette épervière	Sperbergrasmücke	Höksångare	Gestreepte grasmus
Green Warbler	Phylloscopus nitidus	Pouillot vert	Kaukasus Grunlaubsänger		
Greenish Warbler	Phylloscopus trochiloides	Pouillot brillant (verdâtre)	Grünerlaubsänger	Lundsångare	Grauwe fitis
Arctic Warbler	Phylloscopus borealis	Pouillot boréal	Nordischerlaubsänger	Nordsångare	Noordse boszanger
Pallas's Warbler	Phylloscopus proregulus	Pouillot de Pallas	Goldhähnchenlaubsänger	Kungfagelsångare	Pallas's boszanger
Yellow-browed Warbler	Phylloscopus inornatus	Pouillot à grande sourcils	Gelbbrauenlaubsänger	Vitbrynad sångare	Bladkoninkje
Radde's Warbler	Phylloscopus schwarzi	Pouillot de Schwarz	Bartlaubsänger		
Dusky Warbler	Phylloscopus fuscatus	Pouillot brun	Dunklerlaubsänger		
Bonelli's Warbler	Phylloscopus bonelli	Pouillot de Bonelli	Berglaubsänger	Bergsångare	Bergfluiter

Figure 4 illustrates the dominance or percentage of total pairs in various habitats occupied by four genera of British warblers – *Sylvia* (typical), *Phylloscopus* (leaf), *Acrocephalus* (reed) and *Locustella* (grasshopper). In two of the examples warblers occupy more than 50% of the bird community. In the pedunculate oakwood in Northamptonshire, which provided me with the data for Figure 4, two genera of warblers – typical and leaf – take up 10.5% of the bird community, while in the sessile oakwood I visited in Scotland there is only one genus taking up just 3.3% of the community. In mature willow woodland – a scarce habitat in the British Isles – leaf warblers are the senior partners with reed warblers in the community but the total warbler representation is 32.5% of the whole (Wilson 1978). In a young pine plantation two genera of warblers and the Goldcrest have a 59.7% dominance. In one Suffolk wetland Reed Warblers occupied with Sedge Warblers 64.5% of the community and Grasshopper Warblers 2.5%.

Figure 5 shows the distribution of singing warblers of seven species in a coniferous plantation of unbrashed trees with broad-leaved scrub in south Lincolnshire. I have plotted the territory holding males of seven species of warbler belonging to three genera.

The purpose of Table 5 (p. 36) is to list the breeding species of warbler and the vagrants and migrants to the British Isles with their scientific names and those in use in four European countries.

Sylvia or Typical Warblers

There are certain regions of Europe where the members of the warbler genus *Sylvia* leave the ornithologist with a special memory, because they were perhaps the dominant singers or they formed a significant proportion of the composers of the bird chorus in that part of the world. For me the pure, rich notes of Blackcaps and the even-flowing uniform songs of Garden Warblers are as much an integral part of many Continental forests as they are of pedunculate oakwoods carpeted with bluebells in lowland England. Similarly, I remember with affection Dorset and New Forest heaths, now much reduced, for the musical chatters of Dartford Warblers, dancing above the yellow-starred gorse bushes as I have seen them above other kinds of scrub in France. I have wandered with pleasure across the arid regions of the Camargue in Provence watching the Spectacled Warblers launching their ditties from the clumps of low-growing salicornia. Commons and grasslands and the bramble-brakes, nettle-beds and hedgerows along the dusty roadsides attract the Whitethroats while the high uncut lines of thorn and scrub in Suffolk, overgrown gardens in Kent and even young conifer plantations hold their small quota of Lesser Whitethroats. I have, too, the clearest possible memories of Delphi in Greece on a misty, summer morning presaging a hot day with Orphean Warblers uttering their strong repeated notes from the sacred groves, Sardinian Warblers with their musical songs and Rüppell's 'rattling' in the scrub, Subalpine Warblers sweetly dancing in the air with a few Blackcaps and Whitethroats in the light woodland. The songs of the *Sylvia* warblers help in our identification of them as well as adding in many instances a profound aesthetic experience for us.

The nominate genus *Sylvia* embraces therefore a number of fairly common and well-known European species as well as several less familiar ones. All of them are active insect-eating birds: typical warblers, in fact. The evolutionary centre for this group of warblers apparently lies in the Mediterranean region and, except for one species – the Arabian Warbler – no bird of the genus *Sylvia* can be found breeding in Africa anywhere south of the Sahara. A small number have managed to move eastwards as far as Siberia but this would seem to be an event of comparatively recent date. Lesser Whitethroats may have moved west and north in the British Isles in the last fifty years. The Mediterranean species are somewhat smaller, while the graduated and rounded tails typical of the genus, as well as their legs, are longer than those of the more generalized and larger species that nest in the rather more temperate zones. The Palaearctic members of the genus have apparently experienced what Voous (1977) called 'secondary simplification' in both their anatomy and habits. If we take a Garden Warbler as an example we find that it displays a dull, unadorned plumage, has an uncompressed and unspecialized bill, builds a simple, open cup-shaped nest and lays spotted eggs. The rictal bristles

Fig. 6
*The aggressive display of
a* Sylvia *species; male
blackcap. (Eric Hosking)*

around the gape of the *Sylvia* warblers are not as well developed as in two
other genera – those of the *Hippolais* and the *Acrocephalus* warblers. The
sexes may resemble each other as in the Garden or Arabian Warblers but
more often than not they are different. In some species like the Blackcap
or Tristram's Warbler the sexual separation or dimorphism may be quite
pronounced.

All the members of the group share rather sharp monotonous 'tac-tac'
or 'tzig-tzig' notes and harsh churring calls. Their territorial songs are
warbles often of varied and pleasing notes, sometimes quite musical, while
others are simpler buzzing or scratchy ditties. The range is wide from the
rich soprano phrases of the Blackcap through the drier, sharper yet musical
song of the Barred Warbler to the tuneless rattle of the Lesser Whitethroat
and the hisses of Ménétries's Warbler. For birds that sing in dense woodland, scrub or the prickly *maquis* around the Mediterranean the songs still
remain fairly distinctive and prevent hybridization. Some of the species
indulge in short aerial display flights during which they increase the
advertizing value in open flattish terrain of their territorial songs. The
quality of the songs of some species puts them very high up in the order
of merit among avian songsters.

The genus *Sylvia* consists of a Palaearctic and Ethiopian group of seventeen species of which thirteen breed in Europe, twelve in Asia, eleven in
Africa and five in the British Isles. Eight species are also vagrants to the
British Isles. The following table lists the seventeen species as well as their
distribution and status.

Status of Sylvia warblers Table 6

Species	Breeding Status				Vagrants to British Isles	Status as migrants
	Europe	Africa	Asia	British Isles		
Marmora's Warbler *Sylvia sarda*	●	●			●	RPM
Dartford Warbler *S. undata*	●	●		●		R
Tristram's Warbler *S. deserticola*		●				M
Spectacled Warbler *S. conspicillata*	●	●	●		●	RPM
Subalpine Warbler *S. cantillans*	●	●			●	M
Ménétries's Warbler *S. mystacea*			●			M
Sardinian Warbler *S. melanocephala*	●	●	●		●	RPM
Cyprus Warbler *S. melanothorax*	●					R
Rüppell's Warbler *S. rüppelli*	●		●		●	M
Desert Warbler *S. nana*		●	●		●	RM
Arabian Warbler *S. leucomelaena*		●	●			R
Orphean Warbler *S. hortensis*	●	●	●		●	M
Barred Warbler *S. nisoria*	●		●		●	M
Lesser Whitethroat *S. curruca*	●		●	●		M
Whitethroat *S. communis*	●	●	●	●		M
Garden Warbler *S. borin*	●		●	●		M
Blackcap *S. atricapilla*	●	●	●	●		RM

(Code for last column: R = Resident, M = Migrant, PM = Partial Migrant)

The majority of these seventeen species undergo a complete post-nuptial moult. There is some doubt about the moult of the Cyprus Warbler which seems to experience an incomplete autumn moult. The Garden Warbler moults in its winter quarters, the Barred has a late summer and a winter quarters' moult and, while British Whitethroats have a post-nuptial change, those with an eastern distribution have a moult like that of the Garden Warbler. Since the Garden Warbler and the Whitethroats of the eastern race make a longer flight to the south than others of the *Sylvia* warblers, it is not very surprising that they are the only members of the genus to moult their flight feathers while they are in their winter quarters. A study of warblers wintering at Kampala in Uganda by D. J. Pearson (1973) revealed

Garden Warblers going through their complete moult between December and March; I have seen birds in Uganda in December, both adults with worn plumage and birds in their first winter, with light-tipped primaries. Long-distance migrants have evolved several strategies of wing-moult and Stresemann and Stresemann (1966) listed six – suspended moult, moult after autumn migration, moult before migration (post-nuptial), moult during the breeding season, moult before and after autumn migration (two full annual moults) and periodic step-wise moult. Some species suspend their moult for all or part of their migration. In fact, sixteen species of trans-Saharan migrants were found in Iberia to suspend or be about to suspend their wing-moult (Mead and Watmough 1976). Orphean Warblers and Common Whitethroats had largely renewed their feathers before

Table 7   *Dimensions and Weights of Sylvia warblers*

Species	Wing Range	Wing Mean	Tail Range	Tail Mean	Bill Range	Bill Mean	Tarsus Range	Tarsus Mean	Weights (gm)
Dartford Warbler	48–54	51.30	55–68	62.53	10–12	11.00	18–21	19.70	9.4
Spectacled Warbler	50–58	53.65	45–56	49.96	$10\frac{1}{2}$–13	11.66	$17\frac{1}{2}$–19	18.58	8.0–9.2
Subalpine Warbler	53–62	57.80	49–59	53.64	9–12	10.50	18–20	19.07	10.8–11.4
Sardinian Warbler *S.m. melanocephala*	53–62	57.49	54–65	59.38	$11\frac{1}{2}$–$13\frac{1}{2}$	12.58	19–22	20.86	10.8 (1st winter)
S.m. momus	53–59	55.54	51–60	54.79	$11\frac{1}{2}$–13		19–22		
Rüppell's Warbler	64–71	67.61	54–64	59.33	$13\frac{1}{2}$–16	14.52	20–22	21.08	
Desert Warbler	52–61	56.59	44–53	48.79	$9\frac{1}{2}$–$11\frac{1}{2}$	10.19	18–21	19.20	
Orphean Warbler	72–83	77.76	60–71	65.53	15–18	16.25	$22\frac{1}{2}$–25	23.46	19.4–21.2
Barred Warbler	83–90	86.33	64–79	70.44	$15\frac{1}{2}$–18	16.74	24–26	24.92	22.8
Lesser Whitethroat *S.c. curruca*	61–68	64.48	52–58	54.77	$10\frac{1}{2}$–13	11.66	19–21	20.42	10.9–12.4
S.c. blythi	59–69		52–62		11–13		20–22		
S.c. minula	58–65		50–58		11–$12\frac{1}{2}$		20–23		
S.c. margelanica	63–71		57–60		11–$12\frac{1}{2}$		20–23	21.18	
S.c. althaea	63–71		52–61		11–13	12.21	19–22		
Whitethroat	65–74	69.15	54–66	60.00	12–$13\frac{1}{2}$	13.17	21–$22\frac{1}{2}$	21.55	13.00
Garden Warbler	73–84	77.53	50–61	55.41	$12\frac{1}{2}$–15	13.76	20–22	20.76	16.6–17.2
Blackcap	68–78	73.00	53–65	59.06	13–15	14.31	20–$22\frac{1}{2}$	21.40	16.6–16.8

(after Williamson 1976)

migrating with only a few old ones remaining, while Garden Warblers had renewed very few. The whole strategy of moult has to take account of the bird's energy requirements, and suspending moult may be a compromise to maximize its resources. The timing of the moult is very much affected by the length of journeys undertaken and so a delay in undergoing moult until the birds have reached their destinations at the equator or in southern latitudes is to be expected.

Birds of the *Sylvia* group occupy a wide range of habitats – deep forest (both deciduous and mixed), open woodlands, forest edge, tall scrub and plantations, low shrubs with scattered trees, thickets, orchards, hedges, heathland, rocky hillsides, *maquis*, arid growth along water courses and even coarse vegetation in semi-desert regions. In their selection of breeding habitats these warblers are in essence birds of natural scrub. Some, such as the Blackcap and Garden Warbler, have become birds of open and mixed woodland but the latter is more regularly found away from large, maturer trees and in scrub and conifer plantations and the Blackcap in association with evergreens. Barred, Orphean, Sardinian and Subalpine Warblers are to a lesser extent woodland birds. Of the seventeen species, fourteen can be found breeding in scrub and even Blackcaps and Garden Warblers need a shrub layer in a wood for nesting. Where scrub exists in other forms such as hedgerows, gardens, orchards, olive groves and vineyards or even in the spiny *maquis* of the Mediterranean so the species are also well represented. The Dartford Warbler has become dependent in England on a specialized habitat of heaths with heather or gorse, but I have watched birds in France in the *maquis*. Two races of the Lesser Whitethroat and the Desert Warbler are associated with dry, semi-desert regions. Others have favoured hill slopes with few trees like *Sylvia curruca althaea*, or scrub on hill and mountain slopes like Rüppell's, Cyprus and Marmora's Warblers.

The nests of birds in this group are usually built in vegetation some way above the ground. They are in the form of simple cups, not usually woven to stems and branches but resting in a fork. In some instances the male warbler, which arrives on the breeding ground before the female, constructs the outer framework or platform for the nest. Male Blackcaps, Garden Warblers and Whitethroats will build these 'cock's nests' before the females appear from the south. The hen birds will exercise a choice – they may reject them, or select one which they then proceed to line with softer, finer material, or build an entirely new one by themselves. In a number of instances both members of a pair of *Sylvia* warblers will be jointly responsible for building the nest as well as incubating the eggs and tending the young, although in a few species the male plays a much reduced role. Male Blackcaps, Garden Warblers, Whitethroats, Lesser Whitethroats and Barred Warblers are among those that incubate and brood to some extent. All of these five species except the Whitethroat develop an incubation patch which is thought to be equally important in controlling both humidity and temperature (Efremov and Payeysky 1973). Dartford Warbler males do not develop brood patches (Bibby 1979). Clutches usually consist of from 4–5 often very variably-coloured eggs. Incubation takes from 10–11 days in some species but in others it may last for 12, 13 or even 15 days.

Whereas all the *Sylvia* warblers will eat insects and spiders and some like

Table 8   *Habitat selection of the Sylvia warblers in the breeding season in Europe*

Species	Broad-leaved woods	Mixed woods	Conifers	Scrub or *maquis*	Hedges	Orchards, gardens, olives	Heaths, commons	Hills and hill slopes	Arid, semi-desert
Marmora's Warbler				•					
Dartford Warbler							•		
Tristram's Warbler				•					
Spectacled Warbler				•					
Subalpine Warbler	•	•		•	•			•	
Ménétries's Warbler								•	
Sardinian Warbler *S.m. melanocephala*				•		•			
S.m. momus	•								
Cyprus Warbler				•				•	
Rüppell's Warbler				•				•	
Desert Warbler									•
Arabian Warbler				•					
Orphean Warbler	•	•		•		•			
Barred Warbler	•	•		•	•				
Lesser Whitethroat *S.c. curruca/blythi*			•	•	•	•			
S.c. minula									•
S.c. margelanica									•
S.c. althaea								•	
Whitethroat				•	•		•		
Garden Warbler	•	•	•	•	•	•			
Blackcap	•	•	•	•		•			

the Spectacled, Desert, Dartford, Marmora's and Rüppell's predominantly so, others such as the Blackcap, Garden, Barred, Orphean, Sardinian and Subalpine Warblers and both Whitethroats are able to switch in late summer and autumn to vegetable foods: soft fruits including orchard fruits, figs, oranges and grapes, berries, seeds and even peas. Indeed this ability to take vegetable and bird table scraps has enabled the Blackcap to survive in the British Isles during the whole of the winter. However, some of the primarily insect-eating birds have suffered in recent years when there has been a failure of the rains in their winter quarters. The population of breeding Whitethroats in Britain crashed after the winter of 1968-9 with 77% of the previous year's nesting stock failing to return in 1969.

Of the whole genus the Garden Warbler *Sylvia borin* with its failure to display any obvious characters is a difficult species. Indeed, young birds have sometimes been confused with different species of *Acrocephalus* because of a pronounced notch on the inner web of the second primary. A full and comprehensive key to the genus would be difficult to achieve anyway. The eastern populations of the Garden Warbler are somewhat greyer on the back than the western, but the difference is so slight that it seems no justification for regarding them as other than *Sylvia borin*. On the other hand several races of the Blackcap *Sylvia atricapilla* which are greyer, more olive or darker can be distinguished. The nominate race *S.a. atricapilla* occupies the British Isles and Europe south to the Mediterranean and east to Russia but it seems to intergrade with *S.a. dammholzi* which breeds from the Caucasus across to Iran and winters on and around Mount Kenya. There are also several island forms – *S.a. atlantis* in the Azores, *S.a. koenigi* in the Balearic Islands, *S.a. heineken* in Madeira and the Canary Islands and *S.a. paulucci* in Sardinia and Corsica. Of these the first two forms are more greyish-olive, the third darker and the fourth slightly greyer than the typical race.

Both Blackcap and Garden Warbler are primarily woodland species that nest quite commonly in England and Wales but less so in Scotland, and somewhat locally in Ireland. They are both very much lowland species breeding below 250 m. The distribution limits of the Blackcap lie somewhat more to the south than those of the Garden Warbler. There are differences in their choice of habitats although they and the two Whitethroat species could conceivably be found nesting in the same area of woodland. The Blackcap is a species of the high woodland canopy while the Garden Warbler favours more a mixture of scrub and broken woods. Blackcaps will also nest closer to the centre of towns, breeding in London's Royal Parks and in the suburbs. The Common Whitethroat is much more of a scrub bird while the Lesser Whitethroat likes tall thick hedgerows and scrub with more of a vertical structure.

The Common Whitethroat *Sylvia communis communis*, often known simply as the Whitethroat, and the commonest of all the *Sylvia* warblers nesting in Britain, is different from others in that the male possesses a unique combination of a pale grey cap reaching to the nape of the neck and below the eye, an obvious pure white throat and rufous wings. The female is duller with a brownish head but she also has the rufous wings and shares with her mate a rather long tail with white outer feathers. The Whitethroat is a restless bird of deeply tangled growth from which it may emerge with raised crest and fanned tail. The male has a brief staccato song quite unlike the rattle of the Lesser Whitethroat as well as various calls. *S.c. communis* breeds from northwest Africa and Europe east to the Crimea but grades into a greyer-brown and slightly larger eastern form *S.c. icterops*, which ranges from the eastern Mediterranean across Asia to the Altai, southwards to Baluchistan and Afghanistan and eastward of Sinkiang and northern Mongolia. Birds of the nominate race move south in the autumn to the Canary Islands and tropical and southern Africa, while the eastern form winters in northeast Africa from Somalia south to Zimbabwe. I have seen birds in Kenya in December. Little is known about another race *S.c. volgensis* from southeast Russia which is thought to winter in East Africa as well.

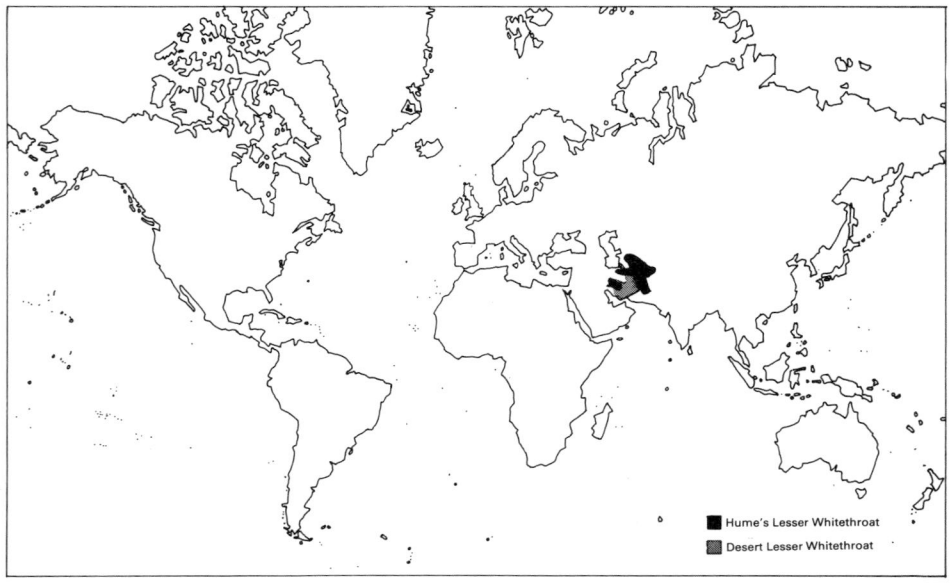

Fig. 7
Breeding ranges of Hume's Lesser White-throat and Desert Lesser Whitethroat.

The Lesser Whitethroat forms in effect a 'group' of small warblers but it is customary and easier to look upon them all as members of the same species. Two of them are typical of lowland trees and scrub – the Lesser Whitethroat of Europe and Caucasia *Sylvia curruca curruca* and the Eastern or, as it is also known, the 'Siberian' Lesser Whitethroat *S.c. blythi*; this last form is browner, more rufous perhaps, and has been drifted from its home in Siberia and other parts of Asia to Fair Isle and England. Two of the forms of Lesser Whitethroat can be found in a much more arid, semi-desert countryside – the sandy-brown *S.c. minula* of Central Asia and *S.c. margelanica*, which intergrades with *minula* but is characteristic of the region from the mountains of Tian Shan across to Mongolia. There is another race known as Hume's Lesser Whitethroat *S.c. althaea* which is a darker grey-brown and a bird of poorly wooded slopes on hills and mountains; it can be found in the Taurus Mountains to Turkestan, Iran and the northwestern Himalayas to 2000 m. *S.c. curruca* winters in Egypt, the Sudan, Ethiopia and Eritrea, *S.c. blythi* in southeast Iran, Afghanistan, Baluchistan, India and Sri Lanka, *S.c. minula* in Southern Arabia and northern India and *S.c. althaea* right through India and to Sri Lanka. The differences between all these races are very difficult to resolve and at least four other forms have been claimed as well. C. Vaurie (1954) looked upon the Desert Lesser Whitethroat, *minula*, and Hume's Lesser Whitethroat as two separate species each with at least two or even more geographical races. K. H. Voous (1977) includes the last two in *S. curruca* as one species and it seems reasonable to do the same here.

Fig. 8
The Desert Lesser Whitethroat (Sylvia curruca minula) *top, Lesser Whitethroat* (S.c. curruca) *centre, and Hume's Lesser Whitethroat* (S.c. althaea), *revealing increasing size and colour saturation in the three forms.*
(D. I. M. Wallace, South Iran, April 1972)

The four species – Garden Warbler, Blackcap, Whitethroat and Lesser Whitethroat – are closely related and breed widely in the British Isles. There are differences which suggest that despite overlaps in some habitats direct competition is on the whole avoided. It was clear from an examination of the succession in a broad-leaved wood (Ferry and Frochot 1970) that Whitethroats were at their greatest density in the beginning when the amount of grass equalled or surpassed that of scrub, and here they shared the ecosystem with Grasshopper Warblers. I found that Whitethroats were at their peak in young conifer thickets about eight years after planting (Simms 1971) and on the Burren in Eire they were the second commonest birds in hazel scrub below 1.3 m in height. The Whitethroats in the young woods preferred the scrub and the Grasshopper Warblers the grass. By the thirteenth year of the succession, as the trees shaded out the grass, both species of warbler disappeared. In the development of a broad-leaved wood the Garden Warbler can be found in the same area as the Whitethroat but at a later state when the scrub and tree growth reach from 1.5–3 m in height. The Blackcap reveals a later peak when the growth is from 3–5 m.

From a detailed analysis of 5066 nest-record cards held at the British

Trust for Ornithology, concerned with the five breeding *Sylvia* warblers in the British Isles, C. F. Mason (1976) was able to show not only these differences that I have described but others in their ecology. Most nests were built in bramble but there were variations in the height at which nests were constructed in secondary sites. Whitethroats nested closest to the ground and more frequently than the other species in grass and nettles, so justifying the vernacular name of 'nettle-creepers'. Lesser Whitethroats built higher, often selecting blackthorn and elder for their nests while Blackcaps showed a stronger preference for elder. I have found Blackcaps often using elders in oakwoods; this shrub was used by a pair that bred in 1958 in the suburban area of Dollis Hill in north-west London. After studying a Welsh oakwood J. M. and M. A. Edington (1972) recorded differences for the breeding warblers in food as well as their horizontal and vertical separation. They suggested that species select a 'refuge' during their habitat selection when there is competition between them. This refuge is an area which a particular species can and does exploit more fully and effectively than any of its possible competitors. If the competitors are not there or the habitat is not full up, then the birds can forage through and exploit the resources of a wider range of habitats. The effects of choosing a habitat or selecting a nest-site may establish such refuges and so reduce or even eliminate competition between species.

The actual recognition of species in the various habitats, which are often very dense and dark where visual clues cannot be easily seen, is achieved largely by calls and in the setting up, defence and maintenance of territories by song. Although for us there may be superficial likenesses between the songs of the Blackcap and the Garden Warbler, the birds themselves show a fine discrimination of the elements in their rapid out-bursts of territorial song: they reject the wrong signals and only respond to the right ones. With application it is soon possible for the ornithologist to distinguish the different songs. The male warblers set up territories and advertise and defend them by song until the females have also appeared. Garden Warblers arrive later than Blackcaps on the breeding ground, perhaps through the demands of food-gathering on migration or in their winter quarters, and they lay smaller clutches and enjoy a lower overall success through a marked reduction in the supply of insect food. There are overlaps and differences, not yet fully understood, in the food which is given to young *Sylvia* warblers. For example, Blackcaps and Whitethroats (Korodi-Gal 1965) feed mainly spiders and the larvae of butterflies and moths to their nestlings (Siefke 1962, Persson 1971) while Lesser White-throats in Bavaria mainly collect aphids for their young, but in the same district Whitethroats seem mostly to ignore them.

The fifth of Britain's breeding *Sylvia* warblers is the Dartford *Sylvia undata*. The species is highly sedentary and very local in its distribution in southern England for a variety of reasons. It also ranges through parts of western and southwest Europe and northwest Africa. Because of the nature of its distribution a number of different forms – up to seven according to some authorities – has evolved but Williamson (1976) chose to divide them into three 'trends'. There is a slate-grey 'Continental' trend *Sylvia undata undata* which can be found breeding in southern France, most of Spain but not the north, southern Portugal, Italy and the islands of Corsica, Sardinia and Malta. Secondly, there is a dark brown 'Maritime' trend *S.u. dartford-*

iensis which embraces the populations of southern England, northern and western France, northern Spain, northern Portugal, probably southwest Spain and the Balearic Islands. Finally, there is a greyish-brown 'Desert' trend *S.u. toni* whose range runs from Morocco in North Africa east to Tunisia. Some birds in Spain that I have seen appear to approach the 'Desert' form, but despite this resemblance they, with birds from Corsica and southeast Italy, are now linked with *S.u. undata*. The mantle plumage of birds on Europe's western boundary is the darkest brown in Portugal while Dartford Warblers from northwest Spain, northern and western France and southern England are much brighter and browner. The species is also dimorphic with two forms: one in which the under plumage is a dark terracotta and the other in which it is pinkish-brown with lighter coloured feather-tips. As most of the former group prove to be males and the latter females it could be an example of sexual dimorphism. Among females those with the pinkest plumage are *S.u. undata*, while *S.u. dartfordiensis* and *S.u. toni* are washed with a buffish-orange on the flanks and breast. Among males the darkest is *S.u. dartfordiensis* while *S.u. undata* is paler and brighter in tone.

Closely related to the Dartford Warbler is Marmora's Warbler *Sylvia sarda* which was reported in South Yorkshire in May 1982. The bird's appearance is similar to that of the Dartford Warbler but it has grey underparts. Its habitat is in some ways like that of the Dartford but its choice suggests a preference for more open scrub in rather more hilly or mountainous country. As both species are sympatric – that is related but sharing parts of their range in northeast Spain, Sicily, northern regions of Africa and some of the Mediterranean islands – they are both granted the status of full species. There is a race *S.s. balearica*, which is less bluey-grey and smaller than the typical, which can be found on the Balearic Islands.

We now come to a group of three warblers, two of which bear some likeness to the Dartford Warbler and one to the Whitethroat. Of these, two have occurred as vagrants in the British Isles. The first two that suggest Dartford Warbler are the Subalpine Warbler *Sylvia cantillans* – a scarce wanderer – and Tristram's Warbler *Sylvia deserticola* of North Africa. To me the Subalpine Warbler, which I have heard singing its musical little song beneath Les Baux, once the home of Queen Jeanne and the troubadours, in the Alpilles, or along the tiny streams among the cistus and heather of the marismas in southern Spain, looks like a small pale Dartford Warbler. The male has a conspicuous white moustache, a pinkish to terracotta throat and a bright eye-ring that is golden in young birds and bright red in adults. It is a bird of thorny scrub and *maquis* in the Mediterranean region. The typical form breeds in Iberia, France, Corsica, Sardinia and Italy. It is a partial migrant travelling to west Africa and a vagrant to the British Isles, where some 100 examples have been recorded. Two of these proved to be of the typical race and one of the race *S.c. albistriata* which breeds from Yugoslavia east through Asia Minor and Syria. In this latter race the male is a dark chestnut-brown on the throat and breast with a broader moustachial stripe, and the second primary is longer than the fifth; it has less colour than the nominate race on the sides and flanks. It is a partial migrant and has been found in Nigeria in winter as well as on the southern edge of the Sahara. Another form, *S.c. inornata*, frequents the cork oaks and cedars in northwest Africa from Morocco to

Tripoli; the male is orange-brown underneath without the normal pinkish colour of *S.c. cantillans*. It seems that this form may also winter in west Africa from Senegal to Chad (Moreau 1961). On migration and in their winter quarters Subalpine Warblers cannot easily be assigned to their correct race.

The other species with a strong resemblance to the Dartford Warbler is Tristram's Warbler which haunts open woodland and scrub in Algeria and Tunisia. It looks like a smaller version of the Dartford Warbler with the male sporting dark brown wings. It can be separated from the Spectacled Warbler by its darker throat and from the Subalpine by the absence of a white moustachial streak. Birds seem to frequent 'the poorest Evergreen oak forests' (Snow 1952) as well as bushy open spaces between the cedars growing in northwest Africa. Snow also found the species commonly in May in bushy places in the Aurès Mountains and the Djebel Amour, especially on scrub-covered hillsides. A race of Tristram's Warbler *Sylvia deserticola maroccana*, somewhat darker on both the upper and under parts, is confined to the Grand Atlas Mountains in western Morocco. The call, a sharp 'chit' or 'chit-it', is different from the note of *S. undata* (Smith 1965).

A somewhat Whitethroat-like warbler in the *Sylvia* genus, which will be treated more fully in Chapter 10, is the Spectacled Warbler *Sylvia conspicillata*. The male has its head rather like that of a Lesser Whitethroat but the mantle is a rich brown and the rump and lower part of the back a greyish-brown. The plumage is completed by a white throat and a pink upper breast which shades below to a paler whitish-pink. Both the paler female and the juvenile display rufous-buff feathers which combine to form a noticeable wing-patch. This is a bird of the western Mediterranean reaching east to Italy, of North Africa and parts of the Near East. The nominate race is a partial migrant wintering in the Sahara, Egypt and Jordan. There is a race *S.c. orbitalis* on the Cape Verde Islands and Madeira which is less reddish-brown and greyer on the head and throat. The birds of this race appear bigger and brighter in the field than the typical birds of the Mediterranean. Dr W. R. P. Bourne (1955) found birds 'occurring throughout the scrub, working the foliage like *Phylloscopus* warblers, and coming freely into the towns and cultivated areas.' To me this is very much the bird of the salicornia, and I first recorded it on tape in 1954 singing its musical ditty from the tops of shrubs of this species or hovering over the sun-baked dried-out mud of the Camargue; when I returned nineteen years later with John F. Burton to make stereo recordings of this species many of the original territories were still occupied by Spectacled Warblers. Examples of this somewhat Whitethroat-like bird have occurred in Iraq, Denmark, and three times in Britain, the latter perhaps as the result of reversed migration (but see Chapter 10).

As long ago as 1962, I. C. T. Nisbet had noticed that the arrival of Barred Warblers *Sylvia nisoria* at Fair Isle was linked with high temperatures and breezes from the southwest or southeast in Germany, but not with the northeast winds in the region of the North Sea which were so often associated with the common immigrants from Scandinavia. He suggested that in warm conditions juvenile birds might easily turn their orientation in central Europe right round from the southeast to the northwest, so that these individuals like Pallas's Warblers might overshoot and turn up in areas far beyond their proper range. Thus an odd Spectacled Warbler might be expected to appear in northwest Europe (Cudworth and Spence 1978).

All the remaining warblers of the *Sylvia* group on the British list are vagrants like Marmora's Warbler, or irregular visitors like the Barred Warbler whose movements have just been described. The Barred Warbler is large and robust with a comparatively long tail and is reminiscent of a Whitethroat. It breeds in eastern and southern Europe, Russia and Asia across to Mongolia and spends the winter months from southern Arabia across to tropical East Africa. It is a regular if not common autumn drift-migrant and birds, apparently nearly always immature, are reported from the Faeroe Islands, Shetland and Fair Isle, less frequently on the east coast of mainland Britain and much more rarely on the English south coast and on islands in the Irish Sea. Williamson (1959) thought that these were random post-juvenile drifted dispersals but, as we have seen, Nisbet suggested that birds reported at Fair Isle arrived through a reversed migration. The Barred Warbler is one of the two largest *Sylvia* warblers in Europe and is a stout, long-tailed greyish bird with barred underparts.

Among the vagrants to the British Isles is the well-built Orphean Warbler *S. hortensis*, stouter than the Blackcap and rather like a large Lesser White-throat with a black cap. It is a bird of open woodlands and scrub with a fluent warbled song, and breeds from Iberia and northwest Africa east to India. It has occurred five times in the British Isles. The typical race breeds from northwest Africa and Iberia eastwards across southern Europe but it reveals an interesting intergradation with another race *S.h. crassirostris* in the Balkans, Cyrenaica and Asia Minor; this form is greyer on the upper parts and has a better defined black cap. A third race *S.h. jerdoni* can be found in Iran and regions east to Afghanistan, is a much purer grey on the back and is adorned with a dark cap which reaches the nape of the neck as well. The western race to which the British examples have been ascribed winters around the Sahara and in tropical Africa, often passing the months in acacia and very arid bush; *S.h. crassirostris* flies south to Arabia and northeast Africa and is very common in Eritrea, and *S.h. jerdoni* to India.

The very secretive Arabian Warbler *Sylvia leucomelaena* closely re-sembles the Orphean Warbler and differs only in certain details of struc-ture. The typical form *S.l. leucomelaena* is an inhabitant of low scrubby thorns and acacias and cannot apparently be separated in the field from Orphean Warblers on passage (Meinertzhagen 1949). However, the sooty head of the male Arabian Warbler does not seem so well defined and the rictal bristles and nasal hairs are finer. Known also as the Red Sea Warbler, the species can be found in Arabia from Midian to Yemen, Aden and also Somalia in northeast Africa. The species was formerly placed in another genus *Parisoma*, but the late Col. Richard Meinertzhagen, who showed me examples of the bird, was able to prove it to have the proper features of a *Sylvia* warbler. This was fully confirmed when the nest, eggs and behaviour were studied in 1971, when a pair bred for the first time in Israel (Zahavi and Dudai 1974). There is a greyer race from the Sudan recognized as *S.l. blanfordi* which exhibits a rather more crisply marked cap.

A few examples of the greyish-brown or sandy Desert Warbler *Sylvia nana* have appeared in the British Isles and also in other parts of Europe from Malta to Sweden and Finland. This is the smallest and palest of the warblers inhabiting scrubby country in desert and semi-desert regions from the steppes eastwards to Mongolia and moving south for the winter to lands ranging from India to the Persian Gulf. All of the British occurrences have been of the nominate eastern race. There is a sandier and whiter race *S.n. deserti* which occurs in the Sahara Desert from Algeria to Tripoli and has wandered elsewhere in North Africa and appeared in Italy and on one of the Madeiran islands. Another race, *S.n. theresae*, described by Williamson (1976) as 'darker and greyer above than the typical race, whiter and less creamy below' has been discerned as a wintering bird in Sind.

We now come to a group of very closely related warblers which have been regarded by some authorities, including Meinertzhagen (1954), as conspecific. Of these the best known is the Sardinian Warbler *Sylvia melanocephala* – a bird that I have heard singing its modulated warbles, rattles and Whitethroat-like ditties in scrub on the left bank of the Rio Tinto in southern Spain, in the juniper woods of the Camargue and around the ancient ruins of Delphi. Remarkable for its jet-black head and red eye and ring, the male looks like a more strongly marked Blackcap or plump Whitethroat. This typical bird of the Mediterranean scrub which often winters in Africa and Iraq is a vagrant to the British Isles and Switzerland while the first bird recorded in the Netherlands – an adult male – wintered in a suburban garden, behaving like a Blackcap and feeding on bread and peanuts! The typical form nests in the Mediterranean region from Iberia east to Bulgaria and Asia Minor with breeding possibly taking place in Romania and the Ukraine, while other forms can be found in North Africa from Morocco to Libya. Of this breeding population some birds winter in Iraq and parts of North Africa. There is a darker greyish brown race *S.m. leucogastra* with less white at the tips of the outer tail feathers in the Canary Islands. An even greyer race *S.m. momus*, which is paler underneath, can be found in Syria, Israel and Jordan; this is a partial migrant with some birds wintering in Sinai, Aden, Egypt and the Sudan. A third sandy-brown race *S.m. norrisae* has been reported from the type locality at El Faiyum in Egypt. A supposed race *S.m. pasiphaë* seems to belong rightly to *S. melanocephala*.

In the Volga Basin, the Caucasus Mountains and in country from Turkestan in Russia to Afghanistan, the Sardinian Warbler is replaced by Ménétries's Warbler *Sylvia mystacea*. This is, of course, very much like the Sardinian Warbler but it is pink underneath and has a pale yellow eye-ring. A white demarcation line also separates the very black cheeks from the pink throat. Although Ménétries's Warbler is now generally regarded as a distinct species (Vaurie 1954), it seems that there is intergradation between the two with Voous (1960) and Harrison (1959) thinking that it was a race of the Sardinian Warbler. After examining many skins S. Marchant (1963) expressed the view that 'I cannot see any valid reasons for the continued recognition of *mystacea* as a separate species.' Until the taxonomists have fuller details, through custom, this warbler remains a full species. It is a bird of the plains and mountain foothills, skulking like the Sardinian Warbler in tamarisks, orchards and riverside scrub. The bird is very restless and flies with its tail held very high. Its call is a sharp 'tack-tack' whilst the song of no outstanding quality consists of various hissing notes and rattles surely different enough in kind from the more musical utterings of the Sardinian Warbler. The species migrates through Iran and Iraq to winter in southern Arabia, Somalia and the Sudan. A first-winter bird was recorded in Portugal in 1967. On the breeding ground the bird is often double-brooded with incubation lasting some fourteen days and the young remaining in the nest for thirteen days or so.

Another close relation, the Cyprus Warbler *Sylvia melanothorax*, is restricted to the island from which it derives its name. It too resembles the Sardinian Warbler but the underparts of the male are quite boldly mottled black and white, and individuals differ in the actual amount of mottling. The female is also mottled underneath but not to the same extent as the male. The Cyprus Warbler behaves rather like a Sardinian Warbler, being a restless lover of cover but cocking its tail at right angles to the body and uttering a harsh call-note 'szack' or 'tzigg-tzigg'. The song is somewhat varied with notes suggestive of those of the Whitethroat. The Cyprus Warbler is a bird of scrub and orange groves, from sea level up to 2000 m in the mountains. Individuals have wandered to Asia Minor, Israel and the Lebanon, but only during the winter period. Vaurie (1954) thought that the question of whether the Cyprus and Sardinian Warblers were con-specific 'is a matter of opinion'. Williamson believed that the former was more closely related to Rüppell's Warbler *Sylvia rüppelli*, and that the two species may have diverged during a protracted period perhaps in Cyprus and Crete, so that Rüppell's then penetrated other islands in the Aegean as well as mainland Greece and parts of Asia Minor and the Near East. Rüppell's is interesting in being the only warbler in the region to have the whole head and throat black, while its white moustachial streak and black throat distinguish it from the Sardinian Warbler. The males of both species have reddish eye-rings. Rüppell's Warbler has occurred in the British Isles and will be treated more fully in Chapter 10 which is devoted to the vagrants of the genus *Sylvia* that have occurred there.

If we look at the ten common species of *Sylvia* warbler by average wing span and average weight we arrive at the following comparison:

Wing spans and weights of Sylvia warblers   Table 9

Species	Average wing span (mm)	Average weight (gm)
Barred Warbler	86.3	23.65
Orphean Warbler	77.7	19.5
Garden Warbler	77.53	17.6
Blackcap	73	16.7
Common Whitethroat	69.1	13.32
Lesser Whitethroat	64.4	11.9
Subalpine Warbler	57.8	10.5
Sardinian Warbler	57.5	10.8
Spectacled Warbler	53.65	8.6
Dartford Warbler	51.3	9.3

Some of the species and forms of *Sylvia* in Europe, especially in the south, are basically sedentary; these include the Arabian Warbler and the race known as Blanford's, four races of the Blackcap, Cyprus and Tristram's Warblers, two races of the Sardinian Warbler, one race of the Subalpine, the *orbitalis* race of the Spectacled Warbler, and the Dartford Warbler and its races. Others like Marmora's or a few Cyprus Warblers may wander a little, while some can be regarded as partial migrants including the Sardinian, Subalpine and Spectacled Warblers. The rest are true migrants and their annual journeys are full of interest to the ornithologist. There is, for example, an apparent migratory 'divide' in the southerly migrations of Blackcaps, Garden Warblers and Lesser Whitethroats, and to a smaller degree of Common Whitethroats. This divide occurs at about 10°–11°E for both Blackcaps and Garden Warblers. Birds breeding to the east of that line travel in autumn to the southeast, while those from the west of that line, including British summer visitors, travel southwest through France to Iberia, where some Blackcaps winter, or on to Morocco and Algeria. However, Norwegian Blackcaps join with the birds from Sweden and central Europe nesting sites to travel to the region of the Lebanon. It is possible that some of the Blackcaps wintering in the British Isles are juveniles carried far to the west in a post-juvenile dispersal of these warblers and are not either local or north European birds.

The Garden Warbler exhibits similar tendencies to the Blackcap with British breeding birds moving southwest to western France and Iberia but birds from Scandinavia, unlike Blackcaps from that part of the world, also join this southwesterly movement. Birds from east of the 10°–11°E divide move southeast to Cyprus, Rhodes and the Lebanon. Most birds finally winter across tropical Africa. The favoured direction for Lesser Whitethroats in autumn, which involves all the European populations, is to the southeast, with autumn migrants from England being recovered in Italy or southern Austria and all the spring records coming from Israel and the Lebanon. The easterly orientation in English birds is clearly shown by the large numbers concentrated on the east coast from Suffolk to Kent compared to those at the south coast observatories. Birds winter in Egypt, Sudan, Ethiopia and Eritrea while more easterly populations travel to Iran, India and Sri Lanka. The situation is nowhere as clear for the Common Whitethroat but examples originating from places in Germany east to about 11°E show a southwest tendency, while those from beyond that point move south or south-south-east to Italy and the shores of Yugoslavia or Albania. On the other hand, Scandinavian birds move more north and south than garden warblers from the same geographical area (Davis 1967). British marked birds have been recovered mostly from western France, western Spain and Portugal together with others from France and Belgium. British birds have been reported in Morocco and Senegal. Since Whitethroats winter in tropical Africa – they are abundant visitors to the thorn-tree savannahs in Nigeria – they are vulnerable to droughts in the Sahel zone of western Africa.

Some of the *Sylvia* warbler species had important parts to play in pioneering experiments in avian orientation and navigation. After a long series of tests Dr Franz Sauer (1956, 1957a, 1957b, 1958) found that nocturnal orientation in night migrants depended on the stars, so establishing the basis of the concept of the 'star compass'. Blackcaps, Garden Warblers, Whitethroats and Lesser Whitethroats were placed in circular cages under clear night skies during the spring and autumn migrations and the birds achieved their bearings very quickly from the stars. Experiments in a planetarium confirmed the results. Later Franz and Eleonore Sauer (1959) took Whitethroats, Garden Warblers and Blackcaps to Africa just before they were due to leave for their winter quarters. The birds first headed south then, reassured by the sight of the sky in Africa, settled to their winter home and lost their migratory restlessness. H. G. Walraff (1960) later questioned Sauer's work.

As a group the *Sylvia* warblers include some of the most familiar birds in the British Isles as well as some of the least known. The following six chapters will consider those on the British list in more detail but the information contained there can be set against the broad backcloth that I have attempted to paint in this chapter.

CHAPTER **5** The Garden Warbler

I first came to know the Garden Warbler – the least well-marked and dis-tinctive of our *Sylvia* warblers – in the oakwoods at Selsdon and Little-heath in Surrey in the years before the last war. Here in the rich choruses of dawn I learned to separate its song from that of the Blackcap by long patient hours of listening and after much effort making visual identifica-tions of the respective performers. Since that time I have met many singing Garden Warblers, rarely in gardens (except very overgrown ones) and more regularly in many broad-leaved woods, in scrub, overgrown hedge-rows and rough growth, in young conifer plantations, northern birch-woods, sparsely wooded Welsh cwms and on wooded islets in Ulster. Here the Greater Pettychaps, as it was known to the ornithologists of the eighteenth and nineteenth centuries, often remains as Sir William Jardine described it as 'a bird of extremely retired and shy habits, seldom appearing out of the thicket and shrubbery.' There is really little of distinction about this bird with its dull greyish-brown upperparts, although its buff throat and larger size help to separate it from the Whitethroat. The absence of a black or brownish crown distinguishes it from a male or female Blackcap. The underparts are whitish with a buff suffusion and the tail is square-ended with the outermost feathers carrying pale edges. The bill is dark brown and the legs greyish-brown.

The Garden Warbler is clearly a bird of the *Sylvia* type but rather

Fig. 9
Garden Warbler at its nest among nettles. (Eric Hosking)

plumper than most, and the combination of dark upperparts and a subtle and pleasing pale buff below provides an effect quite different from that of other warblers. Its short bill and round head help to separate the Garden Warbler from those of the *Hippolais* group and its size and colouring from the *Phylloscopus* warblers. Adults and young have similar plumages. As Jardine remarked, the Garden Warbler is rather a secretive bird and its presence is often betrayed solely by the even-flowing and sustained song. The bird searches actively for food in dense undergrowth and shrubs as well as trees and it will sometimes take insects on the wing.

The typical call of the Garden Warbler is an abrupt, variously rendered 'teck-teck', 'kek-kek' or 'check-check'. When the bird is very alarmed it will produce a run of these notes and one bird I studied produced no fewer than 220 of these calls in a minute! There is also a subdued, rasping 'tchurr-r-r' like the scold of a Whitethroat or of a Blackcap, but its use is much more frequent in the case of the first species. The harsh aggressive note seems to arise especially when the bird is experiencing a conflict between fear and the impulse to flee and a more aggressive tendency (Sauer 1956). When a nest with young is approached it is possible to hear a faint 'phit', 'whit' or 'bit' perhaps the same as the note used by anxious autumn migrants. Finally, H. E. Howard reported hearing a quiet purr 'of sexual or parental emotions' but I am not convinced that this sound is not just a 'mood' of the harsh call, reflecting conflicting emotions in one member of the pair.

Since the habitats of the Garden Warbler and the Blackcap in Britain bear such strong similarities and may overlap, it is logical to compare both them and the vocalizations of the birds and not separate them entirely by species. As I said at the beginning it may not always be easy to distinguish the songs of the two warblers. The song of the male Garden Warbler is a mellow, even warbling, vigorous in quality but lacking variety and set form. It is quieter and more sustained than the song of the male Blackcap, which I have described elsewhere as 'a pure rich warble with clean, musical intervals' being also less rapid, less even and less uniform than the outpourings of the Garden Warbler. The Garden Warbler has a certain 'fruity', often wonderfully beautiful and clarinet-like quality. I once listened in a Lincolnshire wood to a duet between a fine Garden Warbler and a Nightingale, which not only provided an interesting comparison but forced the warbler into long and louder phrasing over the twenty minutes in which the two different species sang against each other. Unfortunately the Blackcap not only indulges in subdued warblings and subsong that may be difficult to distinguish from the full song of the Garden Warbler but the Blackcap may also mimic a Garden Warbler! Even on rare occasions the Garden Warbler has been known to be mimetic. The steadiness, contralto quality and persistence should help the observer to separate the Garden Warbler from the Blackcap which utters pure notes of excellent standard and sings a tune with musical intervals often in the rhythm 'duty day, day of duty' but with a wavy pattern, more definite phrasing and a tendency to become louder towards the end and with a soprano flourish. The full rich territorial song of the Garden Warbler and the subsong of the Blackcap with its high scratchy, coarse, 'wavy' pattern are both much faster than the full song of the Blackcap and lack its obvious tune. A Blackcap that I listened to in April 1984 produced some high notes in its subsong with a pitch range far greater than I have ever heard from a Garden Warbler. It is clear that only extreme vigilance in identification will solve the problems presented by the two species. Workers on *The Atlas of Breeding Birds in Britain and Ireland* (1976) 'were urged to locate and see the singing birds of these two species.'

The actual phrases of Garden Warbler songs are commonly about 3.5 seconds in duration, often up to 6 seconds in length and occasionally even 25 seconds without a break. I have heard an exceptional one in Northamptonshire in May which lasted well over a minute. A typical run of ten

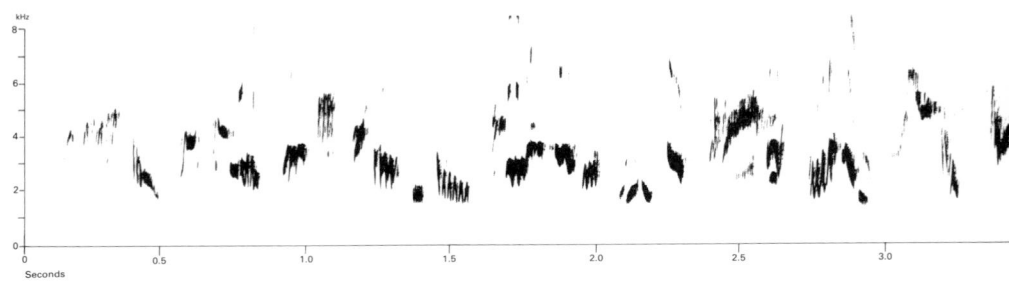

Fig. 10
Typical run of Garden Warbler notes in territorial song. Note less pure notes than those of Blackcap. (Recorded by Eric Simms, Bedfordshire May 1980)

consecutive phrases that I timed over a minute for one Garden Warbler consisted of bursts of 3, 4, 3.5, 3.5, 5, 6, 4.5, 4.5, 6 and 4.5 seconds. With such brief intervals between phrases I have found a song maintained for as long as 25 minutes. In a rich woodland chorus of birdsong the lack of emphasis in the singing and the tonal ranges employed mean that the song of the Garden Warbler may not stand out like that of the Blackcap, even though it can be heard in more favourable circumstances as much as 250 m away. The song may be delivered from dense cover in the shrub layer of a wood or scrub when the singer is static or on the move or occasionally in flight. During a study of Garden Warblers in Lincolnshire I found many individuals singing from songposts at least 9 m high in trees. Another bird that I watched in Cwm Pennant in Wales over many hours spent 49% of its singing time in the day in May uttering territorial song from stations 14 m and 17 m high in ashtrees without leaf and 15 m up in a sycamore; the remainder of its output came from deep in a low bramble or in a small conifer thicket. It also indulged in some invitation or subsong in the bramble which was the only nest site in its territory.

The quality of Garden Warbler song ranges from the merely pedestrian to superb artistry. I have a recording of a male Garden Warbler made in 1951 near Kidderminster in Worcestershire; I am, in fact, glad of the opportunity to point out that in *Woodland Birds* (1971) in this same New Naturalist series I incorrectly gave the county as Staffordshire. This bird uttered an aberrant song made up of extraordinary rattling phrases of Acrocephaline quality over five breeding seasons. The song could be rendered phonetically as 'chirrick, chirrick, chirrick, chit-chit-it-it-it, chick-chick' – very rough and scraping but the final note had some pretension to melody. On average the song lasted from 3–5 seconds and showed little variation. It was known with affection to members of the West Midland Bird Club as *Sylvia laryngitis* and, unsurprisingly, it never in the five years attracted a mate. The full song of normal individuals has been heard in Africa in autumn and spring as a brisk, rather thin, inward warbling which forms the subdued song. Subsong on the breeding ground occurs when both members of a pair are together and it is also used by the male Garden Warbler or Blackcap to entice a female to view a pad or nest-foundation. With its harsh Sedge Warbler-like scraping and thin warblings the subsong of the Garden Warbler is very inferior to the territorial song.

As a breeding species the Garden Warbler occurs in the British Isles, central Portugal, Spain, most of France, Italy, Sicily, Malta, the Balkans and southern Russia and from there across to Transcaucasia and north to about 70°N in Norway, Sweden, northern Finland and Russia. As we saw in the preceding chapter, the eastern populations are somewhat greyer on the back but do not justify division into subspecies. In Britain the range and habitats of the Garden Warbler are very similar to those of the Blackcap but the former is scarcer in the English fens, in southwest Cornwall and eastern Lancashire. In Scotland the range is about the same for both species and the northern distribution extends to Argyll, Aberdeen and Easter Ross with a few singing males in the birchwoods of the extreme north. The Garden Warbler is much scarcer than the Blackcap in Ireland and has its headquarters around Lough Neagh, Lower Lough Erne and the Shannon and Cavan lakes. Although it has nested in a dozen or so Irish counties most of the records are very sporadic.

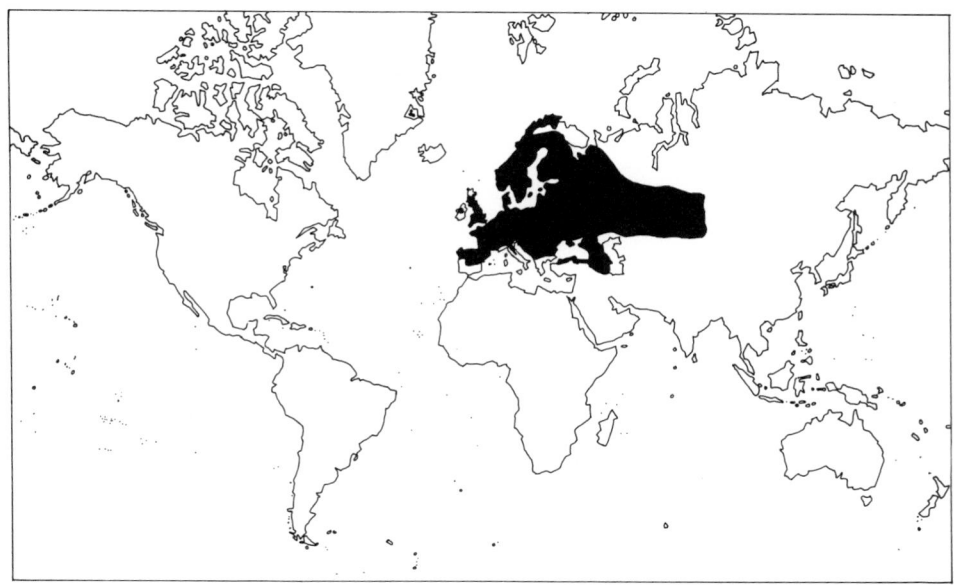

This is a warbler of both broad-leaved and mixed woods with a rich development of shrubs and brambles but growing up to a somewhat lower height than that favoured by the Blackcap. It also occurs in scrub and, unlike the Blackcap, in bushy regions without any trees at all. Some Garden

Fig. 11
Breeding distribution of the Garden Warbler.

Fig. 12
Scrub habitat of Garden
Warbler, Willow Warbler
and Nightingale.
Lincolnshire, May 1983.
(Eric Simms)

Warblers take over dense overgrown hedges, large gardens, osier beds, and even conifer plantations, especially if the latter have a broad-leaved fringe (Williamson 1970). Coppices of oak, alder, ash, hornbeam and hazel, now largely discontinued, favoured Nightingales and Garden Warblers, although they were always forced to disappear for a few years until the wood had recovered from the cutting. After a study of more than 300 British and Irish woods I found that the Garden Warbler was commonest in English woods of pedunculate oak and occurred at lower densities in sessile oak-woods, beech and ashwoods. Although in northern Europe the species nests further north than the Blackcap and even into the birch zone of the sub-arctic, it is scarcer in English birchwoods and pine plantations. Almost certainly the Garden Warbler was one of the dozen or so species which came into Britain with the returning broad-leaved forests after the Ice Age. In those Mediterranean countries where the Garden Warbler occurs the habitat is normally one of high forest. Birds are quite common in Wales and territories are often linear in shape, embracing trees and scrub along field boundaries and rivers; in the cwms they may be much longer than in other habitats. In Ireland I have studied Garden Warblers near Upper Lough Erne where the habitat is one formed from natural woodland, tangles of blackthorn and bramble and almost invariably water nearby, usually a lake.

During an intensive five-year study of a pedunculate oakwood in Northamptonshire I found that on average there were four times as many Garden Warblers as Blackcaps, allowing for slight fluctuations each year. The wood was close-canopied with a dense shrub layer. Here Garden Warblers comprised 3.3% of the summer individuals in the wood; in Finland T. Solonen (1980) found a figure of 6%. In my Midland wood the

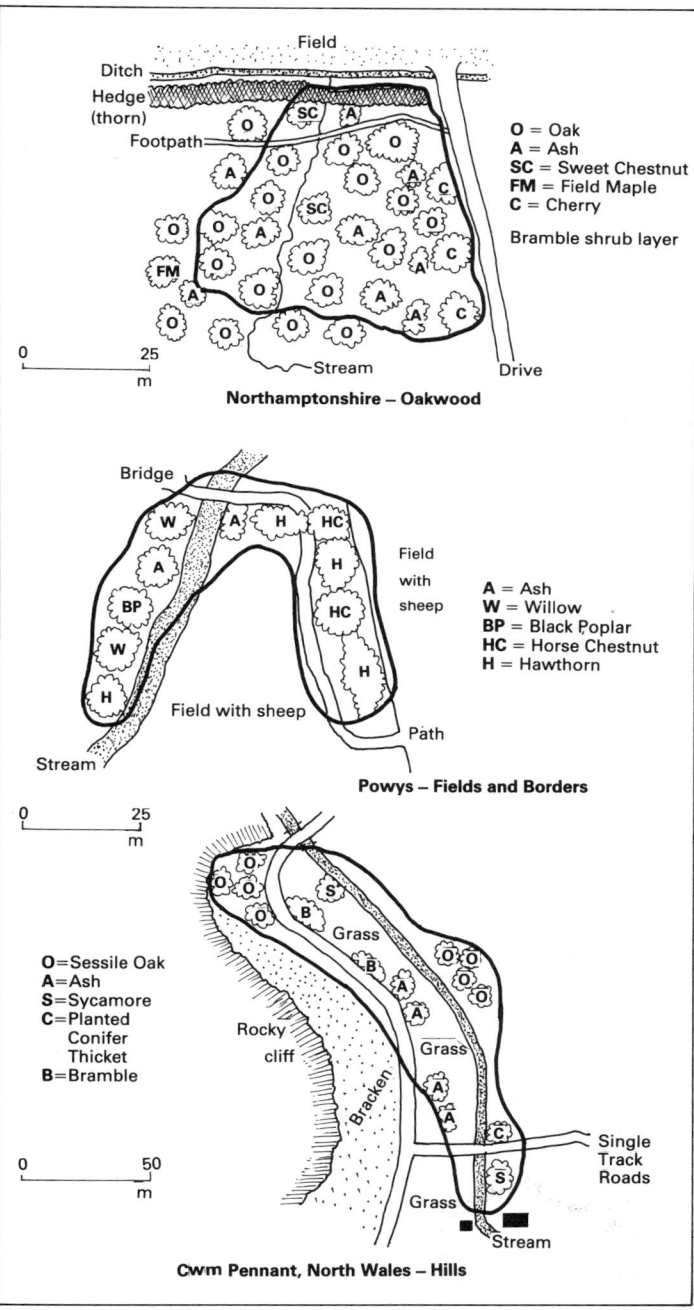

O = Oak
A = Ash
SC = Sweet Chestnut
FM = Field Maple
C = Cherry

Bramble shrub layer

0   25
m

Northamptonshire – Oakwood

A = Ash
W = Willow
BP = Black Poplar
HC = Horse Chestnut
H = Hawthorn

0   25
m

Powys – Fields and Borders

O = Sessile Oak
A = Ash
S = Sycamore
C = Planted
     Conifer
     Thicket
B = Bramble

0   50
m

Cwm Pennant, North Wales – Hills

Fig. 13
*Three territories of male
Garden Warblers. (Eric
Simms)*

percentages of the total population for Blackcap were 1%, for Chiffchaff 1.3%, and Willow Warbler 5.4%. On the other hand a mixed wood that I know in Lincolnshire produced figures of 0.7% each for Garden Warbler and Blackcap, 1.65% for Chiffchaff, 2.7% for Whitethroat and 16.3% for Willow Warblers. In many English woods the Garden Warbler out-numbers the Blackcap – in the Wyre Forest by seven to one, and yet in the Malverns the figures are exactly the other way round, and I found many more Blackcaps in parts of Staffordshire and near Stratford-upon-Avon than Garden Warblers. Yet in other parts of Warwickshire and in Lincoln-shire I have found equal numbers present. The late Dr David Lack (1971) suggested that Blackcaps and Garden Warblers avoided competition by vertical separation with the former feeding higher up in the canopy. That Garden Warblers and Blackcaps maintained mutually exclusive terri-tories was advanced as a theory by Dr R. J. Raines (1945), and Eliot Howard (1948) described interspecific fights and behaviour in which 'excitable outbursts of song are indulged in, tails are outspread, wings are slowly flapped, and feathers raised.' According to *The Atlas of Breeding Birds in Britain and Ireland* (1976), which described the census work needed to make the survey possible: 'Whilst Blackcaps and Garden Warb-lers react to each other's songs, both are able to hold territories and breed successfully in the same area; indeed, on some plots their territories over-lap.' However, Garden Warblers arrive later than Blackcaps and may be synchronizing their breeding activities with one of several prey species as well as exploiting a different stratum in the wood.

Garden Warblers return to the British Isles rather later than Blackcaps, often by as much as $2\frac{1}{2}$ weeks. The average date of arrival for the former over 29 years in the West Midlands was 24 April while that over 32 years

Fig. 14
Island and waterside habitats of Garden Warblers with oak and thorn. Upper Lough Erne, Northern Ireland, May 1967. (Eric Simms)

for the Blackcap was 6 April. Garden Warblers begin their breeding activities quite quickly so that their eggs will hatch when there is the greatest abundance of food available. The males take up territories, begin to sing their advertising songs and to construct simple nest-platforms or cocks' nests. When a female arrives in the territory the male, having chosen a potential nest-site in a bramble or other thick piece of cover and constructed a 'nest' of a few bits of grass with both lateral and vertical movements of his bill, entices her by song and display to examine it. These nest-platforms or 'pads', as they are sometimes called, are low down in brambles, nettles and other cover. Howard said that 'such "nests" do not bear the stamp of genuine effort.' I find that they can easily be overlooked. In an interesting study of Garden Warblers in northeast Shropshire in the spring of 1978, A. S. Norris (1983) recorded five males holding quite clearly marked territories and they 'between them produced at least 13 (3, 2, 2, 5 and 1 respectively) wispy dried grass accumulations sited typically in brambles *Rubus*, larch *Larix* plantations and rhododendron

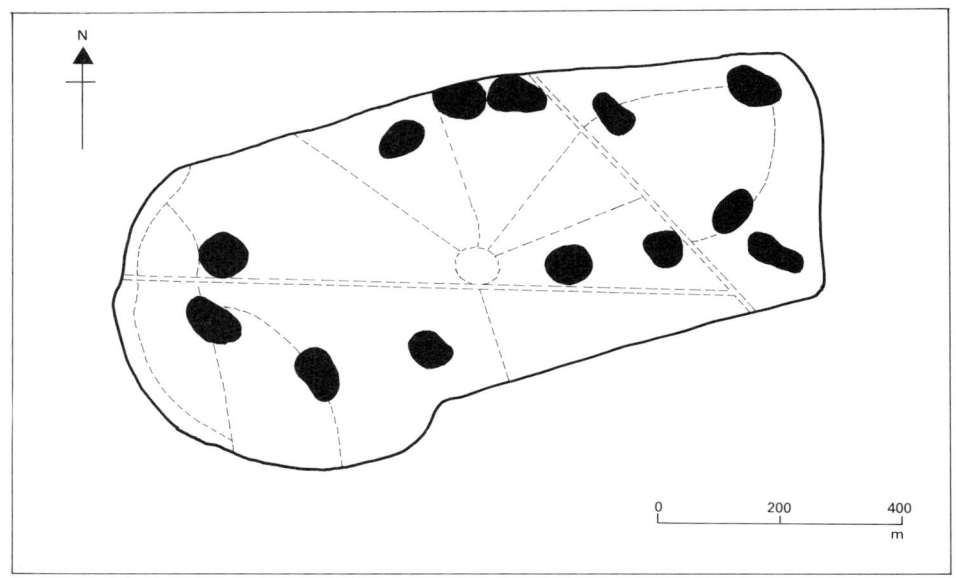

0   200   400
m

Rhododendron ponticum thickets.' I have known females to reject many of these cocks' nests but they will sometimes, after being led by sustained subsong to one, select and largely complete it. Norris, however, found that not one of the thirteen 'pads' was developed into a complete nest. In 1979 he located twelve dummy pads within a dummy territory which led to his suggestion that perhaps they are decoys for predators or merely a reflection of the male's spring exuberance and passion!

Mating pairs demonstrate considerable extravagance in display. While perched on a twig the male will fan his tail and beat his wings so rapidly that they fade into a mere blur. Then he sidles towards the female. Both wings are flapped if the male is facing his mate but, if he is standing alongside her,

Fig. 15
Distribution of 13 Garden Warbler territories in a Northamptonshire oak wood. (Eric Simms)

then he beats only the wing on her side. Before copulation takes place the male lowers his bill.

The nest is usually situated within 60 cm of the ground and is very often at a lower height than nests of the Blackcap. Sometimes nests are reported from 2–3 m up. In half of the 623 nest record cards analysed by C. F. Mason (1976) the reported sites were in brambles. Nests are also built in nettles, roses, willowherbs, hawthorn, elder and grass. They are outwardly formed from dry grass stems, moss or fine twigs, made into a strong cup lodged between twigs or stems of plants and lined with roots, fine grass or hair. T. A. Coward (1944) saw one lined entirely with black goat's hair – 'a goat was tethered close to the nest.' Birds in Switzerland have been known to build in broken reeds and other vegetation growing in water but this is a most unusual site. Both birds take part in the construction of the nest. The eggs are variable in colour being whitish or buffish, even green or pink, with irregular blotches and spots of brown, purple or grey and small enough in number to reveal the ground colour fairly easily. The Garden Warbler is an occasional host to the Cuckoo.

First clutches are laid in early May, later than many of the *Sylvia* warblers, but the overall mean date is 25 May. Whereas most clutches of Blackcaps, Whitethroats and Lesser Whitethroats consist of five eggs, in the case of the Garden Warbler there are as many clutches of four as of five. The incubation period ranges from 10–12 days with a mean of 11, while that for fledging ranges from 9–12 with a mean of 10 days. The incubation range is greater for the Blackcap but the mean is the same, while for the fledging period the Blackcap has a wider range and a mean of 11 days. Mason found that Garden Warblers had a poorer hatching success than Blackcaps and Lesser Whitethroats but better than Whitethroats and Dartford Warblers. However, Garden Warblers reared fewer young per nest than the other species; this is, in part, a reflection of the lower clutch size but 'the overall failure rate of eggs was also higher.' In the British Isles a mean of only 2.1 young fledged from each nest, compared to 2.6 for the Blackcap. In southern Finland T. Solonen (1979) reported more than half the nests being successful (compared to 71% in Britain in low population years and 50% in high). In Finland 1.2–4.9 young (with a mean of 3.3) fledged from each nest. It was interesting that in Finland Solonen found that just over half the males and 82% of the females did not come back to his study area the following year; this suggested that immigration was the vital factor in the population dynamics of the species in that country. If one considers the productivity of nests, which is the product of the percentage of clutches which reach the fledging stage and the mean number of young per succeeding nest reaching that stage, it seems from Mason's detailed

Table 10   *Breeding of Garden Warbler and Blackcap*

Species	%Hatching success	Young fledged as % of hatched	Young fledged as % of eggs laid	Young fledged per nest	Mean clutch size		
					April	May	June
Garden Warbler	71.9	80.1	57.6	2.1		4.5	3.8
Blackcap	75.6	79.9	60.4	2.6	4.8	4.7	4.0

(after Mason 1976)

analysis that the May figure for the Garden Warbler is 2.5, and for June, 2.1 which can be compared to the Blackcap's figures of 2.8 for April, 2.7 for May and 2.5 for June. Table 10 from the same source gives further data on breeding in the two species.

P. Berthold (1970) and other observers have demonstrated the fact that the development of young Garden Warblers is faster than that of Blackcaps. Birds also seem to develop more rapidly if they are hatched later in the season and it is interesting to note that there is a similar acceleration of growth in late hatched Blackcaps. The speeding up of the process in Garden Warblers can be attributed to their lateness of arrival on the breeding grounds and the consequent maturation of the young before supplies of food begin to diminish. While the Blackcap is only a 'middle-distance' migrant, the Garden Warbler has to prepare for its long migration early, even while in the nest. Young captive Garden Warblers often indulge in play during the period between reaching independence and the start of the autumn migration; this might involve picking up tiny stones and dropping them (Sauer 1956). They also show a greater migratory restlessness and degree of nocturnal activity than the 'middle-distance' Blackcaps (Berthold 1973). Indeed the evidence now is that such restlessness is innate in the *Sylvia* warblers with a time-programme in each species to allow them to reach their winter quarters during their first autumn migration.

The Garden Warbler is primarily an insect-feeder taking the caterpillars of the smaller moths and butterflies, as well as small beetles, *Diptera*, *Hymenoptera*, *Hemiptera* including aphids as well as spiders, and occasionally small worms. Later in the summer it turns its attention to fruits and berries. Birds of passage in my garden at Dollis Hill in northwest London fed on blackberries but raspberries, currants, cherries, figs and the berries of elder, buckthorn, honeysuckle, ivy and privet are all welcomed as the year advances. A study in southern Portugal by D. K. Thomas (1979) showed that migrant Garden Warblers in autumn fed very widely on figs and such individuals were heavier than those taking alternative foods. The Portuguese name for the Garden Warbler – *felosa-das-figueiras* or Fig-tree Warbler – and the Italian name – *beccafigo* or Fig-pecker – reflect the bird's predilection for the fruit. Figs were thought to be essential for the deposition of fat reserves necessary to ensure a safe crossing of the Sahara Desert. The timing of the birds' southerly movements could be linked with the abundance of the fruit. When feeding on figs the warblers appeared not to show aggressive tendencies towards each other. Not all the Garden Warblers took advantage of the figs, taking fruits of *Rubus* and the black drupes of *Phillyrea* which abound on the Mediterranean *maquis*. The reasons are not apparent. For a fruit-eating warbler, such communal exploitation of a variable and regionally abundant food source is advantageous, whereas for an insect-eating warbler that depends on a widely spread but not too abundant supply a territorial system would be more appropriate (Snow 1976). Occasionally birds in the British Isles may come to bird tables but not as frequently as the Blackcap. In Uganda the Garden Warblers, mainly of Siberian breeding origin, feed largely on the berries of *Lantana camara*, a plant introduced from Mexico and Central America. As the berries become exhausted, the birds seem to change back to an insectivorous diet (Pearson 1972).

Garden Warblers, like Blackcaps, featured in a number of experiments in the 1950s into migration and orientation. Dr E. G. F. Sauer (1957), pursuing earlier work by Gustav Kramer that indicated that some nocturnal migrants show an orientated migratory restlessness when in circular cages under a cloudless night sky, was able to demonstrate that this nocturnal orientation was dependent upon the stars themselves. Sauer postulated a 'star-compass' that needed a time compensation but S. T. Emlen (1967) showed that the Indigo Bunting used the patterns of the stars to determine its direction – without compensation for time – and this is probably also true for other species as well. Garden Warblers from the British Isles migrate, as we have seen, to Africa, travelling at night. Some may undertake a post-nuptial wing moult before leaving (Gladwin 1969) but evidence for this is sketchy. When the birds leave in the autumn they seem to move roughly southeast on the first part of their journey but then shift towards the southwest to reach Spain, Portugal and North Africa – a feature that they share with some other summer migrants. The birds are common on passage in autumn on the south coast of Portugal and in Tunisia (Moreau 1961). Peter Davis (1967) cites one interesting record of 'reversed migration' in which a Garden Warbler ringed on the coast of Suffolk on 30 August 1965 was recovered a fortnight later in Nottinghamshire at a west-north-west distance of 184 km. The British Observatory records show movement at Fair Isle from the last week of July to the first week of November with the main period from 1–5 September. At other observatories the range of dates and the peaks were, according to Davis, Spurn Point: 14 July–6 November with a similar peak to that of Fair Isle; Dungeness: 20 July–2 November with a peak also at the same time but with a much lower proportion of autumn birds; Portland: 3 August–22 October with ill-defined peaks; Lundy 30 July–27 October with the main peak from 21–25 September; Skokholm: 7 August–13 October with a peak 11–15 September, and Bardsey, 2 August–31 October and a peak from 16–20 September.

Fair Isle and Spurn Point were absorbing birds mainly from Scandinavia, which travel south-south-west in autumn in the region of the North Sea, although some arrivals could be of dispersing rather than truly orientated migrants. Dungeness reveals an early movement of British birds before any of Scandinavian origin begin to come through and Portland seems to experience similar passage. Observation points on the west coast of Britain do show that many large 'falls' or arrivals of Garden Warblers there have coincided with big influxes on the east coast so that it is reasonable to assume that many birds in the west have come from northern Europe.

In the spring, Garden Warblers moving north are common on passage in the Spanish Sahara, western Morocco, Tunisia and Iberia. When we come to examine the spring movements in the British Isles we find that the movements for Fair Isle lie between 2 May–9 July with a peak five-day period from 1–5 June; at Spurn Point 14 April–13 June with two peaks from 21–25 May and 1–5 June; at Dungeness 19 April–6 June with peaks from 6–10 May and 15–20 May; at Portland 6 April–6 June; at Skokholm 6 April–7 June with a peak from 11–15 May and at Bardsey 16 April–9 June also with a peak from 11–15 May. The spring birds recorded at Fair Isle are north European birds shifted northwest from their main north-north-east travels, while Spurn also seems to receive a number of immigrants to

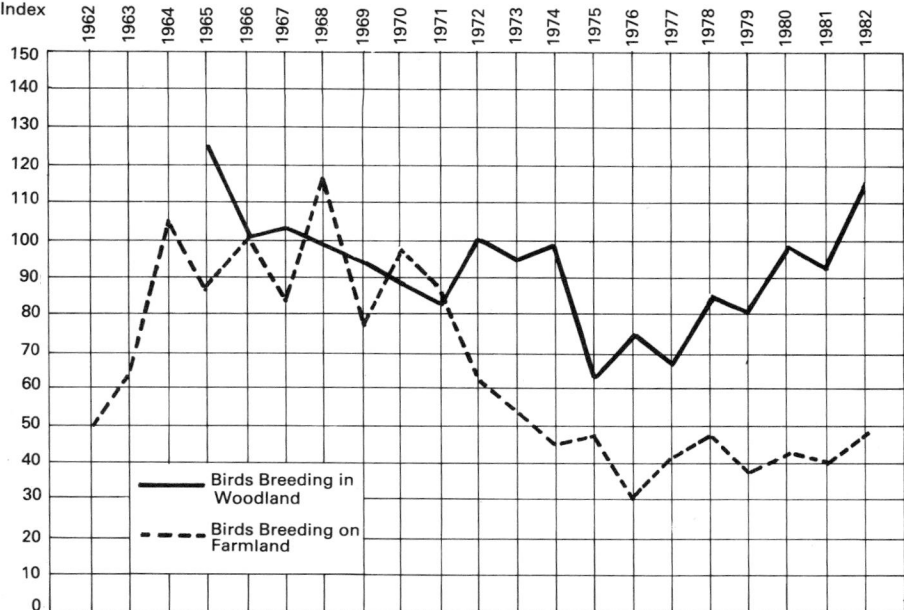

Fig. 16
Population changes in Garden Warbler numbers 1962–82. Based on Common Birds Census of B.T.O. (levels in relation to 1966).

Britain. The noticeable peaks at the other observatories occur earlier and suggest the movement of British birds.

The winter quarters of the Garden Warbler lie in the southern forest areas of Nigeria and the Gambia across the tropical region to Kenya in the east and Damaraland in South West Africa, Natal and the Transvaal in the south. Certain areas such as Eritrea and the northern tropics and even Lake Victoria, where Garden Warblers are one of the most abundant migrants between late October and early December, are stopover regions before further southerly movements to the true winter quarters. These are probably reached before the moult even in birds which are late moving south; we saw in the last chapter that Garden Warblers wintering in Uganda went through their moult between December and March, and departed in spring with fresh flight feathers (Pearson 1973). In their winter quarters Garden Warblers frequent forests, savannahs and gardens, while I have watched birds in the thorn scrub of the Serengeti National Park alongside Blackcaps. In Uganda birds overwinter in bush and forest, and here and in Nigeria in *Lantana* groves. In Cameroon, birds frequent the small woods and forests bordering the bush-savannah. It is strange to hear the subsong issuing from a bush under a tropical sun while even full song may be uttered in March and April, on the African Continent. Subsong was heard on 27 February 1945 and again on 10 March 1945 in London's Hampstead garden suburb: in fact, G. Warburg (whose observations these are) heard what could be described as full song on the later date – a very unusual record reported in *British Birds* 38:255.

It is perhaps firstly the suddenness and clarity of the Blackcap's song and then the rich quality of the performance that so readily focus our attention on the singer, as we walk through a southern or Midland oakwood or the ashwoods of the limestone where the bird is known as 'the northern nightingale'. I have been enchanted by the songs of Blackcaps in the broad-leaved woods of France, Spain and other European countries, while the singers in Switzerland seem to have a contralto quality and rising flourish at the end which are quite their own. Birds sing too in the coniferour forests that start to climb the Alps and I have heard snatches of song

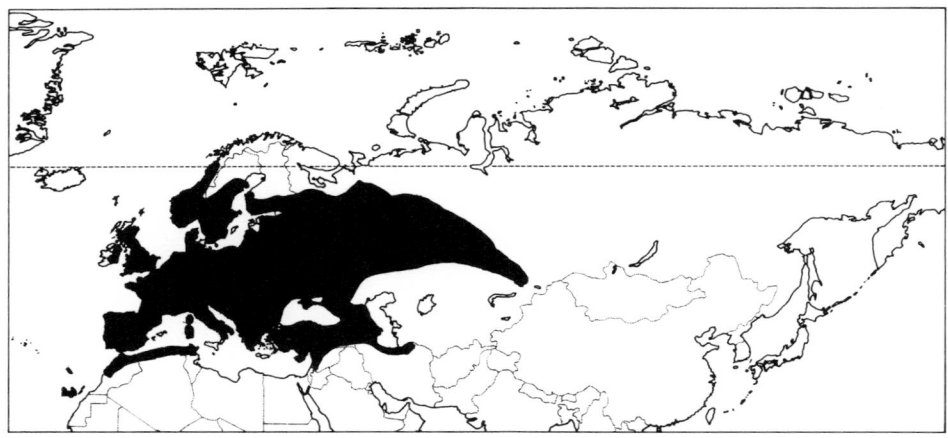

Fig. 17
The breeding range of the Blackcap.

from migrants in East Africa. Better able to tolerate urbanization than the Garden Warbler, the Blackcap has nested not only in the suburban area of Dollis Hill where I lived but even in the central Royal Parks, with as many as half a dozen territories in 1982 in Kensington Gardens and Hyde Park coincident with a more smoke-free London. Being also less retiring than the Garden Warbler and even over-wintering in Europe, this is a warbler that has become increasingly familiar over the years.

Unlike the Garden Warbler, the Blackcap is much easier to recognize in the field because of the colour of the crown. The male has a jet-black crown, dark wings and tail and a brownish-olive back which merges into grey on the nape of the neck. The underparts are a pale grey with an olive suffusion on the breast and flanks. The adult female has much browner upperparts, more buffish underparts and a characteristic rusty or rufous crown. The colour of the legs and feet range from slate to blackish and, while the bill is similar, it has a paler lower mandible. Young birds are

Fig. 18
Blackcap at the nest with head feathers raised.
(Eric Hosking)

much browner above and yellower below, while the males sport a dark brownish crown, sometimes resembling that of the adult female or just showing traces of black in the brown coloration. Whatever the plumage, however, Blackcaps lack any trace of the white on the outer tail feathers that distinguishes many of the warblers of the genus *Sylvia*. As we saw in Chapter 4, eastern populations tend to be larger and paler. Although Sardinian and Orphean Warblers also display black caps, these tend to be more extensive and the birds have white outer tail feathers. Marsh and Willow Tits also have black or brownish crowns and napes but both these

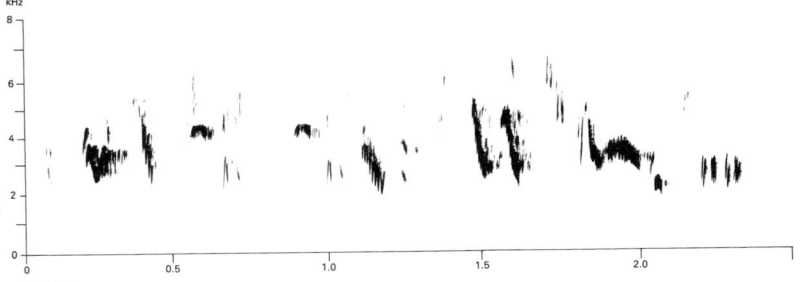

species are smaller than the Blackcap, have black chins and are different in their voices.

The most frequently used of the Blackcap's calls is the contact note which is a hard, rather scolding 'tac-tac', suggestive of the sound made when two small pebbles are knocked together; these calls increase in rapidity when the bird becomes really excited. Care needs to be exercised in separating this particular call from a similar note of the Lesser Whitethroat. One

Fig. 19
Subdued song of Blackcap, with many fewer pure notes. (Recorded by V. C. Lewis, Herefordshire, May 1973)

alarm note consists of a repeated 'churr' with some resemblance to a call
of the Garden Warbler; a second is a scratchy or squeaky 'sweer' and the
third a coarse alto slur 'koo-eh' with a Jay-like quality but less hollow-
sounding than a corresponding call of the Whitethroat. There are also a
soft whistled 'few', low gurgles amongst mated pairs, croaking calls from
aggressive males and strident yells directed against ground predators. A
young fledged bird that I tape recorded in Norfolk had a distinctive hunger
call – 'wee-tchirrruk'.

Comparisons were made in the last chapter between the songs of this
species and those of the Garden Warbler, and I propose to add here only
additional notes and comments. We have seen that the Blackcap's territorial song, when uttered by a top performer, is one of the very best among
all the warblers and in my opinion it is among the top five songbirds in the
British Isles. The song may deteriorate after the females have arrived on
the breeding ground. The full song has definite phrases of rich pure notes,
full of melody and quite free of any slurred or discordant quality, and a
wavy or rippling effect very different from the sustained even song of the
Garden Warbler. After examining the songs of many hundreds of singers
I find that the average length of each phrase is about five seconds but some
may be as short as three or as long as seven. I have recorded as many as
eight phrases in the course of a minute and as few as five. There is a very
full version or elaboration of the basic song early in the summer with an
outstanding beauty and variety which can be sustained for up to two and a
half minutes with only 1–2 second gaps between phrases. Such uninhibited
outpourings may flow almost unbroken for long periods. E. M. Nicholson
(1937) heard a bird in Hampshire that sang 'for more than three hours with
remarkably little variation in the length, pattern and interval, apart from
two or three bursts of particularly intense song.' The end notes of a phrase
are often louder than the rest and possess a rising terminal flourish. Singing
Blackcaps that I tape-recorded in Switzerland often had terminal rising
notes with a woodwind quality, much more distinctive than those of British
birds. F. Sauer (1955) studied in depth the modified ending to Blackcap
songs that he found prevalent in central Europe and came to the conclusion
that this was an inherited characteristic.

The song is generally given from cover, especially the canopies of trees or
dense tall bushes but even occasionally in flight. A bird wintering in Britain
one February was heard to sing on several days (Brown 1976) and such
song in overwintering Blackcaps is not uncommon.

The male Blackcap is capable of proving himself a most accomplished

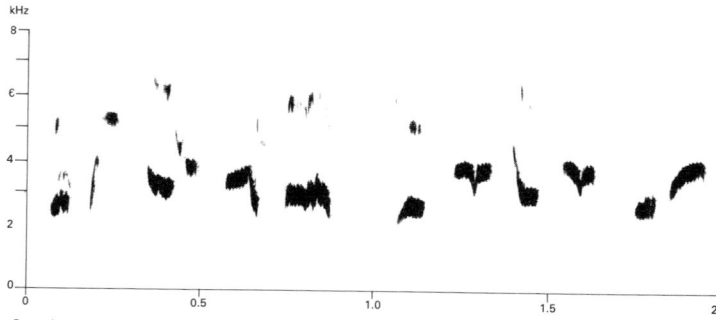

Fig. 20
*Typical phrases from full
song of Blackcap. Note
pure tones. (Recorded by
Eric Simms, Kent, June
1951)*

mimic. He often seems to specialize in the imitations of the songs of Garden Warblers and, where their ranges overlap, of Nightingales. Eliot Howard in his classic work on warblers also listed the songs of Starling, Linnet, Treecreeper, Great and Long-tailed Tit, Sedge Warbler, Whitethroat and Redstart as well as the alarm note of the Blackbird. To this list can be added the songs of Mistle and Song Thrushes, as well as Blackbirds, Chaffinches and Pied Flycatchers. A. A. Wright (1946) added the notes of the Nuthatch. A Hampshire bird was heard to imitate the song of a Willow Warbler very well except that the Blackcap's version was louder and harder (Moule 1966), while other imitations of that particular warbler were also reported by Ronald Kettle in Regent's Park in London and in Surrey. Dr E. Bezzell (1966) recorded two Blackcaps imitating Willow Warblers in southern Bavaria and producing louder and harsher versions of the original songs. A bird near Bath was heard by R. M. Curber (1969) imitating the loud 'pee-pee-pee' call of the Lesser Spotted Woodpecker while other Blackcaps in Spain and Gibraltar were heard making Wryneck-like calls. Such calls seem not uncommon and may be peculiar to the repertoire of local birds.

Subsong in the Blackcap is generally noteworthy for its high-pitched and discordant phrases (*see* Fig. 19); it can often be heard in April and again in September in the British Isles and regularly in the southern winter quarters. In the early part of the breeding season when actual display is taking place the subsong, which can be used to entice a female to a nest-platform built by the male, may consist of sharp squealings and high-pitched notes as well as mimicry (Howard 1907–14). Should a male bird be unable to acquire a mate he will continue like many other species to sing passionately until abandoning his territory in June. Subdued song and quiet warbling may eventually build up into the loud melodious song. The female Blackcap may sing a quiet inward song with the bill closed. E. G. Richards (1952), who listened to a female in song in the Quantock Hills in late April, found that it consisted of 'short phrases of two or three seconds duration and was far more subdued than that of the male although possessing the same rich warbling notes.'

The Blackcap is a bird of the Palaearctic and breeds from northwest Africa and the Atlantic Isles through Europe, except for northern Fenno-Scandia and the extreme north of the Continent, eastwards as far as the Irtysh in western Asia and northern Iran. Apart from Blackcaps in the Canary Islands, Azores, Madeira and the Cape Verde Islands the distribution limits lie between 69°N and 30°N. These limits are somewhat to the south of those of the Garden Warbler and lie between 30°C in the south

2.5   3.0   3.5   4.0   4.5

and 13°C in the north of the range. Here the Blackcap is typically a bird of woods of well-developed trees of various broad-leaved species, with a good but not too dense shrub layer of brambles, willows and elders or of parks and large gardens with tall trees and perhaps evergreen shrubs. In mountainous regions and in the more northerly parts of its range the Blackcap can also be found in coniferous woods such as those of spruce but with a shrub layer of broad-leaved species. In Siberia, birds seem to frequent especially the valleys of rivers, clothed with forests of mixed tree species, that wind their way through wooded steppe country or even the vast taiga itself.

In the British Isles the Blackcap breeds commonly in nearly every English and Welsh county, then more thinly and locally northwards through the lowlands of Scotland and more sparsely still into Inverness-shire. Birds occasionally breed as far north as Ross and nesting has even occurred in Orkney and Shetland. There is a fluctuating population in Ireland concentrated chiefly east of a line from Horn Head and Donegal south to Limerick and Bantry Bay with a few outposts in Co. Kerry. Although there seems to have been some increase in Ireland in recent years birds still tend to avoid the extreme west.

The typical habitats in the British Isles are mature broad-leaved and mixed woodlands with a not too dense shrub layer of brambles and dog-roses, tall overgrown coppices and hedges, sallow scrub, forestry plantations and garden shrubberies all with some tall timber. When a wood is clear-felled and replanted, Blackcaps will continue to frequent the nearby belts of surviving trees until the new plantings have reached some 5–6 m in height after a lapse of about four years (*Atlas* 1976). I found the Blackcap at its greatest density in English pedunculate oakwoods with a relative abundance of 2. It also occurs in sessile oakwoods which I have visited in England and Wales, as well as in the neighbourhood of Upper Lough Erne in Ireland and in Cos. Antrim and Wicklow. I also found the species regular in mixed woods in Ireland, formed from several tree species besides that of sessile oaks. I have also observed birds in many beech woods, in ash woods in both the south and north of England, but their densities there are influenced largely by the character of the understory or shrub layer. In Ireland and to a lesser extent in Scotland Blackcap territories often include rhododendrons and in many areas the bird may show a preference for evergreens. In the pine plantations of Breckland on the borders of Suffolk and Norfolk birds have been found at densities of 1–5 birds per 17 hectares. Without doubt the Blackcap is a common bird in many parts of England especially in the Midlands and the south; in woodlands it may be almost three times more common than the Garden Warbler while on farmland its density is almost four times as great. The Common Birds Census index for farmland Blackcaps has almost doubled since 1966 but the woodland figure shows only a slight increase. I have also come across singing Blackcaps in the alder carrs of the Broads, at Stornoway on the Isle of Lewis and even one year in the sycamores at Kergord in Shetland. Birds that nest in suburban areas may survive and nest without dense cover (Simms 1971).

After taking up their spring territories and indulging in long bouts of full territorial song, male Blackcaps defend their domains against rivals of the same species as well as other kinds of warbler, usually by much aggressive display and even severe bouts of fighting. The plumage is often drawn

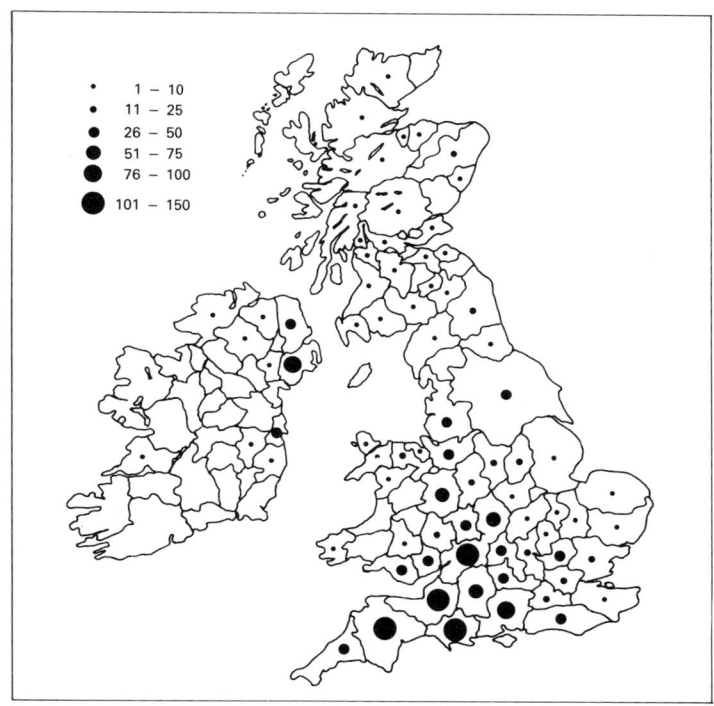

Key:
· 1 – 10
· 11 – 25
● 26 – 50
● 51 – 75
● 76 – 100
● 101 – 150

Fig. 21
Distribution of Blackcaps in Britain and Ireland, winter 1978/9.
(Reproduced from Bird Study, *Vol 28, 1981, by permission of Iain H. Leach)*

tightly down against the body and the black head feathers are raised; this to Eliot Howard in his study of this species seemed expressive of the most intense rage. In fact, I have seen the head feathers rapidly raised and lowered and the body feathers fluffed out, especially those on the back. Sometimes the wings are drooped, fanned out or waved, while the tail moves through various angles, even as much as a right angle to the axis of the body. Some aggressive encounters are sustained for long periods with bouts of aerial fighting so that the combatants break off panting and are forced to rest. Before the females arrive from the south, and this is a few days after the males, the latter become intensely excited, execute a kind of dance leaping up and down from a twig, trifle with stems and sprigs and construct simple nest-platforms. In courtship the male often fluffs out his tail and gently beats his wings before launching himself into flapping flight. The rudimentary nest may be used eventually by the female as the proper nest but some may just be 'excitement' nests for the males – a kind of incubation drive. Dr D. A. Bannerman (1954) recounts the experience of Col. R. F. Meiklejohn who came across 'a male Blackcap sitting on an empty "false" nest two feet from the ground in a clump of brambles some fifty yards from where the female was sitting on the real nest, which contained four eggs.'

Both members of the pair – but seemingly more often the hen alone – help to build the final nest, which C. F. Mason (1976) found in 70% of the Nest Record Cards returned for the species to be below one metre from the ground. Some may, however, be 2–3 m from the ground and occasionally even higher than this. Usually the nest is in a shrub, low bush or tree and in my experience favourite sites are elders, roses, honeysuckle, snowberry hedges, hollies and ivy. Mason recorded that 47.8% of 984 nests were constructed in brambles and 8.5% in nettles, followed in descending order of frequency by hawthorn, elder, elm, rose, willowherb, grasses and gorse. The nest is built of dry grass, roots and bents, slung laterally between two twigs, and the cup is smaller, neater and more compact than that of the Garden Warbler. Wool, down and moss may also be employed while the final inner lining consists of finer grasses or hair.

The breeding season for the Blackcap in England may start as early as late April but more usually it begins in the second half of May – from about 18 May. It lasts long enough in the south of England for a second brood to be raised in most years. The five, sometimes four or six, eggs are very variable in colour but many have a light buff ground, clouded or spotted with brownish marks and a few indistinct dark blotches. Both members of the pair carry out the duties of incubation starting with the second or third egg. Incubation itself may last from 10–15 days but the more likely period

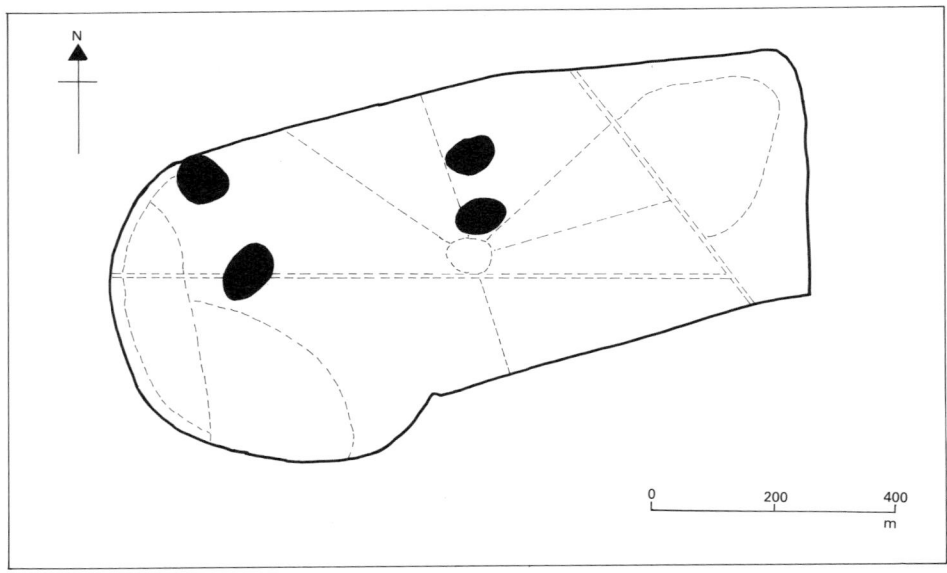

Fig. 22
Distribution of 4 Blackcap territories in a Northamptonshire oak wood. (Eric Simms)

is 12–13. The nestlings are fed by both parents for 10–14 days but, if disturbed, there is a likelihood that the young will leave prematurely; in fact, *The Handbook of British Birds* (1946) puts precocious departure as early as the seventh day. I have not yet witnessed the extraordinary behaviour also described in *The Handbook* where during the incubation period males gather together and perform remarkable movements, twisting and turning together on branches, even hanging head downwards and twisting their heads upwards in a most extravagant, even grotesque fashion. However, similar odd movements may be employed in injury-feigning

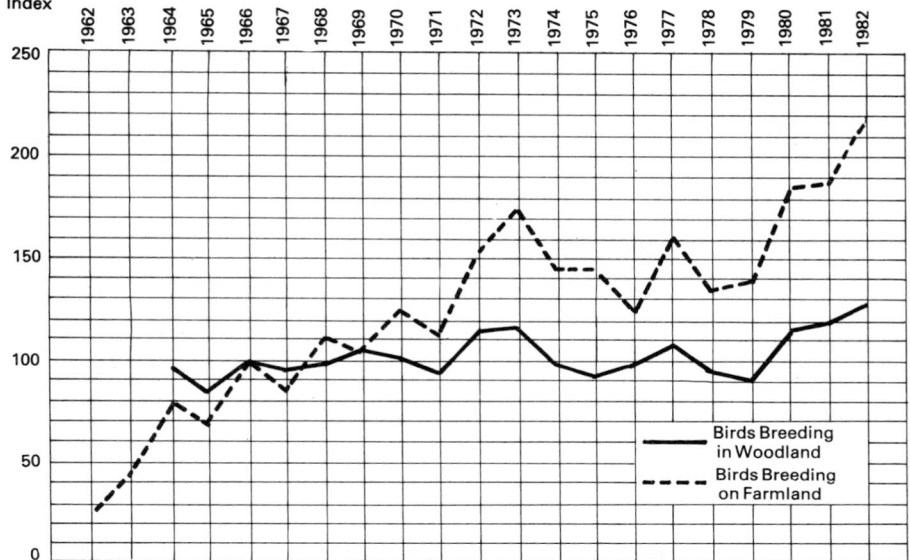

Fig. 23
Population changes in
Blackcap numbers
1964–82. Based on
Common Birds Census of
B.T.O. (levels in relation
to 1966).

displays by parent birds when the young are under threat from a predator; the adults will flutter along the ground with bursts of song and special notes to distract and draw off the intruder. The Reverend E. A. Armstrong (1947) heard a Blackcap giving the alarm note as a cat approached the spot where the young were perched. After the cat had gone and he advanced towards the scene 'the bird performed its deflection display in front of me, fluttering along the ground for some yards.' Young Blackcaps may move up to 25 km from the nest site in July and August while they embark on longer movements in September (Langslow 1979).

The Blackcap tends to feed more in the open and more obviously than the Garden Warbler. It takes insects and their larvae from trees and shrubs usually at a greater height than the other warbler. On their breeding grounds, Blackcaps feed on small *Coleoptera* including dung beetles (*Aphodius*) and rove beetles of the *Staphylinidae*, aphids and bugs like *Halticus apterus* among the *Hemiptera*, the larvae and adult forms of a range of *Lepidoptera*, hairy dipterous flies of the *Bibionidae*, wasps and ichneumon flies among the *Hymenoptera*, the *Macrosiphum* pea louse and small worms. In the province of Cadiz in Spain Blackcaps were regularly seen to land on *Watsonia* plant stems, remove small snails and eat them whole with no attempt to remove the shells (Allen 1968). The young may be fed on various species of spider and H. E. Wright (1949) saw a Blackcap feed the body of a large dragonfly – (*Aeshna cyanea*), the Southern Aeshna – to a week-old chick. In the spring if insects and invertebrates are in short supply adult birds will take any ivy or holly berries that have survived the winter.

It is well known that as summer progresses in the British Isles Blackcaps turn more and more to a diet of fruit, including cherries, raspberries, strawberries, currants, blackberries and apples, as well as many small berries and other fruits such as peas and those of privet, elder, honeysuckle, rose, yew,

Fig. 24
*Male Blackcap feeding
on ivy berries. (J. B. and
S. Bottomley)*

hawthorn, rowan, cotoneaster, snowberry, mistletoe, ivy, asparagus and
Daphne mezereum. Iain H. Leach (1982), who analysed the reports of
Blackcaps over-wintering in Britain, also added to that list *Pyracantha*,
Berberis, spindle, sea buckthorn, dogwood, *Hypericum*, quince (*Cydonia*)
and *Viburnum*. Blackcaps have overwintered in the British Isles for many
years now and there have been many interesting examples of dietary experiment in the species! Frugivory has been well-established and described
for the Blackcap and some examples of foods taken outside Britain will be
given later. As long ago as 1940, K. C. Mackay reported seeing a male and
female Blackcap that spent four days in Co. Waterford in bitter weather
consuming the berries of guelder rose as well as taking suet and scraps.
Dr J. Stafford (1956) commented on a number of records of birds feeding
on stale bread, crusts and scraps, including meat bones put out for starlings,
as well as hawking for insects. In a paper in *Bird Study* Eric Hardy (1978)
reviewed the records of winter foods taken by Blackcaps in Britain in 1976–7
when an unprecedented number of birds overwintered. Many were seen
taking fat and bread at bird tables where they displayed a great deal of
aggressive behaviour to other birds, driving some of them right away. In a
large garden at Llandudno in Gwynedd, three took to ripe mistletoe berries
from which they appeared to extract the juice, and at the headquarters of the
British Trust for Ornithology at Tring, seven fed firstly on yew berries,
then holly and finally ivy. From Gwent came an observation of Blackcaps
taking suet, cheese, apples and the berries of ivy, white bryony and cotoneaster. Some birds fed on the nectar of winter jasmine. In his survey Leach
found that at bird tables bread and fat accounted for 41% of the observations. Many Blackcaps, like Siskins and other species, had also mastered
the technique of feeding from hanging mesh bags containing nuts or fat,
even displaying the agility of tits. During the very severe winter of 1978–9
no fewer than 1714 Blackcaps were reported, especially in the western and

southwestern counties of England. The food preferences for these birds in descending order of frequency were bread, fat, berries of many kinds, apples, peanuts, seed, cooked potato, cheese, porridge, meat scraps, dried

Fig. 25
Blackcap and Blue Tit at feeder. The former takes 'bread' more frequently than any other warbler. (D. I. M. Wallace)

fruit and insects, with miscellaneous items comprising 1.9% of the total. Of the 1714 birds, 76% were in urban or suburban gardens, 19% in rural gardens and only 5% in orchards and woodlands, while 86% of the occurrences were below 92 m above sea level.

In France mistletoe berries are taken and in southern Europe apples, pears, peaches, tomatoes, oranges and figs. In southern Spain Blackcaps are able to subsist for six months almost exclusively on a fruit diet without any obvious ill effects: some of the fruits appear to have a high nutritional value. After an intensive faecal study in several localities in Spain. P. Jordano and Carlos M. Herrera (1981) analysed the fruit content in the diets of wintering Blackcaps: they found it was high compared to the level of insect intake. At least 29 plant species from 18 different families were identified. Those species whose fruit was most consumed were strawberry tree (*Arbutus unedo*), olive (*Olea europaea*), and the mastic tree or lentisc (*Pistacia lentiscum*), while others that appeared less frequently but quite regularly were *Osyris* species – a small broom-like bush with fleshy red pea-sized fruits, wild madder (*Rubia peregrina*) native also to Britain but scarce there, and the climber *Smilax aspera* with globular red berries. Not only do the warblers benefit but certain plants are greatly aided by the dispersal of their seeds. In the Canary Islands the *caparote*, as the Blackcap is known there, also pecks holes in oranges. In winter in Arabia Blackcaps take *Diptera* larvae and *Lantana* berries and dates in Africa. S. E. Linsell (1949) watched numbers of Blackcaps in the winter of 1943–4 feeding outside the galley of a camp near the Algerian port of Djidjelli. In company with Sardinian Warblers, birds fed on scraps of food in the offal bins and were tame enough to take bread, cake, bacon rind, beans and potatoes from the hand.

Records of Blackcaps wintering in Britain and Ireland go back to the early part of the nineteenth century, but a survey by Dr J. Stafford (1956) was the first review of records largely gleaned from local bird reports from 1945–54 and resulted in 256 records being accepted. Most of these birds were found in 'the sheltered lowland areas of southern England.' Many of these birds were also conspicuous visitors to the bird tables which played so important a part in ensuring their survival. A female Blackcap in Cheltenham was present at a bird table on most days from 18 December 1952 to 3 March 1953. Since the review there has been an increase in the number of birds wintering, coincident with a rise in the totals of birds being recorded at the bird observatories. Between 1945 and 1954 the average number of Blackcaps reported wintering was 22 (this figure excluded

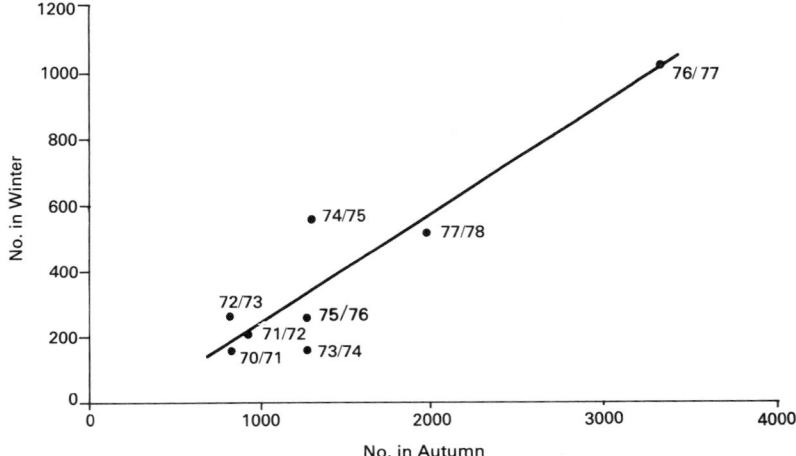

Fig. 26
Relationship between the numbers of Blackcaps on autumn passage and in the following winter, 1970–78. (Reproduced from Bird Study, *Vol 28, 1981, by permission of Iain H. Leach)*

November), while between 1970 and 1977 that average had rocketed to 380. Other increases in winter have also taken place in recent years in Belgium, Denmark, Sweden, Norway, Finland, East Germany and Switzerland (Leach 1981) while at the same time there have been marked rises in the number breeding in Scandinavia but not in West Germany or Sweden. It was also found that the weights of winter Blackcaps were higher than those of summer and reached a peak in January.

As the last paragraph hinted, there is a strong correlation between the numbers of Blackcaps spending the winter in Britain and the numbers recorded on passage at the bird observatories on the east coast. Derek R. Langslow (1978) was able to substantiate this after examining data from ten major British and Irish observatories from 1970–76. To some extent the increase may be due to the better manning of the observatories with more trapping and ringing of birds, and to a larger number of birdwatchers, but the rise in numbers is too great to be attributed to those two causes alone. In late October and November 1976 an exceptional migration of Blackcaps occurred at Dornoch in Scotland: some were killed by flying into plate glass windows (Macdonald 1978) while others died on the coast of Aberdeenshire from the same cause.

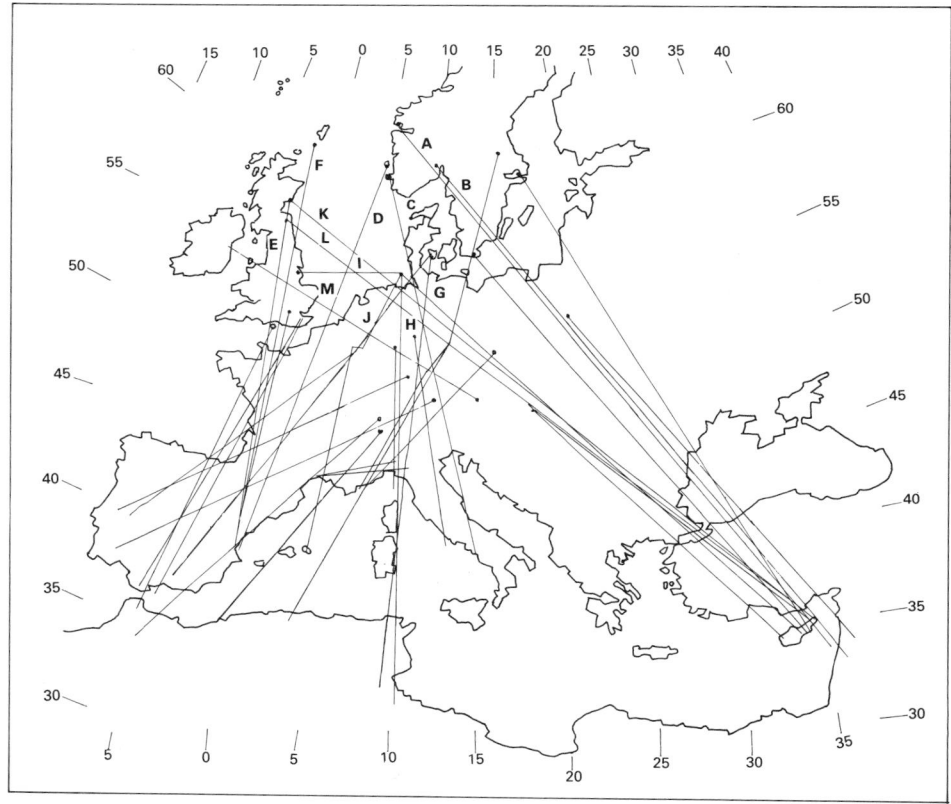

We have already seen with the migrations of the Blackcap that there is a migratory divide at about 12°E with the more eastern populations flying to the southeast in autumn and the western ones to the southwest. The Blackcaps that migrate through Britain include both British and Continental birds. The British birds migrate in the months of August and September and appear in numbers at the observatories on the south coast. Those which arrive on the east coast between the last part of September and November originate from the Continent, and birds occurring in October on the south and west coasts of Britain have a similar origin. As it is not possible to distinguish between British and Continental Blackcaps, ringing recoveries have helped to separate them. The relocation of ringed birds and the entire lack of British-ringed ones in winter confirms the Continental origin of British wintering Blackcaps. The rise in numbers of birds on the east coast may well be due to more easterly movements of air from Europe.

Blackcaps breeding in Britain usually arrive in April and early May and leave again in August and September. Recoveries in April on the northern fringes of the Sahara and the coast of North Africa reveal high concentrations of birds, some of which may have crossed the Sahara. Blackcaps have

Fig. 27
The 'Migratory Divide' in the Blackcap Sylvia atricapilla *as shown by the recoveries of ringed birds. (Reproduced from* Identification for Ringers, no. 3, *a B.T.O. publication by permission of Robert Hudson.)*

been reported wintering in West Africa and they have been observed in
late October in Mauretania. Blackcaps ringed in France and Belgium have
been recovered in West Africa and a bird ringed at Beachy Head in Sussex
on 12 September 1977 was found in Senegal on 19 November of the same
year (Langslow 1979). There is evidence that some British and western
European Blackcaps spend the winter south of the Sahara from southern
Nigeria to the Ivory Coast. Birds also occur in Malawi and the Bight of
Benin but D. J. Pearson (1972) regarded the Blackcap at Kampala in
Uganda as 'very uncommon'. After mist-netting Blackcaps in Tunisia in
July 1978 and March 1980 Brian Wood (1982) handled birds with sizeable
fat deposits which indicated fuel reserves for long migratory flights, perhaps even long single journeys, sufficient to have enabled them to cross the
Sahara; his conclusion was that birds could winter north or south of the
desert 'although whether individual birds use both areas in their lifetime
remains to be proved.' The main wintering areas for Blackcaps is in
southern Europe and North Africa eastwards to Egypt and Ethiopia but
there still remain large gaps in our knowledge of the winter distribution of
these warblers.

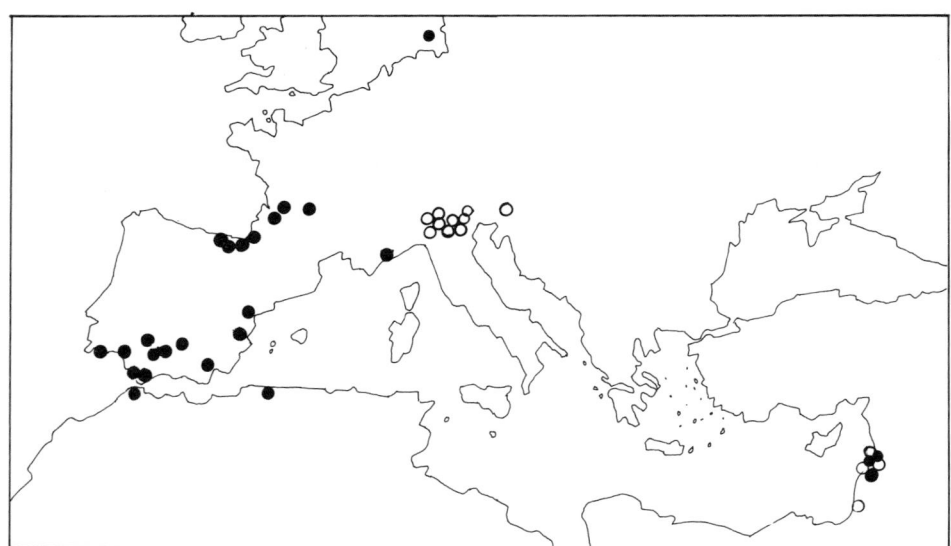

The Whitethroat

Whereas the subjects of the preceding two chapters tend to be rather shy and retiring by nature, the Whitethroat, although skulking at times, is often quite bold and declares its presence with no attempts at concealment. The male sings freely from the tops of hedgerows and even proclaims his territorial rights with an advertising song-flight designed to give him the maximum exposure. The Whitethroat is a restless, lively bird with a short, jerky flight from cover to cover. It is more slender in build with a longer tail than the Garden Warbler and is somewhat larger, browner and longer-tailed than the subject of the next chapter – the Lesser Whitethroat.

Fig. 29
Song-flight of White-throat (see p. 88).
(D. I. M. Wallace)

The Whitethroat often scolds the observer strongly from low cover or a hedgerow and may appear momentarily with a raised crest and spread tail in an attitude suggestive of what Gilbert White called 'a pugnacious disposition'. Whitethroats favour rather more open habitats than either the Blackcap or the Garden Warbler in the breeding season.

When we come to look closely at the Whitethroat we find that the adults are not alike. In the breeding season the male differs from all the other species of warbler in the British Isles and Europe by a unique combination of three features – a pale grey cap that spreads below the level of the eye, an arresting white throat and reddish-brown wings that at all ages contrast with the duller brown of the back. This last characteristic together with a longer tail, more slender build and white outer tail feathers, which are common to both sexes, distinguish the brown-headed autumn male, the female (which occasionally is slightly greyish on the head) and the young from the Garden Warbler. The Lesser Whitethroat lacks the rufous colour on the wings, is both greyer above and white below, sports a darker patch on the ear coverts and is generally smaller and more streamlined in form. During the summer the male Whitethroat has a delicate pink suffusion overlaying his buffish breast and flanks but a few females may display some

Fig. 30
*Whitethroat about to
feed young. (Eric
Hosking)*

pink on their breasts as well. The juvenile always lacks the pink and has a
dull whitish chin and belly. The bill is a brownish-grey in colour and the
feet and legs a paler brown. *The Handbook of British Birds* (1946) gave the
colour of the iris as 'yellowish-brown' but, after trapping Whitethroats on
Skokholm, E. J. M. Buxton (1947) found, when using the colour of the iris
to determine sex, that 'in the males, where the lesser wing-coverts are
tipped with grey, the iris is a clear ochreous brown; whereas in the females,
where the lesser wing-coverts lack the grey tips, the iris is a uniform dusky
brown.' Kenneth Williamson (1976) described the iris as variable, ranging
from yellowish-brown to olive-green and not infrequently with a pale ring.
In a review of albinism in British birds Bryan Sage (1962) included the
Whitethroat as a species for which this condition had been recorded. In
1964 at Dungeness in Kent 543 Whitethroats were trapped and examined
and of this total three showed traces of albinism. One otherwise normal
bird had a white terminal tail-band, one lacked black pigment and was buff
in colour with pale flesh-pink bill, legs, feet and claws, while a third, a
normal first-winter bird, had abnormally pale claws (Scott and Harrison
1965).

Adults of the European populations of Whitethroats undergo a complete
post-nuptial moult between the beginning of July and early September

before they migrate south. Young birds experience a moult of the head and body feathers from early July and of their flight feathers when they are about a year old. Professor Erwin Stresemann (1968) found that Asiatic populations of adult birds moult in their winter quarters during February and March, while the young moult their flight feathers during the first winter. An enquiry by the British Trust for Ornithology indicated that some birds from the European population actually migrated in a state of arrested secondary moult (Pimm 1973). Many birds from Britain seem to pass through the Huelva region of southern Spain and of 64 individuals of *S. communis* trapped in 1967 some 40% were in this condition. It seemed likely that such a flexible moult pattern might be adapted to a fluctuating food supply. In Crete 69.7% of Whitethroats examined in the autumn showed suspended moult of their main flight feathers, or remiges (Swann and Baillie 1979). The recovery of ringed birds indicates that birds passing through the eastern Mediterranean are of eastern origin; these birds appear to have less time available to them to complete their moult before embarking on their autumn migration, and this is most likely due to their experiencing a later breeding season than the birds that pass through Iberia. Indeed British Whitethroats begin laying two weeks earlier than those in north-west Russia.

The Whitethroat is a warbler of open, perhaps tangled hedgerows often in the vicinity of cultivated regions, of scrubby and bushy ground, commons with gorse and heather, osier beds and cliff-faces, and even Welsh heather moor (Roberts 1983). I have also found territories along woodland edges and even in glades in open-canopy forest. After visiting more than 300 woods in the British Isles I have records of territories 'for both pedunculate and sessile oakwoods and for beech, ash and birch' (Simms 1971). Birds can also be found in the native pinewoods, but are uncommon there,

Fig. 31
Territories of White-throats were established in both hedgerows in the picture. Oxfordshire, summer 1962. (F. R. Elwell)

as well as in conifer plantations, but they tend to desert the latter when they are some ten years old after reaching a peak density when the plantations are about eight years old. I also found that Whitethroats preferred the thicket stages of Norway rather than Sitka spruce. The species is distinctly one of scrub such as hawthorn, hazel and other shrubby growth with a rich ground zone. Of some 3040 nests reported 55.7% were in scrub, 18.8% in broad-leaved woodland, 17.7% in hedgerows and 3.1% in coniferous woodland. When I made summer counts in the lower hazel scrub in the Burren in western Ireland the Whitethroat was the second dominant species after the Wren but by the time the hazel had reached from 4–6 m in height the species had disappeared. In Europe the Whitethroat is associated as a breeding bird with cultivated land and, according to Voous (1961), has taken advantage of linear belts of scrub along railway tracks, roads and ditches to extend its range this century far to the east into Siberia. Birds in Europe can also be found on the bush-steppes and in subalpine scrub on dry sheltered mountain slopes.

For me as a boy between the wars the Whitethroat was the common and typical songbird of the roadside hedges and verges. Field and roadside hedgerows in Britain were an obvious and visible sign of the enclosure movement that, particularly from the eighteenth century, replaced the open fields that from Saxon times had been so typical of farming methods.

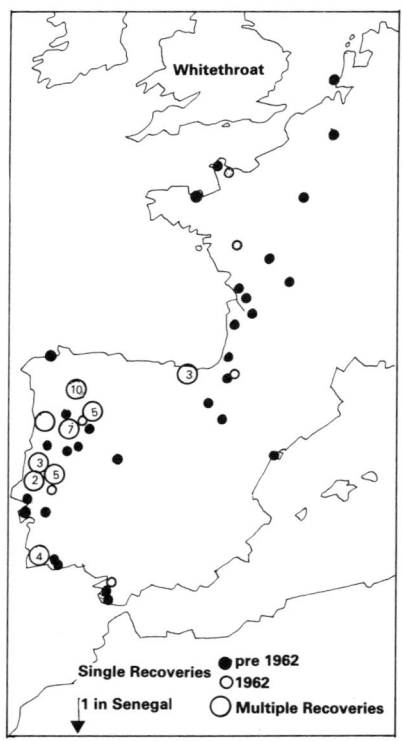

Fig. 32
Recoveries of White-
throats Sylvia communis
1909–62. (With
permission from the
monthly magazine
British Birds*)*

Quickset hedges of hawthorn, blackthorn, elders and crabapples grew up, while trees such as ash, oak, beech, elm and holly were left to develop in the hedgerows. There were some 100,000 hectares of hedge in Great Britain, largely of hawthorn. I wrote in 1971 that, excluding urban and suburban districts, there were probably some 985,600 km of hedge in Britain. Since 1946 we have lost some 200,000 km, and simple extrapolation will show that a reduction in the numbers of breeding Whitethroats was inevitable. The most severe losses have been in parts of eastern England where birds are generally scarce through complete loss of habitat or the flailing or cutting down of hedges to pitiful remnants of battered growth barely half a metre high. Hedge destruction and spraying have also removed the luxuriant ground zone of nettles, brambles, dog roses and other dense or spiny plants that can be found in association with hedgerows, the corners of fields, scrubby grassland, gorse-covered commons and similar country-side. In addition to any losses of birds due to adverse climatic conditions in their winter quarters, it is clear that total loss of habitat has also been taking place in Britain. On the Dorset heaths Dr N. W. Moore (1975) found that Whitethroats were commoner in the more marginal, more complex eco-systems of gorse and birch than Dartford Warblers and Stonechats which preferred the purer habitats of gorse and heather. Birds sometimes breed in suitable places in outer suburban areas such as untidy large gardens, and a pair nested in a bramble on overgrown allotments awaiting develop-ment in 1972 at Dollis Hill in northwest London. Birds have also nested in London's central Royal Parks and even at the Surrey Docks. The habitat distribution of the Nest Record Cards of the British Trust for Ornithology reveal 95.7% from rural habitats, 3.8% from suburban and 0.5% from urban. The species does not adapt well to urbanization. Whitethroats were also not found nesting more than 333 metres above sea level.

Outside the breeding season, Whitethroats in Britain appear more regularly in gardens and parks, while in their winter quarters they favour thorn scrub, ecotones along forest edges and even papyrus swamps. Birds will sometimes overwinter in the British Isles. There were three winter records in the London area between 1948 and 1961 (Meadows 1967), and a female was caught at Attenborough in Nottinghamshire in December 1966 which was 20% below average weight (Hickton 1967).

The distribution of the Whitethroat of the British Isles – *Sylvia commu-nis* – stretches across Europe north to about 65°N in Scandinavia and the northern parts of Russia, eastwards to the Crimea and southwards to northwest Africa and the Mediterranean. In the Near East and Asia Minor it intergrades with *S.c. icterops* – the eastern form – which, as we saw in Chapter 4, breeds across Asia as far as Mongolia and migrates southwest through India, Pakistan, Iran and Iraq to winter in northeast Africa from Somalia to Zimbabwe. British birds winter primarily in tropical and southern Africa. Kenyan and Ugandan birds appear to be of the eastern race but there is probably some overlap in Africa.

In 1969 there occurred a dramatic decrease – actually by as much as 77% – in the breeding Whitethroat population of Britain. This 'crash' was revealed through the continuous Common Birds Census organized by the British Trust for Ornithology (Batten 1971). Some estimates put the drop in numbers from some five million to as low as one million and no real recovery was made in the ensuing years. P. Berthold (1973) reported that

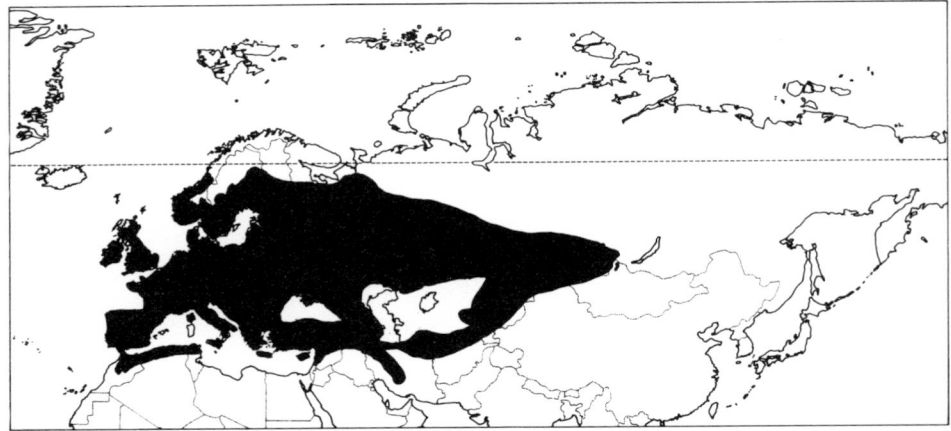

Fig. 33
Breeding range of
Whitethroat.

Whitethroats and several other migratory passerine species had declined
sharply in numbers in western Europe, possibly as far east as 15°E. Observers on Heligoland in the spring of 1969 recorded only 77 Whitethroats
being trapped, showing a drop of 87% on the 1968 figures. At the time
Berthold thought that the crash might have been due to persistent and
harmful pesticide contamination during migration or in the birds' winter
quarters. Although it is impossible to rule out completely poisoning by
organo-chlorine based pesticides, say, from locust-control measures, it
seems that their scattered and intermittent application could not account
for such a major population collapse. Dr W. R. P. Bourne (1974) suggested
also that arboviruses, carried by ticks or other arthropods, might have a
part to play, and reported that 9.3% of the Whitethroats examined in
Egypt in the autumn of 1968 were infected, possibly in eastern Europe or
western Asia. Dr Bourne and other authorities (1976) observed that: 'If
many wintering passerines became concentrated around a limited number
of waterholes by a drought in Africa, this might provide ideal conditions
for the spread of virus diseases by biting insects.'
    In the end it was, in fact, severe drought conditions in the arid Sahel
region of West Africa, lying between 12°N and 18°N, which was thought
to be the most likely cause of the high mortality (Winstanley *et al* 1974).
Migrants from the north arrive at the end of the rainy season when the
plant life is still rich and insects plentiful. Soon the rains retreat to the
south, the ecosystem begins to deteriorate (Moreau 1966) and some species
like the Flycatchers and Willow Warblers remain for only a short time
before also moving south. The Whitethroats seem to stay on the grassy
steppe lands with their acacias and other trees and scrub, taking berries
and arthropods without competition from African species. The lack of rain
upsets the somewhat fragile ecosystem and deprives birds of water, food
and cover while human nomads may also degrade the environment. It is
vital too that birds should be able to build up their fat reserves to undertake
the return crossing of the Sahara but this is necessary at a time when food
is least abundant. In five passerine species weighed in Nigeria, including
Whitethroats, Garden, Reed and Sedge Warblers before their migration

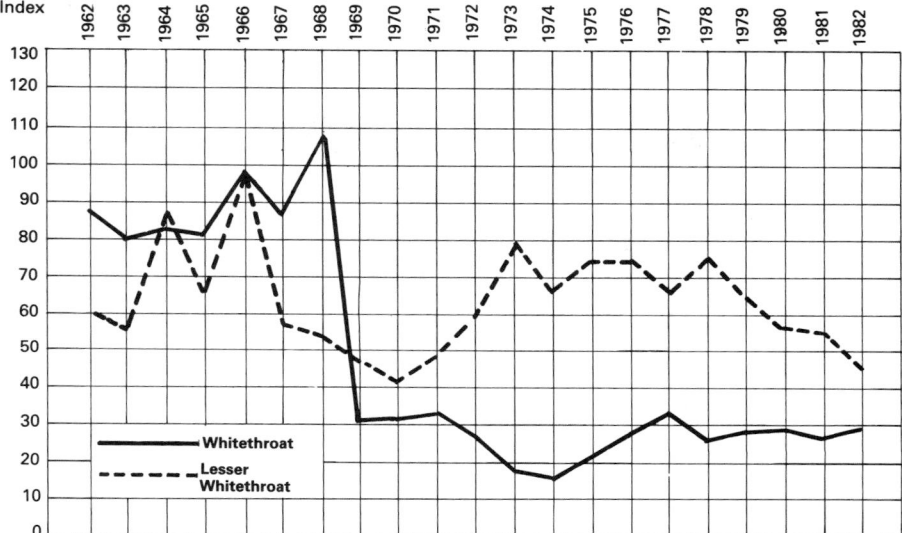

northwards (which carried a great deal of fat), it was found that the same species examined in Morocco revealed weights whose means were 26–44% lower. This meant that birds crossing the Sahara had used up most of their fat reserves (Ash 1969). Such climatic changes may have long term effects and by 1974 the Whitethroat population of Britain was still only one sixth that of 1968. The low population was sustained until 1982 (*see* Fig. 34). In the summers of 1983 and 1984, Whitethroats were much scarcer in the scrubby conifer thickets in Lincolnshire than in the preceding year and low numbers of Swallows, House and Sand Martins and Yellow Wagtails in the breeding season of 1984 seem to indicate another bad period in the Sahel. Although reduced in numbers, Whitethroats can still be found nesting in all the counties of the British Isles except Orkney and Shetland, but the species is decidedly local in northwest Scotland and the Outer Isles.

The vocalizations of the Whitethroat are fascinating and complex. They were studied in depth by Dr Franz Sauer (1954, 1955) and I was present at the XIth Ornithological Congress at Basel when he unfolded an account of his research. He reared seven common Whitethroats by hand, either from the egg or from soon after emerging from the egg, with each bird kept in isolation in a soundproof room. He claimed that the species had a repertoire of twenty-five call notes and three types of song, all of which were innate or inborn. Later he admitted that some learning may occur during the development of the song (Lanyon 1960). In a process of maturation the male's song develops from the twelfth day, beginning more like the food call of the young and reaching its most complex form within a month of hatching. Song is largely confined to the male and an isolated female, whose primitive song consisted of only two sounds of different pitch, stopped on the thirteenth day. The territorial song of the male is a simplification of juvenile song into three types of phrase. Sauer was able to demonstrate that the highest musical differentiation occurred in soft and con-

Fig. 34
Breeding vicissitudes of Whitethroat and Lesser Whitethroat in the U.K. Based on the Common Birds Census of the B.T.O. (levels in relation to 1966)

tinuous juvenile song and in older Whitethroats in autumn and winter singing. In aging and senile birds the behaviour and the call notes regress to those of the juvenile and finally to the stage of the early nestling.

The territorial song is of two types. Males arriving on the breeding ground sing a 'juvenile' type of song or developmental subsong from cover but the full version may be delivered when a female or rival male suddenly appears. When the male is fully stimulated by the arrival and presence of a female in his territory, and after display and coition, he may indulge in a special song-flight which focuses the attention of the female. In the latter part of April a subdued or 'reduced' song may sometimes be heard that can include an occasional rattle reminiscent of the full song of the Lesser Whitethroat while males approaching the nest with food may also sing a subdued song.

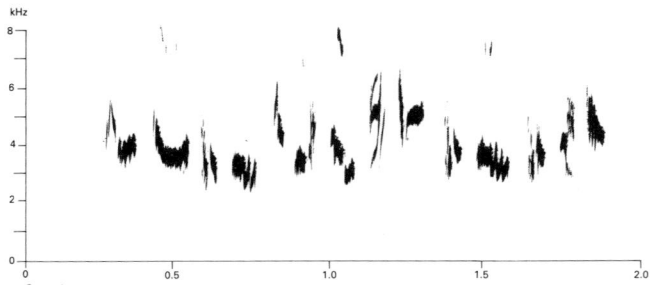

Fig. 35
*Typical territorial song
of Whitethroat.
(Recorded by V. Lewis,
Herefordshire, May
1961)*

But to return to the full typical territorial song: it is vivacious and assured and consists of a short, brisk warble of a dozen or so notes, some fast, some longer, variable in quality and not over melodious. The opening notes are sometimes full and mellow but the song often degenerates into a harsh warbling. Lord Grey of Fallodon (1927) thought the song 'fussy, as if the bird were always in a hurry or slightly provoked.' Each phrase may on average last from 1–4 seconds but I have timed songs of from 5–9 seconds in duration, and one of fourteen. The opening phrase 'che-che worra che-wi' is typical. Six to twelve songs may be uttered in the course of a minute. The song is habitually given in cover, usually from a dense bramble or hedgerow. One summer I listened to a Whitethroat singing full territorial song deep in a clump of brambles barely a metre wide on a cliff-face in the Lleyn Peninsula in Gwynedd; he never once appeared during forty minutes of more or less continuous song and I could detect no movement in the bush. Aberrant songs are occasionally reported: E. V. Rogers (1964) heard a bird in Oxfordshire with three short whistling notes, slightly descending, followed by a trill, lasting just over a second and uttered at intervals of five seconds for as long as ten minutes on end. R. A. Frost (1968) heard an unfamiliar fluted song and H-H. Bergmann (1973) gave a description of a song that incorporated some Blackcap notes in its repertoire, offering confirmation of learning in the Whitethroat. In fact Howard, as long ago as 1900, thought that the songs of Whitethroats differed in various parts of the British Isles. I have heard occasional song in Africa that was somewhat half-hearted in character but K. D. Smith (1951) found song constant in birds on spring passage in Zimbabwe.

Mention has already been made of the Whitethroat's conspicuous song-flight (Fig. 29), which F. Sauer claimed was attractive to a female, but it surely must have some value as a deterrent to rival males. The bird rises up from a bush or hedge top to a height of 1–10 m, raising the feathers on the crown and fanning its tail, before descending with a dancing action, in Howard's words, 'as though suspended on elastic thread.' The song itself is generally uttered towards the top part of the climb and the singer may return to his starting point or land elsewhere in his territory.

The calls include a harsh grating 'tcharr' – a familiar sound amongst Whitethroats – a sharp 'tack-tack' indicating alarm and very similar to the human 'tutting' sound, a conversational intoned 'wheet, wheet, whit-whit-whit-whit' and what E. M. Nicholson (1937) described as a rather Lesser Whitethroat-like 'squeaking, twinkling, shrew-like call.'

The song attracts females and is therefore very common after a male has set up a territory. The hens arrive a fortnight or so later and may present themselves to him. At this he may desport himself amongst them, leaving them until one catches his favour and he will then 'dance' over her, pursue her in a sexual way and finally pair with her. H. E. Howard (1929) deduced from this kind of behaviour that if a female Whitethroat elicits a sufficient sexual response in the male she stays but if she does not then she departs. When excited the birds erect the feathers on their crowns and backs, flutter their wings and droop or flick their tails. During the courtship the male may dash headlong at the female, perhaps carrying bits of dead grass in his bill, only breaking off at the last moment when she fans her wings at him and endeavours to fend him off! The male also gathers simple nest materials and constructs 'cock's nests' or pads which a female may reject or adapt. In one instance a male built a pad before a female arrived in his territory, courted her, built a second pad and then nine days later both began to construct a third nest with the first egg being laid in it two days after that. It also seems that, like the Blackcap, male and even female White-throats may gather at this time in excited groups. Some territories stay constant, others may be changed in as little as ten days, and the pair bond is unstable as well (Diesselhorst 1968).

In his examination of the nest record cards for the *Sylvia* warblers in the British Isles, C. F. Mason (1976) found that well over half the number of Whitethroat nests were built in scrub, while in selecting a site for the actual nest the order of preference was bramble, nettles, grasses, hawthorn, willowherb, rose, gorse, blackthorn, elm and elder. Most were built within 30 cm of the ground but this is likely in a species that lives in scrub with few vertical components in its structure. First clutches are laid in April and the last as late as early August. The species may be double-brooded and occasionally plays host to the cuckoo. The nest itself is a deep, fairly substantial cup of dry grass and roots, lined with finer roots, wool, hair or plant-down, and is snugly embraced by twigs or plant stems without being bound to them. The clutch consists normally of 4–5 eggs – mean 4.67 – but three and six occur and seven, although very unusual, have been reported. The eggs are smooth and glossy and vary a great deal. Many have a bluish or greenish ground and are finely marked or stippled with small ochreous or lead-coloured spots, or even blotched with larger greyish markings. The incubation of the eggs is undertaken by both parents and may last 9–14 days, but with a mean of 11. The fledging period lasts 8–15 days, also with a mean of 11. The following table compares the data on the breeding of both Whitethroat and Lesser Whitethroat.

Table 11   *Breeding of Whitethroat and Lesser Whitethroat*

Species	% Hatching success	Young fledged as % of hatched	Young fledged as % of eggs laid	Young fledged per nest	Mean clutch size		
					April	*May*	*June*
Whitethroat	68.9	85	58.6	2.7	4.8	4.9	4.2
Lesser Whitethroat	77.7	83.4	65	2.6		5	4.1

(after Mason 1976)

In a study of parental care among some 8–10 pairs of Whitethroats in Surrey, R. W. Crowe (1955) found that the eggs were laid before or soon after sunrise and at intervals of twenty-four hours. It appeared that the male started the incubation but I have found that this is not invariably so. In each case the female brooded the nest during the night and also took a greater share in brooding, but after the seventh day this became infrequent. In the feeding of the young at the beginning the male played a slightly greater role but the female made a greater contribution towards the end. The young were consistently fed on green caterpillars and the adults ate the faecal sacs, or took them some 30 m and dropped them or wiped them from the bill on a convenient twig. After fledging, the young were tended

Right: *Chart showing progress of moult in the Whitethroat* Sylvia communis, *based on British examples. The stage reached in the wing-moult (vertical scale) has been assessed by allowing 5 points for each fully-formed new feather, one for a new feather still in pin, and 2, 3 and 4 for intermediate stages of growth as appropriate. The value plotted against time (horizontal scale) is therefore the number of points scored by each bird out of a possible 80 for ten new primaries and six new secondaries. (Reproduced from* Identification for Ringers, no. 3, *a B.T.O. publication, by permission of Robert Hudson.)*

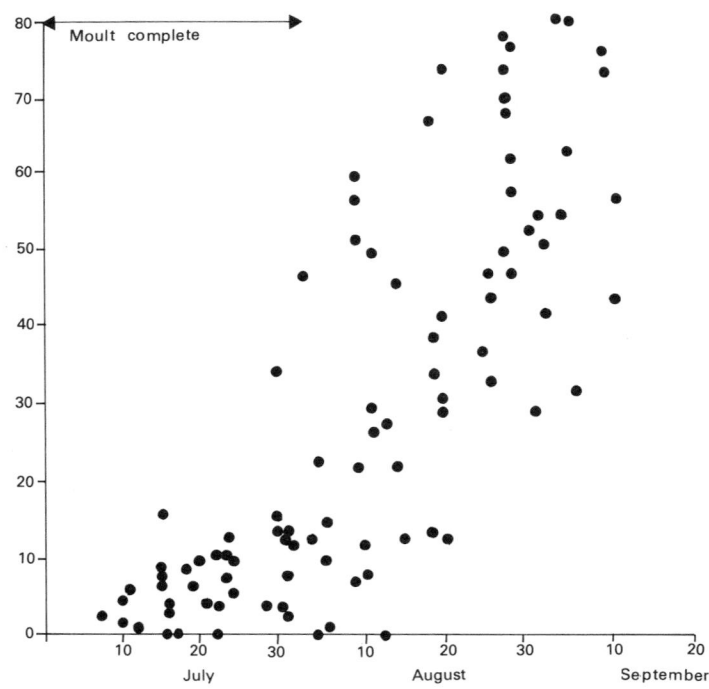

by both parents and in most cases all soon moved right away from the breeding area. There are reports of 'injury-feigning' with female White-throats fluttering along the ground with their wings slowly beating and their tails expanded as a distraction display to lure intruders away from the area.

We have just seen that young Whitethroats in Surrey were fed on green caterpillars and elsewhere they are often given *Aphrophora* cuckoo spit. The Whitethroat feeds primarily on insects and their larvae, especially *Lepidoptera*; a bird at Blakeney Point in May 1955 went for a large prey indeed – a poplar hawkmoth which was pecked to death, had its wings removed and its body carried away in flight (Lloyd-Evans 1955). Other foods include ants, fever flies and St. Mark's flies (*Bibionidae*), stable and house flies (*Muscidae*), aphids, and amongst the *Coleoptera* wireworms, weevils and dung beetles and numbers of spiders as well. A trapped White-throat, which was being held in a ringer's hand at Gibraltar Point, noticed an insect flying by, twisted its neck round and with a sudden dart and snap of the beak took it and appeared to swallow it (Rogers 1967). Birds will search foliage for insects and invertebrates – one was seen picking up small animals from a hedge at Poyle Gravel Pit in Middlesex on 17 January 1948 – and they will also dart up into the air in pursuit of flying prey. I have studied the coastal passage of Whitethroats along the north side of the Lleyn Peninsula over many autumns and can always find these birds assiduously searching broom bushes for animal food to the general exclusion of other shrubs; broom often holds considerable populations of aphids. In the late summer and autumn, birds will also turn to fruit such as raspberries, currants and peas. Gilbert White observed that 'in July and August they bring their broods into gardens and orchards and make great havoc among the summer fruits.' Whitethroats also feed on the berries of wild plants such as elderberries and the fruit of Lords and Ladies (*Arum maculatum*). In August 1974 G. Summer (1975) watched a Whitethroat feeding on thistle seeds in a finch-like manner, in the company of gold-finches and linnets. At Lake Chad Whitethroats take *Salvadora* fruits and flowers, *Tanytarsus* midges and soft- and hard-bodied insects (Fry *et al*, 1970).

Summer resident Whitethroats begin to arrive in England during the last few days of March, but the main arrivals take place from about the third week of April to about the third week in May. However, it is not easy to separate these arrivals from those of birds of passage that travel from late April onwards along both the east and west coasts of Britain. The peak passage in the spring at the observatories at Dungeness and Portland on the south coast and Lundy and Skokholm on the west is from 1–5 May, at Bardsey Island from 6–10 May and Fair Isle 21–25 May (Davis 1967). At Portland as many as a thousand birds were recorded on one late April day. In the autumn breeding birds begin to move south from the middle of July and this emigration becomes intermingled with the passage of non-British birds that begins in late August and continues until about the middle of October. Only small numbers occur at Fair Isle and Spurn in autumn but Dungeness and Portland experience a peak from 21–25 August and Lundy and Skokholm from 6–10 September. Dungeness sometimes has quite large numbers, and between November 1952 and October 1953 no fewer than 554 birds were trapped and ringed. A 'rush' at the observa-

tory there on the night of 5–6 May 1953 resulted in the ringing of many
Willow Warblers, Redstarts, Song Thrushes, Blackbirds, Garden Warblers,
Lesser Whitethroats and exactly 100 of the estimated 300 Whitethroats in
the region. I have been many times to that desert of rounded pebbles with
its stunted flattened broom and blackthorn and its low bushy tufts of gorse,
elder, hawthorn and bramble and watched migrant Whitethroats resting
or feeding in the vegetation. Here in an autumn environment so different
from the breeding habitats in Britain the birds seem to be preparing themselves for another life in the open thorny wastes and bush veld of their
African winter home.

The Lesser Whitethroat CHAPTER **8**

There are many instances of males of this species being reported as singing in a locality for several weeks and then moving on without attracting a mate. This makes some of the breeding records doubtful and *The Atlas of Breeding Birds in Britain and Ireland* (1976) noted that there was a suspicion that some of the records on the fringes of the species' distribution might refer to unmated males. The Lesser Whitethroat is a warbler for which the literature in Britain is rather sparse compared to that for the Whitethroat. It is, of course, absent as a breeding bird from Ireland and the Isle of Man and does not normally breed in Britain north of a line from the Solway Firth to the Firth of Forth. An active but skulking bird of thick cover, it can be found in a number of habitats similar to those chosen by the Whitethroat such as tall scrub, overgrown and bushy hedges and thorns but with a richer, taller growth and quite often with larger trees from which it will regularly sing. It is missing from the small apologies for hedges that

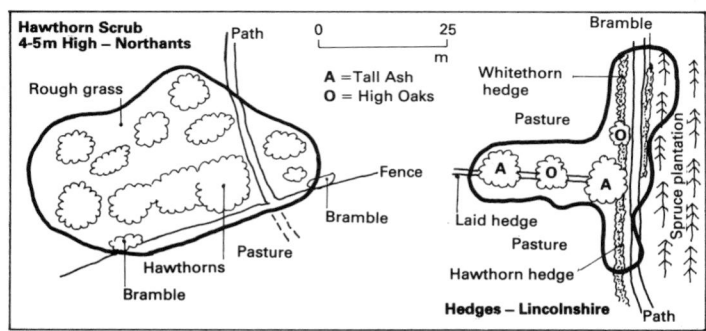

Fig. 36
Two Lesser Whitethroat territories. (Eric Simms)

still attract the Whitethroat. I have occasionally found birds holding territories in pedunculate and even sessile oakwoods and along woodland fringes on the North Downs and in the southern Midlands, but it is not in my view a typical woodland species. Although birds sometimes breed in overgrown gardens they rarely nest in towns. However, a pair raised two young in Kensington Gardens in London and a pair nested in Regent's Park in 1978 and another in Alexandra Park in 1980. I suspected that breeding may have been taking place in the grounds of Holland House in Kenington before the 1939–45 War, and there were regular reports besides mine of singing males.

When one comes to examine the Nest Record Cards for the Lesser Whitethroat it appears that out of 292 nests recorded the majority were in hedgerows and scrub followed by deciduous woodland, parks and only

0.3% in conifers. The clearing of roses, brambles and hedges as well as ash trees adversely affected the number of birds breeding in the late 1940s in the Quorn region of Leicestershire. It was found that of 55 territories, 47 included an ash tree and along one stretch of road three miles in length there were nine nesting pairs in nine bramble clumps each overlooked by an ash. The Leicester and Rutland County Report for 1947 observed: 'When the species is located in a field-hedge away from the road, the field chosen is generally a long narrow grassy field, furnishing conditions somewhat similar to the favourite type of Leicestershire habitat – i.e. the grassy bridle road.' We have seen in the previous chapter that the number of Lesser Whitethroats has to some extent fluctuated over the years, but unlike the Whitethroat the present species remained unaffected by the drought in the Sahel region because it followed different migratory routes and frequented other wintering areas. The highest densities shown by *The Atlas* (1976) were to be found on chalk downland, scrub and then farmland, and it was suggested that in southeast England this species might now outnumber the Whitethroat. Professor E. H. Warmington stated that in 1973 the Lesser Whitethroat was commoner than the Whitethroat in south Hertfordshire and north Middlesex. I found the former holding territories north of the Welsh Harp in Middlesex where the Whitethroat was totally absent.

In Europe, Lesser Whitethroats can be found in conifer plantations and mixed habitats with evergreens as well as scrubby hillsides in Switzerland up to a height of 2500 m. Hume's Lesser Whitethroat lives in scrub up to

Fig. 37
Lesser Whitethroat at the nest – a flimsier structure than that of the Whitethroat. (Eric Hosking)

3000 m and Voous (1961) noted birds as 'common in the scrub vegetation of the Transcaspian and Turkestanian salt steppes and semi-deserts.' We saw in Chapter 4 how Lesser Whitethroats fall into three main types, frequenting respectively bushy grassy habitats, semi-desert and scrubby mountainsides. In the southern half of England in a country where the species is on the limit of its breeding range the Lesser Whitethroat is a not uncommon breeding bird. It is then locally distributed west to parts of east Devon, into the Welsh Marches, the Lake District and Northumbria. It is generally believed without real evidence to support it that the species has moved further west and north during the present century. The bird has bred, though not recently, in the Isle of Man and in over six Scottish counties. In 1977 a pair raised two broods in Aberdeenshire.

The Lesser Whitethroat is slightly smaller and more compact in its appearance than the Whitethroat, and rather more retiring except when with nestlings or fledged young. Thomas Bewick in 1804 commented that 'it is described as darting like a mouse through the interior branches of the brakes and underwood, among which it shelters itself.' When it concedes a fleeting view of itself in a hedge or shrub it looks much greyer than its close relative. Indeed the greyer plumage above and whiter below, the lack of reddish coloration on the secondaries and the darker ear coverts should help in its identification. In Europe, however, some care should be exercised in recognition when the Lesser Whitethroat appears in the same habitat as some other *Sylvia* species. The first winter plumage resembles that of the adult, but as with the juvenile the edges of the wing and tail feathers are generally darker and browner. The bill is slate-black and the legs a rather dark bluish-hued lead colour, while the iris is a pale brownish-grey. The moult is a post-nuptial one, beginning perhaps as early as the middle of July or as late as the middle of August. The Nest Record Cards of the British Trust for Ornithology reveal an interval of some 70 days between the mean date of the first egg being laid and the mean date of the start of the adult's full wing moult (Mead 1976). Young birds moult their body feathers and the wing coverts in the autumn while some first-winter birds seem to change their tail feathers in January and February during their winter sojourn in Africa. Albinism has been reported among Lesser Whitethroats. Birds resembling the Eastern or Siberian Lesser Whitethroat *S. curruca blythi* are regular visitors to Fair Isle and occasionally eastern England, mainland Scotland and Ireland, while two here overwintered.

The chief call of the Lesser Whitethroat is a hard, repeated 'tac-tac' – typical of the *Sylvia* group – and is most often heard after the young have left the nest. A harsh 'chaar' or 'churr' with some Whitethroat-like quality is less frequently employed. Rarer still is a thin 'chit' but I have heard this vocalization run into a series of notes with a somewhat hissing quality during courtship. The desert form of the Lesser Whitethroat, *S.c. minula*, uses contact and alarm notes – 'chee-chee-chee' and 'tirritic' – which recall not the Lesser Whitethroat 'but tits and notably Tree Sparrows *Passer montanus*. Some birds scolded like *curruca* . . .' (Wallace 1973). Hume's Lesser Whitethroat *althaea* has a melodious 'wheet-wheet-wheet' employed sometimes with its song.

It is, however, the repetitive rattling song of the Lesser Whitethroat – a repeated single note 'chicker-chicker-chicker' which most regularly draws the observer's attention to a male holding territory, although I find that many people in the field are either unfamiliar with it or confuse it with some other species. These rattling notes are delivered in bursts of song each lasting from 1.5–2 seconds and with pauses between each outburst of

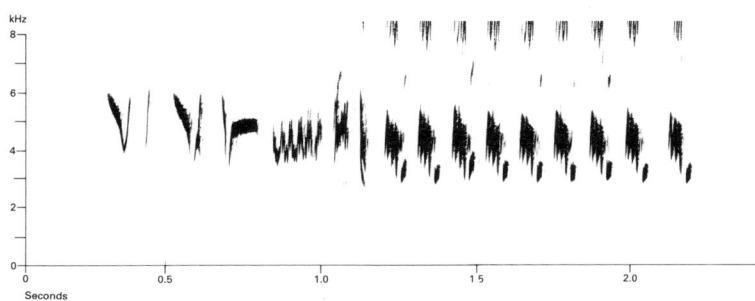

Fig. 38
Typical song of Lesser Whitethroat. Note 3 introductory notes and trill before terminal rattle. (Recorded by V. Lewis, Gloucestershire, June 1965)

perhaps 8–10 seconds. I have listened to singers which have delivered from just six songs a minute to as many as twelve. The loud rattling trill can be heard at quite a distance, perhaps as much as 200 m away. In May 1971 I secured a tape recording of a male in song at Springfields near Spalding which was quite audible above the public address system and the high chatter of human voices. When one is rather closer to the singer it is often possible to hear the rattle preceded and, more rarely, followed by an inward warbled subsong, for example, a swallow-like 'whao-ti-worr'. The soft, varied and rather low warbling may also include a thin squeaking 'week-week-week'. The true subsong is a flowing unbroken sequence of low warblings, uttered especially in April and also in September when full song has ceased. The rattling song without the quiet subdued warble bears some resemblance to the trill of the Cirl Bunting and some observers have even compared it to the songs of Chaffinch and Yellowhammer, yet it remains as a song quite unlike that of any other warbler.

The male sings from cover in tall scrub or in a tree but it has no special advertising flight like the Whitethroat. T. A. Coward (1944) saw a male start to fly across a road 'warbling softly, hover midway and rattle, then continue its journey' before returning and giving a repeat performance. Full song is sustained from late April into July and unmated males may sing for long periods, alternating quiet and loud songs, sometimes in flight. A late bird in the Isles of Scilly in October 1972 sang five or six phrases of the full rattling song before flying away (Summers 1973). At a first glance Lesser Whitethroats may appear to have stereotyped songs but careful analysis by sonagraph has shown that each bird may have several versions. An interesting observation was made by R. A. Frost (1975) who heard a Lesser Whitethroat singing in June near Oberammergau; this individual uttered a strange gabbling song 'longer than, and perhaps twice as fast, as the normal rattle', and later in the same month the observer noted similarly accelerated songs from birds in the Austrian Alps and the Italian Dolomites. Subdued song may be used to induce a female to visit the male's nest-pads and song has also been heard from birds wintering in Egypt. The Desert Lesser Whitethroat *S.c. minula* has a very pleasant and varied warble quite without the rattle of the Lesser Whitethroat, and the song of Hume's *S.c. althaea* is a brief warble with a bright ringing quality easily distinguished from the songs of *minula* and *curruca*. The absence of the rattle does appear to be significant in both cases and would seem to add some weight to C. Vaurie's separation into three separate species (1959), although as I explained in Chapter 4 I am keeping to Kenneth Williamson's treatment of them as races of the same species.

After the male Lesser Whitethroat has arrived back on his territory in Britain, often at night or in the early morning, he then awaits the return of a female; pairing is a fairly rapid process. I watched a male in a region of separate but closely growing tall hawthorns in Northamptonshire which fluttered in a somewhat bizarre way towards a female and displayed extreme emotion by behaving quite erratically and unpredictably. In his close analysis of the warblers, H. E. Howard (1907–14) described how the male Lesser Whitethroat pursues the female closely, creeping in and out of a hedge 'at one moment appearing at the top, then disappearing, or in an excitable way flying up into some tree close at hand, singing, warbling or incessantly uttering his quiet hissing note.' In the typical display the male swells out his breast and the feathers thereon, raises the feathers on his crown, and fans and beats his wings, lowering the bill at the same time. There is an even greater state of ecstasy in which he tumbles and falls about often with a leaf or grass stem in his bill. The bird's abandonment may last for several minutes and in his excitement he often faces up to his partner, rapidly beats his wings, utters the harsh 'charring' note and even makes a grab at her so that in the ensuing mêlée both come fluttering down to the ground. In some ways this frenzied activity reminds me of display in the Song Thrush.

The Lesser Whitethroat has an aggressive display which is used against other species as well. C. J. O. Harrison (1954) saw a bird become aggressive towards a party of Spotted Flycatchers in hawthorns at Mitcham in Surrey in September. The bird 'drew itself up tall and threw back its head until the bill was pointing upwards. The throat was puffed out, presenting a large expanse of white towards the flycatcher and the tail was partly spread and cocked high.' I have seen a migrant Lesser Whitethroat spar up to a Blue Tit when both were searching for insects in the same bush but in less of an extreme posture. R. W. Hayman's record of another bird attempting to copulate with a stone at Dungeness in the autumn reminds me of my own record in 1962 in my garden at Dollis Hill in London, when a Blackbird male displayed sexually and fully to a lump of coal: 'mounted, attempted coition for some ten seconds, dropped down and finally flew off' (Simms 1978). An August bird in Wiltshire was watched by M. W. Tyler (1981) dust-bathing, but this is surely a most unusual activity in *Sylvia* and other warblers.

Earlier in this chapter I described how most Lesser Whitethroats build in hedges and scrub, followed by broad-leaved woods. The nests are usually started by the males while the females add the finishing touches. The actual site for the nest is normally in deeper, darker vegetation than that in which the Whitethroat builds. In an analysis of the Nest Record Cards for the *Sylvia* warblers, C. J. Mason (1976) found nests in a descending order of preference in the following kinds of vegetation: 47.1% in bramble, 21.3% in hawthorn, 9.9% in rose, 8.1% in blackthorn, 1.5% in elm, 1.2% in nettle, 0.6% in both elder and gorse as well as 9.6% in other

Fig. 39
*Territory of Lesser
Whitethroat in hawthorn
and bramble. Northamp-
tonshire, June 1984.
(Eric Simms)*

and miscellaneous sites. There were significantly more nests in hawthorn and blackthorn than were found for the Whitethroat. The late Commander A. W. P. Robertson (1954), writing of East Anglia and its Lesser White-throats, said that the 'usual site is in the low tufts of self-seeded hawthorn at the foot of the hedgerows.' A common site recorded by J. Walpole-Bond (1937) was in dead wood in the depths of dogrose or bramble. The nest site is generally between 0.66 m and 1.66 m above the ground, but one near Ipswich was over 3.3 m and another in Suffolk almost 10 m in the top of a thorn (Payn 1962).

The nest itself is rather like that of the Whitethroat but is somewhat smaller and flimsier and lacks a thick basal platform. It is built from dry grasses, stalks and roots with a few dead leaves, and is lined with finer roots, horsehair, vegetable down or catkins and decorated not infrequently with the cocoons of spiders. The nest is sometimes suspended in the manner of a Reed or Marsh Warbler. Like the Blackcap, the builder uses three simple movements to shape the nest: 'squatting, kicking backwards and tugging' (Deckert 1955). The earliest mean date for laying first eggs proved to be 11 May, six days earlier than that for the Whitethroat, and the latest, 28 May compared to 3 June; in fact, the overall mean for the former species of 28 May was not much different from 3 June for the Whitethroat. The ranges however were slightly greater than those for woodland warblers which may benefit from a more stable structured habitat less vulnerable to climatic change. There are 4–6 eggs normally, occasionally three and much more rarely seven. They are smooth, glossy and with a creamy white ground speckled or blotched with grey or sepia markings; some have a delicate fawn tint. Incubation is carried out by both sexes and the male is one of those warblers that develops a brood patch. The period lasts from 10–14 days with a mean of eleven, and the fledging period is roughly the same.

The young are fed by both parents and leave the nest just able to flutter. At this time the adults are very noisy indeed and often draw one's attention to them. A pair that I came across in a hawthorn frequently showed themselves scolding me all the time. When the young are threatened the female will often resort to a distraction display or 'injury-feigning' to draw an intruder away. She will fall to the ground and dash about with fanned wings and tail in a display which bears the same abandoned character as the sexual display of the male. The nesting success, fractionally poorer than that of the Whitethroat, was examined in the last chapter. It is interesting to note that whereas predation accounted for the loss of 74% of Lesser Whitethroat nests, the figures for Whitethroat was 51%, for Blackcap 55% and for Garden Warbler 51%. Perhaps the overall greater height at which the Lesser Whitethroat builds makes it more vulnerable to crows, magpies and jays which tend to forage through the taller growth. More nests of the Whitethroat sited below 66 cm above the ground produced at least one fledged young. Lesser Whitethroats like the other breeding *Sylvia* warblers will lay repeat clutches if the first are destroyed. The Lesser Whitethroat has been reported as double-brooded at times but not normally so; it is apparently double-brooded in Holland (Erkens 1966).

The food of the Lesser Whitethroat, as one might expect, is made up largely of small soft-bodied insects and their larvae; these include small butterflies and moths and their caterpillars, small beetles, two-winged flies, ants and aphids. An earlier reference was made to young being fed in Bavaria on many aphids. Spiders and small worms may be taken as well so that there is probably little dietary difference from the Whitethroat but there is a spatial feeding difference. Insect food is generally obtained by diligent searches through the vegetation or occasionally by foraging flights. In the summer and late autumn the Lesser Whitethroat will also turn to fruit such as currants, cherries, raspberries and blackberries, and the fruits of *Daphne mezereum* and other berry-bearing shrubs. A Surrey bird in August was observed coming, on two days, to feed on suet on a birdtable (Hayman 1961). The Lesser Whitethroat has a similar winter diet and may take small seeds as well. A bird was seen at Ruxley Gravel Pit in Kent on 9 and 10 December 1961: a most unusual date.

The wintering grounds for the Lesser Whitethroat lie mainly east of the River Nile in the northeastern regions of Africa and west to Chad and Nigeria, in southern Iran and northwest India. Here the bird favours bushy steppe-country with thorns, dry savannah and palm groves generally to the north of the forest belts. Birds regularly visit parts of northern Nigeria every year but are not as common as Whitethroats, although they are frequently reported at Kano (Elgood *et al* 1966). While European birds go to northeast Africa on the whole, the eastern populations travel to India, Sri Lanka, Iran and Afghanistan. The preferred or standard direction of migration for European populations is to the southeast – an orientation reflected in the concentration of birds leaving Britain in the autumn in the southeast of England, so that the observatories from Suffolk to Kent have good numbers of the species. A bird ringed at Eastbourne on 22 August 1965 was recovered at Alexandria in Egypt on 6 September in the same year; in fact, almost all the recoveries of birds ringed in Europe are to the southeast. Autumn returns of English-ringed birds tend to be grouped in Austria and northern Italy and those ringed in spring from the Lebanon and Israel. Birds ringed in Sweden and Finland have been found in Cyprus, Syria and the Lebanon, in Lithuania, Poland, Egypt, Czechoslovakia and in Israel. On migration north of the Sahara Desert the Lesser Whitethroat

Fig. 40
Breeding range of the Lesser Whitethroat.

is practically unknown west of Libya, although R. E. Moreau (1961) thought that it was conceivable 'that a very thin migration takes place to the extremity of West Africa.' Perhaps there is also a migration across the Sahara in autumn between south and southwest (Moreau and Dolf 1970) and it has even been suggested that some birds may make their way westwards to Nigeria from northeast Africa. Birds occur in equal numbers in Egypt on both autumn passage and spring, but at Eilat in Israel the species is commoner in spring than in autumn (Safriel 1968).

Peter Davis (1967) examined the migration seasons of the *Sylvia* warblers at the British bird observatories. In the spring Dungeness in Kent receives British Lesser Whitethroats chiefly between 26 April and 5 May, but the spring totals there are only a fifth of the autumn totals; perhaps, as ringing has shown, because the spring and autumn migrations occur along different routes, or because arrivals are programmed to fly on for greater distances, or because there is dilution in numbers as birds arrive on a broad front. Portland recorded almost as many birds as Dungeness at the same time or a little earlier. The peak of the south coast arrivals is only twelve days before the mean date for the laying of the first egg. On the west coast birds were erratic and small in numbers with minor peaks at Lundy and Bardsey from 11–15 May. At Spurn on the east coast the peak movement was from 6–10 May and seemed largely to concern British birds. The passage at Fair Isle, as one might expect, was later than anywhere else with a clear peak for 16–20 May and fair numbers in early June. This is largely accounted for by German, Danish and Scandinavian birds overshooting since the Lesser Whitethroats of western Europe are orientated northwest in spring.

In the autumn, Spurn and Fair Isle both have similar patterns of movement with a wide spread of records, no real peaks and smaller numbers. Some of the birds may have embarked on 'reversed migration' from Europe and even travelled for some distance on the wrong course. This might account for birds of the Siberian race *S.c. blythi* which have appeared at Fair Isle and on the east coast of Britain. There is considerable migration at Dungeness and I have helped to mist-net quite a few birds there in the autumn. These are birds of essentially British origin with an early September peak. This species has a local migration route through southeast England and the size of its nocturnal autumn passage has been confirmed by regular counts at Rye Meads and in Regent's Park; in fact, it 'is commoner in Inner London than at many bird Observatories' (L.N.H.S. 1964). Portland has an insignificant passage at this time, underlining the southeastern bias to the movements. Actual departure from the southeast seems to take place very soon after completion of the moult. The migratory movements of the Lesser Whitethroat bear some resemblance to those of the Barred Warbler but as a species there is still a great deal that we do not know about its habits and behaviour. Perhaps this is due to what Lord Grey of Fallodon called 'its comparative lack of animation and its quietness.'

CHAPTER 9

The Dartford Warbler

Greatly enamoured as I am of the whole subfamily of the warblers I have to confess to a very special affection for the Dartford Warbler. Refusing, unlike its congeners, to desert the country in spite of severe wintry weather, surviving fierce fires that frequently devastate its gorse-covered heaths and the loss of the unique habitat that it demands, this secretive bird is a most engaging character. I remain quite certain that I saw a young male flitting in and out of a dense gorse bush on Hampstead Heath (north London) on 1 August 1937 – a bird that I watched on and off for half an hour in good light and which gave the characteristic call. At that time the species was thought to be largely sedentary but today we know that young Dartford Warblers can evince a high degree of mobility. Since that early experience I have been able to study the species on Cranborne Chase, where I obtained tape recordings of its vocalizations in June 1952 including one during the feeding of a fledgling, as well as observing it with intense pleasure on the Arne Peninsula. Rare, generally shy, yet on a sunny morning with males perhaps only too ready to propel themselves upwards from gorse bushes in their song-flights, Dartford Warblers provide a considerable stimulus and challenge to the observer. Fortunately through the dedication in recent years of Dr C. J. Bibby, Colin R. Tubbs and Dr N. W. Moore we now know a great deal more about the ecology, behaviour and conservation needs of this scarce resident breeding species which holds an almost unique place among the British warblers.

With a mixture of dark chocolate-brown and slate-grey on its upper-parts and with pinkish or purplish underparts, its small size and long, bobbing white-edged tail, which is often high-cocked or fanned out, the Dartford Warbler, especially as a juvenile, might be confused only with Marmora's Warbler of the Mediterranean region, but this relation boasts grey underparts. The Dartford Warbler has an eye-ring which can vary in colour from brown to orange-red. Living amongst its dense spiny bushes it may often be glimpsed as just a small dark bird with a long tail diving into cover, or emerging from one gorse bush, flying with a typical undulating motion and its long tail bouncing up and down, to gain another nearby. The flight is rather weak and George Yeates (1947) noted that the long tail 'seems almost an embarrassment, too great a load for the small wings to manage.' The tail is often flicked when the bird is perched and the head feathers may be raised. The bird has been reported as 'running across the ground' (Griffiths 1955). In aggressive display the male will stretch out a wing very deliberately, while during courtship both adults will beat their open wings and flick their expanded tails. An amorous male may also erect the slaty feathers on its cheeks, forming a dramatic contrast to the reddish iris, and also droop and spread his tail and drag his half-stretched wings. It is not a very colourful bird but its shape, subtlety of plumage, voice and the nature of its habitat of *maquis* and gorse-covered heaths should make it fairly easy to recognize.

Fig. 41
*Dartford Warbler at
typical nest site.
Hampshire, June 1951.
(Eric Hosking)*

Many times when I have been walking across the southern heathlands it has been the distinctive call of the Dartford Warbler that has first drawn my attention to the bird; for many people it is the only Dartford Warbler vocalization that they hear. Although to some degree the call reminds me of that of the Whitethroat, its coarse, metallic 'tchirr' or 'kurr' has its own special quality that can soon be mastered. One vocalization that I recorded in 1952 was a more complex and contemplative version of this call – 'tchirr-chit-it' or 'kurr-tit-it', which combined the 'tchirr' with a harder more incisive 'chit' or even 'tucc' call. I have not noted the variant of this call – 'tchirr-chi*wee*' with 'the second note clear, liquid, and musical, quite different from the hard "tucc" ', described in *The Handbook of British Birds* (1946). In his study of the species Desmond Nethersole-Thompson (1933) was able to list several calls or their variants when the young were under threat – 'dwa-dee' or 'dwee-day', an abrupt spitting 'dway' and a rarer 'dee-te-dee-dirr'. There seems to be a difference in timbre between the calls of the two sexes.

When we come to the song of the Dartford Warbler we find that it consists of short phrases, somewhat Whitethroat-like but less staccato and deliberately declaimed, slightly more metallic but at the same time more musical in quality. E. M. Nicholson (1937) gave the maximum number of phrases as three in 15 seconds and five in 32 seconds, whereas I have found that up to twenty phrases per minute are not unusual. After timing a number of males in Dorset I found that phrases were normally of only 1–1.5 seconds duration. I have been on heathland, where I know males are holding territories, on grey and windy days when song was completely absent, while on a still sunny early morning birds have appeared all round, launching themselves upwards to heights of even 6 m or more and singing their little ditties with considerable abandon. Early morning is usually the best time for song as well as for obtaining those precious if fleeting views of a small bird with a high-cocked tail perched among the flowers of golden gorse. Yet Dartford Warblers have been observed singing in much more

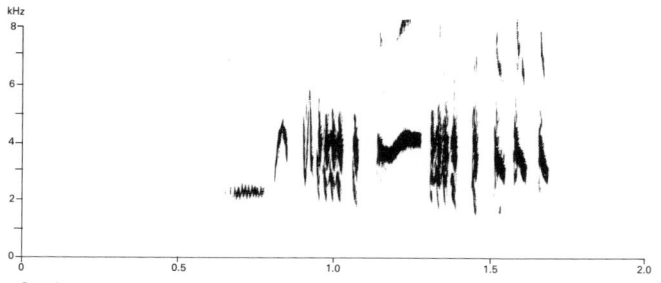

Fig. 42
Song phrase of Dartford Warbler. Note the frequency range and short phrase. (Recorded by Roger Perry, New Forest, May 1960)

exposed sites including trees 20 m high as well as posts and telegraph wires. Song is often erratic and infrequent and I have had many long waits for birds to begin their cheerful notes. In southern France I have heard Dartford Warblers singing among Subalpine Warblers in cistus scrub, and in May 1954 I suspected the former species of sharing a habitat in *Salicornia* with Spectacled Warblers since I heard song but 'the bird did not stay long enough for proper examination' (Simms 1957). The basic song is sometimes uttered with shorter phrases and in a more subdued manner. After studying birds in Surrey L. J. Raynsford (1960) found that at the age of six weeks young males were developing their slate-grey colouring and were 'capable of producing almost mature song'. Blackcaps have been reported singing in the nest but for nestlings this would be subsong. For adults there is a subsong whose quality has been compared by E. M. Nicholson to that of Skylark, Redstart, Stonechat, Sedge Warbler and Redwing. A male may use such subsong to induce a female to examine one of his 'trial' nests. The main period for full song lasts from about the middle of March through to late May, but it can be heard when young are in the nest and some males will warble with their bills full of insects collected to feed the nestlings. Although full song is uttered in July, there is a real revival from September to October after moulting and sometimes when males gather in small parties.

In southern Europe the Dartford Warbler is a bird of the spiny scrubby *maquis* and other thorny Mediterranean vegetation, but in England it is a bird of heathland with dense heather (often *Calluna*) and gorse *Ulex*. The species is the exclusively typical bird of lowland heath in southern England. The requirements of the English habitat were examined in depth by Dr C. J. Bibby and Colin R. Tubbs (1975) on behalf of the Royal Society for the Protection of Birds which was concerned with the conservation of

these birds. The two researchers looked at the physical and vegetational character of 282 Dartford Warbler territories in east Dorset and 190 in the New Forest. They found a predilection for gorse including western gorse in Dorset as well as 'an ericaceous dwarf scrub layer dominated by heather or ling *Calluna vulgaris*, with bell heather *Erica cinerea* and less frequently cross-leaved heath *E. tetralix* or, in Dorset, even Dorset heath *E. ciliaris* subdominant.' Not a single territory was completely without any ericaceous plants but in a few they were scarce and largely replaced by moor grass *Molinia caerulea*, bristle bent *Agrostis setacea* or bracken *Pteridium aquilinum* growing under dense thickets of gorse. One territory in the New Forest included some reeds and a forestry plantation as well as some gorse and grass. Some of the classic Sussex sites on richer soils often embrace a great deal of bramble. When they came to look at the heather and gorse more critically, Bibby and Tubbs found that the heather was generally about 60 cm in height. Raynsford (1960) and Moore (1975) found that Dartford Warblers would not tolerate heather less than that in stature.

The height of the gorse appeared to be even more critical. Although gorse bushes with a height range of 40–250 cm could hold Dartford Warbler territories, by far the largest number fell within the limits of 60–150 cm. Some heathland territories hold a few trees and shrubs while many pairs now occupy pine plantations and sites with trees, especially Scots and Corsican pines up to 6 m in height. Such habitats with small pines appear to have been rather under-recorded in the past, although they were known in both the New Forest and Dorset in the 1930s. In 132 territories investigated, birch was growing quite commonly, whilst willow was present in 37 territories in Dorset and both oak and bramble in 19.

Birds did not reveal any special preference for the direction in which

Fig. 43
Habitat of Dartford Warbler. Dorset, July 1984. (Eric Simms)

territories faced, although about three quarters of those in Dorset lay on slopes or on rolling heathland. The density of territories, always higher on large areas of heath than on fragmented, isolated pieces, was about 42 pairs per square kilometre or a territory size of 2.38 hectares. This last figure can be compared to those of 5.1 hectares per pair (Venables 1934) for Surrey heaths with pure heather, 5.0 hectares per pair in an area of southern French *garrigue* where Sardinian and Subalpine Warblers were also nesting (Blondel 1969), and 2.5 hectares per pair in Brittany (Constant and Maheo 1970). Generally the Dartford Warbler favours larger territories than some of the other *Sylvia* warblers. Data from the British Trust for Ornithology, quoted by Bibby and Tubbs, for Northward Hill in Kent gave territory sizes of 1.04 hectares for the Garden Warbler, 0.51 hectares for the Blackcap, 0.50 hectares for the Whitethroat and 1.02 hectares for the Lesser Whitethroat.

The Dartford Warbler was first described as a species from two birds shot in 1773 at Bexley Heath near Dartford in Kent. It seems that the species was quite fond of the commons around London. Several were shot on Wandsworth Common in 1783 and birds were nesting on Wimbledon Common, but by 1833 they were down to a few pairs. By 1836 the Dartford Warbler was very scarce in Tooting but survived at Blackheath and Shooters Hill (Fitter 1949). Further out it was better established. In 1839 Sir William Jardine quoted a writer in the *Magazine of Natural History* who lived near Godalming in Surrey as stating that 'I have seen them by dozens skipping about the furze, lighting for a moment on the very tops of the sprigs, and instantly diving out of sight again, singing out their angry impatient ditty, for ever the same. While the foxhounds have been driving the furze-fields, I have seen the tops of the furze quite alive with these birds.' J. E. Harting (1866) north of the Thames reported that: 'I have seen this species on Stanmore Common and Harrow Weald Common. A bird catcher residing at Hampstead tells me that he has caught Dartford Warblers on Hampstead Heath.' Others were taken on Old Oak Common and Wormwood Scrubs. A pair was reported from Hampstead Heath in May 1872 and one or two from Putney Heath until 1913. Birds could still be seen on Wimbledon Common in the 1890s and the 1930s and one frequented Richmond Park from 19 December 1937 to 4 February 1939.

Although it always remained a bird associated with heathlands of gorse and heather, it was once much more widely distributed. Numbers were often erratic even where birds were established in quite good numbers. Breeding populations were once in existence in Oxfordshire, Shropshire, Staffordshire and Suffolk, as well as Kent, Surrey and Middlesex and west to Cornwall. Breeding was recorded in Hertfordshire in 1904. By the 1930s the breeding range had contracted and was mainly confined to Surrey and Hampshire with populations still holding on in Berkshire, Sussex, Wiltshire, Dorset and the Isle of Wight. Finally, Dartford Warblers became very much concentrated in Dorset and Hampshire with sporadic breeding in five other counties. In 1981 fair numbers still existed in the New Forest but as it is difficult to assess the population when, as in that year, numbers were high, no exact figures could be obtained. Breeding in that year was also recorded at six other sites in Hampshire as well as ten sites in Dorset, eight in Surrey, six in Cornwall and one each in Devon, west Sussex and the Isle of Wight. Outside the area of the New Forest in 1981 there were from 50–119 pairs nesting at 33 sites. When the population level is high birds may spread locally outside the main headquarters for the species.

For the Dartford Warbler – a western European maritime species on the very limits of its range – fluctuations in its numbers have been a very regular feature. Being extremely susceptible to cold weather the 'crashes' in its population numbers have been only too frequent in the past. These were observed in particular after the severe winters of 1860–61, 1880–81, 1886–7, 1916–17, 1939–40, 1941–2, 1946–7, 1961–2, 1962–3, 1978–9 and probably others as well. After some bad winters the decline may be dramatic. In 1961 it was thought that the total breeding population of Dartford Warblers in England did not exceed 450 pairs; of these 'probably more than

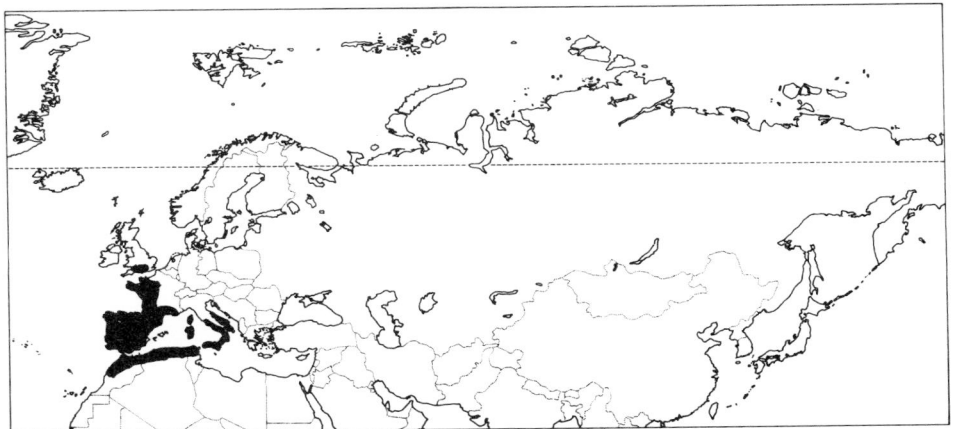

300 bred in the New Forest, upwards of 60 in Dorset and 40–45 in north Hampshire and Surrey' (Tubbs 1967) and there were small populations in Sussex, the Isle of Wight and possibly elsewhere. By 1962 the species was apparently missing from north Hampshire and Surrey, greatly reduced in the New Forest but less affected in Dorset. In 1963, after two consecutive bad winters, only ten pairs were located with four pairs 'in the whole New Forest' (Dobinson and Richards 1964). By 1966 some recovery had taken place but then there was a further drastic reduction after snow in April and of 22 recorded pairs all but six were in Dorset where conditions had been somewhat easier.

Dartford Warblers are significantly associated with gorse and tend to feed more there than in heather especially in the late winter and spring. Through detailed faecal analyses Dr Bibby (1976) was able to show that the adult diet consists of spiders, beetles, dipterous flies, bugs and the larvae of lepidopterous and hymenopterous insects, which are often common on burgeoning birch trees in the spring when food is generally not very plentiful. For the nestlings, insect larvae and large spiders were the most important foods brought to them but some adult insects such as small heath butterflies are sometimes captured for them as well. Interestingly enough the nestlings were often given larger items of food than the adults would take for themselves and much of the nestlings' food was taken not from typical features of the territories but from scarcer ones such as

Fig. 44
Breeding range of the Dartford Warbler.

broad-leaved trees and grassy areas. During the winter, Dartford Warblers seem to subsist mainly on spiders and any other animals they may find in the gorse.

The breeding season may begin as early as the middle of April but usually its inception is towards the end of that month. In the Isle of Purbeck in Dorset the overall span of the breeding season during 1975 and 1976 was 105 days, with the first egg being laid on 23 April and the last young one fledging on 5 August (Bibby 1979). However, a nest which was seen by H. E. Pounds (1937) in Sussex on 16 August 1936 contained three young about 11–12 days old – the latest that this observer had found a brood in the nest. In Purbeck 43% of the nests were built in pure stands of heather and 14% in thickets of gorse, while the remaining 43% were sited in small gorse bushes standing by themselves in the heather: either gorse *Ulex europaeus* or dwarf gorse *U. minor*. Heather generally remained the preferred site. The mean heights of nests above the ground were 25.5 cm for pure heather, 26 cm for heather with young gorse and 41 cm for pure gorse. In both heather and gorse, the nests were usually at a level above the ground equal to about half the canopy height of the vegetation in which the nest was sited. The highest nest that I have seen in Dorset was 45 cm above ground level, but J. Walpole-Bond gave a maximum of 115 cm. Raynsford (1960) found the height of nine nests in Surrey in gorse or heather to range from 23 cm to 37 cm and C. F. Mason (1976) noted that 'the majority of Dartford Warblers nest within 60 cm of the ground.' In Europe nests are often in cistus or bramble.

The nest is a cup of dead grass, heather, roots or moss lined with grass, hair, feathers, thistledown, even according to Raynsford 'knitting wool', and is often adorned externally with spiders' cocoons. Male birds will build cocks' nests of a rather flimsy structural design but the breeding nest is primarily the work of the female. Raynsford also recorded an example of a trial nest being built by a female. The mean clutch size found in Dorset by Dr Bibby was 4, which can be compared to C. J. Mason's figure of 4.08 derived from 24 Nest Record Cards and 3.9 by A. Crowley (1869) for England, and also from 47 clutches collected in Iberia and North Africa. These are the lowest figures for all five breeding *Sylvia* warblers and may indicate a rather lower level of food resource available to Dartford Warblers. Three to five eggs are normal but a clutch of six collected in Suffolk was described by Professor A. Newton in 1894; the main stronghold of the species in that county where the last definite record was in 1939 was in the area between Aldeburgh, Leiston and Southwold (Payn 1962). Seventy percent of the clutches examined by Dr Bibby consisted of four eggs, and there was a very significant rise in the mean clutch size from early May to the middle of June after an initial decline (*see* Fig. 45). Unlike the other *Sylvia* warblers, whose clutch size dropped during the breeding season, the rise in that of the Dartford Warbler indicated that feeding conditions on the heathlands must have improved as the season wore on.

The eggs have a whitish, greyish or greenish ground colour and are finely speckled, spotted or mottled with grey or brownish marks which often form zones or caps around the larger ends. H. M. S. Blair (1965) has described erythrism in the British race of the Dartford Warbler. The incubation period calculated from the morning of the laying of the last egg in

Dorset was in three instances 12 days and in another three 14 days while *The Handbook* (1946) gave the period as 12–(13) days based on studies by three ornithologists. The female appears to take over about 75% of the total incubation commitment, including night duty, whilst her mate assumes responsibility for about one third of the hours of daylight.

The period of time spent by the nestlings in the nest is about twelve days. The period itself falls into three sections of four days each. During the first four days the young are brooded most of the time, largely by the female, while both parents share the task of feeding the young about equally. Then in the second period brooding declines to about 15% of the time and the feeding rate is increased, while during the last four days the male greatly increases his share of the feeding. During this period the adults are sometimes very tame and will feed the young within a few feet of an observer. George Yeates has described how, at a nest near a main road before he was about to take photographs some forty years ago 'the hen bird actually brought food to her chicks on one side of the nest, whilst I was with my hand arranging the gorse on the other.' Young birds will leave the nest before they can fly and will live for a few days quite close to it. Females will resort to injury-feigning to draw intruders away.

About 80% of the nests watched in Dorset by Dr Bibby reared some young birds with the majority of failures arising through predation perhaps by foxes or reptiles. Compared to the other *Sylvia* warblers with failure rates from 36–45%, the Dartford seems to enjoy quite a high nesting success, reflecting perhaps the low numbers of predatory mammals and birds on heathland. Since 10.4% of the eggs laid proved to be infertile – a high proportion compared to 1–3% for the rest of the *Sylvia* warblers in the British Isles – this probably underlines the Dartford Warbler's status as a breeding species on the very limits of its European range. The breeding productivity of the species is 2.3 young per nest. If birds start breeding early then a second brood is not at all unlikely with the two broods being reared within a period of 70 days. *The Handbook* (1946) indicated in relation to the number of broods that there was 'evidence of a third occasion-

Fig. 45
Seasonal variation of clutch size of Dartford Warblers in England expressed as 15 day running means, plotted at 5-day intervals. Dotted bars show 95% confidence limits.
(Reproduced from The Ibis, *1979 by permission of Dr C. J. Bibby)*

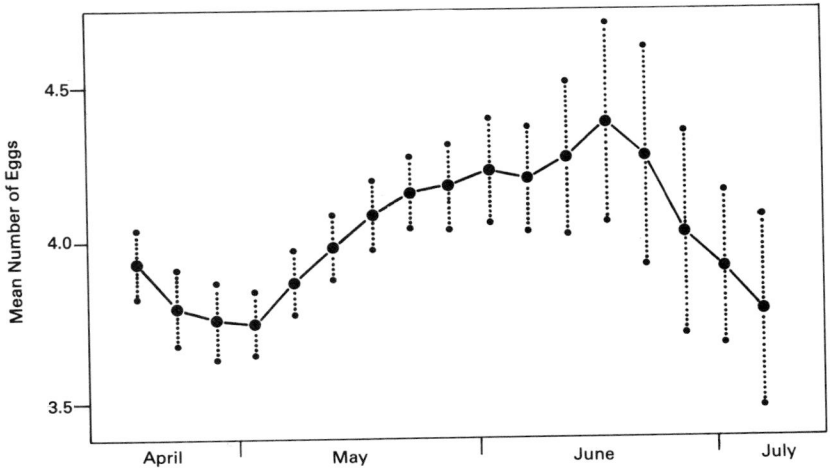

ally'. Dr Bibby was of the opinion that 'it seems unlikely that a Dartford
Warbler could rear three broods in a year in Dorset' but he also referred to
an observation by Bryan Pickess, whom I interviewed at Arne about Dartford Warblers for my Radio 4 Countryside programme on the BBC, that
indicated a possible instance of one pair rearing three broods in a year
with the last brood leaving the nest on about 25 August. Subsequently
P. G. Davis (1980) reported from a heath in southern England an instance
of three broods, spanning a period from the construction of the first nest
on 29 April to the fledging of the final brood about 26 August, and with
intervals between them of 42 and 41 days respectively. What impressed
this last observer was the marked contrast between the quiet retiring nature
of the adults at the time of the third brood compared to the anxious and
close inspection of human intruders and the use of distraction displays
earlier in the season. For this reason Davis suggested that late nests may
be overlooked and third broods go unrecorded.

    As one of the very few wholly insect-eating birds that spends the entire
year in Britain the Dartford Warbler is vulnerable to bad weather and is
dependent upon an ecosystem with a fairly simple structure. A number of
factors have served to bring about an overall decline in the species and
these still remain as an influence upon the survivors. Perhaps the most important of these are the loss of heathlands to farming, afforestation, resi-
dential and industrial development and the extraction of minerals such as
gravel, sand and ball-clay. No one can be sure what oil exploitation and
exploration may mean in the future. In recent years more than half of the
lowland heaths have disappeared. In Dorset a total of 30,000 hectares of
heath at the end of the last century had fallen to 10,000 by 1960 and to only
6000 by 1975 (Moore 1962, Bibby 1975). Some pieces survive as precious
nature reserves, some are incorporated in Ministry of Defence property
where disturbance and protection may take place alongside each other and
some elsewhere lie under the threat of development. In the first instance
these southern lowland heaths arose through man's deforestation of a region,
while grazing and burning prevented the land reverting to woodland.
Much of the New Forest is presently overgrazed preventing the regenera-
tion of gorse, and it is quite clear that the breeding productivity of the
Dartford Warbler is directly related to the abundance and richness of the
gorse growth. As a regular feature of the countryside gorse is disappearing
in an alarming way. At one time it was much used for fodder for the young
shoots are palatable and nutritious while the hard old shoots were ground
up in special mills and used as cattle food in many parts of England. Now
its habitat has changed and it has also been rooted out and burned as it
appears no longer to have any practical value. It may be necessary to re-
establish and cultivate it for the sake of the Dartford Warbler.

    Human disturbance and the trampling of the land may also be detri-
mental to breeding birds while the activities of egg-collectors, illegal though
they are and with the Dartford Warbler protected by special penalties,
may be very severe after a 'crash' in numbers caused by a bad winter. In
any case the very attractive Dartford Warbler will only have a chance of
survival if areas of heathland are conserved, properly managed with
appropriate levels of grazing, burning and the control of invasive trees. It
would be helpful to know more about the behaviour and winter ecology of
the species as well as the causes of mortality. Another study by the inde-

fatigable Dr Bibby (1979), based on his own direct investigations and those of others as well as ringing returns, set out to look at both mortality and the movements among English Dartford Warblers. It was quite clear that adult birds remain extraordinarily faithful to their territories once these had been set up. Even when local adverse weather conditions including snowfalls forced Stonechats and Meadow Pipits to abandon the heaths the Dartford Warblers remained. The depth of loyalty to a territory was well exemplified by a male that was found on Hartland Moor six days after a fire had devastated an area of at least one kilometre's radius from his domain, leaving no heathland vegetation at all! In fact, adult survival stands at 50% per annum, nestling survival at 30% and young birds brought to maturity, as we have already seen, at 2.3 per nest. All these factors should ensure a population growth rate of about 20% a year.

Young birds show a considerable tendency to move away during the first autumn of their lives, even when a local population is actually so low that territories in the vicinity remain unoccupied. Males seem to wander rather further than females. Between 1960 and 1975 a total of 192 birds was recorded away from the breeding areas mostly in coastal regions from Dorset to Kent. One killed by a cat at Castelnau Mansions at Barnes in Surrey on 1 November 1975 was ringed as a juvenile in the New Forest on 1 June in the same year; perhaps my Hampstead bird in 1937 was not so improbable! Other returns and records from the Isles of Scilly and Ireland and a single observation of a bird in the middle of the English Channel in November 1974 seem to suggest that the Dartford Warbler may be a partial migrant in England with some perhaps leaving the country. Spring movements and the absence of records for the middle of winter tend to confirm this supposition. Did survivors of the appalling weather of 1962–3 actually miss it in England and return later? Walpole-Bond (1914) suggested that the bird is 'to some extent truly migratory' because he found Dartford Warblers among the many small migrants near the south coast in spring and autumn.

A considerable question mark must hang over the future of this warbler. The continuing fragmentation of the heathlands may have achieved an isolation of areas and a diminution in size that has rendered apparently suitable habitats too small to be viable any longer. Thus areas like the New Forest and Purbeck in Dorset because of their sheer size might continue with proper conservation methods to give refuge to Dartford Warblers, since their comparative ecological stability and provision of buffer zones as well as their varied fauna are all important in creating optimal conditions for the birds. From these 'reservoirs' might come new colonists to occupy other suitable regions as and when they appear (Tubbs 1967). Research must continue to ensure even better understanding of the species and its needs. Dr Bruce Campbell (1975) suggested that it might be practicable to maintain some birds in captivity during the winter to ensure the survival of some. For the future it may be Dorset rather than the New Forest which provides the best chance for the Dartford Warbler, because of its milder climate and less likelihood of change with well established reserves in the region. To lose the Dartford Warbler through neglect would be unforgivable and we must make sure that large enough regions of suitable lowland heath survive so that in the words of Edward Newman 'the furze-wren is in the height of his enjoyment.'

CHAPTER 10

Rare Migrant and Vagrant
Sylvia Warblers

The purpose of this chapter is to review the status and habits of eight other species of *Sylvia* warbler that have occurred in Britain or Ireland. The first – the Barred Warbler – is a regular if rather scarce bird of passage while the second – the Subalpine Warbler – has appeared at the time of writing in 1984 about a hundred times and has shown a tendency to increase in numbers mainly in the spring. The remaining species are all vagrants – the Orphean, Sardinian, Spectacled, Desert, Rüppell's and Marmora's Warblers. Apart from the Barred Warbler the other seven are unlikely to figure very often in the observations here of many ornithologists but they may be quite common in some parts of Europe.

The Barred Warbler

I have watched the bulky, bumbling Barred Warbler (*Sylvia nisoria*) at several sites on the east coast of England. One September I was walking near the sluice by the sea wall at Minsmere in Suffolk and 'watched more than sixty Blue Tits, a dozen Willow Warbler/Chiffchaffs, six Blackcaps, two Whitethroats and a rare Barred Warbler' (Simms 1979). Others took shelter in the *Suaeda* belts near Cley in Norfolk and in the bushes around Monk's House in Northumberland. Often in anticyclonic weather birds put in an appearance on or near the coast from East Anglia north to Fair Isle where some 80% of the records are achieved, with 'often up to three and rarely up to eight seen on best days' (Williamson 1965). The Barred Warbler is an annual visitor to the area of Shetland in August and September and Kenneth Williamson saw it as far north as Faeroe and as far west as St. Kilda. In 1941 my early mentor and friend the late Colonel Richard Meinertzhagen (1941) saw fourteen in the garden of Lunna House in Shetland on 26 August. Although the species is not a common breeder in Scandinavia, it occurs regularly on the east coast with other favoured regions being the coasts of Fife, Northumberland, Yorkshire, Lincolnshire and Norfolk. Smaller numbers move down the western side of the British Isles through the Outer Isles to Cos. Mayo and Galway. At Fair Isle the peak period is from 1–5 September with birds appearing 'more frequently and rather earlier in the autumn at Fair Isle than at Spurn' (Davis 1967). The Spurn peak is at the same time but there are almost as many records on Humberside from 6–10 September and they also 'tail off' over a longer period. The shortage of records from Holland and northwest France and also from the more southern observatories tends to suggest a proper northwest movement in autumn. Three suggestions have been made to account for the presence of Barred Warblers in the British Isles.

The propositions were, firstly, that a section of the European population travels southwest instead of southeast and some may be drifted to Britain

(Rudebeck 1956); secondly that some juveniles disperse in a random fashion (Williamson 1959) and thirdly that there is a 'reversed migration' towards the northwest related to fine weather with high temperatures in the central parts of Europe (Nisbet 1962). The evidence, summarized by Dr J. T. R. Sharrock (1973), indicated that the last was the most likely explanation for Barred Warbler movements. However, a bird ringed in Finland in August 1972 was recovered in Spain in October 1973 and this may indicate that a few do migrate southwest (Fernández-Cruz 1974). Interestingly enough birds at Fair Isle and on the English east coast tend to dally for only a short time, while Barred Warblers that have reached the west seem to lack purpose and have been known to spend up to eleven days on Lundy and as much as five weeks at Portland in Dorset. In the autumn of 1954 some 30 birds were reported from Fair Isle, the Isle of May, Monk's House, Spurn, Gibraltar Point and Cley with the majority of birds 'in the last eleven days of August, the period when the only large-scale anticyclonic drift of the autumn took place' (Cornwallis 1955). At least 516 birds were recorded in the British Isles between 1958 and 1967 of which only five were reported as adult (Sharrock 1973). All but two of these records fell in the period from August to early November with 77% in the five weeks from 20 August to 23 September and a peak from 27 August to 9 September. The average of records was 51 per year and there were just two spring records in the decade.

The Barred Warbler is a stout, robust bird with a long tail and something of the actions and behaviour of a Whitethroat. It was well described by Miss E. V. Baxter and Miss L. J. Rintoul (1947), who saw the first bird on the mainland of Scotland but knew it well on the Isle of May, as 'heavy in flight, lethargic and skulking'. In Britain juveniles can be distinguished from Whitethroats by size and the absence of extensive white on the outer tail feathers and by the presence of indeterminate wing-bars; barring is usually restricted to the undertail coverts. The bird is very grey, has a square-looking tail, strong legs and bill while the adult has staring yellow irises which give it rather a fierce expression. In Europe the adult male is greyish-brown above with two narrow wing-bars which may be lost through abrasion, and is whitish or pale grey below with the underparts barred with crescent-shaped dark grey marks: these reach as far as the flanks and the undertail coverts. Local names for the Barred Warbler in France, Germany and Sweden, influenced by the barring and long tail, suggest a resemblance to the Sparrowhawk, while the specific name *nisoria* implies the same. There is some individual variation in the degree of barring in the summer which becomes less noticeable in autumn and winter. In both females and juveniles the upper parts are browner and the barring less evident.

Being birds of thick cover Barred Warblers sometimes betray themselves only by their voices. The alarm note is a harsh, chattering 'tcherr', 'terr', 'err-err-err' or 'tch-tchurr-tchurr', diminishing in speed when in series and 'often followed by several softer, subdued notes "tjed, tjed"' (Christie 1975). There is a typical *Sylvia* 'chak-chak' or 'tcheck' while near the nest an adult will launch into a rapid 'ti-ti-ti-ti-tititi' (Melcher 1952). The song shares something of the quality of the Garden Warbler but is hurried, perhaps more musical with its quite rich tones, combining notes of nightingale-like quality with single calls 'dliü, dliü'. The phrases are also shorter than those of the Garden Warbler. After timing a number of phrases I found that they ranged in length from 3–10 seconds with up to seven songs a minute. The territorial song can be delivered from dense cover or from a songpost from which the male will flutter upwards to heights of 12 m or more.

At home the Barred Warbler is, through preference, a bird of scrub and thorny shrubs on rather damp commons and pasture lands. It can also be found by wettish fields with willows, ashes, birches and even scattered firs, in shady broad-leaved forest and woodland clearings, on bushy allotments, parkland and even on peat bogs. Barred Warblers seem to share some of their European habitats with the Whitethroat and the Red-backed Shrike. They will nest close to the last species and the late Dr E. A. R. Ennion (1955) noticed the same relationship being sustained between first-winter birds of both species that fed close together in the same small poplar near Seahouses in Northumberland. In the eastern parts of their range Barred Warblers may nest up to 2300 m above sea level. The nest is built low down in a bush or up to 2.5 m above the ground. Those nearer the ground look like larger versions of the Whitethroat's and are often among twigs inter-twined with grass stems, and include spiders' cocoons in their construction. Around the nest site, birds become quite anxious and raise their crowns and jerk their tails. Birds feed largely on insects gathered by assiduously searching through foliage and very rarely in flight. In Russia ants and locust larvae are taken, while birds shot in the past in Britain have con-tained earwigs, hemipterous bugs, the larvae of Lepidoptera and even once the remains of a small crab. Other birds have been seen to feed on Coleop-tera including garden chafers, click and leaf beetles, and on the whole the prey items are usually larger than those taken by Whitethroats. In the autumn birds will turn to earthworms and soft fruits such as pears and apples, which are pecked at, as well as currants, cherries, bird-cherries and elderberries. In Britain the Barred Warbler can be seen frequenting brambles or ivy where it feeds on fruits as well as insects.

Essentially an east European and western Asiatic species nesting from about 10°E, with small numbers breeding in Scandinavia since the 1960s,

Fig. 46
Breeding range of the
Barred Warbler.

the Barred Warbler can be found eastwards as far as northwest Mongolia. Almost the entire population moves for the winter to southern Arabia and East Africa north of the Equator, and very largely from Uganda to Tanzania where it frequents the thorny acacia savannah, and dry bush country. A bird was obtained at Lake Chad in October 1968 (Dowsett 1969). There is a monograph on the Barred Warbler by E. Schmidt (1981) and valuable papers by R. Melcher (1952), Dr J. T. R. Sharrock (1973, 1974) and D. A. Christie (1975).

The Orphean Warbler

The Orphean Warbler is a species that can be separated from other black-capped *Sylvia* warblers by its large size, stout build and white outer tail feathers and throat. In spring the male has a dark brown mantle but in autumn this becomes a greyish brown with a slight olive tinge. The crown is really a blackish brown also becoming lighter in autumn. The female is browner both on the back and the crown while her buffer underparts are less pink than those of the male bird. Young birds in autumn might be confused with Lesser Whitethroats or young Barred Warblers but they have longer tails. The upper parts and crowns of juveniles are darker than those of females and the underparts are whiter. The species is somewhat larger and more robust than the Blackcap and the white in the rather square tail, which is a characteristic of all the feathers except the middle pair, and the generally pale eyes are very distinctive. In adults the iris varies usually from a straw colour to a yellowish-white. C. H. Fry (1959) saw an adult male in the Camargue with a 'black or very dark brown eye' while other observers have reported spring males with dark and even pale grey eyes.

The Orphean Warbler is a summer inhabitant of open woods of cork, ilex and oak, citrus and olive groves, orchards, gardens and sometimes pine plantations. In these habitats, but not invariably, are some smaller trees and scrubby undergrowth, while birds also occur in rather thin dry Mediterranean scrub; here the birds feed on arboreal insects and their larvae. On passage in North Africa birds can be seen carefully searching the bark of olive trees and in Eritrea (Smith 1957) in winter birds can be found in the acacia scrub from which they will sing in March before migrating. The late H. F. Witherby observed Orphean Warblers busily feeding in central Spain on gypsy moth caterpillars that were attacking the ilex trees, although they needed a great deal of pecking and preparation to make them soft enough for consumption. Feeding has also been noted on other moths and their caterpillars as well as various dipterous flies and grasshoppers. I have watched birds venturing on to marshland to forage where it has bordered the umbrella pine forests of the Coto Doñana, listened to them among the cork oaks elsewhere in Spain, around the *mas* or farmsteads in Provence and in the olive groves of classical Greece. In the poplar groves and tangled scrub along the Rhône I have seen birds foraging for insects often at quite a height. Figs, fruit and berries may be added to the autumn diet. The species nests from Iberia and North Africa eastwards to northwest India. In southern Spain the nests are often in the outer branches of orange trees from 2.6–3.3 m up, in pollarded ilex and oaks from 2.3–3.3 m where they are often parasitized by cuckoos, and in Africa from 2.3 m up in trees or tall scrub. An account of the life style of the

Fig. 47
The ruins of Delphi in Greece where the author heard Orphean, Sardinian, Rüppell's and other Sylvia species in song. (Eric Simms, April 1973)

Fig. 48
Breeding range of the Orphean Warbler.

Orphean Warbler was given by Dr Geoffrey Beven (1971). The typical race winters in northern tropical and northeast Africa, while wanderers have appeared in Madeira, the Channel Islands, Germany, Moravia and Britain. The alarm note of the Orphean Warbler is a hard rattling 'trrrrr' with a suggestion of the Sardinian Warbler but lacking its length and hard metallic quality. There is also a 'tack-tack' or 'tyut-tyut' suggestive of a call of the Blackcap. The song is a short thrush-like warble whose durations I have timed from 3–5 seconds with some six or seven bursts in a minute. The notes are pleasing and repetitive with the same component being repeated and each component formed from similar notes. In this way runs are

established – 'hee-haw-hee-haw-hee-haw', 'chiwiroo-chiwiroo' – with each part perhaps being repeated some 3–5 times. The song may include some imitations. The songs are also said to be more repetitive in the western parts of the range and more thrush-like in the eastern.

The first British record of the Orphean Warbler was of a bird shot on 6 July 1848 near Wetherby in Yorkshire and which may have been breeding. The second was of a bird at Portland in Dorset on 20 September 1955 and the third at Porthgwarra in Cornwall on 22 October 1967. The last bird 'in the hand looked like a large robust *Sylvia* warbler with the same 'staring' eyes and jizz as Whitethroat *Sylvia communis*. The bird cocked its tail while in the hand on several occasions.' (Griffiths *et al* 1970). Subsequent records were at Stiffkey in Norfolk on 17 August 1981 and on St Mary's in the Isles of Scilly from 16–22 October in that same year.

The Sardinian Warbler

The Sardinian Warbler, which nests on the Canary Islands and in the basin of the Mediterranean and east from there to Asia Minor where it may be the commonest warbler (Ogilvie 1954) and to Iraq and Afghanistan, looks rather like a stoutish Whitethroat but with a heavier bill. Although the bird is smaller this may not be easy to determine in the field. It also lacks any rufous colour in the wing and regularly cocks its tail. The male resembles a cock Blackcap but the glossy cap descends below the eye and there are conspicuous red eyes and eye-rings. In fact, the iris may be reddish-brown to yellowish in colour while according to *The Handbook*

Fig. 49
Female Sardinian Warbler at the nest. Spain, May 1957. (Eric Hosking)

(1946) the orbital ring and eyelids in the adult are salmon-pink and pinkish-brown in the juvenile. In bright sunlight I have seen some adults at close quarters with bright reddish eye-rings; other observers have described them as 'crimson' or 'brilliant red'. The male may resemble a Blackcap but with the black below the eye, and its regularly fanned graduated blackish tail with clear white outer feathers, no confusion should arise. The female is much browner in colour both on her back and on the cap. This is a scrub species of open woodlands with thick undergrowth, of thickets, vineyards, gardens and regions with tree heath and cistus. In the western part of its Mediterranean range from Iberia to Greece the Sardinian Warbler can be found where there are tree heath, cistus, *Halimium*, gorse and brambles: here the present species lives alongside the Subalpine Warbler, while in the east it tends to favour tamarisks (Ferguson-Lees 1967). In Libya birds often nest in juniper and *Lentiscus* (Stanford 1954). I have seen males singing from low bushtops or in their aerial dances above low thorn scrub on the Atlantic coast of Spain in a region that they shared with Woodchat shrikes and Andalusian Hemipodes. Another favourite site where I regularly observed them was among the lichen-covered scrub junipers, narcissi and asphodel of coastal southern France.

The Sardinian Warbler is one of the common birds of the scrub and its stuttering harsh alarm one of the commonest sounds – a hard 'stititititititic' thought by some writers to sound like a clock being wound. The bird also employs a double 'treek-treek' or 'treeka-treeka-treek'. These notes as well as a harsh churring call 'tcha' or 'kurr' may be incorporated in the song. I listened to many singers around the Mediterranean and in Spain and the song 'seemed louder than that of the Whitethroat, more prolonged and liberally sprinkled with the loud "tcha-tcha-tcha" alarm call' (Simms 1957). I also timed many phrases and found that some of them lasted for as much as 16 seconds but on the whole seven or eight phrases a minute was a good average. The phrases consisted of not greatly modulated but still quite pleasing notes and in my opinion generally better in quality than the song of most Whitethroats. I have seen birds rise up from scrub to heights of four or more metres and sing, just as they were described by Ogilvie (1954) in Asia Minor, whose performers would 'then glide with high uplifted wings to another bough some 30 to 40 yards away.' This warbler is always active and perky, frequently cocks its tail but will also skulk in thick cover. A bird watched on Fair Isle regularly cocked its tail and erected the feathers on its crown. The nest is built by both members of the pair in scrub and undergrowth from just below to just above a metre from the ground. I have watched birds taking caterpillars and small insects and searching for spiders as well. The bird will switch later in the year to figs, grapes, grass seeds and the seeds of the Californian pepper tree *Schinus molle* in Spain.

The Sardinian Warbler is mainly sedentary but birds have been known to wander south to the Sahara, Egypt, Arabia and Iraq. An adult male was trapped on the island of Lundy in Devon on 10 May 1955 and it was noted by the observer that it reminded her of a Dartford Warbler, 'the tail being held upright at an angle to the body' (Whitaker 1955). A second male was present on Fair Isle on 26 and 27 May 1967 and was trapped; this bird was seen to perch on the rocks or wire netting, cocking its tail and it 'frequently raised and lowered its crown feathers, but did not call' (Dennis 1967). Further birds were reported from Skokholm on 28 October 1968 (the first

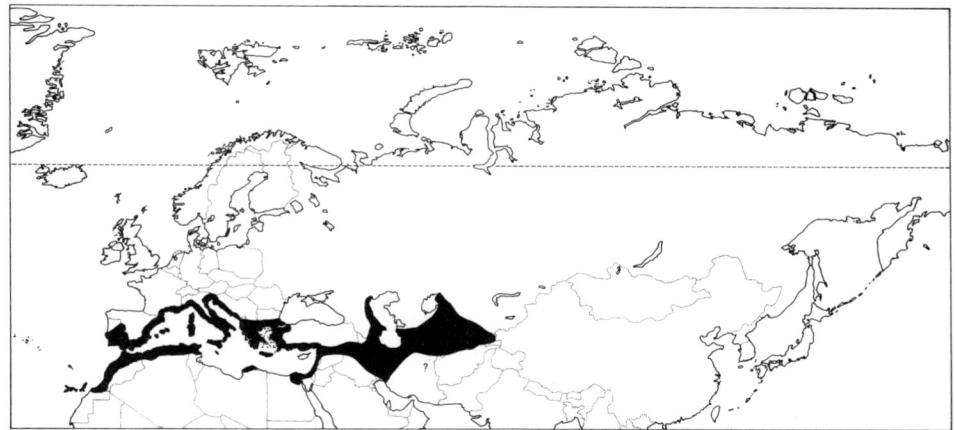

autumn record), at Dungeness in Kent on 17 April 1973, at Waxham in Norfolk on 28–9 April 1973, at Beachy Head from 23 August–30 October 1976, a male at Gibraltar Point from 30 June–15 September 1979, a first-winter male on Tresco in the Isles of Scilly from 25 September to the end of October 1980, one at Weybourne in Norfolk from 1 September–5 October 1980 and a male at Spurn on Humberside from 4–6 June 1982.

Fig. 50
Breeding range of the Sardinian Warbler.

The Subalpine Warbler

The mainly migratory Subalpine Warbler is also a common bird of the Mediterranean scrub and has made many more appearances in the British Isles than the Sardinian Warbler with, for example, as many as 11 records in 1979, 8 in 1981 and 5 in 1982. I consider the Subalpine Warbler to be one of the most beautiful and delicate of this genus of warblers. It looks at first glance like a rather pale Dartford Warbler with a white moustachial stripe and a bright red eye-ring, but this is a dullish gold colour in juveniles. Some males are less bright than others while the females and juveniles are a duller brown on the upperparts and have a buffish white throat. Since Subalpines may nest near Dartford Warblers, it is essential to note the former's paler backs, shorter tails and unspotted throats and the male's moustache. Both female and young Subalpines are buffer and paler on the crown than Sardinian Warblers of the equivalent status. Female and juvenile Spectacled Warblers have chestnut wing-patches, whereas Sub-alpines have pale brown ones, but it has become clear in recent years that trying to separate Spectacled Warblers from Subalpine Warblers in autumn in Britain is more difficult than was formerly believed, so that some reports of Spectacled Warblers here are currently under review.

As we saw in Chapter 4, the typical race of the Subalpine Warbler has a rather restricted breeding range on some Mediterranean islands and around the basin of that sea. It is a bird of the thorny scrub of the *maquis* with spiny-leaved holm oaks, thorny kermes oaks which are hosts to the scale insects that produce red dye known since the time of Pliny, wild olives, myrtles, junipers and strawberry trees often growing in dense thickets, and of the

Fig. 51
Habitat for Subalpine
Warblers below Les
Baux, Les Alpilles,
Provence. (Eric Simms,
May 1973)

garrigue with broom, cistus and other small shrubs, lavender, dwarf palm and fragrant herbs like thyme and rosemary (Beven 1967). I have watched Subalpine Warblers among holm oaks in the south of France where birds sing alongside nightingales, by a stream among dense thickets near Huelva in southern Spain (although the species was only recorded as a scarce passage migrant in the area on three expeditions to the Coto Doñana led by Guy Mountfort (1958)) and among very spiny bushes in the dry Les Alpilles under a blazing sun with nightingales again singing in the background. In May 1973 in this last habitat, which I visited with members of the BBC's Natural History Unit from Bristol, I isolated a Subalpine Warbler that was holding a territory in a scrubby little defile lying amongst acres of arid rock and spiny bushes. Here he sang from the tops or inside of the bushes or in a little song-flight, and we made stereo recordings on tape of his performance. It reminded me of the output of both Whitethroat and Sardinian but to me it was 'more sweet and pleasing without any harsh notes' (Simms 1979). This particular individual sang at the rate of some eight songs a minute with each lasting from only 1-3 seconds and more rarely up to 7 seconds. Yet another that I heard elsewhere uttered sustained bursts of 35 seconds or short ones of only 2, with on average some eight phrases to the minute. When excited the Subalpine Warbler raises its tail like a Dartford Warbler, occasionally, according to Sharrock (1962), keeping it cocked while feeding, and raising the crown feathers into a crest. It also employs a series of very noisy alarm notes – 'chat-chat-chat-chat', 'tac-tac', 'tec-tec' or 'chit-chit' – notes often run together into a rapid clicking or chattering series of notes. The male also has an especially attractive display well described by George Yeates (1946).

Subalpine Warblers hunt for insects and their larvae – the staple food of the *Sylvia* genus – among oaks, olives and other trees. In Portugal they seem to feed on dipterous fly larvae as well as crickets and *Phasmida* stick insects 37–50 mm in length (Beven 1967), while their Mediterranean diet includes spiders, various beetles and occasional grass seeds. A Fair Isle visitor fed untiringly on Chironomid gnats (Williamson 1952) and in their West African winter quarters birds take *Salvadora* berries. Subalpine Warblers may occur in the same habitat as both Spectacled and Dartford Warblers, but the degree of competition between the three species is not known. Nesting takes place in thickets from around ground level to about a metre up. Dr Geoffrey Beven (1967) has written an interesting paper on the biology and habits of this species.

The Subalpine Warbler is usually regarded as a summer migrant to Europe which spends the winter among scrubby acacias along the western and southern fringes of the Sahara Desert west as far as Lake Chad and east to Arabia and northern Sudan. These birds cross the desert and evidently pass through the breeding area of the northwestern African race *S.c. inornata*; they are reported from the Gambia, Niger and Tangier and are common around Timbuktu and some of the Saharan oases. Some birds may winter in the Iberian peninsula, while others are not uncommon on passage in spring from Tripolitania to Egypt where they are rare in autumn, suggesting two different routes during the two seasons. Despite the southern bias in its range birds are recorded much further north, having appeared in countries as widely separated as Switzerland, Holland, Finland, Norway and Sweden, although it was often not possible to determine the race (see Chapter 4).

A fair number of birds have reached the British Isles. There have been records in every month from April to November, largely in coastal counties, and by 1976 of all the occurrences 52% had been in the Northern Isles in spring (Sharrock 1976). Just over half the records were in the period of seven weeks from 16 April to 3 June. What was rather interesting was that 'pairs' of birds were recorded several times in Shetland and on Fair Isle. Some of these northern birds may be of the eastern race. The preponderance of spring over autumn records suggests that spring migrants from the

Fig. 52
Breeding range of the Subalpine Warbler (left) and Ménétries's Warbler (right).

southeast have been 'overshooting' their targets in anticyclonic weather (Williamson 1976). Birds have also shown up around the Irish Sea but more often in the autumn than the spring. With so many records in autumn on the east coast of Britain there is a strong assumption that birds are of a southeastern rather than a southern origin. A bird on Fair Isle in the Observatory laboratory with 'eyes like a miniature Oystercatcher' made a churring noise like a Lesser Whitethroat but on the beach it was only heard to utter a hard 'chep' (Williamson and Hayman 1952), while a bird in Norfolk produced 'a quiet "tec-tec"' (Acklam 1956).

The Spectacled Warbler

The first Spectacled Warbler identified in Britain and Ireland was present at Spurn Head in Humberside from 21–31 October 1968; this bird was mist-netted, weighed and measured and its low weight suggested that it was a new arrival (Cudworth and Spence 1978). It resembled a small Whitethroat 'with greyish head, white throat and rufous patch on the wing'. Its small size suggested a leaf warbler *Phylloscopus* to some observers and a Lesser Whitethroat to others, but the habits were those of a Subalpine Warbler and it often kept its tail cocked. After it was released it frequented some scrubby sea buckthorn *Hippophae rhamnoides* as well as Duke of Argyll's tea tree *Lycium*. A second Spectacled Warbler was seen at Porthgwarra in Cornwall on 17 October 1969 (Jobson 1978). This bird was found in low gorse and 'seemed to combine the best features of Whitethroat and Lesser Whitethroat'. The third British record was of a male on Fair Isle from 4–5 June 1979 (Rogers *et al* 1980), this being the first spring record.

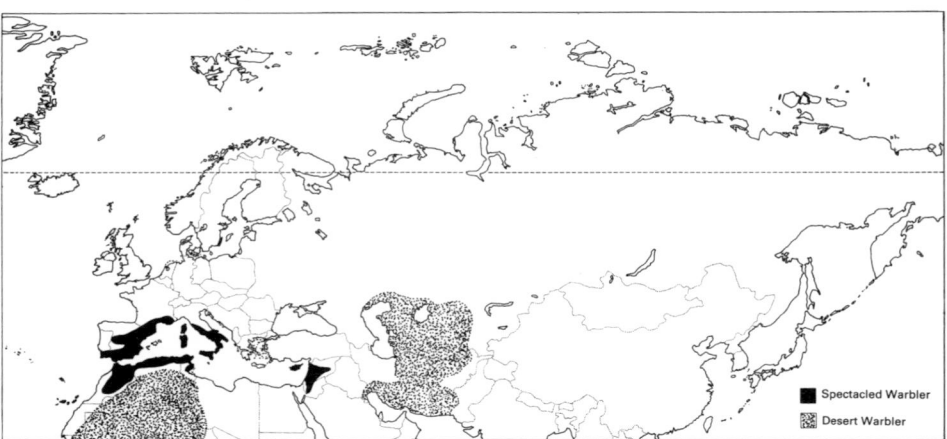

Fig. 53
Breeding range of Spectacled Warbler and Desert Warbler.

As we saw in Chapter 4 the Spectacled Warbler is a typical bird of the *Salicornia* in the Rhône delta yet it also occurs in a wide range of different habitats around the Mediterranean. This range, according to John Gibb (1947), included scrubby desert in Egypt, high mountains in Sicily, inland salt marshes and semi–desert plains in Tunisia, *Thymelaea hirsuta* scrub between the Atlas Mountains and the Sahara, jujube or *Zizyphus* shrubs in Morocco and Algeria, acacia thickets from sea level to the mountaintops in the Cape Verde Islands and the *Euphorbia* brakes in the Canary Islands to heights of at least 2000 m. In Malta the bird is ubiquitous, appearing on rugged coastal cliffs, hillside wastes at 270 m above sea level and on the walls of Valletta city itself and requiring just an open uncultivated patch for nesting. Gibb observed: 'Whether this patch be surrounded by culti-vated land, barren acres of rock or by city buildings as in Valletta, matters not at all.' How different from the *Salicornia* scrub of the Camargue where I first studied the bird in 1954 or of Cyprus where the bird was investigated by Captain P. E. C. Jeal (1970)!

In the breeding season the Spectacled Warbler is not too difficult to identify despite some resemblance to a dark Whitethroat or rather paler Subalpine Warbler. The throat is very white and the head so much darker and the wing browner than those of the first species that separation should be possible. The head of the male may suggest that of a male Lesser Whitethroat but to me the dark patch on the ear coverts of that warbler is much more clearly defined than that of any other European species, includ-ing both Whitethroat and Spectacled Warbler. There may be considerable problems in identifying female and immature Spectacled Warblers and the reader is recommended to consult Swift (1959), Sharrock (1962) and Williamson (1976), the references in the bibliography being listed under the Subalpine Warbler. The whole question of separating these two species with their difficult plumages is under investigation at the time of writing.

The commonest vocalization of the Spectacled Warbler is the alarm, ranging in mood from a gently muttered 'kerr' to a louder, rasping and churring rattle, 'tcharrrr', suggestive of the machinegun-like notes of a Wren. I have listened to many singers in the field and have always found

Fig. 54
Territory of Spectacled Warbler with Salicornia. Camargue. (Eric Simms, May 1973)

the song attractive. It is a high-pitched brief warble with a sweet quality and some deliberation – 'tchirrit-it-it-urritt-chit-chit' – with a suggestion of the Whitethroat's declaimed little ditty but sometimes longer and containing more rambling phrases. A bird that I tape recorded in mono in the Camargue in 1954 sang phrases up to 5 seconds in length while he was performing 'from one of the dwarf tamarisks and tossing himself up into the air, singing all the time. This song flight rather resembles that of the Whitethroat' (Simms 1957). The song excels when it is sung slowly but it is often accelerated into bursts of rather more scratchy notes. In 1973 I was present in the Camargue when another singer was recorded, this time in stereo, and this singer uttered phrases lasting 2–4 seconds at the rate of about eleven phrases a minute. Yet another bird that I timed managed as many as eighteen. The bird nests in low vegetation and one nest of which I have a photograph shows it about 15 cm above the dried mud of a Camargue *étang*. Both sexes help in the construction and the male may build a number of cocks' nests.

The Desert Warbler

The remaining three species of *Sylvia* warbler on the British list are also very rare birds indeed. The first of them is the Desert Warbler – a small sandy or greyish-brown bird with pale legs. It is the smallest and palest of the scrub *Sylvia* warblers and its sandy back with a greyish cast, rusty or russet tail with fairly obvious white outer feathers, yellow iris and pale legs are all useful features in its identification (Britton and Wallace 1980). The sexes are alike. The first record in Britain or Ireland was that of a bird at Weston, Portland, in Dorset from 16 December 1970 to 2 January 1971 (Clafton 1972). This was a bird of the nominate race *Sylvia n. nana*. It fed on the ground among barley shoots and had a sharp 'wee-chur' call with 'something of the rhythm of that of a Partridge *Perdix perdix*'. A second Desert Warbler was at Spurn from 20–24 October 1975 (Cudworth 1979) and a third at Frinton-on-Sea in Essex from 20–21 November of the same year (Harris 1977). The bird at Spurn frequented the stone Humber bank where grass, sea aster, scentless mayweed and oraches were growing from the joints and roosted in a buckthorn near a sandy beach. The Frinton bird also roosted in a sea buckthorn. John Cudworth (1979) writing about the Humberside visitor quoted the observations of one birdwatcher, R. H. Appleby, that: 'On the beach it made short, sharp hops, in the fashion of a Dunnock *Prunella modularis*, continually flicking and cocking its tail, reminiscent of a Dartford Warbler *S. undata*.' This individual also fed under rose bushes in adjoining gardens. The fourth Desert Warbler was reported in 1979 from 28 October to 22 November at Meols on Merseyside (M. J. Rogers *et al* 1980) and this bird, like the previous three, showed all the characters of the eastern population. It seems that the species uses a short rattle or trilled call while the song is pleasant and composed of simple notes, sometimes like jingling bells, sometimes with richer Whitethroat-like notes. The song is delivered from a perch in a low bush or in an aerial song-flight. This desert-loving bird from the Middle East and northwest Sahara and central Asia has been reported from Germany in 1981 for the first time; by 1982 Malta and Finland had their fourth records and Sweden its fifth.

Rüppell's Warbler

Rüppell's Warbler is a bird of thick thorny scrub along the coastal region of the eastern Mediterranean – Greece, Crete, the Aegean Islands south to Rhodes, Turkey, Lebanon and Israel. It can be found in light woods and dry scrub, often in rocky gullies and on stone-covered slopes. The main wintering area is in Chad and the Sudan between 17°N and 20°N, while birds of passage have been observed in Cyprus (in rather small numbers), Egypt, Israel, Lebanon and northwest Arabia, and wanderers have appeared in Italy, Sicily and Finland as well as the British Isles. The bird uses a scolding note somewhat suggestive of a Sardinian Warbler but more

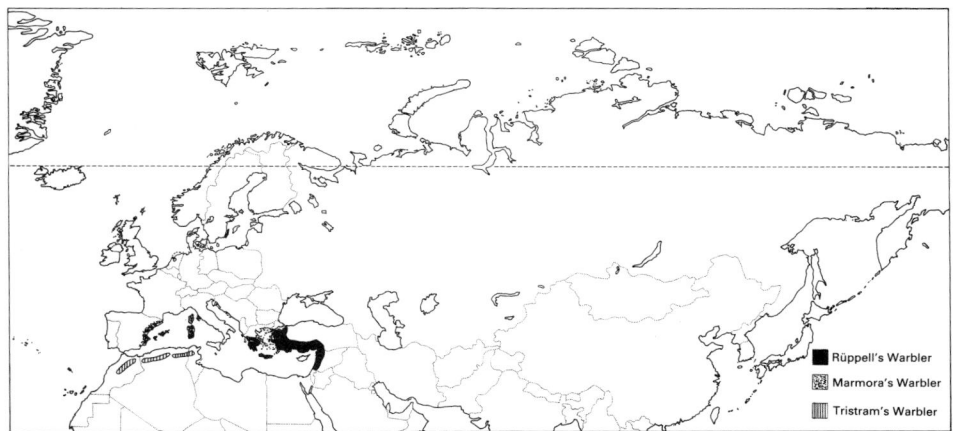

■ Rüppell's Warbler
▨ Marmora's Warbler
▥ Tristram's Warbler

harsh and insistent, but there may be a more musical and terminal 'pit-pit' which, according to *The Handbook* (1946), can be compared to 'a few slow turns of a wooden "bird-scarer".' The song is louder, fuller and more musical than that of the Sardinian Warbler but it is often punctuated with the rattling notes. I find that most of the phrases are short – 2 seconds or less in duration – with up to 16 being produced per minute but the rattle-like 'der-der-der-der' often breaks into the song phrases themselves. The male is the sole warbler in the region with the entire head and throat black with a white moustachial stripe and, although it has a dull orange iris and a red eye-ring like a Sardinian, its black throat and white moustache prevent confusion with that species. The female is greyer and browner with a greyish-brown crown mottled with black, a creamy throat, chin and moustache. The legs are reddish in colour. The flight is more direct and less undulating than that of the Sardinian Warbler with a convex as opposed to a concave back. The male has a strange, heavy Greenfinch-like display flight as he zigzags in the air with slow wingbeats and glides. He also builds many cocks' nests. In the winter Rüppell's Warblers can be found in gardens, canebrakes, scrub and hedges. Food is largely insects, especially small green caterpillars.

An adult male Rüppell's Warbler was discovered in a small willow in a garden at Dunrossness on Mainland in Shetland on 13 August 1977; the

Fig. 55
Breeding range of Rüppell's, Marmora's and Tristram's Warblers.

bird was trapped and ringed – a new species for Britain and Ireland. It remained in the district until 17 September and a full description of this bird was provided by Rodney R. Martins (1981) in the journal *British Birds*. In flight the contrast between the bird's blue-grey upperparts and the black tail was clearly visible 100 m away, even in poor light. It was in full active moult of both the flight and body feathers. The calls of the Shetland bird were a soft, subdued 'tuc-tuc' recalling Radde's Warbler *Phylloscopus schwarzi*, a harsher, more strident 'tac-tac' or 'tchak-tchak' and a rapid series of Wren-like chatters. Full song was heard on two occasions – a 'series of harsh notes in quick succession, rising to and falling from peak of intensity; song considered typical of genus *Sylvia*, recalling Whitethroat in particular.' When singing the bird would often show itself on top of the willow but at other times it was retiring. It was least wary during periods of sunshine. Only two years after the first record another male was present on Lundy Island in Devon from 1–10 June 1979 and was also trapped. It was seen by more than a hundred people who made the annual steamer excursion to the island. The second example fed in sallows by an old quarry, on bracken-covered stony slopes with elder, rhododendrons and sallow; here it appeared rather clumsy in its movements but had a characteristic tail action in which the tail was regularly flicked up into a half-cocked attitude (Taylor and Campey 1981). On 2 June this bird too began to sing, quietly at first, and then progressed into a full song 'which was reminiscent of a Whitethroat's but also contained a distinctive loud harsh rattle'. The bird was adjudged to be in its second summer. R. F. Meiklejohn (1934, 1935, 1936) has written about the ecology and general breeding biology of Rüppell's Warbler.

Marmora's Warbler

At the time of writing there is a report of a Marmora's Warbler from Midhope Moor in South Yorkshire on 15 May 1982, and *British Birds* (75:392) carried two photographs of this rare bird on open heather moorland. As we saw earlier in the book, this warbler closely resembles the Dartford Warbler and is an inhabitant of northeast Spain, Corsica, Sardinia, the Balearic Islands, southern Sicily and the coasts of Tunisia. It occurs in similar country to that favoured by the Dartford Warbler but it seems to prefer rather less dense scrub with more heather, palmetto and grasses in the habitat. In northeast Sardinia Marmora's can be found higher in the hills than the Sardinian Warbler (Diesselhorst 1971). How the Marmora's Warbler became isolated as an ancient form from the Dartford Warbler and how it manages in the same habitats or region is not known. The call note has been described as a single 'tik', 'tsig' or 'tsiig'. The bird scolds at the slightest disturbance, showing itself, then diving out of sight and re-emerging from cover. The song is like that of the Dartford Warbler but is made up of shorter, less grating sounds with faster phrases – up to 14 in a minute. The song can be given from a perch or in a song-flight with the bird dropping sharply into the scrub in which he builds a series of cock's nests. The final nest is made of dry grass, leaves, lichens and spiders' webs. Marmora's Warbler is mainly sedentary but individuals have been recovered in winter in Italy, Spain, Malta, North Africa and Egypt. If Marmora's Warbler – hardly a great traveller – can reach the British Isles then perhaps Ménétries's or even Tristram's may be next!

Locustella or **Grasshopper Warblers**

CHAPTER **11**

For me there have been few greater pleasures than sitting in the late evening concealed by a hedge on a farm in South Warwickshire and listening to the strange reeling song of a small brown bird perched at the apex of a bramble spray. As he sings he fans his tail and his throat pulsates with the energy of his delivery. He also swings his head from side to side so that ventriloquially the song of this Grasshopper Warbler grows subtly quieter and louder. For minutes on end the performance runs on until with his evening utterance complete he slips into dense cover where his dull streaked plumage affords him total concealment. Similarly I have listened with enchantment to the buzzing song of a male Savi's Warbler also borne ventriloquially on a gentle breeze from deep in a reedbed in southern Spain or East Anglia. The warblers of the genus *Locustella*, taking their name from the insect-like songs of some of the species, introduce us to rather special habitats such as the reedbeds, marshes and riverside growth of the wetlands as well as open woods, heaths, plantations and even farmland. Recently J. F. Burton and E. D. H. Johnson (1984) suggested that the reeling songs of some of the *Locustella* warblers evolved from 'acoustic mimicry of the more primitive singing insects because of the additional biological advantage it bestows' but it could also be an example of convergent evolution. Further, continuous songs are possible in species which are comparatively invulnerable because of the density and nature of the habitat.

The genus *Locustella* itself comprises seven species of sleek and rather visually undistinguished birds, often with streaks or mottlings on the back. There is usually a lack of a clear head pattern with a rather obscure pale eye-stripe and perhaps a lower streak which together give members of the genus what was described by P. J. Grant (1983) as 'a rather mean expression which is a general – if subtle – feature of many *Locustella* warblers'. Despite some resemblance to Cetti's Warbler this group sports twelve tail feathers, or rectrices, while the former species has only ten. The

Fig. 56
Flight silhouettes of
Locustella *warblers.*
Note the rather slim head
and chest, followed by
small round wings, but
ending in a broad rump
and tall tail, often
fanned and even cocked
in the air (hence their
alternative name of
'fantail'). (D. I. M.
Wallace)

undertail coverts are long and the tail itself is very rounded in shape and in some species strongly graduated. In flight, which is a rare feature of the birds' life style, the tail appears very heavy. The bill is long, slender and pointed while the feet are strongly developed since all the species live part of their lives on the ground. The wings also seem rather long and this helps to distinguish the *Locustella* warblers from Cetti's and the Acrocephaline group. The sexes also resemble each other.

In addition to their dull plumage the grasshopper warblers are rather secretive, skulking birds, often difficult to detect but also often restless and very agile, clinging to plant stems, creeping through dense vegetation and even running on the ground. As we have already seen, some have sibilant reeling songs especially those that occur at the western end of the Palaearctic but these are not typical of all species in the genus. Some species will sing from dense cover while others prefer more open or exposed song-posts. The scolds or anxiety notes tend to be simple churrs or 'tchicks'. Only two species – the Grasshopper and Savi's Warbler – breed in Britain but others can be found to the east in Europe and across Asia. Of these some have been reported in the British Isles but the main wintering areas are in the southern parts of Asia.

It is interesting to compare the distribution and habitats of the seven species in this genus of which five are on the British list. The Grasshopper Warbler – the most familiar of them – is a western and central Palaearctic species that can be found from temperate through to steppe and desert zones of climate. It occurs in similar habitats to those of Savi's Warbler and I have tape recorded both species singing in reedy, grassy willow scrub at Minsmere in Suffolk. Elsewhere the differences in habitat are very much more marked with Savi's Warbler frequenting marshes and swamps with many reeds and shallow water, while the Grasshopper has preferred bushier fens, rank grass with willows and heaths, commons and fields. This suggests that in general there can be very little competition between the two species. Where both live alongside each other in a wetland habitat there may well be some sharing of the marsh insect food resources.

There are two species – Pallas's Grasshopper Warbler and the Lanceolated, or Lesser Grasshopper Warbler – both vagrants to the British Isles which somewhat resemble the Grasshopper Warbler both in appearance and behaviour. They appear to be eastern ecological replacements for it. Both are birds of reeds, willows and wetland habitats but the Lanceolated Warbler also frequents bushier places and, according to Voous (1960), 'marshy forest'.

The River Warbler of eastern Europe and Russia and Savi's Warbler seem to live alongside each other as 'sibling' species but usually in rather different habitats; the former favours woodland thickets in damp forested areas and meadows with scattered shrubs rather than fens and reedbeds. The River Warbler also has a distinctive rhythmic jingling song quite different from those of Savi's and the Grasshopper Warblers. It has occurred as a vagrant to western Europe and Britain. What competition there may be between the River and Savi's Warblers, when they breed in similar habitats, is not yet clear.

Further across Asia to the east there seems to be no clear ecological substitute for Savi's Warbler but one species – Middendorff's Grasshopper Warbler which breeds around the Sea of Okhotsk and the Yellow Sea –

Table 12 The species of Locustella or Grasshopper warblers

Species	Wing		Tail		Bill (Adults)	Tarsus	Moult	Distribution	Status in British Isles
	Male	Female	Male	Female					
Pallas's Grasshopper Warbler (L. certhiola rubescens) (L.c. centralasiae)	61–71 56–66	58–68 58–66	50–56 44–56	48–55 45–52	15–17 13–16	20–24 20–24	E. Asia (late winter)	C. Asia and Siberia east to Pacific.	Vagrant
Middendorf's Grasshopper Warbler (L. ochotensis)	65–75	62–73	52–58	50–59	15–18	22–26	E. Asia (perhaps completed on breeding ground)	E. Siberia and Sea of Okhotsk. Winters islands of S.E. Asia. (L. ochotensis pleskei) – Korea islands of Yellow Sea. Winters S.E. China.	
Lanceolated Warbler (L. lanceolata)	52–61	51–59	34–49	42–48	12–14	18–21	S.E. Asia (spring)	E. Russia to Kamchatka, Sakhalin, Korea and Japan. Winters India and S.E. Asia.	Vagrant
Grasshopper Warbler (Locustella naevia naevia)	60–66	57–63	47–55	46–55	12.5–15.5	19–21.5	Mediterranean (winter)	Europe to W. Asia and Mongolia. Winters Africa, India and Iran.	Widespread summer visitor
(L.n. straminea)	54–61	54–59	44–58	45–56	12.5–15	18–21	Asia (autumn and winter)	E. Russia to Altai and Sinkiang. Winters Iran, Afghanistan and India.	
River Warbler (L. fluviatilis)	67–78	71–77	53–62	55–61	14.5–17	20–24	E-S. Africa (Jan-March)	Baltic, E. Germany and Balkans to W. Siberia. Winters E. and S. Africa.	Vagrant
Savi's Warbler (L. luscinioides luscinioides)	65–73	63–70	52–62	52–60	15–17	20–23	Africa (Oct-Nov)	Local in Europe east to Turkestan. Winters tropical and NE Africa.	Rare nester
Gray's Grasshopper Warbler (L. fasciolata)	74–83	75–81	67–75	63–72	19–22	26.5–30	S.E. Asia (late winter?)	C. and E. Siberia to Korea. Winters Philippines and other islands of S.E. Asia.	

looks rather like Savi's Warbler but is fractionally larger and has a darkly mottled mantle. It also breeds among reeds, tall grass and low shrubs only on offshore islands and its immediate nesting area is more reminiscent of that of the River rather than Savi's Warbler. The song too is very distinctive and consists of the syllable 'witsche' repeated over and over again: this is said to be like the sound of a scythe being sharpened. This lack of a whirring or reeling-type song distinguishes it at once from Savi's Warbler. *Locustella ochotensis ochotensis* breeds around the Sea of Okhotsk from Kamchatka and the Kurile Islands south to Sakhalin and Hokkaido and winters in Malaysia, Borneo, the Celebes and Philippines. The race *L. ochotensis pleskei* with a longer bill and tail and slightly different wing formula occurs in Korea and the islands of the Yellow Sea and migrates for the winter to south-east China. This species has sometimes been considered to be allied to Pallas's Grasshopper Warbler and some authorities have sought to join the races of both into a single species, claiming that intermediate forms have been reported on the wintering grounds. Since there are differences in plumage, wing length and shape and tail markings as well as song, it seems that the separation should be sustained as recommended by Austin and Kuroda (1953) and Williamson (1976).

Gray's Grasshopper Warbler of central and eastern Asia appears to be the ecological replacement for the River Warbler. This species is rather like a larger version of the River or Grasshopper Warbler being olive-brown with greyish lores and ear coverts, a white eye-stripe and throat and greyish breast, buffish-grey belly with an olive-buff suffusion on both breast and flanks. The undertail coverts are orange-brown and the outer web of the long outermost primary is a dirty white. First-winter birds are browner above and yellower below, with a less clear eye-stripe. This species prefers thick alder and willow brakes and thickets along the banks of rivers. The song of the male Gray's Grasshopper Warbler, heard mostly at night, has been described as '*touti-routi* repeated' (Williamson 1976) but I would favour this version which I have rendered as 'tchee-chit, toi-tu' repeated a number of times. The bird has occurred as a vagrant in France and Denmark, and D. I. M. Wallace (1980) regarded the species as a potential vagrant to the British Isles. It breeds from central and eastern Siberia north to the Tunguska River and east to Manchuria, Sakhalin, Japan and Korea; the species then migrates through China and the Ryukyu Islands to winter in New Guinea, the Celebes, Philippines and other islands in southeast Asia.

An attempt has been made to separate an eighth species of *Locustella* as the Sakhalin Large Grasshopper Warbler (*L. amnicola*) or Stepanyan's Warbler. It was described as a new species by L. S. Stepanyan (1972) (*Zool. Zh.* 51(3):1896) after two adult males were collected in June 1972. It was said to occur on Sakhalin and perhaps the Kuriles and Japan, and was thought also to be most nearly related to Gray's Grasshopper Warbler. Now it is regarded merely as a race of that species and a not very well distinguished one (Voous 1977).

A glance at Table 13 (p. 132) will show that four species possess reeling, whirring or rattling songs of a special kind and that three have much more conventionally phrased utterances. The eastern Palaearctic species include one triller and three traditional-type singers while those of the western Palaearctic produce sustained trills of one kind or another. In the east the separation by voice of the four species is clear even to the human observer while the western species – Grasshopper, Savi's and River Warbler – whose ranges may overlap can still be distinguished since 'the difference in energy peaks and rhythmic beats would ensure the proper separation of the species' (Simms 1979). Alwyn Voight noted that to the human observer the Grasshopper Warbler 'rattles', Savi's Warbler 'buzzes' and the River Warbler 'grinds'. The speed at which the ears of humans can cope with sounds is slow and cumbrous compared with that shown by birds. Indeed, they are ten or more times more efficient at separating sounds than we are. A bird can therefore make a fine discrimination of the notes or elements in a rapid series of sounds and this will help in distinguishing between the species.

The *Locustella* warblers provide an outstanding challenge to the ornithologist. All are excessively plain and for much of their lives feed and nest in such dense vegetation that they vouchsafe barely a glimpse of themselves to the most patient of observers. Some will sing during the breeding season from some conspicuous place but the output is often during the night or around dusk and dawn. The calls are rather unhelpful but each has a song that could be diagnostic. There may be some difficulty at first in distinguishing between the reeling songs of four of the group, but once mastered through field observation or by listening to some of the many wildlife recordings now available, identification problems should be eased. The penalty of increasing age is an inability to hear as well the reeling songs of the grasshopper warblers.

A word of warning needs to be given as well since it is possible to be misled by certain insect sounds. I have described elsewhere how Roger Tory Peterson and I, sitting by a lagoon in the Camargue in 1954, could not at first decide whether a sound to which we were listening was the song of a Savi's Warbler 100 m away or a bush cricket stridulating only a few metres from us. The stridulatory 'songs' of Roesel's bush cricket are very suggestive of Savi's or Grasshopper Warblers, while the rhythmic scraping of another bush cricket that lives in woodland habitats suggests a softer version of the song of another species – the Lanceolated Warbler.

All of the *Locustella* warblers depend on insect foods and so they are forced to migrate south for the winter months in company with other warblers. Savi's and the River Warblers go to tropical and East Africa, the Grasshopper Warbler to regions east from Africa to India, the Lanceolated to India and southeast Asia, Pallas's Grasshopper Warbler to areas from India to China, Middendorff's to Malaysia and islands to the east, and Gray's largely to the islands of southeast Asia. Thus the wintering grounds for the seven species stretch eastwards from central Africa to the Pacific Ocean.

In their winter quarters these warblers seek out swamps and reedbeds, rice fields and waterside vegetation. Some species like Savi's Warbler achieve a rapid moult of their feathers in autumn but the River Warbler moults in Africa between January and March. There are differences in the four eastern species which tend to moult in late winter or spring, although Middendorff's seems to have to complete it on the breeding ground. In Malaysia, Pallas's Grasshopper Warblers, which frequent reedbeds there, time the moult immediately before the spring migration. All the tail feathers and up to 14 wing feathers may be lost at the same time. Yet the popu-

Table 13   *Songs of the Locustella warblers*

Species	Calls	Songs	Duration of songs	Song posts
Pallas's Grasshopper Warbler	Harsh chatter like that of Lanceolated Warbler	Acrocephaline in quality. Opens with chatter which is followed by soft and harsh notes, ending with three musical notes, e.g. *tic, tic, tac-tac, zzz, chack, chack, zzz, chow-chow-chow* (Boswall 1967).	Bursts of about 4 seconds: 11 songs in 1 minute 10 seconds	From top of bush or plant or in song flight
Middendorff's Grasshopper Warbler		Series of repeated syllables – *witsche*-like sharpening of scythe		Largely at night
Lanceolated Warbler	*Chi-chirr* or *chir-chirr*	A vibrating trill suggesting Grasshopper Warbler but slower and sharper like the stridulation of a locust. Ventriloquial.	Quite long bursts	Bush top. Mainly by day
Grasshopper Warbler	A hard *tchick*, a liquid *whit* and a rapid *sisisi*	A long sustained 'rattling' song like angler's reel. Of 23–31 double notes per sec. Range 4.5–7 kHz with energy peak at 5 kHz. Ventriloquial.	A few seconds to 2–10 minutes	Often well exposed. Sings day and night especially dusk and dawn
River Warbler	Low harsh call	Notes softer and slower than of Grasshopper Warbler with rhythmic quality. A metallic 'chuffing' jingle of clear alternate single fast and slow notes. A 'grinding' song.	Short bursts from 4–21 seconds	Often from bush top
Savi's Warbler	A scolding *tzwik* or *tswee*, a soft *puitt* and a chatter	Fuller and lower than that of Grasshopper Warbler. Has energy peaks at 2 and 4 kHz. A 'buzzing' song that often starts with low ticking notes that speed up into a trill. About 50 double notes per second. Ventriloquial.	Short bursts of up to 1 minute or more	Often from top of reed
Gray's Grasshopper Warbler	*Tchirp*	A loud phrase repeated again; *tchee-chit, toi-tu, ter-chit*.	Burst from 1–12 seconds	Song chiefly at night

lation of the same species wintering in Burma moults in the autumn and such a discrepancy in timing may be the result of environmental conditions. A similar situation may also arise with *Acrocephalus* warblers. Pallas's Grasshopper Warbler does not seem to be duly incommoded by losing so many tail and flight feathers together and, according to I. C. T. Nisbet (1967) who ringed 127 near Kuala Lumpur, the birds 'were caught

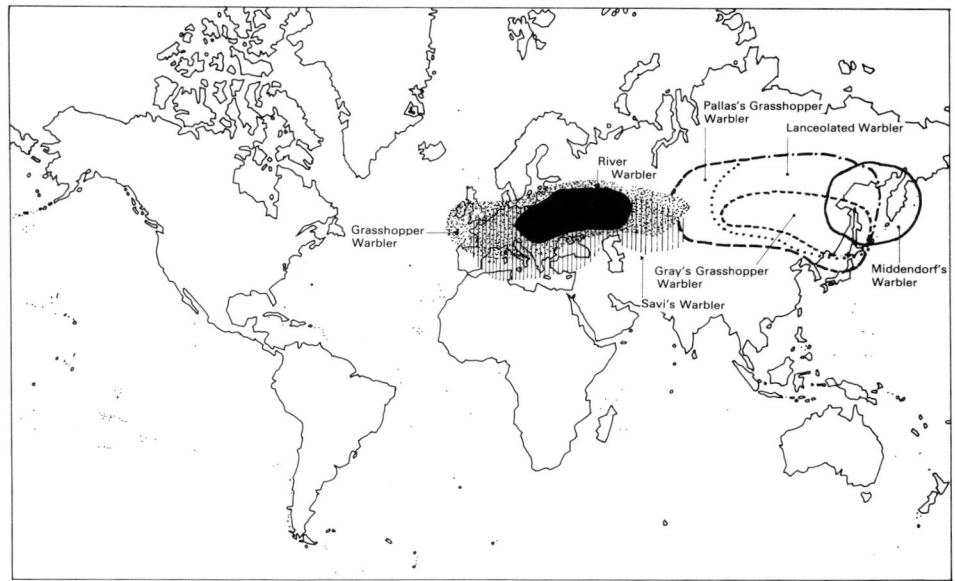

Fig. 57
The westerly and easterly breeding groups of the Locustella *warblers.*

as readily in mist nets and were as heavy or heavier during the moult as before'. This compensation was possibly due to the foraging habits of the birds which involved little flight but in winter quarters the species, like others of its clan, was impossible to observe in the dense cover it lived in and furthermore it was most active at night!

Savi's Warbler has returned to nest in Britain in small numbers after an absence of many years helped by better protection of its wetland habitats. The Grasshopper Warbler, which is the most familiar of the genus to British birdwatchers, is known to fluctuate in numbers due to local habitat changes and perhaps longer term alterations such as climatic changes in its British summer home and in the Sahel region of Africa. The last species was forced on the retreat by the ploughing up or afforestation of its meadows, forest ecotones, heaths and damp places but it has also found refuge in the establishment stages of new conifer plantations. Both species arrive back in Britain from mid to late April. The daily census figures at nine British bird observatories from 1964–81 revealed an appreciable decline in the number of Grasshopper Warblers at these sites in 1973 and subsequently (Riddiford 1983). The reasons for this apparent decrease are not clear. Interestingly enough there were at least twice as many recorded on the coast of Denmark in 1981. Both Savi's and the Grasshopper Warblers will be treated more fully in subsequent chapters.

CHAPTER 12

The Grasshopper Warbler

This mysterious and charming little warbler has intrigued and captivated naturalists for many years. One of the earliest to be entranced by its behaviour was Gilbert White, who after careful observation, wrote in 1768 with great perception and in the most felicitous prose of the habits of this bird:

'Nothing can be more amusing than the whisper of this little bird, which seems to be close by though at a hundred yards distance; and, when close at your ear is scarce any louder than when a great way off. Had I not been a little acquainted with insects, and known that the grasshopper kind is not yet hatched, I should have hardly believed that it had been a *locusta* whispering in the bushes. The country people laugh when you tell them that it is the note of a bird. It is a most artful creature, skulking in the thickest part of a bush; and will sing at a yard distance, provided it be concealed. I was obliged to get a person to go the other side of the hedge where it haunted, and then it would run, creeping like a mouse, before us for a hundred yards together, through the bottom of the thorns; yet it would not come into fair sight; but in a morning, early, and when undisturbed, it sings on the top of a twig, gaping and shivering with its wings.'

It is impossible to improve upon that piece of natural history writing. For those of us who know its subtly changing murmur or its habit of running, mouse-like, under the protection of dense vegetation, the attraction of this bird is most compelling. In his classic study of the warblers Eliot Howard thought also that the species had 'a fascination difficult to account for'.

As we have already seen, in coloration the Grasshopper Warbler *Locustella naevia* is somewhat undistinguished. Its upper parts are a dull olive-brown with broad blackish streaks and a faint barring on the tail. The underparts range from a dull whitish-grey to a more yellowish tinge and this variation in colour is apparently not dependent on age or sex. The sides of the breast are suffused with buff and there is a row of spots or streaks across the lower throat. The chin and throat are white or pale yellow. Both flanks and undertail coverts are pale brown or buff; it is possible to see streaks on the latter when the tail is raised, which is not an uncommon piece of behaviour. In my experience birds rarely have an eye-stripe but one in my collection has just the suggestion of a pale mark. The outer web of the long outermost primary is brownish-white in colour and the tail is well rounded. In the case of a bird netted and examined at Portland in April 1967 'each tail-feather was tipped with buffish-white, markedly so in the case of all but the central pair' (Clafton 1968), and it was thought that the bird could have been mistaken for Pallas's Grasshopper Warbler. However, subsequent correspondence in the journal *British Birds* and an examination of a long series of skins of both species failed to produce any firm conclusions. There have been occasional examples of albinism in the Grasshopper Warbler. The upper mandible has been

Fig. 58
*Grasshopper Warbler
removing faecal sac from
nest. Suffolk, 1951.
(Eric Hosking)*

described as dark brown and the lower as a paler brownish-yellow but five examples looked at by Major R. F. Ruttledge (1955) in the spring of 1954 at Saltee had 'lower mandible bluish-grey in two cases, creamy in two and creamy tinged with yellow in one.' There is evidently some variation in the coloration of the lower bill. Similarly legs were found to be pinkish in colour but ranging through pale flesh, pinkish-flesh, bluish-flesh to yellowish-flesh. The measurements of Grasshopper Warblers can be seen in Table 12.

In the breeding season this warbler can be found from the northern parts of Spain and France eastwards across Europe to southern Sweden and Finland, the Baltic and western Russia as well as in the British Isles and south to North Italy, the northern Balkans and the Crimea. It winters in the region of the Mediterranean but we still do not have a very clear picture about its range outside the nesting season. The western European birds have been reported in southern Spain and France and in northwest Africa west of Tunisia, but records are scarce.

There is an eastern race *L. naevia straminea*, which is smaller and with more of a pale grey or olive colour that reveals the black streaks on the mantle much more clearly. It is also relatively longer in the tail and shorter in the wing than *L. n. naevia*. This eastern race breeds from eastern Russia to western Mongolia and south to Transcaspia and Sinkiang. This race spends the winter in India, Afghanistan and Iran. There are other

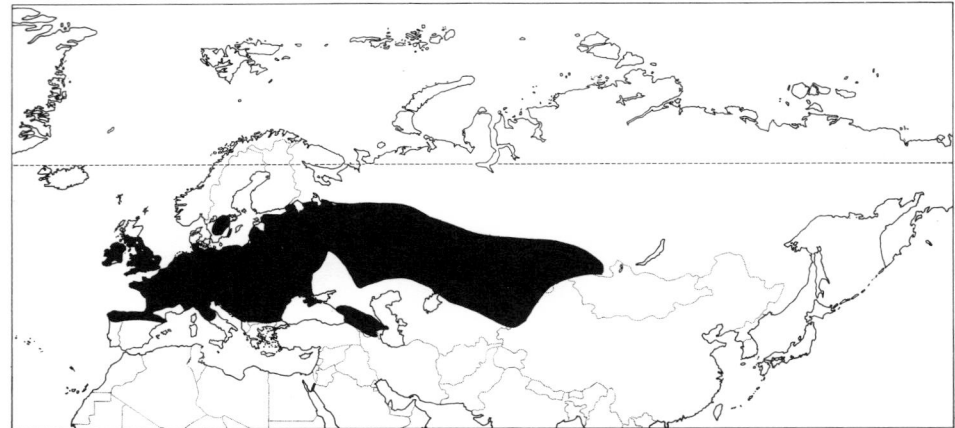

Fig. 59
*Breeding range of the
Grasshopper Warbler.*

races in the Caucasus – the more olive *obscurior* – and in northwest Mongolia is the greyer *mongolica* which winters in Afghanistan and western Pakistan.

In the breeding season the Grasshopper Warbler frequents a variety of both marshy and dry habitats. At one time the species was generally associated with wet meadows, marshes and other wetland sites with tall vegetation and scattered bushes. Sir William Jardine wrote in 1839 that this warbler 'is almost confined to what are called "bottoms", low-lying dells watered by a small stream, and clothed with a tangled thicket of brushwood, blackthorn and brier, bramble and whin, intermixed with the various herbaceous plants and rank grasses which overgrow such retreats.' This kind of countryside remains one of its habitats together with vegetation around freshwater pools, open moist regions in wooded country and willow thickets and cut osier beds. The coppiced willow in the waterlogged fenland reserve at Leighton Moss is a regular habitat and John Wilson (1978), writing of this R.S.P.B. reserve in Lancashire, noted that the birds nest 'almost exclusively in the shrub layer and showed a marked preference for the dense cover provided by tussock sedge.' I have regularly found Grasshopper Warblers in the birch and willow scrub around Lough Neagh in Ulster in a habitat that they share with Willow Warblers, Chiffchaffs, Wrens, Goldfinches and Greenfinches.

Yet the 'wet' quality of the habitat is not essential. Gilbert White wrote of a hedgerow habitat and Thomas Bewick (1804) also noted that the species 'artfully skulks among old furze bushes, or in the thickest brakes and hedges, from which it will not easily be forced away.' Grasshopper Warblers breed amongst light and medium scrub on open chalk grassland, on ground elsewhere with scattered shrubs, scrambling vegetation such as brambles or with tall grasses and nettles, on heaths and heathery moors and even dunes. Birds often move into the spaces in forests when areas are cleared of trees and an increase of the species in Leicestershire was directly attributed to 'the felling of many large woods.' The selection of dry habitats perhaps has some parallels in the way in which both the Reed Bunting and the Sedge Warbler have moved from wetland habitats and adapted themselves to a life in much drier habitats, including field hedgerows and conifer plantations where running or standing water may be absent. Many areas of wetland habitat were lost to the Grasshopper Warbler through drainage, especially from the seventeenth century onwards, of much of the fenland in eastern England. This loss of habitat has to some extent been compensated by the widespread planting of conifers, albeit often exotic alien species, throughout the British Isles and often on wetter, poorer soils or on sands. These conifer plantations with their ground zone and field layer of dry grasses, bramble and willow-herb resemble to some extent the grassland and scrub in which I watched birds in Surrey before the last war. In the early establishment stage of the plantations when the trees are still below a metre in height the region is essentially one of dry heathland with shrubs.

Many of the bird species associated with heaths, grassland, moor and waste continue to live in the plantations – Skylarks, chats, Meadow Pipits and perhaps gamebirds and certain waders – and the provision of this kind of habitat has enabled the species to spread to regions where before there was no suitable countryside for them. This extension of range, following perhaps a move northwards in Europe during the present century, has seen the Grasshopper Warbler make advances in Ireland, Scotland and eastern England, although the bird remains scarce in the fenland areas. Significant extensions have occurred in western Britain and in some southern counties such as Berkshire and Buckinghamshire. I carried out censuses in many regions of Britain and Ireland. In the latter area I found Grasshopper Warblers common in the plantations of young pine, spruce and larch where the trees were up to two metres in height. In fact, the relative abundance in Ireland – the average number of contacts expressed as a percentage of all contacts of species – was as high as seven. On the Continent birds will also nest in fields of cereal, clover and rape and here I have occasionally found birds breeding in field verges where there is still some scrub, hedge or bramble. A male at Bromsgrove sang in dense secondary growth at least three metres high.

Grasshopper Warblers are missing from much of highland Britain and Ireland, although they have been reported at 430 m on Exmoor and 500 m in the Cheviot Hills. Actual breeding records are difficult to come by because of the birds' retiring habits and the species is most likely to be reported because of its reeling song rather than from proved nesting itself. Birds are often heard singing in the north of Scotland but there was only one record of confirmed breeding north of the Black Isle in *The Atlas of Breeding Birds in Britain and Ireland* (1976). The actual number of Grasshopper Warblers seems to fluctuate considerably over the years, which is often due to local changes in their breeding habitats. The total population of the British Isles was estimated in the *Atlas* to be around 25,000 pairs with densities from 3 pairs to 10 hectares, up to 5 in the scrub that flourishes on chalk grassland.

The male Grasshopper Warblers arrive back in the British Isles some ten days before the females. They begin to arrive in the middle of April. In the spring of 1964 birds were reported at Portland on 12 April and at Cley and Spurn on 16 April but the main arrivals were at Portland on 19 April, as well as Beachy Head, Gibraltar Point and Spurn. There were early arrivals at Fair Isle on 20 April and the Isle of May on the following day. On 26 April there were numbers at Portland, Skokholm, Bardsey

Island and Gibraltar Point. The following year Bardsey's main fall was on 2 May. At Skokholm the mean date for the passage in spring is 29 April. There are passage movements on both east and west coasts of Britain, as these records show, but in Ireland the migration is confined almost entirely to the east coast. The main body seems to arrive on the western part of the south coast of England and movements may continue until the third week of May.

It is not unusual to hear birds singing on the coasts as they pass through. I have heard such song from seafront tamarisks and shrubs and brambles on cliff faces. A bird that I came across on the coast of the Lleyn Peninsula in North Wales in early May 1983 sang for more than two hours, hidden deep in a tangled mass of bramble down the cliff, before moving on. Grass-hopper Warblers travel in spring and autumn by night and have often in the past been reported as casualties at coastal lighthouses. Seventy-five were killed at Bardsey in July 1968 while of the 585 warblers that perished there on the night of 29 August, 111 were Grasshopper Warblers with 183 Whitethroats, 153 Willow Warblers and 117 Sedge Warblers. After flying at night, pausing at the coast and then moving on, birds settle quickly on their breeding grounds and tend to wander very little. Males then take up territories and begin to sing. In South Lincolnshire (where I now live) singing males appeared in a conifer plantation on 2 May 1981 although early males had returned to a wood some fifteen miles away on 13 April. In my plantation the song output was high at first, and then a week or so later the females arrived.

No other British bird utters a sound quite like that of the Grasshopper Warbler. The Nightjar, which also has a 'reeling' song, or vibrant trill, has a shriller, more chirping voice as it utters single notes at a rate of some 1900 to the minute (North and Simms 1958). Only Savi's Warbler, which breeds in small numbers in wetland habitats in east or southeast England, is likely to be confused with it. The song of the Grasshopper Warbler consists of two, perhaps three or even more consecutive and rapidly alternating pulses too close together and too quickly uttered to be separated by a human listener. I first isolated the two pulses in 1955 after slowing down a record-ing of the song to one eighth of the recording speed, which brought the sound down three octaves in pitch. At the same time I was able to find out that there were some 1400 of the double notes per minute or some 24 per second. Carl Weismann had also arrived at a figure of around 26 double notes for another individual singer. When Professor W. H. Thorpe (1957) first made sonagrams of the *Locustella* warblers he arrived at '31 double notes' for the Grasshopper Warbler but in his book *Bird-Song* (1961) he wrote that the species 'has thirty-one triple pulses per second.' The Savi's Warbler which I recorded in southern Spain in 1956 was proved to utter 53 double notes per second. Figure 60 illustrates sonagrams from the songs of both species.

The main frequencies for the Grasshopper Warbler's song lie between 4.5–7 kHz with some strong ultrasonic components. There is a strong energy peak at 5 kHz, which is easily within our normal hearing range being not far above top C on the piano. With a somewhat lower pitch, the song of Savi's Warbler ranges from 0.5–6.5 kHz and has energy peaks at 2 kHz and 4 kHz; there are some fifty double notes and a lack of transient sounds such as occur with the Grasshopper Warbler's song. Thus the former sounds lower and more musical. There are tonal differences which we can recognize ourselves and vocal characters which the birds can identify. The song of the Grasshopper Warbler appears to be innate and the same is probably but not necessarily true for Savi's Warbler.

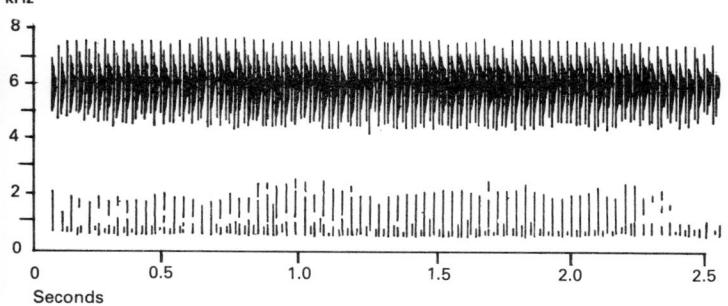

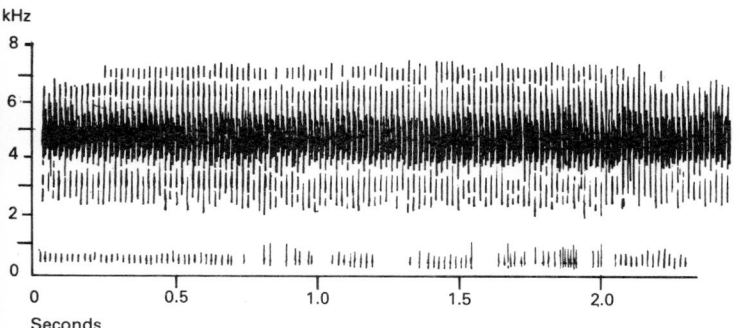

Fig. 60
*Songs of (above)
Grasshopper Warbler;
(below) Savi's Warbler.
The former has 31 triple
pulses per second with an
energy peak at 5kHz
whilst the closely related
species Savi's Warbler
has about 50 double
pulses per second with
energy peaks at 2 and
4 kHz. (Reproduced
from* Bird-Song (1961)
*by permission of Professor
W. H. Thorpe and
Cambridge University
Press)*

The monotonous metallic reeling is given with the bill wide open, the head with its small crest raised and moving from side to side which imparts the strange ventriloquial quality, and the body quivering quite markedly. I once spent a night in 1949 with a singing male on the farm in South Warwickshire where I was then living. It sang from 01.36 GMT to 05.31 with the briefest of 1–2 second intervals between each reeling song. Sometimes the pauses were even shorter. A typical example of the song of that individual comprised bursts of 0 min 28 s, 0 min 15 s, 0 min 20 s, 0 min 14 s, 0 min 3s, 4 min 5 s, and 0 min 32 s all separated by the shortest of intervals. In the time that it was in song that night it uttered more than a quarter of a million double notes! Another male in Staffordshire maintained its song from 8 p.m. on 2 June 1955 to 6 a.m. on 3 June with pauses of only a few seconds and trills sustained frequently for five minutes.

The song is often far-carrying and in still conditions with a minimum of background noise may travel as far as a kilometre but on other days and with different conditions much less. I have listened to songs on hot, dry days but a period of wet and fog may stimulate song which is especially characteristic of the hours from dusk to dawn. There are many times that

I have been within a couple of metres of a singer, as the bird reels from dense cover or from an exposed branch, but the last is always close to dense vegetation in which the performer can seek immediate shelter. D. G. Bell (1960) had the experience of lying under a sapling in the North Cleveland Hills when a bird 'sang within two feet of my face.' It continued to sing into the dark and the observer was actually able to touch the warbler in a very gentle fashion. In 1961 a male was discovered singing under sodium arc lamps in Tamworth Road at Sutton Coldfield in Warwickshire.

A high output of song is maintained until pairing has taken place. Instead of the persistent reeling, there are now erratic bursts of short duration with some song at dusk and dawn; finally the bird becomes totally silent. Song may be heard later in the summer. It has been reported in August (Radford 1969) and there is often a resumption in September. Bernard King (1968) reported short bursts of reeling on 21 October 1967 in Cornwall, while J. H. Taverner (1969) heard a Grasshopper Warbler reeling continuously as it flew round the lantern of the St Catherine's Point Lighthouse on the Isle of Wight.

There is one record of possible singing by the female as well as several instances of unusual songs from males. There is one interesting example of a male singing at Wendover on 14 July 1976 and delivering 'twice a soft sweet jingling song, each time of a few seconds' duration. The song, in its diversity, bore a slight resemblance to the rambling notes of a Dunnock *Prunella modularis*, but, in quality, it was more like a very soft version of the jingling song of a Serin *Serinus canarius*' (Norris 1977). Another produced a similar vocalization at Cap Gris Nez in September 1971 (Milbled 1978). If this was not the performance of aberrant singers but the sub-song of juveniles then there is perhaps a suggestion of the 'jingling' songs of other species in the genus.

During pairing and courtship the male Grasshopper Warbler pursues the female which walks or runs away from him under or through the vegetation. The amorous male indulges in some of the most delightful of courtship ceremonies, which have entranced me, and which Eliot Howard compared to the display of parental anxiety. He fans out his tail which he then raises or lowers, spreads out his wings which are slowly beaten up and down as if by a slowed-down Hedgesparrow or Dunnock. The male also erects the feathers on his neck and mantle and progresses in the most striking manner along a branch; he then presents his mate with a piece of grass or a leaf which he has already found. I have, on rare occasions, seen the male undertake a short display flight but I have not witnessed the aerial excursions such as occurred at Wexford where 'birds often fly an appreciable distance and frequently across open fields' (Ruttledge 1955); here they apparently fly with fast-beating wings and reveal their short wings and long tails.

The male often sings 20 m from the nest site and there are few birds' nests more difficult to find. It is often built close to the ground or just above it in low vegetation, tall rank grass or a tussock, in gorse bushes and clumps of *Juncus* rush. A pair I watched in Ireland shared the building of the nest, bringing in grass, leaves and moss which were then interwoven together. The birds approached the nest with extreme caution, climbing and creeping through the dense vegetation and reaching the structure by means of a kind of run but this approach tunnel is not invariably present.

This makes observation very difficult. A nest built in Surrey was domed instead of the usual cup-shape. There are often six or even seven eggs, sometimes four to five. They are a smooth glossy white, speckled with lilac-blue or purple markings which are often concentrated in a wide zone round the broad end of the egg. Sometimes the eggs have a white ground and large bolder markings of purplish-red. Both parents sit on the eggs and the incubation itself lasts from 13–15 days with 14 as a reasonable average. I have two Warwickshire records of 12 days and there was a Surrey record of 12–13 days (Fincher 1936). Both parents feed the young which remain in the nest for only 10–12 days. The downy nestlings are greyish in colour with yellow mouths, two black spots at the base of the tongue and one on the end, while the flanges on the side of the gape are yellowish-white. The young will abandon the nest while they are still incapable of proper flight and it is possible to come across them away from their natal home being fed by their parents. Under these circumstances an adult may seek to entice the observer away by a distraction display, which suggests injury and in which the parent points the bill upwards to expose the whitish throat to the intruder (Chadwick 1952).

In Europe eggs may be laid in early May, while in the southern counties of England the period from 10–22 May is the most likely time. Further north, many clutches are laid in the last week of May and some not until mid-June. A nest with five fresh eggs was found on 1 August 1950 in Savernake Forest in Wiltshire, while another at Arbury in Warwickshire had five young on 9 August 1956. In southern England Grasshopper Warblers will often raise two broods but this is not so in the north. Henry (1972) who studied a marsh in central France found that whereas Savi's Warblers were double-brooded, the Grasshopper Warblers raised three broods.

The adult warblers feed themselves on insects and their larvae especially *Diptera*, aphids, small moths such as Geometers and their caterpillars, small dragonflies, mayflies and beetles as well as spiders and woodlice but the exact composition will depend on whether they are living in wetland or drier habitats. The young are fed on a range of tiny green caterpillars, flies, aphids and small woodlice.

Birds begin to leave the British Isles from August onwards and the movements will continue until late September. As in the spring, there is a return east and west coast passage with a peak, for example at Skokholm on 7 September and in the middle of the month at other places. Birds appear on the Isle of Wight about 20–21 September, when I have watched small numbers around St Catherine's Point. We still do not know a great deal about the winter quarters of this warbler from Britain or the 'drift' migrants which occur from Fair Isle and the Isle of May to Portland which are probably of Continental origin. In winter, birds have been found in southern Spain and North Africa – Algeria, for example – and as far south as Senegal (Morel and Roux 1962). But where does the bulk of our Grasshopper Warblers spend the winter?

CHAPTER 13

The Savi's Warbler

Had a truly discriminating ornithologist of the sixteenth century – and an obviously affluent one – been able one summer to visit eastern England and much of Europe eastwards from Iberia to the Balkans, Poland and southern Russia, investigating the many regions of fen, swamp and coastal marsh that existed then, he or she would have become quite familiar with Savi's Warbler reeling away amongst the Reed, Sedge and Grasshopper Warblers that shared similar habitats. Yet from the early part of the seventeenth century in England until the middle of the nineteenth century the reedbeds and fens on which this species so depended were drained and turned over to cultivation. Similar changes in land use were also taking place on the Continent. Today's sporadic summer distribution in Europe of Savi's Warbler reflects the way in which man has altered the landscape and so changed the birdlife to be found there.

In England reclamation destroyed most of the natural wetlands, and this process was carried on ruthlessly for 200 years or more to 1850, when Whittlesey Mere was drained. So were removed for ever the great expanses of water, meandering streams, reedbeds and secluded pools lying in the shade of alders, willows and downy birches and the rich growth of fen sedge and many shrubby plants. The earliest poem in the English language recalls these wildernesses of reed and stinking pool which sheltered the monster Grendel whilst the early fenmen lived in fear of the dreaded Black Shuck, descended in ghostly form from the Black Hound of Odin. These human residents – the 'slodgers' or 'yellow-bellies' – lived by grazing stock, fishing and wildfowling, and were familiar with the cranes that bred in Fenland until about 1600 and those other species that disappeared with the draining of the land: Ruffs, Black-tailed Godwits, Bitterns, Black Terns, Spoonbills, Savi's Warblers and rare butterflies and moths. Savi's Warbler was first described as a species by the Italian naturalist Savi in 1824, but the reedcutters of the English fenland could distinguish its song from that of the Grasshopper Warbler until the former became extinct as a breeding species in 1856.

In Europe the surviving breeding populations of Savi's Warbler can be found somewhat erratically from Spain, Algeria, west and southern France, Majorca, Holland, Germany, Poland, the Balkans, Italy, Sicily, Crete, to central and southern Russia, as far east as the River Volga and Kazakhstan and south to the River Amu Darya. The actual geographical limits lie between 33°N and 55°N and the July isotherms of 17°C and 32°C.

I first came to know Savi's Warbler in the reed and sedge beds of the Naardermeer in Holland where in 1947 a local fisherman rowed me around that marvellous sanctuary in a small boat. Neither of us spoke the other's language but with the aid of signs, drawings in a notebook and my copy of T. A. Coward's *The Birds of the British Isles* (1944) we exchanged a great deal of information. Here my particular quarry shared its watery habitat

Fig. 61
*Savi's Warbler at the
nest. Spain, May 1957.
(Eric Hosking)*

with Spoonbills, Purple Herons, Cormorants, Marsh Harriers, Bitterns,
Black Terns and Red-crested Pochards as well as Reed, Great Reed, Marsh
and Grasshopper Warblers. I could appreciate how much of eastern England had once been like this. The species is very common in Poland, while
in the Danube Delta its song mingles with those of Reed and Great Reed
Warblers. It can also be heard in the reeds along the edges of rice fields by
the Costa Brava in Spain, and I made the first sound recordings of the
species by a stagnant lagoon near the coast, not far from Huelva. In this
last site three males were singing in a reedbed, encompassed by dwarf
pines and palmetto and dotted with small patches of open water, where
white ranunculus and water lilies laid a green and white carpet on the
surface. In this lagoon I also found Grey and Purple Herons, a mixed
colony of Night Herons and Little and Cattle Egrets, ten pairs of nesting
Spoonbills, a few Marsh Harriers and small numbers of Coot, Mallard
and Ferruginous Ducks. All the Savi's Warblers were singing from a
sheltered belt of reeds in the lagoon.

    As we have seen in the previous chapter, the song of Savi's Warbler with
its low-pitched reeling and more 'buzzing' voice than that of the Grasshopper Warbler is an aid to identification and a means of separating this
species from other warblers in the same habitat. It often begins with low
ticking notes that quickly accelerate into the sustained trilling song. Much
of the literature about this bird that I read as a schoolboy described Savi's
Warbler as very shy and crawling like a mouse in the reedbeds and 'never
showing itself unless driven out.' This species is less shy than the Grasshopper Warbler and regularly climbs up a reed stem to sing. I have watched

many males showing themselves quite openly, and certainly *The Handbook* (1946) noted that the song is delivered 'with the open beak and vibrating body from top of reed.' In Spain, Holland and East Anglia I found their willingness to show themselves quite intriguing. F. M. Boston (1956) observed that a bird singing at Wicken Fen in Cambridgeshire in June 1954 'had a preference for singing from a small group of willows – in particular one bush where it generally sat in an exposed position in an upright attitude with its tail depressed to an almost vertical position, and the whole body shivering.' The bird moves its head from side to side, producing a similar effect to that shown by the Grasshopper Warbler, and also displays its gape. In my experience the bursts of song in Savi's Warbler are shorter than those of the latter species and many last for fewer than thirty seconds. When I made some forty timings of one bird in the Camargue I found a range from 0 min 30 s to 1 min 3 s, while a Spanish singer had trills over a period of half an hour that varied in length from 0 min 8 s to 0 min 29 s. Yet another bird at Minsmere in Suffolk which I timed over twenty minutes produced bursts of from 0 min 5 s to as long as 5 min 25 s. The first record of a Savi's Warbler at Minsmere in 1964 was of an unmated bird whose utterances lasted 'mostly for one to three minutes and once . . . for more than ten minutes without any apparent pause' (Axell and Jobson 1972). It is to be expected that an unmated bird would reveal a higher and more prolonged output than a mated one. R. G. Pitt (1967) reported that Savi's Warblers in Kent often produced bursts in excess of three minutes. Temperatures may have a part to play as well since better and more sustained performances take place in warm conditions than in cold windy ones. When song comes to an end among several neighbouring males this usually suggests that mating has occurred and breeding is under way. In calm weather I have heard the reeling as much as 300 m away. H. E. Howard (1907–14) wrote that the female may also sing.

I have seen many male Savi's Warblers climb up the stem of a reed calling with sharp agitated 'tswik' notes or making a Starling-like rattle while flicking their rounded tails in a rather anxious manner. The bird sometimes breaks into song when halfway up the stem and gradually works its way to the top. Although a singer exposed in this way may be vulnerable to an avian predator, it enjoys the compensating advantage of a lookout post over a wide area. Its highly continuous song is of more value when given from cover and provides a high degree of advertisement and a lower risk of being approached by a hawk. It is important that a rather dull bird living in a dense habitat should be easily recognizable by its own kind and by other closely related species.

Voice is only one way in which Savi's Warbler reveals its identity and we may have to rely on its appearance in order to recognize it. It is a little larger than the Reed and Grasshopper Warblers and can be distinguished at once from the other British *Locustella* warblers by its uniform upper parts and lack of streaks above and below. It can be told from the River Warbler by its unstreaked breast while Cetti's Warbler, which it superficially resembles, has much less red-brown and more grey-brown or even whitish underparts. The upper parts are uniformly rufous-brown with the head rather darker and the rump paler. Savi's still has a shape reminiscent of the Grasshopper Warbler but the colouring seems more like that of a Reed Warbler, although it is darker and the tail is broader and more graduated.

The bird is whitish below with the side of the breast and the flanks 'washed' with a warm brown; the undertail coverts are similar but with lighter tips. The pale bastard wing shows a marked contrast with the redder greater coverts and dark-tipped primary coverts. The outer web of the outside and longest primary is a dirty white and the wings appear somewhat long in relation to the overall length of the bird. The broad brownish tail often bears narrow rather unclear marks known as 'fault bars' which arise from the way in which feathers protrude irregularly from their protective sheaths.

The side of the head is a dark brown with a thin supercilium or eye-stripe that travels in an arch over the eye, a pale crescent-shaped mark below and a thin, dark moustache which is rather typical of the *Locustella* warblers. The chin is often white and the throat a pale off-white merging into buff on the breast. The bill is dark brown above while the lower mandible is paler, perhaps horn-coloured, and there is a dull yellow colour to the cutting edges of the beak. The inside of the mouth was described by Kenneth Williamson (1976) as puce. The legs seem to range from bright olive-brown to a light flesh-brown, the latter being the colour which I have most observed. There also appears to be a cline of increasing wing and tail length eastwards across Europe.

From numbers of migrants examined in Iberia, some adult Savi's Warblers migrate in autumn with all their old flight feathers, while others travel with fully or partly replaced flight feathers, revealing how different individuals with separate breeding habitats make the greatest use of rich feeding resources. With a moult of the primaries moving in both directions from an originating point around the 3rd, 4th or 5th primaries this could ensure a quicker primary moult which would be of advantage to the birds (Mead and Watmough 1976). The main moult which is a descendant one takes place in Africa and may be accomplished so rapidly between October and November that some individuals may be rendered flightless.

There is a race *L. luscinioides fusca* that occurs in summer from western Siberia south to Transcaspia and the Tian Shan Mountains which is rather paler in colour, less reddish brown and more olive on the upper parts and whiter below. The vital statistics and wing formula do not seem to differ from those of the typical race.

Savi's Warbler is very much a bird at home among reeds and plant stems and its skulking nature may mean that an observer enjoys only the most fleeting glimpse of a slim brown unstreaked warbler with a rather long bill and wings before it disappears from view. I find it a restless bird, making its way skilfully through the reeds, keeping in or close to cover. The bird can run on the ground: one Savi's Warbler, described by M. J. Nicoll, in Egypt, 'waddled along like a parrot.'

We know that both Savi's and Grasshopper Warblers may be found in similar habitats and for me one of the past pleasures of a visit to Suffolk was to listen to both species in song only a few metres apart, suggesting a lack of competition between them. In Europe you may find Savi's alongside River Warblers as well. Generally the habitat for Savi's Warbler is one of reedy fens and swamps with shallow water especially where the reeds are not growing too densely, where there is also a varied underlayer of bur-reed *Sparganium*, sedges and rushes and where scattered sallow bushes and other small trees such as alders and birches may arise from the marsh. It is also a bird of extensive *Phragmites* reedbeds as in the Camargue, and mixed swamps of reed, reed-mace and rushes standing in shallow fresh or brackish water as in Spain and central France. Occasionally it occurs in sedgy marshes without reeds. A typical breeding marsh in France has beds of reed or reed-mace with large patches of *Carex* sedges and grass with ditches bordered by reed and sallows. The Savi's Warblers that breed in Kent have shown a preference for a similar habitat with some sorrel or marsh dock *Rumex* and the reed sweet-grass *Glyceria maxima*, the latter plant species being usually but not always present (Pitt 1967). The Suffolk Savi's Warblers breed in similar sites as well but also with sea club-rush *Scirpus maritimus*, marsh mallow and couch grass. In these habitats the birds subsist mainly on insects, taking the larvae and adults of many marsh-living beetles, moths and flies as well as medium-sized dragonflies and occasionally small worms.

The first records of Savi's Warbler in Britain date from 1835 although the species was unidentified but present long before that date. From that time small numbers nested in the fenlands of Norfolk with the last known survivor of the breeding population there being shot at Surlingham on 7 June 1856 (Stevenson 1866). Birds also nested in Cambridgeshire and Huntingdon; there were breeding records from Baitsbight in 1845, and on about the same date nests and eggs were taken from Milton Fen, Burwell Fen, Wicken Fen and Woodwalton Fen. The bird seems to have been practically unknown in Suffolk. After breeding ended in 1856 the only records in the British Isles until 1960 were of a male shot on Fair Isle and of a male singing at Wicken Fen, from 2 June to August 1956. It was clear that the once thriving summer population had disappeared with the draining and subsequent ploughing of the fens and marshes and the attentions of collectors. Yet there was also some evidence of a decline in the species along the edges of its European range.

Since the year 1960, Savi's Warblers have occurred with increasing frequency in Britain. Before this there was a marked expansion of range on the European Continent with the first records of breeding in Sweden in 1944, a widening range in Germany around 1950 with corresponding increases in Poland and France. Two pairs began nesting in Kent in 1960, although the species may have been present there from as early as 1951 (Pitt 1967). These first breeding records were on marshes formed from mining subsidence at Stodmarsh in the Stour Valley. By 1965 there were as many as twelve singing males. In 1970–71 Savi's Warblers had extended their range as nesting birds to Suffolk, with breeding taking place at Walberswick and Minsmere, while birds were being recorded in summer in Norfolk, Cambridge, Somerset and Hampshire. In the 1970s there were

Table 14   *Savi's Warblers breeding 1973–82*

	1973	1974	1975	1976	1977	1978	1979	1980	1981	1982
Sites	4	5	3	8	13	15	15	14	8	11
Pairs proved breeding	0	1	1	0	3	4	6	2	5	0
Pairs possibly breeding	13	8	3	9	26	28	30	29	15	18

(by permission, from the monthly magazine *British Birds*)

also reports of singing males from Cornwall, Devon, Dorset, Hampshire, Warwickshire, Nottinghamshire, Lancashire, Hertfordshire and elsewhere. The first Irish record was in 1980. By 1981 some 5–15 pairs were breeding at eight sites of which three were in Norfolk, two in Suffolk and one each in Kent, Dorset and Hampshire. Table 14 plots the various vicissitudes of this species between 1973 and 1982. It can be seen that Savi's Warbler has experienced something of a decline in recent years.

In Britain, Savi's Warblers are present from mid-April to late July or early August; the mean date of arrival on their breeding grounds is 19 April. Throughout the whole of the range the breeding season varies from mid-April in the south to late May in the north. Since the bird is such a rare nester in Britain few observers will have been able to see the nest and in any case no disturbance is permissible since Savi's Warbler is protected at all times, with special penalties under the Wildlife and Countryside Act of 1981. I have seen nests in southern Spain in May built in *Juncus* rushes, from a few centimetres to 50 cm above shallow water, and once above damp ground. In northern Israel nests are several times as high as this; perhaps 1 m above the surface (Zahavi 1957). The nest, built by the female, is a deep cup resting in the lower parts of reeds, sedges and even grasses. The outer section is formed from dead leaves such as those of *Cladium* sedge, reed sweetgrass and other aquatic plants, while the interior is not so loosely woven as the outside and is often constructed of grass stems, fine leaves and fibres. The nest is not invariably lined in this way. It is generally well concealed, sometimes with a partial covering and has been compared in shape to the small nest of a Moorhen or rail. Nests of Savi's Warblers used to be found in fenland after the reeds had been cut in the autumn for commercial use.

The clutch usually varies in size from 4–5 eggs but it can be as low as 3 or as high as 6. The eggs themselves are white, glossy and smooth and are often quite heavily speckled with brown, grey-brown, purple-brown or violet markings with the greatest concentration at the broad end of the eggs. In some cases the degree of very fine speckling may give the eggs a clear and distinct pinkish hue. The eggs are incubated by the female for about 12 days and during this time she is fed by the male. The nestling boasts a sparse reddish down and spends 12–14 days in the nest. It is fed in the early nestling stages by the female but the male will help in the later stages. Birds can be observed carrying food or faecal sacs, but they are rarely detected flying from the nest. Juvenile birds resemble the adults but are paler underneath. Where a territory is shared in England with Reed Warblers there seems to be little aggression between the two species (Axell and Jobson 1972), and I have found evidence of such hostility missing from mixed populations in Holland, Spain and France. The species can be double-brooded.

The birds depart from their summer haunts in late July and early August and fly to Africa for the winter. It is not known how extensive their wintering areas are on that continent but it seems that many travel to northeast Africa and some perhaps to tropical regions: there are records in Senegal. Birds have been seen on passage in Egypt and also in swamps in Darfur in the Sudan in October and November. In the last area many young birds were seen, while adults followed later and went into moult, which ended about the middle of November. The bird has been seen in

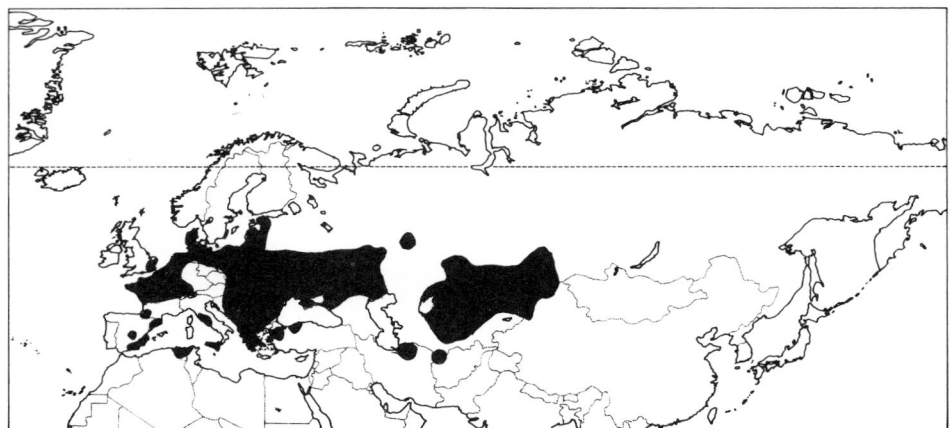

Fig. 62
*Breeding range of the
Savi's Warbler.*

September in Eritrea, where wintering might also occur, frequenting rank grass and docks near streams and dams while *L.l. fusca* has been seen there in grass, crops, acacias and scrub also in the vicinity of rivers (Smith 1957). We still do not know the full extent of the wintering grounds of this species.

The Vagrant *Locustella* Warblers

CHAPTER 14

The Lanceolated Warbler

There are, in fact, three *Locustella* species which have made their way to the British Isles from the east. Of these the Lanceolated Warbler, which to some extent resembles a small Grasshopper Warbler on the upper parts but is drabber with broader darker centres to the mantle and rump feathers, has appeared most frequently. The back does seem to give the impression of a more uniform but darker, greyer hue than that of the commoner species. When seen – and this is a rare phenomenon – its minute size, since it is the smallest of the *Locustella* warblers, and its fan-shaped tail should help in its recognition. It is so small that it has been known to fly several times through a mist net without pausing in its flight! The tail seems to be somewhat smaller in proportion to the body than in the Grasshopper Warbler. The head carries some faint streaks and a narrow buff eye-stripe which barely reaches beyond the eye itself. The chin and throat are both whitish with some dark streaks. The breast and belly are both somewhat variable in coloration but are generally whitish with some spotting, which may resolve itself into a narrow gorget or band on the upper breast. In fact, with this kind of marking the Lanceolated Warbler with its neat, compact shape and breast band has been compared to the Tree Pipit. The outer web of the outside primary is generally a whitish or buffish-brown. First winter birds – all three records of birds on Fair Isle in 1982 were of this kind – are rather more tawny on the back and yellower below. The upper mandible is a dark horn colour and the lower a pale pink with a dark tip. The legs are also pink. Despite an attempt to establish a race *L.l. gigantea* no subspecies are recognized.

In Britain the Lanceolated Warbler has been described as 'an extraordinarily skulking bird' (Davis 1961), finding shelter in the most meagre kinds of cover. It is shyer than even the Grasshopper Warbler; though in 1957 a Lanceolated explored the stubble at the feet of an observer, in full view, which was quite exceptional. It was in all probability a newly arrived and fatigued bird. When in low cover near the ground the bird makes its way through grass with an undulating movement more like that of some small mammal than a bird. The bird will also run quite fast on the ground and one seen in 1982 on Fair Isle was 'strutting around the observatory trap enclosure in the manner of a diminutive Water Rail.'

The Lanceolated Warbler is a breeding bird of the central and eastern Palaearctic regions; it can be found nesting from the Ural Mountains and eastern and central Russia across Siberia to Kamchatka, Sakhalin, Manchuria, northern Korea and north Japan, south to the Russian Altai and Sayan Mountains. Here the species favours wet meadows and grasslands, marshy regions with thick vegetation, liberally sprinkled with bushes, reeds bordering water and grassy clearings in woods. Here the male sings a

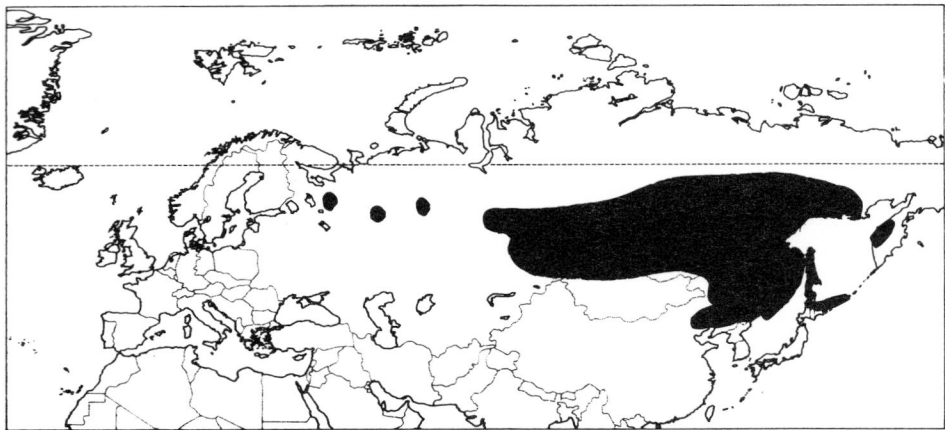

Fig. 63
Breeding range of the
Lanceolated Warbler.

ticking song, sharper and somewhat slower than that of the Grasshopper
Warbler. The nest is built in tall plants or tussocks and is often sited
against the side of a clump of vegetation so that it is concealed from
above. The nest itself is typical of the group and breeding often starts in the
middle of May so a second brood is not possible. The food consists generally of those insects that flourish in watery habitats.

The winter quarters lie in southern Asia reaching east from India to the
Andaman Islands and Burma, Thailand, Malaysia, Indonesia and parts of
Indo-China. Here the habitats are similar to those of the breeding grounds:
reedy areas and marshy vegetation, but they also include ricefields. The
moult is completed in spring and worn birds have been observed in Burma
as late as March. Vagrants have been reported in Yugoslavia, Germany,
Holland, Denmark, Sweden, Heligoland and the British Isles. The first
British record was of a bird at North Cotes in Lincolnshire on 18 November
1909 and, since that time, with one exception, the subsequent records have
been of birds on northern Scottish islands, particularly Fair Isle. There
were six seen between 1908 and 1928; one in 1938; five from 1953–61;
three from 1972–3 and sixteen between 1975–82. Some of the high totals
may be related to good breeding seasons in Russia but such a skulking,
retiring bird must often have been overlooked. Two interesting records
were those of a bird trapped in the Forties oilfield some 145 km off Aberdeen on 14 October 1978, and a first year bird trapped in a mist net in
Hampshire on 23 September 1979. The Lanceolated Warbler is primarily a
vagrant to Fair Isle between the middle of September and the early part
of November.

The River Warbler

I was at Fair Isle in September 1961 when the first River Warbler was
recorded in the British Isles. This too is a rather secretive bird and a
reluctant flier. It differs chiefly from the Grasshopper Warbler in generally
possessing unstreaked and uniform warm rusty-brown or dark olive-brown
upperparts. This is rather a variable species at all ages and some examples
are 'dark earth brown' (Williamson 1976) rather than olive-brown. The

sides of the breast and the flanks of the River Warbler are also olive-brown whereas the underparts are whitish with a buffish-yellow wash. On closer examination it is possible to see blurred, rather indistinct streaks of greyish-brown on the throat and upper breast. H. E. Dresser (1902) observed that 'the young bird has the upper parts more rusty in tinge, the underparts tinged with ochreous, and the throat is also indistinctly striped'; these are characteristic features of the first-year River Warblers on Fair Isle in 1961 and 1969. Yet an adult on Fair Isle on 24 September 1982 'had a distinct rufous tinge to mantle, scapulars, rump and tail' while a first-winter bird there two days earlier was 'a uniform dark olive-brown' (Riddiford 1984). The tail is long, broad and fan-shaped. A vital clue in identification are the under-tail coverts which are grey or buffish-brown but with quite broad whitish tips; those of Savi's Warblers are tipped with buff and much less contrasting. The bill is fairly stout with the upper mandible a horn colour with a fleshy tinge while the lower has a tinge of flesh and a dark tip. The legs and feet are flesh-pink. Gray's Grasshopper Warbler does not have streaked underparts, but the less reddish eastern race of Savi's Warbler *L.l. fusca* may show some mottling on the breast. The River Warbler is very much a terrestrial bird running along the ground or working its way in a crouched or hunched attitude through low-growing plants. When singing from a higher song post it will walk along the twigs.

The breeding range of the River Warbler lies between the July iso-therms of 16° and 23°C. Birds breed from the Baltic States east across Russia to the Ural Mountains at 60°N, and from the region of the River Rhine and East Germany to Poland, Hungary, northern Yugoslavia, the

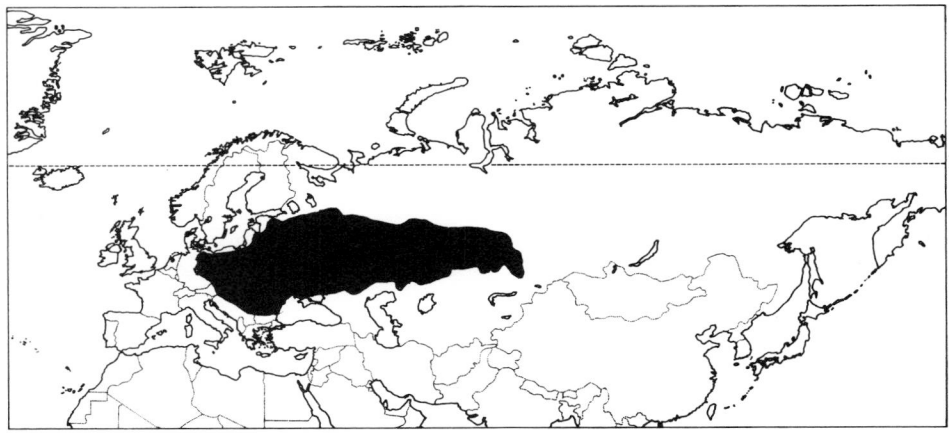

Ukraine, Crimea and lower Volga. The grinding, pulsating sewing machine-like rattle of the male's song can be heard in beech, alder and other kinds of thicket in wet, wooded regions. The song tends to be in shorter bursts than those of the Grasshopper Warbler; of eight that I timed I noted durations of 0 min 5 s, 0 min 7 s, 0 min 10 s, 0 min 9 s, 0 min 12 s, 0 min 17 s and 0 min 21 s in that order. There are some 620 double notes to the minute and the whole performance has a throbbing quality. The singer also seems on

Fig. 64
Breeding range of the River Warbler.

occasion to have a catch in its breath in the middle of a song-burst. As a breeding species the River Warbler is quite common in the sallow woods of the Danube Delta, where its shrub-top song can be heard with those of Collared Flycatchers. Birds also live by rivers and freshwater lakes and pools which boast a fairly dense growth of tall grasses and other plants, and in glades and clearings in forests, including those of coniferous trees, with swampy ground and small trees such as hazel and birch. Voous (1960) also mentions shrubs around ponds in city parks and cornfields as summer habitats for this species. Nests are built on or very close to the ground in dense overgrown thickets and shrubs with often only one route of approach through the vegetation. Nesting often begins in early June, so the species is single brooded. The clutch varies in size from 5–7 eggs, white, smooth and marked in the characteristic *Locustella* way. Incubation lasts about thirteen days. In quite large tracts of country the River and Savi's Warblers overlap, but there are differences in the nature of the habitats and, although competition in the two species might occur, it does not seem to be of much significance. To the east in central and eastern Asia the River Warbler is replaced by Gray's Grasshopper Warbler.

The River Warbler's winter quarters range south from East Africa to the Transvaal; here the bird favours reedbeds and bushes alongside rivers and lakes. Many birds apparently pass the late autumn months in northeast Africa and then travel through eastern Kenya on their way further south. Birds also appear in Kenya between the middle of November and early January as the result of very large nocturnal migrations. Migrants flying from northeast Africa to Tanzania and places even further south are sometimes forced down by rain and mist and are then attracted to the lights around safari lodges. At Ngulia (Kenya) many River Warblers actually enter the Lodge itself and from 1972–3 as many as 185 were trapped (Pearson and Backhurst 1976). Many warblers stayed in the green bush areas for days or even weeks at a time. They then moved south to spend from late January to March moulting in northeastern South Africa, eastern Zimbabwe and possibly Mozambique and Malawi. Many birds seemed to have moulted their outer primaries during the autumn while in Northeast Africa. Birds have been reported moulting in South Africa between late January and early March (Dowsett 1972).

The River Warbler has appeared as a wanderer to Norway, Sweden, Denmark, Heligoland, Holland, Switzerland and the British Isles. Since the first Swedish record in 1937 many more have occurred in that country; indeed, 81 were reported in song in 1981. Another ten were observed in Denmark by the end of May 1983. The extension of range to the northwest has also been reflected to some degree in the British Isles but many occurrences are likely to have taken place without being observed; the bird is shy and not well marked. After the first record in the British Isles on Fair Isle in 1961 other birds were seen at that island site in 1969, 1981 and 1982. Other River Warblers were reported at Bardsey Lighthouse in Gwynedd in 1969, at Spurn in Humberside and Roydon in Norfolk in 1982; after the singleton in 1961 and the two in 1969, five birds showed up in 1981 and 1982. The early records fell in September but in 1981 there were birds in May at Fair Isle and in Norfolk as well as an August occurrence at Spurn. The individual that appeared in 1981 at Roydon in Norfolk was present from 29 May to 6 June, and sang frequently high up in a hawthorn and elder hedge alongside a field of rye and next to a public footpath. When not disturbed it 'sang from exposed perches, giving good views' (Pratley 1984). This bird attracted hundreds of birdwatchers and a certain amount of adverse publicity, since the news was leaked and the ensuing crush of visitors resulted in some damage to the crop.

Pallas's Grasshopper Warbler

The last member of this extremely interesting and demanding genus to be recorded in the British Isles is a vagrant from Siberia – Pallas's Grasshopper Warbler. This small, streaked warbler at a quick glance and when skulking in dense herbage may sometimes resemble a Grasshopper Warbler. When a better view can be obtained, its streaked, dullish yet rather warm olive-brown or rufous upperparts may provide a superficial likeness to that of a Sedge Warbler. The reddish rump and upper tail coverts, however, serve to separate Pallas's from the commoner Grasshopper Warbler. There are pale greyish, sometimes whitish tips to the underside of the graduated tail but these are not reliable diagnostic characters in the field. The typical race bears the heaviest streaking. *L. certhiola centralasiae*, which breeds in Mongolia, is a cool greyish-buff and is also brighter with more contrasting plumage. The third race, *L.c. rubescens*, to which the British and Irish occurrences seem to belong is the darkest and brownest of all; it breeds in the northern part of the range from Siberia to the basin of the Amur. These three races appear to show the more important divergent tendencies within the species (Vaurie 1959) and others that have been described do not appear to be justified.

The crown of Pallas's Grasshopper Warbler is darker and streaked more boldly than that of the Sedge Warbler particularly at the back and on the side of the head. The lower part of the nape and the upper portion of the back are pale enough to form what has been described as a 'shawl' effect – a phenomenon not unknown in Sedge Warblers but without the same degree of contrast. The chin, throat and upper part of the breast are all very pale or whitish in colour and combine to create a gorget or apron. The eye-stripe was described as 'yellowish' (Williamson 1976) but in Mongolia it was regarded as buffy-white, nearly as conspicuous as that of the Sedge Warbler (Kitson 1980) and 'white rather than buffy white and as conspicuous as that of Sedge Warbler' (Densley 1982). The eye-stripe itself is fairly broad and ends abruptly after stretching from the bill to the hind crown. There is a clear contrast in the wings between some of the wing coverts and the rest of the wing; the primary coverts appear so dark in the field that when the bird flies a black spot can be seen on the wing. The juvenile has yellowish underparts and a band of dark spots or blotches across the breast. The bill is a blackish-brown with the base of the lower mandible a flesh colour; the legs are brownish.

This bird is a confirmed skulker and when forced to fly soon dives once more into thick cover. When alighting it may sometimes lift the tail upright at an angle to the back (Williamson 1950). On the ground it runs rather in the manner of a small rodent. Wintering birds may employ the 'chir-chirr' note while the song, sometimes delivered in a fluttering song-flight, was described in Chapter 11.

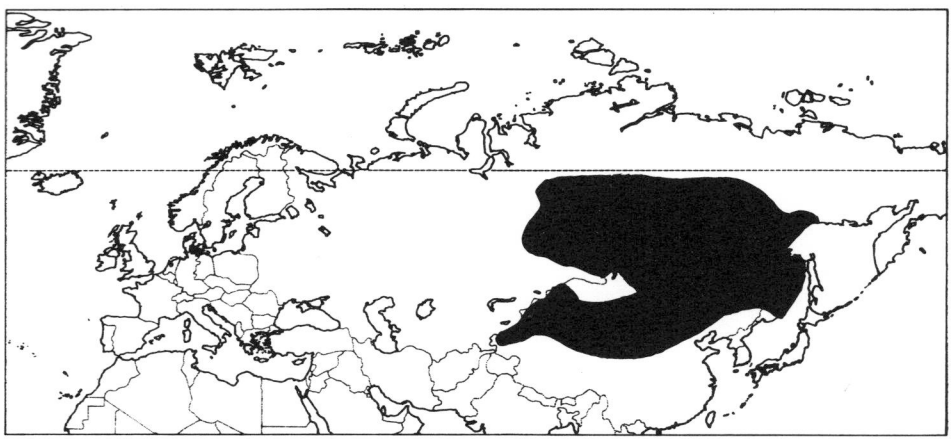

Fig. 65
*Breeding range of the
Pallas's Grasshopper
Warbler.*

In the breeding season Pallas's Grasshopper Warbler has a range over central Asia and Siberia north to about 64°N, and from the River Irtysh eastwards across Transbaikalia, Mongolia and Manchuria to some of the islands off northwest Hokkaido in Japan. Here its habitat is one of reed-beds, rich semi-aquatic vegetation in swamps and rice fields. Kitson (1980) found that the species favoured lakeside reeds and *Juncus* rushes with riparian willows. Other Asian nesting grounds include damp meadows with dense grass and thickets as well as copses bordering streams and swampy ground. The nest is rather like that of the Grasshopper Warbler and is situated in tussocks of grass or rank herbage growing in wet, sometimes mossy meadows. It is well hidden and often has a single side entrance of grass or moss. The clutch of 4–6 eggs, thickly coated with pinkish-brown spots, is laid in Siberia from the middle of June onwards while further east some young birds fledge in early July.

In winter the species moves south to India, Sri Lanka, Burma, Thailand, Malaysia, southeast China, Sumatra, Borneo, Java and the Philippine Islands. In Malaysia one habitat consists of a dense undergrowth of ferns and other plants, fringing beds of tall reeds in the worked out parts of opencast tin mines (Nisbet 1967). The birds are present in Malaysia from mid-September to mid-May, enjoying a largely nocturnal and retiring existence. September birds appeared to be chiefly migrants but later in the year birds were found remaining throughout the winter. Apparently more then 50% returned each year to their wintering grounds. The moult of the wing and tail feathers proceeded throughout March and April and was completed some two weeks before the spring migration. The whole of the tail and as many as four primaries and three secondaries in each wing were moulted simultaneously. Moulting birds were able to sustain and even increase their weight since the period of their moult also coincided with an apparent peak of insect life in the region that also marked the local nesting season.

Pallas's Grasshopper Warbler is a vagrant to Afghanistan, Heligoland, England, Ireland and Scotland. Birds have been recorded at Rockabill Lighthouse in Co. Dublin in September 1908; at Fair Isle in October 1949 and 1956, from 20–24 September 1976 and on 21 September 1981; at Cley in Norfolk on 13 September 1976. All the six records (at the time of writing) fell between 13 September and 8 October. The first winter bird on Fair Isle in September 1976 had only 'a very indistinct, thin creamy supercilium' (Broyd 1983) while the September 1981 bird, also first-winter, had a 'rather well-defined clear-buff eye-stripe' (Page and Greaves 1983).

CHAPTER **15** The Cetti's Warbler

For me Cetti's Warbler is certainly one of the birds in this group to have a great deal of character. It assaults you from dense cover with a robust, abrupt and riveting song, slips surreptitiously away unseen and then suddenly erupts once more into a loud burst of clear notes. It was one of the most challenging and difficult species to record on tape that I encountered in more than thirty years of wildlife sound recording. It reminded me in the mammal kingdom of the Sika deer stag which produces one territorial challenge from cover and then moves some distance, unnoticed and silent, before calling again minutes later. The species is also unique in being the only one of the eleven or so in its genus to occur in Europe and the British Isles. There are, in fact, eight species in the Palaearctic. Cetti's Warbler is also remarkable in three ways: in having only ten tail feathers instead of the dozen in most other warblers; in laying bright brick-red eggs; and thirdly, in living as a resident species throughout the twelve months even as far north as Britain. The latter distinction is shared with the Dartford Warbler, and it therefore also suffers in the same way as this warbler in severe winters when its numbers may be greatly reduced. However, the comparatively mild winters between the late 1940s and 1960 may well have been instrumental in bringing about the remarkable northwards extension of this bird's range – a movement which to some extent coincided with a similar extension in eastern England of Bearded Tits. Taking its name from that of a Jesuit naturalist who lived in the eighteenth century, Cetti's Warbler has become increasingly familiar to ornithologists in Britain.

Fig. 66
Breeding range of the Cetti's Warbler.

It is a bird of the southwestern Palaearctic region, appearing in a wide

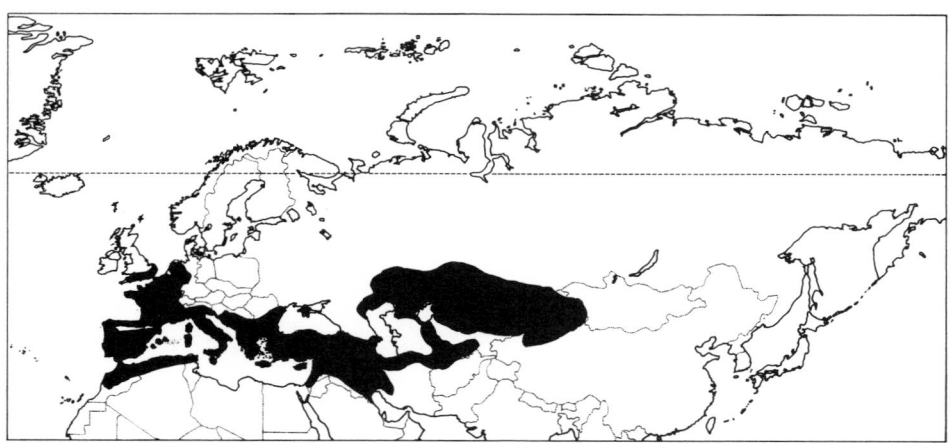

range of climatic zones through temperate, Mediterranean, steppe and even desert (Vouus 1960) and between 30°–53°N. Cetti's Warbler *Cettia cetti*, with a rufous-brown back, breeds in northwest Africa from Morocco to Tunisia, in Iberia, France, Britain, Italy, Greece, Bulgaria, Romania and Crete and other islands of the Mediterranean to the Ukraine and the Crimea. There is an eastern form recognized as *Cettia cetti albiventris*, synonymous with *cettioides* Hume, which is larger and does not enjoy the spring moult undergone by the western race so that it is pale grey-brown on the back and much whiter underneath. This race can be found from the Kirghiz Steppes east to Turkestan and south to Transcaspia, northern and western Iran and northern Afghanistan and appears to spend the winter in eastern Iran, southern Afghanistan, Baluchistan and northwest India. Although some of the populations in Asia Minor and other parts of the Middle East are of intermediate size, there seems to be no real justification for giving these birds any further separation. In eastern Asia it appears that Cetti's Warbler may be replaced by *Cettia diphone*, the Chinese Bush Warbler which ranges from southeast Siberia to Japan and northern China and lives in scrub and reeds. The Asian and Pacific *Cettia* or Bush Warblers occupy habitats ranging from forest including dense bamboo and rhododendron, to woodland clearings, swamp-jungle, scrub, grassland, reeds and tea gardens that stretch from the Himalayas to southeast Asia, Indonesia, China, Taiwan, Korea, Japan and the Philippines with one of the species confined to the mountains of north Borneo and another to Timor. The map on page 156 shows the breeding range of Cetti's Warbler.

Although, like many of the *Locustella* warblers, Cetti's is usually a shy, skulking bird, there are occasions especially in the early morning, less often in the evening and when there are young in the nest, when Cetti's Warblers will show themselves. It is then possible to watch a small, rotund bird with a uniformly dark chestnut-brown back becoming more rufous on the mantle, rump and tail coverts. The chin, throat, breast and belly are a dull white while the rest of the underparts are a warmer greyish or darker brown. Williamson (1976) described also 'sometimes a faint primrose wash on centre of breast and belly', but this is a feature that I have been unable to detect with birds in the field. There is a short greyish eye-stripe or supercilium. The bill is medium in size, horn-coloured on the upper mandible and pink on the lower. The bird has short rounded wings with the third to fifth primary features emarginated (with a narrowing of the web on one side towards the tip), while of 56 birds examined 50% showed emargination of the second primary, about 80% slight emargination of the sixth while 'very exceptionally the 7th is emarginated too' (Scott and Svensson 1972). The tail, which is blackish-brown in fresh plumage and fringed chestnut-brown, is strikingly graduated and rounded. The legs and feet are a brownish-flesh colour. Because the bird is so rufous-brown there may be some danger of mistaking Cetti's for a Nightingale, but this chat-like thrush is considerably larger and has a longer tail which shows up more brownish-chestnut than the rest of its upperparts. Juvenile Cetti's Warblers are less reddish-brown on top and greyer below than the adults, and may reveal 'fault-barring' or starvation marks in bands on the tail showing simultaneous growth of the feathers, whereas an adult would have displayed out-of-phase bars on the tail (Mead 1965). A complete moult is

Fig. 67
Underside view of tail of the Cetti's Warbler.
(Eric Simms)

achieved in late summer when breeding is finished, probably from late July to early September, and there is also a moult of the body and wing coverts in March. The eastern race does not experience this spring moult.

There is a clear sexual dimorphism present, with the males some 12% longer in the wing than the females and also 30% heavier with scarcely any overlap. The significance of this will be discussed later.

Table 15   *Dimensions of Cetti's Warbler (mm)*

Race	Wing		Tail		Bill	Tarsus
	Male	*Female*	*Male*	*Female*		
Cettia cetti cetti	58–64	51–57	54–65	50–56	13–15	20–23$\frac{1}{2}$ (mostly 21–22$\frac{1}{2}$)
Eastern race *C.c. albiventris*	62–73		60–72		14–16	21–25 (mostly 23–24)

I have often found Cetti's Warbler skulking by nature and it certainly is a great lover of dense cover from which it proclaims its identity by its remarkable and characteristic song. Yet, as I mentioned earlier, I have also seen birds perch for a short time on a bush or bramble spray, both at the start and the end of the day and in the vicinity of the nest. In these circumstances and also when on the ground this warbler has a habit of constantly flicking its tail in a downward direction. Its behaviour and actions have been compared to those of a *Sylvia* rather than an *Acrocephalus* warbler. I have experienced many long days in the field when Cetti's Warbler has remained totally elusive and retiring – an enigma – but when it has shown itself it has revealed a dark rufous little bird, active and perky with an engaging tail and with some resemblance to a Wren with a pale breast. In flight its reddish-brown form again suggests a Wren or a round-winged Hedgesparrow with a short untidy tail, diving swiftly towards the next piece of cover. On the ground the bird moves around like a small rodent.

It is indeed fortunate that Cetti's Warbler has the habit of proclaiming its presence in such a forthright and unmistakable way. In *Voices of the Wild* (1957) I described how in the company of M. Henri Lomont, chief warden of the Camargue sanctuaries of the *Société d'Acclimatation*, I made my first acquaintance with this warbler and succeeded in making a sound recording of it for the first time.

'While we were thinking about the best way of approaching Savi's Warbler with a microphone, our ears were suddenly blasted by a violent outburst of music from some tamarisks along the road. It was finished almost before it had started; then again came the sudden impact of song on our astonished ears . . . Twice it flung its passionate phrases at us and then it was gone; but these last two bursts were well and truly recorded. We were never able again to get so close to this elusive warbler whose song of challenge and defiance comes from one spot and is then not thrown out again until the bird is thirty yards further on. I heard the song on many other occasions, and once I was able to watch the singer balanced for a few seconds on the top of a hedge. Once the song of Cetti's Warbler has been heard, it can never be mistaken for that of any other bird. Of the few descriptions of its song that I have read the one I like best is that given by George Yeates; "What-yer . . . what-yer . . . what-yer . . . come-and-see-me-bet you-don't . . . bet you don't".'

The song consists of this sudden brief outburst of notes; of the many that I have timed in the field or from my own recordings the duration is normally from 1.5–2.5 seconds, rarely 3. The interval between each burst of song may easily vary from 15–20 seconds and the daylight outbursts are rarely ever given from the same place twice in succession. A bird that I recorded in Spain in May 1956 sang a simple 'weechoo . . . weechoo . . . weechoo' but the first bird I encountered in the Camargue uttered a much fuller type 'witcher-witcher-witcher . . . too-witch . . . too-witch . . . toowee'. Other versions of this song are 'chee, che-weechoo-weechoo-weechoo-wee' (*The Handbook* (1946)) with minor variations. C. Suffern (1965) in his

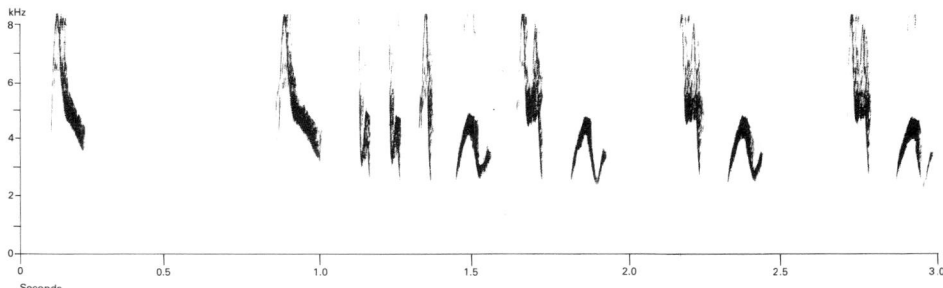

account of the Cetti's Warbler he found at Titchfield Haven in Hampshire in 1961 reported various short phrases introduced by 'a double phrase "chew-to-it; chew-to-it" ', which is reminiscent of the bird that I recorded in Spain, but he also noted other short phrases which to him 'sounded like "is it safe? is it safe? is it? is it? see what you mean, see what you mean",' which also reveals the typical rhythms of the song. Each male bird has his own special variations. I have heard powerful song in November from male birds on the banks of the River Sorgue in the Vaucluse, and in the Camargue, while in Italy regular song can be listened to from February to early July and again from September to October with irregular bouts of song in between. The territorial song is sustained by the male until the female is incubating, after which there is often a decline in output. After the eggs have hatched and the young have fledged song may be resumed. Many males sing loudly in the vicinity of the nest. There is also a subdued form of song which matches the full song in its quality if not its volume.

In Spain, France, Italy and Greece I have heard male Cetti's Warblers sing into the twilight hours, but J. F. Burton (1979) noted a bird at Minsmere in Suffolk which sang continuously from 11.15 p.m. on 25 May 1971 to 1 a.m. on 26 May; he also described how Richard Margoschis had recorded another at Surlingham in Norfolk on 24 May 1977. Both these birds appeared to sing from fixed song-posts which shows a difference from their behaviour in daylight. A male sang from 00.45 a.m. to 02.30 hours on 10 May at Elmstone in Kent, and C. Bignal recorded night singing in east Kent in early May 1976. At the time the habit was thought to be so unusual that it prompted W. G. Harvey (1980), who had exceptional knowledge of Cetti's Warblers nesting in the Middle Stour valley in Kent, to suggest that 'this habit is restricted to unmated males' and its occurrence might provide a useful clue to the nuptial state of the singer. This view was

Fig. 68
Song of the Cetti's Warbler. Note clear-cut nature of phrases. (Recorded by B.B.C. Natural History Unit, Camargue, May 1973)

challenged by D. T. Ireland (1984) who, after studying and sound-recording birds at Radipole Lake, Dorset, proved that 'nocturnal singing by a male Cetti's Warbler cannot be used as a guide to its nuptial status.'

During a study of breeding Cetti's Warblers on Jersey, Frances le Sueur (1980) heard a female on the eighth day of nest building utter a cadence of four very sweet notes five times. Three days later another song, opening with a harsh note 'was followed by seven sweet ones going right down the scale like the final cadence of a Willow Warbler *Phylloscopus trochilus* song. The male was singing excitedly and these female calls were thought to have been associated with mating.'

The call-note of Cetti's Warbler, probably less well known than the song, is a sharp 'twik' or 'chik-chik' of alarm, sometimes becoming a trilling or churring 'twik-ik-ik-ik'. A softer 'twik' may be heard from the male during courtship chases. The soft rather *Phylloscopus*-like 'uit' may be followed by an abrupt opening 'chee-wee' (Trouche 1946) but I have not heard this.

Cetti's Warbler has made an astonishing advance northwards during the present century. In 1900 this warbler was very largely restricted to the shores of the Mediterranean where it was looked upon as a sedentary species. During the 1920s it became clear that a northward expansion was taking place; that by 1924 the bird was seen in Anjou and three years later in Brittany while an eastern prong was advancing up the valley of the Rhône. The Seine was reached by 1932 and the north coast of Brittany and the Channel Islands by 1960. The first bird arrived in the British Isles in 1961. (Three previous occurrences on the British list in 1904, 1906 and 1919, all in Sussex, were rejected during the Hastings Rarities investigation when the authenticity of many early records in that part of the world were discounted.) The first accepted record was of a singing male at Titchfield Haven in Hampshire which was present from 4 March 1961 to at least 8 April; it was trapped for examination on 19 March. A second bird was trapped at Eastbourne on 9 October 1962. The arrival of these two birds

Fig. 69
Northward spread of breeding and territory-holding Cetti's Warblers. (After Bonham and Robertson 1975)

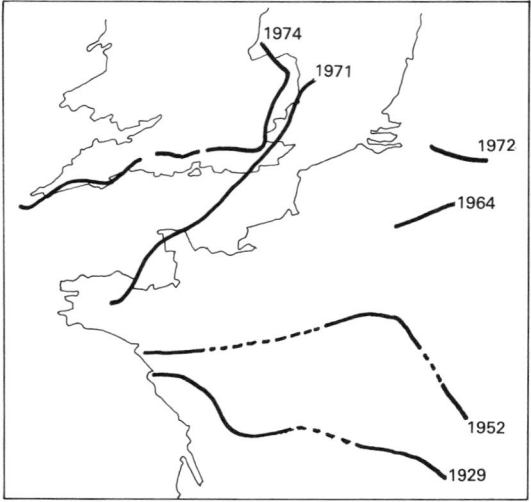

was the logical extension of the northward movement in France. Then followed a bird in Buckinghamshire from July to September 1967 with others in Kent in March 1968, and also that year in Somerset, Sussex and Cork; the last, on 24 August 1968, was the first Irish record. The first bird recorded in Belgium was in May 1962 with breeding two years later, in West Germany in May 1961 with breeding in 1975 and in Holland in October 1968. Nesting was first proved in the Channel Islands in 1973 – it had almost certainly occurred before that year – and in England. Cetti's Warblers were reported in Switzerland and Sweden in 1977. The movements to the north were checked to some extent by the cold winters of 1962–3 and 1978–9, but it was soon clear that the English population survived the second cold spell better even than the Wren, perhaps the only species with which it might have been in competition. A full account of the spread of Cetti's Warbler across northwest Europe has been given by Bonham and Robertson (1975).

By 1972 a growing body of evidence seemed to suggest that Cetti's Warblers might be nesting at two sites in the Stodmarsh area of the Stour Valley near Canterbury in Kent. Birds were also reported from an increasing number of localities in that year including Radipole Lake in Dorset and Hornsea in Humberside. By 1973 there were a dozen birds in the eastern section of the Stour Valley and these included three fledged juveniles. In the next year more birds appeared from Cornwall to Norfolk. Some 70% of the new records occurred in the months of September and October and from March to May. Since 40% of the new records were in the two autumn months it is generally believed that these may well have arisen from the dispersal of juvenile birds from their strongest-held breeding grounds. By 1977 many pairs were breeding at some 41 different sites, and Cetti's Warbler was removed from the *British Birds* rare birds list although it still receives special protection under the Wildlife and Countryside Act of 1981. By 1978 the number of sites rose to 46 but the severe winter of 1978–9 put a check on the colonization and, although there was no really serious decline, the number of sites fell to 39. The following table shows the fluctuations over the years.

Cetti's Warblers breeding 1973–82   Table 16

	1973	1974	1975	1976	1977	1978	1979	1980	1981	1982
Counties	2	3	3	8	10	14	14	11	16	12
Sites (excluding Kent)	1	3	8	14	32	41	33	50	59	58
Pairs proved breeding	1	5	8	8	13	30	46	19	56	29
Pairs possibly breeding	14	16	75	80	153	174	163	198	162	202

(by permission, from the monthly magazine *British Birds*)

Cetti's Warblers can generally be found in dense bushes and hedges with brambles, creepers and tamarisks, on riverbanks and in marshes and scrub growing alongside reedbeds. One favourite site that I know in the Camargue consists of a long dense hedge of thorn and willow with bramble and other straggling plants growing over a ditch; here I found singing males spaced out at about 100 m intervals. Ferguson-Lees (1964) who looked at a similar kind of hedge in Portugal found a pair to every 50 m. A stereo recording that was obtained when John F. Burton and I were near Albaron in the

Fig. 70
Habitat for the Cetti's
Warbler along the Canal
du Rhône, Bellegarde,
Provence. (Eric Simms,
May 1973)

Camargue on 25 May 1973 has a Cetti's Warbler in song with a background of Little Egret, Night Heron, Melodious Warbler, Fan-tailed Warbler, Blackcap, Nightingale, Tree Sparrow and Turtle Dove – a typical and delightful blend of sounds. In Spain I have found birds in habitats similar to those of Provence but in Greece I have come across birds in dryish scrub; in some European sites they occur along the edges of cornfields even if water is not immediately present. However, in Crete they may be located in 'Well-watered gullies at low elevations near the sea' (Bannerman 1954). The song has also been heard in an oleander thicket at 500 m in the south of Spain and at 1450 m in the Sierra Nevada.

In Jersey Cetti's Warblers bred where a small copse of poplar, willow, blackthorn and bramble was flanked on one side by a large reedbed and marshy vegetation along a canal. The favourite habitat in east Kent proved to be marshy scrub or willow carr with three dominant plants: bramble, reed and scrub willow, while the ground zone was often covered with nettles, *Typha*, sedges, rushes, meadowsweet and raspberry. The birds were able to adapt to a wide range of growth in this ecosystem, and the presence of surface water was not apparently an essential feature of the habitat. The favoured terrain at Radipole Lake in Dorset consisted of a shallow lake enriched with large dry reedbeds and scrub formed from blackthorn, hawthorn, willows, bramble and buddleia; Cetti's Warbler first bred in this latter site in 1977. In these habitats birds feed on various small insects, spiders, snails and occasionally small earthworms. I have watched an adult in the Camargue collecting minute caterpillars from a thorn while young birds in Kent were fed on grubs extracted from a rotten branch using a technique similar to that of a woodpecker.

The actual territory of the breeding male can vary in both shape and size. Often it is linear in form with a male taking over a stretch of hedgerow or long scrubby growth, which often border streams and causeways. One territory at Radipole Lake was 450 m long. Territories are regularly patrolled by singing males and it appears that the number of females within them varies considerably. Following preliminary observations by Trouche (1946) and Le Sueur (1980), which suggested that male Cetti's Warblers may be polygynous, Dr Colin J. Bibby (1982) undertook a detailed study of this aspect as well as the breeding ecology of birds nesting in 1980 at Radipole Lake in Dorset. He found that males bred with up to three females at a time and the actual number of hens – or the size of his harem – was correlated to the size of the male.

Male size, territory size and number of females in Cetti's Warblers. Territories were   Table 17
qualitatively assessed for their potential for expansion into suitable vacant habitat
(0 = none, 1 = limited, 2 = extensive) and availability of potential nesting sites within
the patrolled range

Male	Wing-length (mm)	Female/male	Territory perimeter (m)	Potential to enlarge territory	Vacant suitable nesting areas in territory
MRR	64	1	930	0	1
MRL	65	1	480	1	1
MRY	65	1	620	0	1
MRO	65	2	1170	1	1
MRE	67	3	920	1	1
MRG	62	1	130	2	0
MRD	65	2	440	2	0
MRP	64	2	560	2	1
MLR	64	1	330	1	1
MRS	61	0	–	–	–

Notes: Correlations – Female/male; territory size $r = 0.373$ NS
Female/male; wing-length (male) $r = 0.692$. $P < 0.05$
Territory size; wing-length (male) $r = 0.479$ NS
(reproduced from *Ibis*, Vol. 124, 1982, by permission of Dr C. J. Bibby)

The female Cetti's Warblers were thought to be selecting their mates on the basis of their size or perhaps something else that might be associated, such as the quality of the territory. On investigating this possibility Bibby found that six polygynous matings resulted in 'five clutches of five and one of four while all the monogamous pairs had four eggs (first broods only).'

In April and May it is possible to watch males pursuing females in aerial display flights. I saw this taking place in Provence in May 1954 with the larger male chasing a female in a rapid, erratic flight for several minutes on end. To me the flights were revealed as broad sweeps on wide arcs, but in his detailed studies of birds in east Kent W. H. Harvey (1977) saw many such flights where: 'The course is usually roughly circular or oval, but may describe a figure of eight.' Shorter and simpler versions of these chases were also seen in autumn over wintering feeding territories in reedbeds. Another display between members of a pair involved waving alternate wings in a rather hesitant manner, rather suggestive of one of the displays of the Hedgesparrow or Grasshopper Warbler. D. J. Manns (1979) found two Cetti's Warblers standing face to face in the middle of a tarmacadam road in Mallorca waving their wings at each other and slowly circling round, but keeping their distance.

The nests are built by the females, generally in luxurious marsh vegetation, in shrubs and hedges, in brambles close to dykes, often with dead interiors and sometimes reinforced with reeds growing through them. In Israel nests are sometimes built among the bases of reeds, and usually less than 1 m from the ground. All those built at Radipole Lake were 'situated

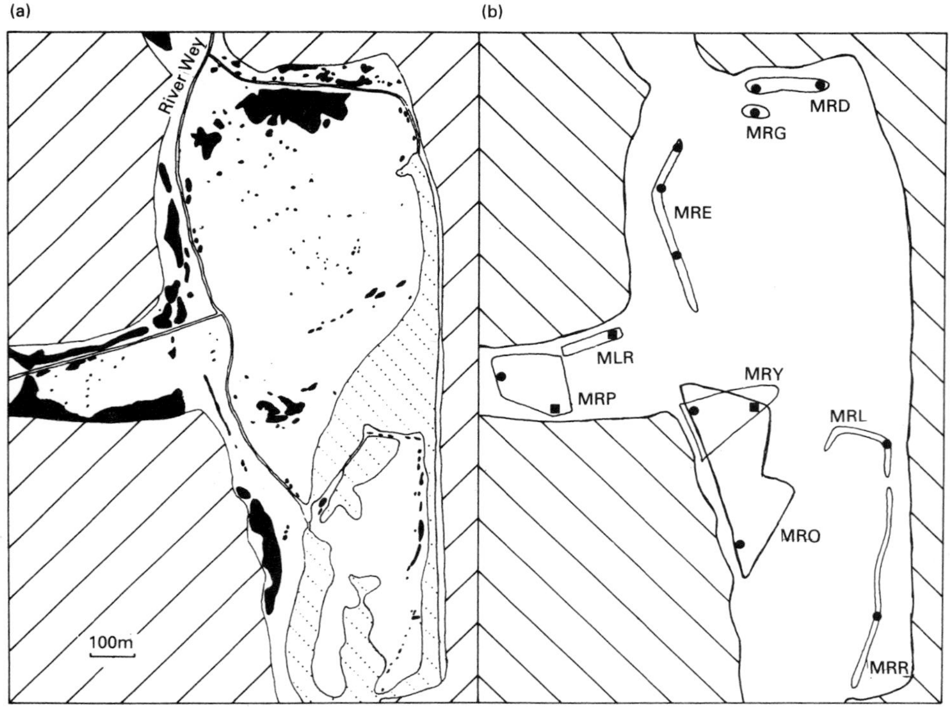

Fig. 71
Vegetation of Radipole Lake and distribution of Cetti's Warblers:

(a)　　　　　　　　　　　　　　　(b)

(a) ▨ urban land; ▦ water; ■ scrub; remainder of site mainly upper marshland. (b) Cetti's Warbler territories identified by colour codes of males. First brood nests shown as dots for those found and squares for those approximately located. (Reproduced from The Ibis, *Vol. 124, 1982 by permission of Dr C. J. Bibby)*

at the edge of a thicket of scrub, in the zone where the ground vegetation tangled thickly among woody stems' (Bibby 1982). I have found nests from 50 cm to 1 m above the ground, sometimes surprisingly exposed for so retiring a bird. The nest itself is a very deep-cupped construction of leaves and grasses, sometimes woven around the stem of a bramble and held up by dead reed or nettle canes, in the fork of a branch or in fallen vegetation in the manner of a Sedge Warbler. The interior of the nest is lined with finely woven grasses, hair, feathers or reed-down. The whole construction in late April or early May takes about eleven days.

The clutches of bright chestnut or brick-red normally consist of four eggs, but three and, as we have already seen, five are not unknown. Should these eggs with their remarkable colour be seen resting on a bed of black feathers in the nest the overall effect is quite dramatic. The female carries out all the incubation and visits the nest from inside the scrub, but the male often sings loudly close by. Of four incubation periods recorded at Radipole Lake the duration proved to be 16 days, and two in the Channel Islands were of 16 and 17 days respectively. The fledging period is also quite long for such a small bird: 15–16 days. Radipole first nests were very successful. Cetti's Warbler is said to be single-brooded (Harrison 1975) but second broods have been recorded on the Continent and in Dorset. The young in the nest are primarily fed by the female on dipterous flies, spiders, small larvae, beetles, moths, snails, caddisflies, worms and other small animals. The male Cetti's Warblers are not regular feeders of the young; the females have the entire responsibility of nest-building and incubation and most of the responsibility of caring for the young. Those males with a smaller number of mates seem to assume a larger role in the feeding of the young, and fledged birds may be fed for up to a month after leaving the nest. Bigamy is known among such marshland breeding species as Great Reed, Reed and Sedge Warblers but polygyny is clearly a feature of breeding in Cetti's Warblers. The food resources of marshy habitats have allowed the male to restrict its function of courtship and pairing, warning and territorial defence. The unequal sex ratios may arise because the larger males find it harder to survive the winter than the females, or because they are excluded by other males. It is likely that the larger size of the male, which assists with breeding success, and the unequal sex ratio evolved alongside each other. Perhaps, as Bibby suggested, Cetti's Warbler once enjoyed a linear distribution in the breeding season along flooded strips of scrub. Here in the ecotone between woodland and scrub and water and marsh the best-equipped males commanded territories of the greatest value and deterred others from coming in. Low levels of predation may have also reduced the need for the male to participate more fully in the breeding cycle. Bibby postulated that after an expansion in range and biotic changes in fens and marshes, Cetti's Warbler was pre-adapted to polygyny in habitats where this remains adaptive 'but historical factors might not have allowed most other marshland birds to have followed such an evolutionary path.' This particular species remains as intriguing and fascinating as ever, but its arrival in the British Isles has enabled people to see and study it who, until recently, would have been forced to go abroad to do so. Recently it has been suggested that the two sexes live in different habitats in the year with the males suffering a higher mortality than the females (Bibby and Thomas 1984). Cetti's Warbler still enjoys the distinction of being the most 'size-dimorphic' passerine in Europe linked, of course, with its polygynous method of breeding.

CHAPTER 16

The Fan-tailed Warbler

To see this, the smallest of the European warblers and that Continent's only species of grass warbler, I had to visit reedy country, marshy grasslands, damp roadside verges and rice fields in the basin of the Mediterranean and along the Atlantic and northern coasts of France. Yet the species has a much wider distribution across the world in Africa and Asia. I first came across the Fan-tailed Warbler *Cisticola juncidis* as barely present in the Camargue in 1954, but it was commoner in southern Spain in 1956. My attention would be drawn by a high-pitched, sharp rasping 'dzeep . . . dzeep . . . dzeep' high in the air and then I might spot a tiny bird with a weak and unwarbler-like undulating flight which dropped lower and began to bob and flutter above the rushes or reeds. If one is fortunate enough to get a glimpse of this shy and skulking species in the

Fig. 72
Song-flight of Fan-tailed Warbler. (D. I. M. Wallace)

wetland vegetation, then it may be possible to see it sliding up and down the stems with legs apart as the feet grasp separate growths, rather in the manner of the Bearded Tit. More often than not, however, the tiny Fan-tailed Warbler remains a disembodied voice in the warm southern skies, only glimpsed from time to time as a diminutive dancing spot against the cerulean blue. To the British Isles the bird is a rare vagrant in spite of recent moves northwards in western Europe.

When this warbler vouchsafes us a view of itself one can see a very small brown bird rather like a tiny *Acrocephalus* warbler; perhaps a small bright Sedge Warbler. The upper parts are rufous brown in colour and the rump is also rufous-tinged but the overall effect is a rather heavily streaked buffish bird. The throat and underparts are whitish and unstreaked, being palest on the throat, shading towards buff on the flanks. Both wings and tail are short and rounded. The tail is rufous, shading into a broader band with the feathers tipped white; these tips are especially evident when seen from below. While the bird is on one of its song-flights the tail is often half open, and when the bird is perched it has the habit of frequently cocking its tail. The Fan-tailed Warbler also has a pale whitish eye-stripe or supercilium. The bill is thin and a pale yellowish colour, similar to that of the legs, and with a darker tip. In the males the interior of the mouth is jet black and in females a pinkish colour; the latter also have darker streaks on the crown. Thus the Fan-tailed Warbler is a small dumpy brownish bird with rounded wings and tail and a high jerky song-flight.

Both adults and juveniles undergo a complete moult between June and November. It seems also that in common with juveniles of many other comparatively resident or partially migratory species in southern Europe, such as the Moustached Warbler, Goldfinch, first-brood Sardinian Warbler and an occasional Spectacled Warbler, many Fan-tailed Warblers enjoy a complete moult in their first autumn. An intensive study on the island of Malta proved that adult males moult in around 92 days, while adult females average about 67 days; male birds in their first year achieved their moult in 81 days and females in 75 (Gauci and Sultana 1981). These are much longer periods than that of 43 days suggested by D. K. Thomas (1979). Fan-tailed Warblers first began to breed on Malta in the early 1970s; a study of them seemed to indicate that the slow moult of the males was perhaps an adaptation to enable them to defend their territories against first-year birds, which are capable of beginning their nesting activities when only 3–4 months old.

The genus *Cisticola*, to which the Fan-tailed Warbler belongs, consists of several score of small, shy, brownish birds often with a dark streaking in their plumage. In his comprehensive review, H. Lynes (1930) sought to bring some order into a very confusing genus, and arrived at some 75 species. It is inappropriate to enter into the problems of separation here but recent listings have reduced this number. Although the systematics of this group offer many problems, including the identification of species which should concern all observers, the British ornithologist is still likely to be concentrating on the one species – the Fan-tailed Warbler or Zitting Cisticola as it is sometimes known. Among the remainder there still exist difficulties in separation as well as those of plumage, voice, habitat selection, food and nest-construction. Members of the group can be found in dry scrub, grassy savannah, bushy fields, and marshes with reeds; they can provide a great challenge to the observer here, and their voices assume great importance. In East Africa I met the Rattling Cisticola of the thorn-bush country which utters a harsh rattling trill from an acacia top, the Trilling Cisticola with a loud utterance from which it derives its name and the Singing Cisticola which I saw in the softer bushlands of Kenya and Uganda; here the songs were most important in species separation. The late Myles North once played me a tape recording that he had made of what he called the 'Boran' Cisticola singing at Marsabit in East Africa. It was discovered in southern Ethiopia by C. W. Benson and North thought that it was new to science; from its appearance it had to be equated with the Rattling Cisticola but its song and habitat were absolutely different!

The genus has been subdivided into grassland species, savannah species and swamp species (White 1960); the Fan-tailed Warbler belongs to the first of these, marked by small species with darkly streaked upperparts. Since *Cisticola* is an African genus with only two species extending to the Oriental and Australasian regions, it is likely that this pair is closely related. The two species are the Yellow or Golden-headed Cisticola *C. exilis*, which ranges from Australia to New Britain, Malaysia, the Philippines and southeast Asia from China to India, and is missing from the Ethiopian region; and the Fan-tailed, which occurs in the same eastern region as *C. exilis* but with a rather different distribution and a range that reaches to Japan, including toeholds in Australia; but it does not extend as far as New Guinea or New Britain. The spotted 'fan-pattern' above and below the tail in the Fan-tailed Warbler not only links it with *C. exilis* but also with the Madagascar Cisticola *C. cherina* and the Socotra Cisticola *C. haesitata*. These three species reveal their spotted fan-tails above and below in both sexes and at all seasons. The island species may, in fact, be insular races of *C. juncidis* which evolved outside Africa and re-invaded that Continent from Asia or Europe. The Fan-tailed Warbler shows little geographical variation throughout its range although somewhat paler northern and darker southern subspecies have been recognized. This warbler also occurs in a wide range of biotopes.

If we look more closely at the distribution of the Fan-tailed Warbler, we find that the species breeds somewhat brokenly in southern Europe around the basin of the Mediterranean, where it was concentrated in Europe in the years before 1970; in parts of western and central Europe; in much of Africa south of the Sahara; in discontinuously isolated regions such as Egypt and the Middle East as well as in India and Sri Lanka; across southern Asia to Japan, China, Malaysia, Indonesia, the Philippines and in isolated stations in northern Australia which may have arisen from Indonesia. Throughout Australia the Golden-headed Cisticicola *C. exilis* largely replaces the Fan-tailed and tends to be found in rather drier situations.

The most interesting feature of the Fan-tailed Warbler's recent history is the remarkable spread that the bird has made since 1971. It recalls a similar one by Cetti's Warbler, which was chronicled in the last chapter, but which with occasional stutters had been going on since the 1920s. However, the Fan-tailed Warbler's European advance really began after 1971. Birds bred for the first time in Malta in 1973 and in Crete in 1975, although singing males had been recorded on both islands in previous years from 1967 onwards. These early arrivals may have been driven south by the severe winter weather in Europe in the early part of that year (Parrott 1977). Birds also spread north along the coast and rivers of France, yet by April 1962 when Dr J. T. R. Sharrock saw one on Cape Clear Island in Co. Cork, birds were still breeding no nearer than 400 km to Cork and these nesters were thought to be sedentary. After 1971 the advance was dramatic with birds establishing themselves across southern France, up the west coast into Brittany and along several parts of the French Channel shore. In 1975 breeding was proved near the mouth of the River Somme and not far from Dunkirk so that Fan-tailed Warblers were now nesting only 80–90 km from the coast of England.

The first bird in Britain was recorded at Cley in Norfolk on 24 August 1976, and a second individual reported from Holme in the same county from 29 August to 5 September was thought likely to be the same bird. The following year the second British bird was found at Lodmoor in Dorset where it remained from 24–8 June. Meanwhile birds were also spreading south in Spain from the Pyrenees into northern Catalonia and Aragon. The Netherlands were reached in 1972, and in 1977 25 singing males were located there; other birds had reached Belgium in 1975. By 1974 some 45 pairs were recorded in Yugoslavia, where previously the species was virtually unknown, and an advance into northern Italy carried birds into Switzerland with other Fan-tails reaching Austria and Germany about the same time.

This truly remarkable advance by a southern Eurasian and African species seems to have been occasioned by the long succession of mild winters which brought about exceptionally high levels of population (Ferguson-Lees and Sharrock 1977). Such a succession of gentle winters led to very high numbers of Wrens and Goldcrests in the British Isles. The prophecy that Fan-tailed Warblers might be nesting in Britain by

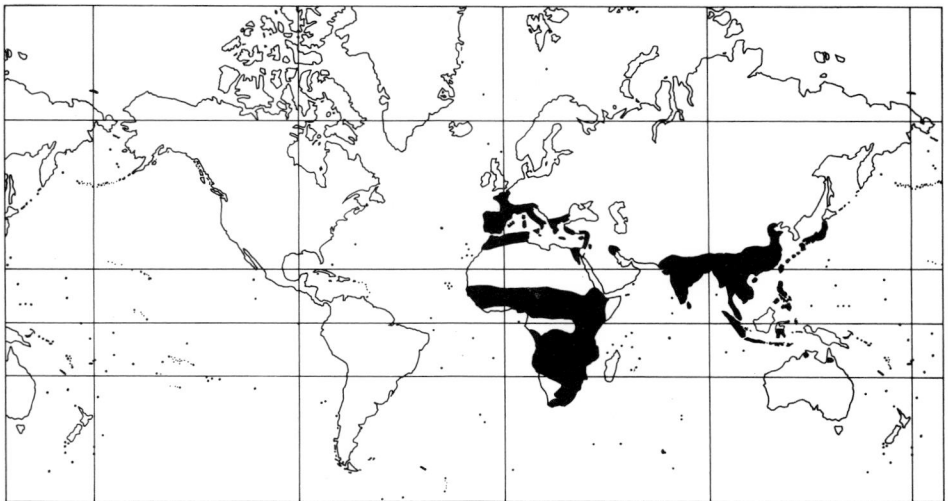

Fig. 73
Breeding range of the Fan-tailed Warbler.

1977 seems not to have been realized. The suggestion has been made that the bird's breeding range would be confined by the January isotherm of 5°C which would limit nesting to the southern and western coasts of England, Wales and Ireland. However, new colonists in Spain are able to breed at 1000 m and remain in a region in the winter where temperatures have been known to fall as low as − 10°C (Brock 1978); of course, Spain has enjoyed milder winters recently and snow cover has not endured for very long.

Professor K. H. Voous noted that Fan-tailed Warblers breeding in eastern Asia migrated mainly to tropical southeast Asia for the winter but the rest were 'sedentary in most of the inhabited regions'. It is interesting to report, however, that Fan-tailed Warblers do move in substantial numbers through Gibraltar in autumn (Elkins 1976); these movements involve both adults and juveniles. It was once thought that these were eruptive movements like those of Bearded Tits, but J. D. Finlayson (1979), who mist-netted birds at Gibraltar from July to October in the years 1977–8, found that all the birds were covered with a thick layer of fat. This strongly supported the proposition that these were real migrants moving south into Morocco. The deposition of fat in this way is typical of many other passerine birds which migrate after the nesting season and moult in their winter quarters. Some Fan-tailed Warblers over-wintered at Gibraltar, moulting over a period of 12–13½ weeks and ceasing to engage in any 'high flying' activities that might suggest eruption immediately after the onset of the moult. In July, Fan-tailed Warblers used to indulge in noisy communal activities ending with a high flight like that of Bearded Tits; I once saw eighty of these birds on the Suffolk coast in autumn circling and then climbing high into the sky until they disappeared. Activity of this kind in the Fan-tailed Warblers of Gibraltar was not seen after the middle of August.

The Fan-tailed Warbler has several calls. There is an explosive single 'tew' alarm note. The call of excitement is a loud sustained 'zip' or 'chip', which can be heard from a nervous bird on a perch, when the wings and tail are often flicked, and also from migrants. The 'zip' or alternative 'zeep' call was heard from the bird seen at Cley and Holme in 1976. There is also a 'plick' call, which may follow the song, be incorporated in it or on occasion be heard alone. N. Elkins (1975) reported a bird at Gibraltar in March which 'uttered this note almost continuously from a perch more than 50 times, interspersed with an occasional "zeep".' I have heard this call at the nest-building stage, and other observers have reported it as well.

The song is often the first clue to the bird's presence; once known it may, in areas where the bird is common, take on a monotonous quality that

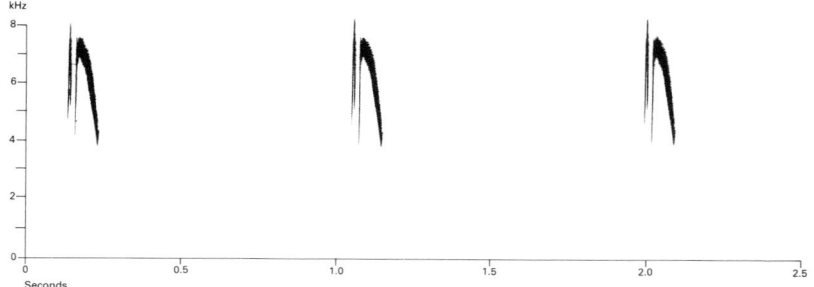

Fig. 74
Three 'dzeeps' in song of Fan-tailed Warbler. (Recorded by Robin Prytherch, B.B.C., Majorca, May 1969)

becomes less and less pleasing as time goes by. It consists of a series of high, rather rasping notes: 'dzeep . . . dzeep . . . dzeep', separated by the shortest of intervals. One bird I timed produced 43 'dzeeps' in 30 seconds. The song may be given in a weak dipping flight with each small climb being synchronized with each 'dzeep'; the song flight may take the bird quite high into the air and the song may be prolonged. A male will flutter up from a tussock or stem, climb to some 15–35 m in the air, uttering the song before dropping down and perhaps employing at the end several of the guttural 'plick' notes. Birds may circle over and cross wide areas of terrain often several hundred metres in breadth. Birds in Elba were seen to perch regularly on overhead wires from which the males sang more often than from aerial song-flights (Rogers 1968), and some of these song-bursts might last for up to two minutes, with the performer turning his head from side to side, thus directing his song across his territory. Singing males may also perch on trees, bushes and fences as well as plants of the ground zone. A Fan-tailed Warbler which I saw in the Camargue sang for 3 min 10 s from a perch before launching himself on a wide singing and undulating tour of his territory.

The Fan-tailed Warbler is a bird of both wet and dry locations, fields of grain and rough grassy places. Although reeds do not provide nesting sites for the bird, the narrow-leaved species often appears in the habitat, growing on the edges of marshes and along waterways and canals. While I was travelling by cabin cruiser in May 1973 along the Canal du Rhône in the Camargue from Aigues-Mortes to St Gilles – a distance of some 20 km – I saw at least ten Fan-tailed Warblers in song as well as eight Cetti's, many Great Reed Warblers, Nightingales, Black Terns, Purple Herons, Night Herons and several Great Spotted Cuckoos. There were many marshy regions of the Camargue with broken grasslands and reeds where the sibilant notes of the Fan-tailed Warblers mingled with the sounds of snorting white horses, booming Bitterns, clamorous stilts and pratincoles, squawking Little Egrets and screaming Black-Headed Gulls, honking Coot, chattering Great Reed Warblers, singing Larks and calling Cuckoos while the high hum of dancing Chironomid midges filled the air. I have only to play a tape recording of this scene in 1973 to realize how much even the Fan-tailed Warblers contributed to this sound picture of the Camargue. Yet in May 1954, when I spent a whole month there, the species was barely present. In 1956 I found birds in the Coto Doñana in Spain, very appropriately on the grasslands crisscrossed with belts of *Juncus* rushes growing along the edges of the marismas – some of the greatest marshland areas in Europe. Here the Fan-tailed Warblers shared their habitat with wild boars, fallow deer, Quail, wagtails and Savi's Warblers. It was a common feature to see the warblers resting on the tussocks of rush between their song-flights and even sometimes singing from them. Birds also favour big open plains (Lynes 1930), rice fields and fallow places in agricultural areas.

Fig. 75
The bushy grassland and wetland habitat of the Fan-tailed Warbler; Provence. (Eric Simms, May 1973)

In Eritrea, Fan-tailed Warblers can be found; in 'rank grass in damp cotton-soil areas, cotton fields, dry savannah grass' (Smith 1957). In Israel the main population in the north breeds in moist habitats, while elsewhere in regions of semi-desert birds nest in very dry ones, according to Amotz Zahavi. Birds at Gibraltar were found by J. C. Finlayson to be roosting in a clump of *Inula viscosa*. The visitor to Holme in Norfolk was found at sea level in a habitat comprising reeds, *Juncus* and stunted thorn bushes. The species feeds primarily on a range of insects, both adults and larvae. Some photographs taken by Eric Hosking in southern Spain revealed young in the nest, chiefly being fed on the larvae of one of the *Decticus* species of bush cricket.

The nest is a pure gem of construction. Shaped, according to view, like a pear, a purse, a cocoon or even an old-style electric light bulb, it is delicately formed from spiders' webs expertly woven around the living stems of grasses, club-rushes and, less frequently, of *Carex* sedges or *Juncus* rushes.

Fig. 76
Fan-tailed Warbler bringing food to the young in the extra- ordinary flask-shaped nest built by the species. Spain, May 1957. (Eric Hosking)

It is well concealed and, built as it is in living sedges or grasses, extremely difficult to find. Many nests are some 30 cm from the ground. The interior is lined with grass flowers or vegetable down, while in Cape Province wool is regularly employed. It is possible to watch both adults ferrying in long strands of spiders' webs to make the nest; during this process they are often very noisy with their persistent 'zip' calls. The nest is often about 22 cm long. H. Lynes described it as 'of soda-bottle type . . . with entrance facing skywards.' There is a small opening towards the upper narrow end of the 'bottle' or 'purse' which allows the adults access, not always without difficulty.

While busily engaged in building the nest and later when feeding the young, the adults can often be observed working their way up to the top of the concealing grass or sedge, pausing to look around and then flying off. The Fan-tailed Warbler in close-up may not be a dramatic sight but its behaviour is both fascinating and challenging. A study by C. Motai (1973) showed the males building the outside of the nests while the females lined them. He also found that one male which he watched from early April to mid-September 'constructed 20 nests during a breeding season of which eight were used by different females.' This successive nest-building was shown by K. Ueda (1984) in a study of Fan-tailed Warblers at Osaka in Japan to have arisen from the long breeding period – April to August – and the male's absence of a parental role. The male constructed many nests but only one was used for his courtship. On the completion of the outer part of the nest the male would induce a female to occupy it by a special song-flight. Of 111 males in Ueda's study which set up territories, 30 had no mate. Fourteen were monogamous 'despite their diligent singing and repeated nest building over a long period' and the rest were polygynous. Breeding females outnumbered the males, which appeared to have become emancipated; after completing the outside of the nest and coition they left the responsibility for incubation and nestling-care to the females. Because nests of living grass do not last very long, nest-building and courtship are recurring events in the life of the male Fan-tailed Warbler. The clutch is formed from 4–6 smooth, glossy eggs, sometimes white or light blue but often adorned with markings of red, purple or even black. Incubation lasts for about ten days. I have seen the female enter the nest with a beakful of food and emerge head first, having managed to turn round inside the flask-shaped nest. This was not the experience of Guy Mountfort who described in *Portrait of a Wilderness* how a film made of a Fan-tailed Warbler in the Coto Doñana on his 1957 expedition showed that a female was 'obliged to come out of the narrow nest backwards'. The method of entry and exit depends on whether the diameter of the nest is greatly constricted by stiff plant stems supporting it or whether thinner, more pliable stems allow a wider, freer nest to be built. It is also worth noting, in case the Fan-tailed Warbler should nest in the British Isles, that nomadic males in autumn, especially those in their first year, may sing and construct nest frameworks in areas quite a distance from those in which breeding has taken place. The bird seen at Holme-next-the-Sea in Norfolk was suspected of carrying nest material – a warning to observers!

CHAPTER 17

Acrocephalus **or Reed Warblers**

The previous chapters in this book are devoted to warblers of the *Sylvia* genus that breed in woodland, shrubs and arid scrub, and the grasshopper warblers of the *Locustella* genus, Cetti's and the Fan-tailed Warblers which frequent marshes, reeds, plantations, damp hedgerows and even agricultural land. The subjects of the present chapter – the reed warblers of the genus *Acrocephalus* – are essentially marsh-loving birds and are widely distributed through many parts of the Old World. They tend to be

Fig. 77
Minsmere, on the Suffolk coast. A habitat for species of Acrocephalus *warbler as well as other wetland genera. (Eric Hosking)*

uniformly brownish or cinnamon in colour but some reveal dark streaking as well. Of the birds on the British list, four fall into the first group of dull, unstreaked birds: the Reed, Marsh, Paddyfield and Blyth's Reed Warblers; three into the second group of streaked birds: the Moustached, Sedge and Aquatic Warblers, and two species into a third group of giants among warblers. This last category includes the Great Reed and Thick-billed Warblers, all somewhat uniformly brown and very large. It is the birds in the first group which pose the greatest problems in identification. Some species are so alike that it may well be differences in their repetitive conversational chattering songs which provide some of the best clues to their identity, although some species are very good at imitating others! However, the mimetic and inventive qualities, for example in the Marsh

Warbler's song, clearly separate that bird from the Reed Warbler with its much more monotonous quality. On the whole the songs of the *Acrocephalus* warblers tend to be harsh, churring, chattering and rapid, sometimes interspersed with more musical notes and imitations.

The main characteristics of this somewhat confusing group of warblers are tails with twelve rounded or graduated rectrices, a long tarsus with its front divided into long scutes or scales which in older birds are often fused on the upper section, a few robust rictal bristles and bills ranging from as narrow as can be seen in some of the slender-billed *Sylvia* warblers to much broader and more depressed ones. The sexes resemble each other, although the Great Reed Warbler females are smaller than males for reasons which we shall examine later, and the juveniles do not differ greatly from the adults. In spring there appears to be a cline in the coloration of the upperparts in certain species, so we find a range of colour from the bright reddish-brown of the Paddyfield Warbler to a duller brown in the Reed Warbler, olive-brown in the Marsh and cooler grey-brown in Blyth's Reed Warbler. Young birds with more subdued colouring can provide real problems of identification. Young Blyth's Reed Warblers and juvenile Paddyfield, Reed and Marsh Warblers may be separable only by a study of their wing formulae as laid out by Williamson (1976). There are also differences in the strength and size of eye-stripes as well as their comparative absence, and in the lengths of wings and bills. In the Sedge Warbler there is also a cline of increasing wing-length from west to east. It has to be remembered as well that the subjects of previous chapters such as Savi's, the Grasshopper and Cetti's Warblers belonging to different genera may also be present in the same habitat as some of the *Acrocephalus* species. The warblers of the *Acrocephalus* group tend basically to be insectivorous but they may, like some other warbler genera, become frugivorous in the autumn. At least four species have been reported taking berries or fruit. In their wintering grounds in Africa, Reed Warblers are known to take *Salvadora* fruits; Sedge Warblers at Lake Chad took insects and spiders but supplemented their diet with about 15% dry weight of plant material, including the nutritious *Salvadora* berries, especially towards the later stages of their pre-migratory fat deposition. The open cup-shaped nests of the *Acrocephalus* warblers, built largely by the females but in some species assisted by the males, are often suspended from the vertical or near upright stems of reeds and other aquatic plants.

In structural characteristics and wing formulae the genus is a very varied one. Whereas the Reed Warbler measures only some 12.5 cm in length, two very large relatives, the Clamorous and Great Reed Warblers measure over 18 cm. Within the general broad assembly of close genera are Cetti's Warbler and some 18 species of *Bradypterus* swamp or bush warblers dwelling in the marshes and forests of the tropical and subtropical parts of Africa and Asia. The genus *Acrocephalus* is widespread and can be described as Palaearctic, Ethiopian, Oriental and Australasian. Of the eighteen or so species, K. H. Voous (1977) lists fourteen on his list of recent Holarctic species. The genus may well have evolved first in temperate Asia with birds moving later into Africa. A population of African Reed Warblers from Lake Chad in Africa recognized as *Acrocephalus baeticatus dumetorum* and having characteristics between those of the Palaearctic Blyth's Reed Warbler *A. dumetorum* and the African Reed Warbler *A. baeticatus* has

Fig. 78
*Clamorous Reed Warbler
(left) and Great Reed
Warbler. (D. I. M.
Wallace, drawn some
years earlier)*

been used to demonstrate that the two are conspecific (C. H. Fry *et al*
1974), although Dr D. W. Snow thought that the two should be treated as
separate species that form a superspecies. Perhaps the link between the
two populations in Africa and Eurasia has only recently been severed.

Of the *Acrocephalus* genus seven species breed in Europe, three in the
British Isles, and six have appeared here as scarce or rare visitors, one
species having bred on a single occasion. The last is the Moustached
Warbler *A. melanopogon*, whose breeding range stretches from Spain and
Tunisia north to Austria and east to northwest India, and which nested
somewhat contentiously in Cambridgeshire in 1946. At one time the
Moustached Warbler was placed in a monospecific genus *Lusciniola*
(Vaurie 1959), partly because the juveniles underwent a complete moult
(Leisler 1972), but reasons for its transfer to *Acrocephalus* were enumerated
by S. A. Parker and C. J. O. Harrison (1963). These included its close
resemblance to the Sedge Warbler *A. schoenobaenus*, primary feather
length, a single annual moult and the distinctive habit of cocking the tail
over the back in a Wren-like manner when at rest. Moustached Warblers
do occasionally cock their tails – not regularly, however – and this custom
may well be associated with alarm and the presence of young (Hollyer 1978,
Oreel 1981, Wallace 1981). A Sedge Warbler may also cock its tail in alarm
(Mellor 1981) but I have never seen this and think it must be rather
unusual.

The typical race of the Moustached Warbler breeds in the region of the
European Mediterranean and as far as Austria, Hungary and Rumania,
wintering around the Mediterranean, in Asia Minor, Arabia and even
reaching areas like Lake Chad to the south of the Sahara. It is assumed that
the accidental occurrences of the bird in the British Isles and elsewhere are
of the nominate race. This form differs from the Sedge Warbler, which is
rather similar, by possessing a reddish-brown mantle and not one of olive-
brown, a rump resembling the mantle and not a contrasting one, an almost
black crown when viewed at close range rather than the somewhat streaked

one of the Sedge Warbler, a whiter, square-ended eye-stripe with a head pattern suggestive of a Firecrest (Dr J. T. R. Sharrock in Bibby 1982), as well as darker cheeks and flanks. However, Sedge Warblers are variable and care needs to be exercised in identification although juveniles are easier to tell apart than adult birds. There is a larger and paler eastern race of the Moustached Warbler *A.m. mimica*, which in summer inhabits the regions from the Black Sea east to Tadzhikistan and south to southern Iran, and spends the winter from Iraq to northwest India; this race is olive-brown and not a russet colour, with a lighter, more clearly streaked crown much like an adult Sedge Warbler. On the breeding ground I find the song very distinctive particularly with its introductory Nightingale-like notes.

The Sedge Warbler, which is also monotypic, is one of the best known of all the *Acrocephalus* warblers. As we have seen, it needs to be distinguished from the Moustached Warbler, and also from the vagrant Aquatic Warbler *A. paludicola*, which is yellower in colour and in addition to long buffish eye-stripes has a noticeable third pale buff stripe across the crown providing a most distinctive head pattern. Most unfortunately light-coloured first-winter Sedge Warblers may be confused with Aquatic Warblers, since they may also show a pale crown-stripe, but this is always somewhat streaked and rather vague in outline. The Sedge Warbler is a common breeding species in the British Isles and across Europe to about 70°N and east across Siberia and the Yenisei, Transcaspia, northwest Iran, Turkestan and the Altai Mountains. In central Europe at the Neusiedler See, for example, where both Moustached and Aquatic Warblers appear in the same region in Austria, the former appear to select wetter habitats and build their nests over shallow water. Elsewhere, since the Sedge Warbler has a more northerly distribution, overlap between the species is barely sig-

Fig. 79
Breeding concentration of 8 Acrocephalus *species on the British list.*

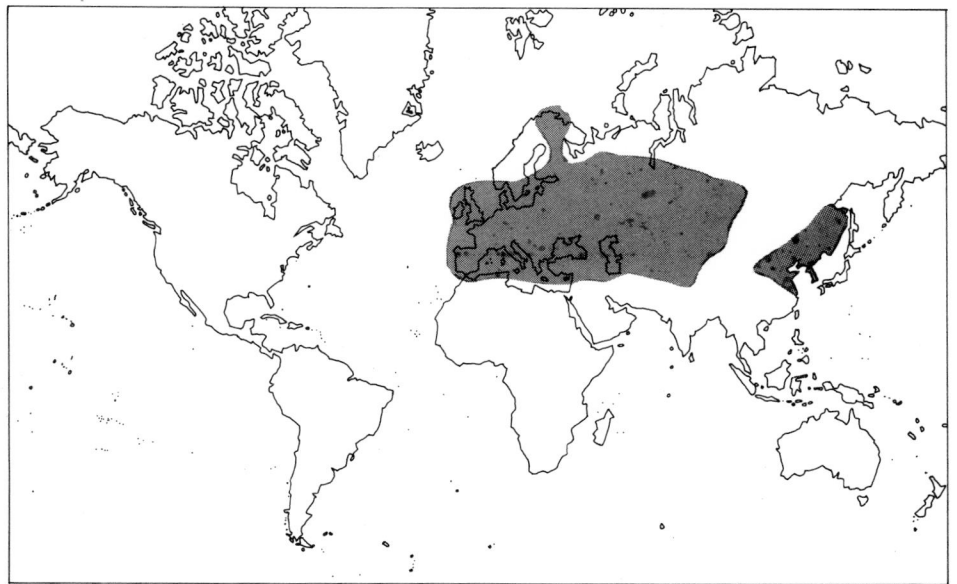

nificant. The Sedge Warbler winters in tropical and southern Africa from Nigeria and Senegal eastwards across the Continent. It is a remarkable bird for accumulating large quantities of body fat before leaving England in autumn, suggesting perhaps a single direct flight to its winter quarters in west Africa (Gladwin 1963). Correspondingly at Lake Chad the fat reserves of Sedge Warblers were sufficient for crossing the Sahara both to the north and the northeast (Fry, Ash and Ferguson-Lees 1970). This prefattening of warblers is often linked to a crossing of the Sahara Desert. It has been calculated by D. J. Pearson (1971) that 'the heaviest sedge warblers trapped at Kampala should have adequate reserves for direct migration to Mesopotamia (3500 km to the north-northeast) or to the Nile Delta (3000 km to the north).' Some Sedge Warblers from Uganda may cross the Sahara but many travel through Arabia.

In the case of the Aquatic Warbler it seems that birds of that species may live alongside Sedge Warblers but the reverse does not seem to be the case (Voous 1961). The Marsh Warbler *A. palustris* has also been recorded in the same habitat as the Aquatic Warbler but what interspecific competition, if any, takes place is not fully known. However, Aquatic Warblers do occur widely in damp marshy regions where *Carex* sedges are dominant, while the Marsh Warbler frequents a wide range of habitats including copses, osierbeds and rank vegetation often near water, and in Europe often on quite dry ground so that overlap would again seem less likely. There are clearly differences in the optimal habitats for Sedge, Reed *A. scirpaceus*, Marsh and Aquatic Warblers. In my experience Moustached Warblers tend to be close neighbours of Reed rather than Sedge Warblers, and are particularly well adapted for life among vertical components of their habitat, such as reeds, fen-sedge and reedmace *Typha*, since their feet are ideally suited for scaling upright objects. Dr Colin J. Bibby (1982) pointed out that the species is absent from drier areas with more tangled, soft-stemmed vegetation where Sedge Warblers might breed or where a walking species like Savi's Warbler might be at home. Moustached Warblers seem to flourish in wet habitats with well-spaced upright plant stems where sometimes only the Great Reed Warbler *A. arundinaceus* can master and exploit the environment. There are also differences in feeding techniques, for the fine-billed Moustached Warbler picks up small items even more regularly than the Sedge Warbler, and takes far fewer flying insects than the Reed Warbler which has a broader bill with a flattened base (Green and Davies 1972).

The Reed Warbler is one of the least distinguished warblers: olive-brown above and becoming darker, especially on the head, after wear, with a reddish rump and white to buff underparts. It occurs in beds of reeds and osiers where in Europe both Sedge and Great Reed Warblers may be found. In Poland it seems that the Reed Warbler is common in the extensive beds of reeds, while the Great Reed Warbler lives more on the fringes of the reed beds; there are also differences in the size and type of food fed to the nestlings (Dyrcz 1974). The Reed Warbler also has a more northerly breeding range in Europe (Voous 1960); it seems likely that the nestlings of Great Reed Warblers are more vulnerable to rain and cold weather. Both species of warbler have spread this century in Scandinavia but the Reed has made much greater advances than the Great Reed Warbler (Eriksson 1969). The Reed Warbler has two main breeding areas –

one that ranges from Britain, Spain and North Africa east to the Black Sea and north to southern Fenno-Scandia, wintering in tropical Africa west to Nigeria and Senegal and east to northern tropical and east Africa; the second group can be found further to the east in a region stretching from the Caucasus, Iran and the Caspian Sea to Kazakhstan and Tian Shan. This last area is the home of the eastern race of the Reed Warbler *A.s. fuscus*, which is paler, less rufous above and more white below, so approaching the Marsh Warbler in its coloration (Pearson 1981). Birds of the eastern race winter in East Africa; I have watched and listened to birds singing on the shores of Lake Victoria and Lake Nakuru in late December. The two breeding areas were presumably the main strongholds in which the species survived during the last Ice Age.

In Britain the Reed Warbler is on the edge of its breeding range, although it made some westerly and northerly advances in the 1960s and early 1970s. The factors which may influence the distribution of this warbler are habitats, temperature (with birds rarely nesting to the north of the 16°C summer isotherm), and rainfall (with birds avoiding regions with more then 77 mm in summer and 1000 mm over the whole year). Where Sedge and Reed Warblers have territories in the same area of marshland, the former tend to feed in the swampy region but nest on dry land close to water, while Reed Warblers feed in willows and nest among the reeds (Catchpole 1972). The Reed Warbler is also very aggressive to Sedge Warblers as well as to its own kind.

The only other *Acrocephalus* warbler breeding regularly in the British Isles is the Marsh Warbler, a species that can pose real problems in identification as well as being a very rare bird. In spring and summer its coloration is one of greenish olive-brown upperparts in comparison with the more rusty-coloured Reed Warbler but some first-summer Marsh Warblers have rusty rumps. In the autumn, when young Marsh Warblers may be more reddish in colour on the upperparts than any adult, they may not be satifactorily separated from young Reed Warblers by plumage alone. D. J. Pearson (1981) drew attention to 'the close similarity between the Marsh Warbler and the eastern race of the Reed Warbler *A. scirpaceus fuscus.*' He found that about 20% of young Marsh Warblers in Kenya were warmer in colour on the back than adults but the rest had a greenish tinge to their uniform, olivaceous upperparts and a yellowish wash below which distinguished them in the hand from Reed Warblers. Pearson also 'tentatively' suggested that the Marsh might be separated from the Reed by its

Fig. 80
Silhouettes of Reed Warblers (left and bottom pair) and Marsh Warblers – their 'multiple image' differs most in the 'pear shape' and long wingpoints of the latter. (D. I. M. Wallace)

shorter bill and 'more rounded, less attenuated head profile.' Blyth's Reed Warbler may also be difficult to separate from the two previous species.

The Marsh Warbler is a species of damp locations with plenty of rank undergrowth and shrubs as well as drier situations, and is certainly far less confined to aquatic habitats than the Reed Warbler. It breeds from southern England and parts of France right across central Europe, north to southern Fenno-Scandia, south to northern Italy and the Balkans, across to the Urals, southeast to Iran and the Caspian Sea. In England, especially after the 1940s, the Marsh Warbler decreased considerably in numbers and is now confined to a few breeding localities in the southwest. It is a marginal species undergoing a loss of habitat. There are often differences in height between the nests of Marsh and Reed Warblers. M. Philips Price (1969) found that in the southwest of England both species preferred to nest in beds of osiers, which were commercially managed and regularly cut, providing stems small enough to support their nests; when allowed to grow uncut the stems soon become too large for the nests and the birds departed. Reed Warblers nested from 2–2.3 m above the ground but Marsh Warblers were rarely 1.3–1.6 m above the ground and sometimes lower than that. The Marsh Warbler winters in southeast Africa. From its nesting grounds in Europe and western Asia the bird enters Africa through the Middle East, spends from September to November in northeast Africa, possibly eastern Ethiopia, and migrates to its late winter moulting area between southeast Kenya and Natal (Pearson and Backhurst 1976).

The Great Reed Warbler to which I made reference earlier in this chapter is a vagrant to the British Isles but there are now many records of Europe's biggest warbler turning up and singing in a wide range of sometimes regularly favoured sites as well as more casual ones. The typical race *A. arundinaceus* resembles a very large Reed Warbler – rufous, long-tailed with eye-stripes, it frequents reeds and the edges of reed beds, *Typha* reedmace and vegetation along watercourses. It breeds in Continental Europe and North Africa, Asia Minor and east to Iran, the Ural Mountains and the eastern Kirghiz Steppes; this form winters in tropical and South Africa but there frequents bush-country and is not confined to water. Birds appear in eastern and southern England and have reached Scotland, Wales and Ireland. Female Great Reed Warblers of the typical and eastern races are on average smaller than the males. Sexual selection on the breeding territory is likely to maintain the large size of the males, which are better adapted to feeding in shrubs in their winter habitat, while the females are more adapted to life amongst reeds. Smaller females probably perform better amongst reeds and also are less likely to collapse their specialized nests in the reeds. Guy Mountfort (1951) has pointed out that many nests break up because of the weight of the female and the young. The nests are built around the supporting stems of *Phragmites* reeds and territories set up by males in regions of reedmace *Typha* or sedge *Scirpus* may either not attract females or result in nests, built in unsuitable vegetation, collapsing (Kluyver 1955). After their investigation of the population ecology of eastern Great Reed Warblers, Ian C. T. Nisbet and Lord Medway (1972) were of the opinion that these factors 'would limit the extent to which the females can join males in utilising scrub habitats, and could suffice to explain their smaller size.'

The Great Reed Warbler *A. arundinaceus* has several races – *zarudnyi*, which is the more olive, less rufous eastern form breeding from the Aral-Caspian basin to Sinkiang; *orientalis*, the far eastern form from Asia which is different in size, wing-shape and migratory movements and *griseldis*, which is smaller and with a more slender bill from lower Iraq. *Zarudnyi* winters in East Africa south to Natal, *orientalis* in a great deal of southeast Asia from Malaysia and Burma to the Philippine Islands and *griseldis* in East Africa. All these birds have been separated from *A. stentoreus* – the Clamorous Reed Warbler with its longer bill, more rounded tail, paler tones and different wing formula which is resident in Egypt, Palestine and perhaps Eritrea. There is also a migratory race *A.s. brunnescens*, which breeds from the Caspian Sea to northwest India and winters

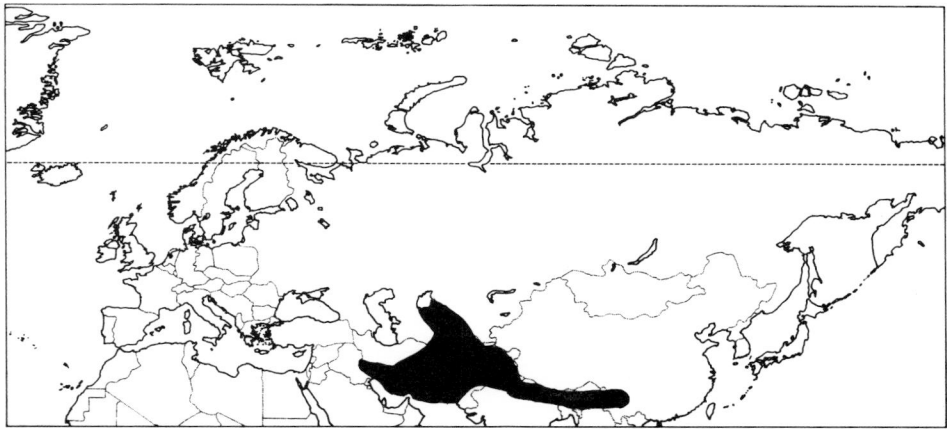

in the Persian Gulf and across India; the eastern form is a more greyish-olive in new plumage and whiter below than the typical race. Both the Great and Clamorous Reed Warblers have somewhat similar calls but their songs are very different. Whereas the song of the former is a rich, throaty croaking series of stereotyped notes, the song of *stentoreus* is thinner and higher pitched. Ian Wallace (1973), who studied the Clamorous Reed Warbler at Azraq in Jordan and Iran, and compared its vocalizations with those of the Great Reed Warbler, found that: 'Its rhythm is more broken, with many grace notes and squeaky cackles, and its most characteristic theme may be written as "ro-do-peek-kiss" with an accent on the third or last syllable.' The Clamorous also evinces a wider tolerance of habitats than the Great Reed Warbler, being often found in papyrus swamps, and in mangroves in Iran. For differences the reader should consult Wallace (1973) and Williamson (1976).

Fig. 81
Breeding range of the Clamorous Reed warbler. (The eastern race).

The other warblers of the *Acrocephalus* genus on the British list include the vagrant Paddyfield Warbler *A. agricola*, which resembles the Reed, Marsh and Blyth's Reed Warblers, and at home is likely to be distinguished in the field by its song and not its plumage. Among the small unstreaked warblers of the genus lie the greatest problems of identification. Although Vaurie (1959) recognized three races of the Paddyfield Warbler, it is usual now to regard the species as monotypic. The average length of wing decreases from the Marsh Warbler through the Reed and Blyth's Reed

Warblers down to the Paddyfield Warbler. As the lengths become less, so the wings become more rounded while the Paddyfield Warbler also has the longest tail. This last species is like a brighter edition of the Reed Warbler but its warm plumage can be deceptive, suggesting a bird of larger size than it actually is. The Paddyfield Warbler has a short, stout bill and longish tail that is often flicked on landing while its crown feathers may be raised as well. Of all the four warblers just mentioned the Paddyfield has the most conspicuous eye-stripe. It is a breeding species of the region that stretches from southern Russia to Mongolia and it spends the winter in Iran, Afghanistan and northern India.

Vagrant Blyth's Reed Warblers have appeared in the British Isles as well. These have rounded wings, a short distinct supercilium, a tail often flicked upwards and, compared to Paddyfield Warblers, look 'cold and olive-grey, particularly in strong sunlight' (Wallace 1973). Blyth's has an eastern range from Finland, the Baltic Sea and Russia south to the Ukraine and east to the Yenisei, northwest Mongolia, Turkestan and Afghanistan; it is also extending its range in eastern Europe. In the breeding season Blyth's is a bird of dryish field and forest edges, gardens with thick under-growth and in Finland nettles, ground elder, rosebay and willowherb (Koskimies 1980). In India on passage and in winter the species feeds in tree canopies with *Phylloscopus* warblers and is also a bird of thick cover of secondary growth where G. Diesselhorst (1965) was reminded 'more of a *Sylvia* of the *borin* type than of a Reed Warbler (*A. scirpaceus*).' It will also feed on the ground not far from cover. For field identification and other information the reader is recommended to consult W. G. Harvey and R. F. Porter (1984).

The last species on the British list is the Thick-billed Warbler *A. aëdon*, which looks like a large Garden Warbler and breeds in southern Siberia from the River Ob east to Lake Baikal, south to northern Mongolia and east to Manchuria and northeast China, and winters from India to China. Somewhat like a Great Reed Warbler it has a shorter, thicker bill, more rounded wings and tail; about the same size, it lacks eye-stripes. There are said to be two forms: *aëdon* in Siberia and *rufescens* with a more easterly

Fig. 82
*Breeding range of the
Thick-billed Warbler.*

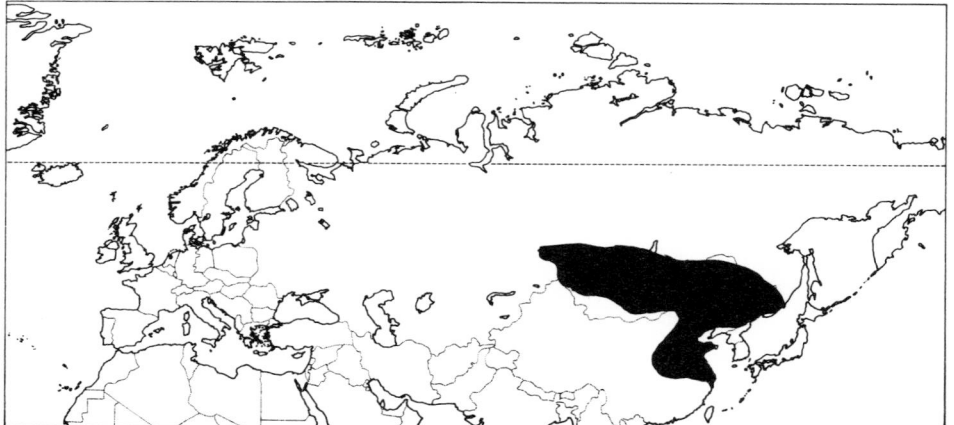

Dimensions and weights of Acrocephalus warblers Table 18

Species	Wing (mm) Range	Wing (mm) Mean	Tail (mm) Range	Tail (mm) Mean	Bill (mm) Range	Bill (mm) Mean	Tarsus (mm) Range	Tarsus (mm) Mean	Weight (gm)
Moustached Warbler	49–61	55.15	42–55	48.64	12.5–16.5	14.48	17–23.5	20.33	11.9
Aquatic Warbler	55–68	61.46	40–54	46.95	11–15.5	13.30	18.5–23.5	21.00	12.0
Sedge Warbler	58–72	64.73	40–56	48.08	12.5–16.5	14.58	19.5–24.5	22.07	11.2
Speckled Reed Warbler	56–59		46–48		14–14.5		20–21		
Von Schrenck's Sedge Warbler	48–58	53.65	40–56	47.64	11.5–16.5	14.04	18.5–24.5	21.31	8.7
Blunt-winged Paddyfield Warbler	50–60	55.17	49–63	56.09	14–16	14.69	21–22.5	21.85	9.8
Paddyfield Warbler	51–63	57.18	45–64	54.36	13.5–16	14.67	18.5–24.5	21.68	9.8
Blyth's Reed Warbler	56–66	61.22	45–58	51.94	14.5–18.5	16.65	20.5–24.5	22.50	
Marsh Warbler	60–73	66.94	45–59	52.32	13.5–18.5	15.98	20.5–26	23.31	11.8
Reed Warbler *A.s. scirpaceus*	58–71	64.80	45–59	52.32	14.5–18.5	16.68	20.5–26	23.36	11.5
A.s. fuscus	59–71		48–58		15–18		22–25		11.5
Clamorous Reed Warbler *A.a. stentoreus*	70–86	78.14	65–84	74.60	23.5–28		27–30.5		
A.a. brunnescens	79–95	86.88	68–91	79.33	21–27	23.83	26.5–33.5	29.88	
Great Reed Warbler *A.a. arundinaceus* ♂	90–101	95.77	73–83	78.67	19–25.5	22.35	26–33.5	29.88	26–33
♀	88–96	91.32	72–80	74.32					
A.a. zarudnyi	87–104	95.59	67–89	78.22	20–25	22.26	27–33	29.81	23.2–34
A.a. griseldis	73–88	80.60	54–72	63.67	19.5–24	21.80	22.5–28	25.22	
A.a. orientalis	72–92	81.98	61–80	70.75	18–25.5	21.77	25.32.5	28.85	17–33
Thick-billed Warbler	71–86	78.66	74–94	84.26	16.5–20	18.45	24.5–32	28.18	22

(after Williamson 1976)

distribution in Manchuria, Ussuriland and northeast China. The species is a vagrant to Japan and Britain.

Species not yet on the British list which might just occur here are *A. bistrigiceps*, the Black-browed Reed Warbler (or Von Schrenck's Sedge Warbler) of eastern Asia from Mongolia and southwest Siberia to Sakhalin, Japan and China, which winters in Indo-China and southeast Asia; and *A. concinens*, the Blunt-winged Paddyfield Warbler (or Swinhoe's Reed Warbler) of eastern Asia from Afghanistan to China, which embraces three races: *concinens* of northern China which winters in the south of that country, *stevensi* of Assam which overwinters in Burma and *harringtoni* of Afghanistan and Kashmir which migrates to northwest India. There is also *A. sorghophilus*, the Chinese Sedge Warbler (or Speckled Reed Warbler) of China and Manchuria, which may winter in southeast China. Another species, *A. brevipennis* (the Cape Verde Islands Cane Warbler) is non-migratory.

All the warblers of the Palaearctic region show a wide variation in the timing of their annual wing moult with differences between genera and species as well, and these discrepancies may be closely linked to the migratory habits of the species. Birds which have to fly far into Africa do not moult their flight feathers until they have completed their autumn journey. Some go through a late autumn moult in their African homes while others delay it until later in the winter; indeed the moult may only be completed in time for the northward return in spring. In Uganda D. J. Pearson (1973) found that most Sedge Warblers arrived there in fresh plumage having undergone the moult elsewhere but many 'trapped between February and April were moulting the feathers of the head, breast and mantle.' Since most Sedge Warblers wintering in Kenya and Uganda have moulted before arrival, these presumably have carried out this change further to the north in late autumn or early winter. With Reed Warblers, the birds can be classified similarly with young birds arriving in worn plumage in November and early December to undergo a local moult – I have seen these moulting in late December in Kenya – while others, probably the majority, arrive in new plumage in December and January having renewed their feathers before reaching Kampala. The usual duration of primary moult in the Reed Warbler is 70–80 days. Most warblers wintering in this part of Africa are of eastern origin. Reed and Sedge Warblers show differences in the timing of their moults in different geographical areas. In the northern part of the tropics moult is generally recorded in late autumn but birds which have to travel further to the south moult much later in the winter. Marsh Warblers, of which many go to southeast Africa, moult in February and March while Reed Warblers aiming only for the equator largely moult in autumn; those that do penetrate further south moult during the winter but not as late as the majority of Marsh Warblers. Most Sedge and Great Reed Warblers moult early during their residence in Africa but the most southerly of the wintering populations of both species renew their plumage just before setting off northwards. Many Great Reed Warblers including adults making for areas north of the equator moult in the autumn but most travel further south for the rest of the winter (Pearson 1975).

It was once thought that young Great Reed Warblers, unlike other members of the genus with plain backs, did not change their flight and tail feathers during their first sojourn on their wintering grounds (Stresemann and Stresemann 1966), but even first-year birds moult in their first autumn or winter. Most of the Acrocephaline warblers in Uganda begin their northwards return journeys with their flight feathers showing some signs of wear. Great Reed Warblers of the *orientalis* race moult their body feathers in March and April while the moult of the flight feathers takes place from July to September in or just to the south of the breeding area (Nisbet and Lord Medway 1972). Both the breeding geography and the age of the different warbler species may affect the timing of moult since the actual onset is determined by certain intrinsic physiological factors reflected in the warblers' endocrine system which has been stimulated by external influences such as light, day-length and temperature. Thus breeding season and area as well as migratory range have to be considered.

CHAPTER 18 The Sedge Warbler

As a breeding species in Britain the Nightingale is chiefly to be found south of a line from Dorset to the Wash. Since the Sedge Warbler – the subject of this chapter – also sings at night it is often confused with the Nightingale by laymen even in northern Britain. The great Cheshire naturalist, Arnold Boyd, described in 1946 how a 'nightingale' had been heard singing at night near Padgate in Lancashire and how in the company of the local worthies he went out in the dark to hear it. It remained tantalizingly silent but was finally stimulated to sing by the sound of a small stone being lobbed into the herbage. At once a Sedge Warbler burst into song and one of Major Boyd's companions exclaimed, 'There it is! That's the Nightingale!' A somewhat amused local farmer who had joined the group knew the truth: 'Why, there's a pair of them by every pit-side on t' farm; we call it "Chattering Billy".' Breeding by the side of many Cheshire marl pits, the bird has also been known as 'razzor grinder' or 'pit-sparrow' to distinguish the Sedge Warbler from the 'reed sparrow' – a name associated with the Reed Warbler since the time of Ray and Willughby. The Sedge Warbler was also known to Gilbert White who knew that it was possible to set it singing 'by throwing a stone or clod into the bushes', that 'it sings for most of the night' and that it can imitate 'the note of a sparrow, a swallow, a sky-lark; and has a strange hurrying manner in its song.'

Besides nesting in sedges and low cover behind reed beds and marl pits in Cheshire, Sedge Warblers are a characteristic breeding species of osiers, marsh dykes, meres, sewage farms, and flooded gravel pits with their rich growth of herbage that flourishes in many waterside habitats. They may share a damp reedy area with Reed Warblers, but they can also be found in rather drier situations near stretches of water. Although common enough in damp areas and rather rank habitats, the Sedge Warbler has in recent times adapted itself to breeding in dry habitats. In 1967 when I was censusing birds in Irish woodlands for my New Naturalist book *Woodland Birds* I found Sedge Warblers to be the dominant species in two totally dry conifer plantations with trees some 2 m high at Cairnwood and Castle Archdale in northern Ireland. In nine Irish conifer plantations the Sedge Warbler was commoner than the Grasshopper Warbler and formed 8% of the total bird populations. Birds have also bred in similar plantations in Scotland. In Suffolk I found a Sedge Warbler singing in a line of thorns at least 600 m from the nearest water, another in Warwickshire 500 m from water and one in south Lincolnshire 350 m away. Birds have also been reported from cornfields, beanfields and fields of rape. Birds have held territories in rape fields without the benefit of prominent song-posts and sometimes as much as 400 m from the nearest water (Bonham and Sharrock 1974). Sedge Warblers have also colonized the dense sea buckthorn scrub at Gibraltar Point in Lincolnshire. Similarly Reed Buntings have also

Fig. 83
*Sedge Warbler territory
by a Northamptonshire
lake. (Eric Simms, July
1984)*

moved out from their wetland habitats into much drier situations, perhaps through loss of wetter sites and a high population level (Kent 1964). Sedge Warblers are more catholic in their choice of habitats than Reed Warblers. In optimal habitats they may be found at a density of 5–6 pairs per hectare, whereas on farmland the figure may be 1.3 pairs per square kilometre (*Atlas* 1976). There may be problems in censusing populations of Sedge Warblers but, although birds nest in dense cover, they can be detected when in song. Since song falls away in its output it is essential to census the birds on their return as well as through the season (Bell *et al.* 1968). The percentage of nests recorded is also lower where birds are densely distributed so slight alterations in population numbers might not be revealed in the annual Common Birds Census of the British Trust for Ornithology. After a five year study of a Welsh marsh D. K. Thomas (1984) concluded that 'habitat selection was more a result of vegetation structure than plant species.'

As a nesting species the Sedge Warbler is very widely distributed throughout the British Isles but is missing from Shetland; it is the most abundant of the wetland warbler species. In Scotland only the Willow Warbler and Whitethroat appear more commonly, but in Ireland, where Warbler species are fewer than those in Britain, the Sedge Warbler is very evenly spread. As one might expect of a wetland species it is missing or scarce in upland and Highland country such as Exmoor, Dartmoor, the Cambrian hills, the Pennines and the Scottish hills and moors. I have located territories at heights of about 260 m above sea level in eastern Scotland, while *The Atlas* mentioned breeding up to 350 m in suitable habitats and Bannerman (1954) referred to nests at over 450 m in the

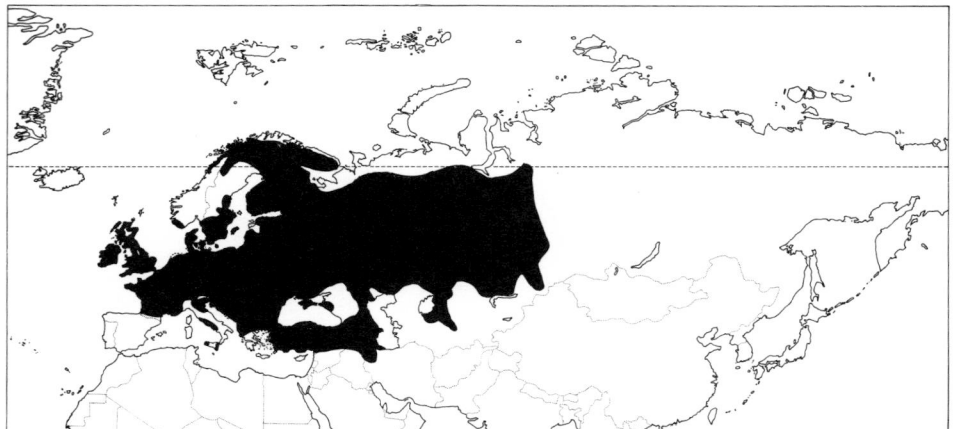

Fig. 84
The breeding range of the
Sedge Warbler.

Scottish Highlands. Nesting has increased in recent years in Orkney while the southern Outer Isles were first colonized in the 1920s. Although the first breeding record on the Isle of Lewis was in 1963, two years later the bird could be described as fairly common (Parslow 1973). Birds have also nested on islands like Lundy and Skokholm; the latter windswept, treeless islet of red sandstone has held breeding birds 'in the dropwort and cow parsnip below the freshwater spring' (Lockley 1947). In some regions of the British Isles the drainage of wetlands may have resulted in local decreases in numbers but these may have been more than offset by the development of clay and gravel pits for construction and other industrial purposes, especially in the south and Midlands (where 60% of the workings can be found), as well as southwest Yorkshire, Lancashire, Durham, Northumberland, the Scottish Lowlands and Wales. There was a significant peak in the numbers of breeding birds in 1968 but a sharp decline the following year after the drought in the Sahel region of Africa, which, as we saw in Chapter 7, also had a serious effect on the numbers of breeding Whitethroats. There was a slight upsurge in numbers in 1970 along with those of Whitethroats, Garden Warblers and Redstarts but the overall level has remained rather low.

In its movements the Sedge Warbler is very lively and active, rarely descending to the ground in the open, and much more often in dense cover. It easily sidles up vertical plant stems, creeps readily through scrub, thick vegetation and nettles and regularly perches on twigs, reeds and other tall plants. On its return to the breeding grounds in spring the Sedge Warbler is more conspicuous, singing from exposed reeds and sprays of vegetation as well as in a rather simple song-flight. Bursts of song may also be uttered from very dense cover. As a species it tends to fly for only short distances and then very low with the tail spread out and depressed. If forced to fly further and in the open it has a rather jerky, random manner. Many times we first become aware of the bird's presence from its song or calls. The call-note is a scolding 'tuk', often rapidly repeated in excitement to form a series of 'tuk-tuk-tuttuttuks' or even 'tuttuttuttuks' in a stuttering kind of rattle. There is also a harsh 'tchurr' which with the scold may be incorporated in the song.

Index

1962 1963 1964 1965 1966 1967 1968 1969 1970 1971 1972 1973 1974 1975 1976 1977 1978 1979 1980 1981 1982

The song is often uttered from conspicuous song-posts which may have a special significance in a region where low-growing vegetation without vantage points seems to hold a lower breeding population of birds than one without them. A song-flight may be used to increase the range of the bird's advertisement; here males will fly up almost vertically, turn rather rapidly and after a circular or semi-circular flight come back to their song-posts, with spread tails and wings outstretched. In April the song-flights of these warblers enliven the marshland sedges and reeds, the tangled edges of meres, lakes and rivers and coastal fenny lagoons, bringing them to pulsating life as bird stimulates bird and vehement song piles upon song. Each year I observe these performances with delight, reminded of the words of a friend, Commander Alec Robertson (1954), who wrote, 'To watch a number of these mercurial little birds at their aerial dance is one of the most charming manifestations of Spring.' The song tails off but can be heard from time to time until the middle of July.

The territorial song is loud, rushed and varied – a medley or babble of harsh and sweet notes mixed together, with utterances that are faster, more full of trills and more musical notes than those of the Reed Warbler. Al-though the song may appear 'garrulous, hurried and erratic', it is liberally sprinkled with imitations, since the Sedge Warbler is an expert and con-sistent mimic although not as good as the Marsh Warbler; all these factors make the song both surprising and exciting to the human listener. A typical section from a song that I recorded by Slapton Ley in Devon could be transcribed 'chit-chit-tuk-tuk-tuk-chit-terwee-terwee-tit-tit-twee-twee-tit-it-it-it-cherwee' and so on. A bird in Sweden was in much more of a hurry in his delivery: 'chit-it-it-it-it, ter-ter-ter-ter-terrichee-terrichee-see-see-see'. Since there is great variety in the songs of this species, indi-vidual performers may also sound very different in their style and execution from each other. A typical run of notes may last from 1 min 10 s to as much

Fig. 85
Population changes in Sedge Warbler numbers 1962–82. Based on Common Birds Census of B.T.O. (levels in relation to 1966)

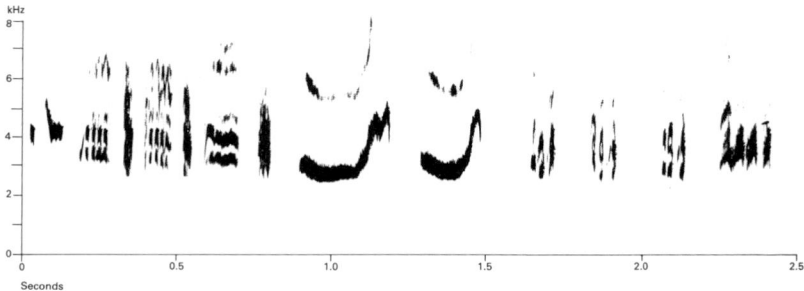

Fig. 86
Part of territorial song of
Sedge Warbler. Note
trills and slurred notes.
(Recorded by Eric
Simms, Devon, April
1959)

as 2 min or more. The peak arrival time for Sedge Warblers in England is about the middle of May, a month before that of the Reed Warblers. Dr Clive Catchpole (1976a) of Bedford College in London recorded singing male Sedge Warblers at Rye Meads in Hertfordshire. He found that there is usually a build up in speed of delivery and loudness of the song, coming to a peak in the middle; the notes slow and fade towards the end. He confirmed that a complete song pattern might last well over a minute but each could contain over 300 syllables. By using sonagrams he demonstrated that there was a recognizable temporal pattern with an opening section full of complex sets of repetitions and alternations, usually involving two-syllabled types, while the middle part suddenly introduced 5–10 new syllable types in quick succession. The end section resembled the beginning but the two-syllabled types were selected from the middle section, and these were used to form the first part of the next song. One performer was still bringing in previously unused syllables in the twenty-sixth consecutive strophe or song-pattern from 32 that were analysed. Some 60–70 types of syllable might appear in the repertoire of one individual. Dr Catchpole (1967b) observed that considering the variable organization involved 'the probability of the same song ever being exactly repeated seems extremely remote.' In the song-flight the structure of the song is even more complex and can involve perhaps twice as many syllable types as normal songs. The function of these elaborate songs is primarily to attract a female and after pairing has been achieved they either cease or are markedly reduced. Dr Catchpole (1981) was also able to show that male birds with more complex songs were able to attract a mate before their rivals, so sexual selection must have played an important role in the evolution of the Sedge Warbler's extremely elaborate territorial song. Committed to long trans-Saharan migrations, Sedge Warblers are left with little time to breed in Europe and so there is considerable advantage to the males in securing females as early as possible.

We have already seen that song tends to diminish or cease after pairing, and experiments by Dr Catchpole with loudspeakers also showed a significant decrease in aggression towards the songs of other males. Rival males are no longer bombarded with song and if one should approach he is warned off with visual signals and perhaps a sharp aerial pursuit. This is different from the courtship pursuit in which a male flies after a female with his wings drooping and his head feathers erected, sometimes bearing a small object like a twig or leaf in his bill.

I have listed many imitations by Sedge Warblers of other species:

Blarkbird alarm, Swallow, House Martin, Pied Wagtail, Reed Bunting, Whitethroat, House Sparrow and Grasshopper Warbler. Victor Lewis tape recorded a male in Surrey in May 1963 and on this recording I heard the flight calls of Linnet, Chaffinch call, Blue Tit song, Blackbird flight alarm and House Sparrow. A bird at Hungerford Marsh in Berkshire was heard by R. G. and R. Frankum (1970) to produce a song rather like that of a Marsh Warbler, lacking most of the grating sounds that characterize the Sedge Warbler's song and containing imitations of five different species in quick succession. The incidence of imitations in the song of a bird gives it a special and easily recognizable character, and its individual idiosyncrasies and wide repertoire show a degree of experience that can attract females and thus have a real biological importance. We saw in the opening paragraph of this chapter that singers may be induced to sing by sudden noises; Charles Dixon (1909) writing of London's birds wrote that 'on several occasions I have remarked how the noisy rowing of some Cockney band on river or canal has called this Warbler into scolding songs of resentment.' I have heard birds singing in December and January at Lake Nakuru and Kisumu in East Africa where the birds feed on many lake flies.

Sedge Warblers tend to feed in the low field layers near water, picking up rather small slow-moving items of prey, unlike Reed Warblers which concentrate more on food in reedbeds and even trees (Green and Davies 1972, Catchpole 1973). The diet seems to include a range of insects and their larvae: Chironomid midges, craneflies, bristly flies of the *Empididae*, long-legged flies of the *Dolichopodidae* family and other dipterous flies. They will also take dragonflies, beetles and aphids while small worms and slugs have been recorded as well. During the breeding season adults will regularly fly out of their breeding territories in marshland to collect food for their young – a fact that suggested to Dr David Lack (1946) that size of the breeding territory did not bear a fixed relation to the availability of food. The defended area of the Sedge Warbler is perhaps five or six times larger than that for the Reed Warbler, a species which arrives later than the Sedge Warbler; it may have to shift some of them around to get territorial room for itself (Catchpole 1972).

Birds begin to breed in Britain at the very end of April and nesting reaches a peak of laying in the period from 15–20 May, just two weeks after their arrival (Bibby 1978). If the start of the breeding season is calculated by taking the mean first egg date of the earliest 10% of Nest Record Cards, Dr Bibby was able to show that the onset of breeding varied from 7–17 May, compared with 16–26 May for the Reed Warbler. Some 2000 cards for the Sedge Warbler – about half the total for Reed Warblers – reveal a great deal about the breeding cycle of both species so that both clutch and brood size could be compared in the two warblers.

From Table 19 it is clear that Sedge Warbler clutches were most frequently of five eggs and Reed Warbler of four. In both species the clutch size dropped fairly evenly throughout the breeding season with an overall reduction of one egg over the long laying period of ten weeks. Brood sizes also declined through the season. In both species the largest broods were seemingly reared from the largest clutches and not from the most frequent clutch size.

The Sedge Warbler generally nests in osierbeds, occasionally reeds and

Table 19   *Frequency distributions of clutch size of Reed and Sedge Warblers*

	Clutch size							Total	Mean	s.d. (standard deviation)
Reed Warbler	1	2	3	4	5	6	7			
Number	11	58	368	1276	299	3	–	2015	3.89	0.70
Percent	0.5	2.9	18.3	63.3	14.8	0.2	–			
Sedge Warbler										
Number	3	6	24	121	493	180	2	829	4.98	0.78
Percent	0.4	0.7	2.9	14.6	59.5	21.7	0.2			

Frequency distributions of brood sizes of Reed and Sedge Warblers

	Brood size							Total	Mean	s.d.
Reed Warbler	1	2	3	4	5	6	7	1959	3.44	0.92
Number	65	233	598	898	164	1	–			
Percent	3.3	11.9	30.5	45.8	8.4	0.1				
Sedge Warbler										
Number	17	62	118	321	520	148	1	1187	4.44	1.09
Percent	1.4	5.2	9.9	27.1	43.8	12.5	0.1			

(Reproduced from *Bird Study*, Vol. 25, 1978 by permission of Dr Colin J. Bibby)

often in rank and tangled vegetation near water, sometimes hedgerows and not only rape and beanfields but clover and cereal crops; in 1948 several Sedge Warblers were heard in song in growing corn on the Isle of Grain (Gillham and Homes 1950). The nest itself is occasionally on the ground but more usually in vegetation not more than a metre tall. Frequent sites are near the foot of an osier, in a thicket of bramble, rose, willowherb or nettle and sometimes in the branches of a willow. The nest is built by the female with, in my experience, the male watching but not helping, and is a deep, rather bulky cup of a cylindrical shape but less long and rounded than that of the Reed Warbler. It is often just supported by stems or bound and woven to them rather than suspended as in the Marsh Warbler but this is not an invariable rule. I have seen a few Sedge Warbler nests with a close resemblance to those of Reed Warblers; Eric Hosking and Cyril Newberry (1944) saw a nest in Hertfordshire 'which looked very much like that of the reed warbler, being woven around, and suspended on, four stems of a stinging nettle.' Provided with a foundation of leaves or moss the cup is built of grass, sedges and other vegetable stems and is lined with willow and other plant down, grass-heads, hair and sometimes a few feathers. An unusually bulky nest was constructed on top of a Song Thrush's nest (Leavesley 1957). Nests are usually well concealed and difficult to find in tangles of vegetation. The eggs are tinged with an olive-buff or pale green but the ground colour is usually obscured since they tend to be heavily speckled with ochreous blotches. Many eggs have black dots or hairlines and a salmon-pink variety has been recorded as well. The incubation period for the Sedge Warbler is about 12 days with 13 and 14 reported, and the duties of incubation are largely carried out by the hen.

Many nest failures arise through the effects of bad weather causing desertion of the eggs but predation on Sedge Warbler nests by mammals is

higher than is the case with Reed Warblers, since the sites of the former are more accessible to them. The B.T.O. Nest Record Cards showed that whereas there were eighty cases of cuckoldry in Reed Warblers, only two cases were logged for the Sedge Warbler. However, a paper in *Bird Study* by Dr David Lack (1963) about the hosts of Cuckoos in England, based on records deposited by zoologists at the Edward Grey Institute in Oxford, showed a rather higher incidence with figures up to 10% of reported nests by A. Whitaker on the Derbyshire-Yorkshire border as well as A. E. Lees in Huntingdonshire. Victims were in part parasitized by Cuckoos that were known to be laying in the nests of Reed Warblers. However, J. H. Owen (1933) claimed that parasitization by what he considered were genuine 'Sedge-Warbler Cuckoos' was high enough to bring about the local extermination of these warblers in the Felsted region of Essex; 'it was', he said, 'hard to find a sedge's nest without a cuckoo in it.' Perhaps successful Cuckoos may over-parasitize their victims: there is some evidence in the case of Reed Warblers, which will be considered in Chapter 20; but other mortality factors might be involved in the case of the Sedge Warbler.

The fledging period of the Sedge Warbler may be as short as 10 days if the nest is disturbed but usually lasts from 11–14 days. The young are fed by both parents, often without much attempt at secrecy. Dr Bibby found that if the young left the nest aged 10 days 'there would follow 15 days to rear them to independence and build a new nest before the first egg of the

Fig. 87
Male Sedge Warbler arriving at nest with food while the female broods the young in the nest. (Eric Hosking)

second clutch was laid.' Allowing for such sampling errors as those involved in less intensive nest-hunting by observers later in the season, and a greater density of vegetation, it still appears that a smaller proportion of Sedge Warblers attempt second broods compared to the Reed Warbler. Despite a shorter breeding season and fewer nesting attempts Sedge Warblers still enjoy a higher breeding success and larger brood size than Reed Warblers. The average number per pair of young Sedge Warblers reared in England is 4.84 compared to 4.09 for the Reed Warbler (Bibby 1978), while in Finland the figure for the Sedge Warbler is 5.57 (Raitasuo 1958). Both a shorter breeding season and a larger clutch size may be related to local and seasonal sources of food, such as Chironomid midges. The actual overall success rate for Sedge Warbler nests was calculated from the Nest Record Cards to be 56%: close to that of 54% found by Dr Clive Catchpole (1972) in a smaller sample. Sedge Warblers seem to suffer an incidence of higher losses after incubation has first attained its peak and the success rate then falls. At the peak they might expect to raise something like 2.8 young (or 3 in Finland) but, if after rearing a first brood the Sedge Warblers started again, the figure fell to 2 and continued to decline. It is clear that an early breeding season has positive advantages for the species. There is a later critical period of aphid bloom, which Sedge Warblers exploit as part of their preparation for the autumn migration, which could be upset if second broods were reared. Bigamy is only known in about 5% of European species (von Haartman 1969) but it occurs among Sedge Warblers as well as Reed and Great Reed Warblers. It may occur when a male, having mated with a female, meets another female when he adopts a new territory.

After fledging it is most unusual for young Sedge Warblers to return to the nest, but D. R. Anderson (1946) found a nest on 26 July 1945 containing four young about 8–10 days old; of these three flew and the fourth nestling was ringed. On the following day two fledglings had returned to the nest and were found asleep in it! In August 1979 Mrs E. S. da Prato (1980) came across two separate broods of Sedge Warblers that had left nests only two or three days before. While it is normal for the young to use their natural camouflage for concealment, hunching themselves up and 'freezing' in dense cover, these fledglings 'adopted a rigid, upright posture which I had previously associated only with Bitterns *Botaurus stellaris*.'

In the autumn Sedge Warblers leave Europe to winter in regions south of the Sahara Desert, some reaching countryside in southern Africa as far north as Kenya, while recent returns of ringed Sedge Warblers from Senegal, Liberia and Sierra Leone indicate that some British breeding birds winter this far west. Birds begin to emigrate from the British Isles in late July with a departure peak in late August and the first half of September. I have watched Sedge Warblers leaving the shelter of tamarisks on the front at Littlehampton and flying directly out to sea. Many British-ringed birds are recovered in northwest France and Iberia, but one reached Heligoland and another ringed at Rye Meads in Hertfordshire on 26 July 1975 was reported from Switzerland on 13 August: the first Swiss recovery. A Sedge Warbler ringed as an adult at Maple Cross Sewage Farm, also in Hertfordshire, on 26 July 1981 was controlled at Lac Aougoundou in Mali on 31 March and 12 April 1982: 3988 km to the south (Hook 1982). Birds have to prepare for this migration as well as the spring journey, involving long flights over the Sahara, by putting on high levels of body fat (Gladwin

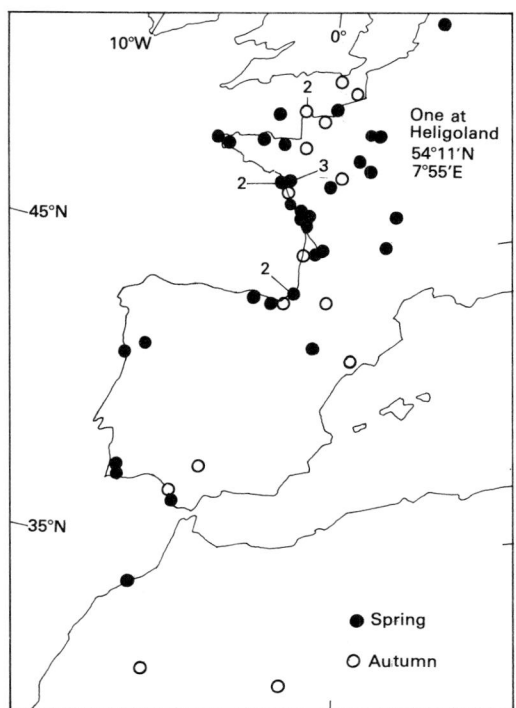

10°W   0°

One at
Heligoland
54°11'N
7°55'E

45°N

2

35°N

● Spring

○ Autumn

Fig. 88
*55 recoveries abroad of
the Sedge Warbler ringed
in Britain. (With
permission from the
monthly magazine*
British Birds*)*

1963, Sitters 1972). For much of the year the Sedge Warbler weighs about
10 or 11 g but before migration it can almost double this figure.

The amount of fat accumulated by Sedge Warblers in southern England
in autumn prompted the view that these warblers might be able to undertake a single flight from England to their wintering grounds; a distance
perhaps of 3800 km. To find out how birds might accumulate fat in
autumn, studies were carried out at Radipole Lake in Dorset over three
autumns from 1973–5 (Bibby *et al* 1976). Many Sedge Warblers from
northwest Britain stay for a short time on their southward migration at this
lake, where few actually nest. The visit has generally been a short one; in
1974, 84% of the birds stayed for two days or less compared with a figure
of 46% for 1973 and 1975. No birds put on any weight in 1974 but in the
other two years the gains were about 0.5 g per day. Although the visiting
Sedge Warblers fed on small flies, beetles and hoverfly larvae, the most
important food source was that of the plum-reed aphid *Hyalopterus pruni*
which occurred on reeds in standing water. The peak of this aphid abundance in 1973 and 1975 from about the 15–25 August also coincided with
the greatest use of Radipole Lake by visiting Sedge Warblers. 1974 was a
very bad year for these aphids, and Sedge Warblers made the lowest gains
in weight. 1975 was the best of the three years; Sedge Warblers not only
stayed longer but they also put on weight much more quickly. As a result
of the B.T.O.'s *Acrocephalus* enquiry it appears that although 'heavy'
Sedge Warblers can be found at most sites the kind of proportions found

at Radipole are largely confined to the south coast from Kent to Cornwall. Yet in that productive year of 1975 less than 10% of the Radipole warblers were thought to have put on sufficient weight for them to achieve a successful non-stop flight across the Sahara Desert. Consequently Sedge Warblers leaving England at normal weights probably add their extra fat in northwest France where many birds ringed in Britain have been recovered (Spencer 1971). The passage of adult Sedge Warblers through Radipole some two weeks before the juveniles, described by Pepler (1976), may indicate the desirability of early movement. The study of the Radipole Sedge Warblers involved 12,000 man-hours of ringing effort compared to 100 man-hours of 'ecological investigation'. The use of the concentrated food resources of Radipole Lake in autumn can be compared to the less successful taking of midges before their spring departure from Africa. At Lake Chad Sedge Warblers fed largely on midges and their average weight gains were only 0.2 g per day (Fry *et al* 1970). In Kenya mean fattening rates were 0.31 at Nakuru and 0.64 at Athi (Pearson *et al* 1979). Insects remain the most regular food source even outside the breeding season but *The Handbook* (1946) reported birds taking elderberries.

Migrants use both east and west coast routes in Britain; there are also night migrants coming to rest and feed in the early morning in many places along the coast, on islands offshore, and many suitable wetland habitats inland including city parks. In fact, Sedge Warblers are likely to appear in a much wider range of habitats than the Reed Warbler. The many passage records indicate a fairly large total population and a wider habitat tolerance. In Africa birds frequent open desert scrub as well as lakeside vegetation. There are often differences in the nature of passage movements in Britain. On Skokholm, off the coast of Wales, Sedge Warblers are the third commonest species of passerine night migrant there, but only the sixth commonest in autumn; the warbler is also commoner in spring at the east coast bird observatories. The birds are probably commoner in spring because these are British summer residents, which when passing over Skokholm are nearer the start of their migratory journey in autumn than in spring; there is better weather in autumn and so birds are less likely to be forced down (Lack 1966). On the night of 29–30 August 1968 more than 500 warblers were killed flying into the lighthouse on Bardsey Island; this total included no fewer than 117 Sedge Warblers (Hudson 1968).

The spring arrival in England begins chiefly in the middle of April and goes on until the early part of May, and may then be rather mixed up with the movements of passage birds. The average date of arrival in the Oxford Ornithological Society's area was 20 April, in that of the West Midland Bird Club 22 April and for Worcestershire (according to Eliot Howard) 25 April. Birds sometimes appear in London's Royal Parks, even St James's Park and Hyde Park, and odd birds could be seen on migration on the old bombed sites.

There are still many unsolved questions about the food of both adults and young of the species, the effect of weather on food supplies, the relation between brood size and the later success of the young, the survival rate and even the incidence of polygamy. The Sedge Warbler remains one of the most attractive and intriguing of all the British warblers: 'small brown birds', wrote the poet Edward Thomas, 'wisely reiterating endlessly what no man learnt yet, in or out of school.'

The Moustached Warbler

CHAPTER 19

About the same size as a Sedge Warbler and rather similar to it, the
Moustached Warbler earns a chapter to itself because of the very unusual
but fully documented instance of a pair breeding at Cambridge in 1946. A
full account of this warbler's appearance and distribution was given in
Chapter 17 but a map is provided in this chapter to show the breeding
range. The Moustached Warbler has been compared to a rather smart Sedge
Warbler with a darker crown to its head, redder mantle, square-ended and
not tapered eye-stripe and occasional but not invariable habit of cocking its
tail. The moustache from which the bird derives its name is a rather faint,
darker streak. The species is about the same weight as the Sedge and Reed
Warblers but has a much smaller wing-length. As we have already seen,
the nominate race breeds in the Mediterranean region, inland and along
the River Danube while there is also a larger, less clearly marked eastern
race. The breeding distribution of its wetland habitats ranges from the
temperate zones to steppe and arid deserts. In winter many birds retreat
towards the Mediterranean; birds from Austria appear to go to Italy and
Dalmatia, some move to North Africa and Asia Minor and even reach
trans-Saharan Lake Chad. The bird is accidental in Denmark and England.
The eastern Asiatic population appears to be more migratory by nature,

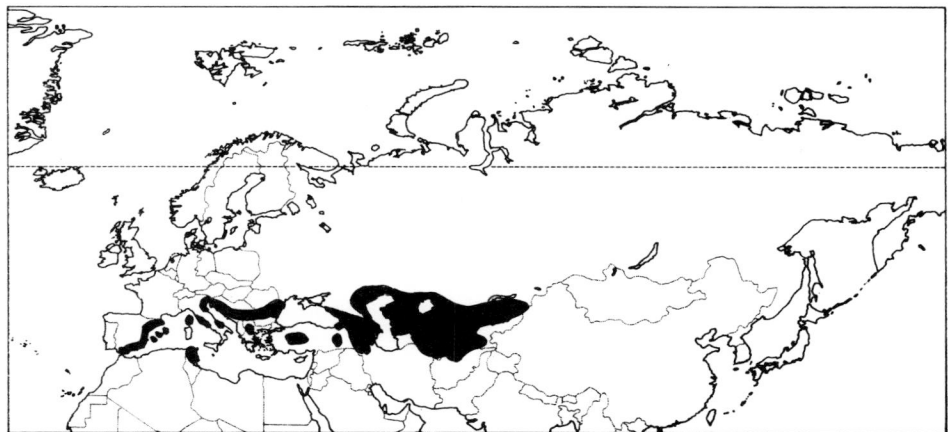

travelling to Arabia and India. It seems to some extent that local movements
in winter are influenced by prevailing weather conditions (Bannerman and
Bannerman 1958).

Fig. 89
*Breeding range of the
Moustached Warbler.*

    The first occurrence of this wetland warbler in the British Isles was that
associated with the remarkable breeding record in 1946; an earlier instance
of a male shot in Sussex at St Leonard's in April 1915 was rejected with a

number of other 'Hastings Rarities' (Nicholson and Ferguson-Lees 1962).
A pair nested at Cambridge Sewage Farm in 1946 and a full account of this
apparently extraordinary event was chronicled in detail in *British Birds*
(Hinde and Thom 1947), while a coloured drawing was also made by Dr
E. A. R. Ennion and reproduced in that journal in December 1948 as
'confirmation of the identification.' That a species whose nearest breeding
range to Britain should be in the south of France had actually nested in
Cambridgeshire seemed so incredible that despite being watched by some
of Britain's most experienced ornithologists doubts were cast upon the
validity of the record, either directly as by Col. Richard Meinertzhagen
(1950) or less so, as by Dr K. H. Voous (1960). However, many years have
elapsed since 1946 and all the original evidence has been re-examined a
number of times and, as Dr Colin Bibby (1982) wrote in a comprehensive
and valuable study of the Moustached Warbler, the original details 'continue to pass the rigorous present-day standards for acceptance of rarity
records.'

The Cambridgeshire birds were discovered on 3 August 1946 when a
single adult was spotted in a sallow on the edge of a large reed bed. On the
following day two adults were observed in the reed bed and also carrying
food into a thick bramble hedge. When they perched in the sallows or
nearby rose bushes they called 'with a soft penetrating "t-trrt, t-trrt,
t-trrt", which all observers agreed was less harsh and readily distinguishable from that of the Sedge Warbler (*Acrocephalus schoenobaenus*).' The
birds uttered each syllable separately but when they were approached too
closely they responded with 'a rather harsher "t-chik", which was repeated
rapidly with the syllables sometimes run together.' On 4 August a young
bird was seen and on 8 August a total of three juveniles was observed of
which two were quite strong on the wing but the third could not fly very
far. The breeding territory was bounded on the west side by a bramble
hedge, on the north by willows and to the east it stretched out over the reed
bed. Reed Warblers and Garden Warblers that intruded into the territory
were presented with a threat display involving extended wings and fanned
tails, accompanied by rapidly repeated 't-chik' notes, but Sedge Warblers
were ignored. When excited the birds cocked their tails, and one display
was carried out with vibrating, half-raised wings and fanned tail. (This
tail-cocking was discussed in Chapter 17.)

Several high sweet notes were heard from a bird thought to be about to
go to roost and on 6 August, provoked by the close presence of a Reed
Warbler, the male uttered one sweet, rather high note and chased the visitor
away. On its return it gave three more high calls followed by low notes:
'trt, trt, trt, rdl, rdl, rdl'.

The Cambridge birds were last seen on 20 August. This quite extraordinary event still remains unique, since this is the only breeding record
in the British Isles of this short-range migrant from southern Europe, and
also because of the high degree of improbability of two birds of the opposite
sex turning up in the same distant place! Yet we now know that the
appearance of certain vagrants in the British Isles is less surprising than it
once seemed to be; earlier we noted 'pairs' of Subalpine Warblers that
were recorded in the Northern Isles on three occasions. Bearded Tits also
seem to like travelling in pairs.

The next record in Britain is that of two birds in spartina on Eling Great

Marsh at Totton near Southampton on 13 August 1951 (Wooldridge and Ballantyne 1952). The calls of these birds were described as a Stonechat-like 'tuc-tuc', a pebble-like 'tac-tac' or sometimes 'tac-tac-tac', uttered occasionally with a slight churring quality but not with the sharpness of two pebbles being knocked together. Another Moustached Warbler was observed on 14 April 1952 in a dyke bordered with sedges and grass near Cliffe in North Kent (Gillham and Homes 1952); a bird was heard to call with a soft 'tack'. On 31 July 1965 a bird was trapped at Wendover in Buckinghamshire, the first to be examined in the hand in the British Isles (Harber *et al* 1966). Fourteen years were then to elapse before the next Moustached Warbler was reported, on 18 August 1979 at Angmering in West Sussex (Rogers *et al* 1980). Even with a vast increase in mist netting in the British Isles the Moustached Warbler remains a rare visitor indeed.

There are other references to the calls of the Moustached Warbler besides those quoted in the last paragraph. One heard by G. R. M. Pepler and described by Dr Bibby (1982) was a tick like the soft alarm of a chat or *Sylvia* warbler and quite distinguishable from the note of any other reed bed warbler. Another call that has been described as a churring flight note 'trrrp' is clearly the same note as that used by the Cambridge birds; also the 'trrrt' that I transcribed from the calls that I often heard from birds in the Camargue; it is quite different from any call of the Sedge Warbler.

In my experience the habitat of breeding Moustached Warblers in Europe is one of dense *Phragmites* reed beds. One such territory in the Camargue which I studied in 1954 was also occupied by Moustached Warblers in 1937 when the same region was visited by George Yeates (1946), but in 1973 it was unoccupied. The reedy nature of the habitat tends to ensure the nearness of Reed rather than Sedge Warblers to the nesting Moustached Warblers. B. Leisler (1973), who has widely studied the present species, found the typical habitats to be reeds with *Cladium* sedge and beds of *Scirpus* rush and *Typha* reedmace. The Moustached Warbler is an agile climber and can cope easily with upright stems in a very proficient manner. It appears to climb and clamber down stems to feed near the water. The result of a study of 22 faecal samples from Moustached Warblers gathered at Capestang in France (Bibby 1982) showed that the most numerous and frequent food items were beetles, especially small leaf beetles *Chrysomelidae* and very small caterpillars and *Hymenoptera*, usually less than 5 mm in length. Dipterous flies made up only 7% of the food taken. In fact, the Moustached Warbler is an assiduous searcher after small items of food and was compared in this respect by Dr Bibby to two other insectivorous birds which do not migrate away from the northern winters: the Dartford Warbler and the Wren. The Cambridge fledglings appear to have been fed with small Dipterous flies but the adults were seen bearing caterpillars, beetles, adult dragonflies, a greyish grasshopper and a gold-tail moth (*Euproctis*).

On its normal breeding ground the Moustached Warbler begins nesting quite early. In the region of the Camargue an early male may start singing on sunny days in February but T. Williams (1983) believed that 'it some-times sings in January'. Early in the year the species is not too difficult to find in the reed beds, since it is the only bird singing there before the arrival of the many southern migrants. Later in the year the bird is more elusive even though it resumes song in the middle of May. Perhaps the two song-periods are indicative of double broods which are claimed by both *The Handbook* (1946) and Dr Colin Harrison (1975). To me there is some suggestion of the Sedge Warbler in the song of the Moustached but it sounds rather thinner in quality, somewhat sweeter in tone and usually without the sharp rattles or jarrings of that species, although harder notes may sometimes occur. The song is often but not invariably introduced by some very characteristic soft 'lu-lu-lu' notes, rather like those of a Nightingale or Woodlark, although Bannerman (1954) thought that they were 'like the cry of a redshank.' It has been suggested in a number of publications that four is the usual total of these preliminary notes (*The Handbook* 1946, Bannerman 1954, Williamson 1976, Moore 1983). Although the

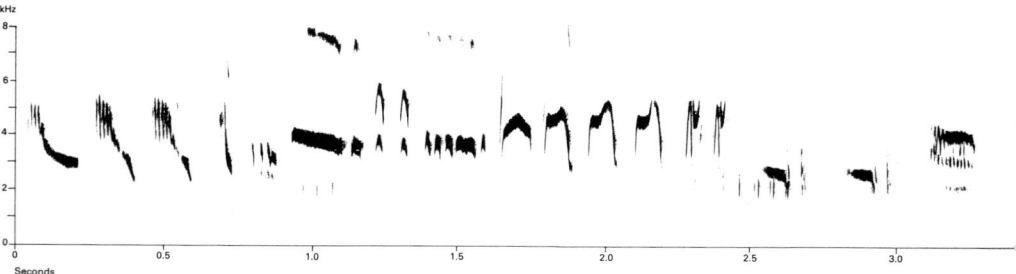

Fig. 90
First part of song of Moustached Warbler. Note introductory Nightingale-like notes followed by typical mixture of rambling notes. (Recorded by Eric Simms, Camargue, May 1954)

song may have a prelude as short as this, I have heard many songs with longer introductions. In 1954 I obtained tape recordings of a male in the Camargue and wrote in *Voices of the Wild* (1957) that I was 'able to watch it singing while its performance was recorded on the tape. Afterwards I played this recording over to myself carefully, as I always do after a recording trip, and I found that our Moustached Warbler used anything from five to twenty-two of the introductory notes before the chattering song. In 95% of the songs used the introductory notes were employed; I would say that the use of these notes is regular but not invariable. Further, I usually heard ten to fifteen introductory notes, which is at variance with the "four musical, high-pitched notes" described by *The Handbook of British Birds*.' The Nightingale-like notes start slowly and softly at first but then rise in pitch and volume and full song follows at once. The introductory notes take on average 4–6 seconds while the rest of the song is often sustained for a minute or more. The song may sometimes contain mimicry. Some birds sing from deep in the reeds but even so I have been able to approach to within a few metres of them. Dr Colin Bibby (1982) quoted instances of birds singing frequently from the tops of reeds in Austria, Mallorca and the Camargue. I watched several in the last region singing from reed-plumes, but one male I studied never showed itself in this way.

The nests are generally built over water up to a height of about 0.6 m above the surface. They are often placed in reeds, reed-mace, sedges and even willows growing in water. With their untidy, loosely constructed character they lack the artistry and execution of the Reed Warbler. The nests are deep cups in *Acrocephalus* tradition, built of dry reed leaves, sedges or grasses, knotted and bound together between tall stems and with their rims plaited down. They are often lined with reed flowers. In Sicily

Admiral Lynes, quoted by Dr David Bannerman (1954), found nests built chiefly of rotting vegetation plucked from the water which subsequently dried into a rigid framework, while others were of softer materials with an outside decoration of tamarisk fluff. Some of these nests were graced with little lining at all but 'one was beautifully lined with a profusion of large soft feathers of the water rail and little bittern, placed loosely around as in a swallow's nest.' Fr. Haverschmidt (1939) wrote that it was a well-known fact in Hungary that Moustached Warblers often built their nests among reeds under the knots made by fishermen tying the reeds together. While visiting Lake Velencze in June 1928 he also found some nests 'immediately under heaps of reeds which had been cut and thrown into the reed-bed at the sides of narrow waterways by fishermen.' The eggs are white or greyish-white with very fine speckles of ash-grey or olive. The clutch size is small; generally 3–4 eggs, although 5 or 6 are known. The young at Cambridge were fed by both adults although it is not known how characteristic this is in view of other evidence from Dementiev and Gladkov (1968). After the breeding season the juveniles undergo a complete moult (Leisler 1972); this may be an indication of the species' southern European origin and lack of great migratory drive, and is not typical of the genus. There are still many unanswered questions about the behaviour of this warbler, including the variety of food taken, details of breeding, mortality and so on. This skulking inhabitant of the reed beds still retains many of its secrets.

CHAPTER **20** The Reed Warbler

The very name of this *Acrocephalus* warbler immediately evokes clear pictures of the green forests of reeds that this bird inhabits, where its continuous chatter is probably the commonest summer sound. I have happy memories of countless hours spent among the tall waving reeds in England, where the honking notes of Coots, the quack of Mallard, the squeal of Water Rails, the pinging of Bearded Tits, the crackle of Garganey, the distant boom of Bitterns have sharply punctuated the sibilant chorus of Reed Warbler songs. As many as ten pairs to a hectare have been recorded in mature beds of *Phragmites* reeds but very large reed beds such as those in the Camargue are not all that common. It is also difficult to census birds in this kind of habitat. Like the Whitethroat, the Reed Warbler suffered a decrease in numbers between 1968–9; the breeding population in England then remained at quite a low level until 1974 when a sharp increase was recorded. The improvement continued until 1977 but a decrease then ensued in the following year. On waterways the rate of increase was still somewhat less than half that recorded for Sedge Warblers (Marchant and Hyde 1979). With both Sedge and Reed Warblers, the timing of visits to their breeding areas is very important in order to check times of arrival, the growth in the nesting population and the output of song (Bell *et al* 1973). We have seen already that in the case of the Sedge Warbler the spring arrival and consolidation of territories are very rapid, but with the Reed Warbler the arrival and build-up of numbers are more protracted (Catchpole 1972). With a slower accumulation and a wider period of song the Reed Warblers require less accuracy in the timing of visits by human observers. Where Reed Warbler colonies are high in the number of territories occupied, the accuracy of censusing cannot be very high either. Mapping territories is not a very effective way of arriving at the numbers in a particular habitat. Birds may nest outside the reed beds, change their territories and indulge in polygamy; all are factors which make censusing difficult.

As long ago as 1946 Philip Brown, in a classic paper, described the way in which Reed Warblers would feed outside the reed beds in which they were nesting. He reported how birds in the colony which he was studying at North Cotes in Lincolnshire were 'feeding in the adjacent corn and clover fields and in rushy ground to the south of the reeds.' Reference has already been made in Chapter 18 to Dr David Lack's observations on Sedge Warblers feeding outside their territories in the same way in which Reed Warblers forage. Stimulated by these records and by work on sympatric breeding populations of *Acrocephalus* species by Dr C. K. Catchpole (1973a), another investigator, T. P. Milsom (1982), studied twelve Reed Warbler colonies in North Humberside to see whether the numbers of singing Reed Warblers could be correlated either with the actual area of the reed beds or with the length of their edges. As Sedge Warblers were missing from ten of the sites and apparently not breeding in the other two there was no question of the Reed Warblers being affected by competition from the other Acrocephaline species. Although there might be some competition for the edge of the reed bed, because it bridged the ecotone between the nest and the feeding grounds or acted as a 'gate', data collected by the B.T.O. indicated that several Reed Warblers could readily share a common departure point on the edge of the reed bed when feeding in a nearby habitat. Milsom advanced the hypothesis that the overall perimeter length was not important itself but that 'it is a good predictor of the size of the feeding area, and hence it is a reflection of the carrying capacity of the reed bed.' It is also true, of course, that the size of a foraging area could be influenced not only by the length of the reed bed edge but also by the nature and variety in the habitats.

Since reed *Phragmites communis* is traditionally the English home of the Reed Warbler, it seems sensible to have a look at this habitat before any others. Yet it should be remembered that these warblers nest in other habitats: roughly half of the total of breeding Reed Warblers at Attenborough Nature Reserve near Nottingham – some 63 pairs – nested outside the reed habitat. However, reed as a plant is most frequent in lowland swampy areas less than 200 m above sea level and south of a line drawn on a map of Britain from about Filey to Preston, down to the Gower in South Wales and on to Start Point in Devon. This is also the area that encompasses the largest number of Reed Warblers nesting in Britain. Although reeds do occur farther north these may be of poorer growth and so unsuitable for Reed Warbler nests. Despite the possibility that there are also as yet undetermined factors affecting the distribution of Reed Warblers, it seems that temperature and rainfall have important parts to play. The limits for breeding birds appear to lie between the July isotherms of 16°C and 32°C

with a few nesting north of the 16°C isotherm (Voous 1961). The Reed Warbler also exclusively selects breeding areas with less than 1000 mm of annual rainfall and less than 75 mm in July (*The Atlas* 1976). There have been few changes in the species' distribution in Britain apart from some advances into Devon and West Cornwall and perhaps North Wales and

Fig. 91
Breeding range of the Reed Warbler.

Yorkshire. The Reed Warbler breeds widely in central and southern England and East Anglia and then more locally to the Isles of Scilly, South Wales, Anglesey (with nesting proved in 1968), Cumbria and Northumberland. Birds have nested in Co. Down in Ireland in May 1935 (Ruttledge 1966) and in a snowberry hedge in Shetland in June 1973 (Bundy 1975). The last of these records was the first for Scotland and the northern or outer isles and could have involved birds with an eastern rather than a southern origin, since Reed Warblers colonized southeast Norway in 1947 (Voous 1961).

Because the Reed Warbler may share a habitat with both the Sedge and Marsh Warblers there is a need to separate one species from another. One way is by song (a subject which will be discussed later in the chapter) and the other by visual recognition in the field or by examination in the hand. As one of the streaked species of *Acrocephalus* the Sedge Warbler obviously presents less of a problem than the other two. It is true that ornithologists with a wide and intimate knowledge of both adult Reed and Marsh Warblers may be able to distinguish between the two by certain characters in their plumages; the Reed Warbler, however, may present a spectrum of variability in its plumages so that it may be unsatisfactory to rely on these characteristics alone. Generally the upper parts of the Marsh Warbler are paler with a greenish tinge, and the throat is white; the Reed Warbler is more rufous on the upper parts and rump, but some first-summer Marsh Warblers have a rusty suffusion on the rump that makes them indistinguishable from young Reed Warblers. The separation of the two species is very critical and, as we saw in Chapter 17, the eastern race of the Reed Warbler is very close to the Marsh Warbler in its coloration. The notch on the inner web of the second primary, which usually falls between the tip of the eighth primary and secondaries but usually not as high as the seventh primary, can help to identify the Reed Warbler, while the Marsh Warbler has the notch falling between the tip of the sixth and eighth and exceptionally ninth primaries (*The Handbook* 1946), but since that time N. Sischka has demonstrated that some Marsh Warblers may have the notch as high as between the fifth and sixth primaries and even exceptionally as low as below the ninth. Since young birds in autumn cannot be separated by plumage it is necessary to rely on properly described and measured wing formulae. Following the ringing work of H. Springer (1960) in Bavaria on colour-ringed Reed, Great Reed and Marsh Warblers, E. Bezzel (1961) showed that of fifteen Reed Warblers colour-ringed near Munich and whose wing formulae were recorded in 1959 and 1960, six revealed different formulae over the two-year period! The nature of the identification problems has been well expressed by John Crudass and T. R. E. Devlin (1965), Peter Davis (1965) and Kenneth Williamson (1976); these should be consulted for their detailed studies. An odd juvenile Reed Warbler trapped at Leighton Moss in Lancashire in July 1978 had its normal rufous coloration replaced by a Lesser Whitethroat-like grey and its underparts were very white (Marsh 1982).

It is perhaps by its voice that the Reed Warbler offers the best chance of identification since it is normally a shy, retiring bird, living much of the time amongst reeds and other dense cover. Here it clings expertly to the plant stems with one leg extended and one foot drawn up nearer to the body; it sidles up and down the stems in a sudden, jerky manner or hops and flits from plant to plant. When singing the male may perch in the open and so reveal its somewhat slender appearance; this contrasts very much with the bulkier form of the Marsh Warbler which has what D. I. M. Wallace called 'a plumper, belly-down appearance, that *scirpaceus* normally lacks.' G. M. Ireson (1965) thought that the Reed Warbler was much sleeker and not 'jowled' like the Marsh Warbler, which seemed to the observer like a heavy Whitethroat. J. A. Walpole-Bond was of the opinion that the Reed was 'not so bottle-bodied' as the Marsh Warbler. The Reed Warbler tends to fly short distances with a fanned and drooping tail.

Reed Warblers feed on many kinds of fenland and marshland insects and their larvae, dipterous flies including craneflies and Chironomid midges, male damselflies such as *Agrion virgo*, small dragonflies, stoneflies, butterflies and moths as well as aphids, spiders and sometimes small slugs and worms. In its feeding habits the Reed Warbler is quite aggressive. It visits trees and shrubs as well as reeds and marshland vegetation, actively catching insects in the air and making fewer changes of perch than the Sedge Warbler (Green and Davies 1972). Even naive hand-reared Reed Warblers are just as capable of catching flies as birds introduced and exposed to them from a very early age (Davies and Green 1976). The busiest feeding time is in the morning and late evening. Although the actual abundance of insect life seems to alter little during the day, insects are more easily caught when it is cooler. Outside the breeding season birds may feed on currants, elderberries and the fruits of dogwood and bird-cherry.

When we come to look at the vocalizations of the Reed Warbler, we find that the usual note is a quiet low 'churr', which will lengthen into a protracted grating scold or rattle when the bird is under stress or excited. I have occasionally heard a quieter version of this scold which is not dissimilar from a churring note of the Bearded Tit, and where both species share a reed bed habitat care needs to be exercised in separating them. To some extent the territorial song of the Reed Warbler is based on the call note. It is slower and more subdued than the song of the Sedge Warbler, and more even in tempo. Although notes such as 'kerr-kerr-kerr', 'kek-kek-kek' and 'chirruc-chirruc' are repeated over and over again, they are low in pitch and of the same overall reedy timbre as the rest of the song, so that the contrast in timbre that one finds in the duetting style of the Great Reed Warbler's performance is absent (North and Simms 1958). Sequences of low churring phrases follow each other: 'kerr-kerr-kerr, chirruc-chirruc-chirruc, kek-kek-kek, chirr-chirr' or 'tuk-tuk-tuk, tcher-tcher,

Fig. 92
Part of song of the Reed Warbler. Note sounds of short duration and considerable frequency range. (Recorded by V. Lewis, Herefordshire, May 1962)

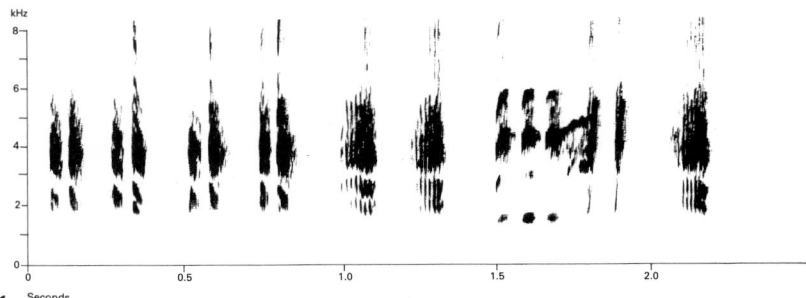

kHz

Seconds

tee-tee-tee, tit-tit' and so on. Each phrase consists of 2–4 notes, delivered in erratic bursts or passages lasting from 5–20 seconds, up to a full minute. The whole effect is somewhat mechanical and, although higher and more musical notes may be inserted, the song is still less varied and powerful than the songs of Sedge and Marsh Warbler and lacks the emphasis of the performance of those two species. It can be indistinct to a human listener at 30 m distance and it can be heard 300 m away, although the average territory is about 300 m² (Brown and Davies 1949). Some individual singers are better than others but, however varied the Reed Warbler's song may be, it still retains a two or three-syllabled character and its own fundamental rhythm. In a study of the sound-pressure levels of the Reed Warbler's song Heuwinkel (1978), who was interested in performance in open habitats, after registering the low frequency and small dynamic range of the song, showed that the average sound pressure level of five singers at 3 m was 58.1–67.7 dB (decibels); this was a measure of the intensity of the sound but when he came to record birds in reed beds he found there was a 5 dB drop over 3 m.

At one time it was thought that the Reed Warbler, unlike the Sedge or Marsh Warbler, rarely included imitations of other species' vocalizations in its song. Philip Brown and Gwen Davies (1949), in their detailed study of Reed Warblers, noted that during the four seasons of their investigation they only once recorded mimicry by a Reed Warbler. Since that time it has come to be realized that Reed Warblers in the south of England are capable of developed songs with mimicry which are suggestive of those of the Marsh Warbler. K. Atkin and A. D. Townsend (1965) reported how a Reed Warbler at Bardney in Lincolnshire that was evicted by a Marsh Warbler from its territory began to imitate a few phrases from the Marsh Warbler's song. Within two days the Reed Warbler had developed its song 'until it was always singing with a "Marsh Warbler" type song', – one that included high-pitched musical trills and a nasal 'chay'. Later it added the notes of Redshank and Common Tern that shared the habitat and, although the Marsh Warbler departed, the Reed Warbler retained its newly acquired utterances.

Thus the Reed Warbler has been proved to be strongly mimetic. G. A. Pyman (1965) reported one amongst Marsh Warblers in Gloucestershire which, in about a quarter of an hour imitated, sometimes several times over, the calls or notes of no fewer than sixteen other species and for long periods 'there was scarcely a trace of the thin slow phrases of the Reed Warbler.' A Reed Warbler in Essex in 1963 imitated fifteen other species and, having mastered the 'yaffle' of the Green Woodpecker, reproduced it five times in quick succession. It appears that many examples of mimetic Reed Warblers have occurred where reeds and dense stemmed plants are few and far between. Outside the traditional reed bed habitat birds are much more likely to come into contact with other species which they could copy. Some instances of mimicry seem to occur late in the breeding season after weeks of conditioning and possibly late arrivals may benefit from a more complex song in setting up territories or attracting mates. E. A. Armstrong (1963) believed that 'in most species mimicries are learned mainly in the first two years', but they may be abandoned later. A Reed Warbler, ringed in 1963, mimicked Blue Tit, Swallow and Blackbird but in the following two years it uttered only normal song having forgotten what it had learned (Crudass and Devlin 1965). Yet one might have thought that a Reed Warbler with a more varied repertoire, suggestive of greater age and experience, would have had an advantage at the beginning of the season in establishing a territory and obtaining a mate, as seems to happen with male Great Tits. Unlike the Sedge Warbler, for whom the spring arrival and build-up in numbers are rapid, the male Reed Warbler has more time to advertise himself. Of course, a too varied or ambitious song which has lost its normal dynamic range, its slow phrases and basic rhythm can become so deprived of its basic cues, which inform other members of its species of its presence, sex and identity, that it becomes biologically worthless. In Chapter 5 on the Garden Warbler we read about a male with so aberrant a song that over several years it failed completely to acquire a mate. Although a brilliant and exceptional Reed Warbler may approach a Marsh Warbler in its performance, a desultory or substandard Marsh may be difficult to distinguish. D. I. M. Wallace was of the opinion that Austrian Marsh Warblers lacked the high musical quality of birds in western Europe and England; there was always the possibility that some of the central European birds might overshoot in spring and reach England, where they could present problems for ornithologists. Unusual songsters should be trapped for a detailed examination in the hand. A Reed Warbler that was caught in a mist net on 1 June 1970 near Tring sang and continued to defend his territory against a second male (Spencer 1971a); the initial drive had been to sing and it was presumably so strong that the shock of capture and the inconvenience of hanging more or less upside down were not enough to end it.

The male Reed Warblers arrive back in their territories in early May before the reed growth of that year has attained any great height. Here they establish themselves and oppose the intrusions of rival males with song and raised feathers. In courtship the male birds indulge in little emotional extravagance. Although the restricted nature of the habitat forces Reed Warblers to nest colonially, they are not basically social birds. H. E. Howard (1907–14) noted that the somewhat haphazard return of birds was typical: 'not that the time of advent of the first male varies much, but that males and females intermingled continue to arrive, and to pair so long as there is sufficient territory for some weeks after the arrival of the first male.' Territories sometimes overlap and both males will sing in the 'no-man's-land' with the bird in temporary occupation evoking song from the second male but not being dispossessed. As more birds come into a reed bed so territory size may shrink since 'territories are elastic and can grow or shrink according to the pressures and the nature of the habitat' (Simms 1971). Even during the nesting season a territory may be so compressed that the result proves fatal. In their study of Reed Warblers, Brown and Davies (1949) were able to show that if a male did not respond vigorously enough to the singing of other unmated intruders he would be deserted by *his* mate. A lack of response or only a weak one meant marital disaster! There is strong evidence that hens will desert their cocks for new mates. Dr C. K. Catchpole (1971) reported polygamy at Attenborough near Nottingham with a male bird attending two females but this is not thought to be a significant feature of the species. At the Attenborough Nature Reserve, 83% of Reed Warbler territories were in marshland and 17% in dry areas of land in the neighbourhood (Catchpole 1972); the latter

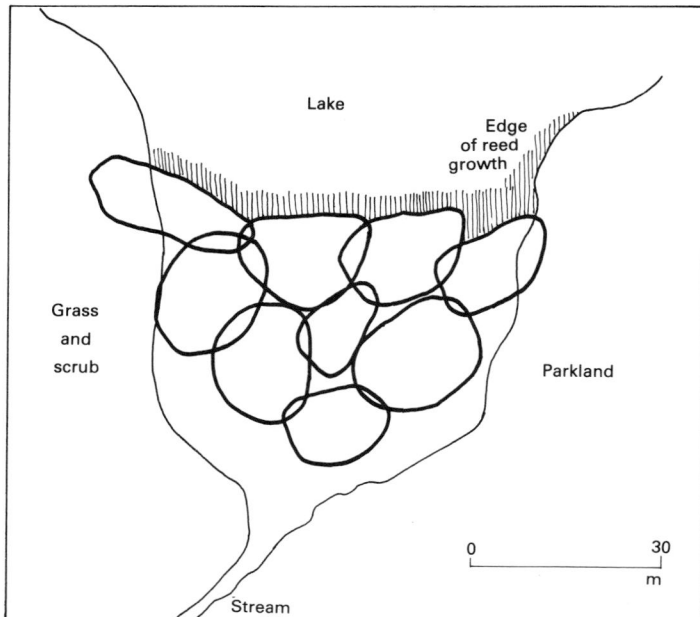

Fig. 93
9 Reed Warbler
territories in a reedbed in
a bay of a Northampton-
shire lake. Assessed
roughly by song and
territorial behaviour.
(Eric Simms)

suffered no decrease in breeding success. Some 74% of males returned to
the same small reed bed but only 40% of the females. Here Dr Catchpole
calculated that the mean territory size of the Reed Warbler was 332 m^2
compared to 1811 m^2 for the Sedge Warbler. At Coate Water near Swindon
a pair was formed from members of the same brood actually bearing
consecutively-numbered rings (Webber 1964). D. K. Thomas (1984)
found that in pure reed marshes on the Gower, Reed Warblers bred earlier,
produced heavier young and enjoyed a higher invertebrate population
than in other habitats.

After pairing has been accomplished there is a sudden stop to singing in
the daytime, but singing at night is continued throughout the season.
Unpaired males often build cocks' nests in the manner of *Sylvia* warblers;
these can vary from a few strands of dead reed or moss to more ambitious
ones which become untidy platforms between points of suspension in the
reeds. Some of these constructions built by males may reach the stage of
half-completed 'proper' nests but are less tightly woven together. Reed
Warblers start to nest on average in England between 16–26 May and the
final nest appears to be built almost entirely by the hen. It is quite often
above a cocks' nest but not woven into it or necessarily supported by it.
G. Trelfa (1959) found a rather flimsy early nest with four eggs at Marbury
Mere in Cheshire on 9 May 1958; other early records listed by the journal
British Birds include a partially-built nest on 4 May, clutches of four eggs
on 14, 15 and 16 May, and one of five eggs on 15 May.

At the start of the construction of the nest a few strands of dead reed leaf –
perhaps six or seven – are loosely woven around some three to five reed

stems. Then strands of fine moss from 75–200 mm in length are fitted to
the top of this platform to form a kind of cushion. Philip Brown (1946)
who watched many nests being built described how 'dried grasses, reed-
leaves and sedges were woven round the outside of this mossy lump, thus
forming the lower outside portion of the cup. At about this stage the main
suspensions were put in, usually considerable lengths of dead reed-leaves.'
These suspensions were fixed by weaving actions to a reed, then pulled
downwards and threaded through the structure of the cup while the other
end was then woven around another stem. How well this last task was
performed would determine later how the nest would survive high winds
and storms. After a few days the base platform or cushion tends to fall
away, so leaving the base of the nest looking rather untidy. As a result of
his survey Philip Brown (1946) gave the average dimensions of nests as
7.8 cm wide and 8.5 cm deep, while the cup inside had an average width
of 4.8 cm and a depth of 5.3 cm. Of 19 nests examined the average height
above the water level, measured to the rim of the cup, was 63 cm while the
extremes were 32.5 cm and 110 cm. The average depth of water below the
nests was 10 cm but the maximum recorded was just over 32 cm. Reed
Warblers evince a habit of stripping nests of material with a pair removing
the material to build another nest somewhere else or suffering destruction
from a territorially-intruding pair.

Birds may use both old and new reeds for the nest site. Although the
growth of new reeds among old canes may tip the nest out of the vertical,
Philip Brown observed that the tilt was not more than 10° to 15° and so
posed no problems for the eggs or young of the Reed Warblers. Major A.
W. Boyd (1951) dissented from this view expressing the opinion that in
Cheshire when the nests became askew as the new reeds grew 'the young
have difficulty in staying inside, despite the depth of the cup.' Occasionally
a nest is built on to the side of another (Billet 1952), a feature brought about
by a rival male disturbing a pair during the laying of the first clutch so that
the hen then builds a second nest alongside the first. It usually takes
3–6½ days for the nest to be built with an average time of 4½ days. However,
in Czechoslovakia the construction seems to take longer – 11 days – a
duration little affected by prevailing weather conditions (Lukeš 1973). All
the Lincolnshire nests studied by Brown were lined 'with dead reed-heads,
usually arranged in crossed spirals.' I have occasionally found wool or
feathers used to make the lining. In the dry summer of 1938 seven pairs of
Reed Warblers in the osier beds of Sedgemoor in Somerset built nests
double or treble the normal size and 'constructed almost entirely of wool
with a few bents interspersed, and lined with fine bents' (Pring 1938)
while another unusually large one at Cley in Norfolk in the same year was
'largely composed of sheep's wool with a lining of fine grass' (Boyd 1938).

Reeds are not the only breeding habitat for the Reed Warbler in Britain.
Birds may be found nesting in many other kinds of vegetation near reed
beds. *The Handbook* (1946) listed osier beds – a habitat also described by
M. Philips Price (1969) in the southwest of England and shared with
Marsh Warblers. Here the nests are built 'round shoots of the basket
willow, generally incorporating nettles. Sometimes they use only nettles,
but then their nests generally come to grief in thunderstorms.' The osier
beds became neglected and were no longer cut every four or five years; as
a result their thickened stems became quite unsuitable for carrying Reed

and Marsh Warbler nests which required thin willow shoots for support. Both species have decreased in southwest England and, although other factors may also be involved, the failure to manage osier beds must have had an adverse effect. In the Attenborough colonies near Nottingham 46% of the nests were in vegetation other than reeds, including dry land habitats (Catchpole 1974). A large proportion of the birds nested in both rosebay and great willowherb as well as purple loosestrife, *Glyceria*, docks and willows (Bell *et al* 1968). The *London Bird Report* (1948) recorded eleven nests in willowherb, nettles, mallow, woody nightshade and docks; nests suspended in willowherb were able to support nests with growing cuckoos in them as well. Nests may also be built in reed grass *Phalaris* and these tend to be rather untidy in appearance; they may be slung from basket handles but this particular plant is 'easily laid by wind and heavy rain with disastrous results to Reed Warbler nests built in it' (Crudass and Devlin 1965). On Rainham Marsh, some ten miles east of St Paul's Cathedral on the north shore of the River Thames, Reed Warblers have become established in nearly dry sea aster on the lagoons (Dennis 1982). Nests have also been reported in meadowsweet, hawthorn, alder, and rhododendron. Reed Warblers were also recorded in the London area from the early 1860s to about 1879 nesting in lilac bushes. Whether these were Reed or Marsh Warblers has never been completely settled (Fitter 1949). There is a record of a lilac being used by Reed Warblers in Suffolk. Exceptionally,

Fig. 94
Courtship feeding in a pair of Reed Warblers.
(Eric Hosking)

the European Reed Warbler has been known to breed in cornfields and even parks quite distant from any water.

When the final nest has been completed by the female she lays the eggs every 24 hours until the clutch is complete. In a comparison with the Sedge Warbler in Chapter 18 I indicated that Reed Warbler clutches were most frequently of four eggs. Out of 99 broods marked by A. W. Boyd (1951) in Cheshire between 1913 and 1936 there were 11 with one egg, 18 with two, 29 with three, 34 with four and 7 with five, giving an average of 3.08. The mean clutch size drops fairly uniformly as the season progresses from about 4.21 in June to 3.38 in August. If a clutch of five eggs appears it is more likely to be in June when a clutch of three eggs is rare. In Holland clutches of five eggs are said to be common although four is also the rule (Haverschmidt 1949); four is also general in Czechoslovakia (Lukeš 1973) and 4.14 in Finland (Raitasuo 1958). The eggs are smooth and glossy, being also a pale green or greenish-white and densely blotched or mottled with greenish-brown, grey and olive, and with a concentration at the broad end which may produce a noticeable capping. One egg in my possession has a single wide band of dark colour around the larger end. In each clutch the eggs are all slightly different and in a clutch of four or five eggs the last to be laid is lighter in colour and often appreciably larger. From a close study of a number of clutches of normal size it is possible to detect a gradation in colour depth starting with a dark egg as the first laid, and each following one being correspondingly lighter than the one before. The eggs are incubated in turn by the adults and it seems that the duty may be shared equally (Hosking and Smith 1943) or the male's share may be very much less than half that of the female (Brown 1946). From my own experience there is some variability among pairs. Incubation lasts 11–12 days and appears to start before the completion of the clutch. Males may sing quite loudly on the nest and there may also be a loud burst before nest-relief. Sometimes at the relief a male may utter 'a very low inward warbling' (Brown and Davies 1949). An incubating male will also sing at an approaching rival male and there are sometimes short bursts of song from a female; Brown (1946) noted this six times from four different hens but 'in no instance more than five seconds in duration.' In heavy rain the male may shelter his incubating mate with his body.

Both parents will bring food to the young Reed Warblers but the male takes on the larger part of this work while the female broods the nestlings. The young birds are fed on insects and other invertebrates crushed into a pulpy lump. C. Henry (1977) found that the adults fed no fewer than fifty different arthropod taxa to the young, of which twenty constituted more than 80% of their diet. The size of the prey was important with the commonest animals brought in measuring 1–4 mm in size. The hen often eats the faecal sacs at the nest while the male removes them some distance. The fledging period is usually 11–13 days but 10 and 14 have also been recorded. The largest broods seem to be reared from the largest clutches but young from broods of three were more likely to survive than those from bigger broods (Bibby 1978). Overlapping broods have been reported for the Reed Warbler. Young raised early in the season have a better chance of survival despite brood sizes being larger then than later in the summer. In an interesting comparison between the breeding success of the Reed and Great Reed Warblers nesting in an area of reed and reed mace at Milicz in

Wroclaw Province in Poland, Andrzej Dyrcz (1974) showed that the former species was better able to rear young in the habitat than the latter species. Young Great Reed Warblers lost more weight in bad weather with whole broods sometimes starving, which suggested that the adverse conditions affected the prey food of the Great Reed Warbler more markedly. Hatching was also spread over a longer period for the Great Reed Warbler. There was apparently some overlap in food for the two species in Poland and this was perhaps confirmed by the low nestling weights recorded when the nestling periods overlapped each other. There was a tendency for the Reed Warbler to favour extensive areas of reed bed and the Great Reed Warbler the edges of the reed growth. When young are in the nest and after fledging, the enticing of intruders away seems to be very exceptional and I have not recorded it. However, there is an account by Chappell (1949) of a female fluttering through the reeds in a helpless manner; when the observer picked up a young one the hen fluttered onto the path with both wings outspread, dragging them in turn.

Out of 1021 Reed Warbler nests logged by the B.T.O. some were tilted, blown over or flooded, some were stripped by other Reed Warblers and 80 were parasitized by Cuckoos. Investigations by Havlin (1971) and Catchpole (1974) made it clear that Reed Warblers had a more successful breeding record in habitats other than dense reed beds and this difference was attributed to higher levels of predation on nests in reed stands. Not only might the Cuckoo be one of the chief causes but avian predators like jays also had an effect. This being so Dr Colin Bibby (1978) observed that, as many Reed Warblers nest outside reed beds 'it is a mystery why they do not all do so as they seem to be more successful.' To this no answer can yet be offered. Perhaps the open nature of Reed Warblers' nests and their accessibility may be more important than Cuckoos.

' It was demonstrated by Chance (1940) and Baker (1942) that each hen Cuckoo restricts herself to a particular host species. If, however, the nest in which she intended to lay her egg was destroyed or she was prevented from reaching it for some reason, then she might have to turn her attention to another species. A review by Dr David Lack (1963) of Cuckoo hosts in England quoted from a long study by A. Whitaker from 1911 to 1944 of a colony of Reed Warblers at Nottingham. The proportion of cuckolded nests varied from none in ten different years to as many as ten out of eighteen nests in 1930: 56%. In the twelve years from 1929 to 1940 inclusive he found 39 cuckolded nests out of 112 – 35% – reflecting a serious loss of young Reed Warblers. Schiermann (1926) found a percentage of 55 near Berlin. An examination of the B.T.O.'s Nest Record Cards for the Reed Warbler revealed 85 cuckolded nests from a total of 2826, or 3% of the total (Glue and Morgan 1972). In Cambridgeshire Ian Wyllie (1975) located 54 pairs of Reed Warblers and 136 nests; 'Of these, 28 were deserted; 25 were cuckolded; 80 were robbed; 11 produced fledged young (one, a young Cuckoo); and 19 were not followed up.' Besides being associated with a remarkable television film made by Maurice Tibbles about the cuckoos, Wyllie made a series of very interesting observations. Twenty-seven Cuckoo eggs were laid between 22 May and 11 July with the maximum number laid by one female being twelve. Eggs were laid at two-day intervals in nests with just one egg as well as two or three, or none at all, and once in a nest with four incubated eggs. To illustrate the variation in the colour of Cuckoo eggs six females in one colony could be identified by pink Robin-like eggs, brown Skylark-like eggs, spotted House Sparrow-like eggs, grey Pied Wagtail-like eggs as well as eggs with a bluish tinge and one hen with oversized grey eggs. At the time of writing I have before me five clutches of Reed Warblers' eggs with Cuckoo eggs collected near Eton at the turn of the century. Four of the Cuckoo eggs are greyish and finely, almost translucently speckled like those of a House Sparrow; a fair match with the eggs of the Reed Warbler. The other two eggs have sharply delineated speckles on a reddish ground suggestive of the 'Meadow Pipit' Cuckoo and a poorer match. All these Cuckoo eggs are on average 21% greater in length than those of their foster parents.

The productivity of early Reed Warbler nests was calculated at about 1.8 young reared but falling to a low of 1.4 for nests begun in the second half of June (Bibby 1978). After an early nesting success a fair proportion of Reed Warblers – larger, in fact, than of Sedge Warblers – will attempt a second brood. Adult survival rates have been placed very high at 56% by R. Long (1975) and at 51% by R. E. Green (1976) with a quarter of the juveniles growing to maturity. From a figure of 4.09 chicks reared per pair the recruitment may be 0.98, so that in spite of a low nesting success and a

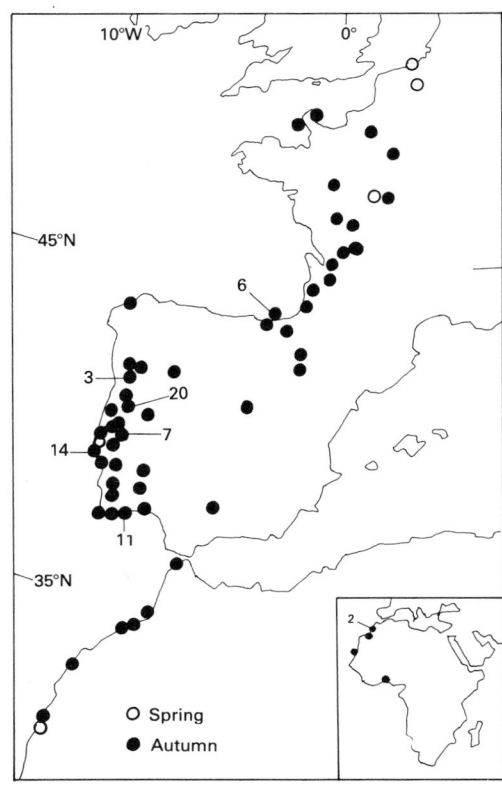

Fig. 95
117 foreign recoveries of British-ringed Reed Warblers. Open circles are those found in spring, and solid dots those found in autumn. (With permission from the monthly magazine British Birds*)*

small clutch size Reed Warblers with a high adult survival succeed in maintaining their populations. Figures for longevity in Reed Warblers include two birds reaching 11 years (one was ringed as an adult), three attaining 10 years (one also ringed as an adult), two ringed as adults living 8 years and two 7 years (Long 1971).

Our summer-breeding Reed Warblers begin to abandon their nesting grounds in early August and their departure continues until the end of September. Passage birds also occur in autumn with most being observed in southern England but some may be found as far north as Shetland and as far west as Ireland. In the past large numbers used to be reported in the reed beds and bean fields in Romney Marsh in early September 'when on certain days the numbers which can be beaten out of a field of standing beans is astonishing' (Bannerman 1954). Reed Warblers ringed in Britain and recovered in Europe in autumn are most frequent in western France, western Iberia and the northwest coast of Africa (Spencer 1971b). Birds pass the winter in tropical Africa and have been seen or collected in Nigeria, the Ivory Coast and Senegal. The bird is a 'common spring passage migrant' in Nigeria (Elgood *et al* 1966) and the spring migration in Senegal is 'pronounced though the species does not seem to winter there' (Moreau 1966). According to the *London Bird Report* (1981) a Reed Warbler ringed at Rye Meads in Hertfordshire on 24 June 1978 was recovered on 1 May 1980 after being killed by a catapult at Lakamene, Diena, in Mali, 4235 km to the southeast. At Lake Chad, which lies in the Sahel savannah with its thin acacia woodlands and other shrubs, many Palaearctic migrants overwinter; these include certain wader species, Sand Martins, Yellow Wagtails, Whitethroats, and Sedge and Reed Warblers. The last two species both feed extensively on the tiny green midge *Tanytarsus* as well as other insects and spiders in the Sahel. They also take *Salvadora* berries which are especially rich in soluble fructose and sucrose (Fry *et al* 1970). At Lake Chad only a short period of time is needed for migrants to increase their mean weight from a mid-winter level to a high fat level ready for the long migration to the north. Some Reed Warblers were so heavy that they had difficulty gaining height on release and must have been extremely vulnerable to predators.

In Uganda, Reed Warblers are inhabitants of dense bush from which I have heard bursts of song issuing in December. D. J. Pearson (1972) noted that in Uganda 'song was commonly heard during December and January, and increased from February onwards.' The earliest records both of song and completed moult were of a bird trapped there on 18 November. The wintering Reed Warblers of East Africa are eastern birds, largely *A. scirpaceus fuscus*, which are larger and paler than our birds. The complete moult takes place in Africa, and in Uganda birds can be found in a variety of plumage states. One group composed mainly of young birds arrived in worn plumage and moulted in the region, while others appeared in fresh plumage in December and January having moulted elsewhere (Pearson 1973). After studying Reed Warblers in the Queen Elizabeth Park in Uganda, Dr M. P. L. Fogden (1972) found that birds wintering in dry thickets of *Euphorbia* and *Capparis* may become dehydrated before their migratory return northwards. This was particularly acute in 1969 when there was a shortage of food but the birds still attained a high fat index. One result of dehydration may be to increase the birds' migratory range or length of journey, but whether the Reed Warbler actively dehydrates as a response to food shortages, to increase its range, is a matter for speculation.

Early arrivals of birds take place in England in the third week of April; the average arrival date over twenty-six years in Warwickshire, Worcestershire and Staffordshire is 30 April. Immigration reaches its peak from early May to the end of the month. Like some other riverside and fenland plants reed burgeons late and so the warblers most closely associated with it appear later than other species. By midsummer the reed beds have become a dense cover for the birds and they ripple with their monotonous babblings. With the advancing season the reed beds stretch into deeper water and birds may nest further from the shore. Second nests are built in late July or August and young may hatch as late as the third week of August. Song may be sustained until August or even September but it falls away as autumn approaches although a sudden noise may result in what T. A. Coward (1944) called 'a short burst of expostulatory song'. Thus the cycle is completed once more and the birds leave for the south.

From 1949 to 1951 I lived at Welford-on-Avon in south Warwickshire. I was therefore within easy reach of the osier beds along the River Avon in the neighbouring county of Worcestershire where Marsh Warblers were nesting. In June 1950 there were at least six males in song. It was an interesting and strange experience to visit the osier or 'withy' beds – dense and mysterious and full of rushes, nettles, iris and meadowsweet. Here Reed Buntings 'jinked' away, Sedge and a few Reed Warblers chattered incessantly and late in the season Marsh Warblers gave vent to their remarkable songs. Willows, especially the osier *Salix viminalis* and the purple willow *S. purpurea* were often planted for their wands, which are used in basket-making. They were grown, certainly from the middle of the seventeenth century, on a coppice system on land close to rivers. After two years' free growth they would be cut back. Then they might be harvested annually or, as in many parts of southwest England, every four or five years. The wands or rods grown in this way could either be left with their bark on or stripped. At one time the withy beds of Sedgemoor provided about 80% of the entire English crop with the production reaching a peak about 1900 (Hawkins 1973). The growing and preparation of the crop were technical and complex matters. The average life of a bed was about twenty years and optimal results were expected from the seventh to the fifteenth year of its life. Some beds were untouched for years, becoming wildlife sanctuaries, but the stems of the willows were too large for the nesting warblers to attach their nests to them. At one time many districts had their withy beds and the wands were made into baskets and fishtraps. Eventually cheaper imports and the advent of plastics and other synthetic materials spelled the decline of the withy industry although today there is still some demand for a 'natural' product. In some regions, sections of osier bed have been cut by volunteers from County Naturalists' Trusts to make them attractive once more to warblers but although Whitethroats, Reed and Sedge Warblers have returned, Marsh Warblers have not (Price 1969). Some Marsh Warblers spurned the River Avon in Worcestershire two or three miles away and sang in beanfields near Sheriff's Lench.

Birds were known to visit the Avon valley as long ago as 1860 but breeding was not proved until 1892 when a nest with eggs was found 'in some rank herbage in a stone quarry near Littleton' (Harthan n.d.). Forty years ago the Marsh Warbler was not uncommon in the Avon valley and along the Severn up to Worcester, but since that time both the range and numbers of the species have contracted. My first impressions of this warbler were of a secretive, cover-loving species with its colour tones shifting in contrast and quality as the light changed; it might suddenly show itself on a conspicuous song-post. It was its voice – often musical, always varied, well sustained and full of imitations of arresting fidelity – that drew my attention to its presence in the rank rambling vegetation of the osier beds. Yet the song, if delivered by a mediocre performer, may not be easily distinguished from an accomplished mimetic Reed Warbler, although I feel that the Marsh Warbler's vocalizations with their ease and imitations still have a special character.

The Marsh Warbler was not separated in Britain from the Reed Warbler until 1871 when it was discovered by Edward Blyth near London; it may have nested in the Hampstead area as well. Marsh Warblers have bred for some time in southern and western England but they were always rather scarce and local. Parslow (1973) noted that nests had been recorded in twenty counties in the south and west but regular breeding was more or less confined to seven or eight: Oxford (1893–1904, 1960), Kent (1926–c. 1946 and at intervals since), Sussex (1920–47 with up to 20 pairs, 1966–7), Dorset (c. 1893–c. 1954 and irregularly since), and sometimes Wiltshire, Somerset, Hereford, Worcester and Gloucester. In the last sixty years the most regular nesting records have come from the counties listed with the fewest from Oxfordshire and Wiltshire. Today the species is really restricted to Worcester, Gloucester and the southeast where it is very scarce indeed. In 1981 outside the Marsh Warbler's main headquarters in Worcestershire, where in 1977 46 singing males were counted, only three possibly nesting pairs were reported from three sites; the worst year for almost a decade. The recent vicissitudes of the Marsh Warbler as a breeding species outside the county of Worcestershire are clearly shown in the following table.

Breeding of Marsh Warbler   Table 20

	1973	1974	1975	1976	1977	1978	1979	1980	1981	1982
Sites	9	6	3	5	6	15	15	8	3	8
Pairs proved breeding	5	0	0	0	2	4	1	2	0	2
Pairs possibly breeding	15	7	5	5	11	15	23	12	3	9

(By permission, from the monthly magazine *British Birds*)

Britain is on the very western fringe of the Marsh Warbler's range; further the destruction of the osier bed habitat, the difficulty of pairs managing to get together when population levels are low, with land drainage schemes, and perhaps longer term climatic changes, have put the Marsh Warbler at a growing disadvantage where it is already at the limit of its range. There are perhaps some 75 pairs still breeding in the Avon valley but at the time of writing these are threatened by a scheme of the Severn Trent Water Authority for flood alleviation and the allocation of land to greater horticultural use; that would bring about the lowering of the water level in the soil and plant changes inimical to these warblers. In Europe Voous (1961) gave the breeding limits as the July isotherms of 16°C and 26°C, but with the species having extended its nesting range northwards with a rise in the mean spring temperatures. After the first breeding record in Sweden in 1930 the estimated population by 1943 had reached 300; a 1977 census in that country put the figure at 10,000 (Cavallin 1979).

Although closely related to the Reed Warbler, the Marsh Warbler in Britain is thus very much rarer – elsewhere it is only a vagrant – and, although nesting often near water it prefers rather drier areas, yet some-

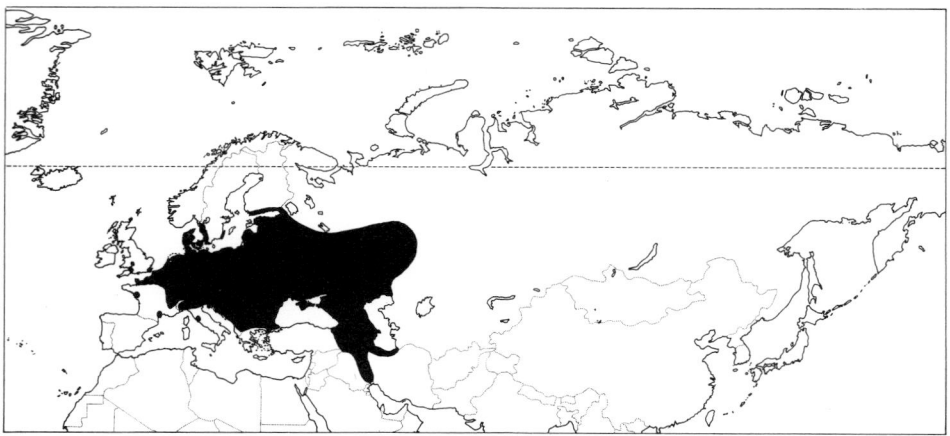

Fig. 96
Breeding range of the
Marsh Warbler.

what damper and ranker than those of Blyth's Reed Warbler. Although Marsh Warblers favoured osiers to which they could attach their nests with 'basket handles', the alternative sites tend to include strong growths of nettles, hoary willowherb and meadowsweet with perhaps a few taller shrubs or small trees dotted around that could serve as song-posts. Lowland copses, bushy places with elder, ash and hazel, hedgerows, banks of streams and other places with sufficiently dense vegetation have been used. According to S. H. Cooke (1948), a Wiltshire nest was in a water meadow among tall reeds, slung between the stems of a reed and a meadowsweet, but this is a less common situation. *The Handbook* (1946) also noted breeding in 'orchards, corn, rye, bean and other cultivated fields' but these sites were generally near water of some kind. I made an earlier reference in this chapter to bean fields; A. J. Harthan (1938) reported five pairs holding territories in such fields in the Avon valley. On the Continent Marsh Warblers quite often appear in standing crops of corn with belts of low bushes nearby, in hopfields and, in Germany, in gardens with peas and beans. Yet they will also share a habitat with Reed and Sedge Warblers and with Sedge and Aquatic Warblers.

Here the problem of identifying visually a small unstreaked *Acrocephalus* warbler raises its head once again. Earlier in the book I compared this species with other closely related ones with which the Marsh Warbler might be confused since several have few definitive plumage differences, and to complicate matters can display variations according to race, age, season and even individual character. Yet the dilemma is further increased since hybrids between Marsh and Reed Warblers have been recorded in Belgium (Lemaire 1977) and between Marsh and Blyth's Reed Warblers in Finland (Koskimies 1980). To the very end, even after being trapped and examined, a few *Acrocephalus* individuals will defy identification. Generally in good light and with a fair view of the bird the adult Marsh Warbler will show a uniformly cold olive-colour while the Reed Warbler has a rufous lower back. The Marsh Warbler also tends to look the heaviest of the small unstreaked warblers and 'may appear pot-bellied, probably because of its stance and its long wings' (Harvey and Porter 1984). It may also suggest a *Sylvia* warbler like a Blackcap in its form, not coloration, but does not carry a typical bill for that genus. It often perches with an upright posture and moves with its tail in a depressed state. Marsh Warblers seem to have the longest wings, and least 'fan-shaped', with their folded points extending to the end of the upper tail coverts; a very close inspection would reveal at least seven spaced primary tips. The birds also show some pale edges on the tertials, secondaries and tips of the primaries. The Marsh Warbler is also strongly yellowish buff below with a clearly contrasting creamy white throat. The bill is pale with the upper mandible horn and the lower a fleshy-pink or pale flesh-brown. There appears to be no real difference between the bills of the Marsh and the eastern Reed Warblers. There can be considerable variation between adult and first-winter plumages with some first-winter birds showing a contrasting rump: a feature of all members of the western and some of the eastern races of the Reed Warbler. (For fuller examinations of plumages the reader is advised to consult Wallace (1978), Dowsett-Lemaire (1979), Grant (1980), Pearson (1981) and Harvey and Porter (1984); other references dealing with the problems of separating Marsh from Reed Warblers were given in Chapter 20.)

Fig. 97
Marsh Warbler at nest which reveals its characteristic 'basket handles'. (Eric Hosking)

The normal call of the Marsh Warbler which I heard from birds by the
River Avon I transcribed as a repeated hard 'tic' or 'tchic' with the vowel
quality changing to 'tcheck' or even 'tchuck' perhaps reflecting differences
of mood. The chief alarm call is a high-pitched grating or churring note
without the extreme harshness of the Sedge Warbler but capable of being
developed into a rattle. Other notes include a more subdued 'tic-tirric', a
triple 'wheet' sometimes followed by 'tics', a Reed Warbler-like 'churruc'
and a sharp 'tweek'. Some of these notes may be incorporated in the long
outbursts of song of which the Marsh Warbler is capable.

At its best at the start of the breeding season the song of the Marsh
Warbler is full of vivacity and variety, speedy and extremely mimetic. So
rich in warblings, low buzzes, high notes, trills and imitations the performance has a wide dynamic range and evinces a variety and invention
that cannot be matched except perhaps by an outstanding Blyth's Reed
Warbler. A top singer among Marsh Warblers has no real peer among the
Acrocephalus warblers but a poorer songster or one singing later in the
season may utter a far less varied song, more reminiscent of a Reed or
Sedge Warbler yet still perhaps retaining the 'silvery' quality. There are
sometimes notes suggestive of other *Acrocephalus* warblers in the song but
few of them match the harsh nature of many of them. Notes that I made on
an early singer in the southwest of England revealed many high 'zit-zits'
(which I have found in many singers in England and Europe), buzzes and
long rattling trills as well as Nightingale-like 'jugs' and 'churrs', 'tser-wees',
'choo-ees', 'peeoos', 'fit-phews', 'chirrups', 'plooees', 'tchee-wits', 'turrup-
tsee-tips', 'jack-jacks', 'tcho-tchoos' and so on. Some of these were obviously
imitations, others more typical of many songs. This was a far more exciting
and rewarding song to listen to than I could have heard from any Reed or
Sedge Warbler.

For a sustained and rich solo perhaps only the Nightingale, Song Thrush
or Skylark could have come near the Marsh Warbler for richness and variety
of notes. One Marsh Warbler that I timed sang non-stop for 2 min 20 s,
paused for ten seconds, sang for 0 min 30 s, paused another 20 s, sang for
1 min 35 s, rested for 15 s and sang again for over 3 min – a not untypical
performance early in the breeding season. In some songs a nasal Greenfinch-like 'za-wee' may be prominent and this feature was described by
Walpole-Bond (1938) as 'never absent from the song if of any duration.'
This is an imitation of the Greenfinch, in fact (North and Simms 1958)
and, although audible with other Greenfinch-like notes in some songs, it
may be completely missing from others. The range of mimicry in the Marsh

Fig. 98
*A remarkable trill from
song of the Marsh
Warbler. (Recorded by
V. Lewis, Worcestershire,
June 1975)*

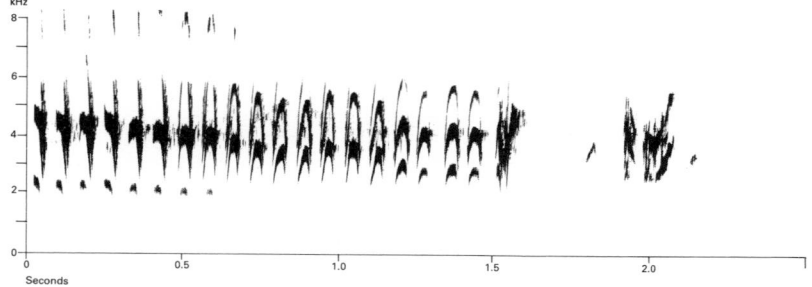

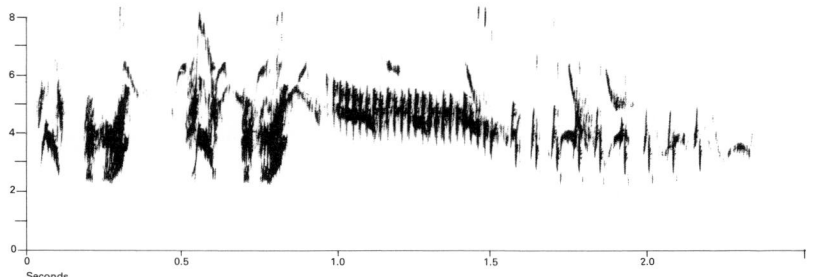

Warbler's songs is very wide indeed and this adds enormously to its fascination. The song structure was studied by Lemaire (1974) who listed imitations of no fewer than 93 European species with the repertoires of individual birds averaging some 30.5 imitations each; the total was later raised to 99 (Dowsett-Lemaire 1979). In England Walpole-Bond (1933) identified 39 species imitated by Sussex Marsh Warblers, including the songs of Starling, Greenfinch, Goldfinch, Linnet, Chaffinch, Yellowhammer, Reed Bunting, Woodlark, Skylark, Tree Pipit and several warbler species; these were added to the song which was one moment slow and subdued, the next rapid and abandoned producing 'a hurried flow of tune, loudly effusive, brilliant, and intensely passionate even to the verge of delirium.' To Walpole-Bond's list I would also add the songs of Swallow, Blackbird and Song Thrush. A recording by Victor Lewis of a Marsh Warbler in Worcestershire in June 1975 revealed a bird whose song was remarkable for its trills some of which had an intriguing diminuendo; this bird is represented in the sonagram (Fig. 99). It produced thirty vocal elements from thirteen different species. When I first watched Marsh Warblers I was impressed by the way in which a singer might appear rather in the manner of a Blackcap and sing from some quite conspicuous post on top of a bush or osier with its creamy white throat puffed out and its mandibles wide apart. High song posts are not uncommon; up to 8 m or more, even on telegraph wires. When the males sang I could sometimes see a yellowish mouth exposed. It appears that a claim by Cantelo (1984) that the colour of the mouth is a useful guide to the identification of *Acrocephalus* warblers was challenged by Harvey and Porter (1984) on the grounds that there is considerable overlap between species and that the colour in the Marsh Warbler ranges from yellow to orange, while in the same species 'the inner edge of the gape can, irrespective of mouth colour, vary from yellow to orange.'

Territorial song tends to ease off or finish about the time of the hatching of the young. Shorter versions may be uttered later on – but the singing season is only from early June to early July – and the record of a bird in song in Wiltshire on 10 September 1948 is quite exceptional (Southern 1949). Singing on the wing and at night does occur but seems rather uncommon, while females have been known to utter a somewhat inferior version of the male's song. The transition of juvenile Marsh Warbler song to that of the adult has been described by Dowsett-Lemaire (1981b); it seems that young birds are still learning song motifs on their way to their wintering grounds but may cease to learn after their arrival in Africa when

Fig. 99
A diminuendo from the same singer as Fig. 98. (Recorded by V. Lewis, Worcestershire, June 1975)

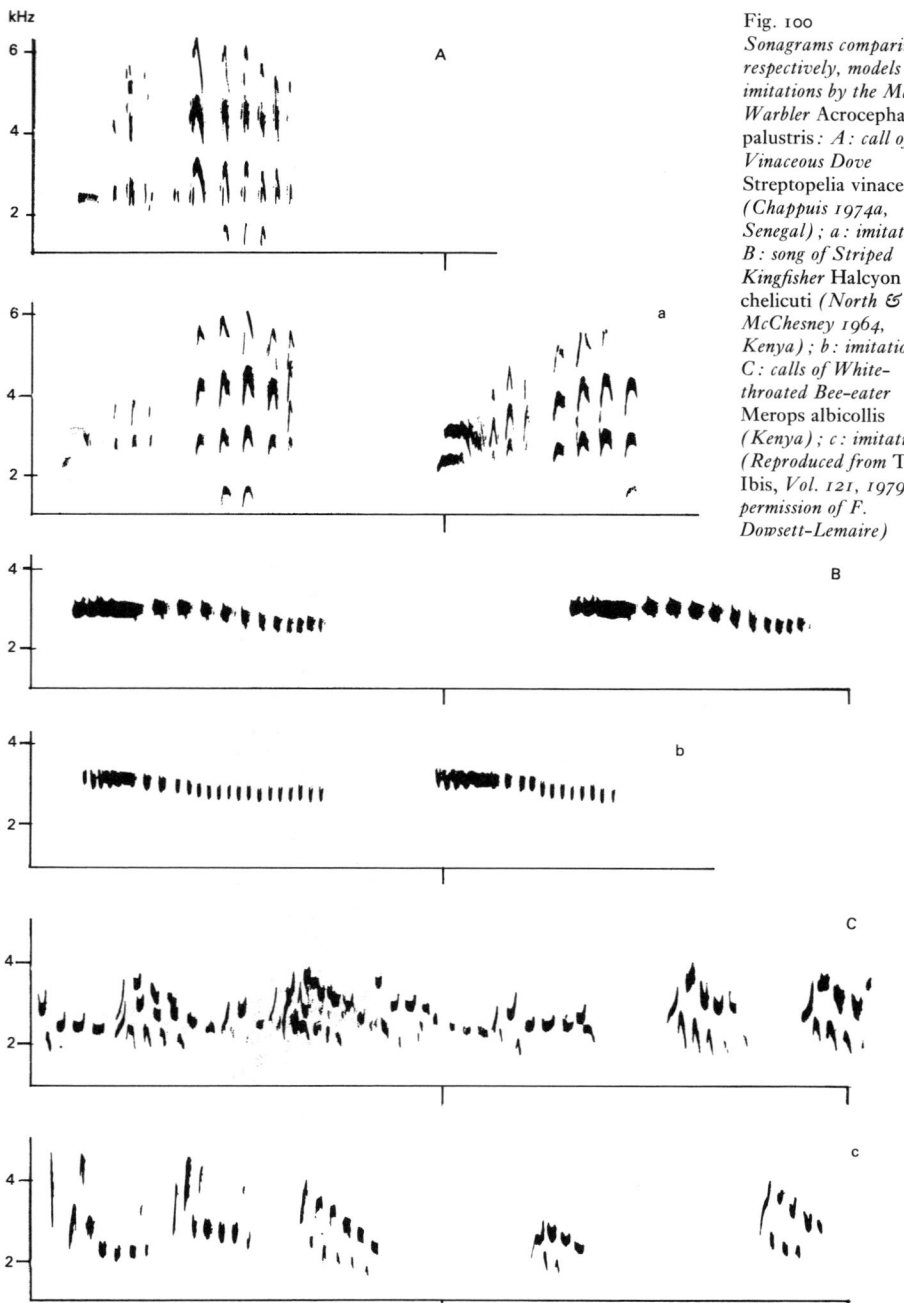

Fig. 100
*Sonagrams comparing,
respectively, models and
imitations by the Marsh
Warbler* Acrocephalus
palustris*: A: call of
Vinaceous Dove*
Streptopelia vinacea
*(Chappuis 1974a,
Senegal); a: imitation;
B: song of Striped
Kingfisher* Halcyon
chelicuti *(North &
McChesney 1964,
Kenya); b: imitation;
C: calls of White-
throated Bee-eater*
Merops albicollis
*(Kenya); c: imitation.
(Reproduced from* The
Ibis, *Vol. 121, 1979, by
permission of F.
Dowsett-Lemaire)*

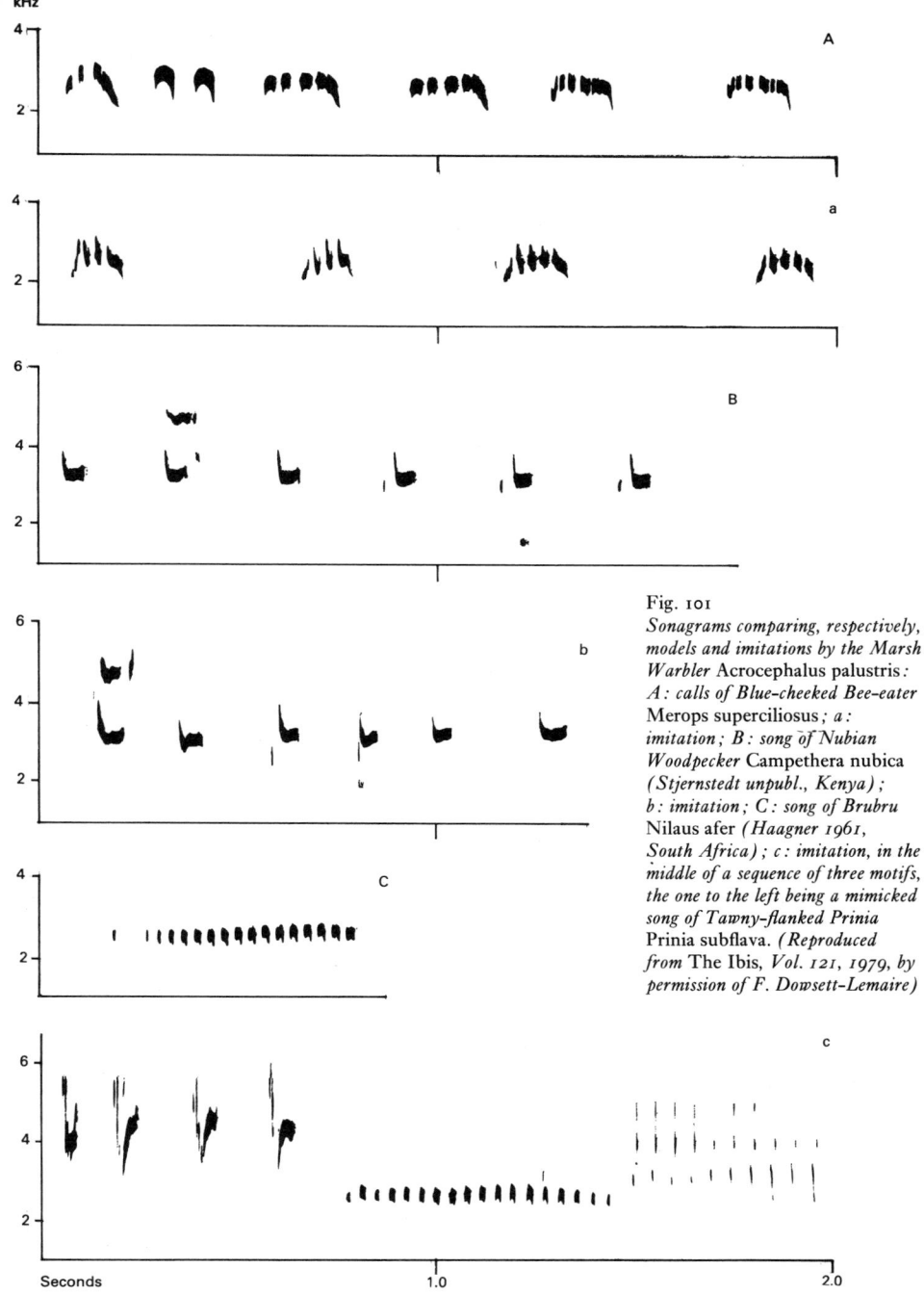

Fig. 101
Sonagrams comparing, respectively, models and imitations by the Marsh Warbler Acrocephalus palustris: *A: calls of Blue-cheeked Bee-eater* Merops superciliosus; *a: imitation; B: song of Nubian Woodpecker* Campethera nubica *(Stjernstedt unpubl., Kenya); b: imitation; C: song of Brubru* Nilaus afer *(Haagner 1961, South Africa); c: imitation, in the middle of a sequence of three motifs, the one to the left being a mimicked song of Tawny-flanked Prinia* Prinia subflava. *(Reproduced from* The Ibis, *Vol. 121, 1979, by permission of F. Dowsett-Lemaire)*

they are 6–7 months old. Françoise Dowsett-Lemaire (1979b) who studied the imitative song of the Marsh Warbler with special regard to the vocal imitations of European birds and mimetic range, fidelity and dialects, found that half of the motifs remained unidentified. This encouraged an investigation in Zambia and Kenya to see if the unrecognized motifs were imitations of birds heard in Africa in the winter quarters rather than on the breeding grounds in Europe. By comparing sonagrams of recordings of Marsh Warblers in Belgium (made by Dowsett-Lemaire), and including the complete repertoire of an individual bird as well as other recordings from France, Sweden and Finland obtained by other sound recordists with models of African species, Françoise Dowsett-Lemaire arrived at a list of African birds imitated by European Marsh Warblers. In fact, there was a total of 133 African species, from 80 passerines and 33 non-passerines, bringing the grand total imitative range for the Marsh Warbler to 212 different species! Individual repertoires contained an average of 76.2 imitated species of which 45 were African and 31.2 European. Noisy African species figured high on the lists and Marsh Warblers did not seem to be very selective in their choice. The frequency of imitations of such African species as the Vinaceous Dove *Streptopelia vinacea* and two species of *Cisticola* suggested that the Marsh Warblers had their autumn quarters in northeast Africa, support for the suggestion by Pearson and Backhurst (1976) that Marsh Warblers 'spend the period September to November, in north-eastern Africa', before migrating to their late winter moulting grounds between southeast Kenya and Natal.

Marsh Warblers are amongst the very latest migrants to arrive back in England in the summer. Early birds may arrive from 20 May but over a period of twenty years the average arrival date in Worcestershire was 3 June. Most birds arrive in Belgium in the second half of May (Dowsett-Lemaire 1981a) and about 20 May in Switzerland (Wiprächtiger 1976). At the time that territories are being taken up song is particularly intense while the males await the arrival of the females over the next ten days or so. Most males are paired within one or two days of the females' arrival and unpaired males may have to defend smaller territories within the community. Where there is a group of birds nesting, the size of the territory can affect the speed with which a male acquires a mate. The density of 8 pairs per hectare, leading to seven nests, found by Wiprächtiger in a mixed strip of land with reeds some 150 m × 5 m seems quite high. Like Reed Warblers, the Marsh Warbler does not care much for the too-close proximity of intruders in a territory but the latter species is more demonstrative, more emotional and more aggressive in its response. Eliot Howard (1948) described encounters between male Marsh and Sedge Warblers in a willow tree that stood in both territories. The Marsh Warbler was generally dominant in these meetings and 'when it attacked, it uttered a peculiar harsh scolding note, raised the feathers on its back, spread out its wings, and betrayed the usual symptoms of emotional excitement.'

Marsh Warblers may find themselves sharing a habitat with other *Acrocephalus* warblers and listening to their songs; we saw in the last chapter how Reed Warblers were induced to mimic Marsh Warblers. Lemaire (1977) found three Reed Warblers in a Marsh Warbler colony uttering songs with phrases from both species' repertoire. Dual-type songs brought reactions from both Marsh and Reed Warblers, while the singers of mixed songs themselves reacted to both species. Birds with only one song type reacted only to their own species and the singers of mixed songs but never to songs of other species in the habitat. In fact, a male Reed Warbler with a mixed or dual-type song mated with a Marsh Warbler and young were hatched. Bigamy is not unknown among Marsh Warblers. During a three year study of colour-ringed Marsh Warblers only five out of 120 males lived bigamously and three adopted this way of life for only a short time; one female shared two males (Dowsett-Lemaire 1979a). Breeding success proved higher for males that lived in a monogamous rather than a bigamous fashion.

When courtship is taking place the male has a 'yawning' kind of display with the bill wide open and the neck outstretched, similar to the displays of Blackcap, Yellowhammer and Tree Sparrow (Turner 1924), while Eliot Howard (1907–14) has described how the male may fan and jerk his tail and extend alternate wings above his back when sexually aroused, often singing in a most passionate and vehement way. I have seen members of a pair fly at each other beating their way up and down in the air with slow exaggerated movements. In his classic work on the warblers Howard also describes how a female displays before coition by quick wing-beats, sometimes with wings alternately extended, and the raising of her tail.

The actual construction of the nest is chiefly the work of the female and in some cases wholly her responsibility. The breeding area is usually one of bushes close to or even over water, although G. K. Yeates (1947) observed that 'I have never found the marsh warbler nesting over water.' Other sites are damp overgrown thickets, hedgerows near standing crops, on the edges of woodland and in the more eastern parts of the bird's range up slopes with scrub and tall plants of a dry rather than aquatic type. The nest may be some 30 cm above the ground in tall plants or even up to 3 m in osiers and shrubs with thin pliable twigs. In Switzerland nests may be within the range of 25–70 cm above the ground. Nests in Worcestershire were often amongst meadowsweet *Filipendula*, and Walpole-Bond who examined 144 English nests in position recorded 51 attached to this plant, 12 to nettles, 8 in willows, 5 in hawthorns and the rest to other plants such as guelder rose and elder. The predilection for meadowsweet was made clear to me also at Villeneuve in Switzerland where I found a nesting colony; this spot had been previously visited many years before by Col. R. F. Meiklejohn, who found a dozen nests in a morning 'all but one in meadowsweet clumps 18 inches (*45 cm*) to 2½ feet (*75 cm*) from the ground. The exception was attached to four slender reeds at the edge of a reed-bed' (Bannerman 1954). On Sedgemoor Marsh Warblers seemed to favour the edges rather than the centres of osier beds.

Much of the nest building is done in the early morning. It starts immediately after pairing and the nest is normally finished after 4–6 days. It is an untidier, flatter and more loosely fashioned construction than that of the Reed Warbler, more suggestive of a *Sylvia* than an *Acrocephalus* warbler. It may be somewhat cylindrical with a depth of 11.5–12 cm. It is built from plant fibre, stalks and grass, often in flower, with the rim of the nest lashed to a stem or twig by strands of material looped out and forming characteristic 'basket handles'. The outer diameter of the cup can vary from 9–11.5 cm with the cup itself from 5–6 cm wide and some 4–5 cm deep. The lining is formed from finer vegetable material, hair and occasionally wool. In

England the breeding season lasts from about the first or second week of June throughout the month, and with such a late start the Marsh Warbler is naturally single-brooded. In southern Europe the peak of laying may be in May, but in Belgium it is late May and in Switzerland late June; but the start may be affected by ambient temperatures several days before. In England the clutch size ranges from three (not all that common) to four or five, with six being very unusual. The average clutch size in Belgium is 4.3 – a figure that declines as the season progresses – although, according to Dowsett-Lemaire (1981a), late and small clutches appear to be as successful as early and large ones. The average clutch size in Switzerland is 4.64 with a slight seasonal decline as well.

The eggs have a pale ground colour and large blotches which make them quite distinctive and less easily mistaken for Reed Warbler eggs which are greenish-brown and less contrasted. Heavier markings may be zoned at the larger end of each egg. In some ways they look rather like small versions of the eggs of Great Reed Warblers. Occasionally erythristic eggs and unmarked ones with white or lavender ground are reported. The eggs are incubated by both parents over a period of about twelve days or somewhat longer. In Switzerland 84% of the eggs being incubated hatched. In his study of Marsh Warblers in the central region of that country Wiprächtiger never came across any instances of Cuckoos, plentiful though they were in

Fig. 102
Pair of Marsh Warblers engaged in feeding and tending a young Cuckoo. Gloucestershire, summer 1951. (Eric Hosking)

the area, parasitizing the warblers. There are, however, some instances of
English Cuckoos laying in Marsh Warbler nests, including a nest at Wrays-
bury in Berkshire in a dense nettle bed with two eggs of the host and one of
the Cuckoo; two weeks later another in the same location had four Marsh
Warbler eggs and a Cuckoo's egg (*Zoologist* 67:397). Two cases were listed
by Lack (1963). Probably these were strays placed in Marsh Warbler nests
because they were in the same habitat as the more common hosts.

It is quite clear that males feed the chicks as often as the females. The
adults are meticulous in the care of the young, removing faeces in their
bills from the nest and maintaining it in a hygienic condition. The success
rate from laying to fledging in Belgium averages 58% with a mean of 2.5
young produced from each nest. Much of the food for the young is collected
outside the domain originally assumed and defended by the male (Dowsett-
Lemaire 1981a). The young are extensively fed on green caterpillars,
chrysalises and Dipterous flies especially Chironomids. The adults pursue
insects of wetland habitats and their larvae such as *Diptera*, small dragonflies, mayflies, beetles, aphids, butterflies and moths as well as spiders,
by searching leaves and twigs rather in the manner of a Willow Warbler or
Chiffchaff. In the autumn birds may change to a vegetarian diet taking
currants and the berries of dogwood and elder (*The Handbook* 1946).

When the young have been reared the adults soon begin their departure
southwards. By the middle of August many have left their few English
breeding grounds. Away from these areas the Marsh Warbler is only a
vagrant from late May to June (and not uncommonly on Fair Isle), and
from August to October, but very fitfully and in small numbers on the
south coast of England as far west as Cornwall and in the Isles of Scilly.
On passage the species is reported in the eastern parts of the Mediterranean
and in southwest Asia and the Middle East. Western populations move to
the southeast arriving in a limited area of northeast Africa to spend 2–4
months before going to the southeast of that continent. The Marsh
Warbler is an abundant migrant across eastern Kenya which it traverses
in December. At Ngulia most birds involved in 'falls' were first-winter
birds but it seemed likely that adults figured more prominently earlier in
the season (Pearson and Backhurst 1976). The species is very scarce in
Uganda, where it is greatly outnumbered by Reed Warblers, but commoner
in Tanzania where, on 13 July 1942, five birds came to lighted windows in
a grassy clearing. R. E. Moreau described the spot at 1000 m above sea
level as 'not like marsh warbler country at all.' Marsh Warblers do not
appear to reach western Zambia or Botswana although a few have appeared
in the extreme southeast of Zaire. There are many recent records from
Malawi and Mozambique but hardly any west of the Rift Valley. A single
bird was ringed near Kano in Nigeria on 28 October 1962, the first record
for that country (Elgood *et al* 1966). Singing males have also been reported
in riverine vegetation in southwest Africa in March with their songs including mimicry of several European species not known in southern Africa
(Becker and Lutgen 1976). Birds also frequent dry scrub and open bushy
habitats in Africa.

The Marsh Warbler is a very rare but distinguished member of the
British avifauna; a bird of the miniature jungles by one or two rivers with
a remarkable song and a distinctive nest. Protected by special legislation
its nest and privacy must continue to remain inviolate.

CHAPTER 22

Rare and Vagrant *Acrocephalus* Warblers

In this chapter we turn our attention to five rare or unusual species of *Acrocephalus* warblers on the British list. These are the Great Reed Warbler, a regular visitor to Britain in small numbers especially in May and June; the Aquatic Warbler, which is a regular autumn visitor in small numbers mostly to southern England, where more than 50% of the records have been of birds taken in mist nets; Blyth's Reed Warbler, an exceptionally rare vagrant in the autumn from the east; the Paddyfield Warbler from Russia and Asia with half a dozen records, and, finally, the Thick-billed Warbler from the Far East – the rarest of them all – with just two records. It is the first two species – the Great Reed Warbler and the Aquatic Warbler – which offer the best chance of being seen by birdwatchers in the British Isles.

The Great Reed Warbler

The Great Reed Warbler is the largest of the European warblers – 19 cm in length – bigger indeed than a Corn Bunting or a Skylark. It resembles a large Reed Warbler but has a narrow creamy-white eyestripe which is sometimes conspicuous, sometimes less distinct and a longer, stouter bill; it also seems more rufous in colour and longer-tailed as well. Although the actions and habits of this giant warbler may suggest those of the Reed Warbler, it is very much heavier in its movements and flight. When airborne it appears almost weighed down, progressing with fanned tail, frequent wingbeats and an erratic movement low over the reed beds which it inhabits. So robust a bird and one which skulks less than its relation should not be easily overlooked. It may be rather retiring on some days but on others I have found it much more willing to show itself, perching on trees and bushes, reeds and even overhead wires. I first became acquainted nearly forty years ago with the Great Reed Warbler on the Naardermeer Reserve in Holland where I used a local fisherman's boat as a hide for observing the species. This wetland was an important wildlife sanctuary and among the pools, reed beds and remote channels I watched Marsh and Montagu's Harriers. 'Both reed and great reed warblers churred and chattered away among the tall stems while I could see great crested grebes, teal, mallard, garganey and red-crested pochards floating quietly on the small secluded lakes. I was particularly thrilled to see eight spoonbills and seven purple herons' (Simms 1976) – a reminder of England's long-lost fenlands!

The Great Reed Warbler is a common bird in Holland in the breeding season. It prefers reed beds as a nesting habitat, like the Reed Warbler, but I also found, as Dr H. N. Kluyver (1961–2) noted, that it 'exhibits a much greater liking than the smaller species for tall reeds growing close to an area of open water.' I have also watched Great Reed Warblers in Provence,

Fig. 103
*Great Reed Warbler at
the nest. (Eric Hosking)*

along stagnant reed-fringed channels in southern Spain and in Italian and
Greek marshes. In 1954 I obtained mono sound recordings of the songs of
Great Reed Warblers performing along the reed-fringed dykes or *roubines*
around Salin de Badon, a regular habitat for them. In 1973 I returned with
a team from the BBC's Natural History Unit on an expedition to obtain
stereo recordings of Great Reed Warblers as well as more than twenty
other bird species that I had recorded in 1954. One of these stereo recordings is of a Great Reed Warbler singing along a reed-fringed *roubine* near
Albaron with Bitterns booming and frogs croaking in the background.
Many lagoons in the Camargue held breeding Great Reed Warblers and
as we made our way along the Canal du Rhône in a cabin cruiser we passed
countless singing males which dominated the sounds of other singing
warblers and small songbirds. Nests are not too difficult to find, but I was
disturbed to see on my last visit that an English birdwatcher had so
stamped his way through the thin curtain of reeds along the dyke that his
only too obvious path had left the nest open for all to see.
    It is the loud croaking song of the Great Reed Warbler that unam-

biguously draws our attention to a male holding a territory: 'kar-kar-kar, karra-karra-karra, keet.' The call note is a harsh 'tchack' or 'tack' while the bird may also utter a deep croaking churr and a harsh alarm. The male may also squat in the nest while the female builds, and utter a special note to stimulate and encourage her in the task of constructing the nest herself. The song is remarkable, dominating and easy to recognize. It is also loud, harsh and croaking in quality with some notes repeated several times. One example from a sound recording that I obtained in the Camargue can be transcribed as 'kar-kar, keet-keet-keet, karra-karra, orre-orre, tchu-tchu-tchu, karra-kee'. Two of the commonest of the deep throaty elements are 'karra-karras' and 'kar-kars' or 'gurk-gurks'. The bird's popular name in Holland is Groote Karekiet. A Great Reed Warbler heard singing in May in a small reed bed in Kent produced a whole range of notes (Houston and Robinson 1951): 'uk-uk' (very low and subdued), 'gerruk-gerruk' (louder and guttural), 'ee-ee' (a very high-pitched almost pig-like squeal), 'sweedle-sweedle', 'tu-ee-tu-ee', 'kuk-kuk', 'wee-wee-wee' as well as low croaking 'turrs' and grating rattles. After listening to many birds in the field and on recordings I find that the pauses between song-bursts vary on average from 1–3 s, while bursts of song can range in duration from 20 s to as long as 20 min or more without a break. The bill is opened very wide during

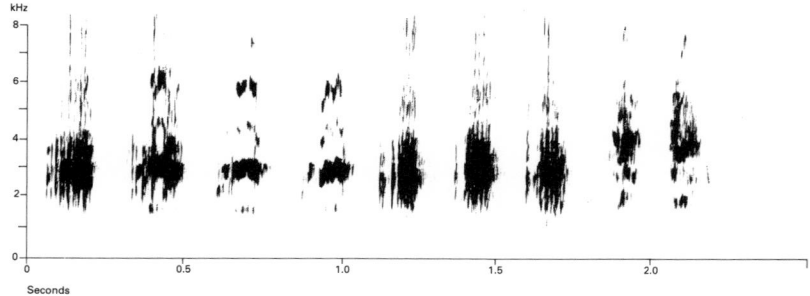

Fig. 104
*Song of Great Reed
Warbler. It begins with
'kar', is followed by an
intermediate 'kiet-kar'
note and then runs 'kiet-
kiet-kar-kar-kar-kiet-
kiet'. (Recorded by Eric
Simms, Camargue, May
1954)*

singing while the bird often braces itself between two reed stems with one leg straight and the other folded, or takes up a position on a spray or bush-top in the more traditional way. Imitations may sometimes be included but a subsong described in *The Handbook* (1946) as 'extremely attractive' I have not heard. Guy Mountfort (1951) wrote how 'the pre-dawn chorus is of remarkable volume' and to wake up to this sound on a boat moored along the edge of a reed bed or dyke is a real aural experience. I have sometimes heard bursts of song during the night. As a singing male swings his head from side to side there may be something of a ventriloquial quality about his song but even the low notes may be audible as much as 450 m away. Birds are known to sing spasmodically in Africa (Lynes 1938) and I have experienced short bursts from birds on the Serengeti Plains and in Uganda in late December.

In Europe Great Reed Warblers often breed socially. The first males come back to Holland from Africa in late April or early May, with the females making their appearance some 7–10 days later. At this time song is sustained by the males for long periods and Dr Kluyver wrote that 'I hardly know of any other song-bird that sings so incessantly from dawn to even-

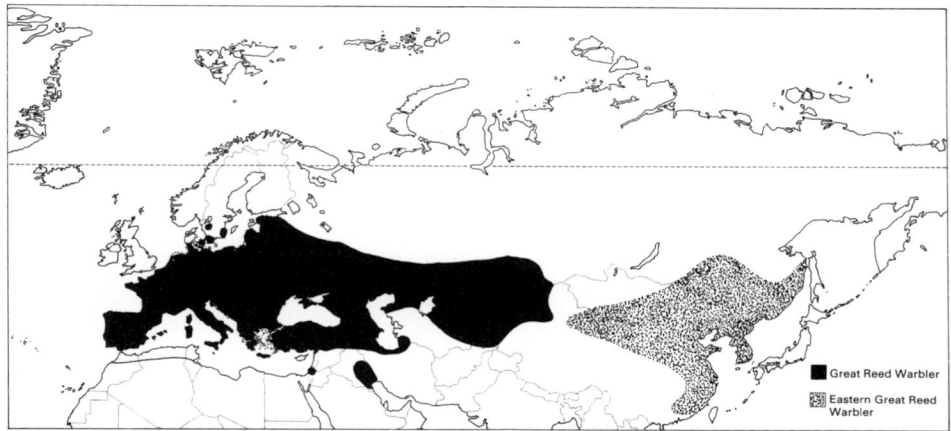

Great Reed Warbler

Eastern Great Reed Warbler

tide.' Song declines after the females have joined the males and ceases when the former begin to incubate the eggs. After this the male will sing only at a rival or intruder or when he comes to feed his mate on the nest.

The nest itself is suspended from four or five, sometimes up to eight reed stems, 0.6–1.3 m above the water. Some nests have been recorded almost 3 m above the surface of the water. The materials include reed and plant stems and fibres, down and spiders' webs. The nest is larger than that of the Reed Warbler, often with a depth of 13–14 cm, an outer diameter of 9 cm and a cup inside with a width of 5–6 cm and a depth of 5 cm. Some nests are deeper than this so that the back of an incubating Great Reed Warbler may barely be visible above the edge of the nest. The nest is coarser and less a work of art than that of the Reed Warbler, but being rather small in proportion may collapse under the weight of the young; we have seen earlier that nests in *Typha* often disintegrate. In order to prevent the nest slipping down the stems of the reeds, the female dredges up damp material from the water which she then weaves around the stems. The structure may be so waterlogged at first that the reeds break, especially in high winds, but after the nest has dried out this danger is lessened to some extent. The eggs are usually 4–6 in number with bluish or greenish grounds and boldly marked with umber and black. Incubation is carried out by both parents and lasts 14–15 days. The young are fed by both male and female and remain some twelve days in the nest. The species is normally single-brooded. Cuckoos will parasitize Great Reed Warblers and the egg match is extraordinarily good in both size and colour.

In a study of Great Reed Warblers in Poland, Andrzej Dyrcz (1977) over a period of five years located 345 broods; of these 12% were polygamous. It had previously been suggested by Kluyver (1955, 1961–2) that polygamy in Great Reed Warblers 'occurs most frequently where reed beds adjoin a habitat (e.g. *Typha*) which is attractive to males but unsuitable to females' since the nests collapse. After vainly trying in the company of her mate to build nests in an unhelpful site, she may then desert and attach herself to another neighbouring male even if he has already mated. Dyrcz suggested that polygamy among these warblers could be considered as 'an adaptation to a local and short-lasting abundance of food'. He found

Fig. 105
Breeding ranges of the Great Reed and Eastern Great Reed Warblers.

Fig. 106
*Habitat of the Great
Reed Warbler along reed-
fringed channel near a
gardien's cabane in the
Camargue. (Eric Simms,
May 1973)*

quite a high mortality from starvation among nestlings in polygamous broods, particularly in cold, wet spells, but polygamous birds were slightly more successful in the size of the clutch, the average weight of nestlings and rearing success than monogamous ones. Great Reed Warblers can be quite aggressive birds – one in Warwickshire attacked breeding Reed Warblers, actually grasping one and falling into the water with it (Jackson and Stone 1983); Dyrcz was often attacked by birds which even struck his head. When three birds from a polygamous group were involved rather than two they provided what he called a 'reinforcement of defence'.

In Holland and the Camargue I have watched Great Reed Warblers hunting large *Aeshna* dragonflies as well as damselflies. These are hammered to death against a stem, but I have not seen them washed before being given to the young, as has been reported. Guy Mountfort (1951) vividly described how 'the sight of a bedraggled nest, sagging under the weight of five large nestlings, each with the wings or bodies of half-digested dragon-flies protruding like moustaches on either side of their bills, is unforgettable.' Other foods taken include many wetland insects and their larvae: craneflies, mayflies, stoneflies, aphids, the larvae of *Lepidoptera* and beetles, including *Donacia*, the adults of which frequent the leaves of pondweeds and water lilies, and whose larvae feed on aquatic plants. Large spiders, freshwater shrimps and small fish have also been recorded. The Great Reed Warbler also feeds regularly on the ground not far from its reed bed home in the manner of a thrush or pipit when it assumes a chat-like and 'alert, upright position' so unlike the stance of a warbler that it might be mistaken for a Rufous Bush Robin (Sharrock 1984). In the autumn berries may be added to the diet including those of elder. In the winter quarters across tropical and southern Africa the bird may frequent reed beds and papyrus swamps, but it also occurs and feeds amongst bush and tall grass not necessarily close to water.

The Great Reed Warbler has increased its range in Sweden especially in the 1960s (Holmbring 1973) and there were earlier expansions of range to Denmark and Finland. These movements have been attributed to rises in the mean spring and summer temperatures in the north of Europe (Voous 1961) but since then the mean summer temperature has dropped: a factor that may have induced northern and arctic birds to become established as breeding species in Britain. Since the species breeds as near as Holland and in much of France and Belgium, it seems odd that it has not yet begun to breed even in small numbers in England. Since this may yet happen, although there seem to be some factors at present militating against this, I have deliberately given some space to the ecology and habits of the Great Reed Warbler. Records in the British Isles extend chiefly from May to November but it is significant that up to 1972, 71% fell in the six week period from 7 May to 17 June (Sharrock 1976); a bird appeared at Slapton in Devon on 13 April 1981, the first record for that month. Although birds appeared in spring as far west as Co. Cork and north to Shetland, 43% of the total were in the counties of Suffolk, Essex, Kent and Sussex with the highest number in Kent. Many birds have frequented reed beds in late spring and summer with males taking up territories for a short time. Frensham Great Pond was a favoured site in the 1960s and another was Fleet Pond in Hampshire, visited in 1970 and 1975, with a singing male there from 26 May to 4 June 1980. There may be no records in one spring and in another as many as eight, as occurred between May and July in 1978. The average number of records per year is about four, and there is a small autumn peak in late August with birds again being reported from southern parts of England.

The Aquatic Warbler

The second of the rare visitors – the Aquatic Warbler – breeds across central Europe from the Baltic to the Black and Caspian Seas, reaching westwards as far as west Germany and eastwards across Russia to the Ural Mountains as well as in Hungary and northern Italy. The range lies between 44°N and 60°N but the bird is not a regular breeder in Holland as has been widely suggested by many of the field guides; M. J. Tekke (1973) listed only three breeding records for that country. There is a discontinuous pattern to the breeding range, due probably to a contraction of range brought about by the draining of suitable habitats (Voous 1961); the species has also declined in the Soviet Union. It is a bird of the marginal zones around freshwater lakes and marshes, preferring open tracts of *Carex* sedges, iris and low vegetation to large reed beds and tall growths. Aquatic Warblers can be found in similar habitats to those of Sedge Warblers. Here the first species needs careful identification especially as bright young Sedge Warblers – juveniles or first-winter ones – bear a superficial resemblance to Aquatic Warblers. Both species are about the same size and also occur in similar habitats on migration.

The Aquatic Warbler is yellowish-buff on the upper parts but is duller in adults, and there is a brighter orange-yellow on young birds. It is dis-

Fig. 107
*Breeding range of the
Aquatic Warbler.*

tinguished by 'long, black, almost continuous streaks on back creating a "tiger stripe" pattern. Down the edge of the mantle, on either side of the central black stripes, are two broad, pale "tram lines"' (Porter 1983). Birds seen in Britain have been described as 'more yellow than the sedge warbler' (Moule, Harber 1950), as resembling 'a very buff-coloured sedge warbler' (Meiklejohn and Reed 1955) and 'even sandy' (Williamson 1950). Other features are the bold head pattern with buff eye-stripes and crown stripe, although the last character was noted in a Sedge Warbler in the Isles of Scilly (Flumm 1984), and a streaked rump and upper tail coverts. The legs are a bright flesh or pearly-pink colour whereas they are light brown in Sedge Warblers. Another difference is that the Aquatic Warbler has pointed tail feathers, which give a 'spiky' effect to a graduated tail while the Sedge Warbler has rounded tail feathers. Apparently adult Aquatic Warblers reveal much greater tail abrasion in autumn than do adult Sedge Warblers (Rumsey 1984).

   Among the Aquatic Warblers recorded in Britain the call has been described as 'a distinct hard single note' (*Somerset Birds* 1963), 'a sharp and rather low note ... "chut"' (Wilkins 1939), 'a soft "tucc tucc"' (Keighley 1950), and 'a short rather loud "teck"' (Warburg and Warmington 1956), all suggestive of the Sedge Warbler but rather deeper. When nearing the nest the female utters a low 'tze tze' rather like a Lesser Whitethroat. Since Aquatic Warblers have been known to sing in England, the song is worthy of attention. To me it is very different from that of the Sedge Warbler, being simpler in pattern and with shorter uncomplicated phrases, which are separated by appreciable pauses, without the invention or musicality of that bird. Many phrases are really short. One German singer produced six phrases whose durations in seconds were 4, 6, 4, 3, 8 and 6, while another had a run of eleven phrases lasting 2, 3, 1, 7, 4, 5, 3, 4, 5, 2 and 3 seconds; these strophes are very different from the long runs of the Sedge Warbler. I have transcribed one burst of song as 'chirr-tee-tee-tee, chirr, titee-tsitee-chirr-titítit' and another from a second German singer as 'err-err-errer, twee-twee, choo-choo-choo, tee-tee-tee, chirr-err-err.' Two further examples are 'err-dididi-err-dududu' and 'tsrr, de-de-de, tsrr du-du-du, twrr, tweet-tweet-tweet.' These four examples show the singular lack of variety in the Aquatic Warbler's song and these short, slow phrases could be diagnostic. There is a song-flight but this is employed far less often than that of the Sedge Warbler. A bird sang in some sallows near the old Dungeness lighthouse in Kent on 19 April 1949, uttering a typical song in short bursts with some trills and notes like those of a Yellow Wagtail and a Blackbird for half an hour (Manser and Owen 1950). Another Aquatic Warbler sang in May 1963 at Blagdon Reservoir suggesting a poor, less harsh Sedge Warbler. The bird is also a great skulker.

Aquatic Warblers breed in marshes favouring clumps of sedge, generally avoiding reed beds and willows. Here they build nests of grass, plant fibres, down and cobwebs, smaller and deeper than those of Sedge Warblers, and sometimes lined with feathers. The site is usually just above ground or water level, tucked amongst stems but not attached or woven to them. The bird is single-brooded and begins to nest about the middle of May. Clutches are usually of five or six eggs with a white, buff or olive ground and covered with many speckles and mottlings of olive-buff. Incubation may be carried out by both parents but the female takes the greater share; the young are tended by both parents. Males and females, according to Heise (1970), who studied the breeding biology of this warbler, hold separate territories and are probably promiscuous.

The Aquatic Warbler is a regular autumn visitor to southern England but it is a vagrant to Wales, Ireland, Scotland, Denmark, Norway (the second record here was in 1981), southern Sweden, Finland and Latvia. The bird probably winters in tropical Africa but its true winter distribution is not properly known. The autumn passage is southerly through the region of the Mediterranean to Iberia. Small numbers were recorded in the southwest of Iberia in autumn by C. J. Henty (1961). Birds appear to cross the Mediterranean to the north of Nigeria but by 1964 there had been no records from west Africa (Elgood et al 1966).

Up to 1940, some 35 Aquatic Warblers had been reported in Britain and Ireland. By 1958 the total had risen to 50 and, after a marked rise in numbers dating from 1969, the years 1958–1972 yielded 215 more. Until 1972, 94% of the records of Aquatic Warblers in Britain had been very much compressed into the months of August and September with the main peak from 13–19 August (Sharrock and Sharrock 1976). By 1975 the overall total had reached at least 360, of which nearly 66% had occurred in the preceding six years. The records for the ensuing years were as follows: 1976: 93 (a remarkable year!); 1977: 34; 1978: 13; 1979: 25; 1980: 20; 1981: 18; 1982: 16 and 1983: 0.

All the records up to 1972 were carefully examined and analysed by Dr J. T. R. Sharrock (1974). Almost 80% of them could be attributed to the eight English coastal counties ranging from Kent to the Isles of Scilly with the distribution as follows: Kent 3%, Sussex 6%, Hampshire and the Isle of Wight 15%, Dorset 18%, Devon 13%, Cornwall 9% and the Isles of Scilly 6%. There were very few records from the east coast counties from Yorkshire down to Essex but there were some autumn records from Ireland, the Channel Islands, Shetland and elsewhere. If these Aquatic Warblers had originated in the east then a much more southeasterly bias might have been expected in England; Dr Sharrock tentatively suggested the possibility that 'the autumn occurrences of Aquatic Warblers result from reverse migration on a north-westerly course of birds from Italy.'

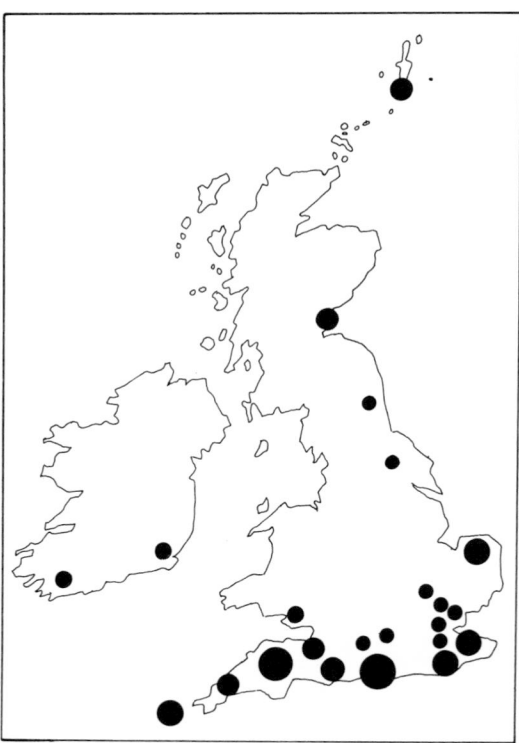

Fig. 108
Autumn concentrations of
Aquatic Warblers
1958–67. Circle size in
proportion to number of
records. (After Sharrock
1973)

C. Joiris (1975) found a dead Aquatic Warbler on a research ship in the
North Sea and he believed that this record was more consistent with an
earlier theory (Sharrock 1973) of the 'displacement of birds migrating
south-west from the northern part of their breeding range.' Dr Sharrock
(1975) was of the opinion that, although vagrancy from north European
Aquatic Warblers was a possible explanation for their appearance mainly
on the south coast of England, 'yet the pattern of British and Irish records
just does not fit it.' There was the possibility that a bias towards ringing
work on the south coast compared to the east was influencing the figures,
and B. Pattenden (1976) pointed out that when there were no sight records
of Aquatic Warblers at Radipole in Dorset, 22 had actually been trapped.
In fact, the increased use of mist nets by 1969 meant that no fewer than 45
of the 94 Aquatic Warblers recorded in the British Isles had been trapped
largely by mist nets. Ringing showed that Aquatic Warblers occurred
among Sedge Warblers in a ratio of 1 in over 1000 at Chew Valley Lake in
inland Somerset, 1 in about 450 at Slapton by the sea in Devon and 1 in
fewer than 30 in the Isles of Scilly (Sharrock 1973). Pattenden also held the
view that, due to the east to northeast winds which prevail from July to
September because of anticyclonic conditions, British Aquatic Warblers
do not come from southern Europe but originate in central Europe. This
matter has not yet been resolved.

Blyth's Reed Warbler

Blyth's Reed Warbler is a very much rarer visitor to Britain with only twelve or thirteen accepted records up to 1982. These are of one on Fair Isle from 29–30 September 1910, and then a batch of records for 1912: one at Spurn Point 20 September, one on Holy Island 25 September, four or five single birds on Fair Isle 24 September–1 October and one on the Dudgeon Lightship off Norfolk; one on Fair Isle 24 September 1928, one on Cape Clear Island in Co. Cork from 13–19 October 1969, at Filey Brigg in Yorkshire on 30 August 1975, and in Orkney on 5 and 13 October 1979.

Others have also been claimed in recent years but not so far accepted. The species breeds from Finland, where it has hybridized with the Marsh Warbler, east across the Baltic States, including Latvia where the bird is common, and then through central Asia to Siberia and southern Asia, to the Aral-Caspian region, eastern Iran, northern Afghanistan and northwest Mongolia. The breeding range stretches from 35°N to 63°N and from the July isotherm of 10.5°C to 32.5°C. This warbler winters in India, Sri Lanka and Burma. In fact, numbers are apparently so high in the Soviet Union that it is now one of the commonest wintering warblers on the subcontinent of India. Birds appear to moult in autumn in northwest India, where like Pallas's Grasshopper Warbler some suffer an almost total loss of flying ability for a time, before spreading across the subcontinent (Gaston 1976). Breeding birds from the most westerly parts of the range migrate to the southeast but the westerly drift of many eastern breeding species is now well accepted and may account for records of Blyth's Reed Warbler in the British Isles.

Fig. 109
Breeding range of Blyth's Reed Warbler.

There is insufficient room to give here all the details of how to identify this very rare warbler, but a long and valuable paper on this subject, richly illustrated, was published in *British Birds* by Harvey and Porter (1984). This makes it clear that emphasis on various structural features of Blyth's Reed Warbler in recognition such as tail, wings and bill may have been too emphatic in the past and the authors state that 'There is, however, a *tendency*, and it is not more than that, for Blyth's Reed to *appear* structurally different.' What follows now is a synopsis of the authors' detailed writing. In colour Blyth's Reed Warbler is 'a uniform, cold, earthy olive-grey-brown above' with a slight greenish wash in spring, while first-winter birds are 'a cold, grey-olive-brown, with a faint rufous wash but no contrasting rump colour.' On the head there is a slight dusky eye-stripe and a short, dirty white supercilium which always 'bulges' or widens before the eye, although it may either stop at the eye or fade away just behind it. The combination of dark tapering bill with the dusky eye-stripe and contrasting supercilium, the long flattened forehead and upward inclined head may help in the identification of this difficult species. There are also several postures adopted by Blyth's Reed Warbler which may be helpful. The bird 'frequently cocks, flicks and fans its tail, drawing attention to itself by these actions' while in the company of other individuals it often assumes a 'banana' posture, especially when feeding, with the neck stretched out and the head and bill turned upwards, forming with the raised tail a smooth and gentle curve. It has been compared by some observers to a small Clamorous Reed or Cetti's Warbler with rounded wings and a fanned tail. When singing, the bird raises its crown feathers and the combination of angular crown and low forehead gives the impression that the bird has a long bill. Blyth's Reed Warbler perches in and progresses horizontally through trees and shrubs, but does not apparently clamber up and down reeds which have little attraction for it. On the ground it hops with a flattened profile, both head and tail somewhat raised.

The breeding habitat for Blyth's Reed Warbler consists usually of the dry scrubby edges of woods and fields, orchards and even gardens with a rich shrub and field layer. This field layer is quite luxuriant as we saw in Chapter 17 (Koskimies 1980). The bird is not a typical wetland species and the thickets and bushes in which it nests are not necessarily near water. The nest is compact and built of grasses and leaves with a deep cup and an outer coat of spiders' webs and plant down. It may be built on to stems or be partially suspended from them, up to a metre above the ground. Nesting is often about the middle of June and the species is consequently single-brooded. The clutch is usually 4–5 eggs, sometimes 6, which are very variable in colour and may sometimes resemble those of the Marsh Warbler but they tend to be much browner or redder. The young are fed by both parents and fledge after about eleven days in the nest. On migration, Blyth's Reed Warblers often appear in the canopy of trees and in tall shrubs where they are not at all retiring and also in lower growth. They sometimes roost in tall bamboo clumps. Diesselhorst (1965) found the species in Nepal in thick cover of secondary growth but he never met with it 'in swampy localities in the same area and season.'

The contact or feeding call of Blyth's Reed Warbler has been variously described as a soft 'tt-tt-tt', a distinctive 'chek', a sharp 'tchik, tchik' ('a sound like flint and steel being struck together'), a double 'tshuk-tshuk', a penetrating 'thik', and in the case of the bird on Holy Island a double 'tup, tup' which, according to *The Handbook*, was 'something like the alarm of Lesser Whitethroat, but much softer and less harsh.' There is also a harsh churring of alarm which is so similar to the churrs of Reed and Marsh Warbler that it is of little help in recognition.

The song is very rich and varied but in comparison with that of the Marsh

Warbler is louder, mellower, slower and more dignified and with an obvious deliberate spacing of the motifs. The call notes 'tchek, tchek' are regularly incorporated in the song itself. A recording made in Finland in June 1958 by my friend and fellow wildlife sound recordist Nils Linnman, of a very fine male Blyth's Reed Warbler, well illustrates the clear and separate motifs each of which is singularly well articulated. A transcription of part of this song can be printed as 'chip-chip-chip, tchek-tchek, ziteree-ziteree-ziteree, cheeoo-cheeoo, tulit-tulit, wit-wit-wit-wit-wit, tchek-tchek, tchirp-tchirp, pit-pit-pit, zitsee-eroo' and sustained with variations for two minutes or more. Such stanzas of two, three or four notes are much commoner in the song of Blyth's Reed than in the performance of the Marsh Warbler. E. S. Ptushenko (1951–4) observed how birds in the Soviet Union 'constantly interpolated more and more notes, perfectly imitated from the songs of other birds.' During the time of pairing, the male will sing day and night but the daytime song is hurried and frequently interrupted while the bird forages and attends to other matters. The night song is given from a definite song-post such as a projecting branch or the canopy of a bush and is much louder, more relaxed and deliberate while, according to Ptushenko, 'Males sing particularly well and frequently on quiet, moonlit nights.' A number of accounts of the song were drawn together by Boswall (1968). Birds will also sing in their winter quarters and M. D. Lister (1952) heard song in India for minutes on end, sometimes as a whisper, sometimes as a crescendo that lasted several seconds. In its winter song varied, sweet and pure notes were combined with more discordant ones.

The Paddyfield Warbler

The fourth subject of this chapter is the Paddyfield Warbler with nine records in the British Isles so far at the time of writing in the autumn of 1984. The occurrences so far are as follows; Fair Isle, 26 September–1 October 1925 and 16 September 1953: Hartlepool in Cleveland, 18–22 September 1969: Isles of Scilly from September to 15 October 1974; Hauxley in Northumberland, 12 October 1974; Priors Park in Tyne and Wear, 27 September 1981; Tring in Hertfordshire, (the first inland record) on 9

Fig. 110
Breeding range of the Paddyfield Warbler.

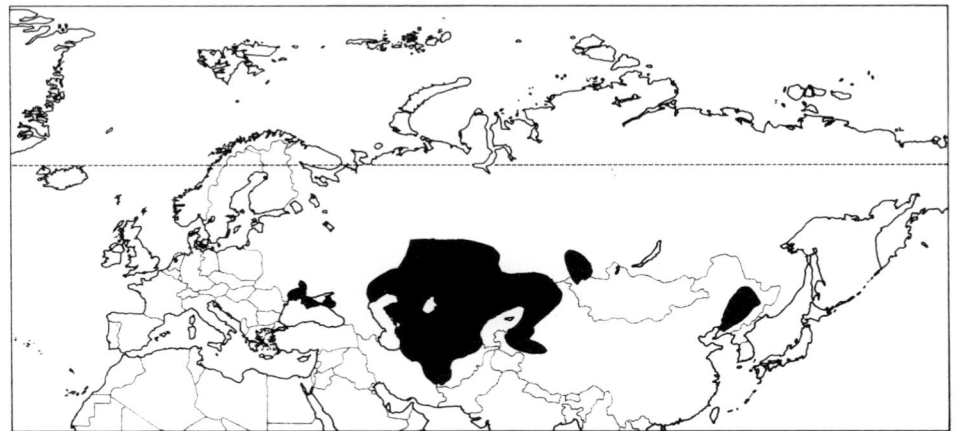

November 1981 (which came to light as the result of a coloured photograph taken to the British Trust for Ornithology headquarters at Tring in
the same county being submitted to an annual B.T.O. conference!). The
last records were at South Walney in Cumbria from 11–13 September 1982,
and Scilly on 26–7 September 1983. The Paddyfield Warbler is a bird of
the central and western Palaearctic, breeding in southern Russia and Asia
from the Caspian Sea east to central Mongolia, south to Iran and Afghanistan and probably northern India as well as Manchuria. The breeding limits
lie between 25°N and 60°N or the July isotherms of 20°C and 32.5°C.
The distribution is a discontinuous one and the breeding rather sporadic
but according to Voous (1961), 'Only in Kashmir is the Paddy-field
Warbler known as an abundant breeding bird.' It frequents the shore
vegetation of rivers and lakes in steppe country with reed, sedges and
willows, but few sizeable bushes as well as grassy wetlands in the valleys of
rivers, and in Kashmir up to heights of over 2000 m. The male will often
climb a tall reed and utter a song suggestive of the Marsh Warbler, but it is
said to be softer and without any jarring notes (Sushkin 1908). Certainly
the species nests in reed beds in Mongolia (Kitson 1980).

The Paddyfield Warbler spends the winter in southern Iran, east across
to northern India. It is a common winter visitor to Sind, especially favouring
any area of water with reeds, sedges, grass and tamarisks as well as the
fringes of swamps, marsh grasslands and flooded rice fields. It may often
skulk in India but it is a noisy, active bird, calling 'chik-chik' as it creeps
amongst thick cover near water, often moving close to the ground where
it feeds on small marsh-haunting insects, taking them also near or even
on the surface of water. It may also sing in its winter quarters uttering a
rather hurried little ditty, softer and less harsh than the song of the Marsh
Warbler. Equipped with a short bill and sporting a long palish supercilium,
which often widens beyond the eye, with a darker lateral stripe above on
the crown and with a tail even longer and wings shorter than those of
Blyth's Reed Warbler, the Paddyfield Warbler is less difficult to recognize
than some of its congeners despite some variations in plumage. The bird
is rufous or sandy brown. Full plumage descriptions have been given by
Flumm and Lord (1978), Bell (1979) and Meek and Little (1979); these
are very helpful for anyone seeking specific identification of this rare
warbler. The last two authors listed seven diagnostic features for the bird
seen in Northumberland: a short wing (57 mm), wing-point formed by
third and fourth primaries, blunt wing with the outside secondary just
10 mm shorter than the wing-tip, an emarginated fifth primary, a rufous
rump that contrasted with the pale sandy-brown back, a distinct supercilium and a short bill, only 9 mm from tip to feathers.

On its breeding grounds in the Kirghiz steppe country the Paddyfield
Warbler arrives back about the third week of May (Sushkin 1908). The
nest is in reeds and sited from 0.6–1.3 m up, suspended between four or
five stems, as well as sedges and other plants growing in water. It is a tight
structure of closely woven grass stems and leaf fibres, perhaps 13 cm in
height and with the cup about 6.5 cm deep, formed from reed flowers and
down. The breeding season ranges from May to July so that the species
may be double-brooded. The clutch is usually of 4–5 eggs, occasionally 6.
The eggs resemble those of the Reed Warbler but are more heavily marked
and darkly spotted with the markings tending to form a cap at the end
(Harrison 1975).

The Thick-billed Warbler

The final character in this chapter on rare and vagrant *Acrocephalus* warblers in the British Isles is the Thick-billed Warbler, *Acrocephalus aëdon*, formerly in the genus *Phragmaticola*. Its world distribution was described in Chapter 17. This bird, the size of a Great Reed Warbler, from southeast Asia is a great rarity indeed with only two recorded appearances in the British Isles, both in the extreme north. One was captured on Fair Isle on 6 October 1955 and a second was trapped on Whalsay in Shetland on 23 September 1971, taken to Lerwick on the island of Mainland and

Fig. 111
Thick-billed (top) and Great Reed Warblers in flight – at first glance very similar but the former trails a narrow, almost pointed tail quite unlike the broad paddle of the latter. (D. I. M. Wallace)

died there on 25 September. The first bird on Fair Isle gave the impression of a large bird with a long rounded tail, and a rufous rump contrasting with the uniform olive-brown colour of the mantle and wings. It was flushed from a turnip-rig and took cover in a dense patch of hogweed. The bird had no eye-stripe and showed a deep bill with a curved culmen (Williamson *et al* 1957). There was a general resemblance to a Great Reed Warbler but the longer tail, bill-shape, rufous rump, blue legs and lack of eye-stripe were all helpful in identifying it. It was seen 'threading its way dexterously through the reedy grass and other cover along the burn' (Williamson 1965). In the hand the bill is diagnostic as well as the long, broad rounded first primary. The sexes are alike.

In the field the bird recalls a large Garden Warbler rather than an *Acrocephalus*. Dr J. T. R. Sharrock (1983) watched Thick-billed Warblers wintering in Thailand and found the most distinctive features to be, firstly, a head like a Garden Warbler with no supercilium or eye-stripe but a conspicuous black eye, and, secondly, a slow heavy demeanour in the bushes reminiscent of a Barred or Orphean Warbler. Birds can cling well to stems but rarely sidle up and down them in the way that many *Acrocephalus* warblers do. On the ground the bird behaves like a thrush or shrike. When disturbed the Thick-billed Warbler often calls with an abrupt 'tschok-tschok' (Neufeldt 1967), clearly the same notes as were quoted by Hollom (1960): a loud harsh 'chok-chok' or 'tschak-tschak'.

When really excited this warbler utters a loud chattering 'cherr-cherr-tschok', and also raises the long feathers on its crown into a crest.

The breeding habitat consists of thickets, which the Thick-billed Warbler prefers to reed beds, and it does not demand the presence of water in the environment. In Amurland it can be found in dense hazel scrub on hillsides, in more open woods of birch with a shrub layer of hazel, oak and *Lespedeza* (bush-clover), while in the southern parts of Ussuriland the habitats include groves of oaks on hillsides where earlier fires and clearance have ensured a rich scrub growth. Other sites are bushy regions alongside woods, damp meadows with isolated trees, bushes and thick grass as well as gardens, roadside verges, the edges of cornfields, in river valleys and sometimes near standing water. The breeding area also includes terrain in southern Siberia, Manchuria and northern Mongolia. Here the species is entirely a day-singer even during the hottest parts of the day. Miss Neufeldt (1967) has provided a great deal of information about the vocalizations, habitats and breeding behaviour of the Thick-billed Warbler. The male sings from exposed song-posts on the tops of trees and shrubs, uttering 'a loud and sonorous song' unlike that of the Great Reed Warbler. It begins with repetitions of the typical 'tschok-tschok' calls followed by a hurried chatter mixed up with melodious motifs and imitations. The song has been compared to that of the Icterine Warbler but with loud fluty notes suggestive of the Nightingale. Miss Neufeldt found that birds in Amurland would imitate the notes of the Brown Shrike, Gray's Grasshopper Warbler, Von Schrenck's Sedge Warbler, Siberian Rubythroat and Black-tailed Hawfinch. In its wintering area the bird still looks for bushy terrain and is often recorded in tea and coffee plantations. Birds will sing here in their winter homes in Yunnan, southeast China, Burma and Thailand and parts of India and Pakistan as well as on passage.

In Amurland nests may be finished by 8 June, but this is an early date. They are built of coarse grass by the females alone, and are rather untidy in form. Their diameters may range from 93–130 mm and their depths from 67–92 mm. All the nests that Miss Neufeldt found were at heights of 60–100 cm above the ground and in 'the forked crowns of shrubs of hazel, oak, *Spiraea* spp., willow *Salix spp.* and rose.' The nest is never lashed to upright stems in the way that the Great Reed Warbler builds its nest. The cup is lined with fine grasses and rootlets and she did not find a single nest out of twenty that was lined with wool or horsehair, materials described for the species by Taczanowski (1872). The usual clutch is formed from five eggs which are strikingly beautiful, being a rose or slightly pinkish-violet colour and inscribed with veins or fine pencilled lines of chestnut, brown or black. According to E. P. Spangenberg (1965), the Thick-billed Warbler is the main fosterer of the Cuckoo in the Iman region of Ussuriland. The eggs are incubated by the female alone and she may be fed on the nest by her mate. Hatching takes place in about fourteen days and the young depart from the nest after about the same period. Nestlings from 5–7 days old are fed on tiny caterpillars, spiders and their cocoons. Young birds about twelve days old are given the caterpillars of hawkmoths as well as both adult and larval noctuid and geometer moths, grasshoppers, crickets and *Neuroptera*. During the summer months the adult Thick-billed Warblers consume large numbers of grasshoppers.

Hippolais or **Tree Warblers**

CHAPTER **23**

Sometimes called the Tree Warblers, the genus *Hippolais* is quite closely related in its physical characters to the *Acrocephalus* warblers, the subjects of the last six chapters. Indeed the Marsh Warbler bears some resemblance to the birds of the *Hippolais* genus, which consists of only six species. These are birds of the Palaearctic and also of the fringes of the Oriental and Ethiopian zoogeographical regions. Five of the species breed in Europe and none in the British Isles, although there is an isolated nesting record for one of them. Two of the species, the Icterine Warbler *Hippolais icterina* and the Melodious Warbler *H. polyglotta*, occur as annual visitors to Great Britain and Ireland and two others, the Olivaceous Warbler *H. pallida* and the Booted Warbler *H. caligata*, are merely vagrants. The two remaining species are not yet on the British list but might well appear there in time. These are the Olive-tree Warbler *H. olivetorum* and Upcher's Warbler *H. languida*. These are somewhat unfamiliar warblers to many British ornithologists although all but Upcher's breed in Europe; the Booted comes no further west as a breeding bird than Russia.

At the outset it has to be said that the identification of any of these warblers can be extremely difficult and demands records of every detail of plumage, shape, voice and behaviour which always need to be rechecked. Any previous knowledge and understanding of this genus with habitat preferences, life styles and variations will all help in the difficult matter of identification. It may not be too difficult to arrive at a generic identification but specific determination may be another matter and depends on the amassing of as much information as possible. D. I. M. Wallace (1964) with his outstanding knowledge of the genus recommends standing still while observing a *Hippolais* warbler since 'stalking a *Hippolais* is usually a fruitless manoeuvre and the odds definitely favour the person who is sitting on his bottom with a mounted telescope to hand.' The issue can be complicated further by variations in the plumage not only between species but in different members of the same species.

In the matter of plumage the six species can be roughly divided into three groups: green and yellow (Icterine and Melodious), brownish (Olivaceous and Booted) and greyish (Olive-tree and Upcher's). However a special problem may arise with the Icterine and Melodious Warblers with a dull plumage in the case of adults and young, in which both may lack any visible yellow, and the greenish tone to their upperparts may be suppressed. There can be variations in tone among the other four species as well. These reservations and full descriptions have been provided by Wallace (1964) who pointed out that: 'Plumage characters are patently unreliable, only one action is unique to a particular species and most recorded calls are common to more than two.' Each bird provides a very special challenge to the observer. With somewhat similar morphological characteristics they can be most difficult to separate from each other, especially at a distance and in poor illumination. Although close to *Acrocephalus*, the *Hippolais* warblers tend to possess longer wings and tails with the latter square-ended or almost square but with rounded corners rather than well rounded or slightly graduated. They also have short undertail coverts which help to provide the body shape; this seems to be belly-down giving the impression of a plump, pear-shaped bird, while the back and tail assume a distinctive flat appearance. The heads carry short supercilia and also eye-rings. All the species with their continuous pale area linking the supercilium and throat also have a 'bare-faced' appearance (Grant 1978, Beaman and Woodcock 1978). The heads are prominent and foreheads are steeper than those, say, of *Phylloscopus* warblers. The bills of all the six species have dark upper and paler lower mandibles and a distinctive breadth which, appreciated only with difficulty in the field, is one of the most important keys to the genus.

They are quite large, heavily built warblers except for one species – the Booted Warbler – and when perched the greater part of the body seems to be forward of the legs. When moving about, *Hippolais* warblers may assume both lateral and vertical attitudes and seem rather careless and pushing in the way that they negotiate foliage. All the species when feeding display a diagnostic habit of stretching up after berries and dislodging them with a tug. All six species will flick their tails, but Upcher's Warbler has the most pronounced tail movement, opening it and regularly cocking it as well while the other species employ only shallow actions. All the warblers also seem to possess prominent legs and feet suggestive of the larger *Acrocephalus* warblers; the Olive-tree appears to have the largest. It also has the longest tail of the six warblers with Upcher's coming second; but the latter bird, in the field, seems to own the longer because of the regular flicking movements which naturally draw an observer's attention to it. In order of descending tail length the rest of the warblers can be placed as follows: Olivaceous, Icterine, Sykes's Warbler (a race of the Booted Warbler from Turkestan), Melodious and Booted Warbler from the south Russian steppes. With the exception of the Booted Warbler, the *Hippolais* warblers appear rather heavy fliers somewhat like the *Sylvia* warblers. The flight characteristics are controlled by the length and formation of the main flight feathers. Icterine, Olive-tree and Upcher's Warblers, with long wings, fly with confidence and what Wallace called 'a characteristic fluid wing beat', while the short-winged Melodious and Olivaceous Warblers seem to have to work rather hard with fluttering movements or intervals when taking off or flying low.

We owe much of our present knowledge about these warblers to D. I. M. Wallace who is responsible for the helpful and sympathetic line drawings and paintings in this book. He summed up the general character of the *Hippolais* genus as 'possessing neither the grace of *Phylloscopus* nor the irascible alertness of *Sylvia* and borrowing only some of the actions of *Acrocephalus*.' He also drew attention to the problem of the Garden Warbler which, glimpsed only momentarily or in shadow and capable of displaying a range of different shades, may by body-shape, tail and leg-colour suggest a *Hippolais* warbler. However, this *Sylvia* warbler has a short bill and 'chunky' head, lacks a defined supercilium and also the wash of yellow on the throat, lores and supercilium 'shown by even the drabbest "grey-and-white" Icterine and Melodious Warblers' (Grant 1978).

Dimensions and weights of Hippolais warblers   Table 21

| Species | Wing (mm) | | Tail (mm) | | Bill (mm) | | Tarsus (mm) | | Weight (gm) |
	Range	Mean	Range	Mean	Range	Mean	Range	Mean	
Olivaceous Warbler H. pallida opaca	61–75	68.18	49–65	57.37	16.5–19.5	17.90	21.5–25.5	23.32	12.3
H.p. elaeica	60–72	65.86	47–59	52.99	13.5–18.5	15.93	19.5–24.5	21.85	9.15
Booted Warbler	54–65	59.60	41–54	47.90	11.5–14.5	13.15	18.5–23.5	21.05	8.4–9.8
Upcher's Warbler	68–81	74.81	55–68	61.63	15.5–19.5	17.60	21–25	22.92	
Olive-tree Warbler	79–93	85.71	59–76	67.55	17–22	19.47	21.5–27	24.08	
Icterine Warbler	69–85	76.87	46–60	52.82	14–18.5	16.20	19–23.5	21.32	12.4–15
Melodious Warbler	59–70	64.69	45–57	50.65	13–18	15.54	18.5–24.5	21.33	12.7

(after Williamson 1976)

The songs of *Hippolais* warblers are varied, babbling, often harsh and somewhat Acrocephaline, sometimes mimetic and usually delivered from a prominent song-post. These will be discussed more fully under the accounts of individual species. The calls are various kinds of click, teck or churr, and as they tend to be rather similar and even to resemble those from birds of other genera they are not very reliable. However, some are thought to be diagnostic. Here are the main calls.

Types of call in Hippolais warblers   Table 22

Species	Short, sharp 'tics', 'chicks', 'tschicks', 'trrks', 'bicks'	Short, Sylvia-like fuller 'teks', 'cheks', 'chacks'	Low prolonged churrings	Diagnostic notes
Olivaceous Warbler	●	●	●	
Booted Warbler	●	●	●	
Upcher's Warbler	●		●	loud 'chuck'
Olive-tree Warbler				'tr-trik'
Icterine Warbler		●	●	'biberoy' or 'dideroid' : rare 'hooeet'
Melodious Warbler	●	●	●	sparrowlike chatter and rare 'hooeet'

(after Smith 1959, Wallace 1964 and Simms unpublished)

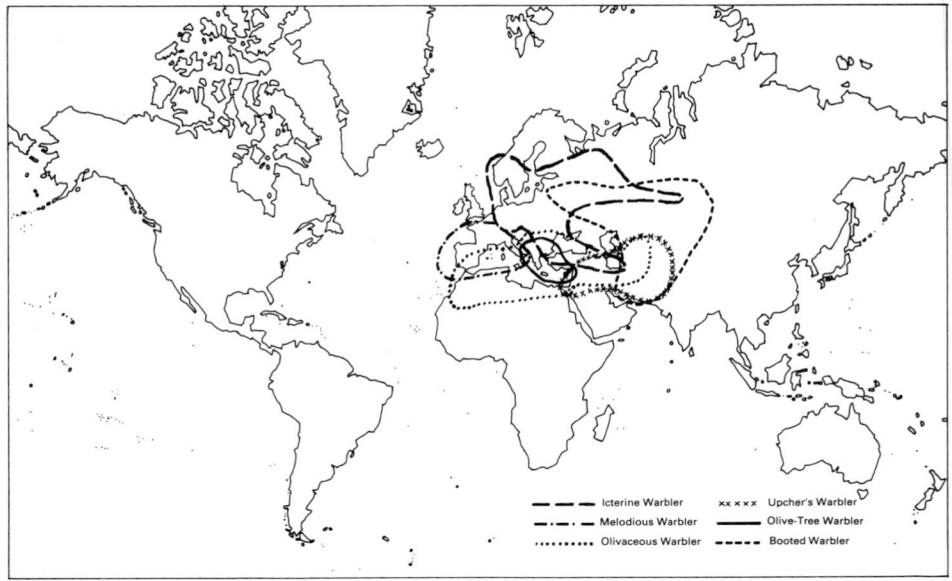

▬ ▬ ▬ Icterine Warbler	xx x xx Upcher's Warbler
▬ ∙ ▬ ∙ ▬ Melodious Warbler	▬▬▬▬ Olive-Tree Warbler
∙∙∙∙∙∙∙∙∙∙ Olivaceous Warbler	▬ ▬ ▬ ▬ Booted Warbler

Fig. 112
Breeding range of 6
Hippolais *species*.

A simple identification key is provided at the end of this chapter (Table 23).

The six species which breed in Europe and western Asia tend to replace each other geographically, but there are some overlaps. The monotypic Icterine Warbler is the most widespread of the six 'ranging from 67° in Norway, 61° in Sweden, 63° in Finland and 64° in Russia southwards to the Alps, northern Yugoslavia, Bulgaria and the northern Caucasus' (Beven 1974). In Asia the species breeds as far as the Altai Mountains as well as in western Anatolia with an isolated population in Iran. The Melodious Warbler complements the distribution of the Icterine by enjoying a more westerly range in Iberia, France but not the north and east of that country, the south Tyrol, Italy, Yugoslavia and northwest Africa. It may be that the Melodious Warbler was the southwest European form of the Icterine Warbler with the geographical isolation occurring during the last period of glaciation. Voous (1961) was unaware of any instances of interspecific competition between the two species, but where the range overlaps as it does in Burgundy along a strip some 20 km wide, Ferry and Deschaintre (1966) were able to demonstrate that each male keeps out other males of both species from his territory, reacting to the song of the other species in the same fashion as to that of his own but in a less intense way. The Olivaceous Warbler also shares the more westerly part of its breeding range with the Melodious Warbler, the more central part with both Icterine and Olive-tree Warbler and the more easterly part with both Booted and Upcher's Warblers. How these different species from the same genus live alongside each other is not fully known.

The Olive-tree Warbler is not yet on the British list. It is the largest member of the *Hippolais* genus being some 15 cm in length, compared with 11.5 cm for the Booted Warbler and 13–14 cm for the other four species. It is a bird with a prominent long, deep bill. The adult is a brownish-grey in colour with a 'dusty' appearance. The head has something of a hooded aspect occasioned by a pale grey patch in front of the eye and an area of dark grey around the ears and sides of the head. There is a broad dirty-white supercilium and a whitish eye-ring. The primaries are dark grey and the tail a lighter grey but both are darker than the rest of the plumage. The tertials and inner secondaries are clearly edged with white. When the bird is at rest, and up to the middle of June, a light-coloured panel may be seen on the wing. The underparts are a dusty white. First-winter birds are more olive. The legs and feet vary in colour from greyish-ochre to dull slate with a bluish tinge; the upper mandible is a dark greyish horn and the lower light horn or yellowish. Its bulky build, its greyness and large bill are all useful as guides in identification, but to make it more difficult the bird is rather skulking by nature.

The Olive-tree Warbler is a nesting bird of southeastern Europe and southwest Asia, breeding in Yugoslavia, Albania, Greece, Bulgaria,

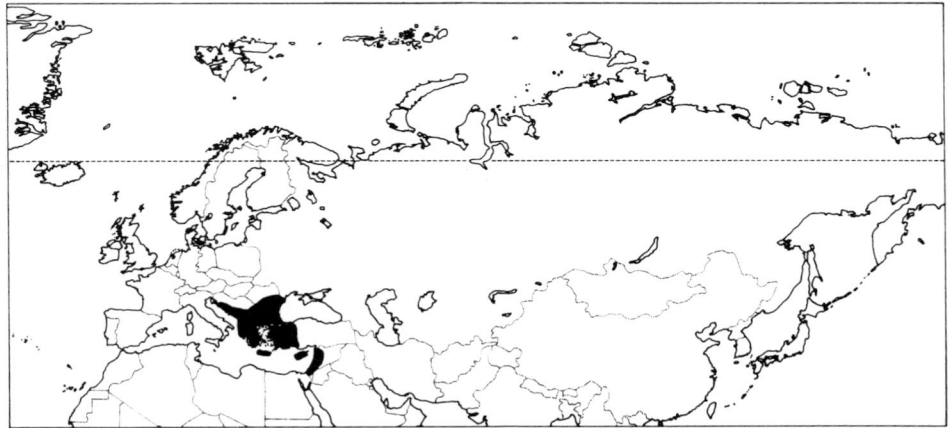

Romania (from 1977), western Asia Minor, Syria, Israel, Iran, Crete and perhaps Cyprus. It is a bird I associate in Greece with olive groves and vineyards, scrubby vegetation and brushwood, often on hillsides; it apparently likes almond orchards as well. The species is quite common in northern Greece from early May to August and fairly well spread across much of that country. The nest is built in the forks of olive trees or oaks, 1–3 m up and is constructed of grass and wool. The 3–4 eggs are an attractive pale pink with fine spots. The bird calls with a repeated 'took-took' or a 'tr-trik' (Nisbet and Smout 1957) but one of the other species quickly doubling up its monosyllabic 'trrk' might prove a complication. To me the song seems to be a combination of the 'took' or 'tchook' notes with 'tchoos'; it is rich and rounded, altogether more contralto in quality than the songs of the other *Hippolais* warblers, and delivered with a slow but sustained pace. It has sometimes suggested to me something of the character of the Great Reed Warbler. I have timed bursts of song from three to as much as fifteen seconds in duration.

Olive-tree Warblers have appeared as vagrants in Algeria and Italy. They are migrants that fly south for the winter to the savannah woodlands

Fig. 113
Breeding range of Olive-tree Warbler.

from East Africa to the Transvaal. The species appears in dry bush country in northern Kenya, and fourteen were trapped and examined at Ngulia in Kenya from 28 November to 11 December 1972 (Pearson and Backhurst 1976). Birds may begin to moult in northeast Africa where they spend some time from as early as late November but the moult 'certainly occurs later than in most Olivaceous and Upcher's warblers.'

The other species not yet on the British list is, in fact, Upcher's Warbler. The adult has a dusky or olivaceous grey quality to the upperparts with perhaps something of a bluish tinge on the mantle, head and rump. The head is slightly darker than the mantle and there is also a thin pale greyish-white supercilium and obvious whitish ring around the eye as well as dark lores and ear coverts. The grey wings have unmarked greater coverts but the tertials and inner secondaries, with dark centres and whitish edges, combine to produce a dull but visible wing panel. The tail is a dusky grey and, unlike that of the other *Hippolais* species, contrasts clearly with the bird's paler rump. The outer tail feathers are brownish-white, tipped with white on the inner web while the penultimate feathers are only slightly tipped with white. The immature bird is less brown than a worn adult and has a more obvious wing panel. The prominent tail is frequently flicked up and down and this tends to make the wings seem shorter than they actually are. The high crown, size and colouring might suggest a *Sylvia* warbler or a chat but the Garden Warbler – perhaps the closest candidate – is more olive-brown in first-winter garb, has a different wing formula and lacks the characteristic tail markings. The call-notes of Upcher's Warblers are a loud 'chuck', said to be diagnostic, as well as a sharp double 'tchik-tchik' and a low sustained churring.

Upcher's Warbler is a bird of hill scrub, wooded valleys, bushy plains and gardens up to 2000 m and is said to be commoner than the Olivaceous Warbler 'in open and semi-desert country' (Williamson 1976). The breeding range stretches from the Near East across northern Iran, Afghanistan, the Aral-Caspian region and Turkestan to the Tian Shan range of mountains and Tadzhikistan. Birds apparently winter in Kenya and Tanzania in dry thornbush country and in Somalia. Many birds pass through Arabia;

Fig. 114
Breeding range of
Upcher's Warbler.

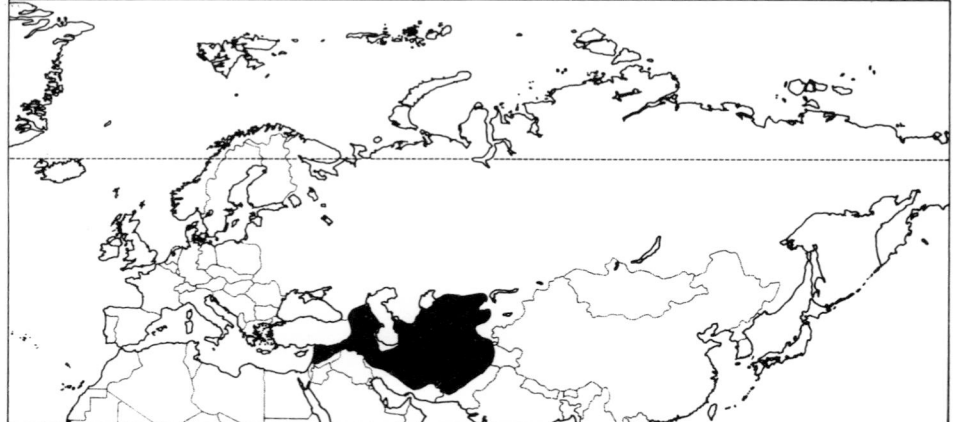

Smith (1957) found birds common in any woodland below 1650 m as well as arid acacia near the coast; many could be heard in song in Eritrea in late September. The moult of this species appears to be very protracted.

We have seen that the monotypic Icterine and Melodious Warblers are the two *Hippolais* species most likely to be seen by observers in the British Isles. Both can be classified as scarce vagrants. Before 1951 only three Melodious Warblers had been recorded in Britain and Ireland but from 1953 onwards the species was recognized every year, with as many as 48 being reported in 1962. This increase in the number of records could be attributed to better methods of trapping in the field as well as the improved identification of birds in a difficult genus. Between 1958 and 1967 a total of 646 Melodious or Icterine Warblers was recorded and almost 82% of these could be subdivided into the two different species (Sharrock 1969). In fact, 217 Melodious Warblers or 41% of the identified birds were listed with the overwhelming majority occurring from August to October and only eight in the spring – between the middle of May and June. The peak was from 27 August to 16 September, a period of three weeks that accounted for 53% of the autumn records. All these were in the south and west with six counties – Dorset, the Isles of Scilly, Pembrokeshire, Caernarvonshire and Cos. Wexford and Cork – providing 74% of the autumn records in the decade. Such a pattern was believed to reflect the western breeding range of this warbler. Possible explanations for this pattern of birds in the autumn were displacement in strong winds from the south or southwest, or by a random dispersal after the breeding season, or by reversed migration. The evidence at first seemed to suggest that the last of these three causes was the most likely, but since some of both the Icterine and Melodious Warblers recorded are first-year birds there may be random post-juvenile scatter in anticyclonic conditions. The autumn arrival was generally synchronous through Britain and Ireland but there was a slight tendency for birds to arrive earlier in the east, with a peak from 20 August to 16 September in southeast compared to the peak in southwest England. Most of the rather few spring records were from Pembrokeshire but others were also reported from Kent, Lancashire and Shetland.

In the same ten-year period from 1958 to 1967, 311 Icterine Warblers were recorded with 85% of the reports being in autumn but with rather more spring records than the eight for the Melodious Warbler: 45, in fact. Most spring records were in Shetland with scattered occurrences of one or two birds from southern Ireland, Pembrokeshire, Dorset, Sussex, Yorkshire, Fife and Angus. The autumn pattern for the Icterine Warblers was very different from the spring one with most records on the east coast of England from Northumberland down to Norfolk but there were also numbers from Kent, Dorset, the Isles of Scilly and Co. Cork, the last county providing as many records as Norfolk. The lowest autumn total was in 1961 with 16 birds and the highest in 1966 with 52. Again it was thought that the spread of British and Irish records could be accounted for by the easterly breeding distribution of the species.

However, Co. Cork posed an interesting problem. Here the number of Icterine Warblers exceeded the total of Melodious and, as we have seen already, rivalled Norfolk on the east coast of England. Yet the Isles of Scilly received three or four times the number of Melodious Warblers to Icterine. A. R. Dean (1984) examined all the autumn records for the

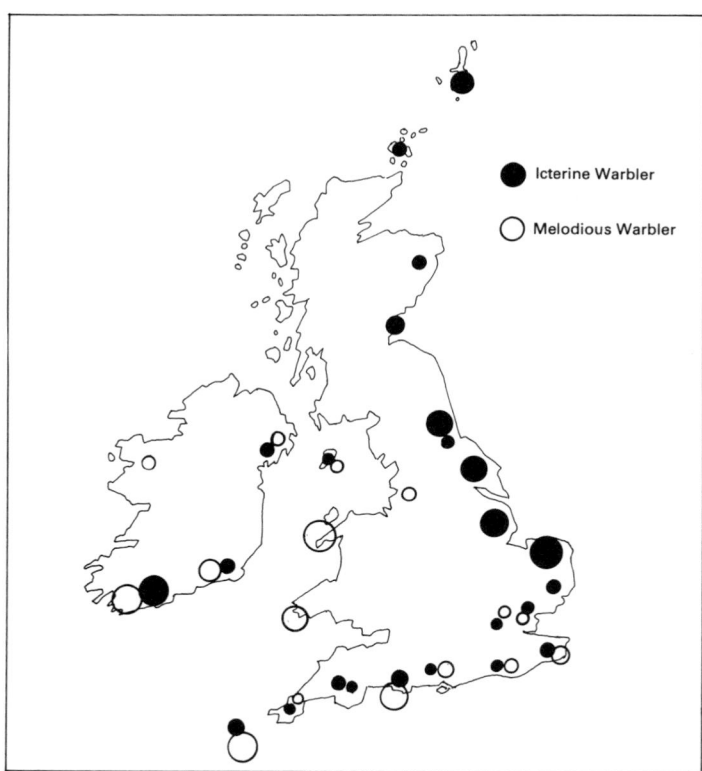

Fig. 115
Autumn concentrations of Melodious and Icterine Warblers 1958–67. Circle size in proportion to records. (After Sharrock 1969)

period 1968–81 from the local bird reports for Cornwall and the Isles of Scilly. His analysis showed that from 1968 to 1973 with 41 Melodious and only 14 Icterine Warblers the relative position of the two species was unchanged. Then from 1974 onwards the number of records increased with many more human visitors making for the islands in the autumn but the relative positions changed dramatically. During the period from 1974 to 1981, according to Dean, 'there have been 80–90 melodious (an average of 11 per year and an increase of 60%), but about 110 icterine warblers (an average of 14 per year and an increase of 500%).' So the Isles of Scilly have joined Co. Cork as rivals to the east coast of England for Icterine Warblers. The peak period in Scilly for both *Hippolais* species is from the second half of September through the first half of October: a month after Sharrock's national peak. Records for Cape Clear Island in Co. Cork from 1959–1967 are of 24 Melodious and 33 Icterine Warblers, from 1968–1973 of 13 Melodious and 12 Icterine, and from 1974–1981 of 11 Melodious and 34 Icterine Warblers. What has brought about this change in the proportions of the two species is not yet known.

The Olivaceous Warbler has several races, two of which have been recorded in Britain. Both have upperparts of greyish-olive colour with brown wings and tail, brownish-white outer and penultimate tail feathers with whitish tips and creamy or pale buff underparts. The race *Hippolais pallida opaca* breeds in southeast Spain, Morocco, northern Algeria and northern Tunisia; a first-winter bird of this race was identified on Skokholm. Birds of the eastern race *H.p. elaeica*, recorded in Fife and Donegal, are greenish in the first-winter plumage; however, adults in fresh plumage in Africa have this suffusion reversed! The eastern race has a breeding distribution in southeast Europe and southwest Asia, nesting in southern Hungary, Greece, Yugoslavia and the Balkans to the Near East and then through Transcaspia and Turkestan to Tian Shan, Iran and northern Afghanistan. The typical race *pallida* is Egyptian, while another race *reiseri* is confined to the oases of southern Algeria and Tunisia. A possible fifth race *laeneni* which is on average 'a little smaller and paler' from Maidugari and Lake Chad is so close to *pallida* that separation seems hardly

---

Key to the Genus Hippolais   Table 23

---

1. *Species with long wings*

Folded wings with longest primary tips either reaching or falling behind the end of the upper tail coverts; also slim point of bunched primaries occupying about a third of the total wing-length visible.

A. Prominent long, dagger-like bill; grey; large size and heavy build; tertials and inner secondaries with clear white edges; broad pale supercilium; crown slightly peaked at the back	Olive-tree Warbler
B. Long bill; dusky grey; quite large body; dark tail, often cocked with white edges and contrasting with pale rump; dull 'wing panel'; pale grey-white supercilium; loud 'chuck' call	Upcher's Warbler
C. Fairly long bill; medium size; greenish-olive upperparts, often yellowish; tertials and inner secondaries edged with golden yellow forming a distinct wing panel; yellow supercilium; nervous and prone to fly in dashing manner. Song with 'biberoy' call	Icterine Warbler (adult in normal plumage)
D. As C but upper parts greyish; tertials and inner secondaries white-edged, not providing a distinct 'panel' effect	Icterine Warbler (immature and variant adult)

2. *Species with short wings*

Folded wings have longest primary tips either not reaching or only just reaching the end of the upper tail coverts; also the point of the bunched primaries occupying about a quarter of total wing-length visible.

A. Prominent pointed bill with apparent length accentuated by flat crown to head; medium size; whitish eye-ring; dull white supercilium; no wing patch	Olivaceous Warbler
B. Strong bill but apparent length decreased by high rounded crown; greenish-brown upperparts; underparts strong yellow; pale edges of tertials and inner secondaries not producing a wing-panel; 'quiet' feeder, not prone to fly.	Melodious Warbler (adult in normal plumage)
C. As B but upper parts brownish and wings not marked	Melodious Warbler (immature and atypical adult)
D. Short bill suggestive of *Phylloscopus*; small body; rounded head; no definite features in plumage	Booted Warbler

---

(after Wallace 1964, Sharrock 1965 and Williamson 1976)

justified (White 1960). Somewhat like a Melodious Warbler with short wings, the Olivaceous is larger and duller, lacking the greens and yellows of that species; it has also been compared to a greyish-brown Reed Warbler with a long bill and flat crown. Before 1958 there were only two records (in 1951 and 1956 in Britain and Ireland) of the Olivaceous Warbler, but eight were recorded between 1958 and 1972. (There will be a fuller discussion of this warbler in Chapter 26.)

The last of the *Hippolais* warblers is the Booted Warbler: a lesser edition of the Olivaceous with a thin weak bill and a seemingly closer relationship to the *Phylloscopus* leaf warblers than to the *Hippolais* tree warblers. There are two races; the first, the Booted Warbler, *Hippolais caligata caligata*, breeds in Russia eastwards to the Yenisei and south to the Kirghiz Steppes and southern Urals, wintering in northern India. The second, Sykes's Warbler, which is more grey and less olive, *H.c. rama*, can be found in Iran, Afghanistan, Transcaspia and east to Tian Shan and Sinkiang and winters across India to Sri Lanka and in southern Arabia. The Booted Warbler also has a finer bill and shorter tail than Sykes's Warbler. Central Asia seems to contain a number of hybrid populations with one, *annectens*, recognized in the Soviet Union as a proper subspecies. The species has appeared in Sweden, Finland (where a bird sang near Helsinki), on Heligoland and in Scotland and England.

For the winter the Melodious Warbler and the *opaca* race of the Olivaceous fly to west Africa, while the *elaeica* race of the Olivaceous, the Olive-tree and Upcher's Warblers make for east or southern Africa. The Booted Warbler of Russia and Asia winters in northern India, and Sykes's goes to India and Sri Lanka.

The Icterine Warbler

The Icterine is a striking warbler indeed, with a very dramatic song to which I have listened in central Europe, and also in England. It bears some resemblance to a rather stout *Phylloscopus* or leaf warbler with generally olive-brown upperparts and lemon-coloured or bright yellow underparts. In the last chapter I drew attention to a variant plumage in both adult and immature birds in which the upperparts were greyish and the yellow pigment below almost completely missing. The typical Icterine Warbler, as

Fig. 116 *Melodious (top) and Icterine Warblers in flight – longer wing point of latter often obvious in flight, as is the former's round-winged fluttering action. (D. I. M. Wallace)*

its specific name *icterina* suggests, is olive and yellow. The Greek word *ikteros* appears to mean either a greenish-yellow bird or jaundice, and indeed in his *Natural History* Pliny suggested that just a glimpse of an Icterine Warbler would be enough to cure jaundice in a person. The Icterine Warbler was once looked upon as a rare vagrant to Britain but in recent years it has been observed and trapped for ringing much more often. The species is now regular in Britain from May to June and also in the autumn. A nest with three eggs was said to have been found near Marlborough in Wiltshire in May 1907 and placed in Marlborough College Museum. There are references to this unique record in *Bull. B.O.C.* 46:74 and *Brit. Birds* 19:311.

From 28–30 May 1947 I watched an Icterine Warbler which was singing in Badby Wood near Daventry in Northamptonshire. It was frequenting the canopy tops of oaks, sycamores and Scots pines for most of the time but sometimes came down to the shrub layer of hazel and Spanish chestnut. This bird was clearly stockier and heavier in appearance than a nearby Wood Warbler, and had very yellow underparts with no suspicion of white underneath. Its back was olive-green, the wings and tail brownish while the head carried a yellow eye-stripe and was itself quite prominent. At the time I wrote: 'In flight it displayed a square tail and rather thin

angular wings. It was continually on the move and its trips in flight backwards and forwards were made in a somewhat hesitant and erratic manner.'
Its calls, of which there were two, I wrote down on the spot as 'biberoy'
and an occasional 'bik, bik'. 'The first call was also incorporated in each
phrase of the song but twice only in each phrase as "biberoy, biberoy".' The
song itself was very powerful and compelling with notes of Garden Warbler
mixed up with the rattle of the Lesser Whitethroat and the chatter of the
Starling. The song was audible from 150 metres. It was usually delivered
from the top of a tree and on one occasion it sang as it flew from one tree
to the other.' This bird showed all the nervous excitability of birds that I
have seen in Holland, Switzerland and Italy.

I have also heard mimetic songs on the Continent. In character the song
is rather like a more powerful and rapid version of the Marsh Warbler's
song. Col. Richard Meinertzhagen thought that the song of the Icterine
Warbler was 'startling in spirit and volume'; James Ferguson-Lees (1954)
described it as 'a long-sustained muddle of many discordant and some
musical notes', while Dr Geoffrey Beven (1974) wrote that: 'Loud and
vehement, sometimes almost explosive, it is long sustained with rich
musical notes and much harsh chattering, shrieking and churring.' These
descriptions help to convey the variety and passion shown in the song. I
have listened to males singing for minutes on end with repetitions of such
notes as 'wee-choo', 'choo-choo-choo-chit', 'tchee-oo-tchoo', 'weea-choo-
choo' and 'chee-chee-wee'. Many have included the musical 'biberoy' or
'dideroid' notes of my bird in Northamptonshire. A singer recorded by
Ludwig Koch in Germany in 1934 used the 'biberoy' note and a sonagram
shows how this note was recorded (Fig. 117). A nasal 'zneer' has been suggested as a regular component of some songs and Sture Palmér thought

Fig. 117
*The 'biberoy' note
characteristic of many
Icterine Warbler songs
(above). 'Tee-up' note
from same singer (below).
(Recorded by Ludwig
Koch, Germany,
May/June 1934)*

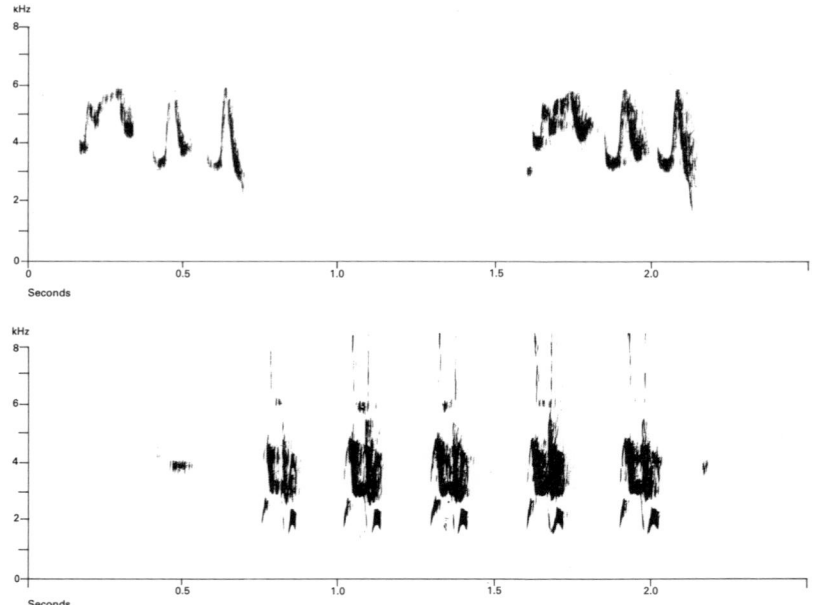

that a wheezy series of 'geea, geea, geea' notes, perhaps the same as the 'zneer', might be distinctive. The latter notes were recorded by Palmér in Sweden but I have heard birds on the Continent that did not include such notes. Perhaps they indicate the variety in the songs, a local tradition or just imitations. In my experience the song can range from a brief phrase of two to three seconds' duration to sustained bursts of up to two minutes or more.

The song often includes mimicry and the German name for the bird – *Gelbspötter* – means the 'yellow mocker'. I have heard birds imitate Skylark, Song Thrush, Blackbird, Whinchat, House Sparrow, Goldfinch, Garden Warbler, Lesser Whitethroat, Starling, Lesser Spotted Woodpecker, Wryneck and Tawny Owl. A bird recorded in Sweden by Palmér mimicked Fieldfare, Thrush, Nightingale, Willow Warbler, Blackbird, Curlew, Common Gull and Common Tern and, having listened to the recording, I am impressed with the faithfulness of the imitations in Scandinavia just as I have been when listening to singers further south.

A singing Icterine Warbler was present in Cambridgeshire from 16 June to 20 July 1980 and, because of the site and much discussion over its identity, came to be known as 'the Wandlebury warbler' (Grant and Medhurst 1982). The song was recognized as that of an Icterine Warbler, although atypical and not 'full song', but the identity was put in doubt by the fact that it appeared to show the wing structure of a Melodious Warbler as well as a pale wing-panel. The conclusion in the end was that the bird was an Icterine Warbler with a diagnostic song and an atypical wing structure. The possibility was also raised that the Wandlebury warbler was a hybrid Icterine × Melodious Warbler. A paired male Melodious and female Icterine Warbler raised two young from a clutch of five eggs in France in 1980; the second instance of a mixed pair among 80 pure pairs (Dr C. Ferry 1981; *Le Bièvre* 3:100–101). Another singing male Icterine Warbler was reported in Huntingdonshire from 6–30 June 1981. Singing birds often assume a rather characteristic stance on a twig with their legs firmly apart, while they raise their crown feathers vigorously from time to time. Many employ high song-posts like the Badby bird as well as telegraph wires and even a 'tall flagpole in a village square' (Beven 1974). Others often sing from dense cover or foliage as E. M. Nicholson (quoted in Bannerman 1954) said 'just within the outermost leaves of some high tree, especially one a little apart from the rest.' Some birds sing in flight and others at night. There is an occasional display flight in which, according to Nicholson, the male Icterine Warbler parachutes down rather in the manner of a Tree Pipit. In Africa, where the moult occurs late in the year, birds often sing before leaving their winter quarters for the north. Besides the 'biberoy' note which I have described which is often a component of the song, there are also a sharp 'teck-teck' or 'bick-bick' suggestive of a *Sylvia* warbler and sometimes accelerated into a kind of chatter, and a churring alarm, while Nicholson noted a plaintive *Phylloscopus*-like 'hooeet' in the autumn which I have not heard.

I would describe the Icterine Warbler as fairly lively and active but less so than the leaf warblers. It moves and jumps about in the canopy and foliage searching for insects yet in the breeding season and on migration it can prove quite elusive. It perches in a fairly upright manner and its flight suggests something of the Spotted Flycatcher. The bird is rarely seen on

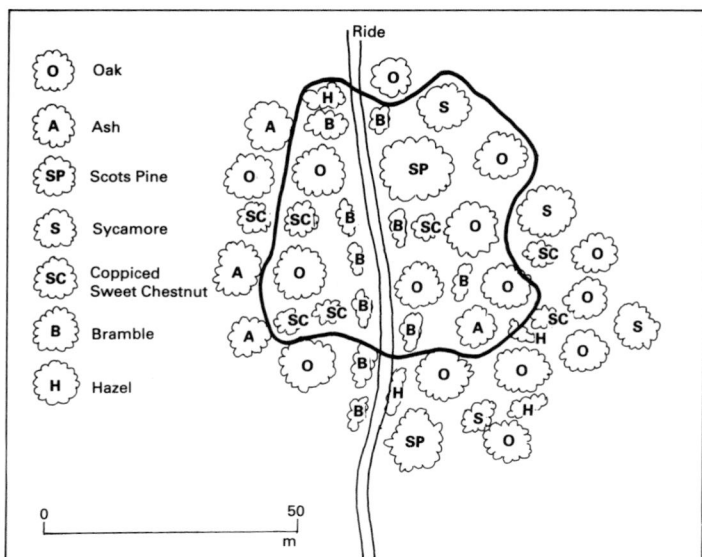

Fig. 118
*Territory held by an
Icterine Warbler in a
Northamptonshire wood,
28–30 May 1947. (Eric
Simms)*

the ground. In the breeding season the Icterine Warbler can be found in
open canopy woodland often with oaks and sometimes with little or no
shrub layer, in parklands with groves of trees, avenues along rivers and
across farmland, as well as orchards, parks and gardens. In fact in Switzerland, where I know the species best, it occurs in small woods and large
gardens very commonly. Since it does not have to depend upon shrub
layers or scrub, it is very much a bird of the parklands of central Europe. It
certainly likes isolated trees in the middle of cultivation, often favouring
the neighbourhood of houses or water. It is a common garden bird in
Germany ranging from small patches to the gardens of large mansions and
parks. In Sweden the Icterine Warbler appears in many broad-leaved
woods but it also occurs in pure conifers (Durango 1948). Voous (1961)
has pointed out that in western Siberia 'it originally inhabited bushes in
wooded steppes, and succeeded in greatly extending its range to the east
simultaneously with the progress of land cultivation in these areas.' Birds
have been spreading in northwest Norway in recent years from which
they might perhaps reach the birch woods of eastern Scotland.

   On migration, Icterine Warblers can be found in vineyards, olive groves
and dry scrub in the Balkans (Lambert 1957), while in North Africa they
appear in palm groves, oleanders, eucalyptus, arid scrub and grassland in
desert terrain. In Egypt birds frequent gardens, palm groves, orchards
and many cultivated areas where they often sing loudly. In Eritrea, Smith
(1957) reported birds as high as 1300 m amongst the plateau scrub and
Combretum woodlands. Many birds winter in western Arabia, and in
Africa from Kenya south to the Orange Free State, but the exact winter
distribution is not yet known. Although Dr David Lack (1971) thought
that most Icterine Warblers wintered south of Zambia, birds occur in
Uganda and one individual sang in a garden in Kampala during three
successive winters (Pearson 1972). Birds have been seen passing north-

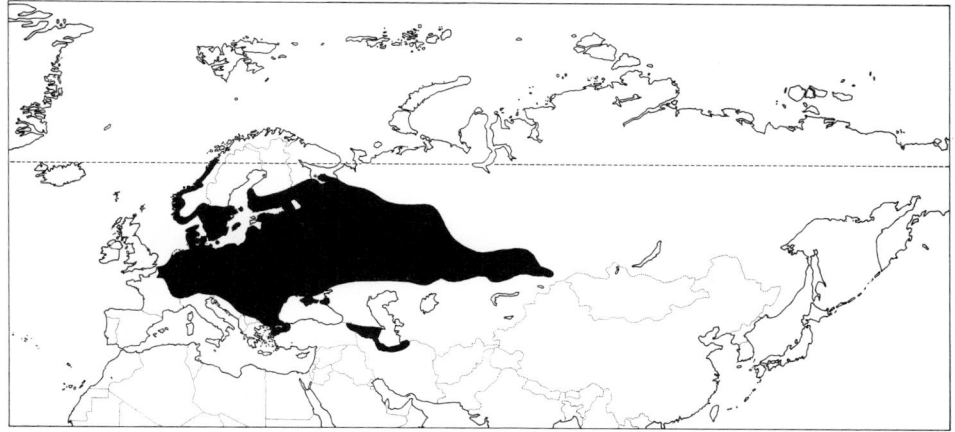

Fig. 119
*Breeding range of the
Icterine Warbler.*

wards through Nigeria in April and May (Elgood *et al* 1966). V. W. Smith (1966) noted a well-defined passage in April and May in central Nigeria with a peak in the last week of April; many presumed Icterine Warblers were seen 'high up in the tall eucalyptus trees searching the canopy for insects and uttering a weak discordant chattering.' Birds have arrived at Lake Chad in early spring with fat already laid down for the northward journey (Dowsett and Fry 1971) and some appeared at the Kufra Oasis in the middle of the huge Libyan desert by the end of March (Cramp and Conder 1970). Icterine Warblers begin to arrive on their European breeding grounds in the middle of April and in May (Scott 1970). Many birds probably undertake very long migratory flights.

Icterine Warblers feed extensively on insects and their larvae especially dipterous flies, beetles, small moths, earwigs and aphids as well as spiders, earthworms and small snails. In summer and autumn the species will turn towards a vegetarian diet of fruit, such as cherries and currants, and berries including those of elder and bird cherry *Prunus padus*.

The breeding season may begin just after the middle of May in Switzerland, in late May in Germany and Belgium and in early June in the Baltic States. Some 121 nests of Icterine Warblers near Turnhout in Belgium were studied by W. Paulussen (1950) from 1942–50. The first egg was laid between 12–20 May, and during the nine years of the study 23 clutches were begun in the last ten days of May, 40 clutches from 1–10 June, 26 from 11–20 June, 14 from 21–30 June and 9 during the month of July. Late clutches were thought to be repeats and the species is single-brooded. The nest is generally constructed in the fork of a tree or small bush, especially of lilac, elder, currant, pear or other fruit tree, at a height usually of 1–4 m but occasionally as high as 5 m. The nest is a deep, well-constructed cup and is built by both parents. The actual building techniques were well observed and described by Van Dobben (1949) who watched the adults fixing sheep's wool and spider cocoons with webs of gossamer to form a platform or base at the nest site. An adult then squatted down on this foundation, turned around and added more material thus shaping the cup. More cobwebs were added to the exterior and pulled up over the rim. The bird then lay flat across the nest, supported by its wings and tail, and

Fig. 120
The finely constructed nest of the Icterine Warbler in the fork of a pear tree in Holland. (Eric Hosking, summer 1952)

with its throat resting on the rim of the structure. In this posture it scrabbled away with its feet. Plant fibres, down, stems, grasses, leaves, roots and more webs were thus pushed up from the base of the cup into the walls of the nest. As the exterior rose in height, the original cobweb binding stretched to accommodate this movement. The outside of the nest may be adorned with pale pieces of birch bark, moss, wool, rags, lichens and cocoons, bound round with fibres like 'barrel-hoops' or attached by loops of grass to the forks of shrubs. In Switzerland I have seen birch bark often used but if there are no birch trees in a territory the birds will resort to paper instead, and even rags. The lining usually consists of roots, fine grasses, wool, hair, fur and sometimes feathers. Nests may bear a general resemblance to those of Chaffinches (Ferguson-Lees 1954). The nest found at Marlborough in May 1907 was built in an alder just over a metre above the ground and decorated on the outside with pieces of birch bark.

There are usually four or five eggs laid at daily intervals. Paulussen (1950) found a rather constant clutch size in Belgium with a hundred clutches of five eggs, one of six eggs, two of three eggs and seventeen of four eggs. The eggs vary in size but are rather glossy with a ground colour ranging from grey-pink to salmon-pink or even pinkish-violet, with a few spots or lines of deep-purplish or even black and resemble those of the Melodious Warbler. However, Icterine Warbler eggs have an average size of 18.3 × 13.4 mm (maxima 20.6 × 13 and 19 × 14.1) and Melodious Warbler of 17.72 × 13.22 mm (maxima 19.2 × 13.6 and 18.6 × 14.5). For the Icterine, the minima are 17 × 13 and 18.1 × 12.4 mm and for the Melodious 16.1 × 13.6 and 17 × 12.3 mm (*The Handbook* 1946). To see a nest with eggs is certainly one of the most satisfying of all ornithological experiences in Europe. Other warbler nests may press for recognition as fine examples of bird architecture but I must to some extent share the opinion of Major Anthony Buxton, quoted in Bannerman (1954), who watched birds incubating under shellfire at Ypres in the First World War but saw a nest near Geneva which he thought to be 'the best that any warbler builds, silvery white with pink eggs in a perfect goblet cup.'

The incubation of the eggs is carried out by both parents and lasts sometimes slightly under 13 days but also any time from 13 to 14. The female will sit very closely, and since the nest cup is so deep be forced to carry her head very high. She will scold very loudly at an intruder. It seems that where both Icterine and Melodious Warblers breed in regions of overlap, the clutch size of the former remains unchanged but the presence of the Melodious Warbler reduces the breeding success of the Icterine and may thus prevent it from expanding more to the west (Ferry 1974). The nestlings remain in the nest for thirteen days.

With its mannerisms, élan and arresting song the Icterine Warbler, so common in many parts of the Continent, is an adornment to the avifauna of much of Europe. To the British Isles it remains a regular visitor and, despite a few singing males in spring, not a breeding species. Apparently, near the northern and western limits of its range, large population fluctuations sometimes take place and despite the spread of the Icterine Warbler in Scandinavia conditions in the British Isles are not yet to its liking.

The Melodious is a very slightly smaller species than the Icterine Warbler which to some extent it resembles in character and general habits. However, the Melodious is rather more compact in shape and has short, rounded wings, not long ones. This last feature gives to the flying bird the appearance of a weak, fluttering flight similar to that of a young bird flying from site to site. On 31 August 1982, while watching newly arrived migrant warblers, especially Willow Warblers and Whitethroats on the seacliffs at Nefyn in the Lleyn Peninsula in North Wales, I became aware of the presence of another warbler. This bird was a clear bright yellow as far as the underside of its tail and had an eye-stripe of the same colour, a heavily pointed head and broad bill; there was no sign of a wing-panel. It was certainly larger than the Willow Warblers and closer to the Whitethroats in size. It was fairly nervous and flitted in and out of the brambles, elders and montbretia growing on the cliff-face. The species was very familiar to me on the Continent of Europe but this was the first Melodious Warbler that I had seen in the British Isles. The bird has occurred on nearby Bardsey Island and one which was trapped there on 27 August 1954, when handled, 'made three or four harsh, almost grating notes, at the same time raising and lowering its crown-feathers' (Thearle 1955).

Before 1951 only three Melodious Warblers had been recorded in the British Isles. Whether the Melodious Warbler had actually bred earlier in Britain depends upon reports of eggs being taken at Lancing in Sussex about 1893 and near Croydon in Surrey in 1884. As we saw in the last chapter the eggs of this species, although slightly smaller than those of the Icterine, are very similar to them and the two nesting records could apply to that species. After 1953 Melodious Warblers were identified annually

Fig. 121
Breeding range of
Melodious Warbler.

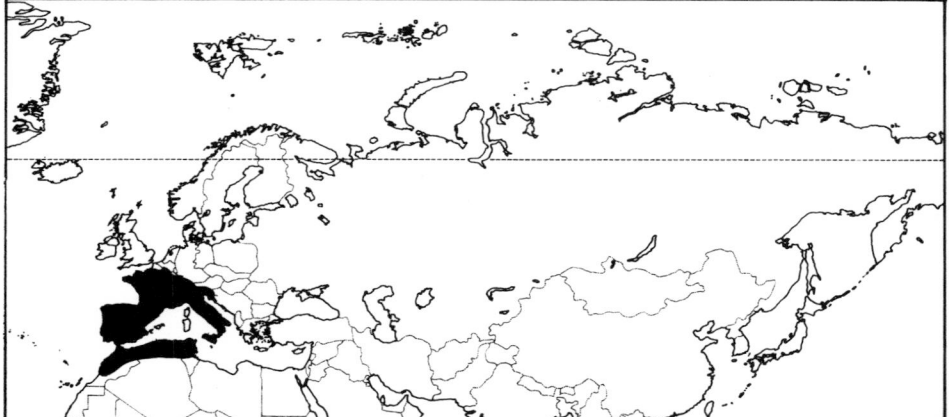

and in the decade from 1954–63 there were at least 130 records chiefly in
the months from August to October. Over 50 were reported at bird
observatories in the Irish Sea and English Channel in the autumn of 1962.
By 1965 James Ferguson-Lees was able to describe the status of the Melodious Warbler as that of 'an annual autumn wanderer here in small numbers, chiefly on the south coasts of Ireland and England and around the
Irish Sea, but this increase is doubtless only another reflection of improved
observation and trapping.' (The increase in numbers of both Melodious
and Icterine Warblers was traced in Chapter 23 and more fully discussed by
Sharrock (1969, 1974).)

The bird that I watched at Nefyn made no call but I have been able to
study breeding birds at Salin de Badon and elsewhere in the Camargue.
The most familiar call was a sparrowlike chirping or chatter quite unlike
any notes of the Icterine Warbler – a 'ter-cheek' or 'tiss-cheek' – which is
in my opinion diagnostic. An Icterine Warbler might imitate a House
Sparrow a few times and in a random manner in his song but not so fully
and regularly as the Melodious employs the sparrowlike calls. I have also
heard a quick 'tit-tit-tit' and *The Handbook* (1946) quoted a description
by E. M. Nicholson of a call used in the autumn: 'a brief, musical "hooeet"
not unlike Icterine Warbler, Chiffchaff etc.'

In the Camargue I obtained a number of sound recordings of territory-
holding male Melodious Warblers. They were all very restless, excitable

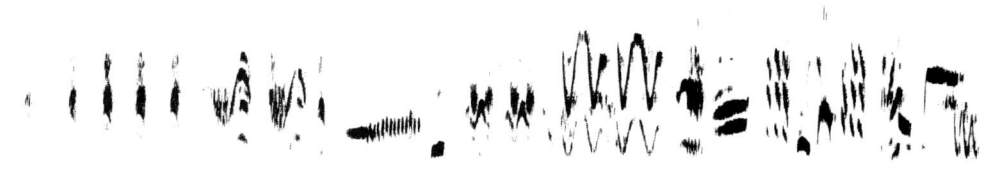

and constantly on the move which made tape recording quite a challenge.
The songs lacked the vehemence and power of Icterine Warblers, being
audible only up to 70 m. They had some variety but much less than that
of the Icterine Warbler, occasional musical notes and a very fast, sustained
delivery. I noted imitations of Goldfinch and Nightingale. In 1957 I wrote
about the Camargue Melodious Warblers: 'The typical call note is a
twitter, sometimes very much like the "chizzick" of the house sparrow,
sometimes a more musical "whit-tchu" or "whi-whi-tchu". These notes
regularly introduce the song which is varied, rich and very quickly delivered.' There may be from three to ten of these chattering introductory
notes. Some songs progressed little further than the introductions but a
fine singer might follow them with a fluent, musical and well-sustained
performance. In 1956 I stayed in the State Albergue at Beilen in Spain and
awoke to a magnificent dawn chorus of Melodious Warblers and Cuckoos.
The ornithologist H. F. Witherby thought that the song of the Melodious
Warbler in central Spain was 'as unmusical as a jazz band' but I cannot
really accept this stricture on many of the birds that I have heard singing in
Spain and elsewhere. Furthermore, many people find jazz musical! In

Fig. 122
*Part of song of Melodious
Warbler. (Recorded by
Eric Simms, Salin de
Badon, Camargue, May
1954)*

Fig. 123
Habitat of the Melodious Warbler at Salin de Badon in the Camargue with hedge, garden and dyke. (Eric Simms, May 1973)

1973 I returned to the Camargue to help make stereo recordings of Melodious Warblers and again I heard some good performers. I timed the durations of many song bursts and found that they might last from as little as 5 seconds to an average of 14 seconds; some singers would continue their performance for two minutes or more. The birds sang from deep cover in the hedges around the garden at Salin de Badon against a background of Willow Warblers, Cetti's Warblers, Nightingales and migrant Bonelli's Warblers, Turtle Doves, Cuckoos, Bee-eaters, Pied Flycatchers, Tree Pipits and Ortolan Buntings. Some Melodious Warblers sang from amongst clumps of tamarisk and on occasion a singer, stirred by passion, would mount in a series of jumps right to the exposed summit of a bush and finish his song there before leaving to seek cover elsewhere in his territory.

In the breeding season the Melodious Warbler favours woodland ecotones, groves of broad-leaved trees, wooded fringes of rivers, streams and *roubines* in southern France, and rough hedges where it occurs with Cetti's Warblers. It can be found in coppiced woods of oak, alder and acacia with taller isolated trees as well as thickets of tamarisk and oleander. With some birds nesting in dampish woodland and vegetation, the Melodious Warbler does not, however, demand the presence of water. It cannot tolerate the small gardens and rather fragmented habitats that the Icterine may occupy, and also needs rather denser bushes and a shrub layer. In southern Spain the species can be found on low ground with wood and scrub, in cork woods with open glades, in citrus groves and in the Coto Doñana in pine woods with bushes. While concealed in a whole range of habitats in Spain and France, and making sound recordings of egrets and herons, orioles, Hoopoes and other birds, I was often startled by the hurried phrases of a Melodious Warbler which had arrived close by and not seen me in my place of concealment!

In fact, the Melodious Warbler breeds in northwest Africa, Spain, Portugal, much of France, Italy, the south Tyrol and Sicily. The species has also recently spread into northeastern France and first bred in Belgium in 1981 after a number of years in which singing males had been reported in that country (Blankert 1981). Birds have also colonized parts of southern Switzerland – there were fifteen territories in 1980 near Verbois – and the extreme west of Yugoslavia (Landenbergue and Turrian 1982). It seems clear that the Icterine Warbler on the whole is keeping the Melodious Warbler at bay, just as I noted in the last chapter how the Melodious was preventing the Icterine from pushing westwards. In southern Europe Melodious Warblers begin to breed from late May onwards, and in France from about the third week of that month. Eggs are known in June and July and the species is sometimes double-brooded.

Because the Melodious Warbler is less closely associated with tall trees and more with scrub composed of bramble, gorse, willow, *Cistus*, hawthorn, arbutus, *Cornus* and oleander, the species nests in shrubs from riversides up the hillsides. Many nests that I came across were in bramble, both in the broad-leaved areas of the Camargue and in the drier parts of the Coto Doñana with yellow-flowering *Halimium* shrubs, pistachio, gorse and broom. In southern Spain nests have also been found in crab apples and a fig (Bannerman 1954). The nest is built in or woven to a fork in a shrub, sometimes as low as 45 cm or as high as 1.3 m. In Algeria birds may nest in small olive trees. Most of the Camargue nests were about 0.6 m above the ground. The nest, constructed by the female, is a deep cup, fashioned from fine flowering grasses, plant stems, and vegetable down; it is lined with grass, plant seeds and down, hair and sometimes feathers. Birds in Portugal will use wool, and nests in southern Spain have sometimes had a whitish appearance due to an outer covering to the nest of dead ash-coloured thistle leaves. In other cases spiders' webs may be employed in the building of the nest. The clutch consists of usually four eggs, sometimes three or five. These, as we have seen earlier, are like those of Icterine Warbler but smaller, and are pinkish with black spots and dark or faint hair-lines. Only the female carries out the duties of incubation which lasts 12–13 days. She arrives to stand on the rim of the nest with a rather flattened crown, but while brooding the eggs, tucked down into the cup of the nest, her head appears very rounded. The nestlings are fed by both parents and spend about twelve days in the nest. The main diet is one of insects and their larvae, including dipterous flies, ants, small beetles and grasshoppers while it is said that fruit may also be taken (*The Handbook* 1946). After the breeding season is over birds are more likely to be seen frequenting gardens. A bird in Devon was found amongst peas and beans and old apple trees (Smith 1957). I have often watched Melodious Warblers in trees picking off small insects in the manner of *Phylloscopus* warblers.

For the winter the Melodious Warbler migrates to tropical West Africa. In this region to the west of the Icterine Warbler's winter range the Melodious Warblers undergo an early moult. Bannerman (1939) gave the dates for the capture of Melodious Warblers in tropical Africa as ranging from 18 October at Timbuktu to 4 May for a late bird in Niger. He also examined examples from the Gambia, Sierra Leone, Ivory Coast, Ghana, southern Nigeria and Cameroon as well as Niger. Melodious Warblers are regular winter visitors to southern Nigeria, living in scrub and forest clearings from early December to the last week of April, and birds were regularly heard singing in gardens in Ibadan (Elgood *et al* 1966). However, at Vom in central Nigeria, V. W. Smith (1966) heard birds singing in March but only 'three birds were caught during five years'. The bird is said to winter in Senegal as well. Melodious Warblers appear in Morocco in August, some migrate over the Sahara while others follow the coast; birds arrive by December in tropical west Africa to disperse through the bush country and even gardens and plantations where they are much less shy and can be more easily observed. Birds often sing quite well before abandoning their winter quarters. Passage birds have also been recorded in the Canary Islands.

The Vagrant *Hippolais* Warblers

CHAPTER **26**

The Olivaceous Warbler

The subjects of this chapter – the Olivaceous and Booted Warblers – are two truly great rarities in the British Isles. In Chapter 23 we saw that the Olivaceous Warbler has several races, two of which have been recorded in Britain – *Hippolais pallida opaca* (once called the Opaque Tree Warbler), which breeds in southeast Spain, Portugal and North Africa, and *H.p. elaeica* which nests in southeast Europe and southwest Asia. Some of the Olivaceous Warblers in Britain and Ireland could not be racially determined but the former was identified off the coast of Wales and the latter in Dorset as well as Ireland and Scotland. Both races are greyish-olive in colour but *opaca* is more grey and *elaeica* more green; this dominant coloration is reversed when adults reach their wintering grounds. The species bears some resemblance to the Garden Warbler but has a flatter forehead, longer and broader bill and more clearly defined eye-stripe and, although the wings and tail are brown, this last feature has its penultimate and outer feathers brownish-white with whitish tips. These tips are especially visible in fresh plumage and are still present even in birds with worn plumage. There is no wing-panel and the underparts are creamy or buff, sometimes with the throat whiter than the rest. After their close study of Olivaceous Warblers in southeast Europe, I. C. T. Nisbet and T. C. Smout (1957) summed up their differences from the Garden Warbler by suggesting that

Fig. 124
Breeding range of the Olivaceous Warbler.

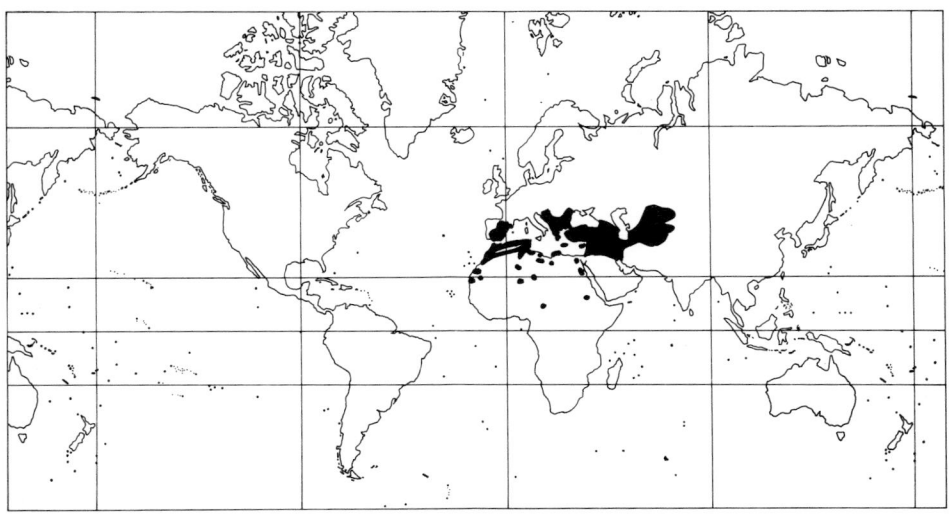

the Olivaceous could be distinguished by the 'combination of the paler grey upperparts, whitish orbital ring, *Hippolais* shape and stance, long, broad bill and "trrk" call.' The head shape of a bird seen in the Isles of Scilly was compared to that of a miniature Starling (Wallace 1966). In contrast the Booted Warbler is some 2 cm shorter than the Olivaceous, has a shorter, more slender bill and is more buff in the breeding season and whiter or paler in the winter.

The Olivaceous Warbler is somewhat nondescript in form and behaviour, rather restless like other members of the genus but not quite as skulking or shy. I have watched birds of the race *opaca* in Spain, where birds frequenting olive groves as well as dense cover in gardens and orchards, would show themselves from time to time and erect the feathers on their napes and crowns. To my mind the birds of the *elaeica* race in Greece were less confiding, occurring in bushy, wet valleys up to 200 m; they can be heard around Delphi. Birds of the race *pallida* from Egypt are said to be even shyer.

The first accepted record of the Olivaceous Warbler in the British Isles was of a bird on Skokholm in Pembrokeshire from 23 September to 3 October 1951 (Conder 1953). The second was of a bird at Portland Bird Observatory in Dorset on 16 August 1956 (Bourne and Smith 1960). From 1958 to 1972 eight more were recorded (Sharrock 1976). Six of these were in the southern counties of England from Kent to the Isles of Scilly. They are as follows: Isles of Scilly (October 1961, September–October 1962); Dorset (September 1962, August 1967); Kent (September 1967) and Cornwall (September 1968). The other two records in that period were in Donegal (September 1959) and Fife (September 1967). Subsequently there was a second Irish record on Dursey Island, Co. Cork, on 16 September 1977 and another English record at Flamborough Head in Humberside on 22 October in 1976. All the records fell between late August and October with many in the last week of September. This peak was much later than the peak for the Icterine Warbler (from 27 August to 9 September) or for the Melodious (from 27 August to 16 September) (Sharrock 1976). These records show how rare a vagrant this warbler is in Britain and Ireland.

The Olivaceous Warbler is a summer-breeding bird of quite a wide habitat range. In southern Spain, where it is locally common, I have found birds in olive groves, gardens and orchards, while at Jerez de la Frontera the bird is present in wooded gardens from which I heard birds in song. Stanley Cramp, who stayed in a hotel at Algeciras, reported in 1959 how he watched a pine in the garden where on 'the lower branches an Olivaceous Warbler often perched, uttering its chattering song.' The Eastern, or Balkan race, as it has sometimes been called in the past, is common in northern and central Greece but less so in the south. After the middle of the 1930s the species extended its range from the Danube north and west. It is essentially a bird of Mediterranean, steppe and desert areas with the limits of its breeding range lying between the July isotherms of 22°C and above 33°C. Voous (1961) has suggested that the Olivaceous Warbler selects lower bushes and shrub layers than the other *Hippolais* warblers and favours more arid climatic conditions. It likes bushy regions in semi-desert areas and steppes, thickets of tamarisk, groves of open canopy broad-leaved and coniferous trees often near water, riverside vegetation and dry valleys, olive groves, orchards, parks, gardens and in the case of the race *reiseri* in North Africa palm oases. In northern Iran it is the commonest warbler around Tehran and also occurs in numbers in the lower parts of the mountains (Passburg 1979). In Iraq the species nests up to a height of 1830 m (Chapman and McGeogh 1956). All the Olivaceous Warblers in Eritrea are *elaeica* which may mingle with resident Olivaceous Warblers in the coastal mangroves (Smith 1960). In Nigeria the resident *pallida* birds may also mix with the migrants from western Europe.

I find that my notes on Spanish Olivaceous Warblers have given the call of these birds as a sharp, clearly repeated 'bec-bec' or 'tec-tec'. This call has also been rendered variously as 'teck-teck', 'tack-tack' or 'tchak-tchak', sometimes 'trrk'; there are also a ticking 'tchick-tick-tick-tick' and a Housesparrow-like chatter, based on the single syllable 'chut'. The bird on Skokholm in 1951 had a note similar to the 'churr' of a Whitethroat but shorter and harsher as well as a 'yilp', similar to a Housesparrow's call but quieter and higher-pitched (Conder 1953). The bird at Portland in Dorset in 1956 was described by Bourne and Smith (1960) as having an alarm note that was a rather sparrowlike 'chut' or 'chek' repeated 2–6 times. To me, listening to songs in the field, the note 'tchick' formed the essential part of the male's territorial song. It was repeated over and over again: 'tchick-tchick-tchick-tchick-tirrit-tchick-tchick'. It had some suggestion of a Sedge Warbler about it, was quite vigorous and loud and came in phrases lasting from about five seconds up to a minute or more. It sometimes seems more Acrocephaline in nature than the songs of either the Icterine or Melodious Warbler. The Greek birds of the *elaeica* race seem to have slightly better songs but a recording of a bird in Hungary, made by Peter Szöke and Michael Orszag, to which I listened, showed a performer little different from the *opaca* race. The simple repetitive song is rather in keeping with the bird, and it is generally given from thick cover. In Egypt, Simmons (1952) found the song of the typical race *pallida* to be vigorous and uneven like that of a Sedge Warbler but sweeter and lacking harsh notes – 'A stuttering succession of reeling notes interspersed with slower ones of varying degrees of sweetness' – and with song phrases lasting from about 6–30 seconds.

On the breeding ground the male will sing intermittently while foraging in the manner of other warblers. The diet of the Olivaceous Warblers appears to consist largely of small insects such as dipterous flies and aphids picked off the heads of flowers and foliage. When feeding, this warbler may flick its tail with a shallow movement. The bird seen in Co. Donegal in 1959 perched on wall tops and also had a Wagtail-like habit of flicking its tail.

In Egypt the males return to their breeding grounds during the last week of March and the first week of April, while in the Balkans and Spain nesting may begin from late May to June. Early arrivals among the males begin to sing intermittently, become more aggressive as further males arrive and then sing much more. Dr K. E. L. Simmons (1952) made a short study of Olivaceous Warblers in Egypt and I am indebted to his paper for the information that follows. Songs were more sustained in the mornings; this had earlier been remarked upon by R. H. Greaves (1936) who noticed the significant contribution made by Olivaceous Warblers to the dawn chorus in Cairo. Gradually the females, which arrived after the males, located the males in their established territories. Unmated birds sang a great deal and were seen by Dr Simmons to shiver their closed wings so that the tips of the primaries crossed over the back 'while the tail was also shivered slightly and continually fanned open and shut'; an outlet for unfulfilled sexual drives. Males may also begin to build rough nests, then later strip them and use the material again in another site. In fact, nest building was regarded as 'undoubtedly a male function only'. The males also had a courtship display in which they followed females, crouching down with ruffled body feathers, drooping wings and an erratic flicking of both wings and tail. The females sometimes responded with a less intense version of the display but both members of a pair were seen to sway from side to side while the male indulged in bursts of subsong.

The nest is a strong cup, typical of the genus and often a very attractive structure, formed from fine twigs, grass stems, sedges and hair, woven to the surrounding plant stems, and lined with fine fibres, vegetable down, hair or feathers. Spiders' webs are sometimes used to bind the nest material together. Nests are built in the outer twigs of shrubs or small trees, from 0.3 m up to heights of over 1 m and, exceptionally, as high as 3 m. The race *pallida* often builds in creepers, thick hedges, small palms, garden plants and grape vines. The clutch size of the Olivaceous Warbler seems to observe in general the north–south and west–east trends explained by Dr David Lack (1947). General observations, summarized by Simmons, indicated 2–4 eggs, but 3 was the usual size of clutch in Egypt, 4 or 5 in Tunisia, while in Spain 4 was normal, 3 less common and 5 rather unusual. The eggs are a pale greyish-white but sometimes pinkish or lilac, with a few black speckles and spots. As with the Icterine Warbler, the incubation is carried out by the female alone but the singing male uttering a kind of subsong will visit her on the nest and, as photographed by Stubbs (1947), even feed her. The output and vehemence of song which has been dropping, with shorter and softer phrases being employed, since pairing took place, is at its lowest level when the nestlings are being fed. The task of feeding the young birds in the nest is carried out by both parents. C. J. Gent (1946) gave a possible incubation period of 13 days for a *pallida* nest near the Great Bitter Lake in Egypt, while Dr Simmons gave 11 days ±1 day for another in Egypt; these figures can be compared with 13 days given for the *elaeica* race in the Balkans. The nestling period in *The Handbook* (1946) for *pallida* was given as probably 15 days which is similar to the 15 days ±1 day found by Simmons in Egypt. After the breeding season the birds remain in the area for some time but are rather silent and retiring. S. Marchant (1963) gave an incubation period of 12–13 days in Iraq and a nestling period of 11–13 days.

In the autumn the western Mediterranean race *opaca* of the Olivaceous Warbler flies down to West Africa where it winters from Senegal to northern Nigeria. It appears in the more arid parts of this latter country where it cannot be distinguished in the field from the resident *pallida* race (Elgood *et al* 1966). On the other hand the Balkan race *elaeica* winters in East Africa. It is common in many of the drier regions (Pearson 1972). Birds arrive in some numbers in the arid parts of Tsavo in December and January where they spend the winter. Birds from the central part of the breeding range also arrive in Africa about December. The races moult in their winter quarters and also seem to undergo quite a protracted change of plumage.

Since birds turn up in fresh plumage in December in eastern Uganda this indicates that they, like some other warbler species, have made a temporary stop on their flight south, where food is readily available, and renewed their plumage before resuming their southwards journey to their actual winter quarters.

The Booted Warbler

The second of the vagrant *Hippolais* warblers in the British Isles is the Booted Warbler. This was described in Chapter 23 as a small edition of the Olivaceous Warbler with a thinner, finer bill. It is, in adult plumage, greyish-brown above and white below with some buff suffusion on the breast, flanks and undertail coverts. The head is slightly darker than the back; it has a fairly clear buffish-white supercilium, which, unlike that of any other *Hippolais* warbler, extends the same distance behind the eye as in front; there is a narrow eye-ring. The two outer tail feathers on each side are a brownish-white with white tips. First-winter birds are greyish-olive or even paler. One on Fair Isle was described as 'milky tea' in colour (the same phrase used by Davis (1960) of a bird on Fair Isle) with a fresh olive tint, and another on Whalsay as 'even paler, almost sandy above' (Chapman 1979). The two Shetland examples were also described as 'small, pot-bellied, long-tailed and very pale' with gleaming white underparts, indistinct dark eye-stripe and supercilium, orangey-flesh bills and bluey-flesh legs. The combination of facial features, long tail and fine proportions induced a number of observers who saw the birds to comment on their dainty and attractive appearance and on the ease of identification. As the Booted Warbler lacks a pronounced dark eye-stripe it does not sometimes have the 'bare-faced' look of the other *Hippolais* warblers (Grant and Colston 1979). The long tail is quite noticeable in flight, which is rather weak and generally carried out close to the ground. Chapman (1979), who watched two individuals in Shetland in the autumn of 1977, was reminded 'sometimes of an *Acrocephalus*, but more of a *Phylloscopus* warbler especially a Bonelli's warbler or even at a distance a lesser whitethroat.'

The first record of the Booted Warbler in the British Isles was of a female on Fair Isle on 3 September 1936 (Stout and Waterston 1936), which was determined as belonging to the race *caligata*. The other records at the time of writing in the autumn of 1984 are as follows; Fair Isle (August 1959, August–September 1966, August 1977); Isles of Scilly (October 1966, October 1980 with characters of *caligata*, September–October 1981); Isle of May (September–October 1975); Whalsay (September–October 1977); Humberside (September 1978, September 1981); Lincolnshire (October 1980 with characters of central Asian form *annectens*); Dorset (September 1980); Out Skerries, Shetland (September 1981), and Norfolk (September 1982). A full account of the Lincolnshire bird was given by M. Boddy (1981) in the *Lincs. Bird Rept.* for 1980.

The usual call of the Booted Warbler has been given as a sharp 'click' note common to many small warblers (*The Handbook* 1946 and Williamson 1976) and also as 'chrek-chrek'. The Russian wildlife sound recordist Boris Veprintsev sent me a recording of the call and song of Sykes's Warbler – the eastern race which breeds from Transcaspia and Iran east to Sinkiang. The call on this recording can best be transcribed as 'tt-ttrk' or 'tr-ttrk'.

The song of Sykes's Warbler is quite strong and musical without a great deal of variety; 'Chit-chit-chit-chit-tchee-chee-chee-chee-chee-see-see-see-tit-tit-tit'. From a run of ten songs in succession the durations of each in seconds were 3, 4, 3, 2, 3, 5, 3, 5, 6 and 2. The song of the Booted Warbler has been described as powerful and sweet, or loud and babbling with similarities to the songs of both Icterine and Sedge Warblers. The song is uttered at night as well as in the daytime. In India in October the Booted Warbler sings subsong of varying intensity and volume while foraging for insects (Lister 1952).

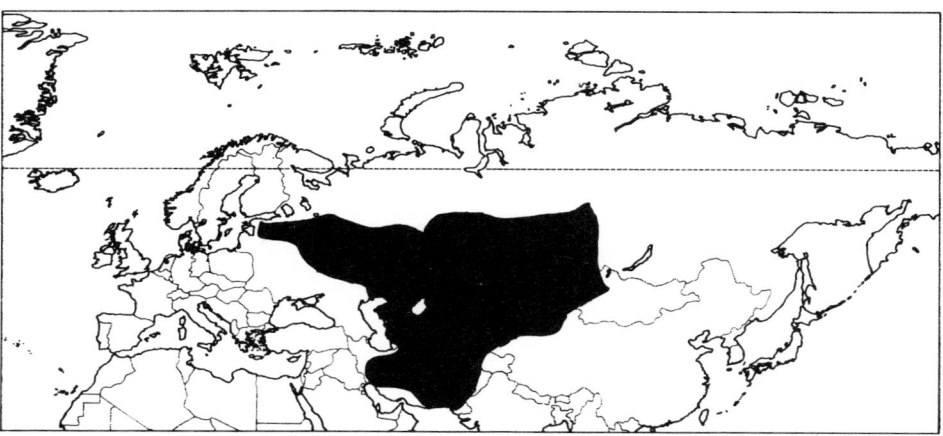

Fig. 125
Breeding range of the Booted Warbler.

In the breeding season the species favours shrubby habitats near water as well as the shores of salt lakes in dry steppe country, birch woods, willow and tamarisk thickets, cane brakes, high field layers in farming country, cornfields and rose hedges around fields of lucerne, which lie between the July isotherms of 17°C in the north and 32°C in the south (Voous 1961). In the winter quarters of the Booted in northern India and of Sykes's in India south to Sri Lanka, the birds frequent low thick scrub rather than forest, scrub-jungle, gardens and babul or acacia trees. They are very skulking birds, keeping to the undergrowth or hunting insects in the foliage of trees from which they may sally forth to take an insect on the wing. The 1959 bird on Fair Isle spent a great deal of time hawking for flies, including craneflies *Tipula*, around the rockfaces and in the scattered clumps of vegetation (Davis 1960).

The Booted Warbler begins nesting in early March in north-central Siberia (Demetriades 1977) but elsewhere it may be not until late March and the breeding season goes on until June. The nest is usually in a depression in the ground amongst tall grass, mugwort, tansy and other plants of the ground zone or field layer. Sometimes it is built in the stems of shrubs, such as rose or tamarisk, or low twigs not much above 30 cm above the ground. The nest is a compact cup of plant stems, leaves, roots, fur and feathers as well as perhaps rotten bark and even string, constructed on a framework of grass and lined with finer grass stems, vegetable down, feathers or even cotton. The clutch may be of five or six eggs, or more rarely four; the eggs are a dirty purplish-pink with a few dark markings. Sykes's Warbler appears to have eggs of a greyish-white ground colour with a heavy region of dark blotches and whorls around the broader end. The average size of 45 eggs quoted in *The Handbook* was 15.57 × 12.24 mm with maxima of 17 × 13 mm and 15 × 13.5 mm, and a minimum of 14 × 11.3 mm. There is normally one brood. The incubation period lasts 13–14 days and the incubation is carried out by the female who may be relieved by the male in the middle of the day. The young remain in the nest about 13 days and leave it still unable to fly, being fed by the parents in the region of the nest for another fortnight or so (Dementiev and Gladkov 1951–4). After the breeding season birds are sometimes reported on passage in Iran, Afghanistan, Baluchistan and northern India and the species has occurred as a vagrant in Europe in Romania, Germany, Norway, Sweden and Finland (with a bird in song in June near Helsinki) as well as the British Isles.

In 1936 one of my brothers gave me as a present an 1833 edition of Gilbert White's *The Natural History of Selborne*. Not only was this classic book to have a profound effect on the rest of my life as a naturalist but it also introduced me to the observations from which White was able to confirm the difference, already suspected by William Derham in 1718, between the Willow Warbler and its two other summer-visiting congeners – the Chiffchaff and Wood Warbler, all members of that large genus, *Phylloscopus*, the leaf warblers.

Many years later in 1977 I revisited Selborne with my copy of *The Natural History* in my hand; I walked around the village and on Selborne Hanger and Common, describing the scene, reading passages from the book and listening to all three species of leaf warbler in song – all in aid of a BBC Radio 4 feature entitled *Gilbert White – Curate Extraordinary*. That programme was for me the culmination of an ambition. Early in my life I had been attracted by the magic not only of the leaf warblers – some with lively songs and personalities – but also of the other genera of these delightful birds.

The Willow Warbler, Chiffchaff and Wood Warbler are the only species of leaf warblers that are both common and regular visitors to the British Isles, but eight species have been recorded as well at various times and in differing numbers. The total is still only just over one third of the recognized species in the world. In his classic *A Systematic Review of the Genus Phylloscopus*, published in 1938 but now out of print, C. B. Ticehurst listed 30 species and 67 forms, some of which were easy to separate and others much less so. Williamson (1976) also listed thirty species but omitted such Far Eastern species as the Philippine Leaf Warbler (*Ph. olivaceus*) and the Mountain Leaf Warbler (*Ph. trivirgatus*) with a wide range across the tropical forests of Indonesia, New Guinea and the Solomon Islands. In his list Williamson was able to group the species into 'clusters' but the relationships among many of them have yet to be fully determined. Voous (1977) in his list of Holarctic bird species (see page 26) gave 32 species which included *Ph. umbrovirens* – the Brown Woodland Warbler – which has often been regarded as synonymous with *Seicercus*, the flycatcher warblers and *Ph. ijimae* which Williamson regarded as an insular derivative of the Pale-legged Leaf Warbler *Ph. tenellipes*, which is described more fully later in this chapter. I propose in the present chapter to review the main groups of the thirty *Phylloscopus* warblers, discuss their identification, distribution, evolution and adaptations in the broadest possible way as an introduction to the genus and the ensuing chapters. It is possible only to attempt to draw the main threads together while later chapters will examine more closely the species on the British list – Willow Warbler, Chiffchaff and Wood Warbler – with a fourth chapter devoted to the seven or eight vagrants to the British Isles.

In general, the genus *Phylloscopus* can be said to consist of slim, graceful, small birds largely of greenish, yellowish or brownish hue with twelve tail feathers and a lively demeanour which frequent the branches and foliage of bushes and trees of both broad-leaved and coniferous groups. They are not basically sociable but may join forces with foraging groups of other species. Their songs tend to be specifically different, thus aiding identification, but their plumages are very similar and the birds can be very confusing and difficult to separate from each other even when examined in the hand. Their evolutionary centre is more difficult to determine than in the case of *Sylvia* or even *Hippolais* warblers but it was probably in south-central Asia (Snow 1978). They are chiefly birds of the Palaearctic and Oriental regions while their habitats are mainly alpine or subalpine in character and 'the great mountain systems surrounding the Tibetan plateau show the richest variety of forms' (Williamson 1976). Today when fifteen species breed

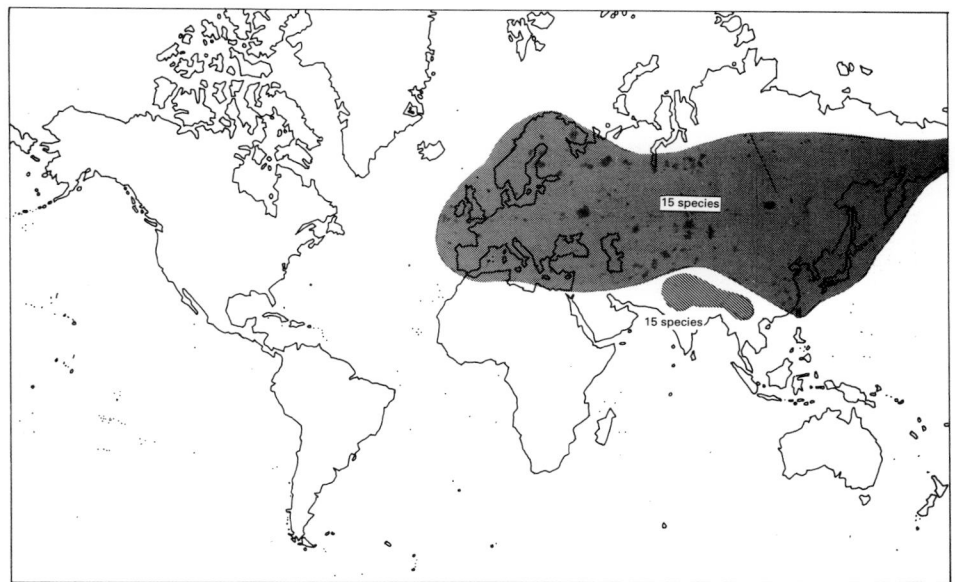

from the British Isles across to the Bering Straits another fifteen are concentrated in the mountainous regions north and northeast of the Indian subcontinent. There are many species in the montane forests of the Himalayas and Burma. The continent of Europe, less well endowed in both the extent and variety of its alpine habitats, has many fewer species, but three species: the Arctic (*Ph. borealis*), the Greenish (*Ph. trochiloides*) and the Yellow-browed (*Ph. inornatus*) have steadily been invading Europe from the continent of Asia. In the tropics and subtropics members of the subfamily *Sylviinae* are mostly skulking birds of low vegetation and field layers and have rounded wings, whereas the temperate species with the needs of migration before them tend to have longer wings and are less able to exploit the lower scrubby and dense layers of vegetation (Gaston 1974).

The taxonomy and distribution of the small insect-eating *Phylloscopi*

Fig. 126
Distribution of breeding Phylloscopus *species showing concentration around the Himalayas.*

have been examined and discussed by Ticehurst (1938) and Williamson (1976). Ticehurst treated the *Phylloscopus* warblers on the basis of several structural features including the bill, which was thin and pointed or sometimes wider, suggesting a flycatcher; the rictal bristles which were always present even if small in some instances; the length and breadth of the tarsi and the ratio of wing to tail. Williamson, however, placed a greater emphasis on 'primary plumage characters – such as the presence or absence of wing-bars, dark coronal bands, a yellow rump-band and pale edges to the tertials' and in this way achieved a more natural grouping of species. Later, A. J. Gaston (1974) took the variations among species in the genus in relation to weight, relative lengths of bill, tarsus, wing and tail, wing formula and roundness of wing, emargination and colour of plumage and compared all these with various niche preferences, feeding methods and morphology.

Table 24   *Moult in Phylloscopus warblers*

Species	Post-nuptial moult (breeding ground)	Body moult		Complete moult Winter
		Winter	Spring	
Green Warbler	● (body and tertials)			●
Greenish Warbler	● (body)			●
Arctic Warbler	● (body)	● (complete)		
Pallas's Warbler	●		●	
Yellow-browed Warbler	● (complete)		●	
Radde's Warbler	● (complete)		● (tail)	
Dusky Warbler	● (complete)		● (body)	
Bonelli's Warbler	● (body and some others)			● (partial)
Wood Warbler	● (body and some others)			●
Chiffchaff	● (complete)	● (body and some others)		
Willow Warbler	● (complete)			●

These will be discussed later in the chapter. The nature of the moult can be seen in Table 24.

It is clear that among the species of the genus *Phylloscopus* there are two colour-types, depending on the amount of melanin – the commonest pigment in birds – in the plumage. The first, and more usual of these types, is greenish or olive above and yellowish below, while the second with more melanin in the plumage has brownish upperparts and whitish-buff underparts. In some instances one or other of these types is exclusive but in others there may be a cline showing a gradation in plumage from one to the other across the full extent of the bird's range. Many races in this genus have been determined by the amount of melanin in the plumage, and there may be intermediate and indeterminate forms where a species has a continuous range. The cline may be irregular and Williamson cited one form of the Chiffchaff and one of the Willow Warbler as examples. There are also two broad geographical groups, one with a good number of species occupying Asiatic regions and wintering in the area from India to the lands and islands in the southeast of that continent, and the other European with wintering grounds chiefly on the African continent. The movements of the species on the British list will be discussed in the chapters on individual species. The following table is a broad key to these two groups and is based on Williamson (1976).

A. *Asiatic leaf warblers*   Table 25

1. *Yellow-rumped leaf warblers and relatives*

Characters	Species	Status in British Isles
Small size; arboreal; greenish above, yellow or whitish-yellow below; round-winged. Clear double wing-bar and supercilium. Dark coronal bands, separated by pale crown stripe (obscure in *inornatus*). Tertials with pale edges and tips. Yellow rump band (less clear in *subviridis* and even less in *inornatus*). White in tail of *pulcher* and *maculipennis* but not others.	Orange-barred Leaf Warbler (*Ph. pulcher*)	
	Ashy-throated Leaf Warbler (*Ph. maculipennis*)	
	Pallas's Warbler (*Ph. proregulus*)	Scarce vagrant
	Brooks's Leaf Warbler (*Ph. subviridis*)	
	Yellow-browed Warbler (*Ph. inornatus*)	Rare vagrant

2. *Crowned leaf warblers and relatives*

Characters	Species	Status in British Isles
Medium to small; arboreal; largely greenish above and yellow or yellowish white below; round-winged. Double wing-bar (single in *coronatus*). Clear supercilium. Dark or dusky coronal bands divided by pale crown-stripe. No pale edges or tips to tertials. Tail with varying amount of white on 3 outer tail feathers.	Slater's Leaf Warbler (*Ph. ricketti*)	
	Yellow-faced Leaf Warbler (*Ph. cantator*)	
	Oates's Crowned Leaf Warbler (*Ph. davisoni*)	
	Blyth's Crowned Leaf Warbler (*Ph. reguloides*)	
	Eastern Crowned Leaf Warbler (*Ph. coronatus*)	
	Western Crowned Leaf Warbler (*Ph. occipitalis*)	

Table 25   *Continued*

3. *Arctic/greenish warblers and relatives*

Characters	Species	Status in British Isles
Large to medium; arboreal. Greenish above (but brown in *tenellipes*). Long-winged in migratory and round-winged in mountain forms. Double wing-bar (lower faint in *tytleri*). Well-defined supercilium. Crown often darker than mantle. No coronal bands or stripes or pale edges and tips to tertials or yellow rump band. Whitish margin to inner webs of 3 outer tail feathers.	Pale-legged Leaf Warbler (*Ph. tenellipes*)	
	Slender-billed Leaf Warbler (*Ph. tytleri*)	
	Green or Green Leaf Warbler (*Ph. nitidus*)	Vagrant
	Two-barred Greenish Warbler (*Ph. plumbeitarsus*)	
	Greenish Warbler (*Ph. trochiloides*)	Vagrant
	Large-billed Leaf Warbler (*Ph. magnirostris*)	
	Arctic Warbler (*Ph. borealis*)	Vagrant

4. *Other Asiatic species*

Characters	Species	Status in British Isles
Large to medium; ground or low vegetation birds. Plumage greenish or browner when more melanin present. Round-winged. No wing-bars. No markings of crown. Supercilium clearly evident in *fuscatus* and *schwarzi* but less in mountain forms. No pale edges or tips to tertials. No yellow rump-band. No white in tail except in *affinis*. Possess none of primary characters of 3 preceding sections.	Radde's Warbler (*Ph. schwarzi*)	Vagrant
	Milne-Edwards's Leaf Warbler (*Ph. armandii*)	
	Dusky Warbler (*Ph. fuscatus*)	Vagrant
	Smoky Warbler (*Ph. fuliginventer*)	
	Sulphur-bellied Leaf Warbler (*Ph. griseolus*)	
	Tickell's and Ogilvie-Grant's Leaf Warblers (*Ph. affinis*)	

B. *European leaf warblers*

Characters	Species	Status in British Isles
Large to small; arboreal. These lack the characters in A1, A2 and A3 except for a less strong supercilium. No wing-bars, no crown marks, no pale edges or tips to tertials. No white in tail. No yellow rump (except in some examples of *bonelli*). Bill weak. Plumage varies from brown above and buffish white below to greenish on upperparts and yellowish colour below.	Bonelli's Warbler (*Ph. bonelli*)	Vagrant
	Wood Warbler (*Ph. sibilatrix*)	Summer visitor, passage
	Plain Leaf Warbler (*Ph. neglectus*)	
	Mountain Chiffchaff (*Ph. sindianus*)	
	Chiffchaff (*Ph. collybita*)	Summer visitor, winterer, passage
	Willow Warbler (*Ph. trochilus*)	Summer visitor, passage

For all these species the wing formulae, measurements and details of moult can be found in Williamson (1976) but as a handy source of reference I am listing dimensions and weights for eleven species and eight forms of *Phylloscopus* warblers in the British list, compiled from Williamson, *The Handbook* (1946) and Simms (unpublished).

Some dimensions and weights of Phylloscopus warblers   Table 26

Species	Wing (mm)		Tail (mm)		Bill (mm)		Tarsus (mm)		Weight
	Range	Mean	Range	Mean	Range	Mean	Range	Mean	
Pallas's Warbler	43–58	48.35	30–45	37.78	9–11.5	10.12	15–19	16.83	4.5–7.5
Yellow-browed Warbler	50–61	55.36	33–46	39.49	9.5–12	10.73	16–21	18.60	4.3–7
Arctic Warbler	57–74	65.42	38–55	46.33	12–16	13.82	17.5–22	19.74	7.5–13
Greenish Warbler (*Ph.t. viridanus*)	53–68	60.34	39–54	46.41	11–13.5	12.21	17–21	19.21	6.5–10.5
(*Ph.t. trochiloides*)	51–72	61.45	40–60	50.03	11–14	12.54	17–21	19.21	–
Green Warbler	55–69	61.94	40–53	46.16	11–15	12.87	16.5–21	18.84	–
Dusky Warbler	50–70	60.10	43–59	50–18	11.5–13	12.43	19–23.5	21.78	8.7–11.5
Radde's Warbler	53–71	62	42–65	33.52	11–14.5	12.84	20–25	22.53	8.5–13.5
Chiffchaff (*Ph.c. collybita*)	50–68	58.54	39–56	47.36	10–13	11.58	18.5–21.5	19.97	5.7–9.2
(*Ph.c. abietinus*)	50–72	60.63	39–58	48.14	10–13	11.58	18.5–21.5	19.97	5.9–9.1
(*Ph.c. tristis*)	50–70	60.37	39–59	49.04	10–13	11.58	18.5–21.5	19.97	6.2–9.3
Willow Warbler (*Ph.t. trochilus*)	57–74	65.22	41–58	49.18	9.5–14	11.73	18.5–22.5	20.55	6.3–11.9
(*Ph.t. acredula*)	59–76	67.38	42–60	50.98	9.5–14	11.73	18.5–22.5	20.55	8.5 (av)
Wood Warbler	68–82	74.74	42–56	48.89	11.5–15	12.98	17–20.5	18.67	8.2–11.8
Bonelli's Warbler (*Ph.b. bonelli*)	56–69	62.44	42–54	47.95	11–14	12.55	16.5–21	18.96	6.4–10.6
(*Ph.b. orientalis*)	58–73	65.53	41–55	48.08	10.5–14	12.20	16–20	18.08	–

With its many species the genus *Phylloscopus* utilizes a wide range of habitats from the tropical rain forests north to the dwarf birch zones of the Arctic. Some populations are sedentary, some migratory and others are in the process of extending their ranges into Europe. A special study of adaptation in the genus *Phylloscopus* by A. J. Gaston (1974) led to the conclusion that 'evolution within the genus has taken place mainly through the development of different feeding strategies, to suit the structural properties of different niches, without altering the range of size of the prey.' Birds will take flying insects on the wing, snatch insects from the surface of vegetation whilst in flight, and hover in front of foliage. Some species can indulge in 'multiple hovering' with this action carried out several times in succession. Other techniques of food gathering involve flitting with short flights being undertaken to investigate potential sources of food on the ground or in foliage and also the searching of tree boles, branches, twigs and even the ground without regular flights but hopping movements instead. Gaston made a tentative division of 28 species of *Phylloscopus* into 'niche-groups' based on the type of vegetation preferred and the height at which foraging took place. There was also some correlation between the colour of the upperparts of these warblers and the niche that they favoured. The broad niche-groups proposed by Gaston were as follows:

Table 27   *Niche–groups for Phylloscopus warblers*

GROUP A. Arboreal; deciduous trees	Eastern Crowned Leaf Warbler, Green Warbler, Two-barred Greenish Warbler, Arctic Warbler, Wood Warbler, Willow Warbler
GROUP A/B Arboreal; deciduous or coniferous trees	Blyth's Crowned Leaf Warbler, Western Crowned Leaf Warbler, Large-billed Leaf Warbler, Yellow-browed Warbler, Bonelli's Warbler
GROUP B Arboreal; coniferous trees	Oates's Crowned Leaf Warbler, Slender-billed Leaf Warbler, Orange-barred Leaf Warbler, Ashy-throated Leaf Warbler, Pallas's Warbler, Brooks's Leaf Warbler
GROUP C Arboreal in summer, ranging to the ground in winter	Pale-legged Leaf Warbler, Greenish Warbler, Chiffchaff
GROUP D Scrub-dwellers or terrestrial	Radde's Warbler, Milne-Edwards's Warbler, Dusky Warbler, Smoky Warbler, Sulphur-bellied Warbler, Tickell's and Ogilvie-Grant's Warblers, Mountain Chiffchaff

With relation to the shape of the wings the index of roundness was lower amongst those species classified in Group A and highest amongst birds in Groups B and D. The shorter wings of species living in dense cover or near the ground are probably the result of selection (Hamilton 1961), but Gaston was of the opinion, in relation to the longer wings of migratory species or races and the shorter ones of non-migratory ones, that wing length is resolved more by the differences in ecological niche in association with weight, than to factors in migration such as distance flown. There was a marked difference in weight between birds in Groups A and B. The mean size of arboreal *Phylloscopus* warblers is smaller amongst those living in conifers than those frequenting deciduous broad-leaved trees; the foliage of conifers is more difficult to negotiate than that of broad-leaved trees and a smaller size would convey advantage together with flitting and hovering techniques of feeding. Species living in Groups A, A/B and B also have relatively shorter tail-lengths than those placed in Groups C and D. Two of the species with the shortest tails – the Sulphur-bellied Warbler, which behaves amongst trees rather like a nuthatch, and Tickell's, which moves around its rocky terrain like a chat, probably reflect the nature of their preferred habitats. Generally the tail shape of the *Phylloscopi* is square at the end, but Radde's and the Dusky Warbler have slightly extended central tail feathers that give a suggestion of roundness to the tail. It may be remembered that rounded tails are typical of *Locustella* and *Acrocephalus* warblers – grasshopper and reed warblers – as well as some *Sylvia* or typical warblers, while the *Hippolais* or tree warblers tend to have squarish or slightly notched tails. The species that live on or near the ground most of the time have relatively longer tails and legs and more rounded wings than those living in trees. Flycatching and snatching of insect prey was commoner among the arboreal warblers of Groups A, A/B and B, while hovering, and particularly multiple hovering, could be found most commonly among the members of Group B. In a most interesting and stimulating paper Gaston (1974) pointed out characters in the groups which suggested convergence with other genera of the *Sylviinae*. Species in Group B were close to the genus *Regulus* – the kinglets – including the Goldcrest, in Group A with the *Ficedula* flycatchers and in Group D to the genus *Sylvia*. The Wood Warbler *Ph. sibilatrix* resembled other members of the genus in breeding habits and song but was most removed from the generic mean which might suggest evolution into 'a separate adaptive zone' – a bird that, still in the early stages of its development, may be free to move into other areas at present outside its range.

Members of the *Phylloscopus* genus are always hard to observe as they spend much time in tree canopies or in thick vegetation in the field layer. The sexes are also alike and the young differ little from the adults. Although they spend so much time under cover, they nest on or near the ground and most of them construct round, domed nests with a side entrance. The building of the nest and the duties of incubation are the responsibilities of the hen alone, although in such species as the Chiffchaff and Wood Warbler the male may occasionally feed the female on the nest. The eggs are white and generally speckled lightly with brown. It is probably by voice that observers in the field are most likely to separate the different species, not by calls which are often alike, but by the territorial songs. The generic quality of the songs may lack the persistence of phrase of the Garden Warbler, the invention and passion of the Icterine Warbler or the sheer magic of the Marsh Warbler, yet most of them are sweet and pleasing to our ears: musical warbles and ditties which are really quite distinctive and serve to keep similar species apart. The songs may appear on the surface to be very stereotyped but the study of sonagrams often reveals alternative songs in use by one individual. Call notes can help with recognition but it is often difficult to separate even distinct species by ear alone; and yet there may be clear differences between races as can be found with the Chiffchaff. In a study of the calls of several species in the genus it was shown that the attack calls of Willow and Wood Warblers were transmitted genetically (Schubert and Schubert 1969); most calls appear to be innate anyway.

It is my intention to make some reference to the Asiatic Leaf Warblers and Crowned Leaf Warblers, the Arctic/Greenish Warblers and other Asiatic species as well as European ones; those on the British list will be given fuller treatment in subsequent chapters. Firstly we have to consider the yellow-rumped leaf warblers of Asia. The Orange-barred Leaf Warbler (*Ph. pulcher*) is a yellow-rumped warbler with a striking double orange wing-bar which ranges in the breeding season from the Himalayas east to Szechwan, northern Burma and Yunnan. The bird nests at heights

of from 2300–4600 m and comes down to lower levels for the winter. A form
Ph.p. kangrae, which is brighter and yellower below, has been described
for the northwest Himalayas but these birds are frequenters of coniferous
and oak woodlands and scrub, singing high Wood Warbler-like trills and
calling with a thrush-like 'zip' or 'twik'. With a similar distribution to that
of the last, another yellow-rumped species, the Ashy-throated Leaf Warbler
(*Ph. maculipennis*) with a lot of grey on the head, face and neck, lives in the
canopies of tall trees and utters a repeated 'zip' call; there is a race *virens*
in the northwest Himalayas. Brooks's Leaf Warbler (*Ph. subviridis*), named
after the rather forgotten ornithologist, W. E. Brooks, who studied the
Phylloscopi in India in the 1870s, has a pale yellow rump and double wing-
bar; it is a breeding bird of the high coniferous forests from 2300–4000 m
on the borders of Afghanistan and Pakistan. It has a very distinctive song
'pi-pi-piazz-z-z-z' and the call-note is a shrill tinkling 'tiss-yip'. Pallas's
Warbler (*Ph. proregulus*) is a scarce vagrant to Britain from the region that
stretches from southwest Siberia to eastern Siberia and Sakhalin; it will be
one of the subjects of Chapter 31. There are, however, two races that inhabit pine forests and deodar; *chloronotus* is greyer and not so bright and
lives in the belts of trees from 2600–4300 m in the eastern Himalayas,
coming down in the winter and moving south to Burma and Thailand,
while *simlaensis* is brighter and more yellowish-green and lives in Nepal
and on the borders of Afghanistan and Pakistan. Finally, in the yellow-
rumped group is the Yellow-Browed Warbler (*Ph. inornatus*) of Siberia
which is a regular vagrant to Europe and Britain and will also figure in
Chapter 31. There are the races *mandellii* with browner, darker upperparts
and a greenish rump that live in forests of poplar, willow and spruce in
mountain ranges in the Himalayas and has two calls: 'tjiss-jipp' and a soft
'si-si', and *humei*, once known as Hume's Yellow-browed Warbler, that
lacks a yellow tinge on the head, underparts and wing-bars and has a loud
ringing 'chil-ip' or 'te-twee-up' call quite unlike the loud 'weest' call of the
typical Yellow-browed Warbler.

There are six species of crowned leaf warblers, forming what would
appear to be a proper species group. The Western Crowned Leaf Warbler
(*Ph. occipitalis*) is a bird of conifers and scrub breeding from 2000–3300 m
in the Himalayas, Kashmir and on the borders of Afghanistan and Pakistan;
sometimes known as the Kashmir Warbler, this species has 'a pale yellowish occipital streak along the crown between broad and dusky coronal bands'
(Alexander 1955). The Eastern Crowned Leaf Warbler (*Ph. coronatus*) is
green and white with yellow undertail coverts, a Far Eastern version of the
Wood Warbler – and has a more easterly distribution from Siberia and
Manchuria to Korea and Japan. It migrates south through China to Malaysia, Indonesia and other countries in southeast Asia, and has been recorded
on Heligoland (Gätke 1895). D. I. M. Wallace (1980) suggested that this
species was a possible future vagrant to Britain. It has been described as
less volatile than most other *Phylloscopus* warblers. Blyth's Crowned Leaf
Warbler (*Ph. reguloides*), known also as Baker's Warbler, is a bright little
bird with yellowish wing-bars but no yellow on the rump. *Ph. r. reguloides*
lives in Nepal, Bhutan, Sikkim and southern Tibet from 2000–3330 m
where it constantly utters its call 'kee-kew-i'. The race *kashmirensis* frequents groves of oak and rhododendron growing over 2600 m in the Himalayas; *claudiae*, which lives at a similar height as the last, sings a Wood

Warbler-like trill and can be found in Kansu, Sikang and Szechwan; *fokiensis* that breeds in southeast China and has a song of three syllables 'chi, chi, chi', and *ticehursti* from Annam. The rather uncertain race *assamensis* has a single 'cheep' call and occurs in broad-leaved patches in coniferous woodland in autumn. Oates's Crowned Leaf Warbler (*Ph. davisoni*), which Alexander in 1955 called the White-tailed Warbler, is near to *reguloides* but the actual tones of green and yellow vary with the populations, the species is smaller and also has conspicuous white in the three outer tail feathers. The most white can be seen on *Ph.d. davisoni* which lives in open high altitude evergreen forest in Burma and Laos. There are several other races: *disturbans* south from Szechwan possibly to Yunnan, *ogilvie-granti* from Yunnan, Annam and Fukien and *klossi* from southern Laos and Annam. Finally, there are the Yellow-faced Leaf Warbler *Ph. cantator* of the Himalayas east to Burma and Slater's Leaf Warbler *Ph. ricketti*, or Rickett's Warbler, which has, according to Alexander, 'a face-pattern like a small tiger, with black lateral coronal streaks contrasting with a pale yellowish central coronal band and bright yellow superciliary.' This is very much an arboreal species frequenting light evergreen forests in southeast China, Fukien, Annam, Tonkin, Yunnan, Laos and Thailand; a smaller race, *Ph.r. goodsoni*, has been reported from south Hainan.

When we come to the Asiatic leaf warblers we find seven species of large to medium-sized warblers with a lower wing-bar present in all the forms but rather faint in *Ph. tytleri*; the upper bar is present in some species but it may be lost through abrasion. The Arctic Warbler *Ph. borealis*, once known as Eversmann's Warbler, is a variable species and although Vaurie (1959) claimed five races and supported earlier authorities in this arrangement, Williamson (1976) reported that: 'Over the whole of its continental range in Eurasia, except perhaps for Kamchatka, I cannot see that any advantage is to be gained by recognizing other than nominate *borealis*.' This species has been recorded in Europe into which it has extended its range and also in Britain. It breeds in damp forests and scrub across northern Eurasia from arctic Fenno-Scandia to the Bering Straits and Alaska, north to about 75° on the Taimyr Peninsula, south to about 68°N in Finland and 61°N in Siberia and in Asia to Mongolia and the Sea of Okhotsk. The race *xanthodryas*, which is a brighter greener-olive, lives in high birch and conifer forest where it sings with a penetrating 'chi-chirra' song rather like that of a Chiffchaff and has a rather metallic 'chink' call; this race may be confined to a few Japanese islands but it possibly also occurs in the south Kurile Islands and Kamchatka. The Alaskan race *kennicotti* is similar to *borealis* and is unique in being the only *Phylloscopus* to have entered the New World; it migrates in a backwards direction to the Philippines and other parts of southeast Asia. (We shall be returning to the Arctic Warbler and the next species, the Greenish, in Chapter 31.)

The group of Greenish Warblers is interesting in that various subspecies once isolated for long periods have joined together but the characteristics that appeared during the separation now militate against their interbreeding so that they now act as true species. The Greenish Warbler (*Ph. trochiloides*) breeds from the Baltic eastward to the Yenisei and southeast to the Himalayas. Looking rather like a greyish Willow Warbler it has a pale wing-bar and well-marked yellowish supercilium. Some of the more than one hundred Greenish Warblers that have reached Britain have been identified as *Ph.t. viridanus* and, in fact, all were probably of this race. The nominate *trochiloides* is a forest bird of the Himalayas from 2000–4600 m, migrating to India or Burma, or even just descending from the high mountain ranges; it is rather like the Large-billed Leaf Warbler but lacks the hook at the end of upper mandible in that species. Another race *ludlowi* seems to link *viridanus* with *trochiloides* and can be found in the Himalayas from Kashmir to Kumaon, while a rather less distinct form *obscuratus* has been described from the mountains of Tsinghai and Kansu. The Green Warbler (*Ph. nitidus*), known also as the Bright Green Leaf Warbler, is rather like a small Wood Warbler with a purer, cleaner green; this species is a bird of the Caucasus, Iran, Afghanistan regions and migrates through India to the south of the subcontinent and to Sri Lanka. It is said to have been taken in the Crimea and on Heligoland, and at the time of writing one has been reported in Britain. The Two-barred Greenish Warbler (*Ph. plumbeitarsus*) is greener and less grey than the Greenish Warbler and greener too than a first-winter Willow Warbler. It has a yellow supercilium and mottled cheeks. This arboreal bird of forested mountains breeds from Siberia northwards to 64°N, from the Yenisei to the Sea of Okhotsk and south to Mongolia and Manchuria. It is replaced by the Greenish Warbler *Ph.t. viridanus* in the Khangai Mountains in Mongolia and it breeds alongside that species to the west; it migrates through Korea and China to southeast Asia. It is slightly larger than the Yellow-browed Warbler and might be mistaken for it but the latter species has yellowish edges and tips to the tertials while the Two-barred Greenish Warbler has these feathers uniform with the secondaries.

The Pale-legged Leaf Warbler (*Ph. tenellipes*) has a golden brown rump and pure white underparts, a double wing-bar and a whitish edge to the outside tail feathers. This is a denizen of broad-leaved forests in river valleys in Japan, the Kurile Islands, Sakhalin and North Korea, migrating to Malaysia and Burma. The song consists of a thin trisyllabic note and the calls are 'tik-tik' and a tit-like 'hee-tsu-pee'. The race *ijimae*, which is restricted to the Seven Islands east of Honshu, was regarded by Ticehurst (1938) as a race of the Eastern Crowned Leaf Warbler *Ph. coronatus*, by Vaurie (1954) and Voous (1977) as a full species, while Williamson (1976) believed it to be 'an insular derivative' of *Ph. tenellipes*. There is also the Large-billed Leaf Warbler *Ph. magnirostris* of high wooded valleys in the Himalayas; this species is olive in colour with a yellow-white supercilium and a single wing-bar. The bill is long, stout and in the adult equipped, as we have already seen, with a small hook-like process at the tip which distinguishes it from the Greenish Warbler. Lastly in this group of Arctic and Greenish Warblers and their close relatives is the Slender-billed Leaf Warbler (*Ph. tytleri*) which inhabits pine forests at heights between 2600–3300 m in the Himalayas.

There are six species in the *Phylloscopus* genus known as Dusky Warblers. These are greenish or more often dark brown above and brownish-yellow or olive below. They can best be recognized by the marked absence of features – no markings on the crown, no wing-bars, no yellow rump-band and no white in the tail. The supercilium may be well developed or in some mountain forms indistinct. There has been a great deal of speculation and discussion in the past about this group and the specific or racial status of its members. However, Williamson and Voous both agreed on six species. Two have occurred as vagrants in the British Isles and will reappear in Chapter 31; these are the Dusky Warbler *Ph. fuscatus*, which does not apparently breed west of the River Ob in Siberia, and Radde's Warbler *Ph. schwarzi*, which is an even more easterly species breeding in Siberia east to Sakhalin, north to Lake Baikal and south to Korea. The Dusky Warbler also has a race *weigoldi*, which is darker and inhabits the mountains of Szechwan, Tsinghai and Sikang. The Smoky Warbler *Ph. fuligiventer*, which is a sooty brown on top and a dusky yellow below, has a call 'tak' or 'tek' like that of a Lesser Whitethroat; it breeds amongst the rocks and boulders in and above the rhododendron forests and scrub in Bhutan and probably Nepal at heights of 4000–4800 m; it is a species that flicks its wings and tail incessantly. There is a darker race of the Smoky Warbler *tibetanus* from Sikang, which lives in the alpine zone above the conifers as well as in rhododendrons and junipers (Ludlow 1944), where its movements and alarm notes suggest those of a European Wren.

Another species of the high mountains is the Sulphur-bellied Warbler, or Olivaceous Leaf Warbler *Ph. griseolus*, which is dark brown with a clear orange-yellow supercilium and sulphur-yellow underparts. This bird can be found up to 5000 m on open stony ground with thin scrub such as juniper and here it is a skulking bird of low undergrowth and rocky terrain as well as trees. The breeding range embraces the mountains of south-central Asia, perhaps the point of origin of all the *Phylloscopus* warblers – of Afghanistan, Pakistan, the Himalayas across to Mongolia and Tsinghai, while birds go to winter in India. Milne-Edwards's Warbler *Ph. armandii*, variously known as the Buff-browed or Streak-breasted Leaf Warbler, has brownish-olive upperparts, yellowish-white underparts and a whitish throat streaked with bright yellow; it is a skulking bird of poplar, willow and spruce groves as well as scrub at altitude in the mountains of China, Mongolia and perhaps Burma (where it winters) and northern Indo-China.

Finally, in the group of other Asiatic warblers is Tickell's or the Chinese Leaf Warbler *Ph. affinis* which is now recognized as also including Ogilvie-Grant's or the Buff-bellied Leaf Warbler which was once regarded by Ticehurst (1938) and Vaurie (1959) as a separate species: *Ph. subaffinis*. The two forms are distinct from each other over most of their range but interbreed where they meet geographically in Yunnan, Szechwan and Sikang. Tickell's is olive-green on its upperparts and bright yellow on the belly, undertail coverts and supercilium. It breeds up to heights of over 5000 m in the Himalayas where it is also a ground feeder in alpine scrub, bushy and rocky valleys and open country, but never in forests. It intergrades with Ogilvie-Grant's in the mountains of North Yunnan, Sikang and elsewhere. This latter form has a more slender bill and lives in pinewoods and open scrub at heights of 2000–4000 m from Yunnan to Fukien in China but comes down to 1300 m in winter to the bushy or grassy jungles of southeast Asia such as those in Burma, Laos and Thailand.

We come now to the last group of *Phylloscopi*, that of the mainly European leaf warblers; the Chiffchaffs, Willow Warbler, Plain Leaf Warbler, Wood and Bonelli's Warblers, four species of which are on the British list. On the upperparts these species tend to range from greenish to brownish, and yellowish, and whitish-buff on the underparts. They have rather thin weak bills and are variable in size; they also lack crown markings, wing-bars, yellow rumps, pale edges and tips to the tertials as well as any white on the tail. The Willow Warbler *Ph. trochilus* is the commonest and most widely spread of all our summer-visiting breeding birds. *The Atlas* (1976) suggested a population in Britain and Ireland of at least 3 million breeding pairs, while in Finland a figure of 11,400,000 breeding adults was given by Merikallio (1958). This species, which nests in a wide range of habitats as we shall see in the next chapter, is dimorphic over most of its world range. With a southwestern distribution – and that includes Britain – there is a regular olive and yellow form, while a brown and white one replaces it progressively towards the northeastern breeding range of the species. This second type appears to be the exclusive morph in north Siberia from the Taimyr Peninsula east to the Kolyma and Yana Rivers, south to about 60°N on the Tunguska and Vilui Rivers. However, this form *Ph.t. yaku-tensis* has as yet an unplottable range but embarks on a remarkable migra-tory journey of 9600–11,200 km, flying round the desert regions of Asia to reach its wintering grounds in East Africa. Of forty Willow Warblers examined in Uganda three appeared to be identical to the east Siberian form *yakutensis*, five grey ones could be matched with a series from the valley of the Yenisei and the rest proved to be more typical of the race *acredula* (Pearson 1972). This last race is paler on the upperparts and a brighter yellow and olive, but with less yellow on the breast, than *trochilus* – the western form – and breeds in Norway, central and northern Sweden and then east to the Yenisei River in Siberia, south to the Ukraine and Kirghiz Steppes; the wintering grounds are in Africa from the Sudan south to Natal as well as Angola and eastern Zaire. Here this form undergoes a complete post-nuptial moult up to a month later than the western Willow Warbler *trochilus*, whose breeding range stretches from the British Isles, Denmark, Holland, Belgium, France (except for the southwest), through Switzerland, Germany, Austria, Czechoslovakia, Hungary, Romania, northern Italy, Yugoslavia and east to southern Poland. This race winters both in tropical West and East Africa.

As Williamson (1976) indicated, 'the eastern races, however, have no monopoly of the "brown-and-white" type and in fact many Scottish breed-ing birds are of this kind': a feature described earlier by P. A. Clancey (1950). Many birds that I have seen nesting in Argyllshire and elsewhere in northern Scotland have been of the 'brown-and-white' type; I also watched birds of this kind around Appleby in the Pennines when my home was there from 1941–3. Scottish birds are apparently impossible to separate from grey-brown Willow Warblers in Scandinavia. In Britain a series of spring birds from Sussex north to Sutherland 'shows a reasonably constant green form in the South of England, a small number of clear-cut grey-brown and white birds from Scotland (Perthshire, Inverness and Fife) and a steadily intergrading population from Lancashire northwards into Scotland' (Hazelwood and Gorton 1956). A series of ten birds from the Yenisei River could be matched with some Scottish breeding birds (Williamson 1976). It is likely that the two populations of *Ph. trochilus* were two separate forms which survived the last Ice Age in different regions and which spread northwards differentially with the retreat of the glaciers.

Closely related to the Willow Warbler are two species of chiffchaff. The first – the Chiffchaff *Ph. collybita* – has six races some of which have been identified in the British Isles. *Ph.c. collybita* is the breeding bird of western Europe: the British Isles, Holland, Belgium, southern and western Germany, France, Denmark, Switzerland, Czechoslovakia, southern Poland, Austria, Hungary, Romania and the hills of Italy, Bulgaria and Yugoslavia. This is a bird with brownish-olive upperparts, a slightly yellowish-olive rump and a dirty white underside, streaked with yellow on the breast and with a slight yellowish-white supercilium. The call note is a plaintive 'houeet' rather like that of the Willow Warbler but higher-pitched, more emphatic and slurred, while the song is a repetition in rhythmic form of two notes: 'chiff-chaff-chiff-chaff-chaff-chiff' and so on. The Chiffchaff of the Iberian Peninsula and northwest Africa is the race *ibericus*, which is more greenish-olive above and a deeper yellow below and on the undertail coverts, giving altogether the impression of a brighter bird. A bird of this last race in northwest London employed a call like that of a young chicken, quite distinct from that of Willow Warbler or *Ph.c. collybita*. The song of *ibericus* is strikingly dissimilar from that of *collybita*, sharing some of the features of the Willow Warbler and Chiffchaff but also differing from both; there is a clear division of strophes in the song into sections. In southwest France there is a region of overlap between *collybita* and *ibericus* where birds may sing normal songs, those of the Iberian Chiffchaff and a mixture of both. When samples of Chiffchaff songs in northern and central Europe were analysed there was a striking lack of geographical variation (Thielcke and Linsenmair 1963).

Another race of the chiffchaff *abietinus* – paler and greyer on the upperparts and whiter below – breeds from Scandinavia and west Russia to the Caucasus and northern Iran. Vaurie (1959) showed that there was a recog-

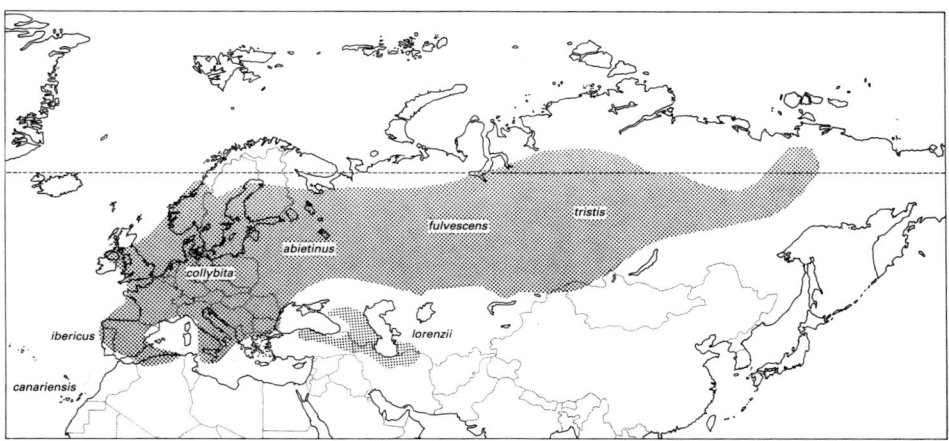

nizable cline of decreased colour-saturation from North Africa through Iberia to Norway. The call of *abietinus* is also said to resemble 'the cheep of a young chicken in distress'. This race also intergrades in the eastern parts of its range with another race *tristis* or the Siberian Chiffchaff. This form is brownish to greyish-brown in colour, lacking olive coloration except on the edges of the wing and tail feathers, wing coverts and rump, and is buff on the flanks and sides of the breast as well as in the eye-ring,

Fig. 127
Distribution of 7 races of the Chiffchaff.

cheeks and supercilium. This race breeds in conifers and mixed forests usually not far from water in northern Siberia from the Pechora River and Ural Mountains across to the Kolyma River as far north as trees will grow, to the Russian Altai and Mongolia. Vaurie (1954) claimed another form *fulvescens* but this has a very broken distribution and rather unstable status and is generally regarded now as *tristis*. Mention should be made perhaps of a rather difficult Chiffchaff in western and northern Turkey, which G. E. Watson (1962) redescribed as *Ph.c. brevirostris* and regarded as being closest to a form of *abietinus* and the race *lorenzii* of the Mountain Chiffchaff *Ph. sindianus*. Both share the region, are geographically sympatric but altitudinally allopatric – that is with contiguous and not overlapping habitats.

There are, finally, two island races of the Chiffchaff. *Ph.c. canariensis* is a distinctive bird with the upperparts darker and more olive-brown than in *collybita* and with a deeper tawny suffusion on the underparts. It is resident on the West Canary Islands where it can be found from sea level to the highest vegetation levels in the hills, including pinewoods, overgrown gardens and orchards. The song, according to Bannerman (1963), is briefer, harsher and lower-pitched than that of *collybita* and lacks the clear differentiation between the high and low notes of that form. Another race *exsul* is smaller, lighter on the upperparts and more fawn-yellow below, and is a scarce bird confined to cultivated regions in the Haria Valley on Lanzarote.

The Willow Warbler and Chiffchaff must have diverged in their evolutionary history from some ancestral form whose populations were separated by various physical barriers during the Ice Ages. This was for a period sufficiently enduring for forms to develop with differences in their plumage and leg-colour which could distinguish them. They may also, in part, have evolved their distinctive types of song. The Chiffchaff has a steady monotonous repetition of two notes with little dynamic range and some quieter chirps added, while the Willow Warbler utters a silvery descending cascade of notes with a purity of tone and lack of effort that delight many people living in the temperate zone. The species are siblings that do not usually interbreed in the wild. Their songs are so different and contain a sufficient number of aural clues for easy identification. Playback of sound recordings has shown that the two species are kept apart primarily by differences in the songs. During the period of glaciation there were two refuges for birds in southern Europe: one in the west and the other in the east. Rosemary Jellis (1977) has described how the 'normal' Chiffchaff and Willow Warbler were probably confined to the eastern refuge 'where, as sibling species, they may have continued to differentiate vocally even more strongly.' However, Chiffchaffs that sought sanctuary in the western redoubt in northwest Africa and the islands kept much more of the features of the ancestral form of song which was probably closer to that of the Chiffchaff than that of the Willow Warbler (Schubert and Schubert 1969). In their western stronghold the Chiffchaffs' song may well have gone on developing but when the ice had retreated and the two forms met, although they had not yet reached specific divergence, their songs were sufficiently different to keep them apart. In an experiment in which sound recordings were played back to Willow Warblers and Chiffchaffs in Germany, both warblers responded well to recordings of the songs of their own species and hardly at all to those of their siblings, but both reacted much more strongly to the Spanish Chiffchaff *ibericus* than to the sibling type; strong evidence indeed that both species identified elements in it that corresponded more nearly to those in their own songs.

The difference in habitats between the two species has not been very clear in Europe but in Britain I have seen a much greater tendency for Chiffchaffs to feed higher up and to show a stronger preference for taller trees; in the eastern parts of the range there are rather greater differences in habitat. However, in a study of habitat selection by both Willow Warblers and Chiffchaffs in grey alder forests in central Norway, B-E. Saether (1983) found that both species occurred in all the stages of tree succession but the Willow Warbler appeared slightly more regularly in the younger stages. Saether's research supported an earlier study by Cody (1978) and the contention that, although a considerable overlap existed, the Willow Warbler chose a greater variety of habitats. In my own observation of the two species in several hundred woods in the British Isles, as well in close studies of birds in oakwoods in the Midlands of England and mixed woods in Lincolnshire, it became clear that Willow Warblers were to be found more regularly in open habitats with low tree heights. This was also found to be true in Finland (Haila *et al* 1980). Saether found both species horizontally well segregated and the pattern of spacing was thought to be more likely a 'result of mutual avoidance and thus not related to differences in habitat preferences.' The species were found to occupy almost mutually exclusive territories. There is often considerable interspecific aggression among the various Phylloscopid species. Indeed Eliot Howard (1948) described much aggression between Willow Warbler and Chiffchaff while, although little occurred in lowland woods between Willow Warbler and Wood Warbler, much sparring took place between these last species in the fell woods of Wales (Edington and Edington 1972). There is quite an overlap in food between Chiffchaff and Willow Warbler and Saether reported that 'in areas of joint occurrence the foraging niches of the two species were very similar.' It was suggested that a greater ecological divergence had not taken place because of competition from other species in the ecosystem.

The second species of chiffchaff is the Mountain Chiffchaff *Ph. sindianus*, which is isolated in the mountains of Sinkiang, the northwest Himalayas and the Pamirs with a closely allied race *lorenzii* in the Caucasus. The Mountain bears some resemblance to the Siberian Chiffchaff *Ph.c. tristis* but in spring it is an even greyer warbler. It is a bird of scrub and willow woodland from a height of 2650–4600 m. The song is a weaker, less rhythmic version of the song of *Ph.c. collybita* and the call-note is a loud 'tiss-yip'. In winter the Mountain Chiffchaff can be found among the acacias and tamarisks that grow in Sind and the Indus valley where it mingles with Siberian Chiffchaffs and Plain Leaf Warblers. The race *lorenzii* is a bird of the subalpine and higher forest zones of the Caucasus coming down into the foothills for the winter.

Several small greyish-green or greyish-brown warblers that frequent high scrub from 2000–3000 m in the Himalayas, Afghanistan, Turkestan and Baluchistan have been brought together in one species: the Plain Leaf Warbler *Ph. neglectus*. This warbler is about the size of a Goldcrest and lacks all trace of yellow or green in its coloration; the upperparts are a greyish olive-brown, there is a indistinct whitish supercilium and the underparts are buffish-white. The call is said to resemble that of the Gold-crest. However, in winter the species visits the Indian plains and even the shore of the Persian Gulf and here the bird employs a harsh churring call.

Whereas the Chiffchaff is a warbler of the western and central Palaearctic and the Willow Warbler a bird of the Palaearctic, the Wood Warbler *Ph. sibilatrix* which is the third breeding species of *Phylloscopus* in the British Isles, is a species of the western Palaearctic region. It is the largest leaf warbler of the region and has yellowish-green upperparts with a slight brownish or greyish tinge, a clear yellow supercilium, throat and upper breast, and white underparts. The Wood Warbler is a bird of woodland canopies with little shrub or field layer, and here it sings two different songs quite unlike those of Chiffchaff or Willow Warbler. It breeds in Eurasia from the British Isles, France and central Scandinavia east to the Ural Mountains; southeast to the Balkans and the Crimea; south to Italy with a small isolated population in the Pyrenees. It is the least common of the three breeding leaf warblers in the British Isles with a total breeding popu-lation of 30,000–60,000 pairs compared to 300,000 pairs of Chiffchaffs and three million pairs of Willow Warblers. The Wood Warbler winters around the Equator or just to the north of it, from northeast Kenya and northern Uganda through northern Zaire and Cameroon to Guinea and the Ivory Coast. (A fuller history of its movements will be given in the species account in Chapter 30.)

The last of the *Phylloscopus* warblers is rather like a grey Willow Warbler; it is Bonelli's Warbler *Ph. bonelli* and it has some affinities, including that of song, with the Wood Warbler. It breeds in montane woods with climax forest and little ground vegetation and in this respect also resembles *Ph. sibilatrix*. The breeding range of the typical race includes northwest Africa, Iberia, France except for the north, southern Belgium, Germany, Austria, Czechoslovakia, Switzerland, Italy, Sicily and Corsica. It winters in west Africa. There is also a greyer race still of Bonelli's Warbler – *Ph.b. orientalis* – which occurs in Yugoslavia, Greece, Turkey, Israel and perhaps southern Syria, the eastern race of the species. This form winters in the Sudan. *Ph.b. bonelli* is an irregular drift migrant and has appeared in Britain.

The Willow Warbler

Of all the species of warbler that occur in the British Isles and most of northern Europe, the Willow Warbler is by far the commonest and most widespread. Its songs make up an important part of the bird choruses of woodland and scrub from April to July; and again, but more spasmodically and with less passion, in the autumn. The Willow Warbler is quite likely to be the one species of warbler that attracts the attention of the layman as he walks through the woods due to the persistence and volume of its delicate and charming warblings. Thomas Bewick noted that many naturalists called it 'the Liquid-noted Willow Wren'. As we have seen earlier, it is a

Fig. 128
Willow Warbler chasing House Sparrow – even migrants will cease feeding to make such aerial sallies. (D. I. M. Wallace)

bird with olive-brown upperparts and whitish-buff underparts tinged with yellow in the breast, but there is also a plumage-type in which the green and yellow colours are suppressed. There is a supercilium, sometimes fairly clear but not always distinct. First-winter birds have uniform bright yellow underparts with a buffish tinge over the breast as well as whiter chins and undertail coverts; they are also a brighter yellow on the cheeks and supercilium. The Willow Warbler is a slimmer and perhaps more graceful bird than the Chiffchaff with generally brighter colouring and a better defined supercilium. The legs are usually a pale horn colour but they may be as dark as those of the Chiffchaff and are not reliable diagnostic features. Edwin Cohen (1951) found that the legs of newly fledged young were 'greenish-grey, whereas parents' legs, viewed at very close quarters, were light reddish-brown.' Occasionally partially albinistic birds are reported and a Nottinghamshire example had white wings.

It is by the wing formulae that Willow Warbler and Chiffchaff are usually separated in the hand. I include two drawings of the wings of both species in my own collection which came from Cheshire (Figs. 130 and 131). For many years it was understood that in the case of the Willow Warbler the second primary was usually between the fifth and sixth in length, very occasionally as short as the sixth or as long as the fifth. However, after R. E.

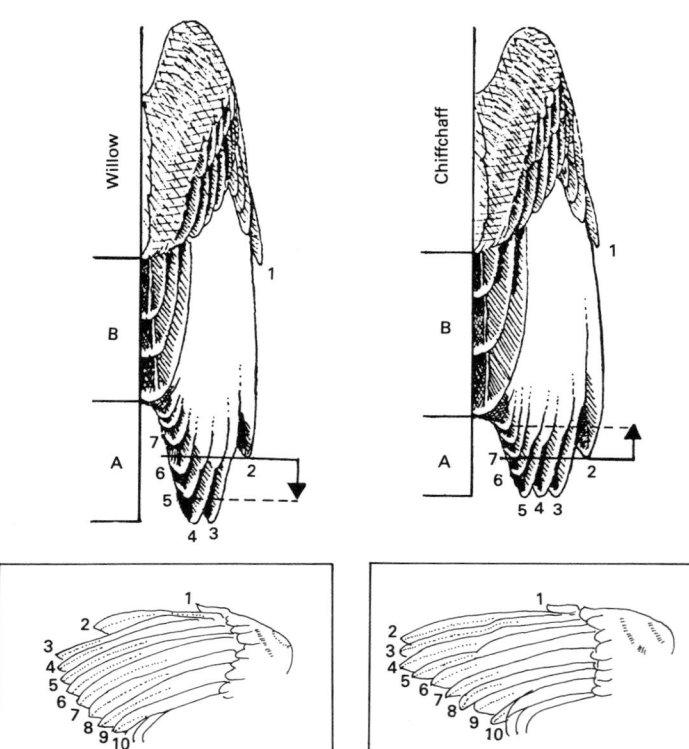

Fig. 129
Wing formula of Willow Warbler and Chiffchaff. (Reproduced from Bird Study *Vol. 16, 1969 by permission of R. E. Scott and P. J. Grant)*

Fig. 130 (left)
Wing of Chiffchaff. Roscote, Cheshire. (Eric Simms)

Fig. 131 (right)
Wing of Willow Warbler. Heswall, Cheshire. (Eric Simms)

Scott (1969) had measured 296 Willow Warblers at Dungeness in the spring and autumn of 1966 and 1967 he suggested that the wing formula should now read '2nd primary longer than the 7th.' A drawing by P. J. Grant (1969) to illustrate an article by Bob Scott in *Bird Study* is reproduced here (Fig. 129).

The distribution limits of the Willow Warbler lie roughly between the July isotherms of 10 °C in the north and 21.5°C in the south. In the last chapter I showed how this species reveals a more catholic choice of habitat than the Chiffchaff and occurs in lower scrub and plantations as well. The latter warbler tends to feed in rather taller growth. I listed in *Woodland Birds* (1971) a wide range of habitats that Willow Warblers will occupy: 'open broad-leaved woods, scrub and bushy regions, moorland with bushy patches and no trees, coniferous woods and plantations, hedges along roads, parkland, gardens and many other areas with grass tussocks and a few bushes or trees.' During a survey of more than 300 British and Irish woods I found Willow Warblers to be the dominant species in the birch woods of Scotland, and co-dominants with Robins in Irish birch woods. They also came first in English ash woods but took second place to Blackbirds in Irish ash woods and were regular amongst ashes in Scotland. Willow Warblers had a relative abundance figure of 15 in the thicket stages of Irish conifer plantations and were often dominant in young plantations

in both upland and lowland regions. I found that Willow Warblers were
the second-commonest species of bird in the birches of Cumbria, the
Pennine Hills and Wales.

Willow Warblers were dominant among the ancient pine woods by Loch
Maree in northwest Scotland, and in the old Speyside forests in the east of
Scotland they might form one third of the bird community. In the sessile
oak woods of England and Wales they were the third commonest species as
they also were in the coniferous and mixed woods of Ireland. I also listed
them in fourth place in the alder woods of Scotland and in fifth in English
pedunculate and Scottish and Irish sessile oak woods. I found birds quite
commonly on the southern heaths of England, in Scottish ash woods, in
English beech woods, the mixed broad-leaved woods of Ireland and in
many areas of scrub and thicket including the hazel scrub of western Ireland
which grew 4–7 m in height. Yet those tangles of hazel, rich in primroses, wood anemones, celandine and early purple orchids, were enlivened
not only by the songs of Willow Warblers but also by commoner species
still: Wrens, Whitethroats, Robins, Chaffinches and Great Tits (Simms
1979). With the advance of afforestation in many parts of the British Isles
the species has increased, coming into the plantations in their fourth and
fifth years of life and reaching their peak in numbers about the eleventh
year in the late thicket stage of the plantations. Another favourite habitat
is a damp one of alders, willows and poplars growing along the banks of
lakes and streams. The greatest height at which I came across a singing
male in Britain was at 566 m in Glen Tromie and in Switzerland at 1450 m.
Birds will breed in the central Royal Parks in London and in many suburban areas.

There has been little change in distribution in the British Isles in recent

Fig. 132
*Territory of the Willow
Warbler along the edge
of a conifer plantation,
with meadowsweet.
Lincolnshire, July 1983.
(Eric Simms)*

years apart from the move into the new State Forests. Willow Warblers breed almost everywhere except on mountains and moors, but breeding in Shetland is sporadic and birds are scarce in the flat fenlands around the Wash. The Common Birds Census showed density figures of up to 425 pairs per km^2 in birchwoods in Wester Ross, 100–200 pairs per km^2 in woodland and scrub, and 8 pairs per km^2 on farmland. We saw in Chapter 27 that in the high fell woods of Wales there was often a positive reaction between Wood and Willow Warblers sharing the same habitat so that the two species established mutually exclusive territories. Following a study by Bo Evenman and Sven. G. Nilsson (1981) on islands in a Swedish lake, these two authors suggested that abundance of food and competition probably amongst the Willow Warblers themselves accounted for an interesting correlation that clearly existed between the physical size of the warblers and their habitat selection. It was found that 'the biggest willow warblers occurred where potential competitors were most frequent' and this suggested that the larger warblers were more successful in interspecific encounters. The larger Wood Warbler might be expected to be socially dominant over the Willow Warbler (Morse 1974) but large Willow Warblers might also be better able to set up territories among the Wood Warblers (Nilsson 1977). Ebenman and Nilsson also found that Willow Warblers living on the larger islands in the lake were bigger than those on the smaller islands.

Willow Warblers will contend with Chiffchaffs when both occupy the same ground but, as Eliot Howard (1948) pointed out, 'In size and strength they are equal, and the "will to fight" is as strong in the one as the other, so that it is seldom, if ever, possible to point to this one as the victor and that one as the vanquished.' Yet constant warfare could affect the health of one contestant, the size of a territory and thus the welfare of the young. Willow Warblers are quite aggressive birds and at Ashbourne in Derbyshire an individual attacked two Robins singing against each other which were also posturing in an aggressive manner (Lomas 1962). This kind of aggressive behaviour is also known amongst migrants and wintering birds, as we shall see later.

Total numbers have remained fairly stable in Britain although M. Philips Price (1961) described a significant drop in the numbers of Willow Warblers near Gloucester from 1927–1960, perhaps through changes in habitats. The chart (Fig. 133) based on figures from the Common Birds Census shows little change from 1962 to 1982. Fluctuations in population levels seem more frequent in Fenno-Scandia. On an island in Finland a population with a density of over 80 pairs per km^2 in 1943 and 1944 plummetted to little over 5 pairs per km^2 by 1948; such changes have occurred in other years as well (Siivonen 1949).

The food of Willow Warblers consists of quite small insects, especially Dipterous flies which may be caught on the wing or skilfully taken from the surfaces of leaves and twigs with delicate movements. Other items of food include small beetles such as weevils, moths, aphids, and the larvae of *Tortrix viridana* as well as spiders and tiny earthworms. Some birds will take ants and F. Fincher (1947) observed a bird near Bromsgrove taking winged forms of these insects. Two Willow Warblers and a Whitethroat were watched flying out over a reservoir in Leicestershire, hovering a few inches above the surface and then perching on the leaves of pondweeds

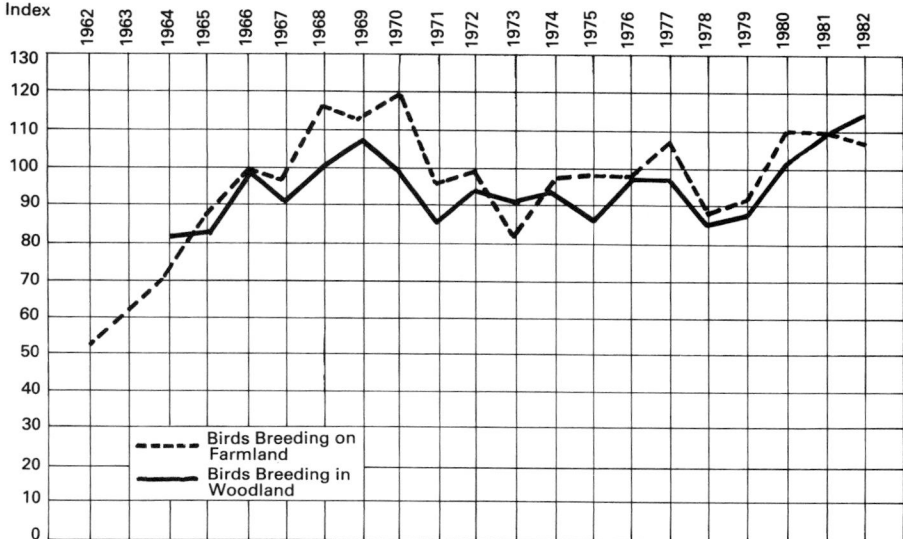

Index

| Birds Breeding on Farmland |
| Birds Breeding in Woodland |

from which they appeared to be picking up insects with their bills (Row-bottom 1952). In the autumn Willow Warblers will also take elderberries and currants as well as the berries of lords-and-ladies and honeysuckle, and in bad weather even breadcrumbs.

The contact and alarm call of the Willow Warbler is a plaintive Chiff-chaff-like 'hooeet' but this note is lower in pitch, less strong and tends to be more disyllabic in its nature than the corresponding call of the Chiffchaff. These are only broad tendencies and not hard and fast distinctions. As the result of widespread variations in this call, largely perhaps according to mood, its use in specific separation can be inordinately difficult. There is also a thin shrew-like note made with a closed bill and shivering wings used in display (Smith 1950), a thin 'sweez-sweez', a plaintive 'cheep' in another display flight (Dunt 1946) and a Wryneck-like and laughing 'pee-pee-pee', described by E. M. Nicholson (*The Handbook* 1946). A harsh rasping note has been heard before coition took place (Brown 1946). As long ago as 1941, O. Kuusisto pointed out that the Willow Warbler uses different calls when alarmed by a Cuckoo from those employed when confronted by a man. Dr Stuart Smith (1946) described how a Willow Warbler when presented with an artificially produced call of the Cuckoo gave vent to 'a queer chittering note' and then fluffed up the feathers on its neck, erected its crown feathers, waved its wings about and 'with a wide gape uttered a long hissing sounds'. S. M. Butlin (1946) also described the Willow Warbler's display and calls against the Cuckoo as 'a harsh squeaky chittering'. Later Dr Smith, George Edwards and Eric Hosking (1949) proffered a stuffed Cuckoo to a Willow Warbler which uttered a rapid chittering 'chee-chee-chee' while continuously flicking its wings and gaping its bill very wide. The three authors in a detailed study in 1950 described how, during nest building, a pair of Willow Warblers reacted to a stuffed Cuckoo with wing-waving and chittering notes but without attacking. As soon as egg-laying

Fig. 133
Population changes in Willow Warbler numbers 1962–82. Based on Common Birds Census of B.T.O. (levels in relation to 1966).

had begun a more violent reaction was seen and after incubation had started real attacks began; with young in the nest the response of the warblers was 'immediate, violent and sustained'. The reaction of the birds to the imitation of the Cuckoo's call was thought to imply some appreciation by the Willow Warblers of an association between the call of the male, who never comes near a nest, and victimization by the female (Smith and Hosking 1955).

When a normal male Willow Warbler is singing no other specific distinction is required. The song is a liquid, silvery succession of notes, gaining volume but then on a descending scale and with changing rhythm falling in a soft cascade of sound into a gentle cadence: 'soft as summer rain' wrote Lord Grey of Fallodon. The strophe is short – usually from two to four seconds in length – but pure and sweet in tone and repeated perhaps as many as nine times in a minute. Sometimes the strophes are separated by low 'tchirrs' or 'tchirrips' and even a slightly wheezy 'tchee'. The song with its limpid notes is not loud but can be heard by an observer 75 m away.

In an interesting analysis of Willow Warbler song H-W. Helb (1973), who played back recordings of real and artificial song to birds, found that increasing the number of notes or changing the sequence had little effect on the responsiveness of birds, and a 30% alteration in pitch in either direction did not decrease the response, while an unmodulated artificial song and imitations of Willow Warblers by other species produced the same reactions; the song of the Chiffchaff produced no response. Every Willow Warbler has a repertoire of songs, each with slight differences from the rest. The song is a very common sound throughout the woodlands and scrub of

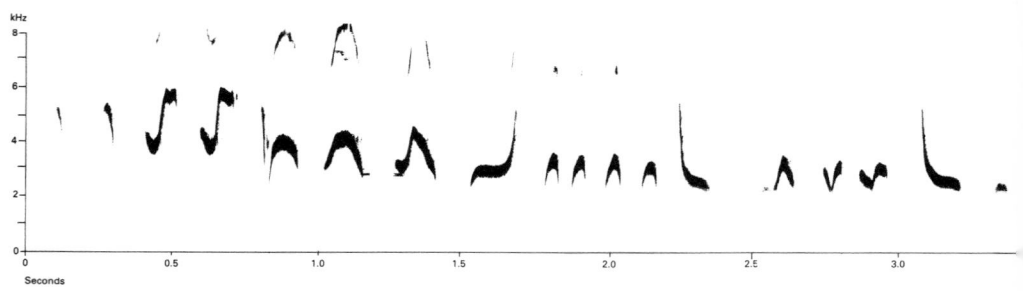

Fig. 134
Complete song-strophe of a Willow Warbler made up of different elements. (Recorded by Eric Simms, Lincolnshire, May 1981)

Europe as far north as the Arctic Circle. The newly arrived males on their nesting grounds start off with short song-patterns to match the fast-moving events at the beginning of the breeding season, but later in the summer the strophes become 'longer, lower in pitch, with new elements inserted, and there is a more fluid pattern' (Jellis 1977). In the midlands of England males start to sing around the time of sunrise but in the continuous daylight of Finnmark birds do not sing all the time; in late June and July they begin to perform between 22.45 hours and 01.45 hours with the start getting later as the season progresses (Brown 1963). In England the song reaches a peak in early and mid-May and falls off towards the end of May or early June with the young hatching out. By early July the full song is infrequent but it may be resumed in August and September, with less verve and volume. The singer often forages for insects and moves about while singing at heights of 1–10 m above the ground. The male may also sing on the wing and with a bill full of insects.

Variations in the song of the Willow Warbler are reported from time to time. I have heard Chiffchaff-like variants in Northamptonshire and south Warwickshire. A male which sang a combined Willow Warbler/Chiffchaff song was successfully paired and when the young, taken at a week old, were reared in isolation they sang normal Willow Warbler song (Gwinner and Dorka 1965). J. H. Barrett (1948) reported a male employing long strophes of 9–16 seconds in length, reminiscent of the outpourings of a Garden Warbler. Sir Julian Huxley (1956) came across a Willow Warbler near Dartford in Kent which opened its song with three typical notes but then indulged at once in a run of Linnet-like notes. A bird observed by Bernard King (1958) had a normal song which trailed off into 'a mixture of sweet and harsh notes' with the quality of a Linnet as well. Another unusual song, including suspected mimicry, was noted by Cheke and Ford (1966) in Abernethy Forest; here the performer sang 3–8 notes rather like those of a Goldcrest but lower pitched and more nasal, or of a Marsh Tit: 'zi-zi-zi' or 'chi-chi-chi'. A bird in Derbyshire was thought by the observer to have imitated a Blue Tit and it sang three almost normal notes followed by eight or nine stuttering ones (Frost 1966). Since the low rippling, rather shapeless subsong of the Willow Warbler includes not only snatches of typical song but other utterances suggestive of Linnet, Garden Warbler, Starling and other birds, some of these variants described may well be examples of subsong and this might explain some of the 'imitations' so far reported. Eliot Howard (1907–14) noted song from a female Willow Warbler, and there are also records from S. E. Brock (1910) in the *Zoologist* 4(14):401–17 and from M. R. Lawn (1984) who reported a female with 'a stammering song like the early attempts of a juvenile in autumn.'

In the spring the male Willow Warblers arrive later than many Chiffchaffs and earlier than the Wood Warblers. In a study I made in Lincoln-

Fig. 135
*The aggressive display of
the Willow Warbler.
(Eric Hosking)*

shire during the last war on the airfield from which I flew I found that early males arrived about 11 April; in the same county from 1981–4 the arrival dates ranged from 7–19 April. In his study of Willow Warblers on a Surrey Common, D. J. May (1947) recorded return dates of 3 and 6 April. The males arrive back at night and then advertise themselves clearly with song. They can be found foraging and feeding, singing in response to each other and when in close proximity engaging in tussles and combat with crown feathers erected. They may also respond aggressively to Chiffchaffs in the same habitat. In the defence of their territories birds will indulge in wing-flapping and, between song strophes, utter hoarse notes: 'ch-ch-ch' as well as wheezy squeaks and 'chees'. C. K. Mylne (1948) experienced a threat display at himself in which the bird faced him with bill half open, neck and head stretched forward, wings arched and raised and with the whole body in an attenuated condition before flying at him.

The actual size of a Willow Warbler territory varies with the nature of the terrain. I agree with Brock (1910), who studied Willow Warblers in a Midlothian wood, that it is difficult to draw exact boundaries to the territories. I have found territories varying in size from 40 m^2 in a Scottish birchwood to 400 m^2 in a midland pedunculate oakwood. The arrival of males and females sometimes overlaps but pairing seems to take place without much difficulty. M. P. Price (1936) observed that 'a certain though fluctuating number fail to get mates each season.' In one wood in Lincolnshire there have been seasons where some males have failed to acquire mates and others in which I could find no surplus birds. There is a very characteristic courtship among Willow Warblers with the male chasing a female through the trees and then pausing with one wing extended, sometimes both wings, before starting a wing-waving display. Both partners will become quite excited and may end up facing each other. There is also a butterfly display flight with quivering wings and tail raised and expanded which I have seen in certain habitats but do not regard as very common. Sometimes there is a little display flight with a burst of song. There is also mutual 'billing' and D. J. May (1947) observed courtship feeding on three occasions. During nest building a male was seen to feed his mate (Dunt 1946) and similar activity was reported by Mees (1946) and Harber (1948). Female Willow Warblers may indulge in slow motion flight and then alight, raise the wings vertically and invite coition which then immediately takes place (Brown 1946). The attitudes of Willow Warblers of both sexes before copulation are identical with the appearance of the female when frightened at the nest; there is also a resemblance between this posture and that of a chick craving food (Howard 1907–14).

The breeding season is comparatively short and there is little difference between southwest and southeast England, but the peak in the north is later with twice as many clutches in June (Cramp 1955). The nest is often built amongst grass at the bottom of a hedge, in a bramble brake or tall herbage in the field layer in open woods, woodland ecotones, groves of trees, hedgerows, scrub, gardens, orchards, quarries, downland, roadside verges, railway embankments – a much wider range of site than that chosen by the Chiffchaff. It is usually on the ground but may be slightly above ground level in a low bush or creeper on a wall. In his study of the Nest Record Cards of the B.T.O. Stanley Cramp (1955) found that most of the nests were 'built on the ground, in grass and herbage, but about 7% were

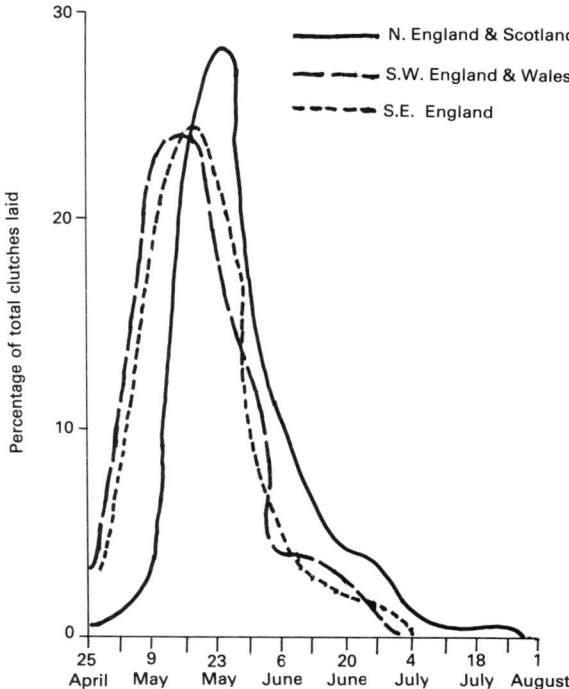

Fig. 136
The breeding season of the Willow Warbler in Britain.

recorded as being more than one foot above the ground – in low shrubs, hedges, and walls covered with ivy and other vegetation.' Nests above the ground were three times as common in June as in May. There are instances of birds nesting in the cavity of a wall at Beccles (Warner 1950) and in a roadside wall at Chewton Mendip. Another nest was built on the occupied nest of a Whitethroat 0.65 m above ground (Woods 1951). Other atypical sites include one in the top of a privet hedge near Uckfield in Sussex over 2 m above the ground (*The Handbook* (1946) gave a top height of 5 m!). The editors of *British Birds*, who published the account of the Uckfield nest, mentioned another nest some 2 m above ground in ivy in an outhouse at Rostherne in Cheshire, as well as nests at heights reaching 10 m; sites included 'the tangled twigs near the bases of low bushes (a not uncommon site), the branches of firs and pines, in crevices or supported by climbing plants against walls, trellis-work or trees, and the disused nests of other species, including once a squirrel's deserted drey.' To me one of the most extraordinary situations was a coconut shell placed in a sapling beech about 2 m from the ground and intended for tits (Harrison 1954). For so adventurous a species there must be other equally fascinating sites as yet unreported.

In my experience the nest is built by the hen alone, although T. A. Coward (1944) wrote that 'the male certainly at times helps in construction.' She starts work within a few days of arrival and pairing, and finishes the nest in about six days. The male may flit around her while she works, showing great interest in the whole process and warning her of danger with the 'hooeet' call. The nest is formed from an outer shell and dome of fairly sturdy grass stems, bracken, leaves, moss, roots or bark, and this is given a lining of feathers with occasional cocoons and hair. A Willow Warbler in Breckland had 'a pleasing arrangement of guinea fowl feathers at the entrance to her nest' (Robertson 1954). May (1947) counted 240 feathers in one nest, but feathers may be absent and the lining can consist only of grass (Brown 1948). The finished nest is normally a spherical construction with a side entrance, but the dome may be missing. May also divided Willow Warbler nests into two categories; the commoner type is built in a hollow under a thick tuft of grass so that the back is invisible and consists in part of living herbage, while the rarer one is fully exposed with the back being entirely constructed by the bird. A nest using dead bracken as a material and built in the leaf-litter among dead bracken fronds is almost impossible to find. Occasionally Willow Warblers will nest close together since they often build on the very edges of their territories and not in the middle. R. A. Frost (1978) found two nests in Derbyshire within 6 m of each other and D. J. May reported two only 'a few yards' apart.

This closeness of nests has sometimes been associated with reports of bigamy (Lawn 1978, Lynes 1979). The Willow Warbler is generally considered to be single-brooded with a small proportion of pairs rearing a second brood. However, Brock (1910) thought that from 15% to 20% of the birds he studied in Midlothian were double-brooded, May considered the figure higher even than that but Cramp (1955) was more inclined to accept a figure that lay between 5% and 10%. These estimates would now seem to have included some bigamous pairings. M. R. Lawn (1978) observed a pattern of behaviour by a colour-ringed male Willow Warbler in Surrey that strongly indicated that he had been the father of two separate broods by different mates. Also, da Prato (1982) had a similar experience in southeast Scotland where one male mated with five different females in two successive breeding seasons. This suggested that some reports of double broods may really be of polygamous relationships which might allow 'a migrant with a short breeding season to produce more offspring without adversely affecting the timing of moult and migration.'

The eggs are usually laid daily and are white with a fine overall speckling of light red or reddish-brown, or larger spots and blotches of pale reddish-brown over the whole surface but concentrated more strongly at the broad end. The average clutch size across the whole country increases from early April, attaining a maximum between 13–19 May in the south, but a week later in the north, and then falls. From 467 records from the B.T.O. Stanley Cramp found an average clutch size over the country of 6.05 eggs. From his interesting paper in *Bird Study* much of the remainder of the information in this paragraph has been gleaned. From the 467 records there were seventeen clutches of eight eggs, 31% of the total were of seven and 44% were of six eggs. The average incubation period was 13 days with a possible range of 10–16 days, but 80% of the records fell at 12–14 days. Most clutches were hatched in one or two days but in the case of eight nests the process lasted three days or longer. The mean nestling period for the whole of the country was longer in June than in May and decreased steadily with increasing brood size; the average figure was 13.2 days. The hatching success was slightly higher in June for all clutches than in May. Out of all the clutches that were laid, the full clutch hatched out in 59% of the cases while almost 10% suffered complete failure. Of 1071 young hatched from 198 broods, 763 or 71.3% flew; if the completely failed broods were withdrawn from consideration this figure leaped to 97.2%. Broods of four were the least successful but those of 5, 6 and 7 had equal success. The overall breeding success rate was 58% with a figure of 59.6% for May and 55.8% for June. The Willow Warbler is occasionally host to the Cuckoo.

The nestlings are fed by both parents. When the female is disturbed from the nest she may embark on a distraction display to baffle and delude potential predators. C. K. Siddall (1910) saw a bird leave her nest and alight on some palings with all the appearance of being wounded with her bill slightly open, left foot trailing and the right wing hanging down as if the humerus were broken. Such feigning of injury seems to vary in its degree of frequency; I find it very uncommon, like some other observers, but it was described as 'frequent' by Southern and Whittenbury (1949). Commander A. W. P. Robertson (1954) observed a female with seven young whose mate had been killed 'having a curious partiality for distraction display at every opportunity.' A Willow Warbler whose leg had been broken by a catapult flew a short distance and burst into song (Dewar 1906).

Nest sanitation, which is mainly confined as a practice to the Passeriformes, is an important part of nest hygiene. An interesting example of sophisticated behaviour was provided when a nestling Willow Warbler failed to deposit a dropping outside the nest, and the nearest youngster picked it up and put it in the right place (Blair and Tucker 1941); this was part of a non-rigid pattern of behaviour. An account of the development of nestling Willow Warblers has been given by Norman (1983). There are several interesting records of young Willow Warblers leaving their nest and returning to it for one night or of nestlings making 'short excursions on their own initiative' (Staton and Hicks 1946).

In June and July there is little adult song and the Willow Warbler enjoys the distinction of having two complete moults in the year. The postnuptial moult in the breeding area may begin in England about the third week of June and end about the middle of August. In Finland the onset of the moult was found to be unrelated to the breeding stage while birds undergoing an early moult attained it more slowly than those starting late (Tiainen 1981). In late summer, birds begin to disperse but with no great urgency, perhaps joining up with nomadic parties of tits to wander through the woodlands. Mixed flocks like these may also contain other warbler species from such genera as *Sylvia* and *Hippolais*, as well as Wood Warblers and Chiffchaffs and members of the *Regulus* genus. By August the southward movement is under way. Perhaps some broods migrate as groups. The Rev. E. A. Armstrong (1947) reported seeing a Willow Warbler feeding fledged young. An interesting observation was made by Nick Riddiford (1982) in which three first-year Willow Warblers trapped at Dungeness in August 1978 in the same net had strands of wool 'entwined round and embedded into the feet.' The wool from each of the three individuals was of the same nature and colour and, having cut deeply into the legs, suggested that it had become entangled when the birds were very young, probably in a nest where the wool had been used as a building or lining material. In the autumn of 1978 more than 400 Willow Warblers were trapped at Dungeness without trace of wool. Willow Warblers are night migrants, when they do not seem to use contact calls, and so it is difficult to see how without using these calls such a group would be able to keep together. There is often some resumption of song in the autumn and both Willow Warblers and Chiffchaffs may even display and copulate on occasion (Brook 1910, Palmgren 1934).

During the August dispersal and southward journey, birds may appear in many places. I kept records of all migrants seen in the region of Dollis Hill in northwest London for 29 years. The main autumn movement was between 17 July and 29 August often with two peaks – one about 6 August and the other from 22–29 August – and birds could be heard in quiet song in street trees, gardens and in the local park. In a study of Regent's Park Wallace (1959) found Willow Warblers were the commonest nocturnal migrants there in the second half of August in 1951 and 1959, and also in the first half of that month in the latter year as well; birds regularly fed in willows, ash trees and poplars. Passage movements also occurred in London and southern England until late September and early October but Chiffchaffs were more frequent in September. Many of the later records on the east coast of Britain and on Fair Isle refer to the northern form – *acredula* – although this race may be overlooked because of the problem of identification.

The Willow Warbler is a rare species to overwinter in the British Isles but A. G. Parsons (1951) reported a bird at Helston in Cornwall from 8 January 1949 to 26 February which roosted regularly in a dense clump of bamboos. Another was observed at Banbury in Oxfordshire in December 1961. There have been a few records of birds wintering in the London area, and one of the more interesting of these was that of a bird that wintered in a garden at Twickenham from 18 December 1982 until 13 March 1983. Another bird was heard in song at Cheshunt Gravel Pit in Hertfordshire on 30 January 1983.

British Willow Warblers winter in tropical West Africa south of 10°N in countries such as Nigeria. In the south of that country the bird is a winter visitor from October to March singing in November and again after February. It is 'never common in central Nigeria' (Smith 1966) but in the southeast song is frequent in January (Marchant 1953). Other birds from

Fig. 137
Breeding range of the Willow Warbler.

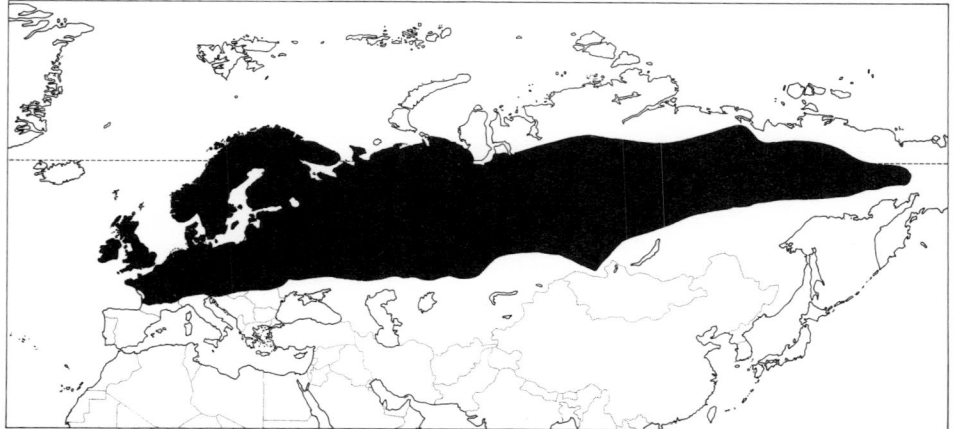

western Europe fly to Cameroon, the Gambia, Senegal, Ghana, Zaire and Angola. Others appear in East Africa from the Sudan south to the Cape. In Kenya the species is scarce in autumn and 'sometimes abundant in spring' (Pearson and Backhurst 1976). The transit migration of the Willow Warbler is something of a problem to unravel. In Egypt and probably in the eastern Sahara, according to Moreau (1961), and certainly in the Sudan (Hogg *et al* 1984), birds are seen in large numbers in autumn but there are surprisingly few in spring. The nominate *trochilus*, which is the only representative in the western regions, is still more common than *acredula* in Egypt (Meinertzhagen 1930). In Cyprus *acredula* is much commoner in autumn than spring, while *trochilus* is commoner in Tunisia on spring passage than in autumn. Examples indistinguishable from *trochilus* have been taken in Eritrea, Arabia and Iraq. *Acredula* can be found from the Sudan south to the Transvaal and Natal as well as in Angola and Zaire. To Uganda the Willow Warbler is a common winter visitor and passage migrant: I have heard snatches of song from birds foraging in low acacias in that country in the first week of January. It occurs 'in open areas with scattered vegetation and low trees, but was outnumbered by other warblers in dense bush' (Pearson 1972). Dr Geoffrey Beven heard song being freely delivered in Zaire in October and in South Africa in November. In Uganda wintering birds moulted completely and song was occasional at first, becoming more frequent from January to the middle of March.

On its breeding ground and even on migration the Willow Warbler often behaves in a most aggressive fashion. Migrant Willow Warblers on passage through Dungeness have been known to attack Starlings and Wheatears and on one occasion a bird made a vigorous assault upon a woodmouse (Riddiford *et al* 1984). In Zimbabwe C. J. Vernon (1965) watched Willow Warblers from 3 October to 27 November one year, and in that period warblers of this species attacked no fewer than ten species of large bird, including a Common Sandpiper, and six species of small birds including not only other Willow Warblers but also Grey Tit Babbler, Grey-backed Bush Warbler, Tawny-flanked Prinia and both Marico and Double-collared Sunbirds. An Icterine Warbler was once observed behaving in a similarly aggressive fashion. The arrival back on the winter grounds is first announced by song. On a sand-veld farm with *Isoberlinia* and *Brachystegia* woodland in Zimbabwe K. D. Smith (1951) noted song from 17 October. Then there was a rise in the number of Willow Warblers so that 'the bush was alive with the songs of these warblers until mid-December, when song became half-hearted and ceased by the end of the month.' Then a period of silence was followed by a remarkable resurgence from early February until the end of the first week of March. The winter quarters may be forest and open-canopy woodland, acacias, scrub in subalpine moorland, from sea level, and (e.g. in Tanzania) to 3650 m.

Early in March the great northward migration starts with birds passing through northwest Africa. The migration across Europe lasts from 5 March at Gibraltar to 1 June in Inari in Finnmark; a period of 88 days in which a distance of more than 4000 km is covered (Southern 1938). The progress is at a rate of about 46.5 km a day with a faster rate of spread up the western seaboard of Europe. There is also a marked correlation between the spread of the Willow Warbler northwards and the isothermal lines which link all the places in Europe where the average temperature on the same day is

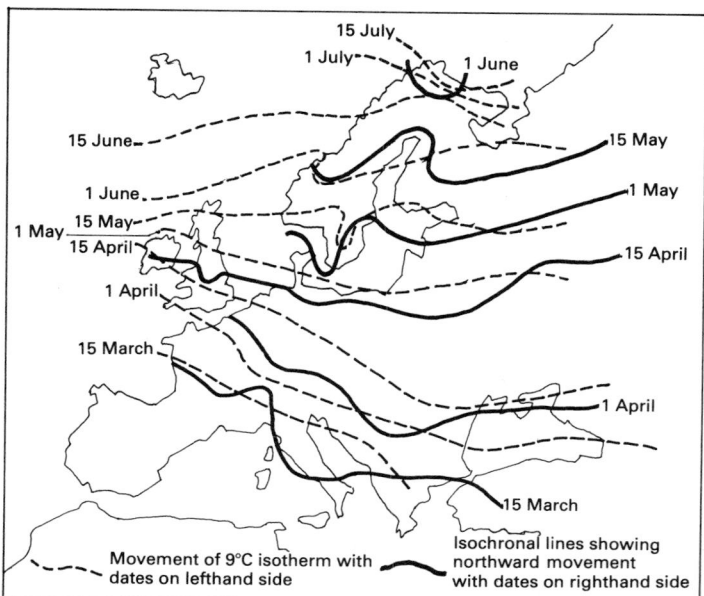

Fig. 138
The rate of spread of the Willow Warbler across western Europe in spring. (After Southern 1938)

Movement of 9°C isotherm with dates on lefthand side

Isochronal lines showing northward movement with dates on righthand side

9°C or 48°F. In the end the spread of the migrants outstrips the northward movement of spring. There is, however, an interesting conformity with the isotherms – better, in fact, than Southern achieved with the Swallow (1938a).

There are early arrivals in England from the third week of March, while the main influx takes place in the first or second weeks of April. After that the movements begin to mingle with those of birds of passage which may be on the move until the very beginning of June. In an examination of the spring movements of Willow Warblers in 1952 Ken Williamson and A. Butterfield (1954) showed that British breeding birds entered the southern Irish Sea in numbers from 9–11 April (males), on 13 and from 15–18 April (females) and again from 26–8 April (males). Passage noticed at the Isle of May during the last two periods was thought to be the residual northward movement of males which had entered the southwest of Britain on 9 April. Later passages at the Isle of May on 1 May (males) and 5 May (females) were attributed to migrational drift in easterly winds. A large influx of male Willow Warblers at Fair Isle on 6 May was due to drift from southern Scandinavia. The large arrivals of females at the Isle of May on 5 May and of males at Fair Isle on 6 May had evidently different sources of origin. All the evidence seemed to suggest that the 'maritime' or *trochilus* stock came sweeping into Europe as far north as Scotland and Denmark with males being in occupation by the third week of April, while the main body of the 'Continental' stock flowed northwards from Italy and the Balkans, not arriving in Sweden until early May. The two groups experience different timings for migration in Europe and it has been suggested that the early arrival of the 'maritime' group is adapted to a slower rate of advance through the coastal regions 'forced upon them by the less frequent develop-

ment of anticyclonic weather favourable for migration in the coastal as
opposed to the Continental sector.'

Willow Warblers are essentially night flyers, and on their northward
spring migration they reach the south coast of England before the dawn
(Parslow 1969). Although they are twice as common there in autumn as in
spring, they are relatively more numerous than most other species. Birds
ringed on migration in spring in southern England have largely been
recovered to the northwest later in the same spring or in the summer of the
same year. For Willow Warblers arriving in spring their whole
pattern of activity 'seemed geared to feeding and consequent weight increase' (Riddiford and Auger 1983). The increase in weight was especially
marked in the morning some two to three hours after sunrise. A weight
increase of from 0.4 to 0.7 g was enough to induce a Willow Warbler to
re-embark on its journey. The spring passage of birds at Dollis Hill in
northwest London takes place between 15–26 April, but some may pass
through until early May.

Such a common migrant with so distinctive a song is not easily overlooked
on passage and many are reported passing through urban and suburban
areas where they do not breed and can only be migrants. The Willow Wren
or 'Peggy Whitethroat', as the Willow Warbler was once known, is one of
the most familiar of all our summer visitors. Its return in spring is always
anticipated with a pleasure which, if not quite equal to that for the Chiffchaff, the first of which arrive earlier, is still quite substantial. The arrival
of the first birds on 27 April in a birchwood by the Kyle of Tongue in the
north of Scotland remains one of my most treasured memories.

In March the English countryside is still in the grip of winter, and appears to be much more so now than twenty years ago. Today we seem to jump straight from winter into summer. There are cold winds blowing and the woodland floor lies deep in mud, carpeted with sodden leaves and bracken fronds. On the calmer days there is some birdsong from Song Thrushes, Blackbirds, Robins, Chaffinches, Blue and Great Tits and the Mistle Thrush clinging to his high swaying song-post in a tall forest or parkland tree. Yet towards the end of the month the walker in the woods may be rewarded by a faint, uncertain 'chiff-chaff-chif-chif-chaff' coming from a copse of bare ash saplings or pussy willow or well down in the canopies of the oaks. The arrival back on its breeding grounds of this unobtrusive little warbler from the south is a milestone in the bird-watching year. As Lord Grey of Fallodon wrote, the first Chiffchaff of the spring is 'a symbol, a promise, an assurance of what is to come.' Yet with so many Chiffchaffs now over-wintering in the southern parts of the British Isles, we cannot be sure that the new singer in the wood has actually moved up north from southern Europe or Africa. It may have passed the winter months in some damp southern grove or garden, along some slow-flowing stream or, less romantically, at a sewage works in the southwest. However, there is evidence that some of the wintering birds breed elsewhere.

We have seen earlier that there are six races of the Chiffchaff and some of

Fig. 139
Wintering Chiffchaff on a sewage filter-bed at St Erth, Cornwall. December 1976. (J. B. and S. Bottomley)

these have appeared in the British Isles. Descriptions of these races and those on the British list were given in Chapter 27; the latter are *collybita* of western Europe, *ibericus* from northwest Africa and Iberia, *abietinus* from Scandinavia and northern Europe, and *tristis* from Siberia. Separation of these races by plumage or even voice alone may be difficult and there are often only small differences in their morphology. A song consisting of two notes with one higher than the other and in an irregular sequence may seem very simple and straightforward, but P. Homann (1960) distinguished at least five forms of song – territorial, rivalry, excitement, display and court-ship – as well as seven call-notes from the adult and eight from young birds! Over much of Continental Europe it is the repeated disyllabic ditty which is the best known of all the vocalizations. It is thought that the song of the Chiffchaff is innate and does not have to be learned. The subsong rather resembles the territorial song of the Willow Warbler which is so closely related. Although breeding ranges overlap, the Chiffchaff with its more southerly distribution has a race whose song is very different from that of *collybita*, and does not employ the 'two sharp piercing notes' that Gilbert White attributed to our bird which he also called 'the chirper'. The *ibericus* Chiffchaffs resemble British birds but have different songs. Dr David Snow (1952) noted in northwest Africa that, although the quality of the notes was similar, the song 'consisted of a set pattern of about ten notes delivered with a halting rhythm, slowing up at the end, and with at least two changes of pitch.' I have listened to many 'Iberian' Chiffchaffs in Spain, where the song is a series of slow 'chips' or 'tits', perhaps in two groups of four and two notes, followed by a rather faster group of five to six notes. This division of the song into sections, ably demonstrated by a range of sonagrams from Thielcke and Linsenmair (1963), is also characteristic of Willow Warbler songs, but the restricted frequency range is more typical of the *collybita* form. I can represent the song that I heard from one 'Iberian' Chiffchaff as 'tit-tit-tit-tit-tit-tswee-tswee-chit-it-it-it-it.' In southwest France 'Iberian' birds mingle with typical ones resulting in the presence of 'mixed' singers.

A Chiffchaff that frequented the Brent Reservoir in northwest London in June 1972 (Batten and Wood 1974) sang and called regularly, uttering a note like that of a young chicken, while the usual song 'consisted of about 10–12 *chips*, the first five-or-six being delivered at a slower rate than the remaining ones. The whole song lasted 2–2½ seconds.' Dr Batten played me his tape recording of this bird and this with a later sonagram of the song left no doubt that the song type had all the characteristics of the Iberian subspecies. Another Chiffchaff singing in Dorset on 17 April 1983 also had a song identical to that of the Chiffchaff of southwest Spain (Paull 1984). Birds in the Canary Islands have shorter, harsher and lower-pitched songs with no alternation of high and low notes. Dr C. J. Henty (*in litt.*) tells me that after studying Chiffchaff song 'over a wide area of the Cantabrian Mountains and coastal strip, roughly just east of Santander to just west of Oviedo, in all cases the song has been characteristic of the typical western European form – the double note with occasional scratchy introduction' and not of the form that ranges from the Iberian Peninsula to North Africa. The song of the Siberian Chiffchaff *tristis* is, according to H. G. Alexander (1951), a musical warbling, more so than that of *collybita* and 'more of a melody' which he expressed as 'wi-di, wee-di, wee-di, wee, widi, wee' and

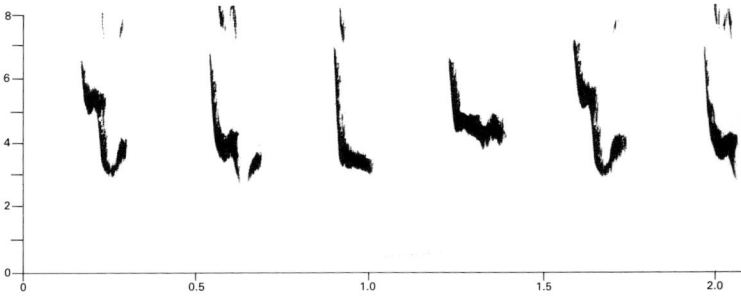

Fig. 140
The last 12 notes of the song of the Chiffchaff. (Recorded by Roger Perry, B.B.C., Suffolk, May 1960)

variants. A recording of this race can be found on the disc *The Voices of Wild Nature* by B. N. Veprintsev and Z. R. Naoomova: *Siberian birds*, Side A. A song of this type was heard by A. M. Heaven (1982) in January 1980 near Cheltenham and another was heard near Hilversum in March 1974 by Rombout de Wijs (1984). This song can be heard not only on the breeding grounds but in April in India before birds leave their winter quarters. The song of *abietinus* or the Scandinavian Chiffchaff is indistinguishable from that of the typical form.

British Chiffchaffs begin to return from the second week of March. Over 31 years the average date of arrival in the West Midlands was 15 March, while other average dates were 20 March for Oxfordshire, Berkshire and Buckinghamshire and 23 March in Cambridgeshire. From this time onwards the male Chiffchaffs can be heard, not quite calling their name but to my mind singing more like 'chip-chip-cheah-chitty-chip-chip' and so on. We have here a clear case of a warbler that does not, in fact warble! British birds utter bursts of song lasting up to twenty seconds with intervals in between of as little as two seconds before the next song begins. These notes may be introduced by or interspersed with low guttural 'chirr-chirrs'. A typical version of the song will include these dry, creaking notes which are only audible at close range. In a minute a run of songs of one bird I heard in Lincolnshire in 1983 had individual durations of 5, 8, 7, 6, 10 and 8 seconds, while a Continental singer had songs lasting 9, 4, 3, 10, 11, 3 and 2 seconds in one minute. From no fewer than 19,144 Chiffchaff songs timed during the summer seasons of 1948 and 1949 in Britain nearly half were found to have lasted from $1\frac{1}{2}$–5 seconds (Brown *et al* 1950). A bird in London ended its song with a Willow Warbler-like phrase but this was probably subsong. In still conditions the song will carry for 100 m or more. It is often delivered from high up in a tree in which the bird is moving restlessly about looking for insects.

R. S. R. Fitter (1957) heard an unusual song from a bird in Ken Wood in Middlesex in June 1942 in which the normal 'chiff-chaff' or 'zip-zap' was intermingled with 'a curious double note *chee-ouee*', a Chaffinch, Redstart or Lesser Whitethroat-like trill and the normal 'chirr-chirr' notes; typical phrases ran 'chee-ouee (thrice), zip-zap (twice), wee (four times), chee-ouee (twice).' Another singer near Radipole Lake in Dorset in April 1959 had its own version of the usual territorial song: 'chi-chi-chi-chi-chi-churru-churru-churru-chi-chi' and so on (Dove 1959). Work by G. Schubert (1971) on the vocalizations of the Chiffchaff by testing the birds

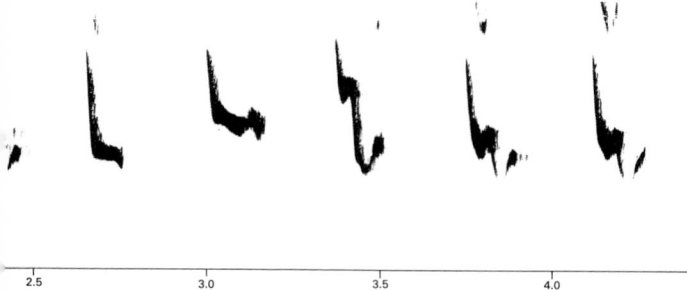

2.5   3.0   3.5   4.0   4.5

with normal and modified recorded signals showed that it was the frequency modulation that contained the most important specific messages for the species. Birds often sing vigorously against each other so that single notes between individual performers may overlap with curious aural effects for the observer. However, Chiffchaffs will sing in duets quite clearly in intervals between other bird songs and E. MacAlister (1936) reported distinctly alternating songs between singing Chiffchaffs and Grasshopper Warblers in Surrey; 'the birds never sang together, and in no case, did I hear a grasshopper warbler before a chiffchaff.' In my own experience I have no instances of female Chiffchaffs singing, but D. W. Taylor (1976) observed a presumed female singing near Maidstone in Kent when the bird dropped some nest material from its bill and sang two or three phrases of normal song before flying off at the same time as a second bird was seen in song close by.

The call note of the typical form is a soft plaintive 'hooeet', 'hooee', 'hweet' or 'whit' and this call tends to be higher in pitch, more incisive and more of a single syllable than the corresponding note of the Willow Warbler. Other notes include a short 'hweep' heard from midsummer onwards, a sustained sibilant 'tsiff-tsiff' in display, and a Lesser Whitethroat-like squeak in the autumn. The call of *abietinus* differs from the usual 'hooeet' of British birds and is a variation of the 'cheet' call rather like that of a chicken in distress. It is not quite clear, however, if the incidence of this call matches the range of the race. The Siberian race *tristis* has a single, very plaintive and 'sad' note which has been compared to one of the melancholy notes of the Coal Tit – a very distinctive 'swee-ooo' (Catley 1981) or 'wheeaa'. On the Canary Islands the commonest call of Chiffchaffs is a metallic note varying from 'chek' to 'chk' and a plaintive 'wheet' (Cullen *et al* 1952).

Birds of some of these races may appear in the British Isles and their call notes may be a partial guide to their identity. This is perhaps especially true for birds showing characteristics of *abietinus* and *tristis*, which are much drabber than British breeding birds but, since both forms intergrade, sub-specific identification can be very doubtful. For this reason these birds have been known in the past as 'Northern' Chiffchaffs. After studying many examples of Chiffchaffs in Lincolnshire and Scandinavia, G. P. Catley (1981), drawing on his own and other observers' experience, suggested that in general birds of the *abietinus* race, in addition to employing a different call note, were a dull brown on the upperparts often with a clearer and more olive or even yellowish tint to the rump, brighter borders to the primaries and with a suspicion of yellow perhaps on the throat and upper breast and a yellowish patch often visible at the carpal joint. On the other hand, birds believed to be of the *tristis* race were usually a drab greyish-buff on the upperparts with markedly creamy-white underparts, lacking all trace of olive or yellow coloration and often displaying a pale, rather narrow wingbar as the result of a lighter edging to the greater coverts; they appeared dumpier than British birds and showed peaked foreheads and uptilted bills. A bird with this kind of light edging to the greater coverts and revealing other characteristics of the *tristis* race, which wintered at Ruxley Gravel Pit in Kent in the late winter of 1976–7, was photographed and its picture appeared in the *London Bird Report* for 1977.

In the British Isles breeding Chiffchaffs are missing from many of the hills of Snowdonia and central Wales, from much of the flatlands of Cambridgeshire and Lincolnshire, from the Pennine Chain as well as the Border counties and the Scottish highlands and islands. In Scotland there was a spread after the 1950s and singing males were reported from Caithness, Sutherland and the Outer Hebrides. In 1959 a pair bred for the first time in the Inner Hebrides. Chiffchaffs are generally less common in eastern Britain north of Yorkshire. In Ireland the Chiffchaff is quite common and widespread. In the middle of the nineteenth century it was known in only 7 of the 32 counties, but by 1900 the species had spread across the island and fifty years later it reached Co. Kerry. Chiffchaffs now occur regularly in Ireland, except for parts of Cos. Mayo, Galway and Roscommon, and in some regions they outnumber the Willow Warblers.

The Chiffchaff breeds in woodlands, coppiced woods, groves, shrubberies with a rich field layer and ground zone, old hedgerows with tall standing timber and, as a species, it often shows a greater dependence on trees than the Willow Warbler. The reasons for its present distribution

Fig. 141
Population changes in Chiffchaff numbers 1962–82. Based on Common Birds Census of B.T.O. (levels in relation to 1966).

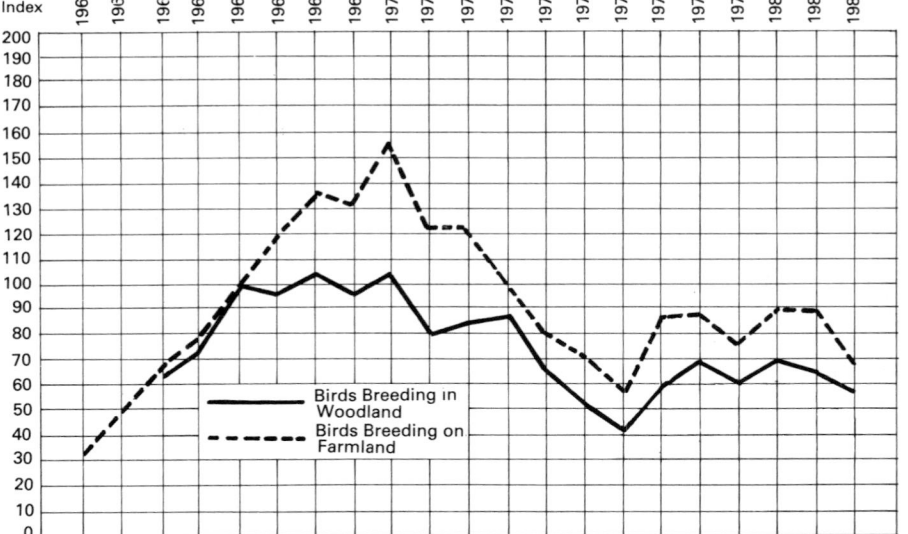

and numbers are not very clear. After a rise in numbers in the mid 1960s, to a plateau from 1966–1973, the population has decreased. I have found Chiffchaffs in most English pedunculate oakwoods. In Badby Wood in Northamptonshire they were outnumbered 4 to 1 by the Willow Warbler, while in a mixed oakwood near my Lincolnshire home, Willow Warblers were eight to ten times as common. In a census of 16 hectares of oakwood at Bookham Common from 1949–1959 Chiffchaffs averaged only 3 pairs annually compared to 13.8 for the Willow Warbler. As the wood became overgrown and the rides narrower the latter species declined but the Chiffchaff maintained its status with little change (Beven 1976).

In my visits over the years to hundreds of woods in the British Isles I have also located Chiffchaffs in sessile oakwoods and woods of beech, ash and birch as well as mixed broad-leaved woodland and plantations of coniferous trees from the thicket stage to maturity. Both species of warbler are equally well represented in Irish beechwoods and spruce forests. However, the proportions in other Irish woods were 4 Willow Warblers to 1 Chiffchaff in old mixed plantations of conifers, 3 to 1 in woods of ash, birch and young conifers, 2 to 1 in sessile oakwoods and 9 to 7 in mixed young broad-leaved/coniferous plantations. In mixed broad-leaved and mature mixed broad-leaved/coniferous woods in Ireland the Chiffchaff was the commoner of the two species (Simms 1971). For example, at Baronscourt I counted 14 Chiffchaffs in song to 9 Willow Warblers during a 25-minute count, and in a sessile wood near Upper Lough Erne I came across 11 singing Chiffchaffs to 6 Willow Warblers in a period of half an hour. Birds are not uncommon in the Scottish beech woods and mixed broad-leaved woods, in Scottish and English conifer thickets and plantations and in mature Scots pine in Ireland. In English beech woods there are often 5 Willow Warblers to 2 Chiffchaffs. On my travels in northern Scotland I have found Chiffchaffs in oak, beech and ash near Ullapool, and on many estates and policies the shrub layer consists of rhododendron which may give protection to the warblers when the weather becomes very severe. When I was counting birds in the hazel scrub of the extreme west of Ireland, the Chiffchaff was the dominant species wherever the growth exceeded 6.6 m in height, followed jointly by Blackbird and Robin, then Willow Warbler, Song Thrush, Chaffinch, Bullfinch and smaller numbers of seven other species. Yet I found the Chiffchaff in many small hedgerows of different shrub species and even in willow scrub less than 1 m high. Birds will also breed in the suburbs, where there are tall trees and good cover, but much less frequently than the Willow Warbler. I found the first nest recorded for Inner London in 1937 (Simms 1976). A pair was reported to have bred in Regent's Park in London in 1972 and in 1981 in the same Royal Park a pair raised two broods with six young in each.

In western and central Europe the Chiffchaff also lives alongside the Willow Warbler but there is an obvious gap on the map for the former species in southern Scandinavia. This was thought by Voous (1961) to result from the fact that after the last Pleistocene glaciation, northern Europe was repopulated from two directions: 'from the south by groups coming from central Europe, and from the east by groups coming from eastern Europe; neither population group has yet reached the other.' The European distribution limits of the Chiffchaff lie between the July isotherms of 10°C in the north and 27°C in the south. The European Chiffchaff is often scarce in woods of birch and willow along lakes and rivers and is absent from the poplar groves along watercourses where the Willow Warbler is often abundant. In the taiga the Chiffchaff occurs in good numbers among both pines and spruces. In the spruce forests of Slovakia Chiffchaffs occur at the rate of 43 individuals to 100 hectares compared to Goldcrests at 56, Wood Warblers at 20, and Willow Warblers at 0 (Turček 1956). In Norway the Chiffchaff occurs more in regions with a less even distribution of vegetation at different height intervals and in areas with a lower diversity of tree species than the Willow Warbler (Saether 1983). Birds also frequent Continental montane oak woods and subalpine coniferous forests to at least 1960 m in the Alps and 2165 m in the Altai Mountains. In Siberia the eastern race occurs in conifers and mixed woodland and in birch groves but seems to demand the presence of water in the habitat.

The first view that one has of a Chiffchaff on its return in spring is often that of a small, active warbler, fractionally smaller than a Willow Warbler and dingier in coloration, flitting on short, rounded wings from twig to twig in a bare ash or willow tree, singing spasmodically. The flight is rather jerky and undertaken over quite short distances. The bird also hops from branch to branch, flicking its wings and tail quite regularly. On the ground

Fig. 142
Tail movement of the Chiffchaff – a unique combination of a drop in angle and then a wag (the species is called Tailwagger in India). (D. I. M. Wallace)

it has a hopping gait. Birds like to bathe but somewhat secretively. Both melanic and albinistic forms occur in the British Isles and J. S. Ash (1961) reported a bird in Dorset that was 'smoky (greyish) brown, the underparts paler.'

While foraging for food birds will inspect twigs and foliage and make short flights. In the spring Chiffchaffs take many Dipterous flies including non-biting midges. Later in the season they feed widely on the larvae of moths and butterflies. These include caterpillars of the winter moth and

Tortrix viridana, the latter being a small moth whose larvae live in abundance in some years in rolled-up leaves. On the Canary Islands Chiffchaffs also feed green caterpillars to their young (Cullen *et al* 1952). Aphids are widely taken as well as the eggs, larvae and imagos of many small insects – flies, beetles, and moths as well as spiders. On the Continent aphids are often fed to the young and even insects as large as the peacock butterfly (Gwinner 1961). Aphids may also sustain birds wintering in England; J. F. Burton (1953) watched a Chiffchaff in Kent in January 1953 which was 'feeding voraciously on the nymphs and adults (scarcer) of an aphid which was numerous on the leaves and stems of Oxford ragwort.' Willow and Wood Warblers may on occasion take berries but these do not seem to attract Chiffchaffs. T. A. Coward (1944) noted that: 'It is said that soft fruit is eaten, but I have not seen this myself.' A bird at Hersham Sewage Farm in Surrey was seen searching for food in partly submerged vegetation (*London Bird Report* 1954.19:36). In Portugal in 1979 B. Gooch (1984) saw migrant Chiffchaffs gorging themselves in his garden on persimmon fruits (*Diospyros kaki*).

In their winter quarters, Chiffchaffs feed in bushy, scrubby places and low vegetation. In the central Sahara in winter birds could be found in all types of vegetation but 'were particularly numerous feeding on the ground in the irrigated grass fields' (Gaston 1970); here they formed loose flocks of 5–20 birds moving on like autumn parties of tits in English woodlands. To the east in 1964 in the Sunt Forest of Khartoum in the Sudan, A. Pettett (1975) came across a Chiffchaff feeding on the gum exudate of the tree *Acacia nilotica*. This bird pecked repeatedly at a crystallized mass of the gum and was seen to swallow some of the particles – a food also taken by White-vented Bulbuls.

Some Chiffchaffs winter in Britain (a subject that we shall return to later in the present chapter) but the main arrival of breeding birds in spring continues from mid-March until the last week of April, although the passage of non-breeding birds that starts in the second week of April may carry on until late May. After arriving by night on the south and east coasts of Britain the male Chiffchaffs distribute themselves across the country to take up their breeding territories which they defend aggressively and advertise by song. The first females begin to appear some 10–14 days after the first males have arrived. They also tend to come by night and the males search them out at first light. The boundaries of the territories are marked out fairly clearly but 'no-man's-lands' often exist between them. Some females appear a bit later than the others and may find that breeding is already under way with the early arrivals. In an elaborate and quite delightful courtship the male Chiffchaff pursues the female who has enticed him into the chase by standing in a very upright posture and calling with a high-pitched note 'tsiff-tsiff-tsiff', while slowly flicking her wings in a wide arc. Dr Geoffrey Beven (1946) watched a male approach a female in the attitude just described and call with a high 'si-si-si', while expanding his wings into a graceful curve almost reaching a semicircle with every feather used in the display. The male may dart at the female so that the bills are actually clicked together in the encounter, or he may approach with a buzzing sound and the aspect of a giant moth with slowly beating wings. Eliot Howard (1907–14) called this one of the most delightful phases of the courtship, since the wings are beaten 'so very slowly as to give the impression that he

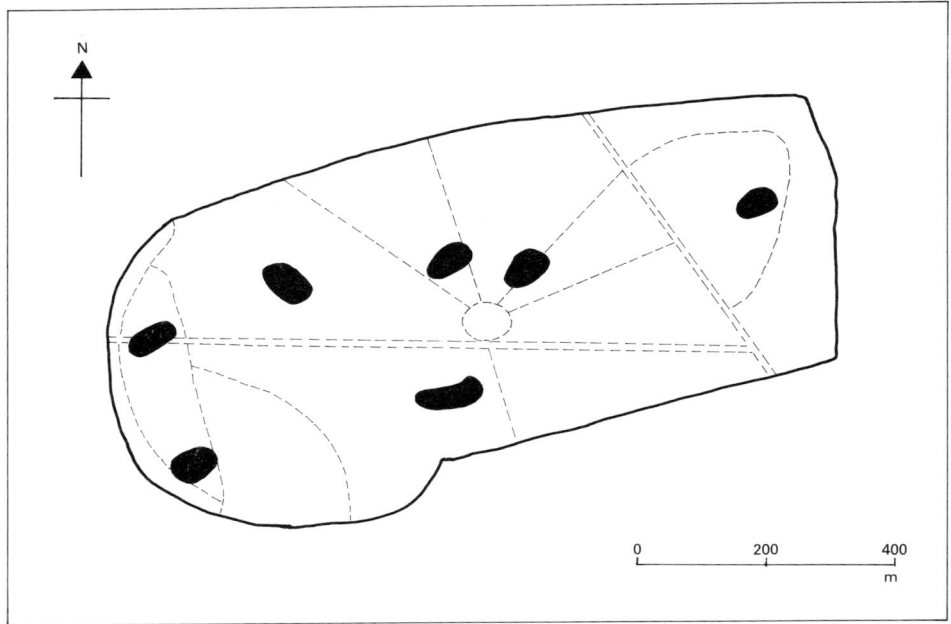

Fig. 143
Distribution of 7
Chiffchaff territories in a
Northamptonshire oak
wood. (Eric Simms)

ought not to be moving at all.' The courtship of the Chiffchaff is one of the most delightful and charming among our British birds. Towards the end of the display the male will leap from twig to twig without beating his wings and the female may then fly towards him in great excitement and copulate with him.

The paired birds nest in woods, scrub, groves of trees with dense undergrowth and even old, well-developed hedgerows. The nest itself is usually constructed in tall growth in the field layer or low shrubs, usually above the ground but sometimes in contact with it. Other sites may be in low tree branches, especially those of yews and hollies, and in ivy and creepers on walls. Two separate nests at Chesterton in Warwickshire were built in a rather unusual site, in sedges over water (*West Midland Bird Report* 18:22). The nest is roughly spherical in shape, having both a domed roof and fairly wide but shallow side entrance. The materials used consist of dead leaves, often employed for the foundation, as well as grass, plant stems and moss. The nest is built by the hen bird and when finished is a looser structure than that of the Willow Warbler. A dense lining of feathers is usually added, such as those from a Woodpigeon or thrush, perhaps plucked or eaten by a predator. A. J. Harthan counted 670 feathers in an abandoned nest at Sheriff's Lench in Worcestershire, all collected in a poultry run some 300 m away, together with a few feathers from a Blackbird and a Greenfinch.

There are regional variations in the size of the clutch but five and six eggs are common, seven are rarer; four, eight and nine have been recorded as well. The number of eggs in second layings tends to fall to four or five. Clutches may be laid as early as late April in the south, to late May further

Fig. 144
*Chiffchaff at its neatly
domed nest. (Eric
Hosking)*

north and even in June in the northeast of the region. In the northern part
of the range there is normally one brood; further south there are two
broods. In Germany there is a record of a successful first brood, followed
by a failure and then a third clutch. The eggs are white, smooth and glossy,
and rather sparsely marked with dark purplish-brown or purplish-black.
Some clutches resemble those of Willow Warblers but even then the eggs
tend to display heavy but scant blotches. The eggs are laid at daily intervals
and incubation is carried out solely by the hen who usually leaves the nest
to feed but may be fed, although very rarely, by the male bird. The incubation period itself lasts 13–14 days. The male shows little attachment to the
nest and may or may not feed the young; if he does so, his share is very much
less than that of his mate (Homann 1960). In a six year study of ringed
Chiffchaffs, Geissbühler (1954) found that the male helped in feeding the
young but his total contribution was always very small. The young spend
12–15 days in the nest and after they have fledged the adults care for only
certain individuals in the fledged group; a practice that I have found
commonly amongst Blackbirds (Simms 1976). The fledged young have no
difficulty in recognizing their mother (Gwinner 1961). There is plenty of
juvenile 'play' among the newly fledged birds involving foraging, chases
and escape movements. Homann (1960), who studied the behaviour and
breeding biology of the Chiffchaff, was of the opinion that the species was
evolving into one in which the male would have no parental responsibilities.
    In addition to any existing problems of separating Willow Warblers and

Chiffchaffs because of regional differences, feather wear and age, there is always the slight and added possibility that hybrids might occur in the wild. In a review of hybridization amongst birds A. P. Gray (1958) described only two cases of suspected interbreeding: one in Germany around 1900 and one in Spain in 1945. An instance of probable hybridization was reported by da Prato and da Prato (1983) near Cousland in Lothian in 1982. In this case a hen Willow Warbler lost her preferred mate and appeared to pair with a male Chiffchaff whose territory was close at hand and in which no female Chiffchaffs were present. Although 'actual copulation was not observed' strong evidence was marshalled for hybridization, including the biometrics of and differences in leg coloration in the resulting chicks.

The emigration of British Chiffchaffs begins quite early, even in the first week of August. A complete post-nuptial moult is undertaken in late July and August, on or close to the breeding ground. As the birds begin to move south, they still continue to sing and indeed Chiffchaffs regularly sing on passage and in their winter quarters. In September and October, movements of British and Irish birds are inextricably bound up with the passage movements of 'Northern' Chiffchaffs. Most Chiffchaff populations are migratory and *collybita* is most frequent on the coasts of southern England and the Irish Sea, but large 'falls' of Chiffchaffs there in late October and November are much more likely to be of Continental birds, some of which remain for the winter. The Scandinavian Chiffchaff *abietinus* appears quite often in autumn on the east coast of Britain, while examples of the Siberian race *tristis* are observed every year on Fair Isle and more rarely in other parts of Scotland, and even less frequently in England and Ireland; some of these may winter as well. The British breeding Chiffchaffs winter in the southern parts of the breeding range; in the British Isles and the Mediterranean basin south to about 13°N in west Africa and to Egypt, Syria and Iraq in the east (Williamson 1976). Birds may also occur in Germany, with

Fig. 145
Breeding range of the Chiffchaff.

more in France (Mead 1974), southern Spain, Portugal, Italy and all southern Europe to the Aegean Sea and the Greek islands, east to Iraq. Wintering birds can also be found on most of the Mediterranean islands and in North Africa from Morocco east to Egypt. The westerly distribution in Africa of the Chiffchaff reaches south to the Gambia, where its range touches that of the Willow Warbler; Senegal, and in northeast Africa to Libya and the Sudan south to the White Nile. Chiffchaffs were noted as passage migrants or winter visitors to Nigeria (Elgood *et al* 1966).

The Scandinavian form *abietinus* winters in the region of the South Caspian, western Iran, Iraq, southern Arabia, the Sudan, Egypt, Eritrea, Ethiopia, Somalia and much more infrequently in Kenya. The Siberian Chiffchaff *tristis* spends the winter months in the Himalayas; then south from that mountain range through Pakistan and the great plains of India to the Central Provinces, as well as Afghanistan, and other countries of southwest Asia. This is a regular drift migrant to western Europe occurring in the British Isles, the Faeroes, Norway, Holland, Italy and elsewhere. At Fair Isle the typical form is a passage migrant in spring and autumn but in somewhat greater numbers in the latter season. In spring birds are mainly of the typical form *abietinus*, and intergrades, while Siberian birds of the *tristis* race have also appeared there in May. For example a 'hold-up' of migrants one May due to fresh to moderate southeast winds was followed by a remarkable 'fall' of birds. George Stout wrote 'there were thousands of willow-warblers and chiffchaffs, of which all three forms were present, from 11th to 16th, viz. British, Scandinavian and Siberian, and an enormous number of pied and spotted flycatchers.' At Fair Isle the early autumn birds include some resembling the typical form, while the main October passage consists of 'Northern' Chiffchaffs, especially *abietinus* as well as good examples of *tristis* in October and November (Williamson 1965).

In their winter quarters Chiffchaffs tend to be rather shy but may become more sociable in certain habitats. Birds can be found in cork woods in Andalucia, pine woods, bushy areas, orchards, vineyards, north African palm gardens, fields of vegetables, irrigated regions and grasslands, marshes and reed beds. In the Balearic Islands when the weather is cold Chiffchaffs 'become exceedingly tame and will freely enter houses' (Bannerman 1954).

On their spring and autumn passage birds are reported from many parts of the British Isles, but the records tend to be much higher in autumn than spring. This was certainly true of the suburban area of Dollis Hill in northwest London where I studied migration for 29 years from 1951. Birds were very scarce in the spring probably because they were undertaking longer nocturnal movements. The regular autumn passage at Dollis Hill lasted from 1 August to 3 October; a later passage there than for the Willow Warbler. D. I. M. Wallace (1961) found that in Regents Park only a few miles away the Chiffchaff was 'the dominant leaf warbler in September'. The Chiffchaff is the first of the warblers to arrive in the British Isles and often the last to go. Migrants often passed through my garden and stopped to feed and sing, while odd birds would appear in the street trees, but on 17 September 1951 I found more than 100 on some allotments and, of these, 10 were in song. I also made some interesting observations on a south Warwickshire farm where I discovered the overland migration route from the Wash to the Severn; three large-scale invasions of the farm took place with 80 on 10 August 1948, 250 on 19 August of the same year and 120 on 10 September 1949 (Simms 1952). There is a long period of migration through the south coast of England in spring and a shorter one in autumn.

Of course, early spring is much more bedevilled by adverse weather than the autumn. It does seem likely that only one population actually passes through southern England in autumn (Parslow 1969).

Not all Chiffchaffs leave the British Isles for the winter. One very early record of a bird wintering in Britain is of a male singing near Evesham on 28 February 1846 (Tomes 1901). In the Channel Isles, Roderick Dobson (1952) listed a February date for a bird in 1917 and other records for 1929, 1931 and 1932 as well as nine between 1940 and 1949. Many of the early records of this overwintering habit came not unexpectedly from the southwest of the British Isles. Up to 8 were found wintering at Clontymon in Co. Cork for three weeks up to 12 January 1940 (Scroope 1940). Fifty or more were recorded at Falmouth from December 1940 to 25 February 1941 when many were in full song (*Devon Bird Watching Society* 1941:48). There were also records from Cornwall from 31 January to 28 February 1941 and again in February 1943, 1944 and 1945. Birds in song were heard in Newton Ferrers in south Devon from 25 January to 17 February 1948 (Hunt 1948) while further instances were noted in Cornwall in 1949 and 1950 (Beckerlegge 1951), and also at Nuneaton in 1950. In 1953 a Chiffchaff was reported at Dungeness in Kent in December. Many of the birds wintering in the southwest of England tended to be rather brown and white and also used the 'hooeet' call, which suggested birds of a western rather than an eastern origin (*British Birds* 75:384).

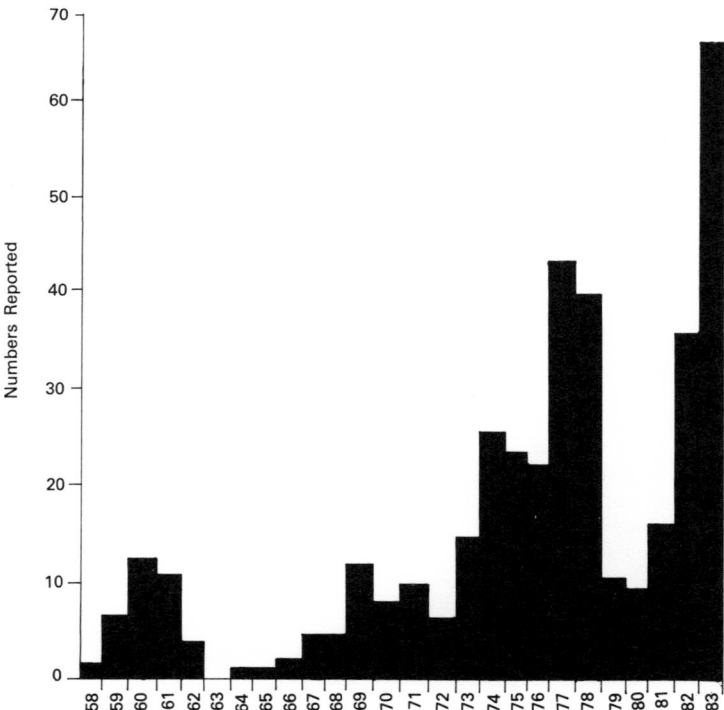

Fig. 146
Numbers of Chiffchaffs reported wintering in the London area from 1958–83. (Taken from the London Bird Report*)*

The number of winter records began to rise. Records of usually not more than one a year were reported regularly in the area of the West Midlands up to 1960 but then became less frequent (Lord and Munns 1970). Six were recorded in Somerset in 1963.

Chiffchaffs were especially numerous in the winter of 1968–9 and ringing showed that some were able to survive the severe weather in southeastern England in February 1969; birds seemed to frequent the banks of rivers and ditches (Gladwin 1969). The first birds in the London area appear to have been one on 1 February 1948 at Walton-on-Thames and others at Stone Marshes on 3 January 1953 and South Norwood on 15 December 1954. A bird sang at Lonsdale Road Reservoir from 27 January to 27 February 1955 and another sang in a garden at Ewell on 1 February 1957. A glance at Fig. 146 will show how numbers have risen in the London area in recent years with a maximum tally of 66 in 1983. A bird in 1965 fed on bread and fat on a bird table.

A favourite site in recent years was in west Cornwall at a sewage works near Treloweth Woods. Here R. D. Penhallurick (1978) counted 23 Chiffchaffs on 24 December 1976 and J. B. and Mrs S. Bottomley saw at least 37 on 29 December and photographed birds feeding on the bacteriological oxidization filters. Most of the Chiffchaffs reported on all Cornish sewage farms appear to have been of the brown and white variety. However, a Chiffchaff which fed in a Cheltenham garden from 23 January to 8 April called atypically and even sang 'a "chiff" note followed by four to six musical bursts of song'; it was thought to be of the Siberian race *tristis* (Heaven 1982). It was grey-brown, buff and white, lacked all yellow in its plumage, displayed a buff supercilium and no wing-bar. It seems that Chiffchaffs have been able to overwinter in some years in apparently less comfortable regions; northeast Scotland had one in 1975, four in 1976 and two in 1977 while four wintered on the Lincolnshire coast and inland in 1980 and one was present at Gibraltar Point on 11 and 14 February 1982.

Fig. 147
Xanthochroistic Wood
Warbler pair in central
Wales, 1954. The female
feeding the young has a
primrose head and back,
pure white underparts,
splashes of darker yellow
on the shoulders and
lower back and two white
outer tail feathers. The
male, departing on the
right to collect more food
for the young, has the
normal colouration of a
Wood Warbler except for
a pale straw-coloured
cap. (Eric Hosking)

One of the easiest and sometimes most reliable ways of identifying a bird is by the auditory clues that it provides. It was by its 'sibilous shivering noise in the tops of tall woods' that Gilbert White was able to distinguish the Wood Warbler – his 'little yellow bird' – and separate it from both Chiff-chaff and Willow Warbler. That song has inspired several writers and poets. An old friend, the late Commander Alec Robertson (1954), thought it 'an image of raindrops scattering among the leaves', while the poet Edward Thomas spoke lyrically of the songs high among the beeches 'as if, over-head in the stainless air, little waves of pearls dropped and scattered and shivered on a shore of pearls.' The Wood Warbler is the largest leaf warbler to be found in Europe, and also has relatively longer wings and a shorter tail. It displays a contrasting coloration of yellowish-green upperparts with a broad golden supercilium, sulphur-stained breast and throat and snow-white belly and undertail coverts. The somewhat brownish wing feathers often carry yellowish edges. It is a stoutish bird and often hangs its wings rather loosely below so that their tips can be seen separate from the outline of the body. It does not flick its tail in the manner either of Willow Warbler or Chiffchaff. The Wood Warbler can be distinguished from the

Melodious and Icterine Warblers by its white underparts, shorter bill, pale yellow-brown legs and feet as well as a less steeply angled forehead, and, of course, its songs. A pair of oddly marked Wood Warblers in June 1954 revealed an unusual condition known as xanthochroism. This arises through an excess retention of yellow and the loss of dark pigment. The male was normal except for a straw-coloured cap but the female sported a primrose head and back, darker yellow shoulders and tail coverts, white underparts and white outer tail. She had a bill and legs the colour of 'dead bracken' but the eyes were dark brown (Sage 1962); both birds were photographed by Eric Hosking, who tells me that the young were atypical with a resemblance to the female. The Wood Warbler behaves like many of the other leaf warblers but is more strictly arboreal.

The Wood Warbler breeds in Europe and Asia from the British Isles, France and central Scandinavia north to about 61° 30′ N in Norway and 64° N in Finland and Russia, then east to the Irtysh River in western Siberia and south to the Caucasus, Crimea, Yugoslavia, Italy, central France with outposts in the Pyrenees and some of the highlands of southern Europe. The distribution limits appear to lie between the July isotherms

of 15°C and 29°C or about 30°N and 64°N. Originally with a European breeding range this species started to nest in the middle of the twentieth century in the wooded steppes of western Siberia (Voous 1961). In mainland Britain this is a not too uncommon species, but it is largely missing from Ireland and the Outer Isles. It is much more frequent on the western side of Britain and is local or missing in eastern England from Yorkshire to Kent. In Scotland the Wood Warbler has been widening its range since the middle of the nineteenth century when it was recorded in Inverness. By about 1950 the species had reached Wester Ross while birds were reported from 1947 in the Tongue beechwoods in Sutherland and by 1949 by Loch Naver and elsewhere in Caithness. In June 1950 Derek Goodwin and R. W. Hayman (1951) found birds singing in birch woods above Loch Merkland and at the foot of Ben Stack in Sutherland, and R. S. R. Fitter (1951) came across birds at Loch Eriboll and Hope Lodge

Fig. 148
Breeding range of the Wood Warbler.

Fig. 149
*Habitat of sessile oak
woods for Wood
Warblers, Redstarts and
Pied Flycatchers.
Central Wales. (Eric
Simms, May 1983)*

in June 1951. The Wood Warbler is still scarce, however, in northern Scotland.

Since the 1940s or even earlier, decreases have occurred in England especially in the eastern counties where the species had always been rather uncommon. Other decreases were reported from Worcestershire, Stafford, Cheshire, Cumbria and Ayr, while Wood Warblers are scarce or missing from northeast Scotland, Humberside, Lincolnshire, Nottingham and many parts of East Anglia (Parslow 1973). However, recent results from the Common Birds Census of the B.T.O. suggest that little further change has taken place. There are often short-term fluctuations in numbers as well as a surplus of males on occasion. Local extinctions have been brought about by tree-felling operations but apparently suitable woods have been deserted and in others the growth of the shrub layer has forced the birds away (Harthan 1961).

Wood Warblers are truly forest birds. I gave the opinion in *Woodland Birds* (1971) that: 'Wood warblers favour fairly open, mature broad-leaved woods especially of oak and beech with very little secondary growth which could, if allowed to develop, exclude the species as a breeding bird.' However, brambles and bracken may be found in the understory of a Wood Warbler habitat but not well-grown shrubs. A typical haunt of Wood Warblers is that of the sessile oakwoods of western Britain. With a relative abundance figure of 7 the Wood Warbler came fourth in my list of bird species for woods of this kind in England and Wales. I have listened to as many as four males singing within earshot in central Wales together with Redstarts and Pied Flycatchers, and I have met many in the Cumbrian

Hills and the oakwoods of Deeside and Argyll in Scotland. Kenneth Williamson (1974) found that even where these sessile woods had been coppiced the Wood Warbler still managed to hold on; he also discovered that in the Glen Nant oak/ash woods in Argyll, Wood Warblers formed 3% of the bird community compared to 8% for the Willow Warbler.

The Wood Warbler can also be found in English and Scottish beech woods with a relative abundance figure of 2 (Simms 1971). I located birds in nearly half of the English and a quarter of the Scottish woods. I have also tape recorded birds in song in the beech woods of the New Forest, where I heard six males in voice on one May day in 1964; I have also recorded them in the mixed oak and beech woods of eastern Scotland. Wood Warblers also nest in many of the birch woods, perhaps up to heights of 480–540 m. From time to time I have come across birds in the heath birch woods of Surrey and Kent. I have known Wood Warblers to breed on Wimbledon Common on the outskirts of London. Besides birch woods, Wood Warblers in southeast England will favour oak, beech, chestnut and mixed woodland that includes some birch and pine. In Glasdrum ash wood in central Argyll, which contains birch, alder and wild cherry with some hazel, hawthorn and elder with a ground zone of bracken, yellow flags, primroses, celandines and violets, Wood Warblers and Willow Warblers each occupied 6% of the bird community.

In Ireland, where I visited almost every wood of consequence between 1967 and 1971, I located only one Wood Warbler and that was in a beech wood in Co. Wicklow. Major R. F. Ruttledge (1966) reported that Wood Warblers had bred in Cos. Cork, Leix, Galway and Down as well as Wicklow but the last time was in 1938 in Cork. Singing, unmated males are discovered from time to time and K. Preston (1980) noted that most of Ireland's few breeding Wood Warblers were confined to the Wicklow Mountains. Although I have seen birds in habitats which contain some scattered conifers amongst oak or birch, I have never seen them in larch and on the whole Wood Warblers in Britain dislike conifers. In Europe, however, birds can be found in subalpine spruce forest and mixed woods of beech and conifer. Undoubtedly the Wood Warbler has more inflexible habitat demands than either the Willow Warbler or the Chiffchaff, although all three species can be found sometimes in the same wood and react aggressively to each other. In 1947 in the 83 hectares of Badby Wood in Northamptonshire I counted 21 pairs of Willow Warblers, 5 pairs of Chiffchaffs and only two pairs of Wood Warblers, both in regions of tall trees and little understory. The best habitat for the Wood Warbler, G. Tiedemann (1971) thought, was one where the canopy of the wood should provide at least 70% shelter from external conditions of weather, such as sun and wind, while low branches not higher above ground than 2.5 m were necessary as perches when the adults were feeding the young.

It is by their songs that we know, more often than not, that the first males have returned to or occupied a territory. The first birds are back in England during the second week of April with the main arrival occurring from the end of that month to the third week of May. The Wood Warbler is of particular interest in that the song of the male has two phases, one of which is more frequently used than the other. The typical part of the song is the repetition of a single note – 'tip', 'sip', 'it' or 'vit' – then hastened into a trill or a grasshopper-like accelerando. After carefully analysing many songs of this type that I have tape recorded in southern England, I list some examples.

1. 15 'vits' lasting 1.6 seconds, followed by a trill lasting 0.8 seconds and containing 25 'vits' = total song of 2.4 seconds
2. 12 'vits' lasting 1.4 seconds, followed by a trill lasting 0.6 seconds and containing 15 'vits' = total song of 2.0 seconds
3. 12 'vits' lasting 1.5 seconds, followed by a trill lasting 1.0 seconds and containing 25 'vits' = total song of 2.5 seconds
4. 9 'vits' lasting 1.0 second, followed by a trill lasting 1.3 seconds and containing 25 'vits' = total song of 2.3 seconds.

An individual singer may have several versions and E. M. Nicholson (1937) observed that: 'The duration of the stuttering preamble and of the ecstatic final trill vary even in successive efforts of the same bird.' Song-trills may last on occasion for more than five seconds (the longest I have heard is 5.3) and one bird I timed in Argyll had trills lasting in order 3, 3.5, 4.5, 3.5, 2.8 and 1.8 seconds. There are often gaps of from 6–10 seconds between the songs which may accommodate the second type of song; at the start and towards the end of the song-period, which lasts from late April to about the middle of June, the songs are less well spaced out or regular.

The second kind of song consists of a series of from 4–17 plaintive, plangent notes: 'pew-pew-pew-pew' or 'püü-püü-püü-püü', either uttered as an independent phrase, or interpolated with brief intervals into the sequence of trills. After timing many of these bursts of piping notes I find that 12 of them last for 3.5 seconds and 17 for 5.3 seconds. This piping is the less common of the two songs and I would suggest that there is often only one example of this type to every 6–10 repeats of the trill. Nicholson (1937) quoted Sir Julian Huxley as saying that the second song 'is usually uttered in a fairly regular proportion of once to every five to twelve repetitions of the trilling song.' There is considerable variation between performers.

The trill can be heard from a bird on a perch or in flight, with the singer perhaps beginning the trill before becoming airborne. In a study of a pair of Wood Warblers at Englefield Green in Surrey, D. J. May and A. Manning (1951) also noted the start of the trilling song from a perched bird and wrote that 'the prelude of shorter notes ("sip . . . sip . . . sip") was invariably protracted until the bird had settled again on another tree. On occasions this prelude was not completed, and the shattering cascade that normally concludes the song was omitted.' When a male launches himself into his song flight he begins slowly yet with a fast wing action, and the

Fig. 150
The more common song of the Wood Warbler—the accelerated trill. (Recorded by Eric Simms, New Forest, May 1964)

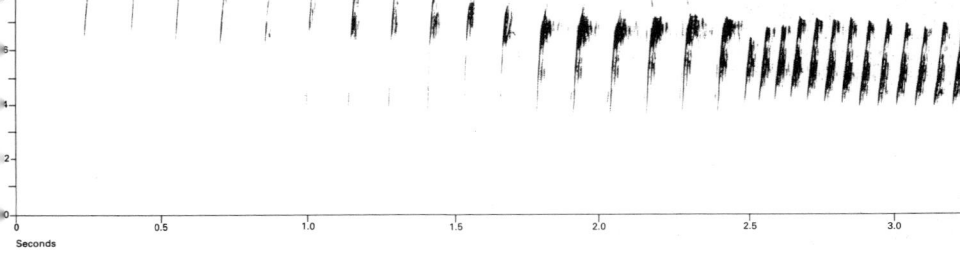

Hz
8-

6-

4-

2-

0-
0   0.5   1.0   1.5   2.0   2.5   3.0
Seconds

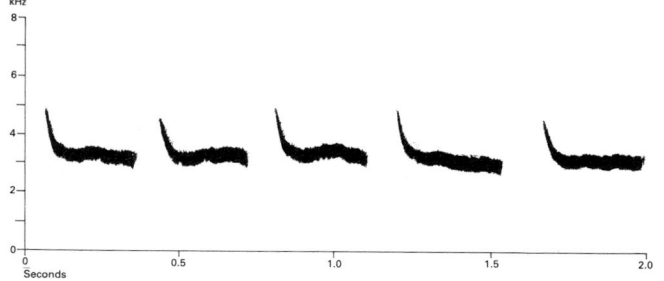

Fig. 151
*The plangent notes of the
Wood Warbler's
alternative song.
(Recorded by Eric
Simms, New Forest,
May 1964)*

vibrating pinions do not drop below the horizontal which gives an exaggerated impression of slow motion. A perched bird will also shiver its wings
at the climax of the trill. There is also a rarer song flight recalling that of the
Tree Pipit. An atypical song was noted by H. J. Hoffman (1949) in which
the vocalization opened normally but the trill, instead of being continuous
and unbroken, came in staccato bursts with a pause between each. The
typical call and alarm note is rather like the 'pew' of the second song-type
but is less clear and liquid although of a similar frequency. Other notes
include a softer version of the trill used in display by the male; a sharp
'see-see-see' with wing-quivering, a softer 'wit-wit-wit' and a call, described
in *The Handbook* (1946) as 'irrr' and used when feeding the young. The
female and young also have a hissing 'ztztzt'.

In some parts of Europe the range of the Wood Warbler overlaps that of
Bonelli's Warbler, a rare visitor to the British Isles. Both species have
trilling songs but that of Bonelli's is slower and less complex. As a result of
a study by J-C. Brémond (1976) in which he used playback methods with
sound recordings he was able to demonstrate that, while the song – the
'signal' in effect – must include enough of the right clues if it is to be
recognized, it must not embrace certain 'wrong' clues. He showed that
some of the characters of Bonelli's songs could be changed quite a bit; for
example, by increasing the length of the trill considerably beyond that of
any known natural song, Bonelli's Warbler still responded correctly.
Another kind of change that he made by shifting the frequency of the trill
upwards into the normal range of Wood Warblers' songs was not only
ignored by Bonelli's Warblers but even elicited responses from some of the
Wood Warblers! Thus the songs of Wood and Bonelli's Warblers could be
distinguished.

The Wood Warbler is a comparatively late arrival in Britain so that the
breeding season is also late and consequently shorter than for many other
species of warbler. According to Elizabeth Lack (1950), 554 nests out of
558 found by Major H. Machell Cox in south Devon between 1922 and
1934 were completed in the six weeks from 6 May to 17 June, and 86% of
them were finished in the three-week period from 13 May to 2 June; the
mean date of clutch completion was established as 24 May. From 83 nests
recorded by A. Whitaker near Sheffield, Mrs Lack found a mean date
of clutch completion eight days later, 1 June, which was a statistically
significant difference. Records from Wales are little different from those
for Devon. While investigating the territorial habits of Wood Warblers,
C. Herman (1971) found that females are more attracted to nesting sites

than to local males which have arrived a few days before the female influx. Because of this attraction he discovered that females would also copulate with strange males. A male may also mate with a female arriving late, while his first partner is faithfully incubating a clutch of eggs. For these reasons polygamy is not at all uncommon and Herman found three cases of this in the ten pairs that he studied. There is sometimes a surplus of male birds so that it is difficult to work out all the territorial interplay that may be going on. In the issue of *Bird Study* for March 1957, L. J. Raynsford reported that near Godalming there was 'an unusual number of unmated wood warblers locally in 1956.' During a period of fifteen years C. Oakes (1953) found in the northeast of Lancashire that some 60% of Wood Warblers were without mates and he knew of other examples elsewhere. This was followed by information from K. G. Spencer (1957) who thought that the disbalance was probably 'regular and widespread'. After observing Wood Warblers in mixed woodlands in northwest Germany in 1951 A. H. V. Smith (1958) located 28 territories of which 10 were held by un-mated males, whilst another three males became established in unoccupied areas later in the season. Later Raynsford (1957) was able to declare that a return almost to normal had taken place around Godalming with only one unmated male. The male is aggressive in the defence of his territory, will attack other Phylloscopid warblers and on the arrival of a female early in the season chases her out as if she were an intruding male.

However, when the male courts a female he embarks on a most attractive display in which he undertakes long sweeping flights around his domain, performed rather in the manner of a dragonfly and descending with wings quivering in a small arc as he spirals down. The female will flutter from

Fig. 152
Territorial flight of Wood Warbler. (D. I. M. Wallace)

branch to branch until the male arrives close to her; he then adopts an attitude with wings opened and quivering and crown feathers raised as he proceeds to swing his body round and back, to nod his head, peck at a branch and open and fan his tail feathers. When she is ready to copulate the female droops and shivers her wings, stretches her neck forward and raises her tail. Coition is often followed 'by a very long and vigorous chase of the female by the male' (May and Manning 1951). I can recall few pleasures greater than watching the Wood Warblers displaying among the most beautiful of forest trees, the beeches, just coming into delicate green leaf.

The female selects the actual site for the nest (White 1931, May and Manning 1951) and she can sometimes be spotted hunting for a suitable place. She also builds the nest alone quite often in a hollow in the ground

Fig. 153
Wood Warbler at nest.
(Eric Hosking)

amongst bracken, brambles or grass. It is of a similar type to that of the
Willow Warbler and Chiffchaff, being normally a domed structure with a
side entrance. A first British record of a Wood Warbler's nest without a
dome appears to be of one near Parkend in Gloucestershire in June 1962;
it was built among dead leaves under a thin cover of low brambles and lined
typically with grass but no feathers. The lack of a dome made it appear
much more like the nest of a Robin or Tree Pipit (Price 1962). John Niles
(1968) reported another domeless nest in the Forest of Dean, found by
Stephen Cooper in July 1967, and his later study of the Nest Record Cards
of the B.T.O. uncovered a third instance of such a nest on Marley Common
in Sussex in June 1966. The normal nest is built of dead leaves and bracken,
grass and sometimes pine needles. In fact, George Yeates (1947) found a
nest in Norfolk – the first that he had ever seen in a coniferous habitat –
which was 'built of fallen fir needles instead of the normal grass bents, and
was consequently even more remarkably concealed than usual.' The
material is collected by the female from the area around the nest site. A
bird in a Surrey wood visited one source of leaves 'exactly 30 times in 20
minutes', spent some five or six seconds at the nest and over 30 seconds
collecting each batch of material (May and Manning 1951). To pull out
grass or bracken the female will lean right back, even beating her wings to
increase the leverage. The male rarely shows the least interest in the actual
work of construction. It takes 3–5 days to finish the building with bouts of
intense activity over twenty minute periods and then an abrupt cessation
of work. One very clear distinction between the nest of the Wood Warbler

and those of Willow Warbler and Chiffchaff is that the Wood Warbler's home is lined with grass or a little hair but not feathers. Why this difference should be is not clear, although it is just possible that, with the protection afforded by a domed nest, the later breeding Wood Warblers feel that in high summer this extra insulation is not necessary.

The normal clutch is 6–7 eggs, rarely of four or five or even eight. In Devon the average clutch size is 6 eggs in late May and 5.6 in June (Lack 1950). In Wales, Derby and Yorkshire the May clutch size is 5.8 and in June 3.6–3.7. These figures can be compared with those from Holland of 6.0, 5.3 from Finland in May, and 5.3 in Holland in June. The eggs are white, smooth and glossy, heavily speckled and spotted with marks of dark-reddish, purplish-brown or -grey. These markings are often evenly spread but they may be larger and more confluent at the broader end of the egg. Incubation is carried out by the female alone and usually takes some 12–13 days. She normally leaves the nest to feed herself but Oakes (1947) described how in 1944 a male approached a nest with young and proffered a small green caterpillar to the female who swallowed it. Courtship feeding was also seen twice in 1946. The young birds spend 11–12 days in the nest and are fed by both parents. While filming a nest with young on 11 June 1947, C. W. Holt observed the young to deposit the faecal sac directly into the bill of the adult who carefully carried it and placed it in the fork of a branch above (*Leic. and Rutland County Rept. of Birds* 1947). The adults will approach a human intruder and utter a single alarm note – a version of the 'pew' heard in the second song phase. A rather odd case of apparent altruism was noted by T. Wesolowski (1981) who recorded two instances of broods being adopted by birds that were probably not the parents. There is normally only one brood but I. J. Ferguson-Lees (1948) found a nest near Handcross in Sussex on 6 June 1947 containing six young about four days old. On 11 June the young were being fed chiefly by the male, and the female started a new nest. On 13 June the young fledged from the first nest while the second nest was completed on 15 June with the first egg being laid in it on 17 June; a clutch of five eggs was seen in it on 20 June 'only seven days after the young from the first brood had flown.' I have not witnessed 'injury-feigning' or distraction display myself, but *The Handbook* (1946) noted that it had been recorded by at least two observers. Ground-nesting birds naturally suffer to some extent from predators. Commander A. W. P. Robertson (1954), who had three nests under observation in a wood in East Anglia, reported that: 'Mice had one, egg-collectors another and a hedgehog was caught in the act at the third.' After the young Wood Warblers have left the nest the parents continue to feed them for about a month. After the breeding season is over, the body feathers are moulted and perhaps the tertials, lesser coverts and even a tail feather or two. A full account of the Wood Warbler in Europe has been given by J. G. Fouarge (1968).

Like other *Phylloscopus* warblers, Wood Warblers feed on Chironomid midges early in the season and caterpillars of various small moths and butterflies later. They forage amongst foliage and in flight for many kinds of insect from eggs and larvae on the leaves and bark to the imagos of flies, Lepidoptera, beetles, aphids and mayflies. Many of these are taken with easy and deliberate actions aided by the longer, more pointed wings than those of either Willow Warbler of Chiffchaff. It will hover efficiently with whirring wings to take an insect from a leaf. It seems that berries may be taken in the autumn, but not regularly, and fruit seems to be shunned.

The departure of the summer residents from Britain begins towards the end of July and lasts to the end of August or a little later. It is generally a little-noticed movement, although I have seen occasional birds on the south coast of England – a few in tamarisks on the seafront at Littlehampton on 2 September 1938, and half a dozen in willows at Studland on 27 August 1984. The autumn migration of the Wood Warbler was described by Professor E. Stresemann (1955) with the western population moving southeast through Europe, and the eastern populations travelling southwest; so the migration is concentrated over the middle part of the Mediterranean and then becomes southerly. This canalizing of the movement between the eastern end of the Pyrenees and the eastern part of southern Greece would, as noted by R. E. Moreau (1961) 'give an autumn front of only one third the width of the breeding range and only half the width of the spring front.' Wood Warblers have been recorded on passage through the countries of the eastern Mediterranean, the Balkans, Cyprus, and in North Africa, Tripoli and the Libyan Desert; yet they seem to miss out Malta, Crete and the Nile Delta. They are common, however, in the eastern Sahara and this region they must presumably reach by what Moreau called a 'transit overhead out of sight' as they overfly the more northerly regions. With regard to the movement from the east this would entail Wood Warblers from the Soviet Union flying in a westerly direction for as much as 40° of longitude. The apparent difference in migratory behaviour between autumn and spring may be explained by the birds undertaking longer direct flights in autumn – the transit overhead and out of sight. Birds that have been ringed in England, Wales, Germany and Sweden have been recovered in Italy confirming the general autumn movement to the south-south-east or south. This 'standard direction' of movement from Britain to the southeast resembles the pattern of autumn migration of the Lesser Whitethroat. In his investigation of the four leaf warblers, Chiffchaff, Bonelli's, Willow and Wood Warblers, E. Gwinner (1969) found that those species making the longer journeys were those with the greater mean body weights and those that showed the greater migratory restlessness.

Wood Warblers winter on the Equator or to the north of it from northeast Kenya and northern Uganda to northern Zaire and Cameroon, the Ivory Coast and Guinea. Birds are often observed on migration through Chad and Niger in both seasons. In Cameroon birds inhabit the forest clearings and edges but not the woodland interiors (Serle 1965). In southeast Nigeria the Wood Warbler was 'commonly noted at edge of high bush and in old farms' (Marchant 1953). It was also described as a common passage migrant and winter visitor in small numbers to Nigeria by Elgood et al (1966). An early arrival date at Lake Chad was netted on 1 October 1961 and a late departure was of a fat bird at Enugu on 6 May 1954. The complete moult takes place on the African continent from about the middle of December until late February. In central Nigeria all Wood Warblers recorded in spring had completed their moult (Smith 1966).

In spring there is clearly a broad-front migration of many species along the whole of the Moroccan Sahara with some evidence that birds fly right over it in good weather conditions. J. A. Valverde (1958), with whom I have spent many rewarding days in the field in Europe, has shown that the hot winds which blow off the Spanish Sahara in spring can push migrants out to sea and cause the irregular arrival of waves of birds in Europe. As someone whose house and car were covered with Saharan dust, once in London and again in south Lincolnshire, I truly wonder what movements of air from north Africa take place without bird-watchers and laymen being aware! In spring the Wood Warbler is very common in northeast Morocco but only fairly common in the southeast (Smith 1968). Here birds often rest and feed in marshy areas with dense tamarisk thickets, oleanders and scattered trees. A few birds have been seen in Algeria between 10–16 April (Blondel 1962). In northern Libya in spring J. K. Stanford (1954) considered that 'next to the subalpine warbler, the Wood Warbler seemed the most common and widely distributed migrant warbler'; a few birds were singing in olive trees from the first week of April to the first week of May. M. H. Rowntree (1943) thought that the Wood Warbler was the commonest warbler in northern Libya throughout April and up to 7 May, while E. Hartert recorded migrants between 23 March and 24 May. To the northwest in northern Tunisia Dr David Snow (1952) found the Wood Warbler common in the cork oak woods at the end of April.

Because of the need for males to acquire territories and with the consequent internal drive to reach the breeding ground, the spring migration is much speedier than the autumn. For the Wood Warbler the return trip takes only half the time needed for the autumn journey. Stresemann (1955) gave an average speed in spring of 179 km per day compared with 89.5 in the autumn. Based on average figures he suggested that for north German Wood Warblers, the annual cycle could be divided up into this form: 100 days on the breeding ground (1 May–8 August), 62 days on the autumn migration (9 August–9 October), 172 days in the winter quarters (10 (10 October–31 March) and 30 days on the spring migration (1 April–30 April). Stresemann concluded that Wood Warblers fly almost direct from their winter quarters to their breeding areas with the most easterly of the birds travelling over the Gulf of Suez and Syria. Still many more are seen on the south side of the Mediterranean than in the autumn.

In spring migrants may arrive along the whole seaboard of England but probably in larger numbers from Portland to Dungeness. Yet the birds seem to pass largely unnoticed and are either missing or not readily trapped. The Dungeness Bird Observatory Report for 1958 listed the grand total of birds ringed there on 31 December of that year. It makes interesting reading since no fewer than 4039 Willow Warblers and 1336 Chiffchaffs had been ringed up to that time, but only 4 Wood Warblers. For me Dungeness is the Whitethroat station, with 5588 ringed there by 31 December 1958. The Wood Warblers are just not there to be ringed. The first that we usually know of the return of the Wood Warblers is their appearance on their nesting grounds, announced by song, while none or only a bare handful has been reported on the coast. The first males can be heard in song in Sussex from the second week of April, sometimes even earlier; in Somerset from about 27 April, while the average date for Oxford, Berkshire and Buckinghamshire is 24 April. For Leicester and Rutland it is about 26–7 April.

On occasion, birds can be found in coastal areas from mid-April to June but, as we have seen already, they are very irregular and usually only in ones and twos. Gibraltar Point in Lincolnshire had 4 in 1979, 2 in 1982 and 1 in 1983. Some of the birds on the south and east coasts of Britain are probably of continental origin. In 1975 migrants were seen on the east coast of Aberdeenshire with 6 Wood Warblers at Cruden Bay on 9 May. This was part of a 'fall' of birds including Chiffchaffs, Pied Flycatchers, Tree Pipits, Redstarts, Whinchats and Wheatears; 2 were at Cruden from 11–12 May and 1 on 13 May, with another bird a few miles away at Newburgh on 11 May (*NE Scotland Bird Rept* 1975). A single bird was recorded at Cruden Bay on 8 May 1977. These scanty records show how unlikely it is for an observer to come across a springtime Wood Warbler on the east coast. A few birds may turn up on the Isle of May in the Firth of Forth. Further north at Fair Isle the Wood Warbler is scarce and irregular in spring but almost annual and in very small numbers in the autumn. Birds were recorded in only five springs but thirteen autumns between 1948 and 1964. The spring records at Fair Isle were between 26 April and 18 June with most of them falling in May; they were nearly always of single birds (Williamson 1965).

The northward passage of birds in spring was compared by H. N. Southern (1940) with that of the Willow Warbler which he had studied and an account of whose spring passage was given in Chapter 28. The migration of the Wood Warbler extends approximately from 1 April from the Pyrenees, Switzerland and Italy, to latitude 60°N on 15 May. This represents a period of 45 days and an average speed of between 35–70 km per day. The Wood Warblers start off behind the 9°C spring isotherm by about 14 days and manage to overhaul it only as they reach the northern limit of their range at 61°N in Norway and 64°N in Finland.

After a lifetime of bird-watching I still remain strangely excited and attracted by the sight of the Wood Warbler, whether as a scarce migrant in those parts of Africa that I know or as a bird on its breeding ground. Its displays and songs have an aesthetic quality of their own quite apart from their fascinating behavioural importance. There is something special too about a warbler that becomes so engrossed with the complexity of its spring displays that it has no time for anything else, not even sometimes a potential predator. 'So occupied in these pursuits,' wrote Lord Grey of Fallodon 'so apparently confident in the security of its own joy and innocence, that it seems not to mind being watched.'

Rare and Vagrant *Phylloscopus* Warblers

Anyone watching at Beachy Head during the period 14–18 October 1974 could have enjoyed the rare privilege of seeing four different species of displaced leaf warbler: a quartet of Yellow-browed, Pallas's, Dusky and Radde's Warblers. Three other species – Arctic, Greenish and Bonelli's Warblers – are also accepted birds on the British list while a single record of the Green Warbler still awaits ratification. The purpose of this chapter is to provide short accounts of the occurrences and behaviour of these warbler species that have visited Britain. Some of these warblers have arrived here perhaps by overshooting their northern European breeding grounds in spring, while autumn arrivals may have been brought by strong anticyclonic conditions in the central U.S.S.R., or been instances of 'reverse' migration in a westerly direction by some elements of Asiatic breeding populations. Some may be the results of drift, and others of tendencies to extend their breeding range west or north. There is still a great deal that we do not know about the reasons for the arrival of these are and vagrant *Phylloscopus* warblers.

The Arctic Warbler

Fig. 154
Breeding range of the Arctic Warbler.

At the time of writing – December 1984 – there are 128 records of this species, once also known as Eversmann's Warbler, in the British Isles. The species has not been recorded in some years, such as 1963, but each autumn

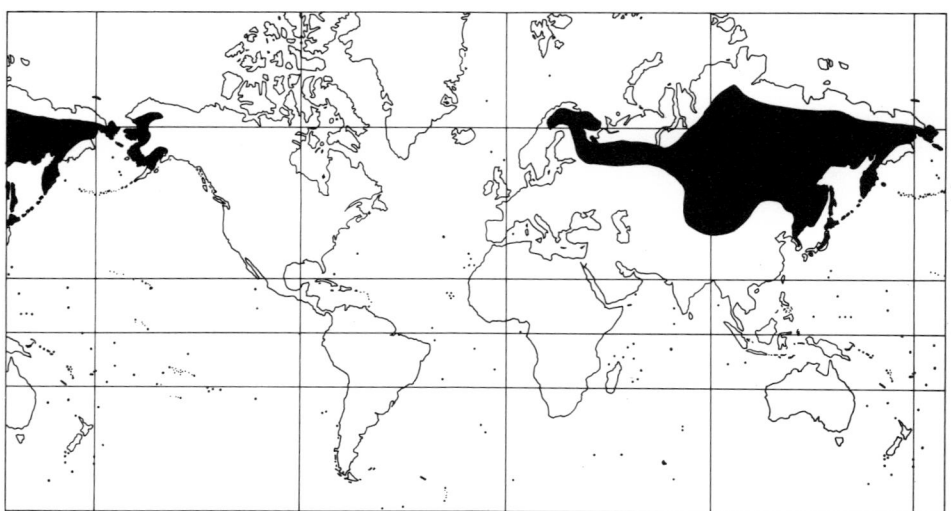

there are generally 1–6 records. Eight were recorded in 1970 and 1976, while 14 were reported in 1981. As we can see from the map, the Arctic Warbler breeds across northern Eurasia from Arctic Fenno-Scandia to the Bering Straits and Alaska. Like another vagrant, the Yellow-browed Warbler, the Arctic effects a more northerly distribution in the British Isles than, say, the Greenish and Pallas's Warblers. Even allowing that weather can induce some random movements, J. Rabol (1969) was of the opinion that 'there is some reversed migration in a westward direction by a part of the population of each species.' Most of the records fall between early August and mid-October and around half in the three week period from 27 August to 16 September (Sharrock 1976). Most of the birds were reported from Shetland and particularly from Fair Isle. The full pattern of records is explained in Sharrock (1974).

The Arctic Warbler is a species somewhat intermediate between the Wood Warbler and the Willow or Bonelli's Warbler. It is largely greenish above – a pure greenish-olive after an autumn moult – and white below; it has pale legs and a rakish superciliary stripe of yellowish-white which is often curved upwards at the hind end. There is a dark stripe through the eye and this warbler has a rather long, spear-shaped pale beak. The outline of the head was described by Williamson (1955) as more like that of a Sedge than a Willow Warbler, while the crown is sometimes ruffled up into a crest. There are also a narrow creamy wing-bar at the tips of the outer

Fig. 155
Variations in head and wing covert patterns of Arctic Warbler (left to right); early September, migrant with 'Sedge Warbler' appearance but no visible wingbars; late October, migrant with 'raked' supercilium and two wingbars still obvious; early June, adult with short supercilium and one broken wingbar; note bold lower eye crescent on all. (D. I. M. Wallace)

greater coverts and a much slighter yellowish bar at the tips of the median coverts, but these can become abraded and disappear. The inner web and tips of the three outside tail feathers have narrow whitish margins. In western populations birds in their first winter are a darker olive-green on the back and yellower below than adults in their autumn coloration, whereas in the eastern populations of the Arctic Warbler there is no such clear difference. It is a restless, active warbler which regularly flicks its wings and tail. A fuller comparison with other Phylloscopid warblers has been given by Robertson (1984).

The call of the Arctic Warbler is 'tzik-tzik-tzik' which is sometimes rendered more emphatically as 'tchik'. Both calls were heard from a bird on Fair Isle, the latter note being evoked by the presence of a cat. Migrants may also use a 'tswee-ip' or 'tswee-ep'. The bird has also been heard to use a scolding chatter or rattle, like that of a Whitethroat or even a Mistle Thrush. The common 'tzik' alarm note also figures regularly in short gaps between the songs which consist of simple distinctive trills of up to fifteen notes. After timing four of these songs I found durations of 3, 3, 3.8 and 2.8 seconds. Birds may sing for periods of an hour or even more, perched high in the canopy of a birch or conifer. According to Bannerman (1954), some Arctic Warblers have songs which end in two abrupt whistles, while there is some evidence that occasional mimicry may occur with the Siberian Tit being a favourite bird to copy. C. F. Lundevall (1952) noted that when the mist descended in Lapland there were longer pauses between the songs.

The breeding terrain consists of subarctic birch woods with a damp ground zone and luxuriant growth of *Vaccinium*, bramble and moss, of the coniferous forests of the taiga up to 1500 m and mixed woods with alder, willow and birch in eastern Asia. Water is often present in the habitat as well. Arctic Warblers feed on many species of mosquito as well as ants, beetles, aphids and many insect larvae. The domed nest with a side entrance is built on the ground often amongst dead vegetation or under rotting tree stumps. The breeding season begins in late June and the species is single-brooded. The incubation is carried out by the female and the young are looked after by both parents. Occasionally nests are reported in scrubby growth up to a metre above the ground. Outside the breeding season birds appear in scrub, mangroves and tall grass. A bird on Fair Isle frequented an enclosed cabbage patch where it hunted for small caterpillars or caught flies from the tops of the plants (Williamson 1951).

In the autumn birds migrate to the Oriental region and the tropical lowlands of southeast Asia. Those from northern Europe and Siberia move east-south-east in quite a different direction from Willow Warblers nesting in the same region. Nesting in the eastern parts of Europe, and northern Scandinavia after a westward move when the Ice Ages were over, the Arctic Warblers migrate eastwards to reach their winter home. The most westerly of the populations have to fly at least 13,000 km to reach wintering grounds in Taiwan, the Philippines, the Java Sea and southeast Asia. Vagrants appear in parts of Europe from time to time – in Holland, Italy and Germany – as well as the British Isles. C. B. Ticehurst (1938) has described how birds from Arctic Norway, northern Russia and northern Siberia travel eastwards 'through E. Mongolia, Dauria and Manchuria, avoiding the deserts of Sinkiang and Mongolia, since there are no records in W. Mongolia, Turkestan, India and Tibet' and reaching the winter quarters by travelling down the eastern side of China.

The Greenish Warbler

Before 1945 there was only one record of this species of the race *viridanus* in the British Isles. In the ensuing thirteen years 11 were reported and between 1958 and 1967 as many as 46. By 1983 the total of records in Britain and Ireland stood at 157. The bird resembles a greyish Chiffchaff with a pale wing-bar. A bird that I watched on 1 October 1964 at Dollis Hill in north-west London – the second record for the London area – was feeding among currant bushes, runner beans and thistles on some allotments. There were also four Chiffchaffs present. The rare visitor was grey, with perhaps the slightest olive suffusion on the back, but especially grey on the head and neck; its overall colour contrasted strongly with the yellow-brown or greenish coloration of the Chiffchaffs. It had a whiter and more striking eye-stripe than those of the Chiffchaffs and a short white wing-bar. It was shy and retiring keeping, unlike the Chiffchaffs which fed conspicuously and chased flying insects in a thoroughly overt manner, quite close to the vegetation. Once however, it emerged to hover and catch a small moth. The bird was restless, occasionally flicked its tail and wings like a Chiffchaff and was once chased by the other warblers. I accidentally flushed it once from cover; the bird called a single time and flew with a direct and rapid flight to a tree. The call was a disyllabic 'tchouee' which at the time I described as 'incisive and "fruity" and unlike the "hou-eet" or "wit" calls of the chiffchaff.' As this bird was not particularly abraded I decided that it must be a young bird. However, some young winter birds are rather brighter than adults and may be a purer greenish-olive than other young birds (Axell 1958).

The call that I heard, 'tchouee', has also been described as 'chew-ee' (Kitson 1979), a loud 'chee-wee' (Williamson 1976), a penetrating 'see-wee' by D. I. M. Wallace, a yellow wagtail-like 'tsweep' (Browne 1953) while *The Handbook* (1946) described the call as 'a double "*tsie*".' Since the song has been heard a number of times in Britain, it is worth listening out for. Often the song opens with a few notes rather like the call, which to me sound rather like 'tit-wheer' or 'tit-tit-wheeur'; then follows a loud, hurried and highly variable medley of notes. It can be transcribed as 'tsi-see-tew, see-tew, see-tee-tee-ti, see'. The song is delivered in short bursts; a typical run of songs might be 3, 4.8, 2, 5.2, 3.2 and 3 seconds and there may be intervals between songs of 5–8 seconds. Vagrant Greenish Warblers to Britain have been heard in song on Bardsey Island in June of 1954 and 1981, Bempton Cliffs and Dungeness in June 1975, at Beachy Head on 19 May 1981, on Lundy Island from 13–14 July 1978 and the Calf of Man in June 1978. R. Thearle (1954), who heard the bird singing on Bardsey Island on 16 June 1954, described the song, which was of short duration, as 'a loud, hurried high-pitched warble, and almost recalled the wren's . . . in its vehement delivery. I wrote it down as "Weedle-weedle-weed-lee-tuee-tuee-tuee" or "Trittit-trittit-tuee-tuee-tu-tu-tuee".'

On migration and in its winter quarters, the bird appears in scrub and secondary undergrowth. In the winter quarters in southern India, where many birds assemble, Trevor Price (1981) found that: 'All birds of both sexes held individual territories throughout the winter.' For the birds of the *ludlowi* race of the Greenish Warbler the call-note 'pitchew' served the function of the breeding season song used in the defence of the nesting territory. Food consisted of insects which were picked off from foliage during a brief flight or taken by hovering or pursuing in flight those disturbed from a leaf or stem. A wide range of insects was taken by the birds.

The Greenish Warbler is a breeding bird of the taiga, where the spruce forests include scattered larches, birches and poplars, of the ecotones in and along the spruce forest as well as montane pinewoods and subalpine coniferous forests (Voous 1961). In the Himalayas birds may breed as high as 1760 m reaching up into the alpine zones of rhododendrons and other shrubs. In Europe birds may also occur in orchards and parkland. They construct domed nests on the ground in hollows, or amongst the plants of the field layer or ground zone, or even in holes in trunks and walls. Nesting begins in June and the Greenish Warbler is single-brooded. Nestlings are fed primarily by the female and it has been suggested that this is another species of warbler in which the male is giving up parental duties (Lilleleht 1963).

Like the Arctic Warbler, the Greenish Warbler has shown a strong tendency to expand its range. A bird of the east and central Palaearctic, breeding from northeast Germany and Finland across to the Sea of Okhotsk, it has been moving steadily westwards. It was first recorded in what

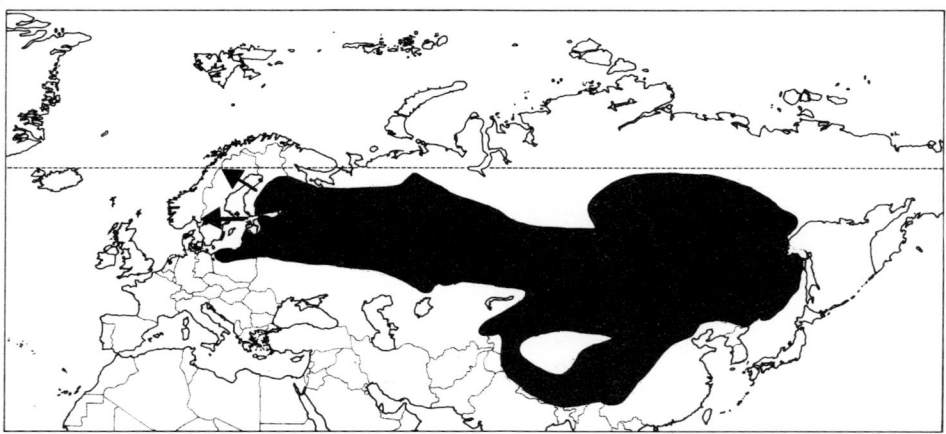

Fig. 156
Breeding range of the Greenish Warbler.

used to be East Prussia on the Baltic Sea in 1905. By 1933 it had reached Danzig (Gdansk), by 1935 Mecklenburg, by 1937 Estonia, Finland about the same time and by 1953 the island of Gotland. This westward movement, together with more competent birdwatchers and an increase overall in the trapping and ringing of birds, was expected to reveal itself in the British Isles as well as in Europe where the advance was associated with a rise in the average spring and summer temperatures (Välikangas 1951). Some of the fresh breeding records in Europe were preceded by instances of males holding territories and singing, but despite examples of singing birds in England the species has not yet nested and would seem unlikely to do so. Most records in Britain and Ireland are in September and October and more than 75% occurred in the 10-week period from 27 August–4 November (Sharrock 1971). The distribution of the records reveals an autumn scatter along the east and south coasts west to Co. Cork and north to Shetland. There was a double peak from 20 August–16 September and from 24 September–21 October, suggesting that the more westerly birds in the late autumn had an origin more from the south and east (Sharrock 1974). The autumn movements are possibly the result of reversed migration as appears to happen with the Arctic Warbler, while the spring occurrences could arise through overshooting by individuals of the north European breeding population. A bird was present at Perry Oaks Sewage Farm in Middlesex from the end of 1960 to 26 February 1961, the first record of over-wintering in western Europe, and a remarkable feat by a bird that normally winters in India (*Lond. Bird Rept* 26:52). A bird has also been seen in winter in Switzerland (Sharrock 1971).

The Green Warbler

At the time of writing, a first-ever record of this species for Britain and Ireland is under discussion. It is of a bird reported from the Isles of Scilly on 26 September 1983 when Greenish and Arctic Warblers were present as well; it remained until 3 or 4 October 1983. This *Phylloscopus* is like a small but greener, brighter Wood Warbler with yellow underparts, a wide eye-stripe and a single pale yellow wing-bar. It has a sprightly call-note 'chi-wee' said to be very similar to that of the Greenish Warbler. The flight call has been described as 'chirr-ir-ip', 'tissick' and 'psew' with a suggestion of the Yellow Wagtail in its voice (Kitson 1979). The song is a repeated

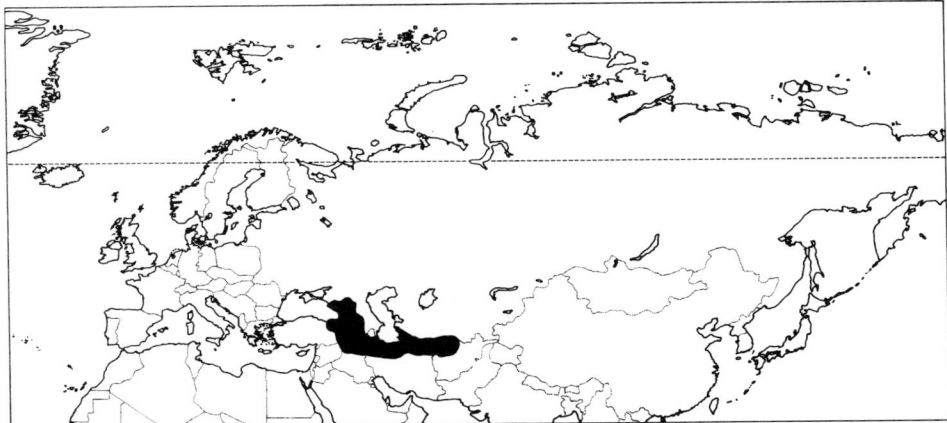

'ts-tri-tsi' with the rhythm of the Willow Warbler. The Green Warbler breeds in the Caucasus from the Black to Caspian Seas, northern Iran and Afghanistan, and migrates for the winter through India to the south of the subcontinent and Sri Lanka.

Fig. 157
Breeding range of the Green Warbler.

The Yellow-browed Warbler

The Yellow-browed Warbler is another vagrant from Asia. It is the most regular of all the Siberian Phylloscopid wanderers in western Europe and for that reason has, for many years, been omitted from the list of rare species' descriptions, which have to be submitted to the Rarities Committee of the journal *British Birds*. This warbler is smaller and greener on the upperparts than the Willow Warbler, possesses a broad yellow supercilium and a conspicuous double yellow wing-bar. There is sometimes a faint pale stripe down the crown but the foregoing details should help in the identification of the Yellow-browed Warbler. It behaves like a *Phylloscopus* warbler; this characteristic together with its eye-stripe distinguish it from the Goldcrest, while it lacks the yellow crown-stripe and rump of Pallas's Warbler. It flicks both its tail and wings and often feeds in the manner of a flycatcher. Its call is a loud 'weest', 'weesp' or 'sweet': a note much sharper and shriller than that of the Willow Warbler. The song is formed by the repetition of a single weak note 'filifilifilifili'. In India the common wintering race is *Ph. inornatus humei*, or Hume's Yellow-browed Warbler from the southeast of the range, and this bird regularly employs a double 'tiss-yip' (Alexander 1951). Birds on Fair Isle have been reported as using this double call.

A bird watched by E. R. Meek (1978) at Low Hauxley in Northumberland in November 1970 showed the external characteristics of *Ph. i. humei*. A similar individual was seen near Beachy Head in East Sussex (Scott 1979) which displayed an indistinct, median-covert wing-bar and greyish-olive upperparts; it lacked yellow on the supercilium, wing-bars and underparts and was said by another observer to have made a loud, ringing call. In the instances of Yellow-browed Warblers that over-wintered in southern England it seemed that individuals on Thorney Island from 10 January to 9 April 1975, and at Titchfield Haven in Hampshire in December 1978, were basically similar to the race *humei* (Quinn and Clement 1979). The two authors thought that the published characters for the supercilium, upper wing-bar and edges to the tertials for the race *humei*, 'are also features of worn, late autumn and winter *inornatus*.' They pointed out that Ticehurst (1938) underlined the importance of the presence or lack of green in the upperparts of the two races, indicating that *inornatus* 'wears to lead grey with green tinge, *humei* to brown with no green tinge.' Writing of his experiences in Mongolia, A. R. Kitson (1980) reported that the bill of *humei* is: 'Blackish or very dark grey-brown' as opposed to brown for *inornatus*. Allowing for any racial differences, the dumpy shape, rather like that of a Goldcrest, the long, dark-edged supercilium, oblong lower wing-bar and smaller upper wing-bar should all help with specific identification. A bird that I watched, which was extremely tame and allowed a very close approach indeed, revealed these features as well as a short tail, active movements and a habit of pursuing flies in the air like a flycatcher.

The Yellow-browed Warbler has three races but *inornatus* breeds across northern Siberia from the Urals to the Sayan Mountains, where it is replaced by *humei*, east to Outer Mongolia and Korea, north to the mouths of the Rivers Lena, Kolyma and Anadyr and south to Afghanistan and the northwest Himalayas. It is one of the commonest birds in Siberia. Migrants pass through China on their autumn journey to India, Malaysia, Thailand,

Fig. 158
*Breeding range of the
Yellow-browed Warbler.*

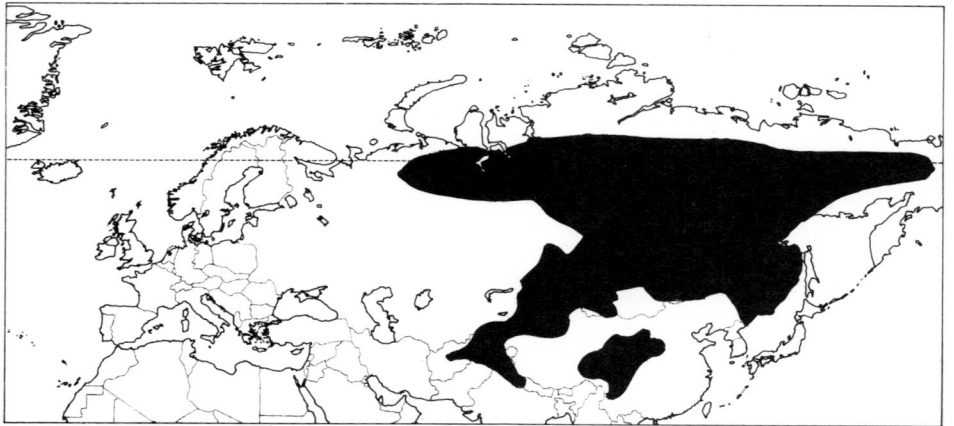

southeast Asia and China. For breeding, *inornatus* favours open groves, light woodlands especially of birch, willow, conifers and mixed species rather than dense forest. In winter it can be found in gardens, where it often joins up with other warblers and tits. It feeds on small insects and may leap up after flying quarry with an audible snap of the bill. Birds may sometimes descend to the ground to feed; one at Porthgwarra in Cornwall remained there for five minutes while catching insects, and another on St. Agnes in the Isles of Scilly fed in the ground zone (Phillips *et al* 1975). The nest is a domed structure with a side entrance and is built on the ground amongst moss, grass or rhododendrons; it is constructed from dead grass or moss and may be lined with hair, perhaps from deer. The breeding season starts in late June. The race *humei* is a breeding bird of mountain slopes with a light cover of trees, particularly silver firs above 2500 m, larch, pine, birch and juniper with the last two species occurring as scrub above the level of pine growth. *Humei* winters in the Himalayas and India.

Together with Richard's Pipit, the Yellow-browed Warbler is perhaps the most regular of the Siberian vagrants to reach the British Isles. It has also occurred in many parts of central and western Europe: Czechoslovakia, Austria, Germany, Italy, Denmark, Norway, Holland and France; I saw a bird near Vevey in Switzerland in October 1959. In September 1984 more than 60 were reported with 12 on Fair Isle, 15 in Orkney, 2 on South Uist, 9 at Spurn and over 10 in Norfolk (Dawson and Allsopp 1984). The species is observed annually at most of the east coast observatories but is much less common on the south coast, in the Irish Sea region and inland. The best sites are Fair Isle, the Isle of May, northeast England, north Norfolk, the Isles of Scilly and Cape Clear Island in Co. Cork. At least 6, possibly 7 appeared on the Lincolnshire coast in 1981 (*Lincs. Bird Rept* 1981).

A total of 275 was recorded in the decade from 1958 to 1967 (Sharrock 1972) but this number included an invasion of around 128 in 1967. The records nearly all fell in the period from mid-September to early December, with 87% in the 6-week period from 10 September to 21 October. Birds were present in 27 counties, all but one being on the coast. The Yellow-browed Warbler is another of the species whose appearance in western Europe has been attributed to reverse migration in a westward direction by part of the population (Rabol 1969). There is also a clear tendency for birds to appear later in southwest Britain and Ireland than in the eastern and northern regions of Britain. Dr J. T. R. Sharrock (1972) noted that '56% of the Scottish records were before the beginning of October, compared with 38% of those in the east of England from Northumberland south to Suffolk and only 13% of those in the south-west.' The peak in the southwest was a fortnight later than in Scotland, a pattern very similar to that for another vagrant, the Greenish Warbler. The large 1967 influx was also reflected in Belgium and Spain – both first records for those countries – and in Holland. The patterns of movement in the British Isles were considered by Sharrock to be due to one or all of three possibilities: birds filtering south after arrival or taking up a standard south direction, later displacement by southeasterly winds or, thirdly, a broad-front reverse migration with the southern portion of the Yellow-browed Warbler population starting later, having more miles to travel and experiencing a southwards shift of the population's centre of gravity. Birds found in the southwest of Britain and Ireland could have arrived there after the main movements, been displaced from northern France by winds from the south or southeast or even been undertaking a northerly course on a reorientated reverse migration.

Records of Yellow-browed Warblers from counties away from the coast are rare. The first occurrence in the London area was that of a bird singing at Sutton on 10 October 1930, while the second was a bird in a garden at Reigate on 28 September 1960, which coincided with a fall at four east coast and two Irish observatories (*Lond. Bird Rept.* 1960). A third was reported from Sevenoaks Gravel Pit in Kent on 8 October 1978. At sea, Dr I. C. T. Nisbet reported a bird on R.M.S. Queen Elizabeth between Cherbourg and Southampton on 12 October, and Dr David Bannerman (1954) tells the story of the Yellow-browed Warbler that settled on the head of a rating during prayers on deck aboard H.M.S. Africa on 10 May 1911, while off Start Point in Devon. The few spring records have been regarded by the British Ornithologists' Union as not fully acceptable because of a lack of sufficient supporting information.

Pallas's Warbler

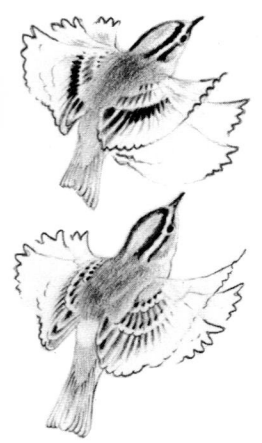

Fig. 159
Firecrest (top) and Pallas's Warbler in hovering flight – their sizes and plumage patterns closely converge but the colours of head and rump allow easy separation.

The diminutive Pallas's Warbler has a yellow crown-stripe and a regular habit of hovering when feeding – features that could cause confusion with the Goldcrest – but the former species has a yellow rump-patch. It could possibly be confused with the Yellow-browed but has a most prominent yellow crown-stripe and supercilium, yellow rump and a greener mantle. Being on the move continuously, it appears a more vivacious as well as a smaller bird than the Yellow-browed Warbler. Pallas's Warbler is more prone to hover than the Goldcrest, and a bird at Monk's House in Northumberland hovered while picking off aphids but remained persistently beneath the canopy of the willow tree in which it was feeding (Ennion 1952). It will also flick its wings like a Hedgesparrow. All races of the species share the fluttering habit, when the yellow rump may be very conspicuous. Birds will hawk after flying insects in the manner of a flycatcher. The little Pallas's Warbler has often been likened to 'a yellow-rumped firecrest' (Clarke *et al* 1961). In thick foliage it may be rather difficult to locate; for example, in conifers or sea buckthorn, and it may be the call which first betrays its presence.

This call has been described as a small soft Phylloscopine 'weesp' (*The Handbook* 1946), a canary-like 'tweet' (Bell 1963), a shrill, high-pitched 'swee' (Wolstenholme *et al* 1961), a 'seep' more prolonged and less squeaky than the call of the Goldcrest (Williamson 1976), and 'shu-ee' (Scott 1964). According to Scott, a bird at St Catherine's on the Isle of Wight in 1963 also employed a single, short Redpoll-like 'choot' and a double 'choo-ee', the last similar to a double note mentioned in *The Handbook*. To me the song is reminiscent of that of a Redstart and is both powerful and pleasant. I have transcribed one singer's performance as 'tirrit-tirrt-tirritt-terchee-terchee-terchee-choo-choo-chee-chee-chee-choo-choo'. The song may last about 2–4 seconds and it can be heard from tree-tops on passage and in the winter quarters. The form *chloronotus* of the high eastern Himalayas and Yunnan has a 'sip-sip' call and a Willow Warbler-like song, while *simlaensis* of Nepal, northwest Pakistan and

Afghanistan has a song consisting of 'a short twittering "wai-wai-wai" repeated quickly with a faint sibilant shivering note' (Williamson 1976).

The typical race is a bird of pine or birch forests where it builds a domed nest of grasses and moss on branches 3–5 m from the ground and often close to the boles of moss-covered trees. In Mongolia, Pallas's Warbler breeds in pine-cedar woods and elsewhere in mixed forests. The nest is often lined with feathers, cow or horse hair. The race which visits Britain, *Ph. proregulus proregulus*, breeds from the Russian Altai eastwards to Sakhalin and travels on passage through Mongolia, Manchuria, Korea and western and central China to spend the winter in southeast Asia. Here it favours tree canopies in light woodland growth, mixed forests and scrub where, like the Yellow-browed Warbler, it mixes readily with other bird species such as tits and Goldcrests. Visitors to Britain have been found in scrub, willows, coastal sea buckthorn thickets and even among the flower-beds around a bowling green on Hartlepool seafront (Bell 1963).

Pallas's Warblers have appeared as vagrants in Russia, Poland, Finland and elsewhere in eastern Europe, in Sweden, Germany, Holland, France, Belgium and, of course, the British Isles. The first three records were of

Fig. 160
Breeding range of the Pallas's Warbler.

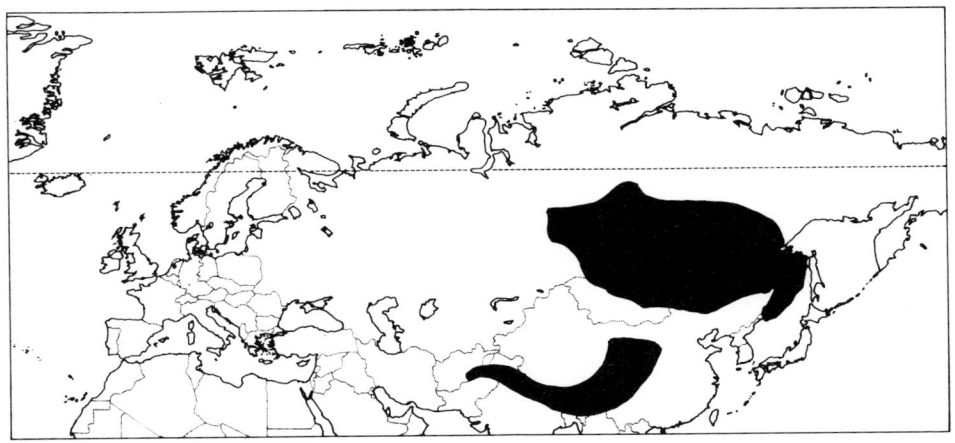

one in Norfolk on 31 October 1896, one at Monk's House in Northumberland on 13 October 1951 and another near Holme in Norfolk (Cambridge Bird Club) on 17 November 1957. Even up to 1963 this vagrant had only occurred on seven occasions, all in October and November and along the east coast of England. During late October and early November 1963 no fewer than six were reported on the south and east coasts of England (Scott 1964); these arrived with Yellow-browed Warblers, Cranes and Little Bunting in anticyclonic conditions. There were also influxes of 18 birds in 1968 and 13 in 1974. Between 1958 and 1972, 44 birds were reported with the records occurring in October and November, 77% of these falling into the period of three weeks from 15 October to 4 November, much later than Yellow-browed Warblers (Sharrock 1976). Nearly three-quarters of these records were from the seven counties from Yorkshire to Sussex; a much more southerly distribution than Yellow-browed and with a breeding range that stretches further north in Siberia. In 1975 there were some 29 birds reported, and in 1981 a total of 33 but the *annus mirabilis* for the Pallas's Warblers was 1982 when 124 were recorded in Great Britain. The arrival of this very large number coincided with haze and a light easterly breeze in the northern part of the North Sea. This brought about a shift in the centre of gravity of the influx to the north, with Fair Isle and Shetland receiving 29 birds compared with their previous all-time best combined total of eight. By 1983 the grand total of Pallas's Warblers had risen to 313. Why so many of these tiny and delightful birds should have moved westwards in this manner remains a mystery unless there had perhaps been a population explosion in Siberia. They are now among the most regularly reported of Siberian passerine species.

Radde's Warbler

At the time of writing in late 1984 there have so far been 44 records of this heavy but secretive *Phylloscopus* – a great contrast to the preceding very dynamic warbler! The first record was of a bird at North Cotes in Lincolnshire in 1898. Between 1958 and 1972 there were 10 records of this warbler, followed by a peak of 5 in 1976 and a total of 14 in 1982. As we have seen earlier, Radde's Warbler is a retiring bird as well as a ground feeder which moves around in a somewhat deliberate and cumbersome manner. On its feet the bird has an 'upright appearance and a curious aggressive darting action' (Britton and Scott 1963). A bird in Norfolk hopped regularly on the sand where it was seen to flick its wings and tail (Richardson *et al* 1962). Radde's Warbler has a distinctive shape and size, being larger and thicker-billed than the Dusky Warbler with which it might be confused; it has a greyish-brown plumage rather than brownish, a longish tail, large eyes, a conspicuous creamy supercilium bordered with black above and below, long and robust yellowish legs and buffish to creamy-white underparts. There is a pale brown mottling on the cheeks and ear coverts and in the autumn the upperparts are olive-green and the underparts suffused or streaked with lemon-yellow on brownish-buff. The call of Radde's Warbler has been described as a musical whistling, nervous 'twit-twit' (Williamson 1976), a double chat-like 'chik' (Richardson *et al* 1962), a soft 'tic' and from *The Handbook* (1946) 'gibout-gibout'. The song is a loud warbling trill, short and not particularly musical. It is variable in quality but quite resonant and can be transcribed as 'a loud whistling "tyee . . . tyee . . . tyee . . . tyee-ee-ee" and finishing with a trill' (Ptushenko, in Boswall 1970).

Radde's Warbler has a narrow breeding range in southern Siberia from the Altai Mountains east to Amurland and Sakhalin and to northeast China and north Korea. It breeds in mixed forests on the lower hill slopes with pines, Mongolian oaks and birches with a dense, impassable shrub layer of stunted oaks, rhododendrons and other bushes and short grass. Birds may also breed in oak and larch forests; here they share the habitat with Siberian Rubythroats, Gray's Grasshopper and Thick-billed Warblers. The nest is spherical with side entrances and is built of dead stems and grass leaves; it is sometimes but not always lined with feathers. Nests can be found in shrubs from 15–70 cm above the ground and breeding starts in the middle of June. The young in the nest are fed with spiders, aphids, flies, mosquitoes, gadflies, small caterpillars and moths, and later, larger insects. Song ceases about 8 August on the breeding grounds; the autumn migration starts about 20 August and continues until the early part of October. A full account of the breeding biology of Radde's Warbler together with many illuminating photographs was provided by Irene Neufeldt (1960).

Birds pass the winter in southern China, Vietnam, Laos, Burma, Thailand and Kampuchea. The distribution of records in Britain is the most southerly for all the Siberian passerines reaching the British Isles with 80% of the records from 1958–1972 south of a line from the Wash to

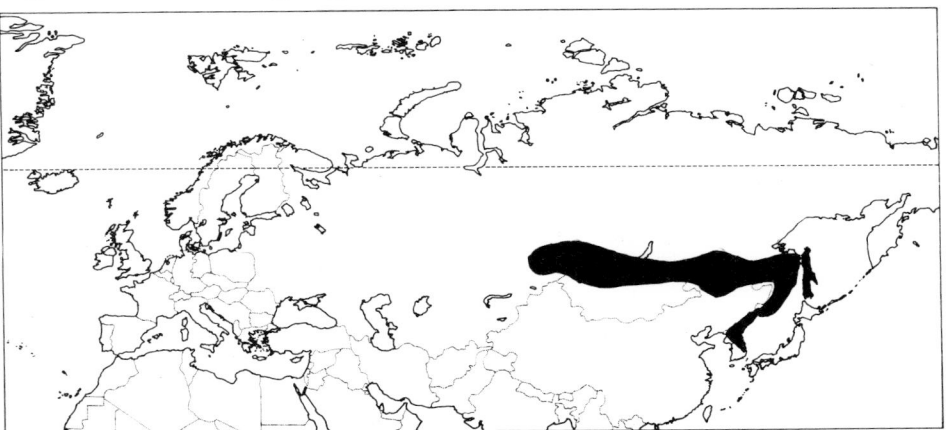

Cardigan Bay. However, an influx in 1982 brought birds to Orkney and Shetland. The records are primarily in October but a bird at Holkham in Norfolk was present in 1982 from 1–6 November. On their return journey in spring from the wintering grounds, birds do not apparently cross central Asia but travel to the north over central and eastern China to Manchuria, where the main pathway then divides into two with some birds moving the short distance to Ussuriland and Sakhalin, and others embarking on a long trek to the Altai Mountains, and along the southern limits of Siberia. On migration, these warblers tend to keep to thick swampy growth of small birch and willow, where the males may sing spasmodically as they forage for food. Although birds like to feed near the ground they may also search canopies of birch trees, 2–4 m above the ground (Lassey and Wallace 1979).

Fig. 161
Breeding range of the Radde's Warbler.

The Dusky Warbler

This Siberian vagrant is unique among the Phylloscopid warblers on the British list in that it lacks all trace of green or yellow in its plumage. It has sometimes been compared to a Reed Warbler but it is not reddish in its coloration; it also recalls a Chiffchaff in its outline and deportment. It is much smaller and thinner-billed than Radde's Warbler, and with its general brownish appearance is the darkest of the British leaf warblers. It sports a buff supercilium but this is much less conspicuous than that of Radde's. The Dusky Warbler tends to be a bird of skulking habits but, like Radde's Warbler, it may also feed in the tree canopy. A bird in Kent on 11 November 1978 fed 6–8 m above ground in a copse of willow, sallow and birch trees; in strong light it appeared green on its upperparts but this effect was attributed to light being reflected from the foliage (van der Dol *et al* 1979). This individual was also seen to cock its tail like a Cetti's Warbler (Cantelo 1979). Yet the species still remains basically a 'cover-seeking, ground-feeding *Phylloscopus.*' A bird on Fair Isle fed openly on short turf, flicking its tail and wings quite noticeably (Davis 1962); another

Fig. 162
Wing and tail movement of Dusky Warbler – a near constant flicking open, almost fanning of flight and tail feathers (perhaps most developed in this species but also common to its congeners). (D. I. M. Wallace)

in the Isles of Scilly spent most of the time 'feeding amongst the leaf litter' (Austin and Milne 1966) and a third in Kent settled on or fed very close to the ground (Scott 1968).

The usual call of the Dusky Warbler is a rather *Sylvia*-like, even explosive 'tchak', 'tak-tak', a single 'tek' or 'tsek', while a bird in an orchard on St. Agnes in the Isles of Scilly had a 'frequently repeated low *chak*' (Austin and Milne 1966). The song has been described as strong and sweet – a repeated 'tia-tia-tia' – with a suggestion of the utterances of the Greenish Warbler. The breeding grounds of this bird range from the River Ob east to Anadyr, north to about 60°N on the Yenisei River, south to the Altai

Fig. 163
Breeding range of the Dusky Warbler.

and the Himalayas, and east to Manchuria and China. The Dusky Warbler nests in sedge and willow swamps near rivers, in water-logged larch forests and in drier subalpine zones of birch, willow and pine. A domed nest is built on the ground, or up to 30 cm above it, is constructed of moss and grass and well-lined with feathers. In the winter quarters, which stretch from north-east India and southern China to Thailand, the bird may be either sluggish in the heat of the day or actively pursuing insects among the canopies of the trees 'from lowly scrub to tree-tops, twisting like tit or tree-creeper from one point to another or occasionally fluttering into air, also often feeding on ground' (*The Handbook* 1946).

The migration of the Dusky Warbler seems to be fairly protracted, with some birds still present on their nesting grounds in September. The first record in the British Isles was that of a bird in Orkney on 1 October 1913. There were 13 records from 1958 to 1972, and of these 12 fell in the period of 28 days from 14 October to 10 November. In 1968, 5 birds were reported at the same time as a large number of Pallas's Warblers. Another 5 appeared in 1976 and 7 in 1982, so that by 1983 the total number of Dusky Warblers recorded in Britain and Ireland had risen to 39. A bird at Sandwich Bay in Kent was trapped on 22 November 1983. Another at Bamburgh on 18 August 1980 may have spent the summer in Britain or western Europe. The distribution of records is rather like that of Pallas's Warbler with most reports coming from the coast of England from Yorkshire to Kent and on the Isles of Scilly. There is an intriguing record of a bird trapped and ringed on the Calf of Man on 14 May 1970 which was found dying near Limerick about 5 December. This individual survived in western Europe for almost seven months and could have drifted west the previous autumn and overwintered before reaching the Isle of Man; its last journey was to provide the first record for Ireland (Smith 1971).

Bonelli's Warbler

I first came to know Bonelli's Warblers in a dark poplar and alder wood on the banks of the River Rhône. Here, many years ago, I was attracted by their trilling songs. From the canopies of the trees came that brief shiver of sound that so intrigued George Yeates (1946), who, on hearing them for the first time in the Camargue, noted that they began like Wood Warblers 'as though working up for that lovely crescendo that on a hot June day is like a freshening waterfall to tired ears. But with these wood wrens the water only bubbled up; it never fell.' In that dense Provençal wood and in bushier regions too I tape recorded numbers of these songs for analysis and one of these is reproduced as a sonagram in this chapter (*see* Fig. 166). I have also watched Bonelli's Warblers in the drier regions of pine and stunted oak on Spanish hillsides, amongst cool beech woods in France, in the pines that spread around Rome and among the open spruce woods of the Swiss Alps. This warbler can be found equally in broad-leaved and coniferous woodland provided the ground cover is sparse and the trees are growing at some altitude. Birds have been reported from woods of birch, larch, mixed open forest of 'sweet chestnut, alder, maple, mountain ash and so on, and even in hawthorn copses' (Ferguson-Lees 1961). I found many birds holding territories in spruce woods in the Grisons, especially on sunny slopes, at 1850 m and their altitudinal range may stretch from around 700–2000 metres above sea level. Birds were not uncommon in southwest France, and Stanley Cramp (1956) reported them in June in the Landes region as the second-commonest birds. In Switzerland they also seem to favour north-facing slopes (Amann 1955). In some habitats, Bonelli's and Wood Warblers can be found living alongside each other.

Bonelli's Warbler breeds primarily in southern Europe and, apart from

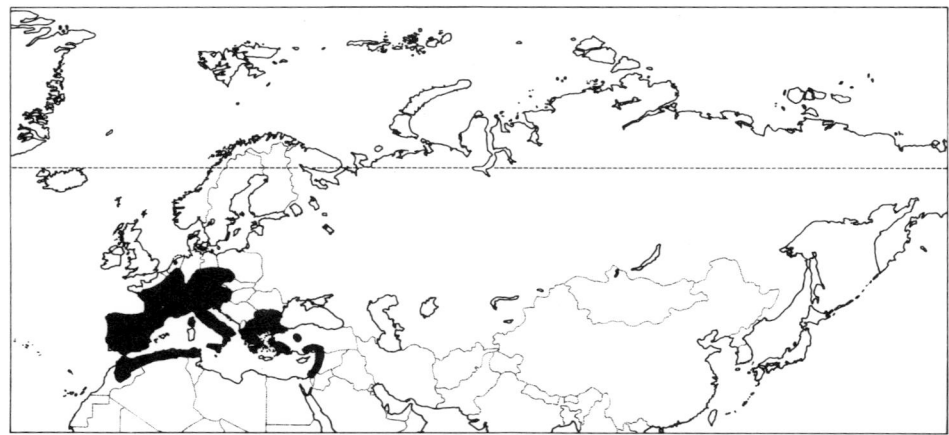

Fig. 164
*Habitat of Bonelli's
Warbler – spruce woods
on mountain slopes in the
Grisons, Switzerland.
(Eric Simms, July 1972)*

Fig. 165
*Breeding range of the
Bonelli's Warbler.*

the three common species of *Phylloscopi* that also nest in the British Isles, is the most widespread and numerous of the European leaf warblers. In Europe it can be found from Iberia east to Syria, north to Germany and in north Africa in Algeria, Morocco and Tunisia. Birds in the Balkans and Near East are greyer in colour and have longer wings, being separated as the race *Ph. bonelli orientalis*. The distribution limits lie between the July isotherms of 18°C and 31°C, or 30°N and 51°N. There are gaps in the European distribution but much of the population is contained in an oblong of country some 4000 km wide and 2250 km deep. In the 1950s there was a tendency for the species to move northwards. Apart from some outposts in Czechoslovakia and elsewhere, Bonelli's Warbler enjoys a rather similar range to that of the Melodious Warbler.

The first record of Bonelli's Warbler in Britain and Ireland was that of a female on Skokholm on 31 August 1948 (Conder and Keighley 1949) – a bird whose second primary fell in length between the sixth and seventh which is an almost 80% characteristic of the race *bonelli* as against 2% for the race *orientalis*. A second bird was trapped on Lundy on 1 September 1954 (Whitaker 1955) and a third was trapped at Portland Bill in Dorset on 29 August 1955 (Tucker 1955). There were 32 records between 1958 and 1972 and by 1983 the grand total had soared to 79. Autumn records have been quite widespread from Fair Isle to the Isles of Scilly with many reports from Cape Clear Island in Co. Cork and from Gwynedd. Birds tend to show up between August and early November with a distinct peak from 27 August to 2 September (Sharrock 1976). A bird in Yorkshire was thought to belong to the race *orientalis* and others in Northumberland, Cork and Scilly may have done so as well. There are differences in voice between the two races, as we shall see later. Most of the spring occurrences, which are rather few in comparison with those in autumn, have been in southeast England, suggesting an overshooting of the usual breeding range. Singing males were reported from Walberswick in Suffolk from 29–30 April 1961 (Pearson et al 1962), and from Delamere Forest in Cheshire from 19 May to 9 June 1963 (Williamson 1976).

Bonelli's Warbler has a light, elongated build, rounded and seemingly big head-shape, short bill and square tail, and lacks any wing-bars. Without a clear or prominent supercilium (it is pale and lacks any bordering with a darker colour above) and a large eye, the facial expression has been described as 'bland' (Grant 1977). There is a general paleness to the bird with light, grey-brown upperparts washed sometimes with a pale olive-green, while a pale yellowish rump, fairly obvious in some individuals, is only seen in others when the bird is hovering. The underparts are a silky white but there is a slight yellowish wash on the undertail coverts. Many birds have their primaries, greater coverts, secondaries and tertials edged with greenish-yellow. The primaries, in fact, extend beyond the upper tail coverts and the secondaries, revealing therefore 'a "pointed-winged" rather than a "rounded-winged" species' (Sharrock 1982). The legs are stoutish and pale and seem 'dull' compared to those of Willow Warblers. Some worn Chiffchaffs and Willow Warblers can look rather like Bonelli's Warblers, but these two leaf warblers through a combination of facial characters possess what P. J. Grant (1977) called 'a special "pinched" expression (best learned through field study rather than by any written description).' To me Bonelli's Warblers, with their eyes of jet and pale supercilia have a slightly sad look about their faces. Even in the hand a Bonelli's Warbler may present a problem, since it could be mistaken for a Booted Warbler. A bird at Portland in Dorset from 22–3 September 1980 was at first thought to be a Bonelli's Warbler, underlining the difficulties facing an observer with the bird in the hand but without the advantage of colour impressions in the field, behaviour characteristics and voice and with those difficult, sometimes subjective observations that form the 'jizz' of a bird. The Portland bird was finally accepted as a Booted Warbler (Rogers 1984).

There is a marked difference in the calls given by vagrants of the western race *bonelli* and the eastern race *orientalis*, and this may be of assistance to observers in the field. The eastern race uses a soft, abrupt 'chip' or, according to Round (1981), a 'chirp', or 'chirrip' or even a loud, sparrowlike 'cheep', while other similar versions include a loud 'tup' or 'chüp' (Kitson and Porter 1983) or 'a loud sharp "chiup"' (Hume 1983). On the other hand, the western race employs a Willow Warbler-like 'hooeet', 'hu-eet', 'clweet', 'hweet' and even 'cloee-ee'. A bird in Gwynedd in August often used 'a single or double harsh and metallic note "chereek" reminiscent of a Wren (*Troglodytes troglodytes*) and, though softer and higher pitched, equally penetrating; and it also had a more typical *Phylloscopus* "hoo-eet" and a ticking note' (Arthur 1960). The song sounds rather simple but sonagrams can reveal a greater complexity than is first apparent and a singer

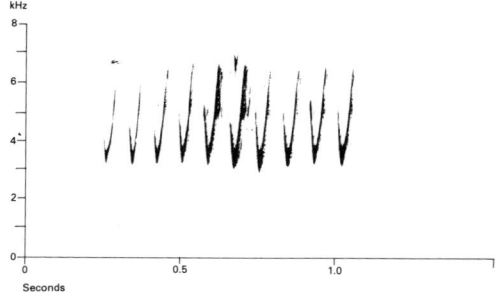

Fig. 166
One song phrase of
Bonelli's Warbler. This
should be compared with
the sonagram for the
Wood Warbler's trill
(p. 322–3). (Recorded
by Eric Simms,
Camargue, May 1954)

may employ more than one version. The song consists of a loose trill on the same even-pitched note. I have found that most songs incorporate 9–11 notes; the sonagram of the bird in the Camargue that I recorded in 1954 shows 10 notes. A bird heard in song in Suffolk on 29 April 1961 was said to have a song consisting of 'a short trill on one note of five to seven syllables, lower pitched and slower than the trill of a wood warbler (*Ph. sibilatrix*) and without the acceleration' (Pearson *et al* 1962). I find that a song of 11 notes lasts 0.6–0.7 seconds. On passage in the Camargue, birds skulking in the tamarisks in May might sing just three strophes in half an hour while they fed (Simms 1957).

Bonelli's Warbler is an active and restless bird, hovering to pick off insects from the leaves of canopies and shrub layers – in Wales reeds, brambles and willows – and flycatching in the air. It breeds in a variety of forest habitats. Ferguson-Lees (1961) found a pair per 0.4 hectares in a region of Spain while Amann (1953) observed a pair per 1.3 hectares in a Swiss habitat. The domed nest is built on the ground in banks, depressions and verges but Zinder (1953) found one in a hole in a wall nearly 2 m above the ground. The side entrance to the nest, which is built by the female, often characteristically has a narrow oval side entrance, rather flatter than those found in the nests of Willow Warblers and Chiffchaffs. It is usually constructed of dried grass and often camouflaged on the exterior with handy local material such as pine needles; it is then very difficult to find like many built by the Wood Warbler. The nest is lined with fine grass or rootlets and not feathers. Nesting begins early in May and the species is normally single-brooded. When incubating, the hen will leave the nest to feed, uttering a typically penetrating Phylloscopid-type 'swee-eet' call which, in the presence of Jays or other predators, becomes much harsher in quality (Ferguson-Lees 1961). P. A. Schneider (1969) has reported a brood of hybrids with the Wood Warbler.

Adults moult the feathers of the body and some of the tertials while on the breeding ground, and finish the wings and tail after they have arrived in Africa. Birds of the *bonelli* race winter in northern Cameroon, northern Nigeria (where they are a 'Common winter visitor' and sing at all hours of the day (Elgood *et al* 1966),) Chad, Niger, Mali and Volta. Two were seen in the Gambia in December 1960 and January 1961 (Cawkell and Moreau 1963). They are often found frequenting the oases and dry country along the desert, and were very common around Timbuktu (Bates 1933). Birds of the *orientalis* race are reported on passage from their eastern European and Middle East breeding grounds in Crete, Cyprus, Egypt and Cyrenaica en route for their winter quarters east of Darfur Province in the Sudan to 9° 30′N. R. E. Moreau (1961) was of the opinion that *bonelli* had a tendency to move west or south, while *orientalis* migrated east of the Tripoli sector. It is not known whether the winter range of the two races actually meets.

In spring *bonelli* has been reported in Algeria, and Smith (1968) described this race as rather uncommon in northeast Morocco but common in the southeast of that country. With a comparatively late breeding season the northwards passage across the western Sahara takes place in late April and May, with many migrants appearing in the large wadis (Smith 1968). Night migrants observed on 22 April 1963 in scrub some ten miles south of Ceuta included Woodchat Shrikes and ten Bonelli's Warblers. Birds have been seen at Gibraltar as early as 1 April but this is unusual. Many birds pass through southern Spain from the last week of April to the middle of May. I have seen considerable passage through the Camargue from 3–20 May, and on 2 May I found a number of migrants – Bonelli's Warblers as well as Blackcaps, Chiffchaffs and Whitethroats – in strips of woodland along the River Pisuerga near Vallodolid in Castile. I did not find Bonelli's Warblers in Spain nesting before the middle of May.

CHAPTER **32** The Kinglets

Rewarded as I have often been by the sight of Goldcrests singing among the Scots pines overlooking the silver mirror of a Highland loch, where the only other sound was that of the gentle plop of trout rising, or of Firecrests in song in an English spruce plantation or broad-leaved wood in France, I have also been fortunate enough to observe their two relations – the Golden-crowned and Ruby-crowned Kinglets – singing in the spruce woods of North America. The kinglets, as this group of birds is known, are minute olive-green arboreal birds that inhabit the circumpolar conifer belts, or more rarely deciduous forests, and breed in both hemispheres from the tree line. They are active and confiding little birds that hunt amongst the foliage for tiny insects and their eggs and larvae. Kinglets are ten-primaried Oscines with slender bills, and nostrils partially covered by a single tiny feather, or, in the case of the Ruby-crowned Kinglet *Regulus calendula*, with bristles. The tarsus is fairly long and 'booted' while the wings too are of good length and rounded at the tips. The first primary is one third or half as long as the second, and among the Palaearctic species the longest primaries are at least the fourth to the sixth. The tail is very slightly emarginated. Bright crown feathers of varying intensity occur in the adult males of all the forms and in the females of all but one. Two, perhaps three, species can be found in the Old World and two in the New, breeding in cool or even cold regions in the northern parts of North America and Eurasia, southwards in high mountain forests.

The best known of the Old World species is the Goldcrest *Regulus regulus* which breeds across Europe east to western Siberia and Asia Minor. Together with the closely-related Firecrest *Regulus ignicapillus* these two birds enjoy the distinction of being Britain's smallest bird species. The British Goldcrest *R.r. anglorum* is a resident and partial migrant in the British Isles, while the Continental bird *R.r. regulus*, adults of which closely resemble the British race but have paler, greyer mantles and hind-necks, is an often abundant migrant and winter visitor to Britain and Ireland. Certain insular populations or races have been described: the longer-billed *azoricus* on the islands of the Azores, the blacker-headed *teneriffae* (considered by some as a race of the Firecrest) on the western Canaries and the grey-necked *interni* of Corsica and Sardinia. The Goldcrest is also so similar to the New World's Golden-crowned Kinglet *R. satrapa* that in the past some observers regarded the two as conspecific. The Goldcrest is more closely confined to conifers and mixed woods than the Firecrest. It can be separated from other warblers and also from the tits by its diminutive size, plumpish form and bright yellow crown with a black border, but the crest is orange-centred in the male, pale yellow in the female and missing from the juvenile bird. The wings carry two white bars and a broad black band. The Goldcrest can be best distinguished from the Firecrest by the lack of black and white eye-stripes found in the latter species. The Goldcrest behaves rather like a warbler, flicking its wings and hovering like a leaf warbler, but it is less acrobatic among the branches than the tits with which it forages in the winter.

The Firecrest is the same size as the Goldcrest but sports a clear white stripe above the eye and a black one through it. The upper parts too are greener and the underparts whiter. This is much more of a broad-leaved woodland bird of the western Palaearctic, breeding in Europe and north-west Russia to the Mediterranean and northwest Africa. *R.i. ignicapillus* nests throughout the whole of the Eurasian range of the Firecrest. The race *minor* in Corsica and Mallorca has a somewhat longer bill and the female a red-orange crest, while the Madeiran form *madeirensis* has the middle of the crown a dull gold and the greater wing coverts black with white tips. The Firecrest behaves rather like the Goldcrest but has a much simpler kind of song. It is mainly European, as we have just seen, but a Firecrest confined to the high montane conifer woods of Taiwan is regarded by some ornithologists as a full species *R. goodfellowi* and by others, including Voous (1977), as conspecific with the Firecrest. The Yellow-rumped or Formosan Kinglet of Taiwan is the most colourful of all the members of the group with a crown that sports the longest crest as well; it is brightly adorned with yellow, orange and red as well as a white line over the eye and a white forehead. Its further decoration includes black and white wing-bars and a yellow rump.

The two species that occur in the New World are the Ruby-crowned Kinglet *R. calendula* and the Golden-crowned Kinglet *R. satrapa.* The first is an olivaceous-grey with the male endowed with an erectile ruby crest, which in my experience is revealed only when the bird becomes excited. A few males may have yellow crowns. Perhaps the best recognition feature is a conspicuous broken white eye-ring which gives the impression of a bird with a large eye. If no crown patch is visible and the bird is quite obviously a kinglet, then it must be a Ruby-crowned Kinglet for the crown patch is quite apparent in both adult sexes of the Golden-crowned Kinglet. The female lacks the coloured crown but still has the broken eye-ring. The Ruby-crowned has a rather stubby tail and two pale wing-bars. This species breeds from northwest Alaska south to Arizona and New Mexico and in eastern Canada as far as Nova Scotia. I found it regularly in open tracts of mixed woodlands in Canada, and it is common in the black spruce bogs around Toronto. A. C. Bent (1964) also found birds amongst fir balsams with red and white spruces, larches and white pines with 'a sprinkling of canoe birches, black birches and mountain ash' in New-foundland. He also went on to say that: 'For its remarkable song the ruby-crowned kinglet is justly famous.' The song is a prolonged and rich warble beginning with 3 or 4 high notes, then several lower ones 5–10 in number, often at least an octave lower but rising slightly in pitch, and the final part with a 3 or 4-note strophe with the last note loudest: the whole phrase is repeated three or four times. It is possible to transcribe it as 'tee-tee-tee-tu-tu-tu-tu-ti-dadee-ti-tadee-ti-tadee'. Another version is 'eee-tee-tee-tee-too-too-tut-tu-ti-ta-tidaweet-tidaweet-tidaweet'. I only heard the eastern race *R.c. calendula* in Canada but it was a truly remarkable performance for so tiny a bird and quite unlike the songs of Goldcrest or Firecrest. The western race sings a somewhat similar song in the first two sections, but the final phrase has the accent on the first note and not the last. The usual call is a rather husky 'ji-dit' or *toute suite* in French. The food of this species is 94% animal but it will also feed on elderberries, dogwood, sumac, cedar berries and wild persimmons.

The eastern Ruby-crowned Kinglet leaves the cold spruce forest belt to winter in the southern United States north to Iowa and Virginia; it is especially common in Florida. The western race *cineraceus* is larger, greyer and less yellow and can be found in the mountain ranges of California usually at heights of more than 1800 m. Two other races that have been recognized are the dark Sitka Kinglet *grinnelli*, which breeds from the moist coasts of Alaska to British Columbia, and the Dusky Kinglet *obscurus* found only on Guadalupe Island. The mainland forms build globular nests high up in conifers, attached to pendent twigs and usually near the end of a branch. They are constructed of moss, tree lichens or plant down and lined with feathers.

The Golden-crowned Kinglet *Regulus satrapa* is a yellowish-olive bird with both sexes having a brightly coloured crown edged with black and white, with the centre of the crown a clear orange-red in the male and yellow in the female. It is a bird somewhere between the Goldcrest and Firecrest. The summer home of the eastern race *R.s. satrapa* is the coniferous forest of the northern United States and the southern provinces of Canada, especially that of spruce, although like O. W. Knight (1908) I found birds in the State of Maine in 'pine, fir, spruce and hemlock woods.' On the whole this species favours rather open kinds of forest. Birds are widespread in the coniferous woods that stretch from Manitoba and the Gulf of St Lawrence south to Minnesota, Michigan, New York and the higher hills of North Carolina. Golden-crowned Kinglets winter from southern Canada to the Gulf of Mexico but as some birds pass the winter months well up towards the northern limits of their breeding range, the spring movement is not easily seen. I found song and nest construction in Nova Scotia well under way in early May. I always found the birds very confiding and tame. The call is a high thin 'see-see-see' very like the high 'zee-zee-zee' of the Goldcrest. The song consists of a series of thin high notes like the normal call but rising up the scale and then descending into a kind of chatter. I transcribed one song as 'see-see-see-see-see-zyzootee-tillee-tillee'. When feeding, birds hover like the European Goldcrest, in front of tufts of pine needles, or perform as expertly as flycatchers taking insects on the wing. These Golden-crowned Kinglets are quite hardy but may suffer like the Goldcrest in very bad winters. The western Golden-crowned Kinglet *R.s. olivaceus* is greener below and brighter above and nests from the Rocky Mountains to the Pacific and from southern Alaska south to northern New Mexico. Another subspecies which is greyer and confined to the mountains of Arizona is *apache*.

Kinglets are primarily insectivorous, often feeding at great heights in the canopies of trees, especially conifers. However, we have seen that the Ruby-throated Kinglet takes some fruit and seeds but the Golden-crowned Kinglet appears not to be frugivorous, although one was seen to peck at a persimmon (Skinner 1928). Goldcrests, unlike Firecrests, seem to show some initiative in their diets in autumn and winter. All the call-notes are high-pitched, thin 'see-sees' or 'zee-zees', so high that they may easily be missed and are amongst the first bird sounds to be lost with increasing age of the observer. Their territorial songs are also high warbles and not easy to hear but the Ruby-crowned Kinglet is the exception, perhaps compensating for a small crown patch by uttering a loud, varied and pure-toned song. Other kinglets rely on their brilliant crown patches for warning rivals, advertising for mates and in courtship. The nests are delightful constructions of moss, cobwebs and plant down, lined with feathers or bits of fur, which bear comparison with those of the Long-tailed and Penduline Tits or some of those of the grass warblers. Both sexes usually carry out the work but the female takes on the greater share, as they fashion their 'procreant cradle' at the end of a branch. The female incubates her large clutch of 7–12 tiny spotted eggs alone. Such a large number of eggs may be accommodated only by the eggs being arranged in the nest in two tiers! For such small eggs the incubation period is quite long: 14 to 16 or even 17 days. The young birds are fed by both parents and may spend up to 21 days in the nest. Outside the breeding season, kinglets often join up in nomadic parties with tits, warblers, creepers, woodpeckers and other species. Two examples of the Ruby-crowned Kinglet in the British Museum, said to have been obtained at Loch Lomond in 1852, could not be admitted to the British list for lack of supporting evidence.

One danger that threatens these tiny birds is that they may be caught up in the burrs of plants. One was so caught when a Goldcrest was entangled in a burdock on the Isle of May (Flower 1958) and J. G. Needham (1909) found scores of young Golden-crowned Kinglets stuck, some fatally, to burdock heads in North America.

This attractive little bird is a typical denizen of coniferous woodland whether it be the scattered 200-year-old Scots pines of the Caledonian Forest, the dark forbidding ranks of alien Sitka spruce in Kielder Forest, the dense shady yew woods of Sussex or the little groups of cypresses in isolated country or suburban churchyards. The Goldcrest is quite a common bird in many parts of the ancient Speyside pine forests, although if silent it can be overlooked, and I have sometimes resorted to giving imitations of the call to elicit responses from birds of whose presence I had been previously unaware. It also forms a significant part of the bird communities of mature pine, spruce and mixed coniferous plantations. In Kielder Forest in the Borders I found Goldcrests to be co-dominants with Coal Tits in the tall Sitka spruce plantations. In compartments of 50-year-old Norway spruce at Dunkeld near Perth Goldcrests, however, outnumbered Coal Tits by almost two to one. Goldcrests enter the new conifer plantations when the trees are about 8–9 years old and then they slowly overtake the Willow Warblers and Chaffinches of the thicket stages until they achieve dominance, or share it with Coal Tits as the trees mature. The highest density figures in England come from the mature State forests with Goldcrests forming up to 20% of the bird community. The greatest densities in

Fig. 167
The mature coniferous stands greatly favoured as a breeding habitat by the Goldcrest. Breckland, Norfolk. (Eric Simms, June 1981)

the British Isles have been found in Irish coniferous plantations. Dr Leo Batten (1976) obtained densities of 591 pairs per km^2 in Norway spruce, 387 pairs per km^2 in Sitka spruce and 160–180 pairs per km^2 in yew, oak and holly woods in Killarney in southwest Ireland.

Other foreign conifers may attract Goldcrests as well. In a western hemlock *Tsuga* plantation at Castlecaldwell in Ireland I counted, in 15 minutes, 17 Goldcrests, 3 Chaffinches, 2 Chiffchaffs and single examples of Blackbird, Song and Mistle Thrush. When I studied the Douglas fir plantations, which form some 2% of our high forest in Britain, I found that Chaffinches, Goldcrests and Coal Tits were the commonest species. In century-old sierra and coast redwoods in Wales the Goldcrest was dominant (Williamson 1971). In their study Lack and Lack (1951) found that Goldcrests formed 62% of the bird community in Douglas fir and 61% in Norway spruce in Wales, 49% in Corsican and 32% in Scots pine in Breckland, 41% in mixed pines in Dorset and 30% in Scots pine in Fife. In winter in the Breckland pines the Goldcrest and Coal Tit are the commonest birds. In the yew wood at Kingley Vale in Sussex the Goldcrest forms 3.5% of the total bird community, where the Chaffinch occupies 11%, the Robin 10.75%, the Woodpigeon 9.5% and the Blackbird 7.75% (Williamson and Williamson 1973). Thus the spread of afforestation with great tracts of land given over to coniferous trees proved of great benefit to the Goldcrest both for breeding and as a sheltered winter habitat. Although the original home of the species must have been the native pine forests, the indigenous woods of yew or mixed oak and yew, the Goldcrest was able to increase after the State conifer plantings of the twentieth century really got under way. I have found Goldcrests regularly in the naturalized pine woods of the heathlands of southern England as well as the yew woods that clothe the chalk slopes, too steep to hold beech trees. Birds also frequent the Surrey heaths and the slopes of the North Downs.

One of the features of some large gardens and many churchyards and cemeteries is the presence of yew trees as well as exotic conifers such as wellingtonias and monkey puzzles, Mediterranean cypresses, Sawara and Hinoki cypresses from Japan and the Chinese arborvitae. Elsewhere I wrote that I was aware of 'at least three instances where in one area the only breeding pairs of goldcrests are in churchyards or large gardens where these trees are present' (Simms 1975). The presence of a few conifers may be all-important; Goldcrests bred in Inner London, in Holland Park in 1972, and Regents Park in 1975 and 1983, while a singing male was present in Kensington Gardens in 1981. In Europe, Goldcrests favour dense coniferous forests of spruce, fir, pine, cedar and *Tsuga* from the lowlands to the high mountain ranges at 4500 m. The highest bird that I have come across in Britain was one singing in stunted pines, 600 m above the River Feshie in Scotland.

One can also find Goldcrests in smaller numbers in pedunculate and sessile oakwoods – I found a relative abundance figure for them of 2 in Irish sessile oakwoods – as well as alders, Irish and more rarely Scottish birch and in mixed woods which are primarily broad-leaved but also have a mixture, albeit a small one, of coniferous species. In some of the sessile oakwoods of Ireland, Goldcrests were in my experience the third commonest species after Chaffinches and Robins. The highest numbers of breeding Goldcrests in broad-leaved woods seem to follow a rise in the general population after several consecutive mild winters and a subsequent high breeding success rate. I have no records for ash woods and only single ones for Scottish and Irish beech woods. Goldcrests also appear more regularly in broad-leaved woods and groves, gardens and even scrub and hedgerows outside the breeding season. In south Lincolnshire, during counts for the winter Bird Atlas, I came across Goldcrests with occasional Great, Blue and Marsh Tits foraging in hawthorn hedges barely half a metre high, since this is a part of England where too-frequent hedge flailing and cutting are carried on.

The species is extremely vulnerable during winters with very severe snow and frost. After the exceptionally bad one of 1962–3 there was a real crash in numbers, involving extermination in many areas, although some birds may have emigrated. Then followed a steady recovery in numbers, especially between 1969 and 1973 (see diagram), which resulted in the

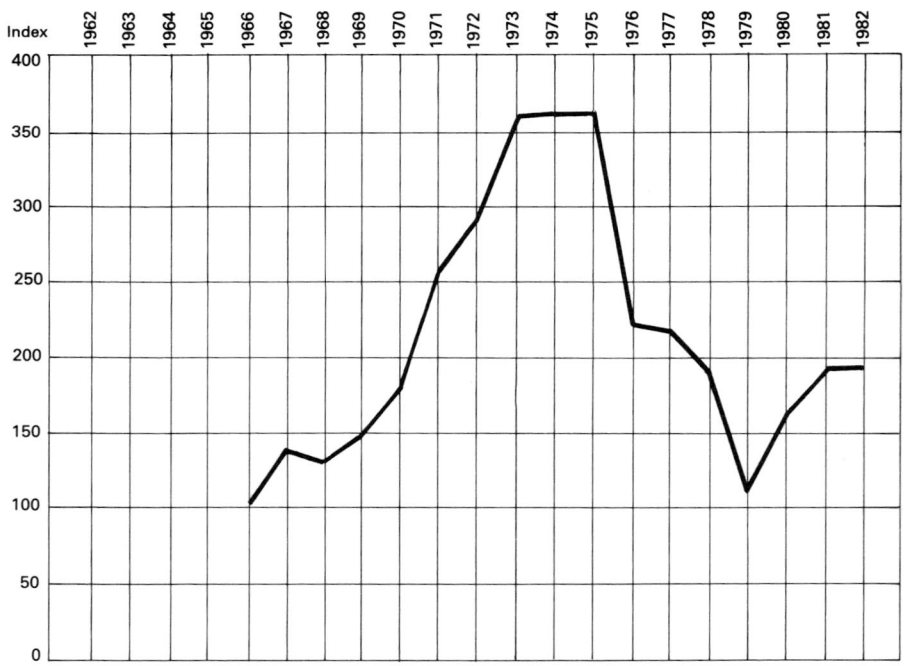

Fig. 168
Population changes in Goldcrest numbers 1966–82. Based on Common Birds Census of B.T.O. (levels in relation to 1966).

population rising 4 or 5-fold from the 1966 total; by 1975 10-fold from the 1969 summer total. An example of how this rise in numbers affected even suburban areas is Dollis Hill, in which I had no records between 1951 and October 1972; no fewer than 10 appeared in my garden between 1972 and 1975, with a final record of a bird on 24 February 1979. All my visitors diligently searched my roses for aphids. Another bad winter ensued in 1978–9 and the population fell to a figure not much higher than that in 1969. The winter of 1981–2 was a white one with some snow but the effects on the Goldcrest numbers was much smaller than expected. A 25% increase in numbers in 1983 was considered to be a continuation of the recovery from the low point of 1979, and Marchant (1983) attributed the high survival rate to the absence of the glazed ice on the trunks of the trees and their foliage which occurred in 1978–9.

The Goldcrest experiences an extraordinarily fragmented distribution in the Palaearctic region, breeding in the Azores and Eurasia from the northern parts of Spain, the British Isles and Scandinavia eastwards but in a discontinuous fashion to Amurland and Japan, north to Finnmark,

central Russia and the region of the upper Irtysh River and south to Italy, the Balkans, northern Iran and the Himalayas. The breeding range lies between 70°N and 25°N and the July isotherms of 12.5°C and 23°C. The northern distribution in Fenno-Scandia appears to be restricted by the ambient air temperature during the breeding season (Haftorn 1978a). Both the Goldcrest and Firecrest have a fragmented distribution pattern and this has not yet been adequately explained. Both Goldcrest and Firecrest behave as sibling species: as two near-relations that are morphologically similar but inhabit the same region without interbreeding: thus they are reproductively isolated. Dr K. H. Voous (1960) knew of no cases of hybridization but two instances of this were reported, in Suffolk in 1974 (Cobb 1976) and in Buckinghamshire in 1978 (Thorpe 1983). Often the two species nest in different kinds of habitat but, even where they may share them, they still remain separated by diet and different foraging techniques (Thaler and Thaler 1982). Outside the breeding season they may share the same food resource.

Fig. 169
Breeding range of the Goldcrest.

Goldcrests are widely spread throughout the British Isles. There was certainly some increase in the last century, due perhaps to the combined effects of mild winters and growing afforestation with coniferous tree species. With the advent of the State forests after 1919, and private plantings, the Goldcrest continued to increase and we have already seen how mild winter weather has also proved of benefit to the species. Certain areas are rather sparsely inhabited and in these there is a general lack of suitable habitat: around the Wash, although birds may have bred in Ely in 1974; on moors and high land above the tree line, and on many of the bare islands around the coast. John Parslow reported in 1973 that nesting occurred throughout the British Isles 'but not in Shetland, only irregularly in Orkney, and locally in the Outer Hebrides, north-west Scotland and parts of eastern England.' Since then Shetland and the Isles of Scilly have been colonized. I have also heard song in Orkney and in the grounds of Lews Castle on the Isle of Lewis.

The typical contact call of the Goldcrest is a thin, high-pitched 'zee' given at intervals of 1–4 seconds. Both *The Handbook* (1946) and M. J. Rogers (1978) described the regular contact and foraging call as a shrill 'zeec' or 'zee'. I spent some time obtaining tape recordings of Goldcrests in Rothiemurchus Forest in Speyside in 1953 and 1957, and found that the softer 'zee' was much more commonly employed than the version with the more clipped ending. I also recorded a more rapid variation with the notes given in quick groups of 3–5 notes – 'zee-zee-zee-zee'. The notes are of the same pitch. I also tape recorded the calls of Firecrests, both migrants at Dungeness and breeding birds in Buckinghamshire, and these are slightly lower and rougher in pitch than those of Goldcrests' 'zit-zit-zit-zit', and again in runs of four or five notes. However, there is considerable stress on the first of the Firecrest's notes, which is longer than the others, while the rest of the group are, as M. J. Rogers (1978) pointed out, of the same length and separated by the same intervals as those of the Goldcrest, but 'on a slightly rising scale'. Goldcrests in Pico on the Azores show no preference for coniferous trees like British birds do and, according to Marler and Boatman (1951), the calls also 'contrast strikingly with those of the British Goldcrest' and include contact calls similar to those of that race as well as 'tsut-tsut' alarm notes, tit-like calls and one that resembled the squeaking of an unoiled gate.

The song of the Goldcrest is an extremely high, thin double note 'cedar', repeated from 5–7 times and ending in a little terminal flourish, e.g. 'cedar-cedar-cedar-cedar-cedar-stichi-see-pee'. It was affectionately described by Lord Grey of Fallodon (1947) as like 'a tiny stream trickling and rippling

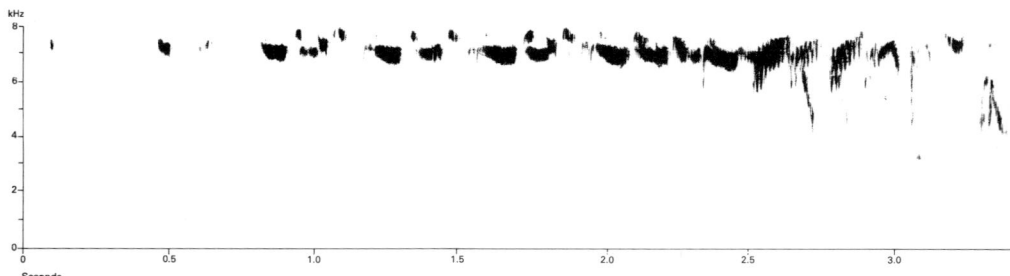

Fig. 170
A complete song of a Goldcrest. Note high frequency and flourish at the end. (Recorded by Eric Simms, Inverness-shire, May 1957)

over a small pebbly channel, and at the end going over a miniature cascade'. The terminal trill may vary in its structure and I have listed some which sounded more like 'diddly-dee' or 'dididee'; *The Handbook* (1946) transcribed the ending as 'stichipi-steeng' and E. M. Nicholson as 'eezeezee'. The entire song lasts 3–4 seconds and is uttered from 5–7 times a minute. Its carrying power is not great – in still conditions perhaps not more than 50 m – but 'it penetrates quite easily the roar of cable winches, tractors and power saws in a Scottish Sitka spruce plantation' (Simms 1971). This delicate fragile little song, often uttered while the male is foraging, can be heard in most months of the year. There is also a sweet, rather subdued rambling subsong, more musical than the full territorial song and suggestive in parts of the song of the Robin. There is a possible complication in that Firecrests seem capable of uttering songs rather like those of Goldcrests, although normally the former do not employ the terminal flourish used by Goldcrests at the end of their songs. However, Goldcrests may omit the characteristic ending and a few Firecrests may complete their vocalization with a tit-like twirl 'tzeeoo-tz'. In May and June both songs are very distinct but later in the season it is difficult to separate the two species by call alone since young Goldcrests have harsher calls than adults (Batten 1971). M. C. Adams (1966, 1980) described how Firecrests breeding in Hampshire between 1962 and 1977 uttered Goldcrest-type songs which almost persuaded him that both species were present; these included one bird that in a period of ten minutes only twice used its own song, and another that produced, in one period of singing, 14 Goldcrest-type songs, 4 'Firecrest', 4 'Goldcrest', 2 'Firecrest', 4 'Goldcrest' and then several short bursts of each. This may not be, as has been claimed, an example of mimicry of Goldcrest by the Firecrest but a case of sibling species that continued to differentiate vocally to an extent that restricted interbreeding, but as with Chiffchaffs and Willow Warblers apparently similar songs may still appear on occasion. The song of the Firecrest is normally more simple in form than that of the Goldcrest.

P. H. Becker (1977a) has described dialects or geographical variations in the song types of both Goldcrest and Firecrest in western, southern and central Europe but could not find that they had any biological usefulness. As we have seen, both species have species-specific calls and Becker (1977b) found no differences in response to playback of recordings, and no difference in the song in sympatry, where both species appear in the same region, compared to allopatry, where they are separated or their ranges are contiguous but do not overlap. Becker suggested that it was largely due to errors in imprinting that might be responsible for interspecific territoriality and mixed singing males.

Goldcrests feed widely on insects and their larvae, especially Dipterous flies, *Hymenoptera*, aphids including American 'blight', many kinds of Psyllid bug, weevils and beetles. These and spiders may be obtained by a diligent search of the foliage or by hovering at the ends of branches, while flying insects may be hunted on the wing. At Dungeness in November 1980 Nick Riddiford (1984) watched eight Goldcrests and ten Firecrests picking off from the underside of common nettle leaves minute nettle bugs *Trioza urticae* (one of the Psyllid species). At Ynys-hir in Wales S. C. H. Smith (1972) saw adult Goldcrests carrying oak bush crickets *Meconema thalassinum*, which are arboreal and only capable of weak flight, to their young on 16 out of 38 feeding visits. *The Handbook* (1946) did not include Lepidoptera in the diet of the Goldcrest but Barry Goater, an outstanding entomologist who taught my son David at Haberdashers' Aske's School at Elstree, watched a Goldcrest in Hampshire swallow a moth complete with wings; it was a variety of the pine beauty moth *Panolis flammea* and must have presented the bird with quite a challenge! Goldcrests and Coal Tits may eat up to 50% of the population of the eucosmid moth *Ernarmonia conicolana* in a habitat and, although Gibb (1960) suggested that such birds may be important in the natural control of forest insects, such a proposition is very difficult to prove. One remarkable observation was made by R. A. Richardson (1950) of a Goldcrest, which had attacked a large dragonfly in flight 'being actually towed along by the insect before releasing it unharmed.' There are several recorded instances of Goldcrests taking bread (Logan Hume 1955, Bottomleys 1961) and also soft fat and bread (*West Midland Bird Rept* 1956, 1961; Huxley 1960). Birds have even been seen examining horse droppings.

In fact, Goldcrests have been known to feed on the ground amongst leaf-litter in the company of Great, Blue and Coal Tits (Radford 1969), whilst one bird, belly-deep in water, was observed picking up items of food from floating mats of vegetation (Stokoe 1980). According to *The Handbook* (1946), Goldcrests may take bud scales but vegetable food seems very rare. A. C. Bent (1964) noted in North America that the Golden-crowned Kinglet had been 'observed apparently drinking the sap that flows from the fresh drillings of sap-sucking woodpeckers but it may be that the birds are after the insects that are also attracted to such places.' However, C. K. Mylne (1959) observed and made a cine film of three species of tit, a Nuthatch and several Goldcrests coming to a birch tree at Minsmere in Suffolk to drink the sap oozing from a broken twig. Although there was again the possibility that the Goldcrests had been drawn to the flies on the sap, the film that he took quite clearly showed 'birds reaching up from below and sipping at the dripping sap, or laying their bills along the bark sideways to drink.'

The breeding season of the Goldcrest may exceptionally begin as early as late March, but it is much more likely to start towards the end of April or in early May and continue until early June. By 1972, according to the Common Birds Census, the average density of breeding Goldcrests in lowland regions and in broad-leaved woods was 12.9 pairs per km^2, while after taking into account the vast tracts of State forests and private plantations the density might rise to a figure as high as 500 pairs. There might be more than 15 million pairs in Britain and Ireland (*The Atlas* 1976) but the total is subject to considerable change because of severe winters and successions of mild ones. Goldcrests are olive-green birds on their upper-parts and dull whitish-buff below, with double white wing-bars, but in the case of both sexes, which are very small and plump, the distinguishing feature is a bright yellow crown with a black border. The crest from which the bird derives its name has an orange centre in the male and a pale yellow one in the female. At the start of the breeding season when males assume their territories the birds are very excitable and in arguments or confrontations with other males the crest is erected and 'spread out sideways in a gorgeous flame of colour' (Lack 1937). Two aroused male Goldcrests spar at each other with their wings slightly lowered and their heads thrust forwards and downwards, while their bodies can be seen jerking up and down from the tarsal joint. Such a territorial dispute may go on for minutes on end. However, as Jacques Delamain (1937) noted, the crest also has a part to play in courtship with the male 'dancing about like a little demon, and an incredibly large crest, a flame of beautiful orange-red colour is raised at short intervals over his head with a vibrating movement when it reaches its full expansion.' At first the female may seem not at all interested but mating is often achieved quite quickly after the display. The habitat

Fig. 171
*Goldcrest displaying at
its own reflection in a
windowpane. Bucking-
hamshire, April 1972.
(Richard Vaughan)*

and spatial relationships of Goldcrests on their breeding ground with
Phylloscopus warblers has been described for a region of southern Finland
(Tiainen 1983).

The nest is normally suspended under thick foliage at or near the end
of a branch of a coniferous tree, particularly spruce, cypress or deodar, but
much less often in pine. When high up – one was recorded at a height of
22–3 m in a wellingtonia (Millard 1938) – it may be almost impossible to
see. On the other hand I have found nests in juniper in Speyside as low as
1 m from the ground. In the North Riding four nests were built against a
trunk on the 'upper surface of a branch' some 1.6 m above the ground (Lord
and Ainsworth 1948), while in some regions nests may even be in ivy
against a tree bole or in evergreen shrubs. One nest in an Exmoor combe
was at a height of 8 m in a hole in an old branch of an oak, covered with
lichen and 'with a small fern sprouting out' (Wootton 1959). More recently
a nest in Northumberland was discovered suspended from a branch just
1 m above the occupied nest of a Sparrowhawk (Heavisides 1984). The
female Goldcrest seems to carry out most of the nest-construction work
but the relative share between males and females seems to vary from pair to
pair. The tiny nest is a deep thick cup of moss, lichens and spiders' webs
with the last material often fixing the structure to the nearby twigs. It is
suspended in a fork in the twigs often so close to the foliage that the cup is
not at all easy of access. A bird was seen removing felt from a mesh con-
tainer full of potential nesting material and taking it away for incorporation
in its own nest (Soper 1972). The Northampton poet John Clare noted that
Goldcrests building in pine trees in Milton Park apparently cemented
their nests 'with the glutinous substance or raisin that oozes from the

grains and were this not to be had it fastens its moss and other substances together like a basket.' The nest is generally lined with feathers, and occasionally down.

The size of the clutch varies normally from 7–10 eggs but as many as 11, 12 and 13 have been recorded. Their ground colour varies from white to buff with faint spots of grey-brown or purple, usually in a zone near the broader end of the egg. The average size of the eggs is 13.6 × 10.2 mm. They were neatly described by T. A. Coward (1944) as resembling 'children's comfits'. Only the female Goldcrest incubates but she may be fed by the male (Pontius 1960). The incubation period varies from 14–17 days – quite a long period for a passerine bird – and the actual nest temperature is maintained at a constant level, according to Haftorn (1978), by altering the lengths of periods spent on and off the eggs. Haftorn found that the period 'on' the nest correlated inversely with the air temperature and the period 'off' with the time of day; and the latter period was shortest at midday. The nestlings are fed by both parents and remain in the nest from 16–21 days. In an extreme spell of hot weather in 1976, when the temperature reached a peak of 28.2°C, a Goldcrest at Omagh in Northern Ireland was seen bringing water to the young, a drop at a time, on the end of the bill (Archdale 1978). When hand-rearing young Goldcrests that had left the nest, Dr C. J. O. Harrison (1969) found that unlike young *Phylloscopus* warblers reared in the same way, an immature Goldcrest reveals 'an innate image of both the location and appearance of its natural food, which is little changed by any later learned feeding behaviour.' The Goldcrest is

Fig. 172
Goldcrest at typical nest, suspended under the branch of a coniferous tree. (Eric Hosking)

double-brooded and, if two broods should overlap, the male is forced to take on the care of the first brood since only the female incubates (Haftorn 1978c). A pair of Goldcrests breeding in a yew tree in Hampshire used the same nest twice in the same season (Moule 1951).

We have already seen that as a species the Goldcrest can suffer badly in severe winters, although dense conifer growths in woods, gardens and churchyards can provide some shelter for roosting at night. One individual roosted in a disused woodpecker hole in an old birch tree in Surrey (Raynsford 1955), and in Finland Goldcrests were reported by M. Lagerström (1979) as roosting in the snow. In Finland it was thought by Österlof (1966) that only one tenth of the wintering Goldcrest population survived to spring. Of course, weather will have an effect on those birds that choose to winter as far north as Finland and central parts of Sweden, and that do not join those migrating southwards. There are other enemies too. Sparrowhawks, Merlins, Tawny and Long-eared Owls, and probably other birds of prey as well, hunt Goldcrests. D. H. Morse (1975) has shown that the erratic movements and flights of small woodland birds, which are vulnerable to attack while away from cover, may confuse their enemies. The random spiralling and looping movements constitute a useful anti-predator mechanism.

The British Goldcrest is primarily sedentary but some, after moving south, may emigrate to the Continent and return in spring, while others travel west to Ireland. Continental Goldcrests also move south and west in autumn. Many leave Scandinavia and this emigration is often reflected in the numbers trapped and ringed at observatories around the Baltic Sea; no fewer than 20,925 were trapped at Pape in Latvia during September and October 1983. These little birds then may continue their autumn movement across the North Sea in anticyclonic conditions in considerable numbers. I well remember one October morning at Boddam near Peterhead in Aberdeenshire, when all the stunted sycamores in the coastal village gardens were alive with these birds, newly arrived overnight. One 2 m high sycamore in a small back garden had over a score of tired birds in its branches. Similarly, Kenneth Williamson (1965) described how Goldcrests arrived in hundreds on Fair Isle on some autumns with birds 'leaping actively among cabbages and salt-blackened turnip-tops in search of insect food.' For him as for me it was a marvel that these scraps of animated life could cross 500 miles of the North Sea in poor weather and in one single flight. In Yorkshire the Goldcrest was regarded as the forerunner of the Woodcock and was commonly known as the 'Woodcock-pilot'. On the coast of Lincolnshire one October J. Cordeaux (1892) described one fall following an east wind, half a gale and heavy beating rain and wrote that: 'During this time the immigration was immense.' More recently, on 2 October 1983 2000 Goldcrests were estimated to be at Saltfleetby on the Lincolnshire coast. These arrivals may occur from Fair Isle down the east coast to Kent and along parts of the south coast of England as well. Stephen Mummery (1844) described how, on about 10 October 1843 every shrub, hedge and garden in Margate in Kent was swarming with Goldcrests for several days.

Once, in October 1957, I spent the night hours on the gallery of the old Dungeness Lighthouse on the coast of Kent with a microphone and a portable radio transmitter. I had stood there before on nights of bird migration with the faint roar of the paraffin lamp behind me and an infinity of blackness around me, swept continuously by the rotating beams of the lantern. I had listened to waders, thrushes and Starlings calling as they passed and glimpsed them like golden wraithes as together with Robins, Skylarks, Chiffchaffs, Wheatears and Short-eared Owls they were picked out by the beams. With me on this particular night was Herbert Axell, then the warden of the Dungeness Bird Observatory, while parked below was a recording vehicle and my colleague Bob Wade. At first the sky was clear, then it became overcast and shortly afterwards we could hear tiny needlepoints of sound far out in the darkness that steadily grew louder. Hundreds if not thousands of Goldcrests that had moved south down the coast of western Europe, had embarked on the Channel crossing to Kent. Probably disorientated by the clouding over of the stars, the birds were being drawn towards the light; this is just as one October I saw hundreds of Redwings around the lamp standards on the sea front at Hastings (Simms 1978). I was able to capture on the tape recorder the calls of these arriving migrants as they flew in from the sea. As they emerged into the light they began to pitch on the gallery rails and on our heads and shoulders. Very gently we picked them off and packed them into boxes for later examination and ringing. One bird sitting quietly on the sleeve of my anorak turned out to be a Firecrest! The arrival of Goldcrests can be traced even in London with birds in Cripplegate and Holland Park in 1959 probably of European origin; a Continental bird was found dead on 11 January 1973 at Sevenoaks. Numbers are often reported in the London area in early winter and D. I. M. Wallace (1961) recorded pronounced autumn passage in Regents Park between 23 September and 19 October 1959. I have seen Goldcrests and Short-eared Owls travelling together at night, and it has been rumoured that Goldcrests arriving on the East Anglian coast may hitch a lift from larger birds, especially the owls, which arrive at the same time. The belief was very strong among old Norfolk wildfowlers, some of whom claimed to have seen the tiny birds spring out from the plumage of the owls that they had shot. No modern evidence is forthcoming to support this charming assertion which has a close affinity with an ancient belief in the New World that hummingbirds travelled on the backs of cranes or geese.

Some of the autumn immigrants may remain in the British Isles for the winter, and there are traceable movements back in March and April. Birds ringed in autumn have been recovered in Norway and elsewhere but we still know very little about the migrations of these birds. Birds that breed to the east in Europe, winter in the more southern parts of their range as far south as the Mediterranean while Asian birds move down to Iran and China. Birds winter singly or in small parties in the Tehran region between 28 October and 10 February (Passburg 1959). Goldcrests have been seen in mixed flocks of warblers, tits and flycatchers in Kashmir in August, feeding at a height of 9.1 m (Macdonald and Henderson 1977).

I have often watched Goldcrests wintering in State forests either as individuals foraging alone or as constituents of mixed flocks. In some spruce and pine plantations the birds seem to move wholly away, or to desert large sections of plantation; similarly I have often walked for long periods in the old Caledonian Forest among the pines before finding a small band of Goldcrests and Crested Tits. Yet although often badly hit by frost and snow in the British Isles their condition may be far worse on the Continent.

We saw earlier how perhaps only 10% of the wintering population in Finland may survive the winter. A recent study of Goldcrests wintering in a predominantly spruce forest near Oslo in Norway showed a decline between November and March of from 76% to 96%; this could be related to snowfall and ambient temperatures. The chief food of the flock studied proved to be spiders (Hogstad 1984). Each flock also seemed to move 'as a unit within a defined winter territory.' The winter survival must depend on the density of the food supply but there is a degree of selective advantage in remaining within their breeding territories during the winter, rather than migrating. It would be interesting to know the respective kinds of fluctuation in population numbers between the migratory and non-migratory birds.

CHAPTER **34** The Firecrest

In 1946 *The Handbook* described the status of the Firecrest in England and Wales as: 'Fairly frequent visitor from Oct. to April along coast from Cornwall to Kent, and considered as annual autumn-visitor Kent and Scilly Is. and nearly so Sussex and Cornwall. Occasional Somerset.' It was also regarded as fairly frequent along the East Coast up to and including Norfolk and more rarely northwards and inland. In 1952 there was an unusually large autumn immigration of Firecrests into the British Isles and Redman and Hooke (1954), who studied the records, suggested that they had arisen through two entirely different movements started in the north and west of Germany in October 1952, within a few days of each other. They appeared to be the result of drift migration arising from the movement of birds through a 'front' or from an apparently redirected passage. These immigrations were followed by reports of 32 different individuals wintering between 16 November 1952 and 13 March 1953. Most of these birds were in Cornwall, Devon, Somerset and Sussex; only 9 were observed in Hampshire, Kent, Suffolk and Worcestershire. In the Channel Islands more than 50 were recorded in just one locality in Guernsey in November 1952. The spring movement in Britain in 1953 appeared to involve birds of Continental origin rather than wintering birds returning through southeast England. Some were thought to have come from the Iberian Peninsula.

From the 1950s there was a steady increase in the number of Firecrests

Fig. 173
Firecrest in display on its breeding ground; Buckinghamshire. (L. A. Batten)

being reported in Britain especially in the spring months. There had been considerable evidence of an expansion of range by the species in western Europe after 1900. Birds nested for the first time in Holland in 1930 and further advances were made to the north in France, Czechoslovakia (where the Firecrest now outnumbers the Goldcrest), Belgium, and Denmark where birds bred first in 1961; there were observations of Firecrests in Norway, Sweden and Finland (Batten 1973). A Firecrest trapped at a site in Lithuania in the autumn of 1982 was only the eleventh between 1966 and 1982, compared to a total of some 73,000 Goldcrests in the same period (*Brit. Birds* 76:276). With this marked expansion in range it was to be expected that Firecrests might breed in Britain in due course. Apart from two early but now discredited breeding records in Berkshire in 1863 and Lancashire in 1927, the first knowledge of Firecrests nesting in Britain was the discovery of three singing males in the New Forest in Hampshire in 1961. After that date several pairs were found in five different localities there and breeding was proved in 1962, when fledged young were seen, and in 1965 when a nest was found (Adams 1966). Singing males were also reported from Hampshire and Kent in 1968 and in Dorset to the west in 1970. Dr Leo Batten (1973) has traced the colonization of England by the Firecrest from the successful New Forest colony to his own discovery in 1971 in Buckinghamshire of two breeding pairs and two singing males. In 1973 two pairs were noted breeding – one in Dorset and one in Hampshire – while a further fourteen singing males were observed as well.

Dr Batten had made his discovery of breeding birds near Wendover while censusing the birds of a Forestry Commission plantation of Norway spruce. In June 1974 I joined Dr Batten so that I could make open-spool tape recordings of the Firecrests' calls and songs. It was a rather misty morning and the bird chorus was clearly dominated by the 'spink-spink' calls and rollicking songs of Chaffinches and the utterances of Wrens, Great and Coal Tits, Goldcrests and the deep, throaty cooings of Woodpigeons being reflected from the nearby hill slopes 'with a strange unnatural hollow quality . . . and some firecrests hissed their high songs from the spruce canopies' (Simms 1979). That year there were at least 24 singing males. A single playback of one song would induce a male to come and investigate from a distance of 2 m above my head, sometimes too close for proper sound recording. This is not a desirable practice since both Jourdain (1937) and Batten (1973) have rightly drawn attention to the fact that as a species the Firecrest is easily disturbed during nest-construction and egg-laying, and special care is imperative if Firecrests are suspected of breeding. The species is given special protection by being placed in Part 1, Schedule 1 of the Wildlife and Countryside Act 1981, and offences carry special penalties. It is an offence to disturb any specially protected bird while it is nesting or with dependent young and a licence should always be obtained from the Nature Conservancy Council to photograph or record any such bird while it is on or near its nest.

By 1974, apart from the New Forest colony, more than 30 singing males had been reported in Buckinghamshire, Berkshire, Bedfordshire and Dorset with probable breeding in both of the last two counties as well. In 1975 there were no fewer than 43 singing males at the main site in Buckinghamshire; out of at least 65 males in song at 23 sites in 10 English counties, only 4 pairs were actually proved to have bred, but 122 pairs might have done so! There was a decline from 1976–8, but numbers picked up again in 1980 and 1981; in the last year 3 sites in Kent, Hampshire and Buckinghamshire held 63% of the breeding population. In the Channel Islands a Firecrest with a brood patch was trapped on Sark in 1977 and one was seen building on Guernsey in 1979 (Long 1981). In 1985 I visited a colony in central Wales. The following table gives the number of sites, pairs actually known to have nested and pairs possibly breeding. The vicissitudes are interesting but the species may well have been overlooked earlier as a breeding bird.

Table 28   *Breeding of Firecrest*

	1973	1974	1975	1976	1977	1978	1979	1980	1981	1982
Sites	5	13	31	14	12	7	25	30	35	21
Pairs proved breeding	2	1	4	4	2	1	9	7	15	4
Pairs possibly breeding	18	37	122	27	31	11	73	78	102	44

(By permission, from the monthly magazine *British Birds*)

It is conceivable that the Firecrest of Europe may have arisen during the ice age as a result of the geographical separation from Goldcrests having an original Holarctic distribution. Today the Firecrest is a bird of the western Palearctic and, like the Goldcrest, it has an extremely fragmented and discontinuous range between 28°N and 55°N, or the July isotherms of about 11°C to 23.5°C. The Firecrest breeds in the British Isles in small numbers, and in Europe from Denmark and northwest Russia southeast to the Balkans and Asia Minor, south to the islands of the Mediterranean and southwest to most of France, to Iberia, northwest Africa, Madeira and the Canary Islands. *Regulus i. ignicapillus* breeds across the Eurasian range of the Firecrest. To the north and east of its range it is very much a summer visitor only, while in the south it is present all the year round.

Fig. 174
Breeding range of the Firecrest (right) and Golden-crowned Kinglet.

I associate Firecrests as breeding species in Europe with groves of broad-leaved trees in France and coniferous and mixed woodlands in central Europe. I have been awakened by a fine dawn chorus of Firecrests near

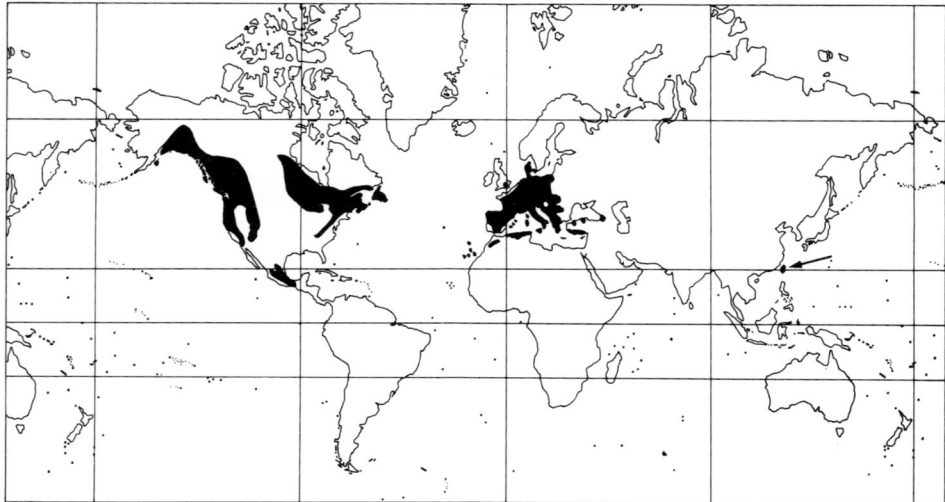

Belin in Les Landes in southwest France, and listened to birds in the Auvergne, in the mixed woods of Andalucia, the spruce forests of the Alps and in the Grecian fir woods above Arakhova in the shadow of Mount Parnassus. Firecrests do not need conifers in the same way that Goldcrests do but they will frequent the subalpine fir woods of Germany, the cedar forests of Morocco and the mountains of the Middle Atlas. Birds also occur in the woods and parks of Europe where both broad-leaved and coniferous trees can be found. Around the Mediterranean I have seen birds in the tree-heath and in the corkwoods of Spain, as well as in ever-green oaks and alders. Nests are often built amongst the ivy hanging from the alder trees but rarely in contact with the boles; here they may suffer predation from egg-sucking reptiles. Firecrests have also been seen com-monly in the cork oak forests of northern Tunisia, in northeast Algeria and in the Aurès Mountains, while nests are often built at heights of 5–12 m 'suspended from underside of cedar boughs' in northwest Africa (Snow 1952). Outside the breeding season, Firecrests can often be found among evergreen oaks and broad-leaved trees as well as scrub and even dead bracken, and less often among the dense canopies of coniferous trees so favoured by the Goldcrest.

In England the most favoured breeding habitat for the Goldcrest is a plantation of Norway spruce over 9 m in height. In Buckinghamshire Batten (1971) found his famous colony in a plantation dominated by 40-year-old Norway spruce trees but with 'a scatter of deciduous trees, pre-dominantly larch *Larix decidua*, but also including beech *Fagus sylvatica* and hazel *Corylus avellana* with some lime *Tilia platyphyllos* along the rides.' Breeding Firecrests in England can be found in a wide range of habitats, involving other conifer species and broad-leaved ones as well. Birds can be found amongst mature Scots pine and Douglas firs, and in Kent western hemlock that has been underplanted with larch. In habitats with well-grown pines there is often a ring of natural scrub or 'thicket' of young developing trees. In Suffolk Firecrests have nested in mixed woods containing mature Scots pine but surrounded on all sides by agricultural land. The greater part of the habitat for one Dorset nest was formed from Scots pine but there was also a luxuriant shrub layer of sycamore, holm or evergreen oak and holly. Scots pine also comprised just over 50% of the vegetative cover at a nesting site in Bedfordshire but Norway spruce and a few silver birches were present as well. The nesting sites in Hampshire investigated by M. C. Adams (1966) were those of 'mature mixed woodland where conifers, perhaps particularly spruce *Picea* spp. are dominant' while conifers were almost totally absent from some sites where the dominants were oak and beech with some holly. Dr Batten (1973) pointed out that holly appeared in all the known broad-leaved habitats and wondered how important the presence of this tree species was. This has not yet been fully investigated.

Firecrests are reported in England in the breeding season, in winter and on passage. On the south coast of England passage birds occur chiefly from the middle of March to April and again from the middle of September to early November. Others in usually smaller numbers may be reported from East Anglia – 50 were recorded in Norfolk between 1836 and 1966 (Seago 1967) – as well as inland in the southern half of England and also on the coasts of Wales and southwest Ireland. Further north, in England, Scot-

Fig. 175
*Habitat for breeding
Firecrests in Bucking-
hamshire, consisting of
40-year-old Norway
spruce. The greatest
concentration of Fire-
crests was at the junction
of the two rides. (L. A.
Batten)*

land and most of Ireland, the bird is a rare vagrant only. It will be remembered from the last chapter how Firecrests were drawn to the Dungeness
Lighthouse with hundreds of Goldcrests on an overcast night in October
1957. In 1958 no fewer than 29 were trapped and ringed at the Dungeness
Bird Observatory. The first Firecrest in northeast Scotland was recorded
at Cruden Bay on 11 May 1974. Wintering Firecrests are most frequent in
southwest England from Dorset to the Isles of Scilly but birds are also seen
quite regularly in the south and Midlands of England. Firecrests may mix
and feed with Goldcrests on passage and in the winter, but I saw a male
Firecrest being fiercely pursued by a Goldcrest in Morkery Wood in south
Lincolnshire on 16 November 1982 (*Lincs. Bird Rept* 1982).

The Firecrests that breed in England are apparently summer visitors
arriving often quite suddenly in numbers on the breeding ground in early
May. The species is resident in southern Europe but is looked upon as a
summer visitor in Belgium and other countries in northern Europe. The
arrival of males in 1972 in Buckinghamshire was quite dramatic with three
birds in song on 9 May where 'none had been heard two days previously,
and by 11th at least seven were singing there' (Batten 1973). This is the
period in which it is easiest to locate singing Firecrests since the output of
song decreases as the season wears on but males stimulated by electronic
playback will sing up to the middle of July.

We saw in the previous chapter that the contact call of the Firecrest is
harsher than the corresponding call of the Goldcrest: a lower 'zit-zit-zit'
rather than 'see-see-see'. The song may be confused with that of the Goldcrest but it lacks the rhythm and normally the terminal flourish; a few
exceptional Goldcrests, particularly in late June and July, may omit the

final twirl. In essence the song of the Firecrest is a succession of the common 'zit-zit-zit' notes assembled in a longer and slightly more varied sequence. The sonagram from a bird that I recorded in Buckinghamshire clearly shows that the final three notes or 'zits' have tiny peaks which are absent from the preceding ones. There are 13 notes in that song and a total

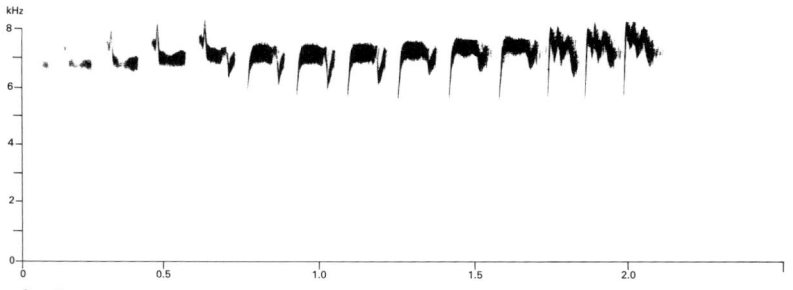

of 11–14 notes per song seems to me to be very typical. One could render this song phonetically as 'zit-zit-zit-zit-zit-zit-zit-zit-zit-zit-zirt.zirt.zirt' with an acceleration and increase in loudness. Other renderings include 'sissisisisisisisisisitt' and 'sisisisi*sisisisisi*'. The whole song usually lasts 1.5–2.5 seconds which can be compared to ranges of 3.5–4.0 seconds for the Goldcrest. Perhaps as many as eight songs a minute may be uttered by an individual singer. In May and June song is most regular after dawn, but it can be heard throughout the day at a lower level of output. Later in the season the song becomes less vigorous, being largely confined to the morning, and is replaced overall by the call. The song of Firecrests may stimulate Goldcrests to sing but the reverse is apparently not true since the songs of the former are simpler in construction.

Firecrests will defend their breeding territories against Goldcrests, and Adams (1966) described how a male Firecrest in the New Forest attacked an intruding Goldcrest, grappled with it and succeeded in ejecting it from his territory. The territories of both species are known to overlap so that the amount of actual competition between the species may not be very great. Aggressive displays of Firecrests involve the raising of the crest and a great deal of wing-fluttering. In his courtship display the male also raises his crest, points it towards his mate and hovers over her before coition takes place. Little is known about the actual size of territories in England but Batten (1971) calculated that one in Buckinghamshire was about 0.5 hectares and a second about 0.4 hectares. In much of Europe the Firecrest raises two broods and the evidence suggests that this is the case in England as well.

The nest is often suspended from the hanging branch of a conifer, in ivy on a trunk or in a juniper bush. In England the heights of the nests examined vary from 2.5 m in a field maple where one was suspended from both a maple twig and the fallen branch of a Norway spruce, to 4.5 m in ivy growing on a sycamore, to 5.0 m in a deodar, 12 m in a Norway spruce, 13.5 m in another deodar and 20 m in a Douglas fir, where the nest was sited 2 m from the tip of a 6 m long branch (Adams 1966, Batten 1973). On the whole the heights are not great but there are problems in locating a nest high up

Fig. 176
One complete song-phrase of the Firecrest. This should be compared with the sonagram for the Goldcrest (p. 356); note high frequency. (Recorded by Eric Simms, Buckinghamshire, June 1974)

in the dense canopy of a very tall conifer. The female Firecrest carries out most of the building of the nest accompanied by her mate. The nest is rather like that of the Goldcrest but it may have a deeper base as well as being smaller and more compact. The base of the nest often consists of twigs from both coniferous and broad-leaved trees, although in Switzerland the majority that I came across were from the former trees. The twigs – up to twelve have been counted in England in a single nest – are brought in but in many nests the birds use twigs on the tree as living suspension points for the nest. The chief materials seem to be green moss interwoven with hair or leaf skeletons and bound together with spiders' webs; the nest is provided finally with a lining of feathers. Two English nests had external diameters of 7.8 and 8.0 cm, internal diameters of the cups of 3.75 and 5 cm, external depths of the nests of 5.0 and 7.0 cm and depths of cup of 4.0 and 4.5 cm respectively. One of the nests had a floor depth of 2.5 cm. Incubation has been recorded from the middle of April to mid-May in Spain and from early May to the middle of that month in France and Germany (Jourdain 1937, Niethammer 1937), while in England first clutches seem to be laid towards the end of the third week of May and second clutches in late June or early July.

The size of the clutch on the Continent, according to *The Handbook* (1946), is 7–12 eggs, while Harrison (1975) gives: 'Usually 7–11, sometimes 12.' The clutch size in England has been inferred at 8 eggs for one nest but data are scanty in this respect. In Spain birds generally lay 5–6 eggs but the clutch size rises further north. The eggs are white, smooth, non-glossy and often carry a warm pinky hue; the indistinct markings are often gathered in a zone at the broader ends like the eggs of many Goldcrests. The average dimensions of 100 eggs examined reveal lengths of 13.5 mm and widths of 10.3 mm, very slightly less than those of Goldcrests. Apparently the Firecrests of Madeira lay eggs more like those of *Phylloscopus* warblers. The incubation is carried out by the female alone and she may sit from 14–15 days. Fledging periods of 19 and 20 days have been recorded in Europe; in the case of one English brood the fledging period was calculated at about 17 days – a similar period to that of the Goldcrest. An extended account of breeding in a pair of Firecrests in Saxony has been given by H. Heft (1965). The young birds are cared for by both parents, which collect small moths, flies and caterpillars for them as well as aphids and their eggs, small beetles and spiders and their eggs. Young Firecrests sport rudimentary white eye-stripes while they are in the nest which are distinct enough to separate them from young Goldcrests. After fledging, when the young birds may take cover in trees and scrub and crouch down on twigs, the eye-stripes may not be so easy to see. In half a dozen cases of nesting in England two nests produced 3 or 4 young, one 4, and another 4 or 5, while the remaining two led to the fledging of 5 young each (Batten 1973). The average of 4.5 young fledged per brood was thought to be higher than the real average. References were made in the last chapter to apparent instances of hybridization between Firecrest and Goldcrest.

Most observers in England will come across the Firecrest, not as a breeding bird but rather as a passage bird or a wintering species. In Lincolnshire in 1979 more than 30 were recorded between spring and autumn and these included several singing males. In 1980 more than 50 were reported in that county and there were overwintering records as well. Birds of passage may appear even in Inner London and there were singing males in Regents Park in April 1977 and 1978. Wintering birds have developed the habit in some areas of coming to feeding stations and bird tables to take bacon fat and bread crumbs (Gush 1976), joining with overwintering warblers such as the Chiffchaff and Blackcap as well as Goldcrests. In 1968 a male came to a garden near the New Forest to take bread crumbs from a table and fat from a hanging feeder, while between 1972 and 1974 up to three Firecrests fed in winter from the same bird table (Glue and Gush 1977). At Ottery St Mary in Devon three were seen and trapped in December 1972 after feeding on beef fat, and four were trapped in the same garden in November 1974 after taking fat that had been pressed into the interstices of an old Scots pine. The Firecrests all fed singly but were actually in competition with Treecreepers, tits, Robins, Greenfinches, Nuthatches and, on occasion, Goldcrests.

The Firecrest may well have been overlooked as a breeding species and winter visitor. A mastery of the calls and especially the songs may ensure that breeding colonies are not missed. The characteristic cleaner-looking plumage overall, white superciliary band and black stripe through the eye with some white below it, the bright orange-red, black-bordered crown in the male and yellow, black-bordered coronal stripe in the female that provide a more dramatic 'face' pattern than that of the Goldcrest, and the bronze-sided neck should ensure separation from the commoner Goldcrest. When these distinctions can be made we should have a much better idea of the breeding range, migrations and overwintering frequency of this little gem of feathered loveliness – one of England's rarer and most appealing birds.

CHAPTER **33 Past and Future**

The history of any group of birds is a dynamic one, and studies undertaken over a period will reveal fluctuations in their breeding numbers, expansions and contractions of range as the result of climatic conditions, the biotic effects of man and density-dependent factors. Climate itself is always in a state of change and has either a direct or indirect influence on the vegetation, birds and other animals. There have also been changes in habitats and farming techniques in recent years as well as a great deal of afforestation. Some have had detrimental effects and others benefits for birds including the warblers. Clean Air Acts seem to have had an effect on some insectivorous birds in built-up areas and Blackcaps and Willow Warblers as well as Goldcrests now nest in some of London's Royal Parks, where once they were absent. Some warbler species in the British Isles such as Savi's, Reed, Marsh, Cetti's and Dartford Warblers are living on the very limits of their breeding range in western Europe where they may be more vulnerable and subject to population changes than those of their species nesting nearer to the centre of their distribution. Some species like the Dartford, Reed and Wood Warblers have specialized habitat demands which limit their range. Others may be in competition with each other while spatial separation through different feeding techniques or foraging niches may reduce this to a minimum except when a local food is abundant or in short supply.

In Chapter 3 we saw how birds had evolved in form and then radiated out from the refuges that they had occupied during the long period of the ice ages. Thus they slowly occupied those regions being released from the grip of the ice. Over very long spans of time, changes in the earth have been brought about by shifts in the continents, by changes in the Sun and the oceans and in the composition of the atmosphere. Ten thousand years ago there were still ice caps left in Britain from the last glaciation while the warmest period since the ice age was past its peak some three to four thousand years ago. The present pattern of bird migration evolved after the ice ages. Long-term changes are notoriously hard to plot but I do wonder whether the present unstable patterns on Earth suggest that we are approaching a new ice age. We have had a long respite but are probably due for another anyway. These unstable patterns have revealed themselves with extremes of cold such as the winters in Britain in 1947, 1961–2, 1962–3 (the worst for 217 years), and 1979, and the severe cold in Europe in 1985, with a drop in our average summer temperature as well as a down-turn in the winter ones as well, a southward shift of the Arctic ice front and recent evidence from core samples in Greenland, with tundra species nesting in Britain perhaps after being displaced by Scandinavian anticyclones, as well as hot summers like those in the British Isles of 1976 (the most remarkable for two hundred years) and 1984; all suggest important changes in the weather.

Professor H. H. Lamb (1975) has shown how the climate of any spot on the Earth's surface is influenced by four main circumstances: radiation from Sun and planet, heat and moisture borne by the winds, heat shifted and moisture supplied by ocean currents and such influences as the nature of the surface, specific heat, thermal conductivity, water content of the soil, presence of hills and forests and human developments at the site itself. It is the differences in heating at varying places which cause movement in the atmosphere; the pressure gradients so formed then give rise to air movement, the wind. A gradient stretches from the high pressures over the tropic regions to those of low pressure above the Poles. Air movements started by the differences of pressure are balanced by the effect of the Earth's rotations so that the winds tend to travel along the isobars – the lines joining points of equal pressure – anticlockwise around 'lows' in the northern hemisphere and clockwise in the southern. Each hemisphere has a subtropical belt of high pressure and there are also subpolar belts of low pressure particularly over the sea. Changes in the strength of the global wind circulation can affect the amounts of rain or snow travelling east across Europe and Asia and into the polar region as well.

At the start of the present century the global wind circulation lessened, with the result that parts of the Arctic were warmed by Atlantic drift water moving further north and causing the sea-ice dramatically to retreat. It also allowed western populations of birds like the Fan-tailed and Cetti's Warblers to remain as residents, and eastern populations to move west. The Arctic amelioration in the first part of the twentieth century was marked by westerly weather and at this time the Sahel in Africa and Ethiopia – so badly affected by drought in the 1970s and 1980s – enjoyed a strong monsoon rainfall. The two decades from 1910–1919 and 1920–1929 revealed a rise in the mean surface air temperature in Svalbard and Franz Josef's Land of over 2.5°C. Northern Europe enjoyed warmer springs and summers and this was marked by the westward movement of Siberian birds, especially young ones, into Fenno-Scandia, Denmark and Germany. Arctic and Greenish Warblers pushed west, Savi's and Bonelli's Warblers moved northwards and the Firecrest expanded its range on the Continent. In the British Isles the Sedge Warbler colonized the Outer Isles from the 1920s, the Wood Warbler reached the extreme north of Scotland in the 1940s and in the early 1950s the Chiffchaff also spread in Scotland. Easterly winds still brought vagrants from Siberia and westerly winds from North America.

However, during the period from 1961 to 1970 the average temperatures showed that the Arctic was getting colder again and 'an area over Franz Josef's Land was 5°C colder than in several preceding decades' (Lamb 1975). The region of Arctic cooling soon embraced Iceland and northern Europe and by 1968 the Arctic sea-ice was further south than it had been for half a century. Between 1967 and 1972 the global snow and ice cover increased by 12%. In the winter of 1973–4 this trend underwent a reversal but it was short-lived; later in 1974 the area under ice and snow was still about 10% greater than in 1967. The mild winters at this time in the British Isles have to be viewed against a very fragile, unstable background. Slow climatic changes may take time to show themselves in bird populations which are not always the best indicators of change; butterflies and moths may be more sensitive barometers of change (Burton 1975). (For further general information on birds and weather the reader should consult

Weather and Bird Behaviour (1983) by a professional meteorologist and experienced ornithologist, Norman Elkins, and also see Williamson (1976).) Chiffchaffs and Blackcaps are able to survive the winter months in the more southerly parts of the British Isles as well as around the basin of the Mediterranean and along the southern fringes of Asia.

R. E. Moreau (1970) indicated that, apart from the raptors and aquatic birds that go to Africa, the entire population or a large part of it of 99 species of bird from Europe and Asia as far as the Bering Straits 'go to spend the winter in Africa south of the Sahara and 30 of these are "warblers".' In all, 92 of the wintering species are insectivorous but some can benefit from temporary and often local supplies of berries. The map, after Valverde (1958), shows the three main ecological zones of the western and

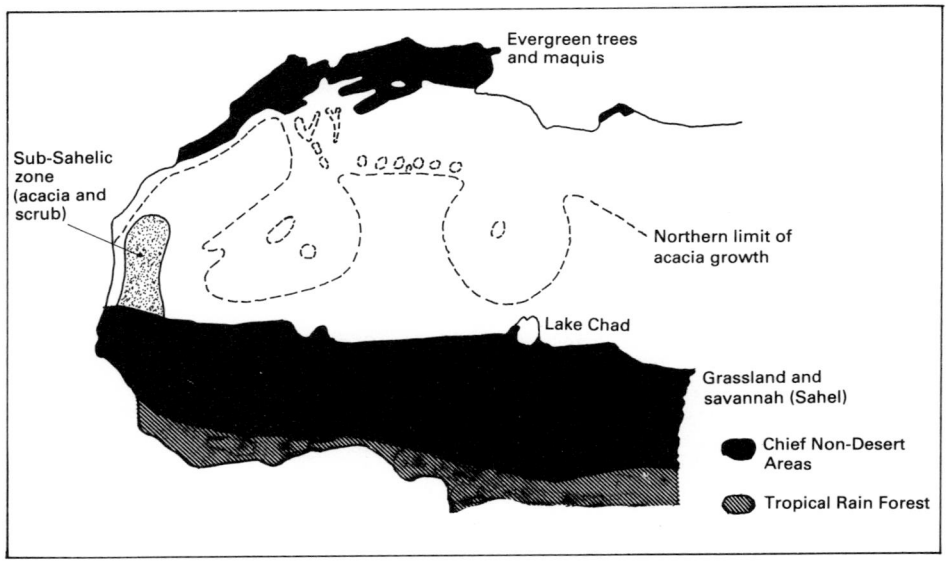

Fig. 177
The western and central Sahara Desert. (After Valverde 1958)

central Sahara. During the ice ages and for some time afterwards the Sahara carried quite an amount of vegetation while the country to the south was covered not by today's tropical plants but those of forest and montane habitats. At this time, with most of Europe in the grip of ice, there would have been few migrants to fly to the African Continent, while Palaearctic Asia would have provided by far the greater part of the migrants flooding southwest to Africa. As late as 5000 years ago both large native mammals and man would have been free to move through the western Sahara because of the richness of its vegetation, Mediterranean in form at first and later more African. This would have been a refuge for the Chiffchaff, which now is forced to winter partly to the north and partly to the south of the Sahara, even being compelled to travel south as far as the equator. Migrants could undertake far shorter migratory flights and there was no need for them to fatten up in preparation for long unbroken journeys. In the Sahel, to the south of the Sahara, the vegetation consists of lowland evergreen forest often along river courses and favoured by Wood

Warblers, montane evergreen forest more open in character than the lowland woods, with ecotones that often hold Blackcaps and Garden Warblers,
and open country of semi-desert treeless land or acacia steppe whose small
scattered trees are inhabited by many Palaearctic warblers, since there is
sometimes a rich insect fauna.

It is rain rather than temperature that controls the very delicate ecological
balance in that belt of Africa between 10°N and 20°N. The rains come
over a limited period from May or June to October so that from the time
that migrants arrive in the autumn the drought is continuous and there is a
corresponding deterioration in the environment. The rains move northwards in the summer months and retreat southwards in the autumn, with
a drop in the mean seasonal rainfall from about 1200 mm or more at 10°N
to only 50 mm at 20°N. When the warblers first arrive from the north the
land is normally still green and Whitethroats remain in the northern semi-
desert or Sahel zone apparently for the winter; but others, including
Willow, Garden and Melodious Warblers, move on south (Morel 1973).
This suggests that the regions cannot provide sufficient reserves of food.
Yet the savannah of the Sahel with acacias, *Balamites* and *Zizyphus* can
support some insectivorous birds. North of the equator the Palaearctic
warblers are absent during the breeding season of African species so that
competition does not occur. Many warblers favour acacia savannah and
south of the equator, for example in the Serengeti, they are present when
African species are breeding, but the former only overlapped with African
species 'where the latter was at medium to low densities, and even in these
areas migrants were outnumbered' (Sinclair 1978). In this southern
tropical savannah migrants will often move from areas of drought to wet
regions where rain has fallen recently, but in the Sahel to the north of the
Equator warblers have to face six months without rain. Yet some migrants
seem able to put on enough fat to accomplish the return journey across the
Sahara.

During the 1950s the rainfall in the Sahel was above average, coinciding
with at first dramatic increases in Britain in breeding Blackcaps, Garden
Warblers and Chiffchaffs which then slowed and were followed by decline
and then an increase. Since 1968 the rainfall has been well below normal,
bringing about severe drought for the next sixteen years and resulting in the
appalling loss of human life in the Sahel, Chad, the Sudan and Ethiopia.
We have seen earlier how the breeding population of Whitethroats in
Britain was reduced in 1969 by 77% of the previous year's level, a downward move that had parallels in Europe (Berthold 1973). The most likely
cause for the steady decline in the rainfall on the southern edge of the
Sahara is 'a decrease in the intensity and northward migration of the
ascending branch of the tropical Hadley cell circulation associated with a
general weakening of the global atmospheric circulation' (Winstanley *et al*
1974). There has therefore been a 200 km southward shift of the Sahara,
with increasing rainfall to the north and severe drought to the south. This
lack of water affected countries from Mauritania across to Ethiopia while
the changing atmospheric pattern in the world may also have brought about
droughts in India, southern Arabia and perhaps even northern South
America. In Africa it seems that the rainfall level may, at the present time,
be on a long downward trend with far-reaching effects not only for the
manner of life and even survival of man and his domestic animals, but also

for the wild mammals, insects and birds. The Whitethroat population has remained, like that of the Lesser Whitethroat, Sedge Warbler and Chiff-chaff, at a comparatively low level since 1969. There does appear to be some evidence that Whitethroats are commoner in suitable habitats in some parts of Britain than in others, which raises the possibility that populations breeding in one area may winter together in another. There is clearly a correlation between high rainfall in the winter quarters and on passage with better survival. There is evidence too that some summer migrants have been arriving later than they did. Mason (1977) has shown how the mean arrival dates for certain warblers have changed in Leicestershire over the years. After comparing the periods 1942–68 and 1969–74 he found that in the second time span the Willow Warbler was late by one day, Blackcap, Sedge Warbler and Chiffchaff by 3 days, Garden Warbler and Lesser Whitethroat by 4, Grasshopper Warbler by 5, Reed Warbler and White-throat by 7 and Wood Warbler by 17 days. Although the lateness was measured in days it was statistically significant. It was thought that colder springs might be responsible for the change.

Within the long-term climatic changes there may be short-term ones as well. Species may or may not be able to adapt to the former, and they may be affected temporarily by the latter. A run of warm winters encouraged the over-wintering of some warblers and Firecrests, while Goldcrests showed remarkable increases through better survival in winter and good breeding seasons. From 1973–5 the Goldcrest was nearly ten times as common as in 1964, but numbers declined from 1976 to a bad low in 1979 after a severe winter. The Common Birds Census of the B.T.O. monitors the annual changes in populations and this project indicates the effects of short-term and long-term weather patterns. Some changes in migrant populations are less easy to explain especially where several parameters may be involved. There was a 54% increase in Chiffchaffs on British farmland and one of 39% in woodland in 1977, while Willow Warblers were at their lowest levels in woods and on farmland since 1965. From 1980–81 the number of woodland Willow Warblers increased and of woodland Chiffchaffs decreased.

When we come to consider the warblers of the British Isles we can see how habitat changes can compound the effects of weather as well as having an independent influence of their own. Two thousand years ago woodland covered more than half the land area of Britain. By 1970, after centuries of clearance by man from the New Stone Age onwards, the figure had fallen to only 6%. With plantings by private landowners and the Forestry Commission the figure now is about 8–9%, far below the figures for Germany, Norway, France and Spain. In Britain in the last 40 years we have lost more of the ancient broad-leaved woods than the amount that disappeared in the preceding 400 years. According to a House of Lords Committee, we have seen the disappearance in the last three or four decades of between a third and a half of our ancient semi-natural woodlands. Some small ancient woods have escaped felling especially those of less than 30–40 hectares. There are many types of ancient woodland and Rackham (1981) listed no fewer than thirty different types in eastern England alone. Large ancient woods have a special value and oak woods especially so, and 'with their open canopies, old trees and rich shrub layer are as rich in bird life as any type of woodland' (Simms 1971). The number of bird species present increases with the size of the wood; a tenfold increase in size doubles the number of bird species present, and woods of over 100 hectares best reveal the potential of this ecosystem.

Many woodland species have adapted to new ways of life in hedgerows and even suburbs but woods remain vital to a number of others. Seminatural woodland is vital for the survival of the Wood Warbler which is commonest in parts of northern and western Britain where large woodlands still survive. In March 1984 the B.T.O. announced a Wood Warbler survey to discover the areas of greatest abundance and the best ways of conserving and improving regions where Wood Warblers are scarce (Cawthorne 1984). In a large broad-leaved wood that I studied for four years in Northamptonshire, five warbler species made up 15% of the total breeding population. Yet small woods and copses also have a part to play, and the process of coppicing small woods gave cyclical advantage to Nightingales and Garden Warblers. Unfortunately 30% of woods of less than a hectare in size were cleared between 1947 and 1972. Clearance has been encouraged by government grants and the Common Agricultural Policy has made farming more worthwhile than forestry. There have also been changes in the style of land ownership with financial institutions taking over from private landowners; in 1977 such bodies purchased more than 10% of all land sold in England and Wales (*H.M.S.O.* 1979). In many instances ancient woods have been sold and replaced by even-aged conifers or by farmland. A simple community is more open to invasion by pests and so it is vital to preserve the greatest variety of natural or semi-natural habitats. Even modern broad-leaved plantations are poorer than the native woods and are felled before reaching their climax and realizing their full potential.

The worsening situation in our native woods alerted conservationists and some landowners to the dangers that were arising. Campaigns have been mounted to identify and conserve the old woodlands. This is an expensive kind of commitment and it would be impractical to seek to preserve all woods as nature reserves. The R.S.P.B. launched a massive Woodland Bird Survival Campaign in 1982 to buy ancient woods, undertake research into management techniques and improve the ecosystems for birds, which would include many warblers. Many old woods have been acquired as reserves at the national level by the Nature Conservancy Council and at the local level by Nature Conservation Trusts. The Woodland Trust has also bought many ancient woodlands since the start of its national development campaign in 1977; up to March 1983 the Trust had spent over £1 million and 'acquired an average of a new wood each month' (James *in litt.* 1983). The National Trust and local authorities have also acquired woodland. The Forestry Commission anticipates a national forest area of 14% of the land area by the year 2025, but Dame Sylvia Crowe, who was the Commission's landscape consultant, indicated that the policy on broad-leaved trees 'should ensure the perpetuation of broadleaves in those parts of the country where they are capable of growing well' and the incorporation of broad-leaved species where possible with those conifers that represented the only viable timber crop. The presence of broad-leaved trees will enhance the woods for small passerine birds including a number of warbler species. A mixed plantation of this kind that I visited in Ulster held at least eighteen different species of birds including warblers and many Redpolls.

Conifers have replaced many of the old broad-leaved woods, bringing favourable conditions for a few years to scrub and grassland warblers and later to Goldcrests and perhaps Firecrests. Woodland and scrub birds replace perhaps the moorland bird species which disappear as the price for afforestation. Yet the Government needs to give stronger encouragement to long-term plans for replanting with hardwoods. Agricultural and forestry grants for timber production have been given to many agencies but the emphasis for broad-leaved planting should be strong. The Countryside Commission has made grants available to plant trees to enhance the country-side and the Nature Conservancy Council has given money for replanting sites of special scientific interest (S.S.S.I.'s) with broad-leaved trees. Bedfordshire County Council has planted some 65,000 trees, mainly oak, ash, beech and hornbeam, in the 1979–80 season, 40% more than in the previous year. The Woodland Trust has launched 'Plant a Tree' campaigns. All this is to be commended but some authorities favour big groves of poplars or lines of *Prunus* or *Acer* species which may have an amenity value for us but little attraction for warblers. Replanting needs care in the selection of trees, according to climate, site and tradition, and I have been only too often appalled by failure to follow up the planting of new trees with proper care and management. I have talked with many foresters; most are concerned about wildlife and some are engaged in a study of the ecology of the woods for which they have responsibility. An empathy with the land and living creatures is essential for there may be a natural inclination to 'clear up' patches of scrub which are regarded as untidy, harbours for pests and so on but where these can be left they have an important role to play. Over-zealous thinning of ash and hazel in one plantation that I know, much of which was for appearance than for any reasons of forestry, resulted in the virtual disappearance of Willow Warbler, Chiffchaff, Garden Warbler and Nightingale. When Willow Warblers decreased over a wide area of woodland at Bookham Common in Surrey (Beven 1963) from 1951 to 1963, the birds were able to maintain their overall numbers by occupying the haw-thorn and rose scrub that had developed on nearby grassland.

Hedgerows, even when tall and overgrown, are not as suitable as mature broad-leaved woodland for some species but Whitethroats, Lesser White-throats, Willow Warblers and, in Ireland, Chiffchaffs are very dependent upon them. However, the loss of hedges has been tremendous. By 1983 more than a quarter of a million kilometres of hedgerow which were standing in 1962, and which largely dated from the Enclosure period of the eighteenth century, had been grubbed up. There has been a corresponding loss of plant species, insects and birds. The destruction of hedgerows, which it is now more widely accepted help to reduce soil erosion, wind-blow and pest-drift and assist in the capture of rain and snow, upsets the ecology of large areas, and reduces the number of passerine birds and use-ful predators like stoats. Certainly some changes are inevitable in a highly mechanized farming world but subsidies have converted much of England into a giant factory. Some hedges go to permit combine harvesters and other machines to operate but many are removed for no real reason. In the autumn of 1983 many surviving hedges were destroyed in South Lincoln-shire by fire from straw and stubble burning – something which need not have happened – and public opinion which held that the land of Britain is held in trust by the farmers brought about a more caring attitude so that in the autumn of 1984 very few incidents in comparison with 1983 occurred.

The remaining hedges are under continuous threat in many areas from mechanical cutters or flails that cut them back, or down to within a metre or less of the ground. The machines often remove saplings that might have replaced, for example, many of the dying ash trees, damage existing trees and, when used as they often are during the breeding season, kill or disturb birds when they are supposedly under some protection from the Wildlife and Countryside Act 1981. Nests, eggs and young may be destroyed or adult birds forced to desert by damage to the hedge from the cutter or to the hedge-foot by the tractor wheels. Many farmers are extremely conservation-minded; here Farming and Wildlife Advisory Groups have an important role in advising and helping farmers towards more realistic conservation methods. Under pressure from conservationists, a spokesman of the National Farmers' Union in March 1984 warned that if farmers were pushed into a corner 'they will go for the throat. Rest assured that a significant proportion will get their tractors out and rip up perhaps a grove of orchids, meadowland and hedgerows out of sheer frustration and annoyance.' It was also said by one with a vested interest in farming that 'hedgerows are not public amenities . . . They are part of a system of farming and any attempt to protect them . . . will fail with absolute certainty.' Farmers own 80% of the land and so a reconciliation with rural decision-makers is absolutely vital for the future of our countryside and its plants, mammals and birds. Indeed the Secretary of State for the Environment in 1979, Michael Heseltine, said that: 'We have . . . to preserve the habitats of wildlife and reconcile conservation of the countryside with the demands of modern agriculture and forestry, and of leisure activities.' In the summer of 1984 I walked along 16 km of truncated hedgerow in Lincolnshire, and only around one field gate, where a short stretch of hawthorn had grown to about 2 m in height, did I find a pair of Whitethroats. Allowing for the losses in Africa this is a poor figure indeed and both Whitethroat species cannot survive where such drastic changes have been made to their habitats. It now seems established that fields of over 40 hectares enjoy no special economic advantage. Even on arable farms where hedges have no value as barriers for stock, or are needed for production, there must surely be an argument for retaining the peripheral hedgerows. Dr Kenneth Mellanby (1982) indicated that by encouraging rather than slandering farmers 'there is some chance that we may retain many more valuable features in our changing countryside.'

Another habitat under threat is that of wetlands which carry a range of plants and animals including some of our most interesting warbler species. For warblers of the *Acrocephalus*, *Cettia* and *Locustella* genera reed beds, fens and marshes are of vital importance. In Britain they are safe in some areas but not so in others. In 1980–81 about £152,000,000 of public money was devoted to land drainage. The R.S.P.B. undertook a survey in 1979 of all the reed beds of more than 2 hectares in size in England and Wales. A total of 109 such reed beds was discovered with the best concentrations in East Anglia and the Norfolk Broads, but overall quite a few of them were senescent. Forty of the sites represented 60% of the total reed bed area and were nature reserves already; another 16% which were in commercial use were thought to be in good heart. Thus about a quarter of the total number were not protected at all. However to maintain the status quo would be insufficient in itself to save the Reed, Sedge, Marsh, Savi's or

Cetti's Warblers that wholly or partly depend upon them. The reed beds will dry out and perhaps in time be replaced by scrub. In the short term they can be improved by irrigation or drainage, additional waterways and control of the reed or scrub but in the longer term the water level may have to be raised or the land lowered, thus extending the life of a reed bed for perhaps fifty years (Bibby 1981). The R.S.P.B. reserve at Titchwell exists as the result of the major empoundment of a watery area.

The Norfolk Broads face a different but no less important threat arising directly from their use for recreation by man. The wash from boats erodes the banks and may swamp nests in the reed beds and sedges. Nitrates and phosphates arrive as effluent from sewage works and as the run-off from agricultural land, which has resulted in eutrophication of the water. With around a quarter of a million visitors each year the Broads have begun to die. The deoxygenation of the water has given it an unhealthy milky appearance and this has had adverse effects on plant life, fish and birds. I wrote in 1979: 'With the development of shacks and shanty towns, the growth of boating and disturbance and the pollution of the water it is rather the confiding common bird species that have survived at the cost of the rarer.' It may be necessary to cut off the Broads with the best conditions for conservation purposes but this would not exclude the construction of new ones as well as other areas where reeds and other aquatic plants could flourish.

If we look at the wetland picture as a whole, we find that only one eighth of the fen and bog present in England and Wales a hundred years ago now remains. To some extent the loss has been made up as the result of mining subsidences and the excavation of marl, sand and gravel-pits which have provided new although artificial habitats. Marl-pits in Cheshire often attract Sedge Warblers while the mining subsidence at Brandon Floods near Rugby which I used to visit when I was teaching in that town provided breeding habitats for Reed and Sedge Warblers, Blackcaps, Whitethroats and Willow Warblers, while others have attracted Savi's and Cetti's Warblers. After the First World War concrete was in great demand as a building material and by 1963 there were some 730 gravel-pits of which 300, or about 40%, were flooded (Simms 1975). From that time something like 1670 more hectares of new sand or gravel extraction were taking place each year. At first the vegetation is slight or absent but after flooding there is often a growth of sedges and reeds; at that time the dominant species are Reed Bunting, Sedge and Reed Warblers. The late Dr Jeffery Harrison who designed and created a management plan for the Sevenoaks gravel-pits, believed that there are 'many opportunities for wetland habitat creation, particularly in conjunction with companies working on mineral extraction, which creates the flooded sand, gravel and clay pits.' Wetlands form one of the most valuable wildlife habitats in the British Isles but we are not always sufficiently aware of their importance in an increasingly urbanized land or of the opportunities to create new ones. The future of some may well depend upon the ability to compensate landowners for loss of income if their drainage should be prevented.

Another rare and fragile habitat is that of heathland, with some of the best examples scattered around Hampshire, Dorset and parts of East Anglia. Because of their special character some have an international significance. Yet between 1962 and 1982 about half of all the heathland in those areas has been converted into farmland or conifer plantation, changed because of different grazing systems, or affected by mineral extraction or urban development. In Dorset alone by 1978 only one sixth of the original habitat in that county still remained. These lowland heaths provided a refuge for all six of Britain's reptile species, many dragonflies and, of course, the Dartford Warbler. Horton Common in Dorset was a Site of Special Scientific Interest; as a Grade 1 site it embraced the whole range of flora and fauna typical of the habitat. It was bought by a private landowner who used bulldozers to convert the land into pasture.

Another threat to Dartford Warblers and other heathland species is fire. Most of the fires are accidental but even the Forestry Commission was guilty of the unfortunate deliberate burning of a Dartford Warbler habitat in the New Forest. Later the following appeared in Notices of Questions and Motions: 23rd July 1980, No 219, The House of Commons; 'That this House congratulates the Dartford warbler on its ability to survive despite the efforts of the Forestry Commission to the contrary.' But this is unusual and it is the discarded cigarette end, the camp fire or sheer vandalism that is the more likely cause.

We know too that Dartford Warblers suffer badly in very severe weather but may recover afterwards. Following the extreme weather in the winter of 1962–3, the population level at only 11 pairs was close to extinction yet by 1974 it had risen to about 560 pairs. Then ensued the dry summer of 1975 and a dry winter too so that the advent of the 'drought' summer of 1976 proved disastrous, with heathland fires devastating vast areas of Surrey with the loss of habitat for Dartford Warblers, Hobbies, Nightjars and Woodlarks, and damaging other regions in the New Forest. Three of the best areas of Hartland Moor National Nature Reserve were destroyed and one third of the Dartford Warblers in Dorset lost their homes. A fire may make a heath unsuitable for a number of years and the burnt region may be colonized by birch and bracken. If such a fire is followed by a bad winter or more fires, then the Dartford Warbler is particularly vulnerable. Perhaps we should declare some rare and valuable habitats 'national monuments' as happens in the United States so that a control of human access and proper schemes of management and protection and adequate fire-fighting precautions can be ensured. Some nature reserves are designed for a high level of visitor use, but others should exist primarily for the species that they are intended to give refuge to, especially where a rare and vulnerable bird like the Dartford Warbler is concerned. There may be cries about personal liberty, and pleas from those who have financed reserves by subscription or gift may not be lightly ignored by any society or organization. Yet it is necessary to preserve a balance between all the contending pressures as the appearance of Sennen Cove, the slopes of Snowdon or Cairngorm and the downland of Box Hill silently demands from us. We cannot unfortunately, as happens in Finland, channel all visitors into one small tundra 'reserve' leaving the rest as true wilderness; we live in too small a country.

I also would like to make a plea for the survival of other rough lands whose grass and scrub used to provide homes for Grasshopper Warblers, Whitethroats and Willow Warblers as well as Whinchats and Stonechats. Some of this country still persists on cliff slopes above the sea, on quarry faces and on land occupied by the military; but its very nature elsewhere often leads to removal, thinning or spraying and being generally 'tidied up' so that it is a diminishing habitat. Willow Warblers often colonize disused allotments and wasteland but rarer species like Whitethroats and Sedge Warblers managed to get a foothold on the neglected and derelict Surrey Docks which became overgrown with grass, weeds, bushes and small trees. This was a habitat with a limited life but other examples may have a better future. Ten hectares of neglected grassland, scrub and woodland on a planned cemetery that was never used by the Welsh Harp reservoir in northwest London and surrounded by houses, gardens and playing fields held seven pairs of Willow Warblers, three of Whitethroats, two of Lesser Whitethroats and one pair each of Garden Warbler and Chiffchaff; a pair of Grasshopper Warblers nested one year (Batten 1972). Although a number of species of warbler find growing urbanization of their habitat distasteful and may move away, the total of 15 pairs of six warbler species just seven miles from the centre of London is worthy of note. This area is now a local authority nature reserve and, if municipal authorities could be persuaded that such habitats deserve conservation, then some security can be given to wildlife in well built-up regions. Yet reserves have to be managed, and scrub and shrub layers treated on proper ecological principles; the decline of Willow Warblers and Chiffchaffs near Gloucester was attributed to an excessive growth of bramble beneath the trees in woodlands (Price 1950, 1961).

We tend now to have a better idea of the ecosystems which birds occupy, and remain only too aware of the gaps in our knowledge; but we have given them in Britain better legal protection and should be able to extend this security to their habitats as well. Much has been done to save habitats through reserves established by the Nature Conservancy Council, the R.S.P.B., the 42 local Nature Conservation Trusts, the National Trust, the Woodland Trust, the Wildfowl Trust, local authorities and so on. This is only part of the answer since some warblers have specific demands: the Dartford Warbler for heathland, the Reed Warbler for *Phragmites* reeds and the Wood Warbler for broad-leaved woods, while others on the limits of their breeding range like the Dartford Warbler, Reed, Marsh and Savi's and Cetti's Warblers and the Lesser Whitethroat may be critically affected by subtle climatic as well as topographical changes which are not easy to monitor.

There is another factor which may be at work as well. Europe's migrant warblers and some of the residents too also have to run the gauntlet of waiting guns, nets and bird lime as they make their journeys across Belgium, France, Spain, Portugal, Italy, Malta and Cyprus. Our summer visitors largely fly southwest in autumn over France and Spain where perhaps the gauntlet is less fierce than it is to the east. It is the breeding birds from Scandinavia and Germany which face the guns in Italy fed annually by 1200 million cartridges. Michael Nicholas (1976) lived for two weeks in a cottage in Tuscany where the lakes and woods for the migrants 'represent an excellent place to break their journey, and the hunter eagerly awaits their arrival.' In fact, in Italy there were 1,701,853 licensed hunters. The legislation for bird protection in Italy reads well but appears to be little observed or applied. The collection of 800,000 names required to hold a referendum in Italy which might abolish hunting was ruled as 'anti-constitutional' by the Italian Constitutional Court in 1981. It is a matter of

Italian persuading Italian, and in that country the position has sometimes changed with the advent of a new government. Countless small birds are trapped in Cyprus and many are pickled and exported in jars as food delicacies. The Smithsonian Institution in America examined 25,202 birds trapped in one Cyprus village in the spring of 1968; there were 100 species represented in the catch and among them were 446 Rüppell's and 98 Cyprus Warblers. If birds are under pressure already from drought in their winter quarters, habitat losses on their breeding grounds, and even the effects of pesticides, such an annual toll of killing might tip the balance. However, the conservation programme of the International Council for Bird Preservation for 1982 carries an item to 'provide financial support through funds raised by a special European Committee for educational and other projects in Mediterranean countries aimed at reducing the killing of migratory birds.' They are surely now no longer the important source of protein that they once were and international agreement must seek to limit this wholesale trapping. A great deal still needs to be done in the protection of not only warblers but many other small passerines. In Belgium in 1981, despite the provisions of the Berne Convention on habitats and the E.E.C. Bird Directive on the Conservation of Wild Birds, permission was given for the capture of 60,000 birds to satisfy songbird fanciers and breeders in that country.

The future for many warbler species will depend upon climatic conditions in their wintering areas – something over which we have no control – as well as weather and habitat conditions in the breeding area. On the breeding ground, animal populations are generally in a state of balance with density-dependent factors tending to suppress the population when it is at a high level and increase it when it is at a low density. Here the most important factors are the reproductive rate, mortality through food shortages, disease, predation and the self-regulating behaviour which is inherent in the territorial system under which many birds live. Food shortages and the taking up of potential nest-sites to the limit may depress numbers. When the population is at a high level there is tendency for birds to disperse into marginal habitats like the Goldcrests, which after the big rise in numbers in the early 1970s, invaded suburban and even urban habitats. In climax broad-leaved woods and other natural communities each of these complex ecosystems is a web of elaborate food-chains and inter-relationships. Thus modern farming methods and those associated with forestry, the loss of habitats whose greatest diversity ensures stability, and the increasing imposition of monocultures and agrochemicals may, if not checked, lead in the end to permanent states of instability in our environment; all this is done in a demand for so-called efficiency and rich short-term profits.

To reconcile the needs of farming, forestry, development, wildlife and amenity with their complex inter-relationships surely cries out for a proper land strategy. With it decisions could then be made about how much land should be devoted to woodland, including both broad-leaved and coniferous trees; to agriculture; to urban development and to the needs of both the human and animal occupants of our countryside. Such a plan put into practice over a 50-year life span could intensify the monitoring and study of habitats, accelerate the ecological research into individual species, expand and improve the level of environmental education, recruit assistance from parish council level to Parliament, allocate money and evolve proper legal and compensatory arrangements for sites of special scientific interest and seek consciously and vigorously to reconcile the many demands upon our countryside. A step in the right direction was the advent of the World Conservation Strategy in 1980, the aims of which were to maintain ecological processes and life-support systems, to preserve genetic diversity and to ensure that we and our children would use species and ecosystems in a proper way. Each nation is expected to apply the strategy according to its own special needs and circumstances. The Conservation and Development Programme for the U.K. (1983) noted that: 'The British public are apparently coming to the view that conservation should be considered and applied across the face of the land and indeed across our coastline to our inshore waters as well.' If this is so then grants over and above those invested in farming should be available for the protection of habitats and wildlife.

There have been no major changes recently in the composition by main species of the avifauna of the British Isles, and indeed there has been an increase in the number of rare breeding species. This condition owes much to serious and sustained efforts in research and conservation, to a growing public awareness and through schemes of monitoring and research to more soundly based scientific inquiry. There are many varied and often beautiful beautiful facets to the countryside of the British Isles with orchards, farms and mountain peaks, oak woods and ancient pine forest, lakes and rivers both in the lowlands and highlands, heathlands and fens, bogs and marshes, chalk downs and heather moors, sand dunes and shingle banks, coastal cliffs and rocky islets. Apart perhaps from some remote stacks and peaks, all these have been largely affected by man and so none are wholly natural. They are therefore subject to change as the result of man's social technological and recreational demands, so it would be Utopian to imagine that one can recreate wildernesses everywhere; we must guard what we have. Conservationists have above all to be informed realists.

In a lecture to Aberdeen University, sponsored by B.P., on 19 October 1983, E. M. Nicholson declared that 'whatever our worries and defeats in conservation generally, the birds dependent on so many diverse habitats and on coping with so many stresses and changes tell us that at least in Britain things are not too bad for them, and are on balance improving rather than deteriorating.' I would like to think that Nicholson's optimistic view will be strengthened in the future by a national strategy for our land that will benefit wildlife including that most attractive family of birds – the warblers – whose delicate forms and often sweet refreshing songs bring delight each year to so many parts of our countryside.

Bibliography

Chapter 1 **Introducing the Warblers**

Bent, A. C. (1953). *Life Histories of North American Wood Warblers*. U.S. Nat. Mus. Bull. 203. Washington D.C.

Bonham, P. F. (*et al.*) (1970). Four American passerines new to the British and Irish list. *Brit. Birds* 63:145–57.

Elkins, N. (1979). Nearctic landbirds in Britain and Ireland; a meteorological analysis. *Brit. Birds* 72:417–33.

Elkins, N., & Allsopp, K. (1977). Falls of Nearctic passerines in Britain and Ireland. *Brit. Birds* 70:399–400.

Durand, A. L. (1963). A remarkable fall of American land-birds on the 'Mauretania', New York to Southampton, October 1962. *Brit. Birds* 56:157–64.

—— (1972). Landbirds over the North Atlantic: unpublished records 1961–5 and thoughts a decade later. *Brit. Birds* 65:428–42.

Gilliard, E. T. (1958) *Living Birds of the World*. London.

Griscom, L., & Sprunt, A., Jr. (1957). *The Warblers of America*. New York.

Nisbet, I. C. T. (1963). American passerines in western Europe. *Brit. Birds* 56:204–17.

Peterson, R. T. (1947). *A Field Guide to the Birds*. Cambridge, Mass.

Robbins, C. S. (1980). Predictions of future Neararctic landbird vagrants to Europe. *Brit. Birds* 73:448–57.

Teale, E. W. (1955). *North with the Spring*. London.

Chapter 2 **The Old World Warblers**

Andrew, R. J. The displays given by passerines in courtship and reproductive fighting: a review. *Ibis* 103a:314–48, 549–79.

Armstrong, E. A. (1956). Distraction display and the human predator. *Ibis* 98:641–54.

Beecher, W. J. (1953). A phylogeny of the *Oscines*. *Auk* 70:270–333.

Cook, R. E. (1970). The sequence of passerine families. *Ibis* 112:118–119.

Cracraft, J. (1973). Continental drift, paleoclimatology, and the evolution and biogeography of birds. *J. Zool.* 169:455–545.

Delacour, J., & Vaurie, C. (1957). A classification of the *Oscines* (Aves). Contributions in *Science*, 16.

Fisher, J. (1966). *The Shell Bird Book*. London.

Gaston, A. J. (1974). Adaptation in the genus *Phylloscopus*. *Ibis* 116:432–50.

Gibb, J. (1947). Some notes on the spectacled warbler in the Maltese islands. *Brit. Birds* 40:298–305.

Gruson, E. S. (1976). *A Checklist of the Birds of the World*. London.

Howard, R., & Moore, A. (1984). *A Complete Checklist of the Birds of the World*. Oxford.

Lack, D. (1940). Courtship feeding in birds. *Auk* 57:169–78.

Lambrecht, K. (1933). *Handbuch der Palaeornithologie*. Berlin.

Leisler, B. (1977). Die Ökologische bedeutung der lokomotion Mitteleuropäischer Schwirle (*Locustella*). *Egretta* 20:1–25.

—— (1977). Ökomorphologische aspekte von speziation und adaptiver radiation bei vögeln. *Vogelwarte* 29:136–53.

Marshall, J. T., & Pantuwattana, S. (1969). Identification of leaf warblers in Thailand. *Nat. Hist. Bull. Siam Soc.* 23:1–8.

Mayr, E., & Amadon, D. (1951). A classification of recent birds. *Amer. Mus. Novitates* 1496.

Mayr, E., & Greenway, J. C. (1956). Sequence of passerine families (Aves). *Breviora* 58.

Moreau, R. E. (1954). The main vicissitudes of the European avifauna since the Pliocene. *Ibis* 96:411–31.

Robertson, A. W. P. (1954). *Bird Pageant*. London.

Sauer, F. (1956). Über das verhalten junger gartengrasmücken, *Sylvia borin* (Bodd.) *J. Orn.* 97:156–89.

Simmons, K. E. L. (1957). The taxonomic significance of the head-scratching method of birds. *Ibis* 99:178–81.

—— (1961). Problems of head-scratching in birds. *Ibis* 103a:37–49.

—— (1974). Types of plumage-scratching in birds. *Avicult. Mag.* 69:143–6.

Snow, D. W. (1978). Relationships between the European and African avifaunas. *Bird Study* 25:134–48.

Voous, K. H. (1977). List of recent Holarctic bird species: passerines. *Ibis* 119: 223–50, 376–406.

Walters, M. (1980). *The Complete Birds of the World*. Newton Abbot.

Chapter 3 Warblers in the British Isles

Andrewartha, H. G., and Birch, L. C. (1954). *The Distribution and Abundance of Animals*. Chicago.

Armstrong, E. A. (1954). The behaviour of birds in continuous daylight. *Ibis* 96:1–30.

Castell, C. P. (1958). The climate and vegetation of the London area in prehistoric times. *Lond. Nat.* 39:5–16.

Curry-Lindahl, K. (1964). *Europe. A Natural History*. London.

Elton, C. S. (1966). *The Pattern of Animal Communities*. London.

Manley, G. (1952). *Climate and the British Scene*. London.

Moore, A. (1984). *A Field Guide to the Warblers of Britain and Europe*. Oxford.

Parslow, J. (1973). *Breeding Birds of Britain and Ireland*. Berkhamsted.

Pfeffer, P. (1968). *Asia. A Natural History*. London.

Simms, E. (1971). *Woodland Birds*. London.

—— (1979). *A Natural History of Britain and Ireland*. London.

Stamp, L. D. (1946). *Britain's Structure and Scenery*. London.

Wilson, J. (1978). The breeding bird community of willow scrub at Leighton Moss, Lancashire. *Bird Study* 25:239–44.

Chapter 4 *Sylvia* or Typical Warblers

Bibby, C. (1979). Breeding biology of the Dartford warbler *Sylvia undata* in England. *Ibis* 121:41–52.

Bourne, W. R. P. (1955). The birds of the Cape Verde Islands. *Ibis* 97:508–56.

Bundy, G. (1976). *The Birds of Libya*. London and New York.

Cudworth, J., and Spence, B. R. (1978). Spectacled warbler: new to Britain and Ireland. *Brit. Birds* 71:53–8.

Davis, P. (1967). Migration seasons of the *Sylvia* warblers at British bird observatories. *Bird Study* 14:69–95.

Dresser, H. E. (1902). *Manual of Palaearctic Birds*. Part 1. London.

Edington, J. M., and M. A. (1972). Spatial patterns and habitat partition in the breeding birds of an upland wood. *J. Anim. Ecol.* 413:331–57.

Efremov, V. D., & Payevsky, V. A. (1973). (Incubation behaviour and incubation patches studied in five species of genus *Sylvia*.) *Zool. Zh.* 52:721–28.

Ferry, C., & Frochot, B. (1970). L'avifaune nidificatrice d'une forêt de chênes pedoncles en Bourgogne; étude de deux successions écologiques. *Terre Vie* 117: 153–250.

Harrison, J. M. (1959). Notes on a collection of birds made in Iraq by F/Lt David L. Harrison. *Bull. B.O.C.* 79:9–13, 31–6, 49–50.

Korodi-Gal, J. (1965). (Contributions to the knowledge of feeding of young Black-caps (*Sylvia atricapilla*) when in the nest.) *Comun. Zool. Bucaresti* 3:67–82.

Marchant, S. (1963). Notes on five species of Iraqi birds. *Bull. B.O.C.* 83:52–6.

Mason, C. F. (1976). Breeding biology of the *Sylvia* warblers. *Bird Study* 23:213–32.

Mead, C. J., & Watmough, B. R. (1976). Suspended moult of Trans-Saharan migrants in Iberia. *Bird Study* 23:187–96.

Meinertzhagen, R. (1949). *Parisoma* in *Sylvia*. *Bull. B.O.C.* 69:109.

—— (1954). *Birds of Arabia*. Edinburgh.

Nisbet, I. C. T. (1962). South-eastern rarities at Fair Isle. *Brit, Birds* 55:74–86.

Pearson, D. J. (1973). Moult of some Palaearctic warblers wintering in Uganda. *Bird Study* 20:24–36.

Persson, B. (1971). Habitat selection and nesting of a south Swedish whitethroat *Sylvia communis* Lath. population. *Ornis Scand.* 2:119–26.

Sauer, E. G. F. (1956). Zugorientierung einer Mönchsgrasmücke (*Sylvia a. atricapilla* L.) unter künstlichem Sternenhimmel. *Naturwiss.* 43:231–2.

—— (1957a). Astronavigatorische Orientierung einer unter künstlichem Sternenhimmel verfrachteten Klappergrasmücke, *Sylvia c. curruca* L. *Naturwiss.* 44:71.

—— (1957b). Die Sternenorientierung nächtlich ziehender Grasmücken (*Sylvia atricapilla, borin* und *curruca*). *Z. Tierpsych.* 14:29–70.

Sauer, E. G. F., & E. (1959). Nächtliche Zugorientierung europäischer Vögel in Süd-westafrika. *Vogelwarte* 20:4–31.

Sharrock, J. T. R. (1968). Migration seasons of *Sylvia* warblers at Cape Clear Bird Observatory. *Bird Study* 15:99–103.

Siefke, A. (1962). *Dorn- und Zaungrasmücke*. Wittenberg Lutherstadt.

Smith, K. D. (1957). An annotated check list of the birds of Eritrea. *Ibis* 99:307–37.

—— (1965). On the birds of Morocco. *Ibis* 107:493–526.

Snow, D. W. (1952). A contribution to the ornithology of north-west Africa. *Ibis* 94:473–98.

—— (1978). op. cit. 2 (25).

Stresemann, E., & V. (1966). Die Mauser der Vögel. *J. Orn. 107 Supp.*

Swann, R. L., & Baillie, S. R. (1979). The suspension of moult by trans-Saharan migrants in Crete. *Bird Study* 26:55–8.

Walraff, G. H. (1960). Does celestial navigation exist in animals? *Cold Spring Harbour Symp. Quant. Biol.* 25:451–61.

Williamson, K. (1959). The September drift-movements of 1956 and 1958. *Brit. Birds* 52:344–77.

Williamson, K., & Whitehead, P. (1963). An examination of blackcap movements in autumn 1959. *Bird Migration* 2:265–71.

Zahavi, A., & Dudai, R. (1974). First breeding record of Blanford's warbler *Sylvia leucomelaena*. *Isr. J. Zool.* 23:55–6.

Chapter 5 **The Garden Warbler**

Berthold, P. (1973). Migration: Control and metabolic physiology. In *Avian Biology* (D. S. Farner and J. R. King eds.) Vol. 4. New York and London.

—— (1973). Relationships between migratory restlessness and migration distance in six *Sylvia* species. *Ibis* 115:594–9.

Berthold, P., Gwinner, E., & Klein, H. (1970). Vergleichen untersuchung der jugendentwicklung eines ausgeprägten Zugvogels, *Sylvia borin*, und eines weniger ausgeprägten Zugvogels, *S. atricapilla, Vogelwarte* 25:297–331.

Berthold, P., Gwinner, E., Klein, H., & Westrich, P. (1972). Beziehungen zwischen zuganruhe und zugablauf bei Garten – und Mönchsgrasmücke (*Sylvia borin* und *S. atricapilla*), *Z. Tierpsychol.* 30:26–35.

Brickenstein-Stockhammer, C., & Drost, R. (1956). Über den zug der europäischen

Grasmücken *Sylvia atricapilla, borin, c. communis* und *c. curruca* nach beringungs-ergebnissen. *Vogelwarte* 18:197–210.

Coward, T. A. (1944). *The Birds of the British Isles and Their Eggs.* London.

Davis, P. (1964). Aspects of autumn migration at the Bird Observatories, 1963. *Bird Study* 11:77–122.

—— (1967). op. cit. 4 (5).

Emlen, S. T. (1967). Migratory orientation of the Indigo Bunting, *Passerina cyanea. Auk* 84:309–42, 463–89.

Ferns, P. N. (1975). Feeding behaviour of autumn passage migrants in north-east Portugal. *Ring. & Migr.* 1 (1):3–11.

Gladwin, T. W. (1969). Post-nuptial wing-moult in the garden warbler. *Bird Study* 16:131–2.

Jardine, Sir W. (1839). *The Natural History of the Birds of Great Britain and Ireland.* Edinburgh.

Lack, D. (1971). *Ecological Isolation in Birds.* Oxford.

Mayaud, N. (1961). Réflexions sur la variation morphologique et les migrations de la fauvette des jardins *Sylvia borin.* Alauda 29:196–204.

Norris, A. S. (1983). Dummy nest-foundation pads of garden warbler. *Brit. Birds* 76:140–3.

Raines, R. J. (1945). Notes on the territory and breeding behaviour of blackcap and garden warbler. *Brit. Birds* 38:202–4.

Sauer, F. (1956). op. cit. 2 (21).

—— (1957). op. cit. 4 (22).

Smith, K. D. (1957). op. cit. 4 (27).

Smith, V. W. (1966). Autumn and spring weights of some Palaearctic migrants in Central Nigeria. *Ibis* 108:492–512.

Snow, D. W. (1976). *The Web of Adaptation.* London.

Solonen, T. (1979). Population dynamics of the garden warbler *Sylvia borin* in southern Finland. *Ornis Fenn.* 56:3–12.

—— (1981). The garden warbler *Sylvia borin* as a member of a breeding bird community. *Ornis Fenn.* 57:58–64.

Thomas, D. K. (1979). Figs as a food source of migrating garden warblers in southern Portugal. *Bird Study* 26:187–91.

Thomson, A. L. (1953). The migrations of British warblers (*Sylviidae*) as shown by the results of ringing. *Brit. Birds* 46:441–50.

Williamson, K. (1959). op. cit. 4 (34).

—— (1970). Birds and modern forestry. *Bird Study* 17:167–76.

Chapter 6 **The Blackcap**

Allen, F. G. H. (1968). Blackcaps eating small snails. *Brit. Birds* 61:374.

Armstrong, E. A. (1947). *Bird Display and Behaviour.* London.

Berthold, P. (1977). The 'Vektoren-Navigations-Hypothese'. Its validity for different populations of the same species. *Naturwiss.* 64:389.

Bezzel, E., Kettle, R. H., & Bullock, D. J. (1966). Blackcap imitating willow warbler's song. *Brit. Birds* 59:502.

Brown, A. P. (1976). Blackcap singing in February. *Brit. Birds* 69:310.

Curber, R. M. (1969). Blackcap imitating song of lesser spotted woodpecker. *Brit. Birds* 62:543–4.

Dachy, P., & Delmée, E. (1965). L'hivernage de la fauvette à tête noire *Sylvia atricapilla* (L.) en Belgique. *Gerfaut* 55:371–83.

Elkins, N. (1978). Calls of blackcap. *Brit. Birds* 71:591.

Fitter, R. S. R. (1978). Do blackcaps have a wryneck-call? *Brit. Birds* 71:189.

Fouarge, J. (1980). (Wintering of blackcaps (*Sylvia atricapilla*) in Belgium). *Aves* 17:17–23.

Gladwin, T. (1969). Weights, foods and survival of blackcaps and chiffchaffs in the British Isles in winter. *Bird Study* 16:133.

Hardy, E. (1978). Winter foods of blackcaps in Britain. *Bird Study* 25:60–61.

Howard, H. E. (1929). *An Introduction to the Study of Bird Behaviour.* Cambridge.

Jordano, P., & Herrera, C. M. (1981). The frugivorous diet of blackcap populations *Sylvia atricapilla* wintering in southern Spain. *Ibis* 123:502–7.

Knight, P. J. (1975). Birds observed at the Banc d'Arquin. *Oxford and Cambridge Mauritanian Expdn. 1973. Rept*: 52–61.

Langslow, D. R. (1976). Weights of blackcaps on migration. *Ring. & Migr.* 1:78–91.

—— (1978). Recent increases of blackcaps at bird observatories. *Brit. Birds* 71: 345–54.

—— (1979). Movements of blackcaps ringed in Britain and Ireland. *Bird Study* 26:239–52.

Leach, I. H. (1981). Wintering blackcaps in Britain and Ireland. *Bird Study 28*: 239–52.

Linsell, S. E. (1949). Winter feeding habits of blackcap. *Brit. Birds* 42:294.

Macdonald, D. (1978). Blackcaps killed by striking window panes. *Brit. Birds* 71: 132–3.

Mackay, K. C. (1940). Blackcaps in Waterford in January. *Brit. Birds* 33:273–4.

Moule, G. W. H. (1966). Blackcap imitating willow warbler's song. *Brit. Birds* 59: 198.

Nicholson, E. M., & Koch, L. (1937). *Songs of Wild Birds.* London.

Palmer-Smith, M. (1955). Wintering blackcaps in Worcestershire. *Brit. Birds* 48: 372–3.

Paull, D. E. (1977). Do blackcaps have a wryneck-call? *Brit. Birds* 70:458.

Richards, E. G. (1952). Song of female blackcap. *Brit Birds* 45:31.

Rodgers, L. F. (1978). Calls of blackcap. *Brit. Birds* 71:591–2.

Sauer, F. (1955). Über variationen der artgesänge bei grasmücken. Ein beitrag zur frage des 'Leierns' der monchsgrasmücke *Sylvia a. atricapilla* (L.) *J. Orn.* 96: 129–46.

Snow, D. W. (1971). Evolutionary aspects of fruit-eating by birds. *Ibis* 113:194–202.

Stafford, J. (1956). The wintering of blackcaps in the British Isles. *Bird Study* 4: 251–7.

Waterston, G. (1957). Blackcaps and other summer migrants wintering in Britain. *Bird Study* 4:108–9.

Williamson, K., & Whitehead, P. (1963). op. cit. 4 (35).

Wood, B. (1982). Weights and migration strategy of blackcaps *Sylvia atricapilla* wintering in Tunisia. *Ibis* 124:66–72.

Wright, A. A. (1946). Blackcap imitating notes of nuthatch. *Brit. Birds* 39:247.

Wright, H. E. (1949). Blackcap feeding young on large dragonfly. *Brit. Birds* 42:246.

Zink, G. (1975). *Der Zug Europäischer Singvögel. Ein Atlas der Wiederfunde Beringter Vögel.* Vol. 1. Schloss-Moggingen.

Chapter 7 **The Whitethroat**

Armstrong, E. A. (1963). *A Study of Bird Song.* New York and Toronto.

Ash, J. S. (1969). Spring weights of trans-Siberian migrants in Morocco. *Ibis* 111: 1–10.

Batten, L. A. (1971). Bird population changes on farmland and in woodland for the years 1968–69. *Bird Study* 18:1–8.

Batten, L. A., & Marchant, J. H. (1977). Bird population changes for years 1975–6. *Bird Study* 24:159–64.

Bergmann, H-H. (1973). Die imitationsleistung einer Mischsänger-Dorngrasmücke (*Sylvia communis*) *J. Orn.* 114:317–38.

Berthold, P. (1973). Über starken Rückgang der Dorngrasmücke *Sylvia communis* und anderer Singvogelarten im westlichen Europa. *J. Orn.* 114:348–60.

Bourne, W. R. P. (1974). Whitethroats and arboviruses. *Brit. Birds* 67:248–9.

Bourne, W. R. P., Bogan, J. A., & Johnson, B. (1976). Whitethroats, organochlorines and arboviruses. *Bird Study* 23:279–80.

Buxton, E. J. M. (1947). Colour of iris in whitethroat. *Brit. Birds* 40:52.

Crowe, R. W. (1955). Parental care in the whitethroat. *Brit. Birds* 48:254–60.

Diesselhorst, G. (1968). Struktur einer Brutpopulation von *Sylvia communis*. Bonn. *Zool. Beitr.* 19:307–21.

Frost, R. A. (1968). Unusual song of whitethroat. *Brit. Birds* 61:468.

Fry, C. H., Ash, J. S., & Ferguson-Lees, I. J. (1970). Spring weights of some Palaearctic migrants at Lake Chad. *Ibis* 112:58–82.

Grey, Lord, of Fallodon (1927). *The Charm of Birds*. London.

Harms, W. (1974). Zum herbstzug der Dorngrasmücke (*Sylvia communis*) in Hamburg. *Hamb. Avifaun. Beitr.* 12:55–61.

Hickton, G. R. (1967). Whitethroat in Nottinghamshire in December. *Brit. Birds* 60:138.

Howard, H. E. (1929). op. cit. 6 (13).

Lanyon, W. E. (1960). The ontogeny of vocalizations in birds. In Lanyon and Tavolga *Animal Sounds and Communication*. Washington D.C.

Lloyd-Evans, L. (1955). Whitethroat capturing hawk-moth. *Brit. Birds* 48:423.

Marchant, J. (1983). Bird population changes for the years 1981–2. *Bird Study* 30: 127–33.

Meadows, B. S. (1967). Whitethroats in London area in winter. *Brit. Birds* 60:302.

Moore, N. W. (1975). Status and habitats of the Dartford warbler, whitethroat and stonechat in Dorset in 1959–60. *Brit. Birds* 68:196–202.

Persson, B. (1974). Degradation and seasonal variation of DDT in whitethroats, *Sylvia communis*. *Oikos* 25:216–21.

Pimm, S. L. (1973). The molt of the European whitethroat. *Condor* 75:386–91.

Richardson, R. A. (1959). Downwind immigration of British whitethroats. *Brit. Birds* 52:131–3.

Roberts, J. L. (1983). Whitethroats breeding on Welsh heather moor. *Brit. Birds* 76:456.

Rogers, E. V. (1964). Unusual song and behaviour of whitethroat. *Brit. Birds* 57: 204–5.

Sage, B. L. (1962). Albinism and melanism in birds. *Brit. Birds* 55:201–25.

Sauer, F. (1954). Die entwicklung der lautäusserungen vom ei ab schalldicht gehaltener Dorngrasmücken (*Sylvia c. communis* Latham) im vergleich mit später isolierten und mit wildlebenden artgenossen. *Z. Tierps.* 11:10–93.

—— (1955). op. cit. 6 (28).

—— (1955). Entwicklung und regression angeborenen Verhaltens bei der Dorngrasmücke (*Sylvia c. communis*) *Act. XI Congr. Int. Orn.* 218–26.

Scott, R. E., & Harrison, J. G. (1965). Notes on variant whitethroats. *Bull. B.O.C.* 85:31–2.

Smith, K. D. (1951). The behaviour of some birds on the British list in their winter quarters. *Brit. Birds* 44:113–17.

Smith, V. W. (1966). op. cit. 5 (19).

Stresemann, E., & V. (1968). Winterquartier und mauser der Dorngrasmücke, *Sylvia communis*. *J. Orn.* 109:303–14.

Summer, G. (1975). Whitethroat feeding on thistle seeds. *Brit. Birds* 68:516.

Swann, R. L., & Baillie, S. R. (1979). op. cit. 4 (31).

Ward, P. (1963). Lipid levels in birds preparing to cross the Sahara. *Ibis* 105:109–11.

Winstanley, D., Spencer, R., & Williamson, K. (1974). Where have all the whitethroats gone? *Bird Study* 21:1–14.

Chapter 8 **The Lesser Whitethroat**

Bewick, T. (1804). *A History of British Birds*. Newcastle.

Brickenstein-Stockhammer, C., & Drost, R. (1956). op. cit. 5 (4).

Coward, T. A. (1944). op. cit. 5 (5).

Davis, P. (1967). op. cit. 4 (5).

Deckert, G. (1955). Beiträge zur Kenntnis der nestbau-technik deutscher Sylviiden. *J. Orn.* 96:186–206.

Erkens, J. (1966). (Two broods per season of the lesser whitethroat). *Limosa* 41:66.

Frost, R. A. (1975). Unusual song of lesser whitethroat. *Brit. Birds* 68:431.

Geyr v. Schweppenburg, H. (1930). Zum zuge von *Sylvia curruca. J. Orn.* 78:49–52, 512–14.

Harrison, C. J. O. (1954). Aggressive display of lesser whitethroat. *Brit. Birds* 47:407.

Hayman, R. W. (1961). Lesser whitethroat feeding on suet. *Brit. Birds* 54:248.

London Natural History Society (1964). *The Birds of the London Area.* London.

Mason, C. F. (1976). op. cit. 4 (14).

Mead, C. J. (1976). The lesser whitethroat *Sylvia curruca* through its year. *Ibis* 118:468.

Moreau, R. E., & Dolp, R. M. (1970). Fat, water, weights and wing-lengths of autumn migrants in transit on the northwest coast of Egypt. *Ibis* 112:209–28.

Payn, W. H. (1962). *The Birds of Suffolk.* London.

Redshaw, K. (1962). Lesser whitethroat attempting to copulate with stone in autumn. *Brit. Birds* 65:127.

Robertson, A. W. P. (1954). op. cit. 2 (20).

Safriel, U. (1968). Bird migration at Elat, Israel. *Ibis* 110:283–320.

Simms, E. (1978). *British Thrushes.* London.

Summers, G. (1973). Lesser whitethroat singing in October. *Brit. Birds* 66:169.

Thomson, A. L. (1953). op. cit. 5 (25).

Tyler, M. W. (1981). Lesser whitethroat dust-bathing. *Brit. Birds* 74:187.

Wallace, D. I. M. (1973). Identification of some scarce or difficult west Palaearctic species in Iran. *Brit. Birds* 66:376–90.

Walpole-Bond, J. (1938). *A History of Sussex Birds.* London.

Warmington, E. H. (1975). Lesser whitethroat. *Lond. Bird Rept.* 38:55.

Chapter 9 **The Dartford Warbler**

Ash, J. S. (1964). Observations in Hampshire and Dorset during the 1963 cold spell. *Brit. Birds* 57:221–41.

Barrington, R. M. (1912). The Dartford warbler in Ireland. *Brit. Birds* 6:220.

Bergmann, H-H. (1978). Étude d'une population des Fauvettes pitchous *Sylvia undata* sur L'ile de Minorque (Baléares). *Alauda* 46:285–94.

Bibby, C. J. (1976). Feeding ecology of the Dartford warbler *Sylvia undata. Ibis* 118:467.

—— (1979). op. cit. 4 (1).

—— (1979). Mortality and movements of Dartford warbler in England. *Brit. Birds* 72:10–22.

Bibby, C. J., & Tubbs, C. R. (1975). Status, habitats and conservation of the Dartford warbler in England. *Brit. Birds* 68:117–95.

Blair, H. M. S. (1965). On erythrism in the eggs of the British race of the Dartford warbler *Sylvia undata dartfordiensis. Ool. Rec.* 39(4):15.

Blondel, J. (1969). *Synécologie des Passeraux Résidents et Migrateurs dans le Midi Méditerranéen Francais.* Marseilles.

Bond, W. R. (1939). The Dartford warbler in Dorset. *Proc. Dorset Nat. Hist. Arch. Soc.* 60:175–81.

Campbell, B. (1975). How wild is our wildlife? *Brit. Birds* 68:37–40.

Constant, P., & Maheo, R. (1970). L'avifaune nicheuse d'une lande xérophile de Bretagne. *Terre Vie* 117:346–55.

Crowley, A. (1869). Number of eggs laid by Dartford warbler. *Zoologist* (Sept. 1869) 1847.

Davis, P. G. (1975). Observations on the nesting of some heathland birds. *Surrey Bird Rept.* 1974:56–63.

—— (1980). Triple-brooded Dartford warbler. *Bird Study* 27:254.

Dobinson, H. M., & Richards, A. J. (1964). The effects of the severe winter of 1962/63 on birds in Britain. *Brit. Birds* 57:373–434.

Fitter, R. S. R. (1949). *London's Birds*. London.

Griffiths, P. R. (1955). Gait of Dartford warbler on ground. *Brit. Birds* 48:373.

Harting, J. E. (1866). *The Birds of Middlesex*. London.

Jardine, Sir W. (1839). op. cit. 5 (12).

Mason, C. J. (1976). op. cit. 4 (14).

Moore, N. W. (1962). The heaths of Dorset and their conservation. *J. Ecol.* 50: 369–91.

—— (1975). op. cit. 7 (21).

Nethersole-Thompson, D. (1933). The field habits, status and nesting of the Dartford warbler *Sylvia undata dartfordiensis*. *Ool. Rec.* 13:49–61.

Newman, E. (n.d.). *Letters of Rusticus on the Natural History of Godalming*.

Newton, A. (ed.) (1894). *Ootheca Wolleyana*. London.

Nicholson, E. M., & Koch, L. (1937). op. cit. 6 (24).

Parslow, J. (1973). op. cit. 3 (8).

Payn, W. H. (1962). op. cit. 8 (15).

Pounds, H. E. (1937). Late brood of Dartford warbler. *Brit. Birds* 30:293.

Raynsford, L. J. (1960). Dartford warblers in Surrey. *Bird Notes* 29:43–4.

—— (1963). A short history of the Dartford warblers in Surrey. *Surrey Bird Rept.* 1961:31–3.

Sharrock, J. T. R. et al. (1983). Rare breeding birds in the United Kingdom in 1981. *Brit. Birds* 76:1–25.

Simms, E. (1957). *Voices of the Wild*. London.

Stone, R. C. (1972). The Dartford warbler in Kent. *Kent Bird Rept.* 20:109–11.

Tallowin, J., & Youngman, R. E. (1978). Dartford warbler associating with stonechat. *Bird Study* 71:182–3.

Tubbs, C. R. (1963). The significance of the New Forest to the status of the Dartford warbler in England. *Brit. Birds* 56:41–8.

—— (1967). Numbers of Dartford warblers in England during 1962–6. *Brit. Birds* 60:87–9.

—— (1969). *The New Forest; an Ecological History*. Newton Abbot.

Venables, L. S. V. (1934). Notes on territory in the Dartford warbler. *Brit. Birds* 28:58–63.

Walpole-Bond, J. (1914). *Field-Studies of Some Rarer British Birds*. London.

Yeates, G. K. (1947). *Bird Haunts in Southern England*. London.

Chapter 10   **Rare Migrant and Vagrant *Sylvia* Warblers**

The Barred Warbler

Baxter, E. V., & Rintoul, L. J. (1947). Barred warblers on Scottish mainland. *Brit. Birds* 40:84.

Christie, D. A. (1975). Studies of less familiar birds. 176. Barred warbler. *Brit. Birds* 68:108–14.

Cornwallis, R. K. (1955). The pattern of migration in 1954 at the east coast bird observatories. *Brit. Birds* 48:429–46.

Davis, P. (1967). op. cit. 4 (5).

Dowsett, R. J. (1969). Barred warbler *Sylvia nisoria* (Bechstein) at Lake Chad. *Bull. B.O.C.* 89:72–3.

Ennion, E. A. R. (1955). Association of barred warbler and red-backed shrike on passage. *Brit. Birds* 48:185–6.

Ferguson-Lees, I. J. (1956). Photographic studies of some less familiar birds. LXXIII. Barred warbler. *Brit. Birds* 49:354–5.

Fernández-Cruz, M. (1974). Recuperación en Barcelona de una Curruca Gavilana (*Sylvia nisoria*) anillada en Finlandia. *Ardeola* 20:374.

Fry, C. H. (1970). Barred warbler. *Birds of the World*. 8:122–3.

Harrison, J. G. (1955). Barred warbler in Orkney in spring. *Brit. Birds* 48:550.
Krampitz, H. E. (1949). Zur verbreitung der sperbergrasmücke (*Sylvia nisoria* Bechst.) in Süddeutschland. *Vogelwelt* 70 (3):65–71.
Meinertzhagen, R. (1941). August in Shetland. *Ibis* 1941, 105:17.
Melcher, R. (1952). Brutvorkommen der spergergrasmücke, *Sylvia nisoria* (Bechst.) im Domleschg (Kt Graubünden). *Orn. Beob*, 49:105–16.
Nisbet, I. C. T. (1962). op. cit. 4 (17).
Rudebeck, G. (1956). Some aspects on bird migration in the western Palaearctic region. *Hanström Festschrift* (Lund):257–68.
Schmidt, E. (1981). *Der Sperbergrasmücke*. Wittenberg-Lutherstadt.
Sharrock, J. T. R. (1973). Scarce migrants in Britain and Ireland during 1958–67. Part 9. Aquatic warbler, barred warbler and red-breasted flycatcher. *Brit. Birds* 66:46–64.
—— (1982). Mystery photographs. 62. Barred warbler. *Brit. Birds* 75:86–7.
Simms, E. (1979). op. cit. 3 (11).
Wartmann, B. (1977). (Distribution and breeding biology of the Barred Warbler *Sylvia nisoria* in Switzerland). *Orn. Beob*, 74:1–11.
Williamson, K. (1965). *Fair Isle and Its Birds*. Edinburgh and London.

The Orphean Warbler

Belman, P. J. (1973). Some notes on the migration and measurements of the Orphean Warbler. *Brit. Birds* 66:72–6.
Beven, G. (1971). Studies of less familiar birds. 163. Orphean warbler. *Brit. Birds* 64:68–74.
Fry, C. H. (1959). Orphean warblers having dark eyes. *Brit. Birds* 52:20–1.
Griffiths, E., Pattenden, B., Phillips, J., & Williams, L. P. (1970). Orphean warbler in Cornwall. *Brit. Birds* 63:178–9.
Smith, K. D. (1957). op. cit. 4 (27).

The Sardinian Warbler

Dennis, R. H. (1967). Sardinian warbler on Fair Isle. *Brit. Birds* 60:483–4.
Ferguson-Lees, I. J. (1967). Studies of less familiar birds. 146. Sardinian warbler. *Brit. Birds* 60:480–1.
Gauci, C., & Sultana, J. (1979). Moult of the Sardinian warbler. *Il-Merill* 20:1–13.
Ogilvie, I. H. (1954). Bird notes from northern Asia Minor, 1946–8. *Ibis* 96:81–90.
Sharrock, J. T. R. (1962). The field identification of Sardinian, subalpine and spectacled warblers in autumn. *Brit. Birds* 55:90–2.
Simms, E. (1957). op. cit. 9 (34).
Stanford, J. K. (1954). A survey of the ornithology of northern Libya. *Ibis* 96:606–24.
ter Haar, G. J., & Kramer, T. (1981). (Sardinian warbler in Amsterdam in winter of 1980–1). *Dutch Birding* 3:102–3.
Tucker, B. W. (1947). Studies of some species rarely photographed. XI. The rufous, Sardinian and olivaceous warblers. *Brit. Birds* 40:335–7.
Wallace, D. I. M. (1968). Distraction display of Sardinian warbler varying according to ground cover. *Brit. Birds* 61:374–5.
Whitaker, B. (1955). Sardinian warbler on Lundy. *Brit. Birds* 48:515.

The Subalpine Warbler

Acklam, G. H., Shepperd, J., & Sutton, R. A. L. (1956). Subalpine warbler in Norfolk. *Brit. Birds* 49:86.
Armitage, J. (1930). Field notes on the subalpine warbler. *Brit. Birds* 24:76–8.
Beven, G. (1967). Studies of less familiar birds. 143. Subalpine warbler. *Brit. Birds* 60:123–9.
Gauci, C., & Sultana, J. (1976). Migration of the subalpine warbler *Sylvia cantillans* through Malta. *Il-Merill* 17:15–20.
Mountfort, G. (1958). *Portrait of a Wilderness*. London.
Sharrock, J. T. R. (1962). op. cit. 10 (31).

Simms, E. (1979). *Wildlife Sounds and Their Recording*. London.
Smith, K. D. (1965). op. cit. 4 (27).
Swift, J. J. (1959). The separation of subalpine and spectacled warblers in juvenile and first-winter plumages. *Brit. Birds* 52:198–9.
Williamson, K. (1952). Subalpine warbler at Fair Isle. *Brit. Birds* 45:260–1.
Yeates, G. K. (1939). Subalpine warbler – colour of legs and display. *Brit. Birds* 32:343.
—— (1946). *Bird Life in Two Deltas*. London.

The Spectacled Warbler

Cudworth, J. & Spence, B. R. (1978). op. cit. 4 (4).
Gibb, J. (1947). op. cit. 2 (9).
Jeal, P. E. C. (1970). Spectacled warbler breeding in Cyprus. *Bird Study* 17:338–40.
Jobson, G. J. (1978). Spectacled warbler in Cornwall. *Brit. Birds* 71:84–5.
Ogilvie, I. H. (1954). op. cit. 10 (30).
Sharrock, J. T. R. (1962). op. cit. 10 (31).
Yeates, G. K. (1943). Some field notes on the spectacled warbler. *Ibis* (1943):68.

The Desert Warbler

Britton, D. J., & Wallace, D. I. M. (1980). The Spurn desert warbler. *Brit. Birds* 73:233–4.
Clafton, F. R. (1972). Desert warbler in Dorset; a species new to Britain and Ireland. *Brit. Birds* 65:460–4.
Cudworth, J. (1979). Desert warbler in Humberside. *Brit. Birds* 72:123–4.
Harris, P. (1977). Desert warbler in Essex. *Brit. Birds* 70:168–9.
Kitson, A. R. (1979). Identification of Isabelline Wheatear, Desert Warbler and three *Phylloscopus* warblers. *Brit. Birds* 72:5–9.
Rogers, M. J., *et al.* (1980). Report on rare birds in Great Britain in 1979. *Brit. Birds* 73:524.

Rüppell's Warbler

Martins, R. P. (1981). Rüppell's warbler, new to Britain and Ireland. *Brit. Birds* 74:279–83.
Meiklejohn, R. F. (1934). Notes on Rüppell's warbler *Sylvia rueppelli* (Temminck). *Ibis* (1934):301–5.
—— (1935). The nesting of Rüppell's warbler *Sylvia rueppelli* (Temm.). *Ibis* (1935): 432–5.
—— (1936). Nesting notes on Rüppell's warbler and black-headed bunting. *Ibis* (1936):377–8.
Rowntree, M. H. (1943). Some notes on Libyan and Egyptian birds. *Bull. Zool. Soc. Egypt* 5:18–32.
Taylor, A. M., & Campey, R. J. (1981). Rüppell's warbler in Devon. *Brit. Birds* 74:528–30.

Marmora's Warbler

Allsopp, K., & Hume, R. A. (1982). Recent reports. *Brit. Birds* 75:391–2.
Diesselhorst, G. (1971). Zur ökologie von Samtkopfgrasmücke (*Sylvia melanocephala*) und Sardengrasmücke (*Sylvia sarda*) im September in Sardinie. *J. Orn.* 112:131–5.
Ferguson-Lees, I. J. (1955). Photographic studies of some less familiar birds. LXV. Marmora's warbler. *Brit. Birds* 48:312.

Chapter 11   Locustella **or Grasshopper Warblers**

Austin, O. L., & Kuroda, N. (1953). The birds of Japan – their status and distribution. *Bull. Mus. Comp. Zool.* 190:No. 4.

Brackenbury, J. H. (1978). A comparison of the origin and temporal arrangements of pulsed sounds in the songs of the grasshopper and sedge warblers, *Locustella naevia* and *Acrocephalus schoenobaenus*. *J. Zool. Lond.* 184:187–206.

Burton, J. F., & Johnson, E. D. H. (1984). Insect, amphibian or bird? *Brit. Birds* 77:87–104.

Collyer, A. A., Beadman, J., & Hill, T. H. (1984). Similarity between songs of two *Locustella* warblers and stridulation of Roesel's bush-cricket. *Brit. Birds* 77:112–15.

Grant, P. J. (1983). Identification pitfalls and assessment problems. 2. Savi's warbler. *Brit. Birds* 76:78–80.

Nisbet, I. C. T. (1967). Migration and moult in Pallas's grasshopper warbler. *Bird Study* 14:96–103.

Riddiford, N. (1983). Recent declines of grasshopper warbler *Locustella naevia* at British bird observatories. *Bird Study* 30:143–8.

Svensson, L. (1975). *Identification Guide to European Passerines*. Stockholm.

Wallace, D. I. M. (1980). Possible future Palaearctic passerine migrants to Britain. *Brit. Birds* 73:388–97.

Chapter 12 The Grasshopper Warbler

Bell, D. G. (1960). An encounter with a grasshopper warbler. *Bird Notes* 29:109–10.

Bewick, T. (1804). op. cit. 8 (1).

British Birds (eds.) (1951). Late nesting in 1950. *Brit. Birds* 44:201–2.

Chadwick, P. J. (1952). Grasshopper warbler: displaying and posturing. *Brit. Birds* 45:77.

Clafton, F. R. (1968). Grasshopper warbler resembling Pallas's grasshopper warbler. *Brit. Birds* 61:269–70.

Fincher, F. (1936). Incubation period of grasshopper warbler. *Brit. Birds* 30:83.

Henry, C. (1972). Notes sur la reproduction et la biologie de la Locustelle tachetée et de la Locustelle luscinioïde. *Oiseau Revue fr. Orn.* 42:52–60.

Hoffman, H. J. (1949). Probable singing by female grasshopper warbler. *Brit. Birds* 42:58–9.

—— (1950). Domed nest of grasshopper warbler. *Brit. Birds* 43:119.

Jardine, Sir W. (1839). op. cit. 5 (12).

King, B. (1968). Late autumn song of grasshopper warbler. *Brit. Birds* 61:136.

Meinertzhagen, R. (1930). *Nicoll's Birds of Egypt*. 2 Vols. London.

Milbled, T. (1978). Unusual song of grasshopper warbler. *Brit. Birds* 71:139.

Morel, G., & Roux, F. (1962). Données nouvelles sur l'avifaune du Sénégal. *L'Oiseau* 32:28–56.

Norris, A. S. (1977). Unusual song of grasshopper warbler. *Brit. Birds* 70:502–3.

North, M., & Simms, E. (1958). *Witherby's Sound Guide to British Birds*. London.

Radford, A. P. (1969). Grasshopper warblers singing persistently in August. *Brit. Birds* 62:498.

Riddiford, N. (1983). op. cit. 11 (7).

Roux, F. (1959). Capture de migrateurs paléarctiques dans la basse vallée du Sénégal. *Bull. Mus. Hist. Nat, Paris* (2) 31:334–40.

Ruttledge, R. F. (1955). Habits of the grasshopper warbler. *Brit. Birds* 48:185.

—— (1955). Leg and bill coloration in the grasshopper warbler. *Brit. Birds* 48:235–6.

—— (1966). *Ireland's Birds*. London.

Taverner, J. H. (1969). Birds singing in lighthouse beams. *Brit. Birds* 62:78.

Thorpe, W. H. (1957). The identification of Savi's, grasshopper and river warbler by means of song. *Brit. Birds* 50:169–70.

—— (1961). *Bird-Song*. Cambridge.

Vader, W. (1977). Notes on the song of a grasshopper warbler (*Locustella naevia*). *Sterna* 16:217–24.

Weismann, C. (1950). Sangen hos Graeshoppesnageren (*Locustella n. naevia* Bodd.) *Dansk. Orn. For. Tids.* 44 (1):19–22.

White, G. (1788). *The Natural History of Selborne*.

Wilson, J. (1978). The breeding bird community of willow scrub at Leighton Moss, Lancashire. *Bird Study* 25:239-44.
Young, G. H. E. (1971). Grasshopper warblers rearing young in exposed and substituted nest. *Brit. Birds* 64:320-1.

Chapter 13 **The Savi's Warbler**

Axell, H. E., & Jobson, G. J. (1972). Savi's warblers breeding in Suffolk. *Brit. Birds* 65:349-55.
Boston, F. N. (1956). Savi's warbler in Cambridgeshire. *Brit. Birds* 49:326-7.
Grant, P. J. (1983). op. cit. 11 (5).
Mead, C. J., & Watmough, B. R. (1976). op. cit. 4 (12).
Pitt, R. G. (1967). Savi's warblers breeding in Kent. *Brit. Birds* 60:349-55.
Sharrock, J. T. R. *et al.* (1975). Rare breeding birds in the United Kingdom in 1973. *Brit. Birds* 68:5-23.
—— (1982). Rare breeding birds in the United Kingdom in 1980. *Brit. Birds* 75: 154-78.
Simms, E. (1979). op. cit. 10 (44).
—— (1984). The songs of three *Locustella* warblers. *Brit. Birds* 77:115.
Smith, K. D. (1957). op. cit. 4 (27).
Spencer, R., *et al.* (1985). Rare breeding birds in the United Kingdom in 1982. *Brit. Birds* 78:69-92.
Stevenson, H. (1866). *The Birds of Norfolk*. London.
Zahavi, A. (1957). The breeding birds of the Huleh Swamp and Lake (Northern Israel). *Ibis* 99:600-607.

Chapter 14 **The Vagrant *Locustella* Warblers**

Boswall, J. (1967). The song of Pallas's grasshopper warbler. *Brit. Birds* 60:523-4.
Broyd, S. J. (1983). Supercilium of Pallas's grasshopper warbler. *Brit. Birds* 76: 89-90.
Davis, P. (1961). Lanceolated warblers at Fair Isle and the problem of identification. *Brit. Birds* 54:142-5.
—— (1962). River warbler on Fair Isle. *Brit. Birds* 55:137-8.
—— (1964). op. cit. 5 (7).
Dennis, R. H. (1973). River warbler on Fair Isle. *Brit. Birds* 66:312-13.
Densley, M. (1982). Identification of Pallas's grasshopper warbler. *Brit. Birds* 75: 133-4.
Dowsett, R. J. (1972). The river warbler *Locustella fluviatilis* in Africa. *Zambia Mus. J.* 3:69-79.
Dresser, H. E. (1902). op. cit. 4 (6).
Harrison, J. M. (1958). River warbler in Switzerland. *Bull. B.O.C.* 78:126.
Kitson, A. R. (1980). Further notes from Mongolia. *Brit. Birds* 73:398-401.
Mather, J. R., *et al.* (1971). Grasshopper warbler or Pallas's grasshopper warbler in Dorset? *Brit. Birds* 64:197-8.
Nisbet, I. T. C. (1967). op. cit. 11 (6).
Page, D., & Greaves, P. K. (1983). Identification of Pallas's grasshopper warbler. *Brit. Birds* 76:88.
Riddiford, N. (1984). Plumage variations and age characteristics of river warblers. *Brit. Birds* 77:214.
Smith, G. (1980). Pallas's grasshopper warbler in Norfolk. *Brit. Birds* 73:417-18.
Williamson, K. (1950). Fair Isle Bird Observatory. Notes on selected species, autumn, 1949. *Brit. Birds* 43:48-51.
—— (1957). Pallas's grasshopper warbler at Fair Isle. *Brit. Birds* 50:395-7.

Chapter 15 **The Cetti's Warbler**

Bibby, C. J. (1982). Polygyny and breeding ecology of the Cetti's warbler *Cettia cetti*. *Ibis* 124:288–301.

Bibby, C. J., & Thomas, D. K. (1984). Sexual dimorphism in size, moult and measurements of Cetti's warbler *Cettia cetti*. *Bird Study* 31:28–34.

Blot, A. (1952). La Bouscarle dans le bassin de la Seine et dans la vallée de la Seille. *Alauda* 20:113–16.

Bonham, P. F. & Robertson, J. C. M. (1975). The spread of Cetti's warbler in northwest Europe. *Brit. Birds* 68:393–408.

Burton, J. F. (1979). Continuous nocturnal singing by Cetti's warbler. *Brit. Birds* 72:184–5.

Ferguson-Lees, I. J. (1964). Studies of less familiar birds. 129. Cetti's warbler. *Brit. Birds* 57:357–9.

Haartman, L. von (1969). Nest-site and evolution of polygamy in European passerine birds. *Ornis Fenn.* 46:1–12.

Harber, D. D. (1964). Cetti's warbler in Sussex. *Brit. Birds* 57:366.

Harvey, W. G. (1977). Cetti's warblers in east Kent in 1975. *Brit. Birds* 70:89–96.

—— (1980). Nocturnal singing by Cetti's warblers. *Brit. Birds* 73:193.

Hollyer, J. N. (1975). The Cetti's warbler in Kent. *Kent Bird Rept.* 22:84–95.

Ireland, D. T. (1984). Nocturnal singing by Cetti's warblers. *Brit. Birds* 77:212.

Le Sueur, F. (1980). Some Cetti's warbler breeding observations. *Bird Study* 27:249–53.

Long, R. (1961). Cetti's warbler in the Channel Islands. *Brit. Birds* 54:208.

—— (1968). Cetti's warblers in the Channel Islands. *Brit. Birds* 61:174–5.

—— (1981). Review of birds in the Channel Islands, 1951–80. *Brit. Birds* 74:327–44.

Mann, D. J. (1979). Cetti's warbler displaying in open. *Brit. Birds* 72:184.

Mead, C. J. (1965). The Sussex Cetti's warbler and the value of fault-bars as a means of ageing birds. *Brit. Birds* 58:227–8.

Mestor, H. (1975). (Biometric features of the west Mediterranean population of Cetti's warblers *Cettia cetti*.) *Ardeola* 21:421–45.

Munn, P. W. (1932). Nesting of Cetti's warbler (*Cettia cetti*). *Oologists' Record* 12:2.

Nicholson, E. M., & Ferguson-Lees, I. J. (1962). The Hastings Rarities. *Brit. Birds* 55:299–384.

Richards, J. H., & Long, R. (1964). Cetti's warblers in Jersey. *Brit. Birds* 57:517–18.

Scott, R. E. (1968). Cetti's warbler in Kent. *Brit. Birds* 61:315–16.

Scott, R. E., & Svensson, L. (1972). Emargination of the primaries of Cetti's warbler. *Brit. Birds* 65:178–9.

Simms, E. (1957). op. cit. 9 (34).

Société d'Études Ornithologiques Aves. (1975). Opération 'Bouscarle de Cetti' (*Cettia cetti*). Réserve d'Harchies. Feuille de Contact. (1975):60–2.

Spencer, R., *et al.* (1985). op. cit. 13 (11).

Suffern, C. (1965). The original misidentification of the Hampshire Cetti's warbler. *Brit. Birds* 58:516–18.

Suffern, C., & Ferguson-Lees, I. J. (1964). Cetti's warbler in Hampshire. *Brit. Birds* 57:365–6.

Tekke, M. J. (1974). Het voorkomen van de Cetti's zanger, *Cettia cetti*, in Nederland van 1968 t/m 1973. *Vogeljaar* 22:280–81.

Trouche, L. (1946). Contribution à l'étude biologique de la Bouscarle de Cetti. *Alauda* 13:27–71.

Yeates, G. K. (1946). op. cit. 10 (50).

Zahavi, A. (1957). op. cit. 13 (5).

Chapter 16 **The Fan-tailed Warbler**

Brock, J. (1978). Spread of the fan-tailed warbler. *Brit. Birds* 71:229.

Cade, M. (1980). Fan-tailed warbler in Dorset. *Brit. Birds* 73:37–8.

Comins, D. M. (1964). Nesting materials used by *Cisticola juncidis* (Rafinesque) *Bull. B.O.C.* 84:141–2.

De Lucca, C. (1967). *Cisticola juncidis* in Malta. *Ibis* 109:623.

Dymond, J. N., & Clarke, P. R. (1978). Fan-tailed warbler in Norfolk. *Brit. Birds* 71:275–7.

Elkins, N. (1975). Voice of the fan-tailed warbler. *Brit. Birds* 68:45.

—— (1976). Passage of fan-tailed warblers *Cisticola juncidis* through Gibraltar. *Ibis* 118:251–4.

Ferguson-Lees, I. J., & Sharrock, J. T. R. (1977). When will the Fan-tailed Warbler colonise Britain? *Brit. Birds* 70:152–9.

Finlayson, J. C. (1979). Movements of the fan-tailed warbler *Cisticola juncidis* at Gibraltar. *Ibis* 121:487–9.

Finlayson, J. C., & Cortes, J. E. (1976). Fan-tailed Warbler passage over Gibraltar. *Bull. Gib. Ornithol. Group* 1:6–7.

Gauci, C., & Sultana, J. (1981). The moult of the fan-tailed warbler. *Bird Study* 28:77–86.

Géroudet, P., & Lévêque, R. (1976). Une vague expansive de la Cisticole jusqu'en Europe centrale. *Nos Oiseaux* 33:241–56.

Gilliéron, G. (1976). La Cisticole des joncs *Cisticola juncidis* aux Grangettes de Noville – Une nouvelle espèce nicheuse en Suisse. *Nos Oiseaux* 33:219–22.

Hermsen, K. (1974). De Waaierstaartrieztzanger *Cisticola juncidis* (Rafinesque) een nieuw soort voor Nederland. *Limosa* 47:163–94.

Lynes, H. (1930). Review of the genus *Cisticola*. *Ibis* (12 ser.) 6 Suppl:1–673.

Motai, T. (1973). (Male behaviour and polygamy in *Cisticola juncidis*.) *Misc. Rep. Yamashina Inst. Orn.* 7:87–103.

Mountfort, G. (1958). op. cit. 10 (42).

North, D. I. (1973). La Cisticole des joncs près de Calais. *Alauda* 41:161.

North, M. E. W. & McChesney, D. S. (1964). *More Voices of African Birds.* Suppl. Notes to LP Disc.

Parrott, J. (1977). The fan-tailed warbler *Cisticola juncidis* in Crete. *Ibis* 119:520–1.

Rogers, M. J. (1968). The song of the fan-tailed warbler. *Brit. Birds* 61:230.

Sharrock, J. T. R. (1972). Fan-tailed warbler in Co. Cork: a species new to Britain and Ireland. *Brit. Birds* 65:501–10.

Sultana, J., & Gauci, C. (1974). *Cisticola juncidis* breeding in Malta. *Ibis* 116:373–4.

—— (1975). The Cetti's warbler and fan-tailed warbler colonising new areas. *Il-Merill* 15:2–3.

Thomas, D. K. (1979). Wing moult in the fan-tailed warbler. *Ringing and Migration* 2:118–21.

Ueda, K. (1984). Successive nest building and polygyny of fan-tailed warblers *Cisticola juncidis*. *Ibis* 126:221–9.

Valverde, J. A. (1958). An ecological sketch of the Coto Doñana. *Brit. Birds* 51:1–23.

White, C. M. (1960). The grassland species of the genus *Cisticola*. *Bull. B.O.C.* 80:124–8.

Yeates, G. K. (1946). op. cit. 10 (50).

Zahavi, A. (1957). op. cit. 13 (13).

Chapter 17 Acrocephalus or Reed Warblers

Bibby, C. J. (1980). Another mystery photograph: Moustached or Sedge Warbler? *Brit. Birds* 73:367–70.

—— (1982). Studies of west Palaearctic birds. 184. Moustached warbler. *Brit. Birds* 75:346–59.

Carlson, K. (1980). Another mystery photograph: Moustached or Sedge Warbler? *Brit. Birds* 73:538–9.

Catchpole, C. K. (1972). A comparative study of territory in the reed warbler (*Acrocephalus scirpaceus*) and sedge warbler (*Acrocephalus schoenobaenus*). *J. Zool.* 166:213–31.

De Roo, A., & Deheegher, J. (1969). Ecology of the great reed warbler, *Acrocephalus arundinaceus* (L.) wintering in the southern Congo savanna. *Gerfaut* 59:260–75.

Diesselhorst, G. (1965). Winter habitat of *Acrocephalus dumetorum*, Blyth. *Bull. B.O.C.* 85:111.

Dyrcz, A. (1974). Factors affecting the growth rate of great reed warblers and reed warblers at Milicz, Poland. *Ibis* 116:330–9.

Eriksson, K. (1969). (On the occurrence of the great reed warbler (*Acrocephalus arundinaceus*) in Finland.) *Ornis Fenn.* 46:80–4.

Fry, C. H., Ash, J. S., & Ferguson-Lees, I. J. (1970). op. cit. 7 (12).

Fry, C. H., Williamson, K., & Ferguson-Lees, I. J. (1974). A new subspecies of *Acrocephalus baeticatus* from Lake Chad and a taxonomic reappraisal of *Acrocephalus dumetorum*. *Ibis* 116:340–6.

Gladwin, T. W. (1963). Increases in weight of *Acrocephali*. *Bird Migration* 2:319–24.

Harvey, W. G., & Porter, R. F. (1984). Field identification of Blyth's reed warbler. *Brit. Birds* 77:393–411.

Hollyer, J. N. (1978). Tail-cocking by moustached warblers. *Brit. Birds* 71:422.

Kluyver, H. N. (1955). Das verhalten des Drosselrohrsängers, *Acrocephalus arundinaceus* (L.) am brutplatz mit besonderer Berucksichtigung der Revierbehauptung. *Ardea* 43:1–50.

Koskimies, P. (1980). (Breeding biology of Blyth's reed warbler *Acrocephalus dumetorum* in S.E. Finland.) *Ornis Fenn.* 57:26–32.

Leisler, B. (1972). Die mauser des Mariskensängers (*Acrocephalus melanopogon*) als ökologisches Problem. *J. Orn.* 113:191–206.

—— (1977). Observations on the moult of the great reed warbler *Acrocephalus arundinaceus*. *Ibis* 119:204–6.

Mellor, M. (1981). Tail-cocking by sedge warbler. *Brit. Birds* 74:444.

Mountfort, G. (1951). Studies of some birds rarely photographed. XXX. The great reed warbler. *Brit. Birds* 44:195–7.

Nisbet, I. C. T., & Lord Medway. (1972). Dispersion, population ecology and migration of eastern great reed warblers *Acrocephalus orientalis* wintering in Malaysia. *Ibis* 114:451–94.

Oreel, G. J. (1981). Tail-cocking by moustached warblers. *Brit. Birds* 74:446.

Parker, S. A., & Harrison, C. J. O. (1963). The validity of the genus *Lusciniola* Gray. *Bull. B.O.C.* 83:65–9.

Pearson, D. J. (1971). Weights of some Palaearctic passerines at Kampala, southern Uganda. *Ibis* 113:173–93.

—— (1973). op. cit. 4 (18).

—— (1975). The timing of complete moult in the great reed warbler *Acrocephalus arundinaceus*. *Ibis* 117:506–9.

—— (1981). Identification of first-winter marsh and reed warblers. *Brit. Birds* 74: 445–6.

Price, M. P. (1969). Nesting habitat of reed and marsh warblers. *Bird Study* 16: 130–1.

Sharrock, J. T. R., Hutchinson, C. D., Preston, K., & Barbier, P. G. R. (1970). The identification of Blyth's reed warbler in autumn. *Brit. Birds* 63:214–6.

Smith, K. D. (1964). *Acrocephalus dumetorum* in Africa. *Bull. B.O.C.* 84:172.

Snow, D. W. (1978). op. cit. 2 (25).

Stresemann, E., & Arnold, J. (1949). Speciation in the group of great reed warblers. *J. Bombay Nat. Hist. Soc.* 48:439–43.

Stresemann, E., & V. (1966). op. cit. 4 (30).

Voous, K. H. (1977). op. cit. 2 (26).

Wallace, D. I. M. (1973). op. cit. 8 (23).

—— (1981). Tail-cocking by moustached warblers. *Brit. Birds* 74:446.

Zahavi, A. (1957). op. cit. 13 (13).

Chapter 18   **The Sedge Warbler**

Anderson, D. R. (1946). Young sedge warblers returning to nest. *Brit. Birds* 39:26.

Bell, B. D., Catchpole, C. K., & Corbett, K. J. (1968). Problems of censusing reed buntings, sedge warblers and reed warblers. *Bird Study* 15:16–21.

Bibby, C. J. (1978). Some breeding statistics of reed and sedge warblers. *Bird Study* 25:207–22.

Bibby, C. J., Green, R. E., Pepler, G. R. M. & Pepler, P. A. (1976). Sedge warbler migration and reed aphids. *Brit. Birds* 69:384–99.

Bonham, P. F., & Sharrock, J. T. R. (1974). Sedge warblers singing in fields of rape. *Brit. Birds* 67:89–90.

Boyd, A. W. (1946). *The Country Diary of a Cheshire Man.* London.

Catchpole, C. K. (1972). op. cit. 17 (4).

—— (1973). Conditions of co-existence in sympatric breeding populations of *Acrocephalus* warblers. *J. Anim. Ecol.* 42:623–35.

—— (1976a). Temporal and sequential organisation of song in the sedge warbler (*Acrocephalus schoenobaenus*). *Behaviour* 59:226–47.

—— (1976b). Song in the sedge warbler. *Ibis* 118:469.

—— (1977). Aggressive responses of male sedge warbler (*Acrocephalus schoenobaenus*) to playback of species song and sympatric species song, before and after pairing. *Anim. Behaviour* 25:489–96.

—— (1981). Sexual selection and the evolution of bird songs. *Ibis* 123:411.

da Prato, E. S. (1980). Bittern-like posture of young sedge warblers. *Brit. Birds* 73:314–15.

Dixon, C. (1909). *The Bird-Life of London.* London.

Frankum, R. G., & R. (1970). Sedge warbler's song resembling marsh warbler's. *Brit. Birds* 63:429–30.

Gillham, E. H., & Homes, R. C. (1950). *The Birds of the North Kent Marshes.* London.

Gladwin, T. W. (1963). op. cit. 17 (11).

Green, R. E. (1976). Adult survival rates for reed and sedge warblers. *Wicken Fen Group Rept.* 8:23–6.

Green, R. E., & Bibby, C. J. (1973). Sedge warblers and aphids. *Wicken Fen Group Rept.* 5:7–11.

Green, R. E., & Davies, N. B. (1972). Feeding ecology of reed and sedge warblers *Wicken Fen Group Rept.* 4:8–14.

Haartman, L. von. (1969). op. cit. 15 (7).

Håland, A., & Byrkjeland, S. (1982). Distribution and breeding habitat of the Sedge Warbler *Acrocephalus schoenobaenus* in western Norway. *Cinclus* 5:65–72.

Hook, J. D. (1982). Ringing report for 1982. *Lond. Bird Rept.* 47:123–7.

Hosking, E., & Newberry, C. (1944). *Birds of the Day.* London.

Hudson, R. (1968). (ed.) News and Comment. *Brit. Birds* 61:535.

Kent, A. K. (1964). The breeding habits of the reed bunting and yellowhammer in Nottinghamshire. *Bird Study* 11:123–7.

Lack, D. (1946). Sedge and reed warblers collecting food outside their territories. *Brit. Birds* 39:97.

—— (1963). Cuckoo hosts in England. *Bird Study* 10:185–202.

—— (1966). Passerine night migrants on Skokholm. *Brit. Birds* 59:129–41.

Leavesley, A. (1957). Unusual nest-site of sedge warbler. *Brit. Birds* 50:78–9.

Lockley, R. M. (1947). *Letters from Skokholm.* London.

Owen, J. H. (1933). The cuckoo in the Felsted district. *Rept. Felsted Sch. Sci. Soc.* 33:25–39.

Parslow, J. (1973). op. cit. 3 (8).

Pearson, D. J., Backhurst, G. C., & D. E. G. (1979). Spring weights and passage of sedge warblers *Acrocephalus schoenobaenus* in central Kenya. *Ibis* 121:8–19.

Pepler, G. R. M. (1976). Autumn passage of sedge warblers at Radipole. *Radipole* 2:25–33.

Raitasuo, K. (1958). The breeding biology of *Acrocephalus scirpaceus* and *A.*

schoenobaenus. *Ornis Fenn.* 35:18–28.

Shepherd, D. (1968). Some studies of sedge warblers at Chew Valley Lake. *Bristol Ornithol.* 1:25–30.

Simms, E. (1952). *Bird Migrants*. London.

Sitters, H. P. (1972). An analysis of the ringing data for the sedge warbler at Slapton Bird Observatory. *Devon Birds* 25:2–20.

Spencer, R. (1971). Report on bird-ringing for 1969. *Brit. Birds* 64:137–86.

Thomas, D. K. (1984). Aspects of habitat selection in the sedge warbler *Acrocephalus schoenobaenus*. *Bird Study* 31:187–94.

Chapter 19 The Moustached Warbler

Bannerman, D. A., & W. M. (1958). *Birds of Cyprus*. Edinburgh.

Bibby, C. J. (1982). op. cit. 17 (2).

Dementiev, G. P., & Gladkov, N. A. (1968). *Birds of the Soviet Union*. Jerusalem.

Ferguson-Lees, I. J. (1954). Photographic studies of some less familiar birds. LIV. Moustached warbler. *Brit. Birds* 47:15–16.

Gillham, E. H., & Homes, R. C. (1952). Moustached warbler in Kent. *Brit. Birds* 45:412–13.

Harber, D. D., & the Rarities Committee (1966). Report on rare birds in Great Britain in 1965. *Brit. Birds* 59:280–305.

Haverschmidt, Fr. (1939). Nest of moustached warbler. *Brit. Birds* 32:306.

Hinde, R. A., & Thom, A. S. (1947). The breeding of the moustached warbler in Cambridgeshire. *Brit. Birds* 40:98–104.

Leisler, B. (1972). op. cit. 17 (15).

—— (1973). Die jahresverbreitung des Mariskensängers (*Acrocephalus melanopogon*) nach beobachtungen und ringfunden. *Vogelwarte* 27:24–39.

—— (1975). Die bedeutung der fussmorphologie für die ökologische sonderung Mitteleuropäischer Rohrsänger (*Acrocephalus*) und Schwirle (*Locustella*). *J. Orn.* 116:117–53.

Meinertzhagen, R. (1950). The record of the moustached warbler breeding in Great Britain. *Bull. B.O.C.* 70:54–5.

Moore, A. (1983). op. cit. 3 (7).

Nicholson, E. M., & Ferguson-Lees, I. J. (1962). op. cit. 15 (21).

Rogers, M. J., & the Rarities Committee. (1980). Report on rare birds in Great Britain in 1979. *Brit. Birds* 73:522.

Simms, E. (1957). op. cit. 9 (34).

Williams, T. (1983). Song period of the moustached warbler. *Brit. Birds* 76:456.

Wooldridge, G. E., & Ballantyne, C. B. (1972). Moustached warblers in Hampshire. *Brit. Birds* 45:219–20.

Yeates, G. K. (1946). op. cit. 10 (50).

Chapter 20 The Reed Warbler

Armstrong, E. A. (1947). op. cit. 6 (2).

—— (1963). op. cit. 7 (1).

Ash, J. S. (1960). Leg coloration of reed warblers. *Brit. Birds* 53:359.

Atkin, K., Townsend, A. D., Pyman, G. A., Swaine, C. M., & Davis, P. (1965). Some comments on the problems of separating reed and marsh warblers. *Brit. Birds* 58:181–8.

Baker, E. C. S. (1942). *Cuckoo Problems*. London.

Bell, B. D., Catchpole, C. K., & Corbett, K. J. (1969). op. cit. 18 (2).

Bell, B. D., Catchpole, C. K., Corbett, K. J., & Hornby, R. J. (1973). The relationship between census results and breeding populations of some marshland passerines. *Bird Study* 20:127–40.

Bezzell, E. (1961). Beobachtungen an farbig beringten Teichrohrsängern (*Acrocephalus scirpaceus*). *Vogelwarte* 21:24–8.

Bibby, C. J. (1978). op. cit. 18 (3).
Billett, D. F. (1952). Double nest of reed warbler. *Brit. Birds* 45:366–7.
Boyd, A. W. (1938). Reed warbler's nest of sheep's wool. *Brit. Birds* 32:83.
—— (1951). *A Country Parish.* London.
Brown, P. E. (1946). Preliminary observations on a colony of reed-warblers. *Brit. Birds* 39:290–308.
Brown, P. E., & Davies, M. G. (1949). *Reed Warblers.* East Molesey.
Bundy, G. (1975). Reed warblers breeding in Shetland. *Brit. Birds* 68:210–11.
Catchpole, C. K. (1971). Polygamy in reed warblers. *Brit. Birds* 64:232–3.
—— (1972). op. cit. 17 (4).
—— (1973a). op. cit. 18 (8).
—— (1973b). The function of advertising song in the sedge warbler (*Acrocephalus schoenobaenus*) and the reed warbler (*A. scirpaceus*). *Behaviour* 46:300–320.
—— (1974). Habitat selection and breeding success in the reed warbler *Acrocephalus scirpaceus. J. Anim. Edol.* 43:363–80.
Chance, E. P. (1940). *The Truth about the Cuckoo.* London.
Chappell, B. M. A. (1949). 'Injury-feigning' by reed warbler. *Brit. Birds* 42:87–8.
Crudas, J., & Devlin, T. R. E. (1965). Letter. *Brit. Birds* 58:476–78.
Davies, N. B., & Green, R. E. (1976). The development and ecological significance of feeding techniques in the reed warbler *Acrocephalus scirpaceus. Anim. Behaviour* 24:213–29.
Davis, P. (1965). Letter. *Brit. Birds* 58:184–8.
Dennis, M. K. (1982). Birds of Rainham Marsh – Ten Years On. *Lond. Bird Rept.* 46:92–104.
Dyrcz, A. (1974). op. cit. 17 (7).
Fitter, R. S. R. (1949). op. cit. 9 (17).
Fogden, M. P. L. (1972). Premigratory dehydration in the reed warbler (*Acrocephalus scirpaceus*) and water as a factor limiting migratory range. *Ibis* 114:548–52.
Fry, C. H., Ash, J. S., & Ferguson-Lees, I. J. (1970). op. cit. 7 (12).
Glue, D., & Morgan, R. (1972). Cuckoo hosts in British habitats. *Bird Study* 19:187–92.
Green, R. E. (1976). Adult survival rates for reed and sedge warblers. *Wicken Fen Group Rept.* 8:23–6.
Green, R. E., & Davies, N. B. (1972). op. cit. 18 (20).
Haverschmidt, Fr. (1949). The clutch of the reed warbler. *Brit. Birds* 42:293–4.
Havlin, J. Nesting behaviour of the great reed warbler on the Náměštske rybníky ponds (Czechoslovakia)). *Zool. Listy* 20:51–67.
Henry, C. (1977). Le nourissage des jeunes chez la Rousserolle Effarvatte (*Acrocephalus scirpaceus*). *Gerfaut* 67:369–94.
Heuwinkel, H. (1978). (The song of the reed warbler with special reference to sound pressure level (loudness)). *J. Orn.* 119:450–61.
Hosking, E. J., & Smith, S. G. (1943). A pair of reed warblers. *Brit. Birds* 37:131–3.
Ireson, G. M. (1965). Letter *Brit. Birds* 58:473–5.
Lack, D. (1946). op. cit. 18 (27).
—— (1963). op. cit. 18 (28).
Long, R. (1964). Exceptional longevity in reed warblers. *Brit. Birds* 57:128–9.
—— (1971). Longevity in reed warblers. *Brit. Birds* 64:462–3.
—— (1975). Mortality of reed warblers in Jersey. *Ringing and Migration* 1:28–32.
Lukeš, S. (1973). Beitrag zur nidobiologie und ökologie des *Acrocephalus scirpaceus scirpaceus* Hermann, 1804. Prírod. čas jihočes. *České Budejovice* 13:161–72.
Marchant, J. H., & Hyde, P. A. (1979). Population changes for waterways birds, 1974–8. *Bird Study* 26:227–38.
Marsh, P. (1982). Grey-and-white juvenile reed warbler. *Brit. Birds* 75:35–6.
Milsom, T. P. (1982). Edge effect on breeding reed warblers in north Humberside. *Bird Study* 29:167–8.
Moule, G. H. (1965). Letter. *Brit. Birds* 58:475–6.
Naylor, A. K., & Green, R. E. (1976). Timing of fledging and passage of reed warblers.

Wicken Fen Group Rept. 8:15–18.

Nicholson, E. M., & Koch, L. (1937). op. cit. 6 (24).

North, M., & Simms, E. (1958). op. cit. 12 (52).

Pearson, D. J. (1973). op. cit. 4 (18).

—— (1981). op. cit. 17 (27).

Price, M. P. (1969). op. cit. 17 (28).

Pring, C. J. (1938). Abnormal nest-building of reed warbler. *Brit. Birds* 32:44.

Pyman, G. A. (1965). Letter. *Brit. Birds* 58:182–3.

Raitasuo, K. (1958). Zur brutbiologie des Teichrorhsängers und des Schiefrohrsängers. *Ornis Fenn.* 35:18–28.

Ruttledge, R. F. (1966). op. cit. 12 (22).

Schiermann, G. (1926). Beitrag zur schädigung der Wirtsvögeldurch *Cuculus canorus. Beitr. z. Fortpfl. biol. d. Vög.* 2:28–30.

Simmons, K. E. L. (1974). Cuckoos and reed warblers. *Brit. Birds* 67:442–3.

Southern, H. N. (1954). Mimicry in cuckoos' eggs. In *Evolution as a Process* (ed. J. S. Huxley). London.

Spencer, R. (1971a). Reed warbler singing in a mist-net. *Brit. Birds* 64:34–5.

—— (1971b). Report on bird-ringing for 1969. *Brit. Birds* 64:137–86.

Springer, H. (1960). Studien an Rohrsängern. *Anz. Orn. Bes. Bayern* 5:389–433.

Thomas, D. K. (1984). Feeding ecology and habitat selection in the reed warbler. *Ibis* 126:454.

Thorpe, W. H. (1959). Talking birds and the mode of action of the vocal apparatus of birds. *Proc. Zool. Soc. Lond.* 132:411–55.

Trelfa, G. (1959). Early nesting of reed warbler. *Brit. Birds* 52:165–6.

Webber, G. L. (1964). Pairing of reed warblers from same brood. *Brit. Birds* 57:253.

Wyllie, I. (1975). Study of cuckoos and reed warblers. *Brit. Birds* 68:369–78.

Chapter 21 The Marsh Warbler

Becker, P., & Lutgen, H. (1976). Sumpfrohrsänger *Acrocephalus palustris* in Südwestafrika. *Madoqua* 9 (3):41–4.

Cantelo, J. (1984). Identification of singing reed and marsh warblers by mouth colour. *Brit. Birds* 77:190–1.

Cavallin, B. (1979). Distribution and density of the marsh warbler *Acrocephalus palustris* in Skane, south Sweden, in 1977. *Anser* 18:243–52.

Dowsett, R. J., & Dowsett-Lemaire, F. (1979). Reed and marsh warbler identification. *Brit. Birds* 72:190–1.

Dowsett-Lemaire, F. (1979a). The sexual bond in the marsh warbler *Acrocephalus palustris. Gerfaut* 69:13–27.

—— (1979b). The imitative range of the song of the marsh warbler *Acrocephalus palustris*, with special reference to imitations of African birds. *Ibis* 121:453–68.

—— (1981a). Eco-ethological aspects of breeding in the marsh warbler *Acrocephalus palustris. Terre et Vie* 35 (3):437–91.

—— (1981b). The transition period from juvenile to adult song in the European marsh warbler. *Ostrich* 52:253–5.

Grant, P. J. (1980). Identification of two first-winter marsh warblers. *Brit. Birds* 73:186–9.

Harthan, A. J. (1938). Some breeding habits of marsh warblers in south Worcestershire. *Brit. Birds* 32:230–2.

—— (n.d.). *The Birds of Worcestershire.* Worcester.

Harvey, W. G., & Porter, R. F. (1984). Field identification of Blyth's reed warbler. *Brit. Birds* 77:393–411.

Hawkins, D. (1973). *Avalon and Sedgemoor.* Newton Abbot.

Koskimies, P. (1980). (Breeding biology of Blyth's reed warbler *Acrocephalus dumetorum* in S.E. Finland). *Ornis. Fenn.* 57:26–32.

Lack, D. (1963). op. cit. 20 (41).

Lemaire, F. (1974). Le chant de la rousserolle verderolle (*Acrocephalus palustris*):

étendue du répertoire imitatif, construction rythmique et musicalité. *Gerfaut* 64:3–28.

—— (1975). Le chant de la rousserolle verderolle (*Acrocephalus palustris*): fidélité des imitations et relations avec les espèces imitées et avec les congénères. *Gerfaut* 65:3–28.

—— (1975). Dialectal variations in the imitative song of the marsh warbler (*Acrocephalus palustris*) in western and eastern Belgium. *Gerfaut* 65:95–106.

—— (1977). Mixed song, interspecific competition and hybridisation in the reed and marsh warblers (*Acrocephalus scirpaceus* and *palustris*). *Behaviour* 63:215–40.

North, M., & Simms, E. (1958). op. cit. 21 (50).

Parslow, J. (1973). op. cit. 3 (8).

Pearson, D. J. (1973). On the wintering of the sprosser *Luscinia luscinia* and the marsh warbler *Acrocephalus palustris* in Kenya. *East Afr. Nat. Hist. Soc. Bull.*, Oct. 1973:140.

—— (1981). op. cit. 17 (25).

Price, M. P. (1969). op. cit. 17 (28).

Southern, J. (1949). Late song of marsh warbler. *Brit. Birds* 42:245–6.

Turner, E. L. (1924). *Broadland Birds.* London.

Wallace, D. I. M. (1978). Mystery photographs. 15. Marsh warbler. *Brit. Birds* 71: 122.

Walpole-Bond, J. (1933). The marsh warbler as a Sussex species. *Brit. Birds* 27: 58–65.

—— (1938). op. cit. 8 (24).

Wiprächtiger, P. (1976). (Breeding biology of the marsh warbler *Acrocephalus palustris*). *Orn. Beob.* 73:11–25.

Yeates, G. K. (1947). op. cit. 9 (42).

Chapter 22   **Rare and Vagrant** *Acrocephalus* **Warblers**

The Great Reed Warbler

De Roo, A., & Deheegher, J. (1969). op. cit. 17 (5).

Dyrcz, A. (1974). op. cit. 17 (7).

—— (1977). Polygamy and breeding success among great reed warblers *Acrocephalus arundinaceus* at Milicz, Poland. *Ibis* 119:73–7.

Esaki, Y. (1981). Female behaviour and pair relation of the polygynous great reed warbler *Acrocephalus arundinaceus* (Aves: Sylviinae). *Physiol. Ecol. Japan.* 18: 77–91.

Haartman, L. von. (1969). op. cit. 15 (7).

Haneda, K., & Teranishi, K. (1968). Life history of the eastern great reed warbler (*Acrocephalus arundinaceus orientalis*). 2. Polygyny and territory. *Japan. J. Ecol.* 18:204–12.

Holmbring, J-A. (1973). The great reed warbler *Acrocephalus arundinaceus* in Sweden in 1971 and a review of its earlier status. *Vår. Fågelvärld* 32:23–31.

Houston, I., & Robinson, W. (1951). Great reed warbler in Kent. *Brit. Birds* 44: 202–4.

Jackson, W. T., & Stone, D. A. (1983). Great reed warbler attacking reed warblers. *Brit. Birds* 76:456.

Kluyver, H. N. (1955). Das verhalten der Drosselrohrsängers, *Acrocephalus arundinaceus* (L.), am brutzplatz mit besondere berücksichtigung der nestbautechnik und der revierbehauptung. *Ardea* 43:1–50.

—— (1961–2). Some observations on the domestic life of the great reed-warbler. *Bird Notes* 30:14–16.

Leisler, B. (1977). op. cit. 17 (17).

Lynes, H. (1938). A contribution to the ornithology of the southern Congo basin. *Rev. Zool. Bot. Afr.* 31:1–122.

Mountfort, G. (1951). op. cit. 17 (18).

Nisbet, I. C. T. & Lord Medway (1972). op. cit. 17 (20).

Pearson, D. J. (1975). op. cit. 17 (26).
Peltzer, R. J. (1972). Notes on the polygamous behaviour of *Acrocephalus arundinaceus*. *Proc. XV. Int. Orn. Congr.*: 676–7.
Reynolds, R. A. W. (1952). Great reed warbler in Sussex. *Brit. Birds* 45:220–2.
Sharrock, J. T. R. (1984). Mystery photographs. 87. Great reed warbler. *Brit. Birds* 77:105–6.
Simms, E. (1976). *Birds of the Air*. London.
Wallace, D. I. M. (1973). op. cit. 8 (23).

The Aquatic Warbler
Ash, J. (1956). Aquatic warbler in Dorset. *Brit. Birds* 49:85.
Axell, H. E. (1955). Aquatic warbler in Kent. *Brit. Birds* 49:85.
Chadwick, P. (1984). Aquatic warbler and streaked sedge warbler. *Brit. Birds* 77:378.
Flumm, D. S. (1984). Letter. *Brit. Birds* 77:377–8.
Heise, G. (1970). Zur brutbiologie des Seggenrohrsängers (*Acrocephalus paludicola*). *J. Orn.* 111:54–67.
Henty, C. J. (1961). Further observations on migration in south-west Africa. *Ibis* 103a:28–36.
Joiris, C., & Sharrock, J. T. R. (1975). The origin of British aquatic warblers. *Brit. Birds* 68:519.
Manser, G. E., & Owen, D. F. (1950). Aquatic warbler in Kent. *Brit. Birds* 43:119.
Meiklejohn, M. F. M., & Reed, L. J. (1955). Aquatic warbler in Middlesex. *Brit. Birds* 48:514.
Moule, G. W. H., Keighley, J., & Harber, D. D. (1950). Aquatic warblers in Norfolk, Pembrokeshire and Sussex. *Brit. Birds* 43:57–9.
Pattenden, B., & Sharrock, J. T. R. (1976). The origin of British aquatic warblers. *Brit. Birds* 69:228–9.
Porter, R. F. (1983). Identification pitfalls and assessment problems. 6. Aquatic warbler. *Brit. Birds* 76:342–6.
Rumsey, S. J. R. (1984). Identification pitfalls: Aquatic warbler. *Brit. Birds* 77:377.
Sharrock, J. T. R. (1973). op. cit. 10 (18).
—— (1974). The origin of British aquatic warblers. *Brit. Birds* 67:443–4.
Smith, F. R., *et al.* (1967). Report on rare birds in Great Britain in 1966. *Brit. Birds* 60:309–38.
Tekke, M. J. (1973). Aquatic warblers breeding in the Netherlands. *Brit. Birds* 66:540–1.
Warburg, G., & Warmington, E. H. (1956). Aquatic warbler in Middlesex. *Brit. Birds* 49:327–8.
Wilkins, J. P. (1939). Aquatic warbler seen in Sussex. *Brit. Birds* 32:273.

Blyth's Reed Warbler
Armstrong, E. A. (1963). op. cit. 7 (1).
Boswall, J. (1968). The song of Blyth's reed warbler. *Brit. Birds* 61:34–5.
Britton, D., Grant, P. J., & Harvey, W. G. (1980). Identification of Blyth's reed and paddyfield warblers. *Brit. Birds* 73:589.
Diesselhorst, G. (1965). op. cit. 17 (6).
Gaston, A. J. (1976). The moult of Blyth's reed warbler *Acrocephalus dumetorum* with notes on the moult of other Palaearctic warblers in India. *Ibis* 118:247–51.
Harvey, W. G., & Porter, R. E. (1984). op. cit. 21 (12).
Hollom, P. A. D. (1960). *The Popular Handbook of Rarer British Birds*. London.
Koskimies, P. (1980). op. cit. 21 (14).
Lister, M. D. (1952). Notes on Blyth's reed warbler in India. *Brit. Birds* 45:328–9.
Merikallio, E. (1958). *Finnish Birds. Their Distribution and Numbers*. Fauna Fennica. 5.
Ptushenko, E. S. (1951–4). In *The Birds of the Soviet Union*. ed. Dementiev, G. P., and Gladkov, N. A. (Vol. VI: 295–300).

Sharrock, J. T. R. (1971). Blyth's reed warbler. *Cape Clear Bird Observatory Rept.* 11:34–8.
—— (1979). Identification of Blyth's reed and paddyfield warblers. *Brit. Birds* 72: 596.
Sharrock, J. T. R., *et al.* op. cit. 17 (29).
Smith, K. D. (1964). op. cit. 17 (30).

The Paddyfield Warbler
Bell, D. G. (1979). Paddyfield warbler in Cleveland. *Brit. Birds* 72:348–51.
Britton, D., Grant, P. J., & Harvey, W. G. (1980). op. cit. 22 (42).
Flumm, D. S., & Lord, N. A. G. (1978). Identification of a paddyfield warbler. *Brit. Birds* 71:95–101.
Kitson, A. R. (1980). op. cit. 14 (11).
Meek, E. R., & Little, B. (1979). Paddyfield warbler in Northumberland. *Brit. Birds* 72:352–7.
Sharrock, J. T. R. (1979). op. cit. 22 (32).
Sushkin, P. (1908). *Die Vögel der Mittleren Kirgisensteppe.* Moscow.
Svensson, L. (1976). op. cit. 11 (8).
Williamson, K. (1954). Paddyfield warbler at Fair Isle. *Brit. Birds* 47:297–301.

The Thick-billed Warbler
Deignan, H. G. (1963). Checklist of the birds of Thailand. *Bull. U.S. Nat. Mus.* 226:175.
Nechaev, V. A. (1963). (New data on the birds of Lower Amur). *Ornitologia* 6:183.
Neufeldt, I. (1967). Studies of less familiar birds. 144. Thick-billed warbler. *Brit. Birds* 60:239–43.
Ptushenko, E. S. (1951–4). In *The Birds of the Soviet Union.* ed. Dementiev, G. P., and Gladkov, N. A. (Vol. VI: 234–8).
Sharrock, J. T. R. (1983). Mystery photographs. 76. Thick-billed warbler. *Brit. Birds* 76:186–7.
Spangenberg, E. P. (1965). (The birds of the Iman River basin). *Sborn. Trudov Zool. Muz. Mosk. Univ.* 9:191.
Taczanowski, L. (1872). Bericht über die ornithologischen Untersuchungen des Dr. Dybowski in Ost-Sibirien. *J. Orn.* 30:353–4.
Williamson, K. (1965). op. cit. 10 (21).
Williamson, K., Thom, V. M., Ferguson-Lees, I. J., & Axell, H. E. (1956). Thick-billed warbler at Fair Isle: a new British bird. *Brit. Birds* 49:89–93.

Chapter 23 **The *Hippolais* or Tree Warblers**

Alexander, H. G. (1955). Field-notes on some Asian leaf-warblers. II. *Brit. Birds* 48:349–56.
Beaman, M., & Woodcock, M. (1978). Head pattern of *Hippolais* warblers. *Brit. Birds* 71:546.
Dean, A. R. (1984). Icterine and melodious warblers in southwest Britain. *Brit. Birds* 77:116–17.
Durango, S. (1948). Om deb gulbröstade Sangarens, *Hippolais icterina* (Vieill.) förekomst och hächningsvanor i Sverige. *Fauna och Flora* 5:186–220.
Ferry, C. & Deschaintre, A. (1966). *Hippolais icterina* et *polyglotta* dans leur zone de sympatrie. *Abstr. Int. Orn. Congr.* 14:57–8.
Grant, P. J. (1978). Head patterns of icterine and melodious warblers. *Brit. Birds* 71:132.
Nisbet, I. C. T., & Smout, T. E. (1957). Field-notes on some birds of south-east Europe. *Brit. Birds* 50:201–4.
Sharrock, J. T. R. (1965). Field-identification of *Hippolais* warblers. *Brit. Birds* 58: 520–1.
—— (1969). Scarce migrants in Britain and Ireland during 1958–67. Part 2. Melo-

dious warbler, icterine warbler and woodchat shrike. *Brit. Birds* 62:300–315.

Smith, K. D. (1957). op. cit. 4 (27).

—— (1959). On the identification of some warblers. *Brit. Birds* 52:31.

Wallace, D. I. M. (1964). Field-identification of *Hippolais* warblers. *Brit. Birds* 57: 282–301.

White, C. M. N. (1960). Notes on some African warblers. *Bull. B.O.C.* 80:18–21.

Williamson, K. (1956). A useful field-character of the icterine warbler. *Brit. Birds* 49:119–20.

Chapter 24 **The Icterine Warbler**

Beven, G. (1974). Studies of less familiar birds. 173. Icterine warbler. *Brit. Birds* 67: 370–6.

Cramp, S., & Conder, P. J. (1970). A visit to the oasis of Kufra, spring 1969. *Ibis* 112:261–3.

Davis, P. (1955). Icterine warbler on Skokholm. *Brit. Birds* 48:550.

Devillers, P. (1964). Les Hypolaïs ictérine et polyglotte. *Aves* 1:5–10.

Dowsett, R. J., & Fry, C. H. (1971). Weight losses of trans-Saharan migrants. *Ibis* 113:531–3.

Durango, S. (1948). op. cit. 23 (4).

Erard, C. (1961). Sur les Hypolaïs (*Hippolais icterina* et *H. polyglotta*). *Alauda* 29: 151–2.

Ferguson-Lees, I. J. (1954). Photographic studies of some less familiar birds. LVI. Icterine warbler. *Brit. Birds* 47:121–3.

Ferry, C. (1974). Fécondité et réussite de la nidification chez le grand Contrefaisant (*Hippolais icterina*) en allopatrie et en sympatrie avec le petit. (*H. polyglotta*). *Jean-le-Blanc* 13:1–10.

Grant, P. J., & Medhurst, H. P. (1982). The Wandlebury warbler. *Brit. Birds* 75: 183–5.

Lack, D. (1971). *Ecological Isolation in Birds*. London.

Lambert, A. (1957). A specific check list of the birds of Greece. *Ibis* 99:43–68.

Lévêque, R. (1957). L'Hypolaïs ictérine en Provence. *Alauda* 25:304.

Paulussen, W. (1950). Nidologische aantekeningen over de spotvogel. *Gerfaut* 40 (3):103–6.

Scott, R. E. (1970). Icterine warbler. *Birds of the World*: 2112–14

Smith, V. W. (1966). op. cit. 5 (20).

Smout, T. C. (1960). Field characters of the icterine warbler in late summer. *Brit. Birds* 53:225.

Van Dobben, W. H. (1949). Nest-building technique of icterine warbler and chaffinch. *Ardea* 37:89–94.

Williamson, K. (1956). op. cit. 23 (14).

Chapter 25 **The Melodious Warbler**

Bannerman, D. A. (1930–51). *The Birds of Tropical West Africa*. London.

—— (1953). *The Birds of West and Tropical Africa*. London.

Blankert, J. J. (1981). (Occurrence of melodious warbler in Benelux). *Dutch Birding* 3:25–6.

Bull, A. J., & Ash, J. S. (1955). Melodious warbler in Dorset. *Brit. Birds* 48:284–5.

Davis, P. (1956). Melodious warbler on Skokholm. *Brit. Birds* 49:233.

Ferguson-Lees, I. J. (1965). Studies of less familiar birds. 131. Melodious warbler. *Brit. Birds* 58:9–10.

Landenbergue, D., & Turrian, F. (1982). (The increase in the melodious warbler, *Hippolais polyglotta*, in the Geneva area). *Nos Oiseaux* 36:245–62, 305–24.

McVail, M. J. (1957). Melodious warbler in Devon. *Brit. Birds* 50:124.

Sharrock, J. T. R. (1969). op. cit. 23 (9).

Simms, E. (1957). op. cit. 9 (34).

Smith, F. R. (1957). Melodious warbler in Devon. *Brit. Birds* 50:124.
Thearle, R. (1955). Melodious warbler on Bardsey. *Brit. Birds* 48:284.
—— (1956). Melodious warbler on Bardsey. *Brit. Birds* 49:232–3.
Whitaker, B. (1955). Melodious warbler on Lundy. *Brit. Birds* 48:284.

Chapter 26   The vagrant *Hippolais* Warblers

The Olivaceous Warbler

Bourne, W. R. P., & Smith, K. D. (1960). Olivaceous warbler in Dorset. *Brit. Birds* 53:312–13.
Chapman, E. A., & McGeogh, J. A. (1956). Recent field observations from Iraq. *Ibis* 98:577–94.
Conder, P. J. (1953). Olivaceous warbler in Pembrokeshire. *Brit. Birds* 46:191–2.
Cramp, S. (1959). Glimpses of Andalucia. *Bird Notes* 28:473–6.
Gent, C. J. (1946). Incubation and fledging period of olivaceous warbler. *Brit. Birds* 39:118.
Greaves, R. H. (1936). Breeding biology of the olivaceous warbler. *Ool. Record* 16:87–8.
Lack, D. (1947). The significance of clutch size. *Ibis* 89:302–52.
Marchant, S. (1963). The breeding of some Iraqi birds. *Ibis* 105:516–57.
Nisbet, I. C. T., & Smout, T. C. (1957). op. cit. 23 (7).
Passburg, R. E. (1959). Bird notes from northern Iran. *Ibis* 101:153–69.
Pettitt, R. G. (1960). Olivaceous warbler in Co. Donegal. *Brit. Birds* 53:311–12.
Pyman, G. A. (1966). Olivaceous warbler in Dorset. *Brit. Birds* 59:197–8.
Simmons, K. E. L. (1952). Some observations on the olivaceous warbler *Hippolais pallida* in Egypt. **Ibis** 94:203–9.
Smith, K. D. (1960). op. cit. 4 (27).
Smith, V. W. (1966). op. cit. 5 (21).
Stubbs, A. (1947). in Tucker, B. W. Studies of some species rarely photographed. XI. The rufous, Sardinian and olivaceous warblers. *Brit. Birds* 40:335–7.
Tucker, B. W. (1947). op. cit. 10 (35).
Wallace, D. I. M. (1966). Olivaceous warblers in the Isles of Scilly. *Brit. Birds* 59:195–7.

The Booted Warbler

Boddy, M. (1981). Booted warbler at Theddlethorpe dunes, 12th October 1980. *Lincs. Bird Rept.* 1980:36.
Chapman, M. S. (1979). Identification of booted warbler. *Brit. Birds* 72:437–8.
Davis, P. (1960). Booted warbler at Fair Isle; the problem of identification. *Brit. Birds* 53:123–35.
Dementiev, G. P., & Fladkov, N. A. (eds.) (1951–4). *The Birds of the Soviet Union.* Moscow.
Demetriades, K. K. (1977). (Nesting of the whimbrel (*Numenius phaeopus*), wood-pigeon (*Columba palumbus*) and booted warbler (*Hippolais caligata*) in the Komi District.) *Ornitologia* 13:189.
Gantlett, S. J. M. (1979). Head pattern of *Hippolais* warblers. *Brit. Birds* 72:82.
Grant, P. J., & Colston, P. R. (1979). Head pattern of *Hippolais* warblers. *Brit. Birds* 72:436–7.
Lister, M. D. (1952). Secondary song of some Indian birds. *J. Bombay Nat. Hist. Soc.* 51:699–706.
Stout, G., & Waterston, G. (1936). The booted warbler on Fair Isle. A new British bird. *Brit. Birds* 30:226–7.

Chapter 27   *Phylloscopus* or Leaf Warblers

Alexander, H. G. (1955). op. cit. 23 (1).
—— (1969). *Some notes on Asian leaf-warblers.* Oxford.

Bannerman, D. A. (1963). *Birds of the Atlantic Islands.* Edinburgh.
Clancey, P. A. (1950). On the racial status of Scottish breeding willow warblers. *Brit. Birds* 43:188–9.
Cody, M. L. (1978). Habitat selection and interspecific territoriality among the sylviid warblers of England and Sweden. *Ecol. Monogr.* 48:351–96.
—— (1979). Resource allocation patterns in Palaearctic warblers (Sylviidae). *Fortschr. Zool.* 25:223–34.
Edington, J. M., & M. A. (1972). op. cit. 4 (7).
Gaston, A. J. (1974). op. cit. 2 (8).
Gätke, H. (1895). *Heligoland. An Ornithological Observatory.* Edinburgh.
Haila, Y., Järvinen, O., Väisänen, R. A. (1980). (Habitat distribution and species associations of land bird populations on the Åland Islands, S.W. Finland). *Ann. Zool. Fennici* 17:87–106.
Hamilton, T. H. (1961). The adaptive significance of intraspecific trends of variations in wing length and body size among bird species. *Evolution* 15:11–13.
Hazelwood, A., & Gorton, E. (1956). On *Phylloscopus trochilus* (Linn.) in Great Britain. *Bull. B.O.C.* 76:11–13.
Jellis, R. (1977). *Bird Sounds and Their Meaning.* London.
Ludlow, F. (1944). The birds of south-eastern Tibet. *Ibis* 86:43–86, 176–208, 348–89.
Merikallio, E. (1958). op. cit. 22 (49).
Saether, B-E. (1983). Habitat selection, foraging niches and horizontal spacing of willow warbler *Phylloscopus trochilus* and chiffchaff *P. collybita* in an area of sympatry. *Ibis* 125:24–32.
Salmonsen, F. (1945). (Notes on the variation and moult in the willow warbler (*Phylloscopus trochilus* (L.)). *Arkiv. for Zoologi.* 36 (17):1–13.
Schubert, M., & G. (1969). Lautformen und verwandtschaftliche Beziehungen einiger Laubsänger. *Z. Tierpsych.* 16:7–22.
Seebohm, H. (1877). On the *Phylloscopi* or willow warblers. *Ibis* (4) 1:66–108.
Snow, D. W. (1978). op. cit. 2 (25).
Thielcke, G., & Linsenmair, K. E. (1963). Zur geographischen Variation des Gesanges des Zilpzalps *Phylloscopus collybita* in Mittel- und Südwesteuropa mit einem Vergleich des Gesanges des Fitis *Phylloscopus trochilus. J. Orn.* 104:327–402.
Wallace, D. I. M. (1980). op. cit. 11 (9).
Watson, G. E. (1962). A re-evaluation and re-description of a difficult Asia Minor *Phylloscopus. Ibis* 104:347–52.

Chapter 28 **The Willow Warbler**

Armstrong, E. A. op. cit. 21 (1).
Arvidson, B. E., & Nilsson, L. (1983). (Breeding biology of the willow warbler *Phylloscopus trochilus* in Swedish Lapland). *Vår Fågelvärld* 42:81–8.
Barrett, J. H. (1948). Unusual song of willow warbler. *Brit. Birds* 41:150–1.
Blair, R. H., & Tucker, B. W. (1941). Nest sanitation, with additions from published sources. *Brit. Birds* 34:206–15, 226–35, 250–5.
British Birds, (eds.) (1953). Unusual nesting site of willow warbler. *Brit. Birds* 46:69.
Brock, S. E. (1910). The willow wrens of a Lothian wood. *Zoologist* (4).14:401–17.
Brown, K. (1948). Absence of feathers in a nest of willow warbler. *Brit. Birds* 41:214.
Brown, R. G. B. (1963). The behaviour of the willow warbler *Phylloscopus trochilus* in continuous daylight. *Ibis* 105:63–75.
Brown, R. H. (1946). Display of the willow warbler. *Brit. Birds* 39:24–5.
Butlin, S. M. (1946). Note of willow warbler. *Brit. Birds* 39:215.
Cheke, A. S., & Ford, H. A. (1966). Unusual song of willow warbler. *Brit. Birds* 59:155.
Clancey, P. A. (1950). op. cit. 27 (4).
Cohen, E. (1951). The leg coloration of the willow warbler. *Brit. Birds* 44:65.
Cramp, S. (1955). The breeding of the willow warbler. *Bird Study* 2:121–35.
da Prato, S. R. D. (1982). Polygamy by willow warblers. *Brit. Birds* 75:406–11.

Dewar, G. A. B. (1906). *The Faery Year*. London.

Dunt, R. H. (1946). Courtship feeding and display flight of willow warbler. *Brit. Birds* 39:25.

Ebenman, B., & Nilsson, S. G. (1981). Size patterns in willow warblers *Phylloscopus trochilus* on islands in a south Swedish lake and the nearby mainland. *Ibis* 123: 528-34.

Edwards, G., Hosking, E., & Smith, S. (1949). Reactions of some passerine birds to a stuffed cuckoo. *Brit. Birds* 42:13-19.

—— (1950). Reactions of some passerine birds to a stuffed cuckoo. II. A detailed study of the willow warbler. *Brit. Birds* 43:144-50.

Fincher, F. (1947). Willow warbler feeding on ants. *Brit. Birds* 40:214.

Fisher, D. J. (1982). Report on roving tit flocks project. *Brit. Birds* 75:370-4.

Frost, R. A. (1966). Unusual song of willow warbler. *Brit. Birds* 59:342.

—— (1978). Willow warblers nesting close together. *Brit. Birds* 71:314.

Gwinner, E., & Dorka, V. (1965). Beobachtungen an Zilpzalp-Fitis-Michsängern. *Vogelwelt* 86:146-50.

Harber, D. D. (1948). Courtship feeding of willow warbler. *Brit. Birds* 41:121.

Harrison, R. (1954). Unusual nesting site of willow warbler. *Brit. Birds* 47:62.

Helb, H-W. (1973). Analyse der artisolierenden Parameter im gesang des Fitis (*Phylloscopus trochilus*) mit untersuchungen zur objektivierung der analytischen methode. *J. Orn.* 114:145-206.

Hicks, N. C. (1946). Young willow warblers returning to nest. *Brit. Birds* 39:178-9.

Hogg, P., Dare, P. J., & Rintoul, J. V. (1984). Palaearctic migrants in the central Sudan. *Ibis* 126:307-31.

Huxley, J. (1956). Abnormal song of willow warbler. *Brit. Birds* 49:154.

King, B. (1958). Willow warbler's unusual song and display-flight. *Brit. Birds* 51:83.

Jellis, R. (1977). op. cit. 27 (13).

Kuusisto, O. (1941). Studien über die ökologie und tagesrhythmick von *Phylloscopus trochilus acredula* (L.) mit besonderer Berücksichtigung der brutbiologie. *Acta. Zool. Fenn.* 31:1-120.

Lawn, M. R. (1978). Bigamous willow warbler. *Brit. Birds* 71:592-3.

—— (1983). Polygamy and double-brooding of willow warbler. *Brit. Birds* 76:413-16.

—— (1984). Song of female willow warbler. *Brit. Birds* 77:488.

Lomas, P. D. R. (1962). Willow warbler attacking posturing robins. *Brit. Birds* 55:239.

Lynes, M. (1979). Bigamous willow warbler. *Brit. Birds* 72:130.

Marchant, S. (1953). Notes on the birds of south-eastern Nigeria. *Ibis* 95:38-69.

—— (1963). Migration in Iraq. *Ibis* 105:369-98.

May, D. J. (1947). Observations on the territory and breeding behaviour of the willow warbler. *Brit. Birds* 40:2-11.

—— (1948). Studies on a community of willow warblers. *Ibis* 91:24-54.

Meinertzhagen, R. (1930). op. cit. 12 (12).

Miles, G. F. (1946). Note on courtship feeding of willow warbler. *Brit. Birds* 39:280.

Morse, D. H. (1974). Niche breadth as a function of social dominance. *Am. Nat.* 108:818-30.

Mylne, C. K. (1948). Threat display of willow warbler. *Brit. Birds* 41:309-10.

Nilsson, S. G. (1977). Density compensation and competition among birds breeding on small islands in a south Swedish lake. *Oikos* 28:170-6.

Norman, S. C. (1983). Growth of nestling willow warblers. *Ringing and Migration* 4:149-53.

Palmgren, P. (1934). Balz als ausdruck der zugekstase bei einem gekäfigten Fitislaubsänger. *Ornis Fenn.* 4:84-6.

Parslow, J. L. F. (1969). The migration of passerine night-migrants across the English Channel studied by radar. *Ibis* 111:48-79.

Parsons, A. G. (1951). Willow warbler wintering in Cornwall. *Brit. Birds* 44:97-8

Passburg, R. E. (1959). op. cit. 26 (10).

Price, M. P. (1936). Notes on population problems and territorial habits of chiffchaffs and willow warblers. *Brit. Birds* 29:159–66.

Riddiford, N. (1982). Do willow warblers migrate in family groups? *Brit. Birds* 75:185.

Riddiford, N., & Auger, R. C. (1983). Weight gains and resumption of passage by willow warblers on spring migration. *Bird Study* 30:229–32.

Riddiford, N., & Chantler, J., & P. (1984). Willow warbler attacking wood mouse. *Brit. Birds* 77:367.

Robertson, A. W. P. (1954). op. cit. 2 (20).

Rowbottom, G. (1952). Unusual feeding behaviour of willow warblers and white-throat. *Brit. Birds* 45:31.

Scott, R. E. (1969). Wing formula of willow warbler and chiffchaff. *Bird Study* 16:60–2.

Siddall, C. K. (1910). Willow wren feigning injury. *Brit. Birds* 4:118.

Siivonen, L. (1949). (Does the willow warbler, *Phylloscopus trochilus* (L.), belong to those species of birds fluctuating greatly in numbers?) *Ornis. Fenn.* 26:89–97.

Simms, E. (1979). op. cit. 3 (11).

Smith, K. D. (1951). op. cit. 7 (33).

Smith, S. (1946). Willow warbler using threat display to artificially produced cuckoo-note. *Brit. Birds* 39:118.

—— (1950). Notes of willow-warbler. *Ibis* 92:151.

Smith, S., & Hosking, E. (1955). *Birds Fighting*. London.

Smith, V. W. (1966). op. cit. 5 (20).

Southern, H. N. (1938). The spring migration of the willow warbler over Europe. *Brit. Birds* 32:202–6.

—— (1938a). The spring migration of the swallow over Europe. *Brit. Birds* 32:4–7.

Southern, J., & Whittenbury, R. (1949). Frequent 'injury-feigning' of willow warbler. *Brit. Birds* 42:245.

Staton, J., & Hicks, N. C. (1946). Young willow warblers returning to nest. *Brit. Birds* 39:178–9.

Tiainen, J. (1981). (Timing of the onset of post-nuptial moult in the willow warbler *Phylloscopus trochilus* in relation to breeding in southern Finland.) *Ornis Fenn.* 58:56–63.

Vernon, C. J. (1965). Incidents of aggressive behaviour by the willow warbler *Phylloscopus trochilus* (Linn.) in its winter quarters. *Bull. B.O.C.* 85:152.

Wallace, D. I. M. (1961). The birds of Regent's Park and Primrose Hill, 1959. *Lond. Bird Rept.* 24:81–107.

Warner, J. G. (1950). Willow warbler nesting in wall. *Brit. Birds* 43:337.

Williamson, K., & Butterfield, A. (1954). The spring migration of the willow warbler in 1952. *Brit. Birds* 47:177–97.

Woods, H. E. (1951). Willow warbler building on occupied nest of whitethroat. *Brit. Birds* 44:279.

Chapter 29   **The Chiffchaff**

Alexander, H. G. (1951). 'Northern' chiffchaffs and kindred *Phylloscopi*. *Brit. Birds* 44:358–60.

Ash, J. S. (1961). A melanistic chiffchaff (*Phylloscopus collybita*) in Dorset. *Bull. B.O.C.* 81:81–2.

Batten, L. A., & Wood, J. H. (1974). Iberian chiffchaff at the Brent Reservoir. *Lond. Bird Rept.* 37:78.

Beckerlegge, J. E. (1951). Winter song of chiffchaff. *Brit. Birds* 44:94.

Beven, G. (1946). Pre-coitional display of chiffchaff. *Brit. Birds* 39:246–7.

—— (1976). Changes in breeding bird populations of an oakwood on Bookham Common, Surrey, over twenty seven years. *Lond. Nat.* 51:7–19.

British Birds (eds.) (1951). 'Northern' chiffchaffs in the British Isles during the winter, 1949–50. *Brit. Birds* 44:94–7.

Brown, P. E., Davies, M. G., & Mytum, E. (1950). Duration of song of chiffchaff. *Brit. Birds* 43:153-4.

Burton, J. F. (1953). Chiffchaff eating aphids in mid-winter. *Brit. Birds* 46:457.

Catley, G. P. (1981). Unusual races of three warbler species recorded in 1981. *Lincs. Bird Rept.* 1981:37.

Coward, T. A. (1944). op. cit. 5 (6).

Cullen, J. M., Guiton, P. E., Horridge, G. A., & Peirson, J. (1952). Birds on Palma and Gomera (Canary Islands). *Ibis* 94:68-84.

da Prato, S. R. D., & E. S. (1983). Probable hybridisation between chiffchaff and willow warbler. *Brit. Birds* 76:248-51.

de Wijs, R. (1984). Chiffchaff in the Netherlands with song resembling Siberian race. *Brit. Birds* 77:24-5.

Dobson, R. (1952). *The Birds of the Channel Islands.* London.

Dove, R. S. (1959). Abnormal song of chiffchaff. *Brit. Birds* 52:390-1.

Fitter, R. S. R. (1957). Abnormal song of chiffchaff. *Brit. Birds* 50:124-5.

Gaston, A. J. (1970). Birds in the central Sahara in winter. *Bull. B.O.C.* 90:53-60.

Geissbühler, W. (1954). Beitrag zur biologie des Zilpzalps, *Phylloscopus collybita*. *Orn. Beob.* 51:71-99.

Gladwin, T. W. (1969). op. cit. 6 (11).

Gooch, B. (1984). Chiffchaffs eating fruit. *Brit. Birds* 77:424-5.

Gray, A. P. (1958). *Bird Hybrids – a Checklist with Bibliography.* Tech. Comm. No. 13. Commonwealth Agricultural Bureaux, Farnham Royal.

Gwinner, E. (1961). Beobachtungen über die aufzucht und jugendentwicklung des Weidenlaubsängers (*Phylloscopus collybita*). *J. Orn.* 102:1-23.

Heaven, A. M. (1982). Wintering by 'Siberian' chiffchaff. *Brit. Birds* 75:384.

Homann, P. (1960). Beitrag zur verhaltensbiologie des Weidenlaubsängers (*Phylloscopus collybita*). *J. Orn.* 101:195-224.

Hunt, O. D. (1948). Winter chiffchaff song. *Brit. Birds* 41:309.

London Bird Reports, 1959-83. Notes on chiffchaffs.

Lord, J., & Munns, D. J. (1970). eds. *Atlas of the Breeding Birds of the West Midlands.* London.

MacAlister, E. (1936). Chiff-chaff and grasshopper-warbler association. *Brit. Birds* 30:131.

Mead, C. J. (1974). *Bird Ringing.* B.T.O. Guide No. 16. Tring.

Meiklejohn, M. F. M. (1952). Habitat of chiffchaff in Scotland. *Scott. Nat.* 64: 114-16.

Parslow, J. L. F. (1969). op. cit. 28 (48).

Paull, D. E. (1984). Chiffchaff in Dorset with song resembling those from Iberia/ North Africa. *Brit. Birds* 77:25.

Penhallurick, R. D. (1978). Chiffchaffs wintering at sewage-works in west Cornwall. *Brit. Birds* 71:183-6.

Pettett, A. (1975). Chiffchaff feeding on acacia gum. *Brit. Birds* 68:45-7.

Saether, B-E. (1983). op. cit. 27 (16).

Schubert, G. (1971). Experimentelle untersuchungen über die artkennzeichnenden Parameter im gesang des Zilpzalps, *Phylloscopus c. collybita*, (Vieillot). *Behaviour* 38:289-314.

Scroope, C. F. (1940). Chiffchaffs in Cork in winter. *Brit. Birds* 33:252.

Simms, E. (1952). op. cit. 18 (37).

—— (1976). op. cit. 22 (20).

Snow, D. W. (1952). op. cit. 4 (29).

Taylor, D. W. (1976). Presumed female chiffchaff singing. *Brit. Birds* 69:64-5.

Thielcke, G., & Linsenmair, K. E. (1963). op. cit. 27 (21).

Tomes, R. F. (1901). In *The Victoria County History of Worcestershire.*

Turček, F. J. (1956). On the bird population of the spruce forest community in Slovakia. *Ibis* 98:24-33.

Williamson, K. (1954). 'Northern' chiffchaffs and their area of origin. *Brit. Birds* 47:49-58.

—— (1965). op. cit. 10 (21).

Chapter 30 **The Wood Warbler**

Blondel, J. (1962). Migration prénuptiale dans les Monts des Ksours. *Alauda* 30: 1–29.

Ferguson-Lees, I. J. (1948). Double brood of wood warbler. *Brit. Birds* 41:274.

Fitter, R. S. R. (1951). see Eds. Wood warblers in Sutherland. *Brit. Birds* 46:114.

Fouarge, J. G. (1968). Le Pouillot siffleur, *Phylloscopus sibilatrix*, Bechstein. *Gerfaut* 58:179–368.

Goodwin, D., & Hayman, R. W. (1951). Wood warblers in Sutherland. *Brit. Birds* 44:98–9.

Grey of Fallodon, Lord. (1947). op. cit. 7 (13).

Gwinner, E. (1969). Untersuchungen zur jahresperiodik von Laubsänger. *J. Orn.* 110:1–21.

Hartert, E. (1923). On the birds of Cyrenaica. *Novit. Zool.* 30:1–32.

Harthan, A. J. (1961). *A Revised List of Worcestershire Birds*. Worcester.

Herman, C. (1971). Évolution de la territorialité dans une population de Pouillots siffleurs, *Phylloscopus sibilatrix*. *Gerfaut* 61:43–86.

Hoffman, H. J. (1949). Variation of song in wood warbler. *Brit. Birds* 42:122.

Lack, E. (1950). Breeding season and clutch-size of the wood warbler. *Ibis* 92:95–8.

Marchant, S. (1953). op. cit. 28 (39).

May, D. J., & Manning, A. (1951). The breeding cycle of a pair of wood warblers. *Brit. Birds* 44:5–10.

Nicholson, E. M., & Koch, L. (1937). op. cit. 6 (24).

Niles, J. (1968). Wood warbler's nest without a dome. *Brit. Birds* 61:175–6.

Oakes, C. (1947). Courtship feeding of wood warbler. *Brit. Birds* 40:116–17.

—— (1953). *The Birds of Lancashire*. Edinburgh and London.

Parslow, J. (1973). op. cit. 3 (8).

Preston, K. (1980). Irish bird sites. *Brit. Birds* 73:62–71.

Price, M. P. (1962). Wood warbler's nest without a dome. *Brit. Birds* 55:446.

Raynsford, L. J. (1957). Excess of male wood warblers. *Bird Study* 4:109.

Robertson, A. W. P. (1954). op. cit. 2 (20).

Rowntree, M. H. (1943). Some notes on Libyan and Egyptian birds. *Bull. Zool. Soc. Egypt* 5:18–32.

Ruttledge, R. F. (1966). op. cit. 21 (59).

Sage, B. (1962). op. cit. 7 (28).

Serle, W. (1965). A third contribution to the ornithology of the British Cameroons. *Ibis* 107:60–94.

Smith, A. H. V. (1958). Excess of male wood warblers. *Bird Study* 5:113.

Smith, K. D. (1968). Spring migration through southeast Morocco. *Ibis* 110:452–92.

Smith, V. W. (1966). op. cit. 5 (19).

Snow, D. W. (1952). op. cit. 4 (29).

Southern, H. N. (1940). The spring migration of the wood warbler in Europe. *Brit. Birds* 34.

Spencer, K. G. (1957). Excess of male wood warblers. *Bird Study* 4:223.

Stanford, J. K. (1954). A survey of the ornithology of northern Libya. *Ibis* 96:606–24.

Stresemann, E. (1955). Die wanderungen des Waldlaubsängers (*Phylloscopus sibilatrix*). *J. Orn.* 96:53–67.

Tiedemann, G. (1971). Zur ökologie und siedlungsdichte des Waldlaubsängers (*Phylloscopus sibilatrix*). *Vogelwelt* 92:8–17.

Valverde, J. A. (1958). Some observations on the migration through the occidental Sahara. *Bull. B.O.C.* 78:1–5.

Wesolowski, T. (1981). (Altruistic wood warblers?) *Notatki Ornitol.* 22:69–71.

White, W. W. (1931). *Bird Life in Devon*. London and Toronto.

Williamson, K. (1965). op. cit. 10 (21).

—— (1969). Bird community in woodland habitats in Wester Ross, Scotland. *Q.J. Forestry* 63:305–28.

—— (1974). Breeding birds in the deciduous woodlands of mid-Argyll, Scotland. *Bird Study* 21:29–44.

Yeates, G. K. (1947). op. cit. 9 (42).

Chapter 31   Rare and Vagrant *Phylloscopus* Warblers

The Arctic Warbler

Lappi, E. (1968). (Occurrence of the arctic warbler (*Phylloscopus borealis*) in northern Karelia). *Ornis Fenn.* 45:89–91.

Lundevall, C. F. (1952). The bird fauna in the Abisko National Park and its surroundings. *Kungl. Svensk. Vetensk. Akad.* 7:1–72.

Rabol, J. (1969). Reversed migration as the cause of westward vagrancy by four *Phylloscopus* warblers. *Brit. Birds* 62:89–92.

Robertson, I. S. (1984). Mystery photographs. 93. Arctic warbler. *Brit. Birds* 77: 415–17.

Swanberg, P. O. (1953). Om nordsångeren (*Phylloscopus borealis* Blas.). *Vår Fågelvärld* 12:49–78.

Swanberg, P. O., & McNeile, J. H. (1953). Studies of some species rarely photographed. LI. Arctic warbler. *Brit. Birds* 46:330–2.

Williamson, K. (1951). Fair Isle Bird Observatory. Notes on selected species, autumn, 1950. *Brit. Birds* 44:117–22.

—— (1955). Arctic warbler trapped at Fair Isle. *Brit. Birds* 48:132–3.

The Greenish Warbler

Axell, H. E. (1958). Greenish warbler in Kent. *Brit. Birds* 51:125–26.

Browne, P. W. P. (1953). Greenish warbler on Great Saltee, Co. Wexford. *Brit. Birds* 46:456.

Browne, P. W. P., & Hitchon, A. (1952). Greenish warbler in Norfolk. *Brit. Birds* 45:413–14.

Bryson, A. G. S. (1956). Greenish warbler in the Isle of May. *Brit. Birds* 49:43–4.

Ferguson-Lees, I. J. (1955). Photographic studies of some less familiar birds. LXVII. Greenish warbler. *Brit. Birds* 48:499–500.

Kitson, A. R. (1979). op. cit. 10 (62).

Lilleleht, V. (1963). (Nesting of the greenish warbler (*Phylloscopus trochiloides viridanus* Blyth) in the middle reaches of the Ahja River.) *Ornitologiline Kogumik* 3:176–94.

Lundberg, S., Hosser, J., & Norbeck, J. (1954). Invasion av Lundsångare (*Phylloscopus trochiloides*) pa Gotska Sandön, 1954. *Vår Fågelvarld* 13:240–4.

Mikelsaar, N. (1963). (The 1937 invasion of the greenish warbler in Estonia). *Ornitologiline Kogumik* 3:148–58.

Price, T. (1981). The ecology of the greenish warbler *Phylloscopus trochiloides* in its winter quarters. *Ibis* 123:131–44.

Sharrock, J. T. R. (1971). Scarce migrants in Britain and Ireland during 1958–67. *Brit. Birds* 64:302–9.

Simms, E. (1964). Greenish warbler. *Lond. Bird Rept.* 29:49.

Thearle, R. (1954). Greenish warbler on Bardsey Island. *Brit. Birds* 47:408.

Välikangas, I. (1951). Die expansion von *Ph. trochiloides viridanus* im nordwesteuropäischen raum, insbesondere nach Finnland, und ihre Ursachen. *Ornis. Fenn.* 28:25–39.

Veroman, H. (1963). (Expansion of the greenish warbler in Estonia). *Ornitologogiline Kogumik* 3:158–74.

Williamson, K. (1951). Fair Isle Bird Observatory. Notes on selected species, autumn, 1950. *Brit. Birds* 44:117–22.

Williamson, K., & Thom, V. M. (1956). Greenish warbler at Fair Isle. *Brit. Birds* 49:42–3.

The Green Warbler
Allsopp, K., & Hume, R. A. (1983). Recent reports. *Brit. Birds* 76:594–9.
Kitson, A. R. (1979). op. cit. 10 (62).

The Yellow-browed Warbler
Alexander, H. G. (1951). The call notes of *Phylloscopus inornatus*. *Brit. Birds* 44: 351–2.
—— (1979). Unusual yellow-browed warblers. *Brit. Birds* 72:130.
Dawson, I., & Allsopp, K. (1984). Recent reports. *Brit. Birds* 77:631–7.
Ferguson-Lees, I. J., & Sharrock, J. T. R. (1967). Recent reports. *Brit. Birds* 60: 534–40.
Hjort, C. (1971). The yellow-browed warbler *Phylloscopus inornatus* wintering in Iran. *Bull. B.O.C.* 91:95.
Kitson, A. R. (1980). Identification of eastern yellow-browed warblers. *Brit. Birds* 73:193–4.
Meek, E. R. (1978). Unusual yellow-browed warbler in Northumberland. *Brit. Birds* 71:464–5.
Phillips, N. J., Wood, V. E., & Bonham, P. F. (1975). Yellow-browed warblers feeding on the ground. *Brit. Birds* 68:249–50.
Quinn, A., & Clement, P. (1979). Plumage of yellow-browed warblers wintering in southern England. *Brit. Birds* 72:484–5.
Rabol, J. (1969). op. cit. 31 (3).
Scott, R. E. (1979). Unusual yellow-browed warbler in Sussex. *Brit. Birds* 72:124–6.
Sharrock, J. T. R. (1980). Mystery photographs. 39. Yellow-browed warbler. *Brit. Birds* 73:158–9.
Shrubb, M. (1979). Sussex yellow-browed warblers. *Brit. Birds* 72:485.
Wallace, D. I. M. (1973). op. cit. 8 (31).

Pallas's Warbler
Baker, K. (1977). Westward vagrancy of Siberian passerines in autumn 1975. *Bird Study* 24:233–42.
Bell, D. G. (1963). Pallas's warbler in Co. Durham. *Brit. Birds* 56:112–13.
Cambridge Bird Club. (1958). Pallas's warbler in Norfolk. *Brit. Birds* 51:197.
Clarke, R. B., Coath, M., Johns, R. J., & Jones, D. B. D. (1961). Pallas's warbler in Essex. *Brit. Birds* 54:73–4.
Ennion, E. A. R. (1952). Pallas's warbler at Monk's House, Northumberland. *Brit. Birds* 45:258–60.
Harle, D. F. (1959). Pallas's warbler in Kent. *Brit. Birds* 52:317–18.
Rabol, J. (1976). (The orientation of Pallas's warbler *Phylloscopus poregulus* in Europe). *Dansk. Orn. Foren. Tidsskr.* 70:5–16.
Rogers, M. J. *et al.* (1983). Report on rare birds in Great Britain and Ireland in 1982. *Brit. Birds* 76:476–529.
Rooke, K. B. (1966). The orientation of vagrant Pallas's warblers, *Phylloscopus proregulus*. *XIV Int. Orn. Congr. 99*.
Scott, R. E. (1964). Pallas's warblers in Britain in 1963. *Brit. Birds* 57:508–13.
Wolstenholme, P. H. G., Butterworth, J. M., & Chislett, R. (1961). Pallas's warbler in Yorkshire. *Brit. Birds* 54:364–5.

Radde's Warbler
Boswall, J. (1970). The song of Radde's warbler. *Brit. Birds* 63:255–6.
Britton, P. L., & Scott, R. E. (1963). Radde's warbler in Kent. *Brit. Birds* 56:420–1.
Clarke, G. L., & Pearson, D. J. (1966). Radde's warbler in Suffolk. *Brit. Birds* 59: 155–6.
Lassey, P. A., & Wallace, D. I. M. (1979). Habitat preference of migrant dusky warbler. *Brit. Birds* 72:82.
Neufeldt, I. (1960). Studies of less familiar birds. 104. Radde's bush warbler. *Brit. Birds* 53:117–22.

Ptushenko, E. S. (1954). Section on *Herbivocula schwarzi* (Radde) in *The Birds of the Soviet Union*. Moscow.
Richardson, R. A., Spence, B. R., Alexander, H. G., & Williamson, K. (1962). Radde's bush warbler in Norfolk. *Brit. Birds* 55:166–8.

The Dusky Warbler
Alexander, H. G. (1955). op. cit. 23 (1).
Austin, B. P., & Milne, B. S. (1966). Dusky warbler in the Isles of Scilly. *Brit. Birds* 59:112–13.
Cantelo, J. (1979). Tail-cocking by dusky warbler. *Brit. Birds* 72:483.
Davis, P. (1962). Dusky warbler on Fair Isle. *Brit. Birds* 55:190–92.
Hubbard, J. P. (1969). *Phylloscopus fuscatus* in Cyprus. *Bull. B.O.C.* 89:116.
Lassey, P. A., & Wallace, D. I. M. (1979). op. cit. 31 (56).
Page, D. (1978). Dusky warbler feeding in open canopy. *Brit. Birds* 71:82.
Scott, R. E. (1968). Dusky warbler in Kent. *Brit. Birds* 61:563–4.
Smith, F. R. (1971). Report on rare birds in Great Britain in 1970 (with 1960, 1966, 1967 and 1969 additions). *Brit. Birds* 64:339–71.
van der Dol, J. H., Batchelor, D. M., & Taylor, D. W. (1979). Dusky warbler feeding high and looking greenish. *Brit. Birds* 72:482–83.

Bonelli's Warbler
Amann, F. (1953). Beobachtungen am Berglaubsänger, *Phylloscopus bonelli*, im Basler Jura. *Orn. Beob.* 50:157–68.
Arthur, R. W. (1960). Two Bonelli's warblers in Caernarvonshire. *Brit. Birds* 53:276–8.
Bates, G. L. (1933-4). Birds of the southern Sahara and adjoining countries in French West Africa. *Ibis* (13) 3:752–80; 4:61–79, 213–39, 439–66, 685–717.
Belman, P. J., & Eddings, P. A. I. (1980). Marsh frogs seizing Bonelli's warbler and yellow wagtail. *Brit. Birds* 73:418–19.
Brémond, J-C. (1976). Specific recognition in the song of Bonelli's warbler. *Behaviour* 58:99–117.
Cawkell, E. M., & Moreau, R. E. (1963). Notes on the birds of The Gambia. *Ibis* 105:156–78.
Conder, P. J., & Keighley, J. (1949). First record of Bonelli's warbler in the British Isles. *Brit. Birds* 42:215–16.
Cramp, S. C. (1956). Summer in the Landes. *Bird Notes* 27:113–17.
Davis, P. (1962). Bonelli's warbler on Fair Isle. *Brit. Birds* 55:278.
Ferguson-Lees, I. J. (1961). Studies of less familiar birds. 114. Bonelli's warbler. *Brit. Birds* 54:395–99.
Göttschi, F. (1944). Vom Berglaubsänger. *Vögel der Heimat.* 14:179–80.
Grant, P. J. (1977). Mystery photographs. Bonelli's warbler. *Brit. Birds* 70:296–7.
Heilfurth, F. (1934). Zur brutbiologie des Berglaubvogels. *Orn. Monatsber.* 42:65–68.
—— (1935). Ueber as verhalten brutpflegender Männchen bei *Phylloscopus b. bonelli* (Vieill.). *Orn. Monatsber.* 43:33–37.
King, B. (1959). Bonelli's warbler in Cornwall. *Brit. Birds* 52:317.
Kitson, A. R., Porter, R. F., & Hume, R. A. (1983). Call of Bonelli's warbler. *Brit. Birds* 76:537.
Lasnier, J. (1952). Note sur la date d'établissement du Pouillot de Bonelli dans la vallée du Loing. *Alauda* 20:117–18.
Luscher, W. (1936). Beitrage zur fortpflanzungsbiologie von *Phylloscopus b. bonelli* (Vieill.) in der Schweiz. *Schweiz. Arch. f. Orn.* 1:299–305.
Pearson, D. J., Boddy, S., & Smart, M. (1962). Bonelli's warbler in Suffolk. *Brit. Birds* 55:277.
Prenn, F. (1932). Beobachtungen am neste des Berglaubvogels. *Orn. Monatsber.* 40:7–12.
Richard, A. (1927). Le Pouillot Bonelli ou Natterer. *Nos Oiseaux* 8:133–41.

Rogers, M. J., *et al.* (1984). Report on rare birds in Great Britain in 1983. *Brit. Birds* 77:506–62.
Round, P. D. (1981). Call-notes of migrant Bonelli's warblers. *Brit. Birds* 74:444.
Schneider, P. A. (1969). Mischbrut zwischen Berglaubsänger – (*Phylloscopus bonelli*) und Waldlaubsänger (*Phylloscopus sibilatrix*). *J. Orn.* 110:101–102.
Sharrock, J. T. R. (1962). Bonelli's warbler in Co. Cork. *Brit. Birds* 55:92–3.
—— (1982). Mystery photographs. 67. Bonelli's warbler. *Brit. Birds* 75:318–20.
Simms, E. (1957). op. cit. 9 (34).
Smith, K. D. (1968). op. cit. 30 (29).
Stadler, H. (1917). Die rufe und gesänge des Berglaubsängers. *Tierwelt.* 27:13–20.
—— (1929). Die stimmen der alpenvögel. Berglaubsänger (*Phylloscopus b. bonelli* (Vieill.). *Verh. Ornith. Ges. Bayern.* 18:308–17.
Tucker, W. H. (1955). Bonelli's warbler in Dorset. *Brit. Birds* 48:551–2.
van den Oord, A. M. (1959). De Bergfluiter, *Phylloscopus bonelli* Vieillot, nieuw voor Nederland. *Limosa* 32:110–12.
Whitaker, B. (1955). Bonelli's warbler on Lundy. *Brit. Birds* 48:285.
Yeates, G. K. (1946). op. cit. 10 (50).
Zinder, J. P. (1953). Curieux emplacement d'un nid de Pouillot de Bonelli. *Nos Oiseaux* 22:18.

Chapter 32 **The Kinglets**

Bent, A. C. (1964). *Life Histories of North American Thrushes, Kinglets and Their Allies.* New York.
Flower, W. U. (1958). Goldcrest caught on hooks of burdock. *Brit. Birds* 51:276.
Jenks, R. (1936). A new race of golden-crowned kinglet from Arizona. *Condor* 38:239–44.
Knight, O. W. (1908). *The Birds of Maine.*
Lewis, H. F. (1920). The singing of the ruby-crowned kinglet (*Regulus c. calendula*) *Auk* 37:594–6.
Needham, J. G. (1909). Kinglets captured by burdocks. *Bird-Lore* 11:261–2.
Palmer, W. (1897). The Sitkan kinglet. *Auk* 14:399–401.
Skinner, M. P. (1928). *A Guide to the Winter Birds of the North Carolina Sandhills.*

Chapter 33 **The Goldcrest**

Adams, M. C. (1966). Firecrests breeding in Hampshire. *Brit. Birds* 59:240–46.
—— (1980). Firecrests mimicking song of goldcrest. *Brit. Birds* 73:477–8.
Archdale, A. (1978). Behaviour and water-carrying of goldcrests at nest in drought. *Brit. Birds* 71:314.
Batten, L. A. (1976). Bird communities of some Killarney woodlands. *Proc. Roy. Irish Acad.* 76:285–313.
Becker, P. H. (1977a). Geographische variation des gesanges von Winter- und Sommergoldhähnchen (*Regulus regulus, R. ignicapillus*). *Vogelwarte* 29:1–32.
—— (1977b). (Behaviour towards vocalizations of the sibling species, interspecific territoriality and habitat in the goldcrest and firecrest (*Regulus regulus, R. ignicapillus*). *J. Orn.* 118:233–60.
Bent, A. C. (1964). op. cit. 32 (1).
Bottomley, J. B., & S. (1961). Goldcrest eating bread. *Brit. Birds* 54:290–91.
Cobb, F. K. (1976). Apparent hybridization of firecrest and goldcrest. *Brit. Birds* 69:447–51.
Cordeaux, J. (1892). Migration in the Humber district. *Zool.* 1892:418.
Coward, T. A. (1944). op. cit. 5 (6).
Dean, T. (1984). Goldcrest trapped in spider's web. *Brit. Birds* 77:569.
Delamain, J. (1937). The function of the goldcrest's crest. *Brit. Birds* 31:82–3.
Gibb, J. A. (1960). Populations of tits and goldcrests and their food supply in pine plantations. *Ibis* 102:163–208.
Goater, B. (1951). Goldcrest eating moth. *Brit. Birds* 44:36–7.

Grey of Fallodon, Lord. (1947). op. cit. 7 (14).

Haftorn, S. (1978a). (Energetics of incubation by the goldcrest *Regulus regulus* in relation to ambient air temperatures and the geographical distribution of the species.) *Ornis Scand.* 9:22–30.

—— (1978b). (Egg-laying and regulation of egg temperature during incubation in the goldcrest *Regulus regulus.*) *Ornis Scand.* 9:2–21.

—— (1978c). (Co-operation between the male and female goldcrest when rearing overlapping broods.) *Ornis Scand.* 9:124–9.

Harrison, C. J. O. (1969). The fixed feeding pattern of young goldcrests. *Bird Study* 16:62–3.

Heavisides, A. (1984). Goldcrest and sparrowhawk nesting in close proximity. *Brit. Birds* 77:569.

Hogstad, O. (1984). Variation in numbers, territoriality and flock size of a goldcrest *Regulus regulus* population in winter. *Ibis* 126:296–306.

Huxley, J. (1960). Goldcrest eating bread and fat. *Brit. Birds* 53:578.

Irvine, J. (1977). Breeding birds in New Forest broad-leaved woodland. *Bird Study* 24:105–11.

Lack, D. (1937). The function of the goldcrest's crest. *Brit. Birds* 31:82–3.

Lack, D., & E. (1951). Further changes in bird life caused by afforestation. *J. Anim. Ecol.* 20:173–9.

Lagerström, M. (1979). (Goldcrests *Regulus regulus* roosting in the snow.) *Ornis Fenn.* 56:170–72.

Logan Hume, W. M. (1955). Goldcrest eating bread-crumbs. *Brit. Birds* 48:286.

Lord, J., & Ainsworth, G. H. (1948). Unusual nest-sites of goldcrest. *Brit. Birds* 41:118.

Macdonald, D. W., & Henderson, D. G. (1977). Aspects of the behaviour and ecology of mixed-species bird flocks in Kashmir. *Ibis* 119:481–93.

Marchant, J. (1983). Bird population changes for the years 1981–2. *Bird Study* 30: 127–33.

Marchant, J. H., & Hyde, P. A. (1980). Bird population changes for the years 1978–9. *Bird Study* 27:173–8.

Marler, P., & Boatman, D. (1951). Observations on the birds of Pico, Azores. *Ibis* 93:90–99.

Millard, H. S. (1938). High site for goldcrest's nest. *Brit. Birds* 32:160.

Morse, D. H. (1975). Erratic flights of goldcrests *Regulus regulus* and treecreepers *Certhia familiaris.* *Ibis* 117:379–82.

Moule, G. W. H. (1951). Goldcrest using same nest twice in same season. *Brit. Birds* 44:21.

Mummery, S. (1844). Note on migration. In *Annals and Magazine of Natural History*, 1844. 13:237–8.

Mylne, C. K. (1959). Birds drinking the sap of a birch tree. *Brit. Birds* 52:426–7.

Nicholson, E. M., & Koch, L. (1937). op. cit. 6 (24).

O'Connor, R. J., Cawthorne, R. A., & Mead, C. J. (1982). The effects of severe winter weather on British bird populations. *Commissioned Research Rept. to CST, Nature Conservancy Council.* 1–53. Tring.

Österlof, S. (1966). (The migration of the goldcrest (*Regulus regulus*).) *Vår Fågelvarld* 25:49–56.

Passburg, R. E. (1959). op. cit. 26 (9).

Pontius, H. (1960). Beobachtungen zur brutbiologie von Winter- und Sommergoldhähnchen. *J. Orn.* 101:129–40.

Rabol, J. (1971). Goldcrests killed by edible frogs. *Brit. Birds* 71:85.

Radford, A. P. (1969). Goldcrests feeding on ground in association with tits. *Brit. Birds* 62:202.

Raynsford, L. J. (1955). Goldcrest roosting in disused boring of woodpecker. *Brit. Birds* 48:285–6.

Richardson, R. A. (1950). Migrant goldcrest attacking large dragonfly. *Brit. Birds* 43:295.

Riddiford, N. (1984). Food of goldcrests and firecrests on autumn migration. *Brit. Birds* 77:367.

Rogers, M. J. (1978). Call-notes of firecrest and goldcrest. *Brit. Birds* 71:318.

Ruttledge, R. F. (1955). Field-characters of the goldcrest. *Brit. Birds* 48:423.

Simms, E. (1976). op. cit. 22 (20).

Smith, S. C. H. (1972). Goldcrests feeding young with oak bush crickets. *Brit. Birds* 65:33.

Soper, E. A. (1972). Goldcrest taking felt for nesting material. *Brit. Birds* 65:303.

Stokoe, R. (1980). Goldcrest feeding by walking on floating vegetation. *Brit. Birds* 73:38.

Thaler, E., & K. (1982). (Feeding biology of goldcrest and firecrest (*Regulus regulus, R. ignicapillus*) and their segregation by choice of food.) *Ökol. Vögel* 4:191–204.

Thorpe, R. I. (1983). Apparent hybridization between goldcrest and firecrest. *Brit. Birds* 76:233–4.

Tiainen, J., Wickholm, M., & Pakkola, T. (1983). (The habitat and spatial relation of breeding *Phylloscopus* warblers and the goldcrest, *Regulus regulus*, in southern Finland.) *Ann. Zool. Fennici* 20:1–12.

Tutt, H. R. (1972). Goldcrest trapped by threads of spider's web. *Brit. Birds* 65:483.

Wallace, D. I. M. (1961). op. cit. 28 (74).

Williamson, K. (1965). op. cit. 10 (21).

—— (1971). The breeding birds of a century-old grove of coast and sierra redwoods in Wales. *Q.J. Forestry* 65:109–21.

Williamson, R., & K. (1973). The bird community of yew woodland at Kingley Vale, Sussex. *Brit. Birds* 66:12–23.

Chapter 34 The Firecrest

Adams, M. C. (1966). op. cit. 33 (1).

Batten, L. A. (1971). Firecrests breeding in Buckinghamshire. *Brit. Birds* 64:473–5.

—— (1973). The colonization of England by the firecrest. *Brit. Birds* 66:159–66.

Cobb, F. K. (1976). op. cit. 33 (9).

Glue, D. E., & Gush, G. H. (1977). Firecrests feeding at garden bird tables. *Brit. Birds* 70:169.

Gush, G. H. (1976). Treecreepers feeding on fat. *Brit. Birds* 69:310.

Heft, H. (1965). Zur fortpflanzungsbiologie des Sommergoldhähnchens (*Regulus ignicapillus*). *Vogelwelt* 86:65–9.

Jourdain, F. C. R. (1937). The birds of southern Spain, Part ii. *Passeres* (concluded). *Ibis* (1937):110–52.

Long, R. (1981). Review of the birds in the Channel Islands, 1951–80. *Brit. Birds* 74:327–44.

Niethammer, G. (1937). *Handbuch der Deutschen Vogelkunde*. Leipzig.

Redman, P. S., & Hooke, W. D. (1954). Firecrests in Britain, 1952–3. *Brit. Birds* 47:324–35.

Rogers, M. J. (1970). Calls of firecrest on passage. *Brit. Birds* 63:179.

Seago, M. J. (1967). *Birds of Norfolk*. Norwich.

Simms, E. (1979). op. cit. 3 (11).

Snow, D. W. (1952). op. cit. 4 (29).

Spencer, R., et al. (1985). Rare breeding birds in the United Kingdom in 1982. *Brit. Birds* 78:69–92.

Thorpe, R. I. (1983). op. cit. 33 (56).

Williamson, K. (1952). Migrational drift in autumn 1951. *Scott. Nat.* 64:1–18.

Chapter 35 Past and Future

Bartlett, G. (1984). 'Do not push farmers too far' warning to conservationists. *Daily Telegraph*, 26 March 1984.

Batten, L. A. (1972). The past and present bird life of the Brent Reservoir and its vicinity. *Lond. Nat.* 50:8–62.

Berthold, P. (1973). (On the marked decline of the whitethroat *Sylvia communis* and other species of songbird in western Europe). *J. Orn.* 114:348–60.

Beren, G. (1963). Population changes in a Surrey oakwood during fifteen years. *Brit. Birds* 56:307–23.

Bibby, C. J. (1975). Blasted heath – or precious heritage? *Birds* 5 (8):20–23.

—— (1976). Unlucky black heather. *BTO News* 82:1–2.

—— (1981). Stopping the clock. *Birds* 8 (6):21–3.

Burton, J. F. (1975). The effects of recent climatic changes on British insects. *Bird Study* 22:203–4.

Campbell, B. (1981). Forestry in the balance. *Birds* 8 (5):32–3.

Cawthorne, A. (1984). Wood warbler survey. *BTO News* 131:4.

Dawson, W. (1982). Action in the parish. *Natural World* 5. Autumn 1982:14–15.

Elkins, N. (1983). *Weather and Bird Behaviour*. Calton.

Flegg, J. J. M. (1975). Bird population and distribution changes and the impact of man. *Bird Study* 22:191–202.

Forestry Commission. *The Landscape of Forests and Woods*. (FC Booklet No. 44).

Harrison, J. (1970). Creating a wetland habitat. *Bird Study* 17:111–22.

Hawksworth, D. L. (ed.) (1974). *The Changing Flora and Fauna of Britain*. London.

James, J. D. (1983). Personal letter. 31 March 1983.

Johnson, B. (1983). *The Conservation and Development Programme for the UK. A Response to the World Conservation Strategy. An Overview – Resourceful Britain*. London.

Lamb, H. H. (1966). *The Changing Climate*. London.

—— (1975). Our understanding of the global wind circulation and climatic variations. *Bird Study* 22:121–41.

Mason, C. F. (1977). Recent late arrivals of summer migrants in Leicestershire. *Brit. Birds* 70:342–3.

—— (1978). Problems in Broadland. *Birds* 7 (2):32–5.

Mellanby, K. (1982). Hedges – habitat or history. *Natural World* 5. Autumn 1982:27–9.

Moreau, R. E. (1970). Changes in Africa as a wintering area for Palaearctic birds. *Bird Study* 17:95–103.

—— (1972). *The Palaearctic-African Bird Migration Systems*. London.

Morel, G. (1973). The Sahel zone as an environment for Palaearctic migrants. *Ibis* 115:413–17.

Nature Conservancy Council (1984). *Nature Conservation in Great Britain*.

Nicholas, M. (1976). The deathly hush. *Birds* 6 (4):34–7.

Price, M. P. (1938). Disappearance of wood warbler in Gloucester and Buckingham. *Brit. Birds* 32:17.

—— (1950). Influences causing fluctuation of warbler population in cultivated lands and oakwoods in the Severn valley. *Brit. Birds* 43:345–51.

—— (1961). Warbler fluctuations in oak woodland in the Severn Valley. *Brit. Birds* 54:100–106.

Rackham, O. (1981). Memories of our wildwood. *Natural World*. Spring 1981:26–9.

Shoard, M. (1981). *The Theft of the Countryside*. London.

Simms, E. (1975). *Birds of Town and Suburb*. London.

—— (1984). 'Land mustn't become featureless prairie!' Article in *Grantham Journal*, 16 March 1984.

Sinclair, A. R. E. (1978). Factors affecting the food supply and breeding season of resident birds and movements of Palaearctic migrants in a tropical African savannah. *Ibis* 120:480–97.

Valverde, J. A. (1958). op. cit. 30 (37).

Williamson, K. (1975). Birds and climatic change. *Bird Study* 22:143–64.

—— (1976). Recent climatic influences on the status and distribution of some British birds. *Weather* 3:362–84.

Sound Recordings

Sound Recordings of Warblers

In Europe the most ambitious set of recordings is *The Peterson Field Guide to the Bird Songs of Britain and Europe* by Sture Palmér and Jeffrey Boswall (1969–73); it consists of 14 electronic stereo discs with more than 1000 recordings of over 530 species, including 40 species of warbler. Highly recommended is *British Bird Vocabulary (An Aural Index)* by V. C. Lewis (1979) with 12 cassette tapes with accompanying text; it includes long clear recordings of warblers and is published by S/Ldr Lewis at Rosehill House, Lyonshall, Herefordshire. *Witherby's Sound Guide to British Birds* by Myles North and Eric Simms (1969) consists of two LP discs and a 104 page book and includes recordings of 17 warbler species. Another set of European birds is a guide by J-Cl. Roché (1964–66) with a range of warblers represented. *The Birds of the Soviet Union: A Sound Guide* (1982) has been launched by B. N. Veprintsev with 3 LP records and in time will include the sounds of 750 bird species and as a publication will parallel the new *Handbook of Soviet Birds*. More than 20,000 bird recordings are housed at the British Library of Wildlife Sounds at 29 Exhibition Road, London SW7, and these can be listened to at that address by appointment with the Curator, Ron Kettle, whose telephone number is 01-589 6603.

Index